The Power of Place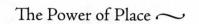

The Power of Place ∼

RULERS AND THEIR PALACES, LANDSCAPES, CITIES, AND HOLY PLACES

David Rollason

PRINCETON UNIVERSITY PRESS

PRINCETON AND OXFORD

Copyright © 2016 by Princeton University Press
Published by Princeton University Press, 41 William Street, Princeton, New Jersey 08540
In the United Kingdom: Princeton University Press, 6 Oxford Street, Woodstock, Oxfordshire OX20 1TR

press.princeton.edu

Jacket photograph: View of the Alhambra, Granada (Spain) from the quarter called the Albaicin. The large, square, tower-like building in the foreground is the Palace of Comares, with the Palace of the Lions to the left of it, and another palace (of which little remains) called the Palace of the Partal on the same side. The palace of Charles V is the large rectangular building on the right. Courtesy of Lynda Rollason

Library of Congress Cataloging-in-Publication Data

Names: Rollason, D. W. (David W.)
Title: The power of place : rulers and their palaces, landscapes, cities, and
        holy places / David Rollason.
Description: Princeton : Princeton University Press, 2016. | Includes
        bibliographical references and index.
Identifiers: LCCN 2015038255| ISBN 9780691167626 (hardback) | ISBN 0691167621
        (hardcover)
Subjects: LCSH: Europe—Kings and rulers—Homes and haunts. |
        Palaces—Europe—History. | Landscapes—Europe—History. | Cities and
        towns—Europe—History. | Sacred space—Europe—History. | Historic
        sites—Europe. | Architecture and state—Europe—History. | Power (Social
        sciences)—Europe—History. | Europe—History, Local. | Europe—Politics
        and government. | BISAC: HISTORY / Europe / General. | ARCHITECTURE /
        History / General. | HISTORY / Ancient / General.
Classification: LCC D107 .R65 2016 | DDC 940.09/9–dc23 LC record available at http://lccn.loc.gov/2015038255

British Library Cataloging-in-Publication Data is available

The publication of this book has been made possible by funding from the Leverhulme Trust, the Scouloudi Foundation in association with the Institute of Historical Research, and Dr. C. P. Graves.

This book has been composed in Minion Pro and Adobe Jenson Pro

Printed on acid-free paper. ∞

Printed in the United States of America

10 9 8 7 6 5 4 3 2 1

In memory of
Philip Rahtz
(1921–2011)
~
a great archaeologist,
an inspirational teacher,
and a warm friend

Contents ⁓

List of Illustrations ⌒

Preface ⌒

The writing of this book was made possible by the support of the Leverhulme Trust, which granted me a Major Research Fellowship, between 2010 and 2013, permitting me to devote all my time to it in the three years prior to my retirement from Durham University. I cannot sufficiently praise the Trust's generosity, supportiveness, openness, and willingness to support ventures such as this. The Trust has book-ended my career, granting me a European Studentship in 1976–77, which allowed me to spend an academic year studying in Paris and absorbing at first hand the ideas of Georges Duby and Jacques LeGoff. It has supported me with grants for developing projects during the course of my career, and now it has supported the writing of a book so risky that only on the verge of retirement could I have attempted it. For this book has involved study far outside my long-standing areas of expertise. On an almost weekly basis over the three years of the fellowship, I found myself tackling royal and imperial sites that were quite new to me, and dealing with a large and often technical literature in a range of languages that was equally new. With my wife, Lynda, I found myself regularly traveling across Europe, exploring and seeking to master the sites themselves, which were often dauntingly complex. The work was extremely exciting, but fraught with danger. The Trust calmly accepted this, and the three years of the fellowship enabled me to do my best to master both the sites and the literature.

In embarking on such a demanding course, I was driven by a deep irritation with divides in the scholarship between periods and between countries. To conduct really intensive research, it is of course necessary to specialize in a particular period or a particular country, or often just a small part of a particular period or a small region of a particular country. Valuable, and indeed essential, as such specialization is, it seemed to me that insights that could be gained from looking much more widely were likely to be lost as a result of it. So the present book was conceived as boldly going across period and geographical boundaries in the hope that interesting parellisms, or indeed contrasts, could be brought out from a wide-ranging approach. I was driven also by a desire to exploit to the full non-written historical sources, which is what the sites considered in this book are, even for periods with rich written documentation. This desire arose partly from the belief that written sources can only ever offer a partial picture of the past, so that we should be making use of every type of source available; and partly from a suspicion that differences of interpretation applied to different periods might sometimes be explained principally in terms of the nature of the source material available or used. For periods for which there are written sources, scholars have largely used these in preference to the non-written sources, so that the differences between human organization in those societies and in those for which scholars had more extensively depended on non-written sources (the early middle ages, for example) might in fact have been much less than appeared. Hence my desire to explore at least one category of non-written sources—royal and imperial sites—across a wide temporal and geographical range.

My wish, more specifically, to explore the nature of power through those non-written sources goes back to the very beginning of my career, to the teaching at Oxford of Peter Brown, David Hinton, and the late L.M.J. Delaissé, but above all to a golden summer evening on the ramparts of the Iron Age hillfort of Cadbury Congresbury, with Somerset countryside stretching away below them. As a young and very fresh student, about to begin my PhD work at the University of Birmingham, I was taking part as a humble troweller in the excavations which the late Philip Rahtz was directing there and which were uncovering evidence for early medieval re-use of the fort. On that evening, we stood around Philip to ponder the results of the day's excavations—myself, Ian Burroughs, Sue Hirst, Peter Fowler, and others—and the discussion flowed, guided by Philip's inimitably light-hearted humor and enthusiasm, over the status of the site in the early Middle Ages. Was it a royal center? Was it a monastery? Was it a hermitage? And how could one distinguish these one from another in the physical record? The effect of the discussion was electrifying, and it stayed with me over the succeeding decades, right up until the time that I began working on this book.

In the course of my fellowship, and in the years after my retirement, I have had movingly generous help and support from many scholars, for many of whom I was a completely unknown quantity, but who were nevertheless unfailingly supportive both with information and with guidance at the sites themselves. They have included my friends at Montpellier, Gérard and Nadia Dédéyan, with whom the exploration of Perpignan was undertaken and who put me in touch with other scholars; their daughter Marina Taub and her husband Marc, who generously provided accommodation and fellowship during visits to Paris; Julien Gallon at the Palais des Papes in Avignon, with whom I spent a stimulating morning in parts of the palace that other scholars cannot reach; Paola de Angelis-Noah and Christina Carile at Ravenna; Aymat Catafu and Olivier Passarius, who welcomed me to the colloquium on the Palace of the Kings of Majorca at Perpignan; Letha and Ingo Böhringer, who generously provided hospitality and friendship in Bonn; Frode Iversen, who received me in Oslo and introduced me to his colleagues; Anne Pedersen, who was generous with her knowledge in Copenhagen; Simon Thurley, who has given encouragement and stimulating comment from a very early date in the project's inception; Kent Rawlinson, whose knowledge of Hampton Court was placed at my disposal in the course of a day spent there; Sally Dixon-Smith at the Tower of London; Antonio Triano, who gave up a Sunday morning at Madīnat al-Zahrā to answer my questions; Mariam Owen-Rosser, who helped me into the world of Islamic palaces; Graham Jones and Jack Langton, who shared with me the expertise of the Forests and Chases project; Tom James, who showed me round the remains of Clarendon Palace, for which he has done so much, on a very wet morning; Chris Gerrard, whose critical appraisal of the original project-draft did much to ensure its success; and, last but not least, my friends at Aachen, Clemens Bayer with whom I first explored the cathedral almost thirty years ago, Harald Müller, and Judith and Karsten Ley. Several scholars have fueled my approach and honed my ideas, either by generously taking part in seminars I organized, or co-organized with Sarah Semple, at the Leeds International Medieval Congress, or by inviting me to speak about the project at various places. I am thinking especially of Thomas Zotz, Simon Thurley, Len Scales, Conor Newman, and Keith Lilley, but there were many others who took part in the seminars at Leeds; and, for their invitations to speak and their hospitality, I am thinking with gratitude of Maria Duggan at Newcastle University, Hugh Doherty at the University of East Anglia, James Clarke at Exeter University, Ildar Garipzanov at Oslo University, Paul Oldfield at Manchester University, and Durham University History Society and Institute of Medieval and Early Modern Studies at Durham itself. Several friends and colleagues have rendered invaluable assistance by reading drafts of all or part of the book: Lorna Watts, whose enthusiasm and encouragement were especially valued; Michael Donithorn, with whom I first discussed history close to fifty years ago; Frank Haylett, who brought to bear an eminently commonsense approach; Alan Thacker, who has helped with so much of my work over many years; John Gilbert, who generously helped with my chapter on forests; and above all my wife, Lynda, who has patiently read the book twice in successive drafts. Other scholars have helped me with particular points or above all with illustrations. They include: Ulrike Heckner, Zoë Opačić, Manfred Luchterhand, John Crook, Tim Tatton-Brown, Mark Johnson, Jim Crow, Warwick Rodwell, Christopher Wilson, Richard Pears of Durham University Library—with whom I have also had many discussions over fish and chips, Gottfried Kerscher, Sally Foster, Julian Munby, and Holger Grewe and his colleagues at the Ingelheim Kaiserpfalz. But, as with all my books, my principal debt is to my wife, Lynda. The often tiring excursions to wrestle with the architecture and layout of the sites that feature in this book were almost always joint excercises, and they could scarcely have been undertaken without her support, engagement, acumen, and expertise. She has also been the project's principal photographer, she has been a stern critic of every stage of the book's development, and what the final version possesses in coherence and clarity owes much to her. In the process of preparing the book for the press, my son Ed has equally been a tower of strength; he applied his GIS expertise to preparing the maps, and he generously placed at my disposal his knowledge of computer graphics to enable me to draw the maps and diagrams. Risky books need risk-taking presses, and I should, finally, like to express my appreciation for the willingness of Ben Tate at Princeton University Press to take the book on, and for the support and help of the Press's staff in bringing it to publication.

David Rollason
August 2015

The Power of Place ⌣

CHAPTER 1

Introduction

This book is about the messages of power that sites created by, or associated with, rulers could send to their subjects, to visitors, to ambassadors, and to anyone who saw or entered them. The rulers it considers were principally, although not exclusively, emperors and kings. The period it considers is that reaching from the early Roman Empire to the beginning of the sixteenth century. The sites it considers are, first, what can loosely be termed palaces, whether elaborate stone- or brick-built complexes of buildings, or timber great halls, or earthworks, the residential centers for rulers in one form or another. Second, artificial landscapes around or near the palaces, whether gardens, or parks, or forests managed for hunting. Third, cities founded, enlarged, or patronized by rulers. Fourth, places that rulers made holy, either by endowing them with holy objects, or by constructing or expanding holy buildings there. Fifth and finally, places where rulers were inaugurated into their offices, and places where their remains were placed and memorials to them created.

The book draws on a range of disciplines, including: architectural history, for the light which it can cast on the form and inspiration of rulers' buildings; archaeology, for its role in reconstructing buildings only partially preserved, for providing a deeper context for them from the excavations of the layers in which they sit, and for making possible the interpretation of earthwork sites, for which there is no—or only very limited—written evidence; garden history, for reconstructing the form and assessing the significance of gardens associated with palaces; landscape history, for the understanding of parks and forests; art history, for approaches to understanding the significance of the decoration and embellishment of rulers' buildings, and of the representation of those buildings in paintings or mosaics; literary history, for the light it can cast on images of palaces and their functions conjured up in poems and other writings; and liturgical studies, for their importance in understanding ceremonies and rituals carried out in rulers' holy places.

The book's guiding discipline, however, is history. Its aim is to examine what can be learned from the sites in question about the nature of rulers' power, or at least about how rulers wished to represent their power. Readers will appreciate that the validity of this aim is open to the question of how far such sites were created or modified simply for the enjoyment and gratification of rulers, rather than being designed to send messages of power in the way this book proposes. Readers, in other words, may conclude that, in creating, modifying, or using these sites, rulers were doing no more than fulfilling their personal taste for magnificence, luxury, and self-aggrandizement, and were perceived as doing this by those who visited the sites. So the palaces, gardens, parks, and forests would have been just the perks of the job of being a ruler and not intended to make any public statement about the rulers' power. The cities founded or enlarged or patronized by the ruler would have been simply for his comfort and convenience. His holy places would have been designed for no more than to guarantee the well-being of the rulers' souls after their deaths. In the end, it is a matter of judgment; for rulers in the period in question have almost never left statements of what their intentions were in building this or designing that. Self-gratification, self-importance, craving for luxury, fears for the fate of the soul after death might have been the real motives for the work undertaken, perhaps even the principal motives.

The case argued in this book, however, is that the sites in question were indeed designed to send messages of power—and consequently functioned as mechanisms by which that power could be consolidated and increased. So, the book argues, the ruler's palace could be an explicit statement of his power. It could be a carefully designed mechanism for presenting him and his power in particular ways and to particular groups, whether his high-ranking subjects or the ambassadors of other rulers (Part I). Gardens could function similarly, especially where they served as open-air stages for courtly meetings and rituals; and so too could parks and forests, especially in what were the ritualized proceedings of the imperial and royal hunts (Part II). The cities built by, or modified by, rulers were similarly expressions of the rulers' power to control cityscapes and the built environment in which some of their subjects lived. And, like the palaces, they were mechanisms for displaying that power. This could be achieved through great buildings and piazzas built in the ruler's name and serving to impress and overwhelm those who saw them. But it could also be achieved through the creation in the cities of processional ways in which the rituals of rulership could be played out to the greatest effect (Part III). The holy places created or patronized by rulers were, the book argues, no less committed to representing and reinforcing rulers' power. In them, a ruler could associate his power with especially holy objects and with divinities themselves (Part IV). Messages of power could be sent too by the places where the rulers were inaugurated, and the places in which their remains were deposited—all the more when inauguration places and funerary places were fixed sites associated with the rulers' dynasties. A ruler's burial place could send a message of power not only about the deceased ruler, but also about his successors in office who were, of course, responsible for the implementation of the funerals (Part V).

In exploring these matters, the book makes no claim to being a definitive statement, for it is by no means a comprehensive survey of the types of site in question, valuable and illuminating as that would no doubt be. Such a survey, examining developments over time and space and the interrelationships of sites over time and space, would require research of many years' duration and a multivolume work much larger than the present study. This book's objective is more limited. It is to bring together the best and most illuminating examples of these sites, in order to examine the most productive approaches that scholars have used to draw significance from them.

These examples are taken from Europe and from a wide range of historical periods. The earliest considered are Roman imperial sites from the first to the fourth century AD, such as the Imperial Fora in Rome and the Palace of Diocletian in Split. These are followed in time by sites from the Byzantine Empire, which constituted the continuation of the Roman Empire in the eastern Mediterranean, such as the Great Palace of Constantinople, and the great church of Haghia Sophia in that city. Alongside these, the book considers sites of the "barbarian" kingdoms that succeeded the Roman Empire in western Europe, such as the mauseoleum of Theodoric, king of the Ostrogoths (454–526), in Ravenna (Italy), and the great palace site of Yeavering (England) in the kingdom of Northumbria. Moving on in time again, the book examines sites of the great empire of Charlemagne (768–814) in western Europe, especially the palaces of Aachen and Ingelheim (Germany). It looks too at sites created or modified by the newly emerged Muslim caliphate in southern Spain in the tenth century, notably the palace city of Madīnat al-Zahrā, and the Great Mosque of Córdoba. Outside the area of the Roman Empire, the book considers sites such as the timber halls at Lejre (Denmark), the massive royal mausoleum of Jelling in the same kingdom, and the earthworks, which gave the Hill of Tara in Ireland its central importance for Irish kingship. For the later Middle Ages, the book examines sites from the kingdoms of France and England as they emerged from the twelfth century onward, especially the great French palaces in Paris and at nearby Vincennes, and the equally imposing Westminster Palace, which became the chief royal palace of the kingdom of England. For less enduring kingdoms, the book ranges across the thirteenth-century kingdom of Majorca, with one of its principal centers at the palace of Perpignan in south-west France; and the kingdom of Naples and Sicily, with royal and imperial sites at Naples itself, at Palermo where a complex of palaces grew up, at Capua where the triumphal gateway built by the king of Sicily and Germany and Holy Roman Emperor, Frederick II (1198–1250), still stands in mutilated form, and at the Castel del Monte, where that ruler's octagonal castle palace still dominates the surrounding landscape. The book also considers the sites created by the kings of Bohemia in and around Prague, especially those built or enlarged by the king of Bohemia and Holy Roman Emperor, Charles IV (1346–78), at Prague itself but also at Karlštejn, the castle developed to guard his collection of relics and his regalia. For sites created for rulers other than kings and emperors, the book considers the Palace of the Doge in Venice, and the immensely important monument which is the Palace of the Popes at Avignon, built by Benedict XIII (1334–42) and Clement VI (1342–52), during the period when the papacy was in exile in France. The intention of ranging so widely is to permit the book to use the work of scholars specializing in different centuries and in different countries. That work and the conclusions the scholars draw from it can be very different for different periods and areas, but they can also be revealingly similar, so that bringing them together to an extent that has not often been attempted before can prove revealing and illuminating.

The book's practical aim is to provide a sort of handbook to how sites created or modified by rulers can yield essentially historical conclusions about the nature of their power, or at least about the power they were claiming to possess. It guides readers around the sites in question, or sometimes around the artistic and literary representations of such sites, in as hands-on a way as is possible without actually taking readers in person to these places. The book attempts to draw to the attention of readers the individual features of these sites, always striving to extract from them the historical conclusions about rulers' power which they might be perceived as offering. It supports descriptions of the sites with as lavish a collection of photographs and diagrams as has been possible. These are often labeled, and always fully captioned, so that they are an essential part of the fabric of the book.

It is also intended that a reader should be able to go on to consider sites that this book has not considered, and to press further the line of historical questioning that the book has sketched out. For this reason, the book largely provides references for the themes and sites discussed in a discrete section entitled "Research and Reading" (below, pp. 391–416). In addition to providing the equivalent of footnotes to the material in the chapters, this section offers a critical commentary on the most exciting scholarly literature, archaeological reports, or collections of sources bearing on the themes discussed in each chapter, as well as providing a similar commentary on the scholarly literature relating to the individual sites examined.

The book nevertheless has aspirations to provide some sort of answers to two fundamental questions about rulership even if, given that it is not a coherent history of the types of site in question, they must be only provisional. First, its wide geographical and chronological scope permits it to address, in the context of the sites with which it is concerned, the question of how unchanging rulership was across the centuries from the first century AD to the end of the Middle Ages; and how unchanging it was also across the wide area this book embraces, from Bohemia to Andalusia, from Sicily to Scotland and Norway. For scholars have often treated the manifestations of rulership in various areas and periods as very different, so that Roman emperors have been interpreted as radically different rulers from kings of France and England, for example, or from caliphs of Córdoba. Irish kings have been seen, at least for certain periods, as a quite different type of ruler from the rulers of Continental kingdoms or even of Anglo-Saxon England. It may be that these differences of perception are justified by the evidence; but it may equally be that they are illusory. They could arise from differences in the type of evidence that has survived from the areas in question; or from modern interpretations of the past which, for example, have sometimes seen Muslim states such as the caliphate of Córdoba as being of completely different origin and type from those of non-Muslim areas of Europe; or from the simple fact that specialists are often focused on their areas of specialization and too rarely look beyond. This book, in short, has a mission, first, to break down the various chronological and geographical—and cultural—divides apparent in the scholarly literature; and, second, to place squarely on the agenda the hypothesis that rulership was in important respects unchanging across Europe in the millennium and a half or so from the early Roman imperial period to the end of the Middle Ages.

If the book's contention that sites created by rulers were expressions of, and therefore tools of, their power is sustainable, it becomes necessary to ask what sort of power was in question, and how far this differed from period to period and place to place. To approach this, it has been necessary to adopt a framework within which to describe the power of rulers, so that like can be compared with like across the book's chronological and geographical range. The framework adopted here is a threefold categorization of types of power. First, the type of power that derives from the exercise of law and the creation of bureaucratic and fiscal machinery to enable the ruler to impose his will on his subjects. It may be given the shorthand label "bureaucratic power." This is the type of power most familiar in the modern period, when people obey their governments, because those governments possess the means to make them obey—that is, the complex record-keeping, all the more developed in the present computerized age, which allows them to follow the affairs of their subjects and above all to extract taxation from them. Then there are the hierarchies of officials that allow the governments' instructions to be made known, and the police or military personnel, authorized to use force to ensure that they are followed. And, finally, the system of prisons and other places of punishment to coerce those who do not obey or to punish those whose actions fall outside the laws. An impersonal system of offices and officeholders, regulated by impersonal procedures, regulations, and laws, is a defining feature of bureaucratic power.

But, even in the present, this is by no means the only type of power in existence, and in the past it may not always have been the dominant one. A second type of power, to which we can assign the shorthand label "personal power," derives from the hold rulers have through their personal relationships with their subjects—a hold which ensures that those subjects (or at least a sufficient number of them) are, as a result of these personal relationships with the holders of power, either constrained to support them, or see it as in their interests to do so. This may have been the type of power that sustained the rulers of the barbarian kingdoms of Western Europe from the fifth century onward, for example, when they developed war bands of military retainers who were committed to them through strong personal bonds, reinforced by oaths of loyalty. Such war bands might thus have been essentially personal in nature, yet they would have assured the power of the ruler in the same way as police forces do in the case of bureaucratic power. It is arguable that throughout the Middle Ages personal relationships created power for lords over their vassals, that is, the military retainers sworn by oath to support their lords especially in warfare. And it is observable too in the early modern period in the relationship between a ruler and the members of his court, like the courtiers of Louis XIV (1643–1715) at his palace at Versailles where they lived, often in personal intimacy with their monarch.

A third type of power is encompassed under the shorthand term, "ideological power," which is not rationally based on bureaucratic machinery or on personal relations with the ruler, but is based rather on a sense, or a belief, that the rulers occupied a special position relative to the gods or to God. It was this that made their position legitimate and meant that they had to be obeyed, for failure to obey risked supernatural retribution at the hand of the divinity that had granted power to the ruler. So, for example, the Roman emperors were closely associated with pagan gods, and were believed to become gods themselves after their deaths. The barbarian kings who ruled in the areas outside the Roman Empire and, after the end of that empire in Western Europe, in the kingdoms that replaced it, may themselves have been believed to have been descended from gods or to have been closely associated with them. There are indications in the first-century Roman writer Tacitus' account of them that barbarian kings functioned as priests as well as rulers, that they were, for example, close enough to the gods to interpret the neighings and snortings of sacred white horses (Mattingly and Handforth 1970, Germania, ch. 10). There are traces of similar ideological aspects of power in the Viking kingdoms of Scandinavia.

Such pagan aspects of ideological power were no doubt disrupted by the conversion of the Roman Empire to Christianity in the course of the fourth century, and by the subsequent conversion of the barbarians to the same religion. But even after this rulers could be viewed—or at least could view themselves—as having received their power from the Christian God, who also guided and supported their rule. For example, the development of the ritual of anointing a king with holy oil developed and represented in symbolic form the idea that the ruler received his power from God.

So, the categorization of power set out above can be summarized as follows:

(1) Bureaucratic power, which came into existence through the creation of bureaucratic machinery, and the development of laws and ideas about them.
(2) Personal power, which originated through circumstances that made it desirable for influential members or classes of society to forge personal relations with the ruler.
(3) Ideological power, which was made possible by ways in which rulers were able to merge their power with existing or new religious beliefs.

There is nothing fixed about this categorization, and the distinctions between the categories are often blurred. Personal power, for example, may shade into bureaucratic power, when subjects of a ruler served him by being appointed to what appeared to be impersonal offices, but still swore oaths of allegiance to him. Were the oaths, then, simply fossilized formalities, or were they the core of the relationship between ruler and subject? Also, some subjects may have perceived and accepted the power of rulers in different ways from others. Some may have devoutly accepted the ruler's divinely given power; others may have been skeptical of this, but nevertheless have felt bound to the ruler by personal bonds, or have been constrained to obey him by virtue of his bureaucratic machinery.

If the aim of this book is to cast light on the nature of rulership across a wide chronological and geographical range, viewing it in the framework of these types of power, readers may object that there are more obvious ways to approach it than through the sites with which it is concerned. It would, for example, be possible to concentrate on how the political theorists of the past explained the power of rulers in their writings. For modern scholars, this has often proved very illuminating, especially for periods like the ninth century, or the thirteenth century, when political theory was an important subject of contemporary scholarship. So it would be possible to study the writings of a scholar such as Hincmar, archbishop of Reims, in the ninth century, or of the English specialist in law, Bracton, or of Thomas Aquinas in the thirteenth century. But such an approach is always dependent on the opinions of these theorists. There is no guarantee that what these scholars wrote was representing accurately the nature of rulers' power, rather than describing or discussing what they wished to exist as distinct from what actually did.

Alternatively, it is possible to examine the archives of administrative documents that past governments have left behind them, and scholars have often done this for particular periods and particular states. They have looked at the law codes that particular rulers and their governments produced, at the tax records, at the treasury accounts, and at the accounts of the rulers' landed holdings. But not all the states this book is concerned with left such archives, and in any case documents of this kind are necessarily going to give the impression that power was primarily bureaucratic power, because the documents are themselves the product of bureaucratic machinery. They may provide an important part of the answer, but not necessarily a complete one.

Another possible source of information is the narrative writings from the past, the histories and chronicles, the biographies and epic poems, that pertain to rulers and their power. These too can be very illuminating, but once again they are always at one remove from the rulers themselves, and it is never absolutely clear whether the writers in question were portraying those rulers and their power as they actually were, or as they wanted or imagined them to be. In short, documents, chronicles, and other written texts from the past—even apparently impartial ones like law codes—can present prejudiced views of the reality of power. And, for some periods and some parts of Europe, there are no documents and chronicles, either because the societies in question were not literate ones, or because little or nothing in the way of written sources for them has survived the passage of time.

So, while still drawing on these sources, this book takes a different approach. Its aim is to get as close as possible to the rulers themselves, and to understand the nature of their power through the places and buildings they themselves created, or that were created for them. A ruler was after all a real person, living and working in particular places, in particular buildings and indeed in particular rooms or apartments within them. Enormous resources were devoted to these buildings, which were often glowing with rich decorations, and embellished with spectacular images and sculptures. Rulers visited or lived in—and sometimes founded or developed—particular cities, often bearing their names, to which equally enormous resources were devoted. They made ceremonial use of forests, parks, and gardens, which were often the product of their own organization of the landscape. They were crowned in particular places, and buried in particular places, often in great monuments or churches, which they themselves had built. These sites were, in other words, very close to rulers, very much part of their own actions rather than of other people's reflections on them. Understanding them in detail, as this book tries to do, may represent a more direct approach to understanding what kind of power rulers exercised, or at least claimed to exercise.

Were the palaces and cities of rulers designed to accommodate and to give precedence to the bureaucratic offices and the courts of lawyers? Were they dominated by strong rooms for the treasury and cubicles for the treasury clerks? Were their principal spaces given over to law courts? Can we identify the sort of government offices that are so dominant an aspect of the modern city? If so, this would point toward the prime importance of bureaucratic power. Or were the planning and the architecture of centers of power primarily designed to provide the contexts in which rulers could meet with their subjects and forge those personal relationships that made up what is here called personal power? Were palaces, for example, dominated by great halls in which rulers entertained their subjects, enjoyed entertainments with them, held meetings with them, and received oaths of loyalty from them? Were cities characterized by places where subjects could be in the presence of their ruler, perhaps as the latter processed through the city, or held meetings in great public concourses? Were forests and parks primarily designed so rulers could fraternize with their subjects, providing contexts in which messages of personal power could be conveyed? Or was the primary intention of palaces, cities, and planned landscapes, as well as rulers' holy places such as temples and churches, to emphasize the divinity of the ruler, or at least his relationship to God or the gods? Did the ruler make his appearances in contexts where he was surrounded by priests, in close association with holy objects, and among images that represented his holiness, or at least his divinely chosen status? Did his throne look out from the gallery of some holy building, allowing the ruler to gaze on images of the divine? Were his palaces and cities dominated by holy places—temples, churches, mausolea—which underlined in more or less explicit ways the ruler's relationship with the deity? If so, this would point toward the prime importance of ideological power.

Of course, in all of this we may still be obtaining only partial clues to the nature of power. Especially in the case of ideological power, what the ruler wanted his subjects to believe about his power may not have been what they actually did believe. Building great churches and palaces to express this power was not a guarantee against their destruction by subjects who did not share his view of his power. For all the resources lavished by Charles IV, king of Bohemia (1346–78), on his palace and cathedral of Prague, much of what he had achieved was swept away in the Hussite Wars of the following century. For all the efforts devoted to the creation of a magnificent church and palace at Westminster by King Henry III (1207–72), none of this stopped an attack on the palace by citizens who destroyed at least some of what the king had created. Perhaps such incidents show that the importance of these sites was accepted by rebellious subjects, even if they had no sympathy for them. Nothing is ever simple. Nevertheless, it is the contention of this book that the study of such sites leads to the heart of what rulers saw the nature of their power as being. It is bringing us as close to them as we are likely to get—to stand in the spaces they made, to look at what remains of the landscapes they shaped, to understand the layout of the cities they conceived and the holy places they created.

PART I 〜

Palaces

This part of the book examines the residences of rulers. It asks whether these residences were intended to convey messages to those who saw them about the power of the rulers for whom they were constructed. Were they in other words, tools of power which rulers used to establish, maintain, and display their positions, or were they just luxurious residences intended simply to pander to the luxurious tastes of rulers? And, if the former, is it possible to be precise about the meaning of the messages of power envisaged as being conveyed? To what sort of power, in other words, did those messages relate?

The word used in this book for such residences is "palaces," which can pose a problem of meaning. That word, or its Latin forerunner, had a very particular origin. According to the Roman writer Cassius Dio, the residence to which it was first applied was that of Romulus, the founder of Rome, near which the Roman emperors from the time of Augustus (d. AD 14) built their own residences. This Romulus' house was on the Palatine Hill, one of the seven hills on which the ancient city of Rome was built. This hill originally had the Latin name *Palatium* (Palace), which only later changed into *Palatinus* (Palatine). So the name of the hill, Palatium, became a term for the ruler's residence. In this way, the Latin word *palatium* (palace) came into existence, and it was from this that the English word palace derived (Carile 2012, 2).

It is not an easy word to use, for it evidently had different nuances of meaning for writers in various kingdoms and during various periods. Modern scholars have often struggled to define it (see, for example, Staab 1990; Renoux 2001). It can be used primarily to mean a residence that was also a center of imperial or royal government, as the Palace of Westminster was in the Middle Ages and has remained to the present day. But it can equally be applied to a complex of buildings that served primarily as a luxurious residence, often set among parks and gardens, as in the case of the Palace of Vincennes in the Forest of Vincennes near Paris, or Windsor Castle, looking out over Windsor Great Park.

In a book as wide-ranging as this one, it must be accepted that the word palace cannot be used in a way that reflects all the nuances of meaning of the past, or even of present scholarly debate. It is used here simply to mean "the residence of a ruler," which embraces many types of residence that would not necessarily have been termed palaces by contemporaries. In other words, what characterizes them is simply their construction for, or use by, rulers. In practice, they range from enormous rural complexes like Hadrian's Villa (*Villa Adriana*), built by the emperor Hadrian near Tivoli (Italy), to palaces dominating their cities like the medieval palace of Nuremberg (Germany); and they include also timber-built palaces like the complex of structures at Yeavering (England), or the sequence of timber halls at Lejre (Denmark).

It must equally be accepted that rulers' palaces, defined in this way, were not necessarily or always different from the habitations of their greater subjects. Or, looked at another way, the term ruler is not a hard-and-fast one. This book concentrates on rulers who were kings and emperors, and to a lesser extent on popes and doges. But the power that they exercised, and from which palaces arose, was inevitably shared to a significant extent by an elite group of powerful men and their families—great lords such as counts and dukes in the lay world, bishops and even abbots and priors in the ecclesiastical world. These men, naturally enough, built themselves palaces in imitation of their rulers, or sometimes in competition with them. While recognizing the importance of this much wider range of habitations for understanding aspects of power, this book must nevertheless be restricted, if only for reasons of practicality, to those of the greatest rulers, that is, the kings, emperors, popes, and doges, rather than embracing more widely those of elite members of society who were in effect lesser rulers.

In asking whether palaces so defined were intended to convey messages of power, and, if so, what those messages were, it is possible to consider two aspects of palaces. The first is that of their component parts, how these functioned as elements of the palace, and what their purposes were. Their design, it will be argued, was intended to transmit to observers messages in stone or in timber about the power of the rulers who built and used the palaces. Through the use of key examples, chapter 2 will examine how these messages can be analyzed, and what their nature may have been. The second aspect is the architectural and artistic style of palaces. The style of palaces' architecture, decoration, and furnishings may equally have been intended to convey messages about the power of rulers, as they were seen in the settings these elements provided. Chapter 3 will continue from chapter 2 in examining how these messages can be analyzed and of what they may have consisted.

CHAPTER 2

The Power of Design

In their design, palaces were often complicated buildings, or sometimes complexes of buildings, with a series of different spaces within them, and with elaborate entranceways and courtyards. Was this design based on nothing more than the need to provide appropriate facilities and amenities for the rulers and their courts? Or was it intended to convey messages of power and, if so, can we discern what messages particular palaces were designed to send? To approach these questions, it is necessary to consider the various elements of a palace's anatomy—in other words, to examine in turn its various components, such as its entrances, its halls, its apartments, and so on.

It must be appreciated, however, that defining the functions of such elements of palaces is almost never straightforward. For Christian churches and Muslim mosques, there exist liturgical texts which give some indications, sometimes quite detailed indications, of how the buildings were used for the various services and ceremonies that took place in them. Even for pagan temples, there is some evidence of how they were used in what is known of the sacrifices and other ceremonies that took place in them. But this is often not the case with palaces. From the later Middle Ages onward, there sometimes exist financial accounts for the building of palaces, which at least give clues to the functions of the rooms that the ruler was ordering to be built; and there are sometimes texts setting out what the etiquette and manners of the ruler's court should be, for example, for the Byzantine emperors in the tenth century (see below, pp. 295–97). These naturally cast some light on the use of various elements of the ruler's palace. Very often, however, especially with earlier palaces such as those of the Roman Empire, there is no real evidence beyond quite general statements. As a result, it is possible to begin to understand the functions of palaces, and why they were designed in the way that they were, only on the basis of their physical remains. And, even then, we must accept that elements of palaces probably had more than one function at any one time, and all the more so across a protracted period.

ENTRANCES AND ENTRANCE-FAÇADES

With these constraints in mind, we shall begin with the element of a palace that would have been the point of first encounter for the visiting official, or the ambassador, or any other visitor, that is the entrance. The sheer size of this component of the palace is already evident in the palace that the emperor Domitian (AD 81–96) constructed on the Palatine Hill in Rome. Here, the principal entrance was at the base of the hill, at the edge of the Roman Forum, which was the civic and religious focus of the city (Figure 2–1). This entrance was an enormous structure, measuring 32.5m in width by 23.5m in length, and it was imposingly high, for the surviving walls still rise to around 27.5m. Even today, the building towers over the Roman Forum, and the effect must have been even more dramatic in Roman times when it stood to its full height. Once visitors had passed through the entrance and climbed up the Palatine Hill to reach the main body of the palace, they would have been faced with an open forecourt, with a high façade on the far side of it, formed by the walls of the main body of the palace. Behind the centre of this façade was the so-called audience chamber, with a basilica (that is a rectangular hall with a rounded end or apse) on one side, and a side chamber of uncertain function on the other. Like the entrance, the audience chamber and the basilica, and probably the side chamber too, must have been impressively tall. The surviving walls of the audience chamber still rise to 8.9m, those of the basilica to 16.25m. Even more than the entrance, which was at the level of the Roman Forum, the great height of this façade must have contributed to the palace's dominating effect, since it was seen by those approaching the palace from the Roman Forum in conjunction with the height of the hill itself. It is not possible to be precise about the type of power being communicated by these arrangements, but it clearly involved the dominance of the emperor over his subjects, rather than any co-equal relationship with them. The entrance to the Palace of Domitian and its façade high on the Palatine Hill embodied the autocratic supremacy of the Roman emperors.

The entrance arrangements of the palace which the emperor Diocletian (286–305) built at Split (Croatia) around 305 are preserved more completely. He was in retirement when he used this palace, and he famously declined his former co-emperor Maximian's suggestion that he should return to power by referring to the cabbages which he grew with his own hands (Wilkes 1993, 1–12). Nevertheless, it seems likely—given the enormous scale of this retirement home—that he was still treated with at least some of the honors appropriate for an emperor. So it is not unreasonable to examine the elements of this palace in terms of the messages of power they could have conveyed.

An imposing gateway, the so-called Golden Gate, led through the outer walls of the complex and into the precinct of the palace. Beyond this, the approach to the palace's inner core was across a peristyle-courtyard (that is a courtyard lined with columns), which survives almost intact. Figure 2–2 shows the view of it that is available to anyone who has just crossed the palace precinct and is facing the entrance to the main body of the palace. This peristyle-courtyard is a very imposing space with its great marble columns supporting arches on either side. Through the arches on the left lies the mausoleum in which Diocletian intended himself to be buried; through those on the right, now blocked by shops and other modern structures, lies a temple. Straight in front is the entrance to the residential part of the palace.

This entrance consists of a series of openings pierced through an imposing façade, topped by a great triangular pediment. That façade is not quite in its original form, because the two openings that were originally on either side of the central opening were converted during the Renaissance into two small chapels with decorative stone structures on top of them. So originally there would have been four openings: the main arch in the center, the two on ei-

Figure 2–1: The Roman Forum, Rome (Italy). The principal entrance to the Palace of Domitian is on the right; the palace buildings on the Palatine Hill rise above it.

Figure 2–2: Peristyle-courtyard, Palace of Diocletian, Split (Croatia), looking toward the entrance to the residential part of the palace. The main arch leads through to the vestibule, the lower arch to a series of basement rooms which reflect what the layout of the palace at its upper level would have been.

ther side of it, and a lower arch below the central arch. Above the central arch, at the apex of the triangular pediment, are the remains of a stone platform, which must once have supported a statue, probably representing the former emperor in a four-horse chariot, a *quadriga*, as was used in triumphal processions (below, p. 205). But otherwise the façade still represents what was built for Diocletian. It seems likely that the façade was intended to provide a visual framework in which the former emperor could appear and greet his subjects, or at least his former subjects, or any visitors to the palace. It is probable that he would have appeared on the balcony located in front of the central opening. In that position, he would have been framed by the great arch above him, and would have looked out over subjects or visitors, who could have used the three steps around the courtyard either as seating or to stand on in tiers to greet him. The possibility that the façade was intended to present the former emperor in this way is strengthened by the evidence of a silver plate of the late fourth century, the so-called Missorium of Emperor Theodosius I (Figure 2–3). This shows the emperor enthroned under an arch reminiscent of the central arch of the façade at the far end of the peristyle-courtyard in the Palace of Diocletian, with his heirs enthroned on either side of him under openings which are themselves reminiscent of the side openings of the façade of that courtyard.

The lack of written evidence explaining how the Palace of Diocletian was used means that it is impossible to be certain that the façade and the peristyle-courtyard it faced onto were used in the way set out above. On the contrary, perhaps, rather than being intended to convey a message of power, they were designed merely for convenience. It is true that the opening underneath the main central opening led (as it still does today) down a flight of steps into a series of basement rooms. So the balcony between this opening and the main central opening above need not have been designed for emphasizing the emperor's power when he appeared on it, but rather just for the convenience of those passing through the palace. So those wishing to reach the upper parts would go up to the balcony and go through the main entrance, those wishing to go to the basement rooms would go through the lower entrance and down the stairs, those wishing to go to the mausoleum would turn off through the arches to the left, and those wishing to reach the temple would turn off through the arches to the right. It is possible. But the basement rooms, which all survive, are themselves of considerable grandeur, although of unknown function, and their scale and character make it unlikely that the lower entrance of the peristyle-courtyard was only utilitarian in function.

An example from a much later period of the comparable use of an elaborate façade as a component of the entrance to a palace is to be found in the Palace of King Pedro the Cruel (1350–69) in Seville (Spain). To enter this palace, visitors would have passed through the imposing Portada del León and across the Patio del León. On the far side of that, they would have faced a great archway, the Portada de la Monteria, pierced through a wall stretching across the courtyard. It is now sadly degraded, but there are still traces in it of the interlaced brickwork arches and the heraldic emblems of the kingdoms that Pedro ruled, those of Castile and Leon, and these would have made it look splendid in its original form. As visitors passed through it and into the Patio de la Montería beyond, the full magnificence of the façade of the Palace of Pedro the Cruel would have been apparent (Figure 2–4).

Figure 2–3: Replica of the Missorium of Emperor Theodosius I, Museo Nacional de Arte Romano, Mérida (Spain).

Figure 2–4: North façade of the Palace of Pedro the Cruel, Seville (Spain), looking from the Patio de la Montería.

The façade has been much restored in modern times, but it seems nevertheless broadly to preserve its original form, with some changes of the late fifteenth or early sixteenth century. It is made splendid by colored tilework and by intricate and delicate plasterwork decoration, forming intertwined geometric forms—the *sebka* work of Muslim art. The broad and highly decorated eaves shelter the façade, with a line of *mquarnas* below them, executed in wood. These hanging decorations, resembling elaborate icicles, were also characteristic of Muslim art. It seems plausible that Pedro the Cruel used this façade as a backdrop to his appearances in majesty, either at ground-floor level, appearing in the central opening, sheltered by the eaves above; or at the first-floor windows below the blue and white tilework, which looked out from the highly decorated and lavish room that is now called the audience chamber, the upper walls and roof of which can be seen rising above the façade.

At the palaces of Domitian and Diocletian, no written sources exist that can help to confirm the functions of their entrances, but at the Palace of Pedro the Cruel there are original inscriptions on the façade that permit interpretation of how it was used. On the wooden frieze running below the main part of the roof is an inscription with the words:

> Happiness, peace, glory, generosity, and perpetual felicity [to the master of the house]. (Hernández-Núñez and Morales 1999, 45)

Since this is set alongside castle emblems of Pedro's kingdom of Castile, it presumably referred to Pedro's reign. It was giving voice to the message of the façade, that the king who appeared against it as a backdrop had brought these immeasurable benefits to his realm. In the blue and white tilework below the wooden frieze is a longer and more explicit inscription in praise of Pedro:

> The highest, noblest and most powerful conqueror, Don Pedro, by God's grace king of Castile and León, has caused these alcázars and palaces and these façades to be built, which was done in the year 1402 [1364]. (Hernández-Núñez and Morales 1999, 45)

The plural, "alcázars and palaces," suggests that this is more than just a statement of the fact that Pedro the Cruel had built the palace of which this was the façade. Rather, it was in praise of his achievements more widely—the palaces and alcázars (the term really also means just palace) across his realm. As with the other inscriptions, it is a statement of the power and the standing he wished to be seen as having. If the king was not present, the visitor to the palace would nevertheless have received the message of his greatness, broadcast by the grandeur of the façade and by these inscriptions. If the king was there and was making an appearance in front of the façade, it would have provided an imposing—and explicit—backdrop to his majesty.

Despite the Muslim elements of its decoration, the Palace of Pedro the Cruel was the palace of a Christian ruler. So it is striking that, in the nearby Muslim-controlled province of Granada, the Palace of Comares, within the complex of palaces of the Alhambra, has an entrance façade of a similar design. The Palace of Comares, built originally by the sultan of Granada, Isma'il I (1314–25), was remodeled by his successor Muhammad V (1354–59, 1362–91). The latter was closely allied to King Pedro the Cruel, and it is possible that the entrance façade of the Palace of Comares was influenced by the façade that Pedro had built

Figure 2–5: Entrance façade of the Palace of Comares, the Alhambra, Granada (Spain), looking across the Cuarto Dorado.

at Seville. The main body of the palace was approached across an enclosed courtyard, the Cuarto Dorado (Figure 2–5), in much the same way that the subject or visitor would have crossed the peristyle-courtyard at the Palace of Diocletian. Just as there, the entrances to the Palace of Comares (the main entrance was the one to the left) were set in an impressive and highly decorated façade on the far side of this courtyard.

This façade, although restored in modern times, seems nevertheless to be basically as it was when Muhammad V built it. Like the façade of the Palace of Pedro the Cruel, it is splendid: with colored tilework around the doors and across the balcony; with elaborate and delicate patterns in plaster around the windows and across the main face; and with mqarnas decoration, here executed in plaster, below the eaves—looking like elegant icicles emerging from the surface of the façade. Moreover, the façade is notable for its wide, overhanging eaves. The two doors and the raised platform above the level of the court are not unlike the arrangement of the balcony in this position at the Palace of Diocletian. It seems probable that the sultan made his appearance in majesty on that platform, sheltered by the overhanging eaves, with the magnificence of the façade behind him.

The likelihood of this is increased by an Arabic inscription in the decorative plasterwork on the façade. This inscription, which is just above the balcony, seems to refer to the majesty of the sultan, for it is the so-called Throne verse from the Koran (II.256). This finishes with the words:

His throne extends over the heavens and the earth; . . . He is the Most High, the Supreme. (Vílchez, Guarde, and Cuenca 2011, 72)

The quotation refers to Allah, but it is easy to see how it could be transferred to the sultan. As the sultan appeared on the balcony or platform, sheltered by the eaves and with the magnificence of the façade behind him, those standing in the Cuarto Dorado would have read above him this reference to Allah's all-dominating position, and would no doubt have felt impelled to apply the words, "Most High," "Supreme," to the ruler who stood or sat in front of them. The message conveyed was one of ideological power: the ruler on a level with, or at least closely related to, Allah as the ruler of the whole universe. The façade could thus have been a sort of stage set for expressing and reinforcing the ruler's power, and even more so when, as here at the Palace of Comares and at the Palace of Pedro the Cruel, inscriptions made explicit the type of power the ruler was claiming.

STAIRCASES

Staircases could be an important part of palaces, especially where the most important rooms were on the first and second floors; and they were another aspect of palace design that could convey messages of power by being used in almost theatrical ways to focus attention on the ruler and to emphasize his superiority. Staircases not only permitted the ruler to place himself above his subjects and visitors, but they could also be designed to facilitate processions involving the ruler which served in their turn to focus attention on him and his power.

Imposing staircases occur already in the earliest palaces with which this book is concerned. The balcony in the peristyle-courtyard of the Palace of Diocletian may, as we have noted, have been intended to present an image of the ruler's elevated power, and it was accessible via a staircase (Figure 2–2). But, from the thirteenth century onward, the staircase became a major element of palace architecture, developing as a full-blown ceremonial staircase (an *escalier d'honneur*).

After James I "The Conqueror," king of Aragon (1213–76), split his realm between his two sons, southwestern France and the island of Mallorca came to form the Kingdom of Majorca. Its first king, James II (1276–1311), began the building of a sophisticated palace at Perpignan (France). This palace, known as the Palace of the Kings of Majorca, to a large extent survives today. It is built around a square courtyard, with ranges on each side. On the west side, there are chambers and a gallery, evidently intended for ceremonial appearances, facing out on to the courtyard. On the south side, there is a substantial hall, with what were probably lodgings on the north side. The focus of the courtyard, however, is provided by the two chapels, one above the other. These formed a sort of chapel tower on the east side, dominating the other buildings and the courtyard. It had the king's lodgings on one side of it and the queen's lodgings on the other, so it was evidently the most important side of the courtyard. The Galérie Sainte-Florentine ran along this side of the courtyard on two storys, the middle section of its first story further raised to allow access to the upper chapel. The gallery had open arches along it so that it offered a view on to the courtyard, while at the same time permitting those in the courtyard to see processions moving along the gallery. It also provided access to the upper chapel which, judging from its lavish decoration, was the more important of the two super-imposed chapels. Access to the gallery was by way of two imposing staircases, leading up to it from either side of the courtyard (Figure 2–6). The width and shallow slope of these strongly suggest that they were ceremonial staircases, designed to accommodate formal processions from the courtyard up to the king's and queen's chambers and to the upper chapel. The balcony immediately in front of the west door of that chapel must have offered an excellent space for the ruler to pause in this elevated position, backed by the power of God as represented by the chapel.

The staircases in the Palace of the Kings of Majorca are modern reconstructions, although the gradient and width of the originals are not in doubt because of the scars left on the masonry when they were demolished. For a nearly contemporary ceremonial staircase in Paris, there are no remains surviving, but there is a visual representation. When Philip IV the Fair, king of France (1285–1314), remodeled and extended his principal palace, the Palais de la Cité on the island in the River Seine at the heart of Paris, the staircase known as the Grands Degrés (Great Staircase) featured prominently in this work. A visitor would have passed through the Grande Porte of the palace into the Great Court beyond it; then almost immediately opposite would have appeared the Grands Degrés, giving access to the main body of the palace. It led up to the Merchants' Gallery, which in turn provided access

Figure 2–6: Courtyard, Palace of the Kings of Majorca, Perpignan (France), looking east toward the chapel tower.

Figure 2–7: Palais de la Cité, represented on the Parliament Altarpiece (*Retable du Parlement*) of *c.*1453–54, Museum of the Louvre, Paris (France). Detail showing the Grands Degrés (1), the exterior of the Merchants' Gallery (2), the statues of King Louis of Navarre (3) and King Philip of France (4), and the niche for the destroyed statue of Enguerrand de Marigny (5). Cf. Figure 2–33.

to the king's chamber to the left, and the great hall and the rooms around it to the right (see plan, Figure 2–33). The visual representation of this staircase is part of a painting of *c.*1453–54 called the Parliament Altarpiece (*Retable du Parlement*) (Figure 2–7).

The painting shows the Grands Degrés leading from the ground level of the Great Court up to the Merchants' Gallery. The double doorway at the top of the staircase was magnificently decorated with sculptures. In the center was a statue of King Philip IV the Fair himself, and to the left, a statue of his son and heir, Louis, king of Navarre. To the right was an empty niche, which originally had a statue of his minister, Enguerrand de Marigny, removed in 1315 after his disgrace and execution. The Grands Degrés represented a very imposing way for a subject or visitor to enter the palace, or for the king himself to move to and from it, or indeed around it. For, when he was to be present at a feast in the Great Hall, it seems likely that he would have come from his apartment along the Merchants' Gallery, down the Grands Degrés, across the Great Court, and up another set of steps leading him into the great hall (Figure 2–33), down which he would have processed to take his place at the high table. The Grands Degrés added grandeur to the king's ceremonial movements, gave him the imposing backdrop of the sculptured door with its figures celebrating his rule, and allowed any of his subjects gathered in the courtyard to observe those movements.

Staircases as ceremonial components of palaces came to be increasingly common. When Charles V, king of France (1364–80), reconstructed the Palace of the Louvre, on the north bank of the River Seine just inside the walls of Paris, this too had a magnificent spiral staircase known as the Grande Vis, which led up from the courtyard to the queen's apartments on the first floor, and then on to the king's apartments on the second floor (see plan, Figure 2–31). This was not a staircase at right angles to the building like the Grands Degrés at the Palais de la Cité, but rather a spiral staircase in hexagonal form. It was innovative by virtue of being built on the outside of the building rather than within it. Although nothing survives of it, it was clearly ornate, for it is known to have been decorated with a number of sculptured figures. These represented: two sergeants-at-arms at ground level; the princes of the blood (i.e., those of the king's family) at first-floor level; and the king and queen themselves with their male children at second-floor level. In the vault of the staircase were carved the royal arms. So, even when the king was not there, the staircase would have conveyed a message in stone about his rule and his family. When he was there, it would have created an imposing way for him and the queen to move between the levels of the palace and to come down into the courtyard, perhaps to process across to the chapel or the great hall on the far side of the courtyard. If the staircase was like the staircase of similar date which survives at the palace of Saumur on the River Loire (France), built by a prince of the blood in imitation of the king's reconstructed palace at the Louvre, then it would have been an open fretwork staircase in stone, with wide window openings, so that it would have been possible to watch the king and queen as they moved ceremonially up and down it (Figure 2–8). The Saumur staircase gives some impression of the richness of the sculptured decoration that must have existed on the Grande Vis at the Louvre, and that would no doubt once have been glowing with paintwork.

One of the grandest of such staircases to survive, however, is the Staircase of the Giants, built shortly after 1483 at the Palace of the Doge in Venice (Italy). The original entrance to this palace was through the towering and elaborate mid-fifteenth-century Arch of Foscari, and so into the courtyard of the palace. From there, the Staircase of the Giants led up to the doge's apartment on the first floor, from which access could be gained via a magnificent internal staircase to the great meeting rooms on the third floor (Figure 2–9). The combination of the Arch of Foscari and the Staircase of the Giants provided a truly stunning entry to the palace. As the doge mounted the sumptuous and elaborately decorated staircase, or descended it to take part in festivals, or received visitors standing at the top of it, no one can have doubted the message it was conveying: the dominance and power of the doge and of the city he represented.

Entrances, whether great gateways or ceremonial staircases, thus seem to have been intended to emphasize the dominating position of the ruler above his subjects. This they did by offering theatrical backdrops to enhance views of him, or by placing him in an elevated position relative to his subjects, or by providing him with a staircase that led him up above his subjects to his apartments and his meeting rooms on the upper floors of the palace. The message of power being projected must surely have been of some form of ideological power.

Figure 2–8: Spiral staircase, Château of Saumur, Saumur (France).

Figure 2–9: Arch of Foscari, Palace of the Doge, Venice (Italy). The arch, under its great superstructure, is on the left, leading from the courtyard of St. Marco to the Staircase of the Giants on the right.

COURTYARDS AND PORTICOED GALLERIES

The courtyards themselves, however, into which the entrances often opened, could convey a more ambiguous message. These courtyards were often peristyle-courtyards, lined with columns providing covered walks along each side, rather like the cloister of a monastery. Such peristyle-courtyards went back a long way in the tradition of ancient Greek houses of greater and lesser grandeur, and they continued as a major feature of the design of Roman palaces. When one of the greatest of the Roman emperors, Hadrian (117–38), built his enormous palace, known as Hadrian's Villa, at Tivoli (Italy), the peristyle-courtyard was one of its features, especially in the section known as the Piazza d'Oro (Figure 2–10). Stone bases still visible in the foreground are those of the columns that would have lined the sides of the courtyard, roofed over against the side walls to provide the covered walks, sheltered from sun and rain. The center of the courtyard was embellished with a water feature, remains of which have been archaeologically excavated and are visible in the turf.

Hadrian was extremely powerful and extremely wealthy, and the construction of his enormous palace was hardly an exercise in humility. The Piazza d'Oro had an imposing entrance in the form of a grand vestibule. Peristyle-courtyards were, of course, a convenient feature of layouts of residences, be they great or small, because their covered walkways provided shaded and sheltered access to rooms on the four sides of the courtyard. But they may nevertheless have been intended to convey a message of power just as much as entrances and stairways did, and the message in this case may have had more to do with personal

Figure 2–10: Piazza d'Oro, Hadrian's Villa, Tivoli (Italy), showing the stone bases of the columns which formed the covered walkways around this rectangular space, and the remains of the elaborate water feature in the now grassy area at the center. The vestibule, which was the entrance to the piazza, is off the image to the left.

Figure 2–11: Courtyard, Palace of the Lions, the Alhambra, Granada (Spain) after refurbishment in 2012, looking west with the lion fountain in the foreground.

power than ideological power. For, the fact that peristyle-courtyards were a feature of relatively ordinary houses as well as palaces raises the possibility that the emperor was making at least a token gesture to represent himself as at one with his subjects. Just as they had peristyle-courtyards in their mostly more modest dwellings, so too did the emperor in his great palace.

A similar message may have been being conveyed by the peristyle-courtyard at the Palace of the Lions in the Alhambra (Spain). Although the style of this palace, built by the sultan of Granada, Muhammad V (1354–59, 1362–91), is superficially different, the fundamental resemblance to a Roman peristyle-courtyard is nevertheless strong, with the covered, porticoed walkways on each side of the courtyard, a water feature at the center, with the water flowing from the famous lion fountain, and rooms opening off the courtyard—just as at the Piazza d'Oro of Hadrian's Villa (Figure 2–11). For all the magnificence of this courtyard, the message of power being conveyed may nevertheless have been one of humility just as at the Piazza d'Oro of Hadrian's Villa. For the basic layout of a courtyard in this way was equally part of traditional Andalusian house design of the fourteenth century, no doubt in itself inherited from the time when Spain was part of the Roman Empire.

In the case of the Palace of the Lions, the issue is complicated by a mystery as to its function—some have seen it, for example, as a scholarly center rather than a residence. But no such mystery applies to the adjacent Palace of Comares, originally built, as we have seen, as a residence for the sultan of Granada, Isma'il I (1314–25). It too has a courtyard, although without covered, porticoed walkways on all sides as at the Piazza d'Oro or the Palace of the Lions. Nevertheless, the effect is similar, with a water feature in the center and rooms open-

Figure 2–12: Courtyard, Palace of Comares, the Alhambra, Granada (Spain), with the Sala de la Barca at the far end and the Hall of the Ambassadors rising behind it.

ing off the courtyard (Figure 2–12). The suite of rooms opening off the main short side, which can be seen in the center of the figure, consists of the Sala de la Barca, which was probably the sultan's apartment, for it had a private oratory, bed-niches, and a privy, and a great reception hall, the Hall of the Ambassadors, beyond it. The latter is visible rising above and behind the porticoed walkway. The rooms along the two long sides of the courtyard constitute four self-contained apartments, with bed-niches at the ends of long rooms, and these were probably the apartments for the sultan's four wives, the maximum number allowed by Muslim law. In this way, the courtyard would have mirrored the more modest courtyards of the sultan's subjects and would have conveyed the message that he was just one of them, despite the magnificence with which he was able to build.

Peristyle-courtyards could, however, convey quite different messages of power. After the end of the Roman Empire in the West in the course of the fifth century, the most powerful kingdom to emerge in Western Europe was that ruled by the barbarian people called the Franks, especially under the rule of Charlemagne (768–814), who was crowned emperor in 800 by the pope in Rome. Imitating the Roman Empire was an important theme of Charlemagne's power, and the lead bulls on his documents even bore the inscription, "Renewal of the Roman Empire" (Nelson 1994, 70). Like a Roman emperor before him, he was—according to his biographer Einhard's *Life*—a prolific builder of palaces, including the Palace of Ingelheim, located close to the River Rhine a few miles from Mainz (Germany) (Halphen 2007, ch. 17). The basic form of what Charlemagne built at Ingelheim, as shown in the reconstruction (Figure 2–13), is still clearly discernible, and, even though it was in subsequent centuries absorbed into the village of Ingelheim, it has been extensively excavated. A mag-

Power of Design   25

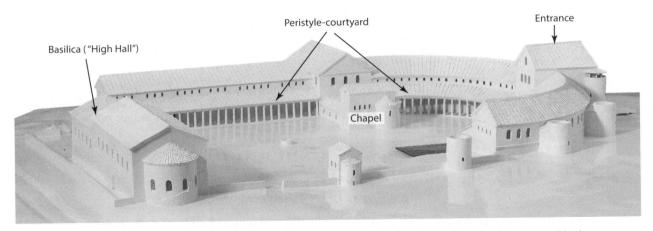

Figure 2–13: Reconstruction model, Palace of Ingelheim (Germany), showing the palace as built by the emperor Charlemagne (768–814). The peristyle-courtyard, which was never completed, extends from the basilica to the stilted semicircle on the right of the image. The entrance, now absorbed into the medieval Heidenheimer Tor, rises above the stilted semicircle.

Figure 2–14: Reconstructed bases of Roman-style round columns and attached piers, Palace of Ingelheim (Germany). These supported the roof of the covered walkway that ran round the peristyle-courtyard. The steps are a reconstruction of those that originally led up to the principal entrance to the palace, which was subsequently absorbed into the twelfth-century Heidenheimer Tor. The battlements belong to that period.

nificent entrance, now absorbed into the Heidenheimer Tor, led into a peristyle-courtyard, apparently unfinished on one side, which terminated in the form of a stilted semicircle. The columns supporting the covered walkway around it on the inner side have been recovered in the excavations and their bases have been restored to show the original arrangement (Figure 2–14).

The historical context for the palace's design and construction, that is, Charlemagne's assumption of the imperial title in 800 and his deliberate harking back to Roman culture in his reforms of education and Church, strongly suggest that building such a palace was a deliberate statement of the ruler's attitudes and aspirations. It was to be the palace of a new Roman emperor, and the architecture used was intended to convey that message loudly and clearly. So it seems likely that the primary message of power conveyed by this peristyle-courtyard was that of Charlemagne as an emperor every bit on a level with his Roman predecessors. The message here was therefore one more of ideological than of personal power.

Peristyle-courtyards as tools of ideological power could be explicit in this respect, as was the case with the courtyard of the palace built at Urbino in Italy by the lord, later duke, Federico of Montefeltro (1444–74). As visitors passed under the decorated archway which formed the imposing entrance to this palace, the first thing to stand out in the imposing peristyle-courtyard beyond would have been the Latin inscription, set in large, clear brass letters (Figure 2–15). This reads:

> Federico, duke of Urbino, count of Montefeltro and Casteldurante, Knight of the Holy Roman Church and Commander of the Italic Federation built this house, raised from its foundations to celebrate his glory and that of posterity. More than once he fought in war, six times he united the ranks, eight times he put the enemy to flight and, winner of all battles, he has increased his dominion. His justice, clemency, liberalism and devotion are equal to and honour with peace his victories. (quoted by Cavalera and Cucco 2007, 23)

Here was an ideological statement of the Federico of Montefeltro's power, deriving from his international status, his military success, and his virtues. Its prominence in the peristyle-courtyard suggests that it was intended to convey a message of power.

Not all Roman palaces were arranged around a peristyle-courtyard, for others consisted instead of a solid block with porticoed galleries (that is, galleries with arches along them) around it, or at least down one side of it. There are two classic examples of this type of Roman palace. The first is the palace built by the Roman emperor Nero on the hill opposite the Palatine Hill in Rome after the great fire in that city in AD 64. This palace, known as the Golden House (*Domus Aurea*), was destroyed after Nero's death, but one wing of it (the Esquiline wing) survives, at least in part, and has been excavated (Figure 2–16). Although a peristyle-courtyard is part of this layout, it is by no means the dominant element, which is rather suites of rooms arranged as a compact mass with a porticoed gallery, providing communication between them. The effect of this mass of masonry, seen from the south in particular, must have been very imposing, especially when one realizes that an element of this view was the polygonal courtyard with most probably a gigantic statue of the emperor.

The second classic example of a Roman palace is the main residential block of the Palace of Diocletian at Split (Figure 2–17). Although the principal rooms survive only fragmentarily, they can be reconstructed on the basis of their basements which survive below ground level, the shapes and size of which must have been followed by the rooms above. Like the Esquiline Wing of the Golden House, they formed a compact block of rooms, with a porticoed gallery serving as the principal means of communication between them. Remains of that gallery are clearly visible in the sea-front façade of the palace as it is at present, and even more so as it was drawn by Robert Adam in the eighteenth century (Figure 2–18).

Figure 2–15: Courtyard, Ducal Palace, Urbino (Italy), with the inscription in brass letters running around it above the arches and above the first-floor windows.

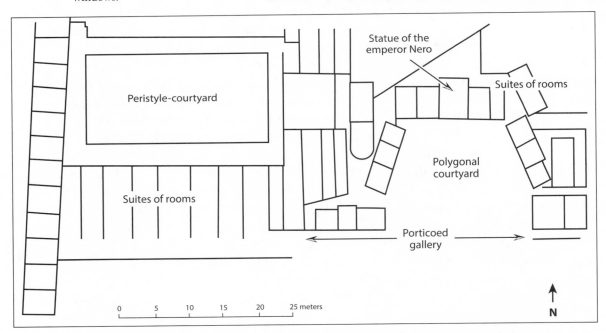

Figure 2–16: Diagrammatic plan, Golden House (*Domus Aurea*), Rome (Italy), showing the layout of part of the Esquiline wing with its porticoed gallery (after MacDonald 1982–6, I, fig. 24).

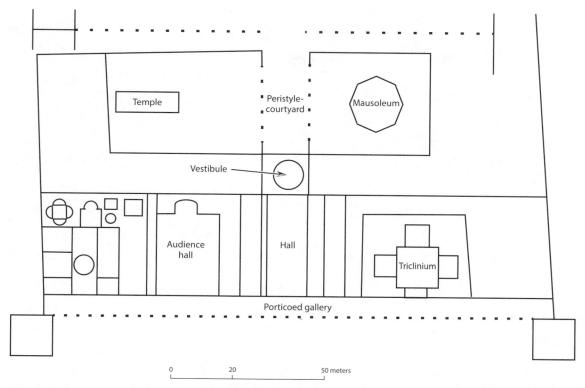

Figure 2–17: Diagrammatic plan, Palace of Diocletian, Split (Croatia), showing the main residential block and the porticoed gallery running along the seaward side of it. The openings between it and the rooms behind it have not been shown. Note also the disposition of the peristyle-courtyard, vestibule, temple, and mausoleum (cf. Figure 2–2) (after Ćurčić 2010, 26, fig. 14).

Figure 2–18: South front, Palace of Diocletian, Split (Croatia), showing the remains of the arches of the porticoed gallery on the seaward side as they were in the late eighteenth century (after Adam 1764, plate VII).

Figure 2–19: Imperial palace, Gelnhausen (Germany), seen from the Watch-Tower, showing the main façade with its porticoed form.

Porticoed galleries were used by the later German rulers, who were—like Charlemagne—crowned by the popes as emperors, or at any rate Holy Roman Emperors, so that they too had an incentive to see their realms as revivals of the Roman Empire and to design their palaces accordingly. The particular drive of the king of Germany and Holy Roman Emperor, Frederick Barbarossa (1152–90), to create such an empire may have been given expression in the palace he built at the trading city of Gelnhausen, which he had founded in the valley of the River Main (Germany).

Figure 2–19 shows the main façade facing the entrance court, with a ground-floor stage, now partly buried, the top of its entrance showing between the two benches, and a first floor with groups of arched openings and with a decorated entrance archway above the ground-floor entrance just mentioned. The striking aspect of this façade is its Roman character, with its Roman-style columns and capitals, and the neatly formed voussoirs (that is, radiating stone blocks) of its arches. The architect's aim surely must have been to create a palace façade reflecting that of Roman portico-type palaces, and conveying the message that Frederick Barbarossa was as much an emperor as his Roman predecessors. Here then the message would seem to have been one of ideological power—the ruler presented as an imitation of his Roman predecessors with a palace in the Roman manner.

TRICLINIA AND HALLS

Another component of palaces that had the capability of reflecting and creating a ruler's ideological power was the *triclinium* (dining room). The Latin word meant in origin "an arrangement of couches on three sides of a central table for the purposes of dining" (Glare 1990, s.v. triclinium), for it was the practice, amongst the upper levels of Roman society, to eat in a reclining position, propped up on one's elbow. By a process of transference of its meaning the word came to be applied to the dining room itself. Dining, however, was certainly not the only one of such a room's functions, which included acting as a hall and a reception-room. The scale of the triclinium could be a striking aspect of the design of the palace. In the Palace of Domitian, a contemporary, Statius, in a poem written in AD 93 or 94, describes what was probably the triclinium as follows:

> I think I recline with Jupiter in mid-heaven . . . An edifice august, huge; magnificent with a hundred columns . . . The view travels upward, the tired vision scarcely reaches the summit, and you would think that it was the golden ceiling of the sky. Here . . . Caesar has bidden the Roman elders, and the ranks of *equites* recline together at a thousand tables. (quoted by MacDonald 1982–86, I, 61)

"Caesar" in this passage is the emperor, while the *equites* were a particular level of the higher reaches of Roman society (Hornblower and Spawforth 2003, 530–32). The room in question is probably the triclinium, because those present are said to "recline," presumably on eating couches. The room that archaeologists have identified as the triclinium in the remains of the Palace of Domitian is indeed enormous, measuring 29.05m x 31.64m. Although its walls are now only stubs, there is evidence to suggest that it was very high and lavishly decorated. It had an apse in its south wall, which would have provided an appropriately prominent place for the emperor's couch, at the center of the attention of the company. Although the number of a thousand for the tables must surely be a poetic exaggeration, the triclinium certainly struck the poet as a very impressive space, and one, moreover, that reminded him of the heavens and of the chief of the gods, Jupiter.

Near Piazza Armerina (Sicily), there are remains of what must have been a magnificent palace, the Villa Romana di Casale, notable for the survival of large areas of its floor mosaics. Although nothing is known of its history, it is clear from its style that it belongs to the early fourth century, and its size and richness point to its having been built for someone who was either an emperor or of comparable status. A prominent part of it consists of a triconch room (that is a room with three conches or apses), interpreted as a triclinium, with a courtyard with rounded sides (a sigma-courtyard) leading into it (Figure 2–20; cf. Figure 6–18). This courtyard, with its own apse, may well have been intended to provide the setting for the emperor (if this was an imperial palace) and his train to enter the triclinium in state.

Although it is not certain that the Villa Romana di Casale was intended for an emperor, it is certain that the Great Palace at Constantinople was an imperial residence. It too had a triconch-room with a sigma-courtyard, built by the emperor Theophilus (829–42). The message of ideological power that could be conveyed by such a room had earlier been carried to great heights in the room in the Great Palace that the *Book of the Ceremonies* calls

Figure 2–20: "Sigma-courtyard," Villa Romana di Casale, near Piazza Armerina (Sicily), looking from the entrance of the triclinium toward the apse of the sigma-courtyard (see also Figure 6–18).

Figure 2–21: Interior of the vestibule. Palace of Diocletian, Split (Croatia), with the entrance from the peristyle-courtyard behind the viewer.

the Golden Triclinium (*Chrysotriklinos*). This was built—or perhaps rebuilt—by the emperor Justin II (565–78). As with most other parts of the Great Palace, no trace of it has survived, but a fair amount is known about it from the *Book of the Ceremonies*. This shows that it was octagonal in plan, with apses on each side, opening on to a central space with a dome lit by sixteen windows. It was in some respects the heart of the palace. Immediately to the left of the main apse opened the chapel of St. Theodore, which served as a vestry for the emperor, and the treasury. On the south side opened the private apartments of the emperor and empress. As befitted a triclinium, the Golden Triclinium was used for feasts, both large affairs and more intimate occasions, and it included a breakfast room, where the emperor's children could come to eat dessert in the company of select guests at the end of feasts. Entertainments, including ballets, might be performed during the meal. It was also used as an imperial reception hall. When it was fulfilling this function, the emperor entered it from his private apartment and sat on a golden chair beside the main throne in the center of the main apse opposite the entrance, where he received those whom his minister, the *logothete*, brought to him. It is true that the Golden Triclinium was a room that provided access to other parts of the palace, so that its octagonal shape might have been simply for convenience, rather than with any intention of conveying a message of the emperor's ideological power. But the scale and decoration of the room, which included a mosaic of Christ over the emperor's throne, make this unlikely.

Indeed, the same argument—that the room was merely a practical access point to other parts of the palace—has been advanced regarding the vestibule in the Palace of Diocletian. This was a room situated immediately behind the central opening in the entrance façade, the one leading to the upper and principal parts of the palace (Figure 2–21). It was, however, an enormous circular room, with a great dome that originally may have covered it entirely or may have had a circular opening, or *oculus*, at its crown to let in light. It has now been stripped of all its decoration and most of the finishing of its windows and doors; but the surviving masonry and brickwork show how impressive it must have been in its original form. As with the Golden Triclinium at Constantinople, this too could be interpreted as merely a useful space, which gave access through its various doors to other parts of the palace. But it is difficult to entertain that interpretation given the vestibule's scale and grandeur. Surely, its principal purpose must have been to send to those coming to the palace a message of power, to reinforce how grand and how dominating was the former emperor who had built it. Perhaps he would even have been enthroned under the soaring dome when important visitors came through the main arch in the façade and entered the vestibule, just as the emperor was enthroned in the Golden Triclinium. As with the vestibule at Split, the grandeur of that room, as the *Book of the Ceremonies* reports it, makes it difficult to accept that it was primarily a utilitarian space.

Triclinia were not found widely outside the Byzantine Empire in the Middle Ages, but they were used in the pope's Lateran Palace in Rome. This was substantially enlarged by Pope Leo III (795–816), who added in particular a triclinium which, according to his contemporary biography, was "greater than all other *triclinia*" (Duchesne and Vogel 1886–1957, 3–4). On the basis of this text and of what archaeology has been possible on the site of the Lateran Palace, the plan and position of this triclinium of Leo III was as shown in Figure 2–22.

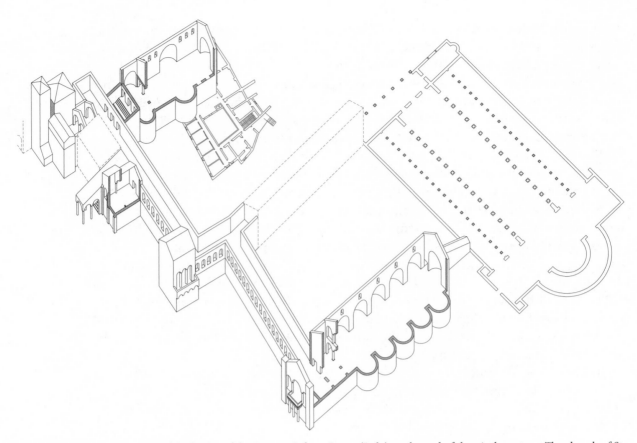

Figure 2–22: Reconstruction of the layout of the Lateran Palace, Rome (Italy), at the end of the ninth century. The church of St. John-in-the-Lateran appears on the right. Next to it is Gregory IV's triclinium, the Hall of the Couches, while the triconch triclinium of Leo III is at the top on the left.

The importance of triclinia at the Lateran Palace was underlined by the construction by Pope Gregory IV (827–44) of another and even larger triclinium there, the Hall of the Couches. This was a long hall with a main apse on one short end and a series of apses down each of the long sides, evidently intended to accommodate eating couches. As with Leo III's triclinium, neither do we have any idea what this enormous room was used for, but the fact that it was directly connected to the palace church of St. John-in-the-Lateran suggests that it was important for ceremonies of a religious character, no doubt as well as for feasts of an equally formal character.

BASILICAS AND HALLS

Not all the great spaces in Roman palaces were in the form of triclinia. There were also basilicas, which were long, rectangular halls with just one apse, on the short side opposite the entrance. We have come across such a basilica as the reception hall at the Palace of Domitian. That one is in ruins, but a basilica still standing to its full height, although restored in

Figure 2–23: The basilica in the former imperial palace, Trier (Germany), now converted to a church, looking from the entrance toward the apse.

modern times and converted into a church, formed part of the Roman imperial palace at Trier (Germany). Figure 2–23 shows the interior, looking toward the apse at the far short end. As so often with palaces, we have virtually no information about what a room like this was used for, but presumably there was judicial business, as seems to have been the case with basilicas that were not located in palaces, such as the Basilica Ulpia in Trajan's Forum in Rome (below, pp. 184, 185). Presumably there were also meetings and ceremonies involving the emperor occupying a throne in the apse, where he could have dominated the hall and been the focus of attention. That the focus of such a building was on the person of the emperor is suggested by the Basilica of Constantine and Maxentius in the Roman Forum, an enormous structure, which had in its apse a colossal statue of the emperor Constantine (Claridge 1998, 115–16). So the emperor dominated the basilica from the apse even in his absence through this stone representation of him.

That one of the functions of a basilica was to reflect and create the ideological power of the emperor, in terms of his relationship to the divine, is suggested by the fact that basilicas were one of the most common forms of Christian church buildings from the earliest period. In his seventh-century *Etymologies*, a work that defined the meanings of words, the Spanish scholar Isidore of Seville (d. 636) wrote that the word "basilica" was first used in the context of royal palaces but was now applied to churches "because in them worship and sacrifices are offered to God, Ruler of all" (Lavin 1962, 17). Just as it is assumed that the apse of a palace basilica held the throne of the emperor, it is certain that in a Christian church the apse held the high altar where the deity was most immediately present, with the decoration of the half-dome above often featuring the Christian cross, or Jesus Christ in Majesty represented as a ruler, just like the secular ruler sitting on his throne in the apse of the palace basilica.

A basilica of Roman type has been excavated at the palace at Ingelheim. Like the basilica at Trier, it was a rectangular stone building with an apse in the short wall opposite the entrance. Apart from the excavations, which have only revealed the lower walls of this basilica and rather more of the apse, a certain amount of information about its use can be derived from a Latin work, *The Poem on Louis the Pious*, written in the early ninth century by a writer named Ermold the Black, who was at the time in exile from the court of the Frankish emperor Louis the Pious (814–40), the son of Charlemagne. Since Ermold's poem was written to praise the emperor and perhaps to reestablish his relationship with him, it can be surmised that it represented the ruler in as favorable a light as possible. Nevertheless, the pictures it paints must have been believable ones. One of those pictures is a remarkably vivid account of how Louis received at Ingelheim a Danish king, Harald, his queen, and a large number of his Danish subjects (Faral 1932, lines 2164–2509). Harald asked to be baptized a Christian, and this was granted to both himself and his queen. Louis is said to have "received him with joy" in his "high hall" (*celsa aula*), presumably the basilica, and ordered that a meal be brought and served. He then arranged the baptisms of his guests and a mass in the church (presumably the palace church at Ingelheim) for them to take part in. There then followed a feast, presumably also in the basilica, at which the newly baptized Harald sat with the emperor, his queen Judith, and his son and heir Lothar. Ermold comments that the Danes admired the feast, the emperor's warriors, his ministers, and the young men around him (Faral 1932, lines 2358–59). Clearly, this was a ceremonial feast with the purpose of impressing the royal visitors, just as we can imagine feasts in Roman palaces being ceremonial and intended to convey such a message of power. The basilica, like the triclinia of Roman palaces, was a dining room, as well as the place where the ruler, as Ermold wrote, handed down judgments to his subjects and considered affairs of state (Faral 1932, lines 2166–67).

The basilica at Ingelheim clearly was built in the tradition of the basilicas of Roman palaces. There was, however, a different tradition of creating grand spaces, which originated in the lands outside the Roman Empire. This was the tradition of building great timber halls as components of the palaces of rulers. These halls are known only from archaeological excavations, which rarely give any detailed information about how they might have been used; and—worse still—the lack of written sources about the Germanic and Scandinavian kingdoms during the period of the Roman Empire and after it came to an end in Western Europe make it difficult even to be sure when we are or are not dealing with a ruler's palace.

There is, however, some information available for the site of Yeavering in the early medieval kingdom of Northumbria, because it is mentioned by the early eighth-century writer

Bede in his *Ecclesiastical History of the English People*. The mention in question is extremely brief, but Bede does at least specify that it was a "royal palace" (*villa regia*), where the Christian missionary Paulinus came to the king and queen, soon after the former's conversion to Christianity in 627, and spent thirty-six days baptizing people in the river there (Colgrave and Mynors 1991, book 2, ch. 14). Fortunately, the name, which Bede gives in the form *Gefrin*, has survived as the place-name Yeavering. Aerial photographs of the place in question showed a complex of structures appearing under the turf, and excavations revealed a series of timber buildings and earthen banks. These left no doubt that, at least in the most developed of its several phases of building, this was a complex palace. So the great timber hall at the center of the site (Figure 6–20) was almost certainly a royal hall with functions that may not have been dissimilar to those of the stone basilicas in Roman palaces and in the Carolingian palace at Ingelheim.

Nor is this the only example of a great timber hall in the context of a royal residence. Another place for which there is some written confirmation that it was such a residence is Lejre (Denmark), which later medieval writers identified as the royal center of the Skjöldung kings of the Danes. There, the remains of postholes discovered in the course of excavation showed that there was an enormous timber hall, measuring no less than 48m long, with curving sides giving it a width varying from 11m in the middle to 8.5m at the ends. Around the walls were postholes for timbers set in a raking way to support the building, and the angle of the rake of the postholes suggested that the roof rose to a height of 10m. Inside the walls were more postholes, suggesting that the interior was divided into three aisles by lines of posts, with some subdivisions across the central aisle. There was a fireplace at one end and a cellar at the other. Dated to the mid-seventh century, this was certainly an imposing building. Later excavations revealed that it was probably the successor to a comparably large hall built nearby in the mid-sixth century, this one measuring 45m long by 7m wide.

There are tantalizing clues in written sources as to how such halls may have functioned. According to the Old Norse *Saint Olaf's Saga*, there was in the royal residence that King Olaf built at Nidaros (Trondheim, Norway) "a large hall for his retinue." Evidently, the hall was used to accommodate the king's retinue (or his war band). His "high-seat" stood in the center of it and "whenever men of importance came to see the king, they were well taken care of." So the hall was also for receiving and entertaining guests, no doubt including guests who could be described as ambassadors. It was in addition a drinking hall, or a mead-hall, for, the saga continues, "fires were lit [in the central hearth] on such occasions when the ale was drunk" (quoted by Niles 2007, 78–79).

That such a hall could in itself serve to convey messages of power for the ruler who built it is most clearly suggested in the epic poem, *Beowulf*, written down in the Old English form in which we know it around the year 1000. The first part tells the story of a hall called Heorot, how it was built by Hrothgar, king of the Danes, how it was attacked by the monster Grendel, and how it was defended by the hero Beowulf. The story, which relates events supposed to have taken place centuries earlier, probably in the sixth century AD, is certainly fictional, and it is unlikely (although not impossible) that the hall of Heorot ever existed. But the image that the poet depicts may nevertheless provide us with clues as to the importance of such halls.

The poet describes the circumstances of the hall's construction. When King Hrothgar, the poet tells us, was successful in battle and increased his position of power, he decided to have built "a huge mead-hall (*medoærn*), a house greater / than men on earth ever had heard of" (Alexander 2003, lines 64–9, Fulk, Bjork, and Niles 2008). There seems to have been a clear link in the poet's mind between Hrothgar's power and the construction of Heorot. When the political situation turned sour, he hints, the hall was burned down. Nor was this link between hall and power exclusive to Heorot in the poet's mind, for of Hrothgar's predecessor, Scyld Shefing, he records that he harrassed his enemies and many nations, specifically by taking away the mead-benches (*meodosetla*) which would have been in their halls (Fulk et al. 2008, lines 4–5). The implication is plainly that the halls were the symbols of the power of Scyld's enemies, and he made them fear him by attacking their halls. Heorot was especially appropriate as a symbol of power, because of the richness of its materials and decoration. Anyone approaching it would see "the ample eaves adorned with gold" of a king's home, the radiance of which "lighted the lands of the world." And, inside it, they would find the walls glowing with "gold-embroidered tapestries" (Alexander 2003, lines 306–11, 995–96).

As *Saint Olaf's Saga* makes clear, King Olaf's hall at Nidaros was used to receive guests and also for drinking ale. The use of Heorot is similarly described in *Beowulf*. It was in Heorot that Beowulf and his followers were received when they came to offer their help to King Hrothgar to deal with Grendel's attacks. There, they were offered "bright mead" when they arrived, and there they were entertained to an evening of drinking, during which Hrothgar's queen herself served mead from the horn (Alexander 2003, lines 491–665). The Roman historian Tacitus, writing in the first century AD, implies that drinking—or at any rate feasting, which certainly involved drinking—was a formal, perhaps a ritualized, activity among the Germanic barbarians, in the course of which there took place discussions of feuds, marriage alliances, and the selection of leaders, and decisions were made as to whether to go to war (Mattingly and Handforth 1970, Germania, ch. 22). Drinking, then, was more than just a convivial activity; it was a social ritual with a close relationship to power. For this reason too, the hall where drinking took place, the hall often referred to by the Old English composite word mead-hall (*meduheall*) to emphasize this function, was a tool of power in the ruler's hands.

Clearly, the stone hall of a Carolingian palace of around 800 could have had a similar function. When Charlemagne received the pope, Leo III, in the hall of his newly constructed palace at Paderborn, he invited him to a great feast with drinking:

In the middle of the high hall they celebrate a great banquet.
Golden bowls overflow with Falernian wine.
Charlemagne and Leo, the highest prelate in the world,
Dine together and quaff sparkling wine from their bowls.
After the joyful repast and much drinking,
Kind Charlemagne gives many gifts to great Leo

(freely translating Brockmann et al. 1966, 96; Paul E. Dutton 2004, 65).

The giving of gifts in the hall of Paderborn was certainly a formal activity, embodying in some way expressions of power, or at least of policy. At Heorot, too, King Hrothgar 'shared out rings and treasure at the feast' (Fulk et al. 2008, lines 80–1).

The hall, as described in *Saint Olaf's Saga*, was also the place where the king's "high seat," or his throne, was placed. In *Beowulf*, Hrothgar's throne was also in his hall. For, the poet writes that even when Grendel took possession of Heorot, he "could not touch the treasure-throne (*gif-stol*) against the Lord's will" (Alexander 2003, lines 166–9). If the "Lord" here is the deity rather than Hrothgar himself as seems likely, the implication of the lines is that the "treasure-throne" was a sacred place within the hall, enjoying divine protection.

Although *Beowulf's* stories are set in a remote period, the poem was certainly being written down, and perhaps even composed, around the year 1000. Before the end of the eleventh century, the Norman king, William II Rufus, whose father had been King William I, conqueror of England in 1066, built an enormous stone hall at Westminster, on the River Thames just upstream from London. If Heorot could be regarded as a symbol of King Hrothgar's power, so much more must this hall have been so regarded. With it, we are literally on more solid ground, because its basic structure still exists as Westminster Hall within the Palace of Westminster (England). William Rufus's hall measured 73m x 20.57 m, and was probably the largest building of its date and type in Western Europe. It is often assumed that it was built as a three-aisled building, but it is more likely that it was of a single span, because there is no trace either from the archaeological excavations or from the documentary records of any pillars or bases for arcades of columns inside it. If it was indeed a single-span building, it must have been still more impressive. Just as Heorot was a mead-hall, so Westminster Hall was, in principle at least, a hall for feasting. Although by the fourteenth century rulers were no longer eating in the hall, at any rate routinely, its character as a feasting hall, very much in the tradition of halls like Heorot, is shown by the fact that it was on ground level, to be accessible to all, and it was heated—just like the hall at Lejre—by open fireplaces located centrally along the long axis below louvers built into the roof to allow the smoke to escape.

The same idea—that this was primarily a feasting hall—was also presumably inherent in the great marble table that dominated the main (southern) end of the hall and to which the earliest reference in documents is in 1253. The recovery of three marble trestles in excavations in the hall has permitted a reconstruction of this imposing table. It continued to be used on ceremonial occasions as a dining table for the kings. When Richard II (1377–99) arrived at Westminster from the Tower of London on the eve of his coronation, he took refreshment of wine and sweetmeats at it; on the morning of the coronation, the king took his seat for the first time on the throne, surrounded by his peers, and the regalia was placed on the marble table to be acknowledged by the king. The table was also the place where the king feasted after the ceremony.

Just as Roman triclinia and basilicas, and to an extent perhaps Heorot too, reflected and helped to create the ideological power of the ruler through his association with the deity, so Westminster Hall may have had a quasi-religious character, at least at certain periods of its history. Surviving masonry discovered at the time of the nineteenth-century restoration of the hall showed that, as built by William Rufus, its windows were deeply recessed and had running at the base of them a wall passage with a barrel vault that opened toward the interior through small paired arches. This may have been inspired by the clerestory of Winchester Cathedral, begun in 1079, and the effect must have been to make the hall look rather like a church, with all that that implied about the sacredness of what took place within it. As the prayer *Prospice*, which was already used by William I, put it:

> Look down, Omnipotent God, with favourable gaze on this most glorious king . . . Grant that the glorious dignity of the royal hall (*palatium*) may shine before the eyes of all with the greatest splendor of kingly power and that it may seem to glow with the brightest rays and to glitter as if suffused by illumination with the utmost brilliance. (quoted by Nelson 1982; citing C. Wilson 1997, 34)

When the hall was rebuilt by King Richard II in the fourteenth century, this quasi-religious character was increased. Internally, this was achieved by the new timber roof that he had built and that survives (Figure 2–24). The use of so many arched elements in the roof and the shield-bearing angels at the end of each hammer-beam must have made the hall feel like a church and likely conferred an aura of ideological power on the ruler who built and used it. This perception of Westminster Hall was enhanced by the new north façade that Richard II added, for several features of this were taken from church architecture (Figure 2–25).

First, there was a "welcoming porch," such as had been first used in the choir screen of St. Paul's Cathedral in London, in which a large outer entrance drew the visitor in through a canted passage to a smaller door. Second, there was a band of twenty-seven niches on either side of the entrance for statues of kings and queens, with further niches for king statues higher up the north face, and an additional four on the great pinnacle. By the time of the hall's construction such figures had become a feature of cathedral architecture, as can be seen, for example, at Exeter Cathedral (England) (Figure 2–26). Third, the tracery of the north window resembled that of the windows in Winchester College Chapel, while the lozenges at the top of the window resembled that of the openings in the cloister of St. Paul's Cathedral. In this way, the hall emphasized the ideological power of the ruler. As he presided over a ceremonial feast in the hall, it was as if he was presiding over a reflection of the heavenly court of God.

The effect was completed by the royal throne, which occupied a focal position behind the marble table at the south end of the hall. In March 1245, Henry III ordered a new marble throne with stone steps in front. This may have been intended to resemble the throne of the biblical king, Solomon, who

> made a great throne of ivory and covered it excessively with tawny gold. It had six steps and the top of the throne was round on the back side. And there were two hands holding the seat on both sides, and two lions standing next to each hand; and twelve little lions standing on the six steps on both sides of it. (I Kings 10: 18–20; Carroll and Prickett 1997, I, 424)

To make the point more clearly, in 1267 the throne had added to it "two small lions" (M. Collins et al. 2012, 209), presumably to echo the lions on the throne of Solomon. Like-

Figure 2–24: Drawing by Eugène-Emmanuel Viollet-le-Duc of the roof of Westminster Hall, Palace of Westminster, London (England), as remodeled by Richard II (after R. A. Brown, Colvin, and Taylor 1963, I, 531, fig. 48).

Figure 2–25: North façade, Westminster Hall, Palace of Westminster, London (England), viewed across New Palace Yard (etching in J. T. Smith 1807, facing p. 30, from an original pencil, pen and ink sketch in Westminster City Archives, Box 58, No. 12).

Figure 2–26: West front, Exeter Cathedral (England), with images of kings and queens placed on the lower parts of the façade.

wise, the stone steps referred to in Henry III's order for the throne in 1245 were no doubt intended to imitate the six steps approaching Solomon's.

So Westminster Hall conveyed a message of power, embodying personal power through its role as a feasting hall, and, especially from the time of Richard II, ideological power through its quasi-religious character. Its varied functions were a feature of halls of other medieval palaces, for example, the Palais de la Cité in Paris. The great hall there was certainly in existence by the early eleventh century, perhaps earlier. In the early fourteenth century, however, King Philip the Fair tripled the palace's surface area, which amounted to five hectares. The existing great hall was rebuilt and more than doubled in size, so that it covered 1785m², well in excess of Westminster Hall's 1440m². The undercroft, which is known today as the Conciergierie and is all that survives, admittedly in a much restored state, is an enormous stone-vaulted space. The great hall on the upper floor, which seems to

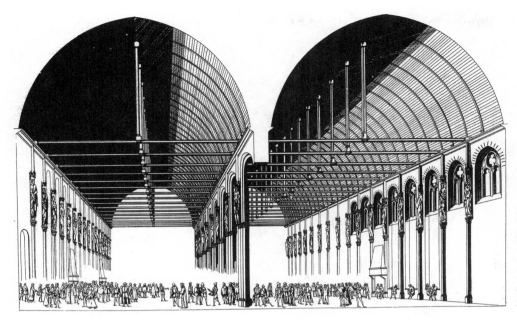

Figure 2–27: First-floor great hall (*Grand' Salle*), Palais de la Cité, Paris (France), as built by King Philip the Fair, shown in an engraving by Jacques Androuet du Cerceau.

have been wooden-roofed, was even more impressive. It was destroyed by fire in 1618, and it is known only from early modern drawings, especially that of Jacques Androuet du Cerceau (Figure 2–27). The functions of this great hall were similar to those of Westminster Hall. As at Westminster Hall, it was the site of formal feasts, and there was a ceremonial table, this one made of nine plates of marble; although no trace of it survives, clearly it was very large. It served as the high table when feasts took place in the great hall as, for example, on the occasion of the visit to Paris in 1378 of Charles IV, king of Bohemia and Holy Roman Emperor. Unlike Westminster Hall, the Paris great hall was not the venue for the coronation feast, which took place at Reims (below, pp. 329–31), but it did serve as a venue for assemblies, such as the one held in 1314 to confirm the grant of the crown to Philip the Fair (Bove 2003, 54).

Impressive as Westminster Hall and the Paris great hall must have been, even more impressive were the halls at the Palace of the Popes at Avignon (France), built by Popes Benedict XII (1334–42) and Clement VI (1342–52). There were two great halls—the Consistory Hall on the ground floor and the Great Tinel above it. Both halls were very impressive, especially the Great Tinel (Figure 2–28). Here the government functions were somewhat distinguished from the functions of a feasting hall, since the Consistory Hall was used for meetings of the consistory, that is, the assembly of the pope and the cardinals to pronounce judgment or to take counsel, while the Great Tinel was used chiefly for feasting, as is shown by the servery at one end for arranging dishes for the waiters to serve them, as well as its links to the buttery on the ground floor (where the drink was prepared) and the kitchen adjoining the hall (Figure 2–30).

As in other halls, the feasting in the Great Tinel could itself convey a message of power. When the pope presided over feasts, he sat alone at a table at the southern extremity of the

Figure 2–28: The Great Tinel, Palace of the Popes, Avignon (France), looking toward the vesting chamber.

Great Tinel, with the cardinals and laity arranged hierarchically around and below him. A visiting emperor would be seated among the cardinal-bishops, and a visiting king among the cardinal-priests. The design of halls such as this, without aisles, and with their long axis the principal axis, may have been intended to facilitate this hierarchical arrangement with the pope at one of the short ends. As in other halls, this was evidently a combination of personal power engendered by feasting, and ideological power engendered by this hierarchical arrangement of it.

PRIVATE ROOMS AND APARTMENTS

Great halls, however, were not the only, and sometimes not the most important, element of palaces. At the Palace of Domitian, the lower level of the part of the palace known as the *Domus Augustana* has been fully excavated to reveal a rather bewildering range of small and differently shaped rooms (Figure 2–29). This complex of small rooms was grouped around a central peristyle-courtyard within which were geometric features that must have been the basis of some sort of a formal garden. That this complex was intended to be a private space is indicated by its relative inaccessibility—only two staircases originally led to it, as the figure shows. Also, the small size of the rooms on the left of the peristyle-courtyard is espe-

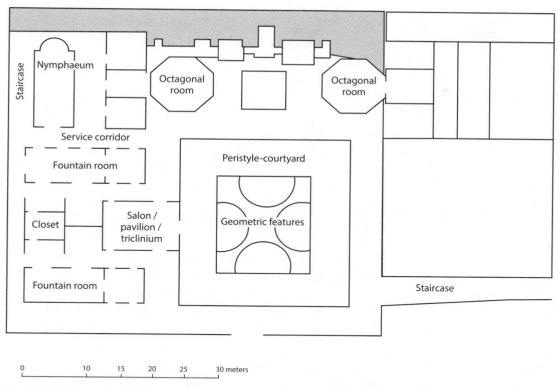

Figure 2–29: Lower level at the southern end of the *Domus Augustana*, Palace of Domitian, Rome (Italy) (after MacDonald 1982–6, I, fig. 58).

cially striking, with a salon (or perhaps a pavilion or triclinium) opening into the courtyard, a small private closet some way behind it, and a series of rooms, which were interconnected, permitting movement between them, that is, an enfilade. The contrast between these and the great rooms of other parts of the palace makes it likely that they were more public areas while this was the more private area. The public areas had the great audience hall for receiving many of the emperor's subjects or perhaps visitors and ambassadors from afar, while the basilica probably served similar functions. The upper-level triclinium was used for feasts with great numbers of guests who were being brought into contact with the emperor, through the practice of dining in a formal, perhaps ritualized way.

The private area of the palace, if that is the correct interpretation of it, is unlikely to have been intended for the emperor literally to have "time to himself" as the idea would be understood today. Much more likely, it would have been for the reception of fewer, more high-ranking subjects, guests, or ambassadors, on a more intimate footing, granting them the privilege of approaching much closer to the emperor by entering his private space. It will thus have been intended to convey a message of power, through its function in giving the emperor the possibility of awarding particular favors to particular people, through their intimacy with him. In the design of the palace, we may then be seeing clues to how personal power functioned, in terms of the relationships that the emperor built up with his subjects and others, either in the great halls or in the more intimate spaces.

Like the Palace of Domitian, Westminster Palace in the thirteenth century had both public spaces, chiefly Westminster Hall, and also private spaces, known as the "privy palace." As its name suggests, this comprised private rooms for the king and queen around a courtyard, and including a queen's chamber and a king's chamber (called the Painted Chamber because of its wall paintings). The importance of this part of the palace is clear from the enormous resources lavished on its building and decoration, and especially those of the Painted Chamber. Built originally in the twelfth century, the private character of this chamber was underlined by its role as a bedchamber, with the royal state bed as its main feature. It was, however, probably only a ceremonial bedchamber, for it was not in fact where the king slept, at least from 1307 when King Edward II constructed a private bedchamber, presumably to sleep in. The Painted Chamber seems to have been designed as a space where the king could favor a select group by receiving them in it, or could give particular prominence to political transactions by having them carried out there. It was the room, for example, where the homage of King Alexander of Scotland was taken by King Henry III in 1279. In the fourteenth century, it was used for more intimate, and therefore higher-level, state feasting; in 1310, the Reforming Ordainers, who were charged by Parliament with reforming the government of King Edward II, were chosen there. And in 1297 the king, who was desperate for money, imposed a tax with the consent of "the people standing around in his chamber."

By the time the Palace of the Popes was built in Avignon, even greater emphasis was coming to be placed on private apartments, and their importance in relation to great halls was growing. This palace was one of the first medieval palaces in Europe known to have had the rooms of the ruler's apartment organized in an enfilade leading from the most public to the most private rooms (Figure 2–30). This enfilade started from the Great Tinel, which was a very public room, through the door in the south wall into the vesting chamber, which was on a smaller scale and suitable for receiving smaller numbers of people, and in which—to judge from inventories showing that it had in it benches, tables, a "console," and a chandelier—smaller feasts could be held. It was also where cardinals, legates, and other dignitaries received their offices and were vested with the appropriate robes—hence its name. It was probably also the place where the pope and his assistants changed their liturgical vestments on Sundays and feast days when the pope was not himself saying mass.

Beyond it lay the pope's chamber, which served as the pope's most intimate, most private reception area, as well as his private bedroom. Alongside the vesting chamber was another room, the Little Tinel, which was certainly used for dining as it had its own kitchen. So the vesting chamber was an antechamber to the pope's chamber, which lay beyond it, while the Little Tinel was a second antechamber. Even the pope's chamber was not, however, the most private and exclusive room. That was probably his richly decorated and intimately sized study in the Study Tower. The study opened off his chamber, although it was also accessible from the vesting chamber. Benedict XII's successor, Clement VI, went on to build a second study, the magnificently decorated Stag Chamber (*Chambre du Cerf*), which was larger than Benedict XII's study, but was also more private, in that it opened off the pope's chamber but not off the vesting chamber.

The arrangement of the rooms in the Palace of the Popes as a public-private enfilade was the future, and with it came a tendency for great halls to become less important than private

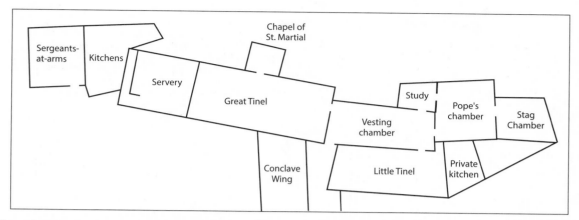

Figure 2–30: Diagrammatic plan of the Palace of the Popes, Avignon (France), showing the sequence of rooms leading from the Great Tinel to the Stag Chamber (after Schimmelpfennig 1994, fig. 5). Note that the position of doorways is not always certain, or in some cases fixed. In particular, openings from the Great Tinel to the Conclave Wing were only available during the election of a pope. At other times, they were walled up.

apartments. The Louvre in Paris, which was originally a fortified palace of the twelfth century, ceased to have any real military function when King Charles V built new walls around the city (below, p. 192). In the years after 1365, that king committed immense resources to upgrading it as a royal residence. Nothing survives above ground but it is possible to reconstruct the palace from archaeological excavations in the courtyard of the Louvre Museum, from pictures of it such as the one in the Très Riches Heures of the Duke of Berry (Figure 6–8), and from descriptions of it before it was demolished to make way for its early modern successor. Although the reconstruction is controversial in detail, it seems clear that what Charles V built had a north wing on four levels, which contained the private apartments for himself and his queen. There were cellars and service rooms at ground-floor level, and attics on the fourth floor. At first-floor level was the queen's apartment, and at second-floor level, the king's apartment (Figure 2–31).

The great hall, which belonged to the period before 1365, rose from ground-floor level up through all four floors. Its measurements are given by an early antiquary as 17.35m x 9.98m, which was rather small, and certainly tiny by comparison with the great hall of the Palais de la Cité. Clearly, then, the Louvre was not a palace focused on its great hall, even before 1365, in the way that the Palais de la Cité was. Nevertheless, the great hall was an important place when the king dined on special occasions with his knights and squires at the great royal table, sitting on a monumental bench, 6.5m long and two steps above the floor. The first rooms to be entered from the courtyard on the north side, from the ornate spiral staircase, the Grande Vis (above, p. 21), were the new chamber of the queen on the first floor, and that of the king on the second floor. These functioned as reception rooms and formal dining rooms. The king's new chamber had a chapel in the central wall tower, a monumental fireplace against the east wall, and an enormous royal table. On its east side, it opened into the council chamber; on its west side was the vesting chamber (*chambre de parement*), in which the king gave audiences to officials and judges. Just as at the Palace of the Popes in Avignon, a study opened off this room, and at the Louvre this was repeated.

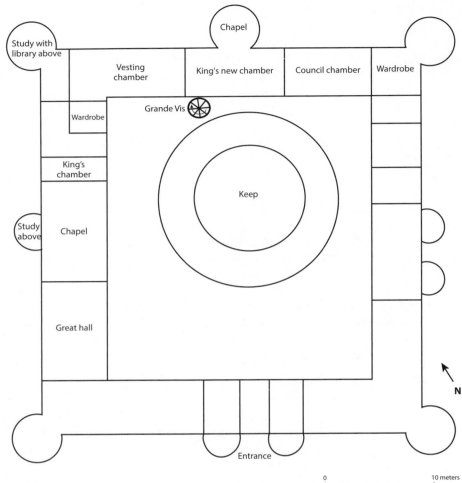

Figure 2–31: Diagrammatic plan showing a reconstruction of the second-floor layout, Palace of the Louvre, Paris (France), containing the king's apartment and surrounding rooms, as the palace was rebuilt by Charles V (after Salamagne 2010, 90, fig. 12).

The relative importance of the apartments is shown by the size of some of these rooms. The king's new chamber had a floor area of 125m², the vesting chamber a floor area of 173m², which made it larger than the great hall. That importance is also indicated by the fact that the Grande Vis led from the courtyard to the queen's and king's apartments. Clearly, at the Louvre the apartments were much more important than the great hall, and they were arranged in such a way as to create, as at Avignon, an enfilade, a sequence, from the more public to the more private. Or, to be more precise, two sequences. The first led from the great hall through the chapel and the wardrobe and so to the king's or queen's chamber. This was probably the route used by the king and queen when they went in procession either to mass in the chapel or to a feast in the great hall. The second began in the new chambers, to which the Grande Vis gave access. This was probably the point of entry for those coming to the court. From the new chamber, they could either enter the council chamber or turn the other way and follow another public-private sequence through the vesting chamber to the king's chamber, if they were very privileged visitors and were being received by the king in a special way.

Figure 2–32: James IV's Great Hall, Stirling Castle (Scotland), showing the large windows at the high table end.

The increasing sophistication of apartments arranged in enfilades like that at the Louvre, and the relative decline in the importance of great halls, must have arisen from changes in the ruler's power, or at least in perceptions of it. The great hall was conceived as a space where the ruler could exhibit a relationship, however formal, with a mass of his subjects gathered in it; it therefore had as much to do with personal power as anything. The private apartments arranged as an enfilade were presumably related to personal power, but in a rather different form. The personal relationships that it both reflected and created were of a much more hierarchical type. Only the most favored could penetrate to the most private recesses of the enfilade; those less favored were restricted to the outermost spaces. The ruler and the circle who had access to him were evidently being seen as forming a more hierarchical elite than that represented by the great hall.

Nevertheless, great halls continued to be an important element of existing palaces, such as the Palace of Westminster and the Palais de la Cité. They could also be elements in newly built palaces. That of Hampton Court (England), a palace built by Cardinal Wolsey and taken over and extended by Henry VIII in the early sixteenth century, had a very magnificent example (below, pp. 69–70), although it also had a ruler's apartment with a developed enfilade. At Stirling Castle too, the most prominent building constructed by James IV (1488–1513) was a great hall, with enormous windows at its high table end to look down over the surrounding landscape, and painted externally—as it has recently been restored—in a dazzling gold to increase its prominence, glowing against the sky as the inhabitants of the city and subjects of the king looked up at the site of his majesty on the ridge above them (Figure 2–32; cf. Figure 6–6). It may remind us of Heorot's "ample eaves adorned with gold" (above, p. 38).

BUREAUCRATIC OFFICES AND TREASURIES

If, in the ways considered so far, the design of palaces could convey messages of ideological and personal power, so too could they convey messages of bureaucratic power. The importance of this type of power could, for example, be indicated by the presence within palaces of bureaucratic offices and apartments for the various officeholders, and by the closeness of the relationship between these design elements and the great halls or the rulers' apartments themselves.

Such arrangements cannot be identified in Roman and early medieval palaces, although they may have existed. It is clear, for example, that bureaucratic officeholders had an important place in the Great Palace of the emperors in Constantinople at least in the tenth century. There, the *Book of the Ceremonies* mentions bureaucratic offices called the *Lausiakos* and the *Eidikon* or Imperial Privy Purse, which seem to have been within the palace. Although the text gives no further details, we must assume that a fair number of people were involved in, and admitted to, these offices every day (Featherstone 2006, 54). From the twelfth and thirteenth centuries, however, we get a view of the financial and judicial functions accommodated in the Palace of Westminster. From at least 1215, the Court of Common Pleas was usually held in Westminster Hall, on its west side toward the north end, while from at least the early fourteenth century the Court of King's Bench met in the southeast corner of the hall, with the Court of Chancery established in the southwest corner by 1281. The link between this judicial function of the hall and its role as a feasting hall is shown most clearly by the fact that the marble table was also where the chancellor, the king's most senior official, was installed, and where he sat when he was acting in place of the king. The Exchequer, the department that controlled the king's finances, seems to have been located in Westminster Hall from its inception in the twelfth century. Purpose-built administrative buildings were soon constructed for it, but these were nevertheless closely connected to the hall. They consisted of the Upper Exchequer or Receipt, where the accounts were presented on the chequered tablecloth, and the Lower Exchequer, where money was received, weighed, and stored in sealed chests. By 1244, it was on a site at the north end of the west side of the hall. During the reign of Edward I (1272–1307), the Lower Exchequer moved to a room on the east side of Westminster Hall.

Provision for judicial functions was also an aspect of the great hall in the Palais de la Cité. Around the walls and against the pillars were the benches of the masters of requests and royal notaries, just as Westminster Hall had screened-off areas for the courts. The great hall also functioned as an antechamber for the *parlement*, and it could be the place where new taxes and military victories were announced. From the beginning of the fourteenth century, more detail about the location of administrative offices in the palace is available, for it is possible to reconstruct the organization of four rooms devoted to judicial functions (Figure 2–33). These rooms, which were built up against the great hall, were, first, the Pleas Chamber, where cases and pleas were heard. It led out of the great hall. Surviving from it are the north gable and two towers on its riverward side, Caesar's Tower and the Silver Tower (Figure 2–34). The Criminal Chamber was on the upper floor of Caesar's Tower. The Chamber of Inquests was to the west. Another series of rooms devoted to financial administration can also be located in the Palais de la Cité as rebuilt by Philip the Fair (1285–1314). These rooms were, first, the Accounting Chamber, housing officers responsible for checking the accounts of royal agents, the Money Chamber, and the Treasury Chamber. The way in which these rooms were attached to the great hall, or adjacent to the king's apartment, is a clear indication of the importance of bureaucratic power in the design of this palace.

But it is, perhaps, the Palace of the Popes at Avignon that offers the clearest evidence for the relationship between the ruler, in this case the pope, and the bureaucratic offices which formed an important aspect of his government. In the fourteenth century, when the palace was built, the pope's government was probably one of the most sophisticated in Europe. It was divided into four bodies. First was the Apostolic (i.e., Pope's) Chamber, which was the most important department and dealt with revenues, budgets, the material life of the pope's court, the minting of money, and the security of the pope's treasury. Its head was the chamberlain, with the treasurer in second place—who was responsible for the movement of money, for accounts, and for controlling agents throughout western Christendom. Second, the Apostolic Chancery, which was responsible for the examination of petitions, for "correction," for letters, and for benefices. Its head was the vice chancellor, with a staff of around 100–130 persons. Third was the Apostolic Penitentiary, with a staff of about thirty to forty persons. And fourth was the Public Audience (or Great Audience), also known as the Wheel (*Rota*), with twelve auditors in 1332 (Vingtain 1998, 27–39).

To accommodate the requirements of this enormous governmental machine, the necessary offices were located both within the palace and in the city beyond. Within the palace, the most striking aspect of the arrangement of the bureaucratic offices was their close proximity to the pope's apartment, for the pope's chamber was on the first floor of the Pope's Tower, above the lower treasury, and immediately below the upper treasury. The pope literally slept sandwiched between the rooms containing his treasure. Between the pope's chamber and the lower treasury, however, was the chamberlain's chamber, to which it communicated via the staircase in the depth of the wall. The proximity reflects the importance of the chamberlain in the pope's government. The chamberlain controlled the finances, was responsible for political correspondence, and was the head of most of the personnel of the papal curia. With the construction of Clement VI's west wing later in the fourteenth century, however, the chamberlain's chamber and offices were moved there, probably because they had outgrown the space in the Pope's Tower. The lower treasury in the Pope's Tower was for the storage of money and documents. In 1343, for example, there were 600,000 florins in forty chests and three sacks, while an inventory of 1369 records church archives being stored in thirty chests (Lentsch 1990, 295). A passage from the Lower Treasury opened into the Great Treasury, which probably had a range of functions pertaining to the financial management of the pope's government, and was perhaps divided with wooden screens to create separate offices for different officials and groups.

The new bureaucratic offices in Clement VI's wing of the Great Dignitaries, built in the fourteenth century, were still more extensive. The chamberlain had a large room divided by screens, a little office adjoining, and—close by—a high room for his scribes and notaries. Accounts of 1363 and 1364 show that, under Pope Urban V (1362–70), the floor area at the

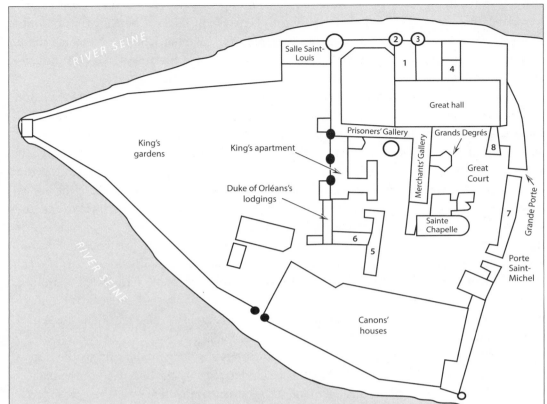

Figure 2–33: Diagrammatic plan showing the arrangement of buildings *c.*1400, Palais de la Cité, Paris (France). The numbered elements are as follows: 1: Pleas Chamber (Great Chamber); 2: Caesar's Tower; 3: Silver Tower; 4: Chamber of Inquests; 5: Accounting Chamber; 6: Money Chamber; 7: Treasury Chamber; 8: staircase to the Great Hall (after Lorentz and Sandron 2006, 83).

Figure 2–34: The north side, Palais de la Cité, Paris (France), showing the twin towers—Caesar's Tower on the right, the Silver Tower on the left. Between them can be seen the gable-end of the Pleas Chamber (Great Chamber). The rest of the façade is modern.

treasurer's disposal was around 320m³ while the chamberlain had at his disposal 210m³ (Lentsch 1990, 300–302).

As for the judicial functions of the pope's government, in the fourteenth century these centered around the two halls built by Clement VI: the Public Audience, which dealt with ecclesiastical elections, and cases concerning marriages, prebends, and the like; and the Little Audience (or Audience of Contested Cases), which dealt with litigation arising from orders and privileges issued by the papal curia. The former was an enormous hall built under the chapel, and the latter was constructed at the same level but in the west façade. The pope's judicial power was especially important, given that so many judicial matters from across Europe were referred to his court. The auditors were in permanent session, apart from vacations, so that a room devoted to their courts had to be provided in any papal palace. In the palace at Avignon, the integration of the Public Audience into the very heart of the palace emphasizes the importance of bureaucratic power in its design. There was, in addition, the Consistory Hall, the room in which the pope met with the cardinals to discuss important juridical affairs such as litigious elections, political trials, and so on, and where he also distributed bishoprics and abbacies. Large receptions could also be held there.

Clearly, the design of the Palace of the Popes reflected, and facilitated, the sophistication and complexity of administrative arrangements which were equally clearly closely linked to the ruler. It represents a remarkable example of the importance of bureaucratic power in palace design, but it is evidently parallelled in the design of Westminster Palace and the Palais de la Cité. This importance, of course, could only arise in states where bureaucratic government had developed sufficiently, and presumably that is why these elements of design are found in these late medieval palaces but seemingly not in early palaces. The exception that proves the rule was—to judge from that brief mention in the *Book of the Ceremonies*—the Great Palace in Constantinople, where bureaucratic arrangements were evidently important in the context of a state that had preserved and developed the governmental sophistication of the Roman Empire. It is, however, puzzling that it is so difficult to identify administrative offices in Roman palaces, despite the bureaucratic sophistication of the Roman Empire as revealed by inscriptions and surviving documents.

The element of bureaucratic power in palace design, however, may sometimes have been greater than appears at first, if we consider palaces in the broader context of their sites. A few miles north of Düsseldorf, the great artery of the River Rhine was overlooked from at least the mid-eleventh century by the fortified palace of Kaiserwerth (Germany). In 1016, the German king and emperor, Henry II (1002–24), gave the place the responsibility for collecting revenues from the area of the Lower Rhine, including tolls from ships passing along the river. The king and emperor, Henry III (1028–56), seems to have developed it as a palace, staying there repeatedly, as did his successor, Henry IV (1056–1106). At the end of the twelfth century, the powerful and successful German king and emperor, Frederick Barbarossa (1152–90), rebuilt the palace with a massive tower and an imposing façade facing the River Rhine. The palace was partially destroyed in 1702, but enough remains to give an impression of the efforts that were made by Frederick Barbarossa's architect to make it as imposing a structure as possible. This was not only in relation to the height and solidity of the buildings, but also to the use of decorative stonework. Great blocks of the dark volcanic

Figure 2–35: Exterior of Emperor Frederick Barbarossa's palace, Kaiserwerth (Germany), viewed from the northeast, showing the use of white limestone and dark dolerite to create an imposing effect.

rock called dolerite, which is naturally octagonal, were used for the bulk of the walls to create a lowering, imposing effect, heightened by their being framed with features made of white limestone blocks, at the corners of the walls, in their footings, and to emphasize openings, contrasting vividly with the dark color of the dolerite (Figure 2–35). Windows looked out over the River Rhine from the halls within, and there were also inscriptions of classical type, done in magnificent chiselled letters, which recorded the date of the building, attributing it to Frederick Barbarossa (Figure 2–36), and also explaining where he had obtained the magnificent stone used in it.

In terms of the design of its buildings, Kaiserwerth appears to have been seriously fortified, and its function was no doubt in large part to defend the shipping route along the River Rhine from attack and disruption, and to provide security too for those charged with collecting tolls. But it was evidently also designed to convey a message of power. Dominating the River Rhine with its tall profile and its use of light and dark stone, it was a building intended to impress. The inscriptions tend to confirm that it was conceived to convey a message of power, a message that must have been closely bound up with the ruler's bureaucratic power involving movements of shipping and goods along the River Rhine and over the tolls payable by those who moved them.

Figure 2–36: Inscription in the palace of Kaiserwerth (Germany), reading in translation: "In the year of the Incarnation of our Lord Jesus Christ 1184, Emperor Frederick dedicated this embellishment to the Empire, wishing to make it steadfast with justice, and so that there should be peace everywhere."

The fourteenth-century royal palace at Kutná Hora (Czech Republic) in the former Kingdom of Bohemia, and especially its construction in intimate proximity to buildings concerned with bureaucratic power, was evidently intended to convey a similar message. Kutná Hora was a town that developed largely because of the rich silver deposits discovered there in the late thirteenth century. As a result of this discovery, King Wenceslas II (1278–1305) brought in minters from the Italian city of Florence to establish a royal mint to produce the silver coins called Groschen, which became for a time the most important coinage in Europe. This mint was established in what is now called the Italian Court, and around 1400 the buildings associated with it were enlarged and reshaped by King Wenceslas IV (1363–1419). These buildings included a palace complex. Although this was greatly modified when it was converted into the town hall in the sixteenth century, the chapel is more or less as it was, and the king's bedchamber adjoins it, with other halls and chambers on the ground floor (Figure 2–37).

The palace itself seems to be nothing more than a luxurious residence for the ruler. But when the wider design of its site is considered, it becomes obvious that it stood in intimate relationship to the royal mint, which was located where the great arch enters the courtyard on the right of the figure, and in the immediately adjacent spaces. The palace would have dominated the mint much as Kaiserwerth dominated the Rhine River route. But, more than that, the rooms of the palace looked out across the Italian court, where a series of openings is still visible in its walls (Figure 2–38). These mark the booths, or workshops, of the metalworkers who prepared the silver from the nearby mines for minting into Groschens in the mint. So, from the windows of his palace, the king could look down over this work in progress, work that was so important to his wealth and consequently to his power. His palace dominated the work of—quite literally—making money in a very intimate, a very direct way. The palace's situation may have been merely practical, in order to facilitate supervision of the minting process; but it seems more likely that a message of power was intended to be conveyed. Just as Kaiserwerth conveyed a message of power about the ruler's dominance over commercial wealth, so at Kutná Hora the palace conveyed a message of power about the ruler's command of silver and the coins made from it.

Figure 2–37: Oriel window of the royal palace chapel in the Italian Court, Kutná Hora (Czech Republic).

CONCLUSION

This chapter has argued that palaces and their sites had the potential to send a message of power in a range of ways. The design of their various elements, which might include, for example, the entrances, the intermediate spaces to which they led such as vestibules, the staircases that led the ruler or his subjects or guests to the upper parts of the palace, the great spaces in the form of halls or similar rooms where feasts could be held or ambassadors re-

Figure 2–38: Booths of metalworkers in the Italian Court, Kutná Hora (Czech Republic) viewed from the palace.

ceived, the private apartments of rulers, and the bureaucratic offices which might equally form components of a palace, may have been intended to create a context—a sort of stage set—for the ruler. In this, he could make formal appearances, or ritual processions, or be visited in the more intimate context of his private apartments. The various parts of the palace could be designed in order to present the ruler's power in particular ways through the functions they served. A great hall, for example, could have been designed for a ruler to mingle with his subjects, perhaps in the context of feasting, so that the message being conveyed was that he was one among equals. The intention would be for his power to be perceived as personal power, dependent on his relationships with his subjects. The private apartments of the ruler could also have functioned as instruments of personal power. They were designed for displaying that power to those admitted to them, and so creating a hierarchy of those with the most privileged admission to them. In this way, the apartments could themselves have helped to create the personal relationships on which this type of power was based. Where a palace incorporated bureaucratic offices, these could both display the ruler's bureaucratic power through their grandeur and prominence. It may be, however, that such differences in the design of palaces reflected less the nature of rulers' power and more the different functions of types of palaces. So, the reason for the emphasis on administrative offices at Avignon, Westminster, and the Palais de la Cité was the result of these palaces being the principal state palaces of the rulers in question, with quite different palaces, such as the Louvre in Paris, being designed alongside them to serve other purposes. In the case of Paris, for example, one could argue that the Palais de la Cité was primarily for government, while the nearby palace, called the Hôtel Saint-Pol, and also the Louvre, were for the ruler to welcome visitors, to discuss, to receive those coming with petitions, and in addition to enjoy and to show off the luxurious living appropriate to his rank (Cazelles 1982, 519–20). This is possible. But it is striking that even palaces like this group of Avignon, Westminster, and the Palais de la Cité also placed considerable emphasis in their design on other types of power, reflected by their great halls and their complex apartments. There were differences of emphasis between individual palaces within the same domains, certainly, but also considerable commonality of functions (Bove 2003).

CHAPTER 3

The Power of Architectural Style and Decoration

The previous chapter argued that the design of the spaces in a palace and their relationship to each other could be a means of conveying a message of power to those who entered the palace, and that this message could have had a specific and comprehensible meaning as to the nature of the power of the ruler whose palace it was. The aim of this chapter is to explore how far this could also be true of the style of a palace's architectural style and decoration. When a courtier or an ambassador or merely a visitor or a subject of the ruler saw that architectural style and decoration, were these intended to impress upon him the extent of the ruler's power? More particularly, what specific image of that power could they be designed to convey? This chapter will explore how messages of power could be conveyed by the manner in which a palace's walls were adorned, or the images in paint or in sculpture with which its spaces were decorated. It will explore too how the features of the masonry or of the timberwork could convey those messages, and how the overarching style of a palace as an architectural concept could achieve the same effect.

MAGNIFICENCE

Almost by definition, palaces were and are magnificent structures. It is natural—and no doubt correct—to assume that the magnificence of a palace fulfilled the ruler's desire that his habitation should be richly appointed. Such a desire no doubt arose from his craving for luxurious living, which his power and wealth made possible. It no doubt arose too from his desire to have a residence as magnificent as, or preferably more magnificent than, the residences even of his wealthiest subjects. It is obvious that such a residence helps conveys a message about its owner's power through the effect it has on those who see and visit it. That message could be a very straightforward one: Here is the habitation of an immensely rich and powerful ruler. Behind this, however, may have been a more subtle message, based on the notion that magnificence was not just a reflection of a ruler's desires and capabilities, but was actually part of the essence of being a ruler. A ruler, in other words, had to be magnificent as a qualification for being a ruler, so that the message conveyed by a magnificent palace was one of the ruler's legitimacy.

This idea finds explicit expression in the work of a sixth-century Roman senator, Cassiodorus. An important figure in the government of the barbarian kingdom of Italy after the end of the Roman Empire in the west, he wrote for the rulers of that kingdom a work called the *Variae*. One passage in this, which relates to the appointment of the palace architect, comments on why rulers' palaces, which he calls "halls," were important:

> Our halls . . . are the delights of our power, the decorous face of our rule, the public testimony to our kingdoms: they are shown to ambassadors for their admiration, and at first sight one believes that as the house is seen to be, so must be the lord. And moreover it is a great delight to the most prudent mind to rejoice ceaselessly in a most beautiful habitation and, amidst public cares, to refresh the tired spirit by the sweetness of buildings. (translated from Mommsen 1894, 204)

While the last sentence presents the palace as an amenity to delight and refresh the ruler, the preceding sentences contain deeper ideas. They make clear the importance of the role of the palace in showing the public face of the king's rule and of his kingdoms, and in making an impact on visiting ambassadors. The palace's magnificence was "the worthy face of our rule, the public witness of our kingdoms." In a similar vein, Cassiodorus's contemporary, Ennodius, commented on the rebuilding of cities by the barbarian king of Italy, Theoderic (471–526), after the troubles of the later Roman Empire: "I see an unhoped-for beauty rise from the ashes of cities and the roofs of palaces gleam everywhere under the fullness of civilisation" (Deliyannis, 2009, 119, citing B. Ward-Perkins 1984). The gleam of the palace roofs must allude to their magnificence, their cladding perhaps of gold like the Golden House of the emperor Nero was in Rome in the first century AD. For Ennodius, they were associated with "the fullness of civilisation." The ruler who had built them had evidently established that desirable state, so their magnificence conveyed the message of the ruler's power as a fount of civilization.

Much later, around 1470, in England, Sir John Fortescue wrote in his book on *The Governance of England* a passage about the necessity for the king to have splendid buildings:

> It is necessary that the king should have treasure, so that he may make new buildings when he wishes to, for his pleasure and magnificence . . . And often he will buy rich hangings and other apparel for his houses . . . for if a king did not do, nor might do, he lived then not according to his rank, but rather in misery, and in more subjection than a private person does. (quoted by Thurley 1993, 11)

The magnificence of the king's palaces was thus a qualification of legitimate rule. Indeed, according to Guillaume Fillastre, chancellor of the order of the Golden Fleece, an order of knights set up by the Dukes of Burgundy in the fifteenth century, it was the ruler's chief virtue. In this, he was influenced by the ancient Greek philosopher Aristotle's concept of the "magnificent man" who "can spend large sums of money with good taste" (quoted by Thurley 1993, 11).

The Renaissance architect, Alberti, summed it up when he wrote in his *On the Family*:

> Men of publick spirits approve and rejoice when you have raised a fine wall or portico, and adorned it with portals, columns, and a handsome roof, knowing you have thereby not only served yourself, but them too, having by this generous use of your wealth, gained an addition

of great honour to yourself, your family, your descendants, and your city. (quoted by Fraser Jenkins 1970, 167)

So the ruler's palace conveyed a message of power through its very magnificence, and that message was to the effect that the ruler was qualified to exercise his power by the magnificence he displayed. That the magnificence of the Painted Chamber in Westminster Palace (England) was effective in conveying this message of power is strikingly shown by the account written in the 1320s by two Irish friars. En route to the Holy Land, they visited London and particularly the Painted Chamber, which was apparently accessible to visitors in the king's absence, and reported it to be

that well-known hall, on whose walls are painted in a manner indescribable all the historical battles of the whole Bible, and in French most completely and most perfectly described in order, to the no little admiration of the spectator and to the greatest regal magnificence. (Hoade 1952, 3)

A similar effect was produced by the court of King Edward IV of England, when a visitor described it in 1466 as "the most splendid court that could be found in all Christendom" (quoted by Thurley 1993, 12). This reaction was no doubt inspired by the king's palace and its decoration, but also by the sumptuous richness of its furnishings and the rich dress of himself and his court. It is striking that Henry VI, king of England (1422–61, 1470–71), one of the weaker of the English kings, was explicitly criticized for the lack of magnificence he displayed in his dress, clad as he always was "in a long blue gown of velvet as though he had nothing else to change into" (Wolffe 1981, 10–13, 95–96).

Little enough of the magnificence that Roman and medieval palaces must have had survives. But there are occasional hints of what there was—for example, in the mosaics of the Villa Romana di Casale near Piazza Armerina (Sicily) (Figure 3–16), in the intricate plasterwork of the palaces at the Alhambra (Spain) (Figure 2–5), in the sumptuous wall painting of the pope's chamber at the Palace of the Popes at Avignon (France), and in the glowing goldwork of the dome of the Hall of the Ambassadors in the palace of Pedro the Cruel in Seville (Spain) (Figure 3–22), or the brightly patterned tilework of the Patio de las Doncellas just outside (Figure 3–1).

Figure 3–1: Dado tiling, Patio de las Donacellas, Palace of Pedro the Cruel, Alcázar, Seville (Spain), showing the richness of the decoration. (See insert for color version of this image.)

Figure 3–2: *Studiolo*, Palace of Federico of Montefeltro, Urbino (Italy), showing the rich and intricate marquetry work. (See insert for color version of this image.)

Much of the effect of magnificence must, however, have been created by the hangings and furnishings of the palace. Occasionally, fragments survive, as in the case of the state bed at the palace of Duke Federico of Montefeltro in Urbino, or the Hunting of the Unicorn tapestries from fifteenth-century France (Figure 5–11). Just occasionally a room survives with sufficient of its original decoration and furnishings to give a clearer indication of the magnificence it once possessed. This is the case, for example, with the intimate study, the *studiolo*, of Duke Federico of Montefeltro's palace at Urbino (Figure 3–2). Here the sense of magnificence is conveyed by the intricate marquetry of the lower walls, the rich tilework of the floor, and the equally rich ceiling. The marquetry in particular conveyed not only magnificence, but also a message of humanist scholarship and culture. The *trompe l'oeil* bookcases and desks which it represents around the walls were evidently intended to convey a sense of the duke as a scholar, while the musical instruments and scientific tools pointed to his cultural pursuits, and the view out over the city and countryside through a series of arches (on the right of the figure) spoke to his power and territory. But the overwhelming impression is one of magnificence—restrained magnificence because the material primarily used is wood rather than precious metal, but magnificence nevertheless in the intricacy of the carving and the richness of the wood.

STYLISTIC IMITATION

The architectural style of palaces could act in various ways as another vehicle for conveying messages of power. First, when that style was imitative of earlier buildings. The message of power being conveyed was that the present palace was one of a ruler every bit as great and powerful as the rulers for whom the palaces of the past had been built. Renaissance buildings like the palace at Urbino were of course seeking to imitate the style and grandeur of buildings of the Roman period, for admiration of Roman achievements and culture was one of the distinguishing aspects of the Renaissance approach to art and architecture. In some palaces, however, the imitations of Roman style seem to have been more specific and the architects and their patrons seem to have had more precisely defined ideas about the message of power they were seeking to convey.

This can be seen most clearly in the various elements of the palace that the German emperor Charles V (1519–56) built at the Alhambra in the 1540s. This consisted, first, of a circular courtyard within a square structure (Figure 3–3). The courtyard, which was colonnaded in the Roman manner, was a conscious reminiscence of Roman imperial palaces, and it was almost certainly a specific allusion to the so-called Maritime Theatre, one of the components of Hadrian's Villa, near Tivoli (Italy). This structure, which was not a theater at all despite its modern nickname, consisted of a circular courtyard with a colonnade, just as Charles V's courtyard was colonnaded (Figure 3–4).

It was not like Charles V's palace in that the center was not simply an open space, but rather consisted of an island, on which sat a building with rooms of unknown function, and surrounded by a channel of water. Nevertheless, it seems likely that Charles V's courtyard was intended to evoke it, and it is in that connection striking that his courtyard had exactly the same diameter as its Roman model did. Admittedly, Hadrian's colonnade was on one story, whereas Charles V's was two-storied, and the order of columns was the Ionic order rather than the Doric order of Charles V's colonnade. But such round courtyards were extremely rare in Roman architecture, and the only known surviving example from antiquity is the Maritime Theatre.

Second, Charles V's palace also had an octagonal chapel. In addition to possibly being intended as a reminder of the emperor Charlemagne's octagonal palace church at Aachen, where Charles V had been crowned in 1526, it also evoked Roman buildings, such as the mausoleum built by the emperor Diocletian at his palace at Split, or the Golden Octagon built by the emperor Constantine at Antioch (below, p. 284).

Third, the outer façades of the palace seem equally to have been intended to convey the message of Charles V's status as a new Roman emperor. They were organized into a hierarchy with the columns above and very large irregular blocks of stone below, such as had been used in Roman walls in the period of the later Roman Republic. This effect of imitation of Rome was increased by the entrance on the west façade, the arrangement of which, with a large central opening flanked by smaller side openings, reflected the characteristic structure of a Roman triumphal arch (Figure 3–5, and below, pp. 218–21).

This imitation of Roman architecture is especially clear in Charles V's palace at the Alhambra, but it is perceptible across the whole period this book is concerned with. We have seen

Figure 3–3: Circular courtyard, Palace of Charles V, the Alhambra, Granada (Spain), viewed from the gallery.

Figure 3–4: Maritime Theatre, Hadrian's Villa, Tivoli (Italy).

Figure 3–5: West façade, Palace of Charles V, the Alhambra, Granada (Spain), with doorways, columns, and tondi in imitation of a Roman triumphal arch.

it in the architecture of Charlemagne's palace at Ingelheim of around 800 (above, pp. 25–27), and in that of the emperor Frederick Barbarossa's twelfth-century palace at Gelnhausen (above, p. 30). Sometimes, however, it is possible to place the imitation of Roman architecture in a more precise context as regards the intentions of the ruler who commissioned it. The Palace of the Popes at Avignon may be such a case. One of its most characteristic features was the tall, chiefly blind arches that line the lower story, dominating every façade of the palace inside and out. On the west façade, they were restored in 1905, but they appear in early drawings, so they certainly existed in the palace as originally built (Figure 3–6).

They resemble machicolations, that is, blind arches that had at their heads slots to allow defenders to ward off attackers by pouring on to their heads noxious substances, such as hot oil or boiling water, or by firing at them through the slots. At the Palace of the Popes, however, it is unlikely that the blind arches were really machicolations intended for defending

Figure 3–6: West façade, Palace of the Popes, Avignon (France), showing the tall, chiefly blind arches. The two on the left mark the palace built by Benedict XII; those to the right of them mark the façade of the new Wing of the Great Dignitaries built by Clement VI.

the palace in this way, since they occur in the interior of courts as well as on the exterior façades. That they were not functional is clear from the Cloister Court of Benedict XII's palace, where the lean-to galleries are original and yet they cut the arches halfway up their height. This must have rendered the latter ineffective for defensive use as machicolations, so they must have been primarily aesthetic rather than defensive.

The clue to explaining why these blind arches were used so prominently in the Palace of the Popes may lie in the situation of the popes at Avignon. When Clement V arrived there on March 9, 1309, it was not intended that the city should be a permanent residence of the papacy in France. Nevertheless, the popes from John XXII (1316–34) to Clement VI were more or less settled in Avignon, where they built the Palace of the Popes in all its magnificence. It seems, however, always to have been part of papal policy for the papacy to return to Rome when circumstances allowed, and this was achieved by Pope Gregory XI (1370–78) (Kelly 1986, 226–28). It would therefore have been understandable if the style of the Palace of the Popes had evoked the city of Rome which the popes regarded as their true home. The blind arches may have been intended to do just this. For their aesthetic effect was to make the palace look, superficially at least, not unlike Roman buildings, such as the fourth-century Basilica at Trier (Figure 3–7).

Contemporary images of buildings in Rome, such as those in the fourteenth-century *Liber Guidonis*, also emphasize this feature (Poisson 2004, 225–27). The style of the Palace of the Popes, then, may have been conveying a specific message about the roots of the pope's power in the city of Rome, and—for the time being—the creation of Avignon as a new Rome where the popes were appropriately installed.

Stylistic evocations of earlier monuments in order to deliver messages of power may also have been a prominent part of building undertaken in Wales by Edward I, king of England

Figure 3–7: Exterior of the side wall of the basilica of the former Roman imperial palace, Trier (Germany), showing the use of arches to articulate the wall-face.

Figure 3–8: Caernarfon Castle (Wales) from the southeast, showing the polygonal towers and the bands of brick in the masonry. The Eagle Tower is on the left.

(1272–1307). After his conquest of the principality of Wales, he founded a new town—one among several—at Caernarfon on the north coast, and there he built a castle that was to be the center of his government in Wales. This was built in an unusual way, with towers that were polygonal rather than round (as was the case with most castles of the thirteenth century), and stonework that was interspersed with horizontal bands of brick or colored stone to give it a striped appearance (Figure 3–8).

These striking and unusual features were surely intended to evoke the great land-walls that had been built at Constantinople by the emperor Theodosius II (408–50). The towers there are reminiscent of the towers of Caernarfon Castle, with bands of brickwork giving the same striped appearance to the walls and towers as seen at Caernarfon (Figure 3–9).

Moreover, at least some of the towers of the land-walls are polygonal, as are the towers at Caernarfon. That Caernarfon Castle was designed to evoke the Roman Empire is confirmed by the decoration of its Eagle Tower, which was surmounted by gilded imperial eagles like those of Roman imperial standards. Also, what was believed to be the body of a third-century claimant to the Roman imperial throne, Magnus Maximus, was found at Caernarfon in 1283, and Edward I himself was responsible for its reburial in the town's church

Figure 3–9: The fifth-century land-walls of Constantinople, viewed from outside the city. Note the banded masonry and the polygonal tower, matching the towers of Caernarfon..

(R. A. Brown, Colvin, and Taylor 1963, 370). Edward I was clearly attempting to create an association between his reign and the Roman past. He was evidently seeking to send a message of power indicating that he was a ruler as great as the emperors of Rome, and his new castle and town in Wales were every bit as grand and powerful as their great city of Constantinople.

A final example of the use of evocation of earlier buildings in this way comes from Hampton Court (England). Although this palace was built in the period of the Renaissance, when imitation of Roman architecture was increasingly prevalent, its style was quite different, harking back to much earlier medieval buildings. The great hall is the most striking component in this respect (Figure 3–10). As we saw, a great hall was no longer an important part of a palace at this period, when increasingly the most prominent part was the private apartment, as at the French kings' palace of the Louvre in Paris (above, pp. 47–48). Yet, not only was Hampton Court's great hall old-fashioned in the very fact of its existence; it was also consciously modeled on earlier halls. The figure shows the doors to the screens passage, at the far end of the hall, which permitted entry to the hall from the kitchen and the buttery for meals to be served—an arrangement that went far back into the medieval period. More-

Figure 3–10: The interior of the great hall, Hampton Court Palace, Kingston-upon-Thames (England), looking toward the screens passage.

over, the hall had no fireplace with a chimney, as would have been expected in a room of its period, but instead had an open fireplace in the center of the room (shown reconstructed in the figure) with the smoke intended to escape through a louver in the roof. This too must have been a conscious archaicism. The roof of the hall is also striking in this respect, for it is a great timber, hammer-beamed roof which seems consciously to imitate King Richard II's hammer-beam roof constructed during his rebuilding of Westminster Hall (Figure 2–24). The Hampton Court great hall must have been intended to convey a message of power relating to Henry VIII's legitimacy as the heir to the line of medieval English kings; and it must also have been part of an attempt to create a world of medieval chivalry which the king and his court could inhabit, and which also added the legitimacy of an aura of antiquity.

The cases of evocation of earlier architectural styles by the builders of palaces examined so far all address a wish to connect the builder with earlier rulers. More complicated is the process of evocation, or rather of adoption, which went into the building of Christian palaces at the Alcázar, formerly the Muslim palace quarter, at Seville (Spain). The Christians' "reconquest" of Spain from the Muslims, who had taken possession of it in the eighth century, had been going on sporadically since the eleventh century, although there had been

Figure 3–11: The Salon Gotico, Gothic Palace, the Alcázar, Seville (Spain), showing the Gothic style of the vaulting.

varying degrees of cooperation and friendship between Muslims and Christians in the interim. In 1248, however, after a two-year siege, the Christian king of Castile, Ferdinand III (1217–52), captured Seville, which up to that point had been a Muslim city, and made it his residence until his death. He probably lived in the Alcázar, which his successor, Alfonso X the Wise (1252–84), turned into a considerable center of culture. In particular, he demolished some of the Muslim buildings there and built the so-called Gothic Palace for himself. Although this palace has been much modified during the Renaissance, it is clear, notably from the remains in the Salon Gotico, that it was a building in Gothic style, with pointed arches and ribbed vaults—hence its name (Figure 3–11).

In light of the fact that, as we shall see, a very different style predominated in new buildings in the Alcázar in the following century, this use of Gothic presumably represents both a statement of a change in culture away from Muslim architecture following the victory of the Christians, and a statement of alignment with the northern areas of Spain, which (as in the cathedrals of León and Burgos) were overwhelmingly influenced by Gothic style. The use of that style in the Gothic Palace was arguably intended to send a message of power relating to the new Christian rulers and their links to other Christian areas where it was the favored style.

Although there were some Muslim elements in the Gothic Palace, notably the arrangement of the living rooms as long spaces with bed alcoves at each end, and the cruciform sunken garden in the courtyard in front of it, the adoption of Muslim features was carried much further in the fourteenth century in the building of the Hall of Justice across the courtyard from the Gothic Palace, and above all in the Palace of Pedro the Cruel (1350–69). It is not certain whether the Hall of Justice was built by Pedro the Cruel or Alfonso XI (1312–50), although the former seems the more likely in view of its similarity to the palace named after him (Figure 3–12).

Like the Palace of Pedro the Cruel, the Hall of Justice is very different in style from the Gothic Palace, and it would not have looked out of place among the Muslim palaces of the Alhambra at Granada. It is a centrally planned hall, decorated with stucco, and with a central water feature in the Muslim style flowing through a channel across the floor and into the courtyard beyond.

Muslim style was even more the keynote of the Palace of Pedro the Cruel. Its main façade resembles the façade of the Muslim Palace of Comares at the Alhambra (above, pp. 16–18). It is, in addition, decorated with stucco decoration forming so-called *sebka* patterns. These might well have been copied from the nearby minaret of what had been the principal mosque, but had by King Pedro's time been converted into a Christian cathedral (Figure 3–13; Figure 3–14).

At the heart of the palace was the Patio de las Doncellas, which was also lavishly decorated with stucco work in sebka patterns. Recent excavations have shown that it had at the center a garden of characteristic Muslim type, including a water feature and sunken beds, which have been reconstructed (Figure 3–15).

The arch on the far side leads into the Hall of the Ambassadors, which was in much the same style as the Hall of Justice. Along the sides were Muslim-style apartments, consisting of long rooms with sleeping alcoves at the ends of them. To the right of the Hall of the Ambassadors was a more private Muslim-style apartment suite (Patio del Techo de las Muñecas). Above the Patio de las Doncellas were rooms lavishly decorated with tilework, equally in Muslim style, such as the Chamber of Audiences, with stucco work and Muslim-style tiling.

The decorative style of the palace was not entirely Muslim, since it incorporated non-Muslim elements such as heraldic motifs, including the castle which was the heraldic emblem of the Kings of Castile, and also pictorial representations of scenes from non-Muslim literature, such as chivalric combats between knights, which appear on the walls of the Hall of the Ambassadors. Scholars generally refer to such a hybrid of Muslim and non-Muslim

Figure 3–12: Interior, Hall of Justice, the Alcázar, Seville (Spain), looking southeast. Note the stone bowl in the center from which a water channel flows toward the opening into the courtyard beyond.

elements as the Mudéjar style and, despite its non-Muslim elements, it was primarily influenced by—and indeed largely derived from—Muslim art.

Why should Pedro the Cruel have adopted this style whereas Alfonso X had been content to construct a palace that was at least superficially Gothic in style? What message of power might this have been intended to convey? It is possible, of course, that no message at all was intended; rather, the style was quite simply that in which the craftsmen and designers Pedro the Cruel had available to him knew how to build. This, however, does not seem likely, since Alfonso X seems to have had no trouble obtaining men able to work in Gothic style to build the Gothic Palace, and in any case an inscription on the doors leading into Pedro the Cruel's Hall of the Ambassadors shows that workers were drawn from a wide area, for it speaks of Toledo as a source of such expertise, and it is clear that workers from Granada were also involved (Cómez 2006, 58–60).

Figure 3–13: *Sebka* decoration on the main façade, Palace of Pedro the Cruel, the Alcázar, Seville (Spain).

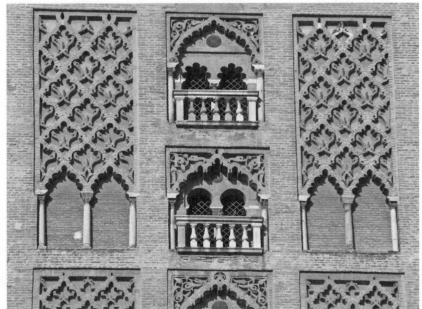

Figure 3–14: La Giralda, Seville Cathedral (Spain), formerly the minaret of the mosque from which the cathedral was converted, showing sebka decoration comparable to that on the Palace of Pedro the Cruel (see Figure 3–13).

Figure 3–15: Patio de las Doncellas, Palace of Pedro the Cruel, the Alcázar, Seville (Spain), as restored following the excavations, looking east toward the Hall of the Ambassadors, showing the sebka patterns and a garden of Muslim type. This latter consists of the central rectangular basin of water, with paved strips to either side, and beyond them sunken beds with trees, edged with walls decorated with patterns in stone.

It seems more likely then that the adoption of Muslim style and its modification into the Mudéjar style were deliberate, so that the style of Pedro the Cruel's palace was indeed intended to convey a message of power. But what message? It may have been a triumphalist celebration of the victory of the Christian monarchs over the Muslims of southern Spain. That it was, in other words, to articulate through the adoption of Muslim style that Pedro the Cruel's dynasty had dominated and absorbed the Islamic inhabitants and culture into their kingdom. This is hard to accept, however, since Pedro the Cruel had a close alliance and even friendship with Muhammad V (1354–59, 1362–91), the Muslim sultan of Granada, who spent a period in exile at the Alcázar and who was restored to his throne with the assistance of Pedro the Cruel.

An alternative interpretation is that Pedro the Cruel was identifying himself, through the use of this style, with a southern Spanish identity rather than demonstrating his triumph over Muslim culture. By his time, Christian rule in Seville was a century or more old, and the conquerors were no doubt absorbing naturally aspects of Muslim culture, and perhaps developing an admiration for Muslim art. This is suggested by the fact that until 1519 they continued to use the prayer hall of the principal mosque of Seville for their cathedral, and even then they kept the minaret, the Giralda, as the spire of the new Christian cathedral (Ruggles 2004, 94–96). So, by the mid-fourteenth century, it may have been natural for a ruler like Pedro the Cruel to have developed a quasi-Muslim style which the Mudéjar style was. He may also have been distancing himself from the dominating Gothic culture of northern Spain, and its close dependence on French culture.

ICONOGRAPHY

Just as the magnificence and the architectural style of palaces could carry messages of power, so too could the iconography of the images or sculptures with which they were decorated. One theme of these was the legitimacy of rulers, either through their achievements or through their family connections and their descent. According to Ermold the Black's *Poem on Louis the Pious*, the basilica of the emperor Charlemagne's palace at Ingelheim had wall paintings that showed the deeds of heroes on one side with those of the anti-heroes of antiquity on the other. The latter included an "unhappy prince who had seized the lands of a woman and whose head was plunged into a bottle of blood," as well as an ancient ruler called Phalaris and "the horrible massacres which he inflicted on his miserable people." Romulus and his brother, Remus, the founders of the city of Rome, were also represented, but not in a favorable light since the paintings showed "how the former killed his brother with a criminal hand." The North African ruler Hannibal, he of the elephants, also made an appearance in paintings showing how he "was endlessly employed in unjust wars and how he himself perished." On the other side of the great hall, Ermold writes, the paintings represented more recent rulers who were "inspired by the Christian spirit." These included the first Christian Roman emperor, Constantine, shown "leaving Rome to found Constantinople," as well as the actual ancestors of Louis the Pious represented in various military exploits. At the head of them all was a representation of Louis the Pious's father, Charlemagne, "with his face radiant and the crown on his head: the Saxons oppose him and try the fortune of arms; but he strikes them down, tames them and reduces them to obedience" (translated from Faral 1932, lines 2128–2163). This was evidently a message of the ruler's ideological power, deriving from his military success (sometimes against pagan peoples like the Saxons) and his virtues compared to the horrid vices and crimes of ancient rulers. The underlying implication is that pagan rulers were bad rulers and Christian rulers, like Constantine and the members of Charlemagne's family, were good rulers.

A similar message, cast in terms of the kings of the Bible, was conveyed by the thirteenth-century paintings on the walls of the Painted Chamber in the Palace of Westminster. These showed scenes of the deeds of various kings from the Old Testament. Rather like the paintings in the basilica at Ingelheim, they showed—lower on the wall—the deeds of tyrannical kings, their subjugation of peoples, and their downfall, while above they showed the heroic deeds of Judas Maccabaeus, whose martial exploits are described in the Book of Maccabees.

Clearly, it was with him that the English king was to be compared. He embraced the virtues of chivalry, as they were painted in the window openings, and eschewed the anger and malevolence of the bad Old Testament kings.

In the early fourteenth century, a series of statues in the great hall of the Palais de la Cité in Paris conveyed a similarly explicit message of power, in this case relating to the king's right to rule deriving from the legitimacy he had through his relationship to past rulers. The hall had long lines of statues of kings attached to the pillars that divided it into three aisles. No trace of them has survived, any more than has the great hall itself, and the details of the figures and which kings they were intended to represent can be reconstructed only from early modern representations, like that of Du Cerceau (Figure 2–27) and an earlier one of Gilles Corrozet, which do not always agree with each other. It seems clear enough, however, that the theme of the sequence of statues was the legitimate heredity of the French kings, for each had a label showing the dates of the king represented and his relationship to his predecessor. This sequence of figures was intended to convey the message that Philip the Fair, the rebuilder of the hall, and future generations of his family, were the legitimate heirs to the kingdom of France. To do this, it had to reach far back in time. It began with Pharamond, mythical king of Paris; then it proceeded through mythical or semi-mythical kings of the Franks, Clodio and Merovech; and so to more historical kings who created the kingdom of the Franks after the end of the Roman Empire in the West, Childeric and Clovis. Then to the emperor Charlemagne's father, Pippin III, and so to Charlemagne himself, and his son, the emperor Louis the Pious. And so on through the sequence of these Carolingian rulers, to the kings of France who emerged in succession to them in the western part of their empire, down to Philip the Fair (1285–1314) himself, the rebuilder of the great hall. This last clearly had an eye to the future of his family, for spaces seem to have been left for further statues, which were added for succeeding kings down to the time of Henry III (1574–89).

Emphasizing continuity with past kings, and especially with the Carolingians, was especially important to Philip the Fair because of the circumstances in which his ancestor, Hugh Capet (987–96), obtained the throne after the demise of the last Carolingian ruler of what was to become France. He had no real hereditary claim, so the legitimacy of his family as the royal family of France depended on establishing a seamless connection with the Carolingian dynasty. King Philip Augustus (1180–1223) had done this by asserting that his family had inaugurated a "return of the kingdom of France to the stock of Charlemagne," specifically by virtue of his mother being Adela of Champagne and his wife Isabel of Hainaut, both descended from Charlemagne. This claim seems to have been given new prominence from the late thirteenth century, so the issue of the legitimacy of Capetian rule was evidently still a live one at the time when Philip the Fair rebuilt the great hall (J. Bennert 1992).

It is in this context that the message of the sequence of statues of kings in the Paris great hall should be seen. It was subtly modified with respect to the known history of the kings to more clearly identify Capetian legitimacy. Three of the later Carolingians, Louis III, Carloman III, and Charles the Fat, were omitted, presumably because they were illegitimate, and their reigns therefore did nothing to support Capetian legitimacy. Kings who were not members of the Carolingian family and had nevertheless had brief reigns were also omitted: Odo (888–898), Robert I (922–23), and Raoul (923–36). Charles the Fat, although a Carolingian, was also omitted, probably because he was an emperor, ruling over the whole of the Carolingian Empire, rather than a king who could be regarded as a ruler specifically of France.

The ruler's relationship to the supernatural was another theme of the iconography of palace decoration. In a pagan context, this probably underlies the subject of the floor mosaics in the triclinium of the early fourth-century Villa Romana di Casale, near Piazza Armerina (Sicily). These show the labors of the mythical hero and demigod Hercules, who was the object of a cult. They include, for example, in the apses scenes of giants being overcome by Hercules' strength (Figure 3–16).

What is striking about these mosaics is that, although Hercules appears in the northern apse, he does not appear in the central square of the room, where one might have expected him to have been represented as the subject of the whole cycle of scenes. Perhaps the purpose of the cycle was to associate the owner of the palace with Hercules and, at whatever dinners or ceremonies took place in the triclinium, it was he who would have presented himself in the middle of the floor as a personification of Hercules, whose labors would have been represented around him. This is made the more likely because the fourth-century emperors were committed to the cult of Hercules, so that associating him with an emperor—or someone of equivalent status—would have been an obvious thing to do. The message would have been that this person's power derived from his association, or even identification, with the hero and demigod.

In a Christian context, a comparable theme of the ruler's relationship to the deity appeared in the mosaics that decorated the main short wall and its apse in Pope Leo III's triclinium in the Lateran Palace at Rome (Figure 2–22). Although the triclinium was destroyed in the early modern period, the subjects of the mosaics are known from descriptions, drawings, and paintings; and there is a modern reconstruction of them outside the church (Figure 3–17).

In the apse itself, the mosaics showed—on the half-dome—Christ giving his disciples the mission to preach Christianity. To the left of the apse, Christ, seated, is shown giving the keys to the Kingdom of Heaven to his disciple, St. Peter, and a banner with a cross on it to the first Christian Roman emperor, Constantine, both of whom kneel before him. On the right of the apse, St. Peter, seated, is giving the white shawl of office (the pallium) to the kneeling Pope Leo III, the builder of the triclinium, and he gives a lance with a banner to Pope Leo's contemporary, the emperor Charlemagne. These mosaics carried a clear message that the pope's power derived from Christ via St. Peter, who had himself received his power directly from Christ, and that the pope was on a level with secular rulers who received their power equally from Christ (in the case of Constantine) or from St. Peter (in the case of Charlemagne). Leo III was the pope who crowned Charlemagne as Holy Roman Emperor in Rome at Christmas 800, so that this view of the ideological character of the ruler's power stemming from the deity through him found appropriate expression in the message of power conveyed by the apse mosaic of his triclinium.

There is an equally clear, although less direct, reference to the ruler's relationship to the deity in the Painted Chamber at the Palace of Westminster. In the thirteenth century, its walls were decorated and its state bed was painted and furnished in ways and with subjects that emphasized the English king's alleged connections with the kings of the Old Testament

Figure 3–16: Mosaic in the central apse of the triclinium, Villa Romana di Casale, near Piazza Armerina (Sicily), showing a giant struck dead by Hercules' dart.

Figure 3–17: Reconstruction of the apse mosaic of Leo III's triclinium. Lateran Palace, Rome (Italy).

of the Bible. For a document of 1244 refers to green textiles for the bed and green paintwork decorating it (Binski 1986, 14), suggesting that it was intended to recall the bed of the biblical king Solomon, which the Bible described as similarly green in color. Solomon's bed is further described in the Bible as being guarded by armed men (Song of Songs I.16 and III.7–8; Carroll and Prickett 1997, I, 761, 762). The bed in the Painted Chamber had such a bed guard painted on the west side of the bed, and there was presumably another one on the east side (although there is no copy of any such painting). The bed's message of ideological power was reinforced by the large wall painting behind it of the coronation of the saintly English king, Edward the Confessor, whose relics were venerated in Westminster Abbey as one of its principal cults (below, pp. 327–28). There was another painting of the same saint on the window opening opposite the bed. The window openings also included painted figures representing the virtues and vices.

HEAVENLY DOMES

The idea that the ruler's power came from the cosmos itself goes a long way back in time. It is found in Central Asia and in the Middle East in antiquity, when the heavens could be represented by a tent decorated with stars. When the Greek ruler, Alexander the Great, conquered Persia he seems to have taken over this tradition, for his historian, Plutarch, refers to how Alexander, whom he calls "the Son of Heaven," "had a magnificent tent made with fifty gilded posts which carried a sky of rich workmanship" (quoted by E. B. Smith 1950, 82). The sky in this passage was presumably fabric patterned with stars and heavenly bodies.

It was no doubt this idea that the ruler's power was cosmic and that he should therefore appear under a representation of the heavens that explains the use of a baldachin, that is, a canopy in the form of a dome, which covered the ruler's throne. Such a baldachin appears over the throne of the emperor Theodosius as it appears in an illustration to a ninth-century Byzantine manuscript (Figure 3–18).

Later kings clearly also used such baldachins, for the Carolingian ruler, Charles the Bald (840–70), is represented enthroned under such a canopy in a miniature in a contemporary manuscript, the Golden Book of St. Emmeram (Munich, Bäyerische Staatsbliotek, Clm. 14000, fol. 5v). That the baldachin symbolizes the heavens is made clear by the emergence from above of the Hand of God, blessing the ruler beneath it.

The ruler's cosmic power could also be expressed by means of covering rooms in a palace, especially triclinia or halls, with domes, since these had the potential to represent the ruler whose palace it was as one so closely in touch with the deity that he was the ruler of the cosmos itself. For the dome, through its shape, represented the heavens themselves, and this representation could be enhanced by its decoration. The message was that the ruler's power stemmed from the heavens, or that he was so great a ruler that he was ruler of the cosmos itself.

A very early account of a triclinium with such a dome in a Roman palace is that by Suetonius in his description of the Golden House built by Emperor Nero at Rome. Among a

Figure 3–18: Throne of Emperor Theodosius the Great (379–95), represented in a miniature from the time of Emperor Basil I the Macedonian (867–86) (Paris, Bibliothèque nationale de France, MS Grec 510 fol. 239r). The emperor is attended by two guards, standing in front of his throne, which is covered with a baldachin. (See insert for color version of this image.)

series of impressive and opulent features of this palace, Suetonius notes that the "main dining hall," which could no doubt have been termed a triclinium, was circular and it "constantly revolved day and night." It seems likely, however, that it was in fact the domed ceiling of the circular room that rotated in imitation of the heavens (Suetonius's words are *vice mundi*, which could equally mean "in imitation of the earth") (Rolfe 1998, II, 136–37, and note c). This ceiling was presumably decorated with images of the sun, moon, and stars to call the heavens to the minds of those present in the room as it turned, just as the sky appears to turn about the earth. Suetonius called this a dining hall, so it was likely used chiefly as a dining hall rather than a throne room. But, as we have seen, dining in the emperor's palace was a very formal matter, and it no doubt offered the possibility of presenting the emperor at the high table, or at least at the high eating couch, as the focus of attention, with the illusory vault of heaven, created by the decoration of the dome and mechanical device driving it, turning above his head. There could hardly be a clearer message of the ideological power of the emperor, placing him in relationship with the cosmos, making him a ruler of the universe and on a level with the deity.

In Muslim culture, domes were found not only in mosques, for example in the Dome of the Rock in Jerusalem, but also in Muslim palaces, in centrally planned spaces which may have been the equivalents of Roman triclinia. Opening off the principal side of the courtyard of the Palace of Comares at the Alhambra is, as we saw, the sultan's apartment, the Sala de la Barca, and beyond that the Hall of the Ambassadors, built by the sultan, Yusuf I (1333–54) (Figure 2–12). This hall did not have a spherical dome, but its ceiling nevertheless was recessed in the form of a cupola suggestive of the heavens (Figure 3–19).

It has a large number of inscriptions worked into the magnificent plasterwork decoration around it. The inscription immediately under the ceiling is from the Koran, and specifically from the *surah* (or verse) known as the surah of the Kingdom (surah LXVII). This has the words:

> Blessed is He in whose hands is Dominion; and He is powerful over everything—He who created death and life . . . and He is the Exalted in Might, the Oft-Forgiving—He who created the Seven Heavens one above another. (Vílchez, Guarde, and Cuenca 2011, 124)

This is a reference to Allah, but in the context of the Hall of the Ambassadors it is hard to escape the conclusion that the message being conveyed was that the sultan's power was closely linked to Allah's and that it derived from the heavens which Allah had created. The message must have stood out all the more clearly because the decoration of the ceiling, which consists of six rows of stars and a central, star-like cupola, actually represents the Seven Heavens. When the sultan received guests or ambassadors here, he was receiving them under a representation of the canopy of the heavens from which his power flowed.

At the back of the room, in the center of the wall opposite the entrance, is a highly decorated alcove with an arched ceiling over it (Figure 3–20).

The inscription along its inner sides reads:

> Through me, both by day and night, mouths salute you
> with wishes of good fortune, happiness, and friendship . . .
> being without doubt the heart and the limbs,
> for it is in the heart that spiritual strength and the soul reside.
> If my sisters are constellations in its heaven [of the cupola]
> it is to me that the honour of bearing the sun falls.
> My lord Yusuf, sustained by God, clothed me
> in dignity with robes of undeniable distinction,
> making me the throne of the kingdom, the grandeur
> of which is born up thanks to the Light, the Seat, and the Throne.
>
> (Vílchez, Guarde, and Cuenca 2011, 126, 30)

The speaker in this contemporary poem is meant to be the room itself describing the glory that the sultan has bestowed on it, decorating it with "robes of undeniable distinction," and

Figure 3–19: Ceiling of the Hall of the Ambassadors, Palace of Comares, the Alhambra, Granada (Spain).

raising it above the constellations. It shows that the alcove was where the sultan's throne was placed, so the point that his power was associated with the stars was made all the more clearly. Together with the decoration on the cupola, it seems quite plausible that the room was a "microcosm," showing the Seven Heavens with below them the throne of the ruler, who derived his power from Allah.

In the adjacent Palace of the Lions, there is another impressive room, the Hall of the Two Sisters. This has more of a dome than the ceiling cupola of the Hall of the Ambassadors in the Palace of Comares and, although it does not have such explicit inscriptions as that room does, its plasterwork leaves no possible doubt that the dome of heaven was again being represented (Figure 3–21).

Domes were also found in Christian contexts, mostly in churches (below, pp. 273–96), but also in palaces. Equally explicit in its decoration was the dome of the Hall of the Ambassadors in the Palace of Pedro the Cruel, a close and nearly contemporary neighbor of the domes in the Alhambra (Figure 3–22). The representation of stars in this golden, glowing space is unmistakable, as is the star shape created by the *mqarnas* plaster decoration around the base of the dome.

Figure 3–20: Decorated alcove in the Hall of the Ambassadors, Palace of Comares, the Alhambra, Granada (Spain).

Figure 3–21: Dome of the Hall of the Two Sisters, Palace of the Lions, Alhambra, Granada (Spain).

Figure 3–22: Dome of the Hall of the Ambassadors, Palace of Pedro the Cruel, the Alcázar, Seville (Spain).

SACRED GEOMETRY

The style of a palace may have carried an even deeper meaning, one that went beyond the mere appearance of the buildings to which it was applied. That style could, for example, have symbolized the ruler's relationship with the supernatural; it could have conveyed a message of power based on nothing less than his standing in the cosmos. Such possibilities are especially raised by one of the most remarkable buildings to have survived from the Middle Ages, the Castel del Monte in Apulia in southern Italy, constructed around 1240 for the German emperor Frederick II (1198–1250) (Licinio 2002a, 5). Despite its name, it can surely be described as a palace rather than a castle. Like other palaces considered in this book, it occupied a high and dominating position; unlike the palaces of Nuremberg and Prague (below, pp. 173, 175) it did not look down over a city, apart from that of Andria in the distance, but rather over the hills of Frederick's kingdom away to the coast of the Adriatic Sea many miles away (Figure 3–23).

Such a hilltop site could have been chosen for its defensibility, but in the case of the Castel del Monte it seems more likely that the views from the building, and the views of it from a distance, were the reasons for the choice. From its principal rooms on the first floor, handsome, two-light windows take in the view; and the road approaching the castle, which is thought to be following its original course, winds in a circle around it, partly no doubt to lessen the incline, but chiefly, surely, to give the best views of the magnificent building it is approaching.

Like other palaces discussed in this book, it is magnificent. Its main entrance, which is at the top of a flight of steps, is largely built of a beautiful red stone with white flecks called brescia rossa and resembles in its style a Roman opening, perhaps a triumphal arch (Figure 3–24). It is fortified, certainly, for it has a slot for a portcullis, but the main purpose of such an entrance must have been to receive the ruler into his palace, and to convey a message in providing a context for that arrival so magnificent and Roman in character.

Magnificence evidently continued as one passed into the interior. The principal rooms were on the first floor, the "noble floor" as it would be called in early modern palaces and great houses. They have been badly treated over the centuries, and stripped of most of their decoration; but enough survives to show that the walls were originally clad in marble or in brescia rossa, they had rib-vaulted ceilings with marble columns, the most important of them had magnificent fireplaces, and some had marble benches (Figure 3–25). Cladding the walls in brescia rossa was also a feature of the ground-floor rooms, which were almost as magnificent, although they lacked the number of fireplaces and windows that the first-floor rooms originally had.

The really distinctive aspect of the Castel del Monte, however, was not its decoration, magnificent as that certainly was, but its plan, which is based with the utmost rigor on the geometrical shape of the octagon (Figure 3–26). The palace consists of two octagons, the first being the outer walls, the second enclosing the central courtyard. At the center of this courtyard, there was once an octagonal fountain. Around the outer wall, and partly merging with it, are eight towers, one at each corner of the outer octagon, and these towers are themselves octagonal in plan, apart from where they merge with the palace's outer wall.

Figure 3–23: Aerial view, Castel del Monte (Italy), showing the octagonal plan of the castle, its towers, and its central courtyard. The approach road winds around the castle from the left.

Figure 3–24: Main entrance, Castel del Monte (Italy).

Figure 3–25: Room VII (first floor), Castel del Monte (Italy), showing the marble columns, marble benches, and remains of the fireplaces with two cupboards lined with brescia rossa on either side of it.

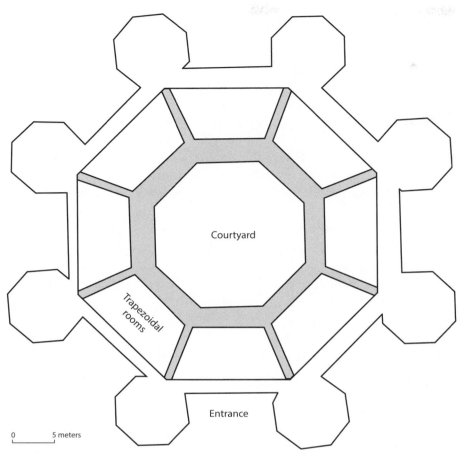

Figure 3–26: Diagrammatic plan of the ground-floor layout, Castel del Monte (Italy), showing the rigorous geometrical planning and centrality of octagons in the design (after Götze 1998, 89, fig. 125).

The palace's octagonal shape meant that the rooms were all trapezoidal in plan. This is not the most practical shape for a room, but it is nevertheless clear that these rooms were meant to be functional. Careful study of the doors into them from the courtyard and the doors communicating between them shows how those on the first floor could have been used as apartments and halls, opening out on to a gallery, now disappeared, which ran round the inside of the courtyard; and as guard rooms and service rooms on the ground floor. Latrines and washbasins were installed in various of the towers, and the remains of them show that in this respect too the magnificence of the palace was upheld.

Clearly, though, convenience was not the primary driving force behind this palace, but rather the wish to build according to a strict application of geometry. Why should this have been so? It is known that Frederick II was very concerned to be a cultured and educated ruler and to have a similarly cultured and educated court. He founded the University of Naples in 1224, and he remained in close contact with scholars, such as Leonard of Pisa, who traveled widely in the Arab lands, introduced the 0 and the X into western mathematics, created a mathematical expression for the harmonic ratio of the golden section which was of importance in architecture, and dedicated his *Book of the Abacus* to Michael Scotus, who was concerned with science at Frederick II's court (Burnett 1994, 116–17; Götze 1998, 27). It is not difficult to envisage a rigorously geometrical style such as that of the Castel del Monte being adopted in such a context. Nor was it the only such building Frederick II had built. The keep of his castle at Termoli on the Adriatic Coast, for example, took the form of a perfect square set within another square, with circular turrets at its corners, with strict concern for symmetry shown throughout. Similarly, the towers he had built for his bridgehead gate at Capua (Figure 7–16) also show concern for geometrical rigor, with the truncated octagons of the lower parts of the towers turning into perfect cylinders higher up.

Frederick II was not the only ruler of his time to have adopted geometrical rigor in his buildings. When Louis IX (1226–70) built his new city of Aigues Mortes on the south coast of France, the castle-palace that he constructed had a keep which stood apart from the rest of the castle and was quite circular in plan, producing circular rooms inside which were of some grandeur. The castle-palace built by the King of Aragon and Majorca at Bellver on the island of Mallorca had not only a circular keep, but also a circular main body, consisting of two concentric walls enclosing curving rooms between them, and with a circular courtyard at the center (Figure 3–27).

This rigorous use of geometry in palaces had a long history. The lower level of what is thought to be the more private part of the palace of the emperor Domitian (81–96) at Rome was notable for the geometrical shapes of its rooms (Figure 2–29). This aspect of style may not have been intended to convey any particular message, but was rather a reflection of scholarly interest in geometry at particular periods. It was certainly the case that this discipline was studied by scholars in the so-called renaissance of Charlemagne's time, as well as in that of the twelfth century. The result was no doubt that architects were familiar with classical works on geometry. So it could be argued that application of geometry to the style of buildings was no more than a natural consequence of having acquired that knowledge. It seems more likely, however, that a building constructed according to strict geometrical principles was intended to convey a message of power. For geometry was more than just a practical subject; it was also a mystical one. Geometrical ratios and geometrical shapes were regarded as reflecting the fundamental structure of the universe and as having a significance in their own right. Thus, the square was regarded as a reflection of the earth, while the circle was a perfect shape, and so reflected heaven. The octagon was a shape intermediate between the square and the circle, and so had a particular significance as a shape tending toward heaven. It was also a shape that could be extended to form the eight-pointed star, itself a sacred symbol in both Christianity and Islam. It may therefore be significant that the eight-pointed star can be neatly superimposed on the Castel del Monte. It can equally be imposed on the octagonal shape of the church of San Vitale in Ravenna, one of the churches the architect of the Aachen palace church may have been evoking, and the eighth-century Dome of the Rock, built in Jerusalem on the site of King Solomon's temple by the caliph Abd al'Malik (Götze 1998, 117, 129–40, 144–46).

The religious significance of an octagonal building was made explicit by Ambrose, bishop of Milan, in an inscription written in the baptistery church of St. Thecla in Milan:

Figure 3–27: Aerial view, Bellver Castle (Mallorca), showing its rigorously geometrical form, based on circles.

With eight niches the temple rises to holy use.
The fountain is octagonal, worthy of the [sacred] gift.
The house of holy baptism had to arise in the [sacred] number eight.

(quoted by Götze 1998, 117)

There are no extant documents or chronicles whatsoever to help in understanding what Frederick II's motives were in adopting geometrical forms for his buildings, including the Castel del Monte. But it is not impossible that the octagonal form of the Castel del Monte was intended to broadcast that here was a ruler in tune with the deepest levels of the cosmos, reaching toward heaven with a palace, the octagonal shape of which approached the perfect circle of the celestial realm.

At the palace church of Aachen, in a sense, the octagon made this transition to a circle. As has been seen, the plan of the nave was octagonal, with the outer wall of the aisle and gallery sixteen-sided; but the elevation of the nave and the aisles was based on the circle (Figure 3–28).

Such a use of geometry as the language of the cosmos may also be found in the recently restored mosaic pavement in the sanctuary of Westminster Abbey, more or less contemporary with the Castel del Monte. This is a pavement in the style of the Cosmati mosaicists of the city of Rome, who produced many works of this type, including some of the finest surviving examples in the papal palace at Agnani (Italy). A Latin inscription, in brass letters, was set into the Westminster pavement. Although it is no longer extant, a copy of it made in the fifteenth century shows that it dated the pavement to 1272 and attributed it to King

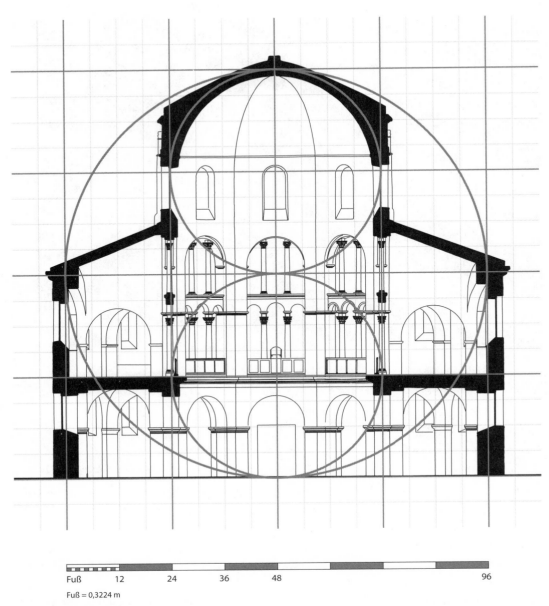

Fuß   12   24   36   48   96

Figure 3–28: Diagrammatic north-south cross-section, St. Mary's Church, the former palace church, Aachen (Germany), showing the use of circles to define the elevation of the nave, aisles, and galleries.

Henry III (1216–72), Richard of Ware, abbot of Westminster, and a certain Odoricus, who was probably a mosaicist from Rome (referred to in the inscription as simply "the city") (Binski 1990, 10; R. Foster 1991, ch. 5). The involvement of the abbot, Richard of Ware, in the laying of the pavement is confirmed by the epitaph from his grave, which was part of the pavement and is recorded as having read: "Richard of Ware, who rests here under these stones which he brought back from the city [i.e. Rome]" (Binski 2002, 120). The abbot was deeply involved in the project to create Westminster Abbey as a royal palace church, and it seems likely that, in bringing the mosaic ready-made (or perhaps the mosaicist to make it in the abbey) from Rome, he was acting at the king's behest, or at least with the king's approval. Indeed, a document of 1269 records that the king paid him for services that included "a pavement which he brought with him from the Roman curia to the king's use, to be put in the church of Westminster before the king's great altar there" (R. Foster 1991, 14). This pavement was presumably the one in the sanctuary.

The pavement is a rare survival of a Cosmati mosaic in a fairly undisturbed condition, and it is very beautiful, making use of a wide range of stones. But the really distinctive aspect of it was the now almost entirely lost Latin inscription around the four innermost circles of its design (Figure 3–29). According to the fifteenth-century copy of this, it read (in translation):

> If the reader wittingly reflects upon all that is laid down,
> he will discover here the measure of the *primum mobile*:
> the hedge stands for three years,
> add in turn dogs, and horses and men,
> stags and ravens, eagles, huge sea monsters, the world:
> each that follows triples the years of the one before.

(R. Foster 1991, 110)

On the face of it, this is deeply enigmatic. What is the *primum mobile*? What is the significance of the hedge? Why this sequence of birds, animals, men, and the world, and why do they "triple the years of the one before" in sequence?

The closest parallel to this inscription is an Irish poem in a manuscript called the *Book of Lismore*, which can be translated:

> A year for the stake. Three years for the field.
> Three lifetimes of the field for the hound.
> Three lifetimes of the hound for the horse.
> Three lifetimes of the human being for the stag.
> Three lifetimes of the stag for the ousel.
> Three lifetimes of the ousel for the eagle.
> Three lifetimes of the eagle for the salmon.
> Three lifetimes of the salmon for the yew.
> Three lifetimes of the yew for the world
> from its beginning to its end, as the poet says.

(R. Foster 1991, 101, quoting Whitley Stokes)

This too appears at first glance deeply enigmatic, but at least the last two lines give some clue to what it is about. They refer to "the world from its beginning to its end," showing that the aim of the poem is to give a method for calculating the period that was supposed to have elapsed since the Creation. This begins with one year, assigned to "the stake," followed by three years, assigned to "the field," just as three years are assigned to the hedge in the Westminster inscription. The poem then goes on with a list of animals, birds, fish, and a tree (the yew), to each of which is assigned "three lifetimes" of the one that comes before in the list.

Since there are nine such "lifetimes," the poem is simply an elaborate way of expressing the mathematical formula 3 to the power of 9 as the number of years from the Creation to the point at which the world will come to an end, that is, 19,683 years.

The Westminster inscription also gives a sequence of nine lifetimes, so that it prompts exactly the same calculation, that is:

Hedge: 3 years
Dog: 3 x 3 = 9 years
Horse: 3 x 9 = 27 years
Man: 3 x 27 = 81 years
Stag: 3 x 81 = 243 years
Raven: 3 x 243 = 729 years
Eagle: 3 x 729 = 2,187 years
Sea monster: 3 x 2,187 = 6,561 years
The world: 3 x 6,561 = 19,683 years

The poem in the *Book of Lismore* is relatively simple in stating that what is being calculated is the date of the end of the world, but the Westminster inscription states that what is to be calculated is the "measure," meaning probably the "end," of the primum mobile. These two Latin words, which mean literally "first moving entity," seem to have referred to the outermost sphere of the universe, which was conceived of as a series of spheres, one inside the other. That outermost sphere had been the "first moving entity" produced by God who caused it to turn with perfect precision in a motion which was that of the heavens turning over the earth. Its end would be the end of the world and of the universe.

It seems from this that the Westminster inscription intended to make those who saw and read the inscription reflect on the end of the universe. It also seems, however, that the mosaic itself was intended to represent that universe schematically as it was envisaged to be. For another inscription around the inner circle of the design read in translation:

Here is the perfectly rounded sphere which reveals
the eternal pattern of the universe.

(R. Foster 1991, 109–10)

This is not very clear, but it seems to hint that the mosaic is a diagram of the created universe, as it was understood as a "perfectly rounded sphere" with layers within it (Figure 3–29).

The circle at the center of the pavement might represent the *silva*, that is, the unformed matter of creation. Around it, the four circles swirling into each other would represent the four elements of earth, air, fire, and water. The circle on the south (the left) has a black disk or dot in the middle, which may mark it as a representation of fire, or perhaps of the sun, for which a circle with a dot in the center was a symbol used in astrology and alchemy. Just within this circle is an octagon, the sacredness of which shape we have already considered. It may also be relevant that, if this circle does represent the sun, the number eight stands for Sunday, the day of the sun, the first and eighth day of the week.

The swirling circle on the north side (to the right of the central circle) has within it not an octagon but a seven-sided polygon. This circle may represent the element of water, and

Figure 3–29: Sanctuary pavement after cleaning and conservation, Westminster Abbey, Westminster (England). (See insert for color version of this image.)

the polygon within it the moon, which was associated with that element. The seven sides of the polygon would have corresponded to the number of phases of the moon, as well as to the numbers from one to seven, which, added together, gave the number twenty-eight, being the number of days in the lunar month. The element of air should probably be identified with the eastern swirling circle (below the central circle), which has in it a second perfect circle—perhaps representing the "breath" or "word" of God. The western swirling circle (above the central circle) would then represent the earth. It has within it a hexagon, the number of the sides of which, six, was a perfect number, and also the number of faces of a cube, the basis of terrestrial geometry. Around these four swirling circles and the square that contained the inscription attributing and dating the pavement was a series of interlocking circles with much more varied shapes and patterns inside them, although these are still expressed in geometrical shapes. These may have represented the outer layer of the universe, which was conceived as more transient and less perfect than the inner layer, which was in turn less perfect than the circular core, the circle of the pavement. So the pavement could be interpreted as a representation of the created universe, moving outward from the silva at its core. But the main inscription indicated that it is in fact about the end of time, so what it may really represent is everything falling into the central roundel of the silva as the universe comes to an end.

If this interpretation of the sanctuary pavement is accepted, what might its significance have been? It would be possible to regard the pavement as intended to do no more than to prompt those learned enough to understand it (or those who were fortunate enough to have it explained to them) to ponder the created universe and its future end. In view of the close royal associations of the church in which it was set, however, and the role of the king in its creation as acknowledged in one of its inscriptions, it may be reasonable to see it equally as an evocation of the created universe and the geometry which expressed it in terms of royal power. Just as the Castel del Monte's rigorous geometry may have been intended to convey a message of power based on the connection between the ruler who built it and the cosmos, so the Westminster pavement may have been intended to convey a similar message of the kings who worshipped, were crowned, and were also buried in Westminster Abbey (below, pp. 327–29, 366). In such ways, the use of geometry in palaces and their churches may represent the deepest aspect of style in transmitting a message of power, and in reflecting and helping to create the most ambitious claims of rulers—that they were in some sense rulers of the universe.

CONCLUSION

Much of this chapter is inevitably conjectural. As we have seen, there are written statements from different periods confirming the importance of magnificence as an aspect of palaces which conveyed a message about the power of the rulers in question. Beyond that, however, we are dependent on deducing conclusions about messages of power only from the architectural style and decoration of the palaces themselves. There are written sources confirming, for example, the importance of geometry, but there are almost never specific commentaries from the past on how palaces were intended to be seen and how they were seen. Rulers must surely have selected the architectural styles and decoration to be used in their palaces, but they never left statements as to why they made those choices. In all the examples discussed in this chapter, and indeed in all the examples that there are, of palaces built according to particular styles and decorated in particular ways, it would be possible to argue these were simply a matter of personal taste or of family taste.

If we accept, however, that the design of palaces was, in many cases at least, intended in itself to convey a message of power, through the elaborate spaces created almost in the form of a stage set for the presentation of the ruler and his court, then it is hard not to proceed to the further conclusion that the architectural style and decoration of palaces must also have contributed to this. Magnificence, as we have seen, was at various periods a compulsory aspiration of rulers, even if it was shared with a wider social elite, and even if it no doubt accorded with private taste as well as with political aspirations. The evocation of earlier styles, especially Roman and Byzantine styles, was evidently an important aspect of medieval and later palace-building, and for this too it seems likely that it was intended to convey a particular message about the ruler's position relative to the rulers of the past, to convey in other words a message about the comparative scale of his power. That message, as we have seen, need not have been restricted to presenting the ruler as an equal of past rulers, but it may have aimed to present him as their superior. The architectural style and decoration of palaces could equally underline the relationship between the ruler and conquered or subject cultures, as may be the case with the adoption of the quasi-Muslim Mudéjar style in the Palace of Pedro the Cruel. As is true of the magnificence of palaces, such a style was not restricted to rulers, for other elite buildings used it too (the Casa di Pilatos at Seville, for example). But it could have had a specific meaning when used by a ruler, like Pedro the Cruel, whose family members were the conquerors of parts of Muslim Spain, and who was himself in close contact with one of the remaining Muslim rulers, Muhammad V, sultan of Granada.

Architectural style, however, could have conveyed a message of power because of its novelty and sophistication. It could also have been intended that the architectural style of palaces should have been studied for the deeper meanings it could convey. As has been argued, the use of geometry may have been intended to convey a message of the ruler's relationship to the cosmos, which can hardly have been other than a message of ideological power.

In considering the possible importance of the architectural style and decoration of palaces, it may be instructive to look beyond the period of this book into the eighteenth century, for which the written evidence for the work of architects, their attitudes, and their relationships to their patrons is much fuller. It is striking that the importance of architectural style and decoration that this chapter has proposed for palaces in earlier periods seems very clearly to have been part of the outlook of eighteenth-century architects. When, for example, Sir John Vanbrugh (1664–1726) built Castle Howard in Yorkshire (England) for the Earl of Carlisle, he used, on the north front of the house, the classical Doric order, which was an order of architecture especially associated with soldiers. Further, on this front all the sculptural scenes are military. The conclusion must be that this façade of the palace was intended to glorify Carlisle's military career. On the other hand, the south or garden front has capitals of the Corinthian order, which Vaughan Hart describes as "the feminine order most appropriate to Venus and Flora according to Vitruvius" (Hart 2008, 132). The kitchen court (and there should have been a matching stable court on the other side) was built in a quite different, quasi-medieval style as if to suggest a medieval castle rather than a classical house. The approach to the house from the York road is also striking in that it leads through a sham curtain wall with medieval turrets and battlements. These features add to the military tone of the house, but they are also a medieval reminiscence. This medieval emphasis was a political statement in stone, reflecting the Whig preoccupation with the Englishness of Whig politics, rooted in the old English past, in opposition to the Frenchness, as it was perceived, of the culture of their political opponents, the Tories.

It may be, of course, that eighteenth-century architects were operating in a quite different way from their predecessors. It may be that their studies of earlier texts, such as the *Ten Books of Architecture*, by the Roman writer Vitruvius, or the more recent works on architecture, created a quite different intellectual world in which their buildings were conceived. But there is perhaps enough evidence in the examples considered in this chapter at least to bring forward the possibility that the architectural style and decoration of buildings was not so differently envisaged in earlier periods, and that it is therefore not unreasonable to regard earlier palaces as conveying messages of power through these aspects as much as through their design.

PART II

Landscapes

This section of the book is concerned with the ways in which the landscapes around palaces could be modified or organized or artificially created, to convey messages of power, just as much as the palaces that were sited in them. Such landscapes are usually divided into three types: the smallest landscape, which is the garden; the medium-sized landscape, which is the park, enclosed by a wall or a fence; and the forest, which could extend for many miles outside the palace. But that threefold division is not a straightforward one. In the period we are concerned with, gardens could range in type from quite small gardens in the courtyards of buildings, to much more extensive affairs, with series of lawns and enclosed spaces. They could also be confused with parks, for parks could sometimes have inside them features such as fountains, normally regarded as typical of gardens, and sometimes too there could be actual gardens within parks.

The functions of designed landscapes can also cause problems for this threefold division. Parks could be largely aesthetic, their layout aimed at creating pleasing vistas; but they could also be places to hunt animals, in which they were related to the much more extensive forests beyond them, which also provided opportunities for hunting. Gardens, on the other hand, could be laid out primarily for their appearance and as places of relaxation, or they could be intended to produce food. The distinction does not seem to have been a sharp one, as is shown, for example, by the use of the Old French word *vergier*, which (like modern French *verger*) can mean "orchard." But it seems to have also meant a place where there were often fruit trees, but which was nevertheless a garden for enjoyment, often enclosed by a hedge, moat, or wall. It could have a fountain, as in the poem written in Old French by a writer called Marcabru in the twelfth century, entitled "At the Fountain of the *Vergier*," which also refers to white flowers growing there (Gesbert 2003, 386). The range of types of garden and park, and the overlap between garden and park, appear in a miniature from the calendar of the Très Riches Heures of the Duke of Berry (Figure –II-1).

This shows a scene of betrothal, in which a young couple are exchanging rings in the presence of their parents. The château, which is recognizable as the Duke of Berry's château

Figure II–1: Château of Dourdan and its garden and park (Très Riches Heures of the Duke of Berry, Musée de Condé, Chantilly, France, fol. 4v, April).

of Dourdan in France, stands in the background with its village nestling close to it. On the right-hand side of the painting appears another building, its large windows showing it to be of high status. This seems to be a pavilion and its garden, set in the park of the château. For it is evidently in the park that the principal action takes place. That this is an artificially created landscape is shown by the regular lines of trees planted, the lake which serves to enhance the view of the château (although the boats fishing on it show that it was also a productive resource), and the smooth green turf, on which the elegantly dressed persons are standing, and from which two girls are gathering flowers. The pavilion, if that is what it is, has around it a walled garden, with grassy areas, flowering trees, a trellis for growing shrubs against, and more trees or shrubs trained against the walls. A line of flowering shrubs has been established around the outside of the walls too, so that the transition from garden to park seems to be made as smooth as possible. The park is larger and more open than the garden, but it is not dissimilar to it in its artificiality and in having been created with the desire to make it beautiful.

So it makes sense not to be too rigid in definitions, and to think more in terms of the function of the artificially created landscapes than whether they were strictly speaking gardens, parks, or forests. The first chapter of this section will look at the aesthetic, religious, and cultural aspects of such designed landscapes, especially gardens and to a lesser extent parks, as they can be perceived as conveying messages of power. The second will look, from a similar perspective, at forests, especially their more practical functions, and especially as regards the practice of hunting.

CHAPTER 4

Gardens, Parks, and Power

Although gardens and parks from the period we are concerned with have not survived the passage of time as well as buildings have often done, there is nonetheless a fair amount of evidence about them. They appear in contemporary poems and other writings; they are mentioned in accounts detailing what was spent on particular work to create or maintain them; they often feature in paintings and manuscript miniatures; and, in recent years, more and more of them have been discovered through archaeological work. Research at the Roman city of Pompeii in southern Italy, for example, has shown the existence of many gardens of various sizes (Jashemski and Jashemski 1979); the excavation of the Roman palace at Fishbourne in Sussex (England) has brought to light a garden, which would probably have been lost if the excavators had not been using the most up-to-date methods of archaeology (Cunliffe 1971, 128–48); and a series of studies of earthworks around palaces and castles has provided more and more examples of gardens and parks as part of artificially created landscapes. We should then probably expect to find gardens, sometimes with a park beyond, as an essential and integral part of palaces at most periods. If a palace was to be a proper palace, it had to have one or more of these landscapes, just as it had to be splendidly decorated, with an imposing entrance, and so on. The garden had to be grander than the garden of an ordinary dwelling, just as the palace had to be grander than such a dwelling.

GARDENS AND PARKS AS INTEGRAL COMPONENTS OF PALACES

The Palace of Domitian in Rome had splendid gardens in at least three of its peristyle-courtyards, which have been uncovered by archaeological excavation. All had sophisticated garden features. Excavation of the peristyle-courtyard in the area of the palace called the *Domus Flavia* has revealed a large, octagonal feature, once richly decorated in different colors of marble, and with a series of channels running around it which will certainly have carried water. As has been seen, the peristyle-courtyard of the lower level of the part of the Palace of Domitian called the *Domus Augustana* has been revealed as a series of geometric features, perhaps beds for plants, which must have constituted a garden of some sort (above, pp. 44–45, and Figure 2–29). Grandest of all was the garden in one of the peristyle-courtyards of the upper level of the Domus Augustana, which has the remains of what was clearly an artificial island set in a lake (Figure 4–1).

Figure 4–1: Artificial island in the peristyle-courtyard of the Domus Augustana, Palace of Domitian, Rome (Italy). The island is the earth mound with a tree on it; to the right, the remains of a stone bridge can be seen leading to it.

Clearly, the intention was to produce a stage set comprising an island set in water, perhaps in the sea itself. This may have been mere caprice, mere diversion. But perhaps the intention was that this garden should convey a message as to the emperor's power over the sea, or perhaps his prowess in naval warfare—especially if this garden feature was used for games representing the emperor's naval triumphs, with ships, or perhaps models of ships, sailing in the water around the island.

That gardens could be an almost obligatory part of palaces is suggested by the Roman villa excavated at Fishbourne, which was rebuilt as a grandiose palace sometime after AD 73. This palace consisted of four wings with a formal garden between them, and another garden beyond the southern wing. The archaeological excavations have uncovered the bedding trenches for plants or shrubs. The importance of the garden between the wings is clear from its position. Visitors entering through the entrance hall would have passed along a path across it on the way to the audience hall in the opposite wing, where the palace's lord would have been waiting to greet them. The garden had colonnaded walks on three sides, and the path across it was lined with geometrically arranged plantings of shrubs, perhaps with flowers between them. The effort required to create this garden must have been enormous, for the whole site had to be leveled with a vast amount of earth-moving, and great care must have been taken to preserve the topsoil in order to create the gardens when the leveling and building works were finished. These gardens were evidently very important to the owner of the palace. That owner may have been a native British king called Cogidubnus, a client of the Romans who had invaded Britain in AD 43, and who gave him the title of "legate of the emperor" on three occasions, in AD 43, 60, and 69 (Cunliffe 1971, 166–69). He must have wanted very badly to prove that he was now a real Roman ruler, and an excellent way to do so was to build Fishbourne palace, and to adorn it with gardens in the manner of Roman palaces such as the Palace of Domitian.

The importance of gardens to palaces is clear from other places and other periods. Although we have no trace of the gardens—and accompanying parks—that the king and emperor Charlemagne (768–814) constructed at palaces like Aachen and Ingelheim in Germany, there are clear indications that gardens and parks were important to him. In the document called the *Capitulare de Villis*, which was issued either by him or his son Louis the Pious and which deals with how the ruler's landed estates and houses were to be managed, clause 40 reads:

> That every steward [in charge of one of our estates] shall always have swans, peacocks, pheasants, ducks, pigeons, partridges and turtle doves, for the sake of ornament. (Loyn and Percival 1975, 69)

Clearly, this must mean that the ruler's houses were to have gardens around them, or perhaps ornamental parks, graced with ornamental birds. Being a great ruler comparable with a Roman emperor, which was what Charlemagne aspired to be, evidently meant having such features as part of his residences.

Elsewhere in the *Capitulare de Villis*, it is stated that there were "walled parks, which the people called *brogili*" (clause 46), while the document closes with a long list of plants and trees that the stewards are to "have in our gardens." This list includes: herbs used in medicine, such as sage, rue, rosemary, and lovage; salads, such as cucumber, lettuce, and rocket; beans, such as kidney beans and broad beans; cooking herbs, such as chicory, endive, and mint; root vegetables, such as carrot and parsnip; plants used in cloth-making, such as madder and teasel; and fruit and nut trees, such as apples, pears, cherries, chestnuts, and hazel—a total of no less than eighty-six varieties. Clearly, these plants were largely intended to produce fruits and seeds for eating or other uses, and this is especially evident in the treatment of the apples:

> The names of the apples are: *gozmaringa, geroldinga, crevedella, spirauca*; there are sweet ones, bitter ones, those that keep well, those that are to be eaten straightaway, and early ones. (Loyn and Percival 1975, 73)

Even if they were productive, however, the gardens could nevertheless have been ornamental and an intrinsic part of the magnificence of Charlemagne's or Louis the Pious's houses. Indeed, the opening of the list strongly suggests this, for it contains roses and lilies. These did have uses in medicine, but not so extensively as not to leave open the most obvious interpretation, namely that they were grown primarily for their beauty. The flag iris (*gladiolus*) was probably also included in the list for the same reason.

That gardens were important in the palaces of Charlemagne and Louis the Pious is also suggested by the fact that one of the court poets, Walafrid Strabo, wrote a poem sometime after 829 entitled "On the Cultivation of Gardens," which comments on the beauty and scent of sage, flag irises, lilies, and roses, and also makes reference to a range of other plants, including violets, hyacinths, and possibly primroses (C. Thacker 1979, 81–82; J. Harvey 1981, 34). In another poem, the same author mentions a park at Charlemagne's palace at Aachen (see below), which is also referred to by another writer in Louis the Pious's reign, Ermold the Black, in the following terms:

> There is a place close to the illustrious imperial palace of Aachen, enclosed by stone walls, planted with trees and green with grass. A river peacefully flows across it, and it is inhabited by birds of different sorts and by wild animals. (translated from Faral 1932, 140–41)

Unsurprisingly, there were gardens and parks also at the palaces of the Byzantine emperors. In the Great Palace at Constantinople, the emperor Basil I (867–86) constructed a small secluded garden called the Mesokepion, between the church of the Nea, which he had also built, and his new polo ground. The garden was evidently part and parcel of the emperor's expansion and embellishment of his palace. As for parks, one called the Philopation was located immediately outside the walls of the city, close to the Blachernae Palace at its northwest edge. The belvedere, or viewing gallery, which stood on top of the so-called Tower of Isaak Angelos, probably offered views across this park. A second park, the Aretai, was located near the city walls of Constantinople at their southern end, and was relatively easily accessible from the Great Palace. Like the Philopation, this park had ornamental buildings and water features, as well as a landscape, inhabited by game, especially hares and roe deer. It may be the park eulogized by the late tenth-century poet John Geometres, who described the earth there as "arrayed like a bride . . . with laurels, with plants, with [young] shoots, with bushes, with vines, with ivy clusters, with fruit-bearing trees." He wrote about its landscape, which included fountains, water courses, wooded and pasture areas, mountainous sections, and caves, and he enthused about its flora, which included "all beauties, every scent, every complexion" (quoted by Littlewood 1997, 37).

Gardens and parks were evidently as necessary to palaces in cities as to rural palaces. At the palace of Nuremberg, looking down over its city, the emperor Frederick II not only laid out a park, but also established hanging gardens on the buttresses of his palace, so limited was the space available. At the Palace of Westminster, which by the thirteenth century was largely engulfed by the urban growth of London, the records mention the creation of covered walks by Master Maurice the gardener in 1312–13, and, when the French chronicler, Jean Froissart, visited the garden in 1397, he found it "very pleasant and shady, for these walks were all covered with vines" (quoted by Colvin 1986, 14). The French kings' palace, the Palais de la Cité, at the heart of Paris, also had gardens, and these appear in the painting of the palace made in the Très Riches Heures of the Duke of Berry (Figure 4–2). Visible in this miniature, beyond the river and inside the wall of the palace, is the pergola for a covered path running from left to right, and leading to a domed pergola, from where it was presumably possible to sit and enjoy the garden.

Figure 4–2: Palais de la Cité, Paris (France) and its gardens (Très Riches Heures of the Duke of Berry, Musée de Condé, Chantilly, France, fol. 6v, June, detail). (See insert for color version of this image.)

That a palace had to have a garden appears most clearly with the creation of a new palace. At Avignon, gardens were established on the east side of the Palace of the Popes. The Old Garden was constructed by Benedict XII, around the foot of the Pope's Tower, on the south side. The New Garden, which was created by Clement VI, lay to the east of the Old Garden, 4m below it and surrounded in 1346 by a new wall. These gardens were evidently quite sophisticated in design. Later fourteenth-century popes, Innocent VI and Urban V, built a two-story gallery called the Roma. This opened out of the Study Tower at the corner of the Pope's Tower, in which Benedict XII located his study, and provided a covered and shaded walkway to the Garden Tower at the edge of the enclosing wall of the Old Garden. It would have provided the opportunity for the pope and his most intimate associates and guests to take exercise under cover and with views of the garden. From the time of Innocent VI and

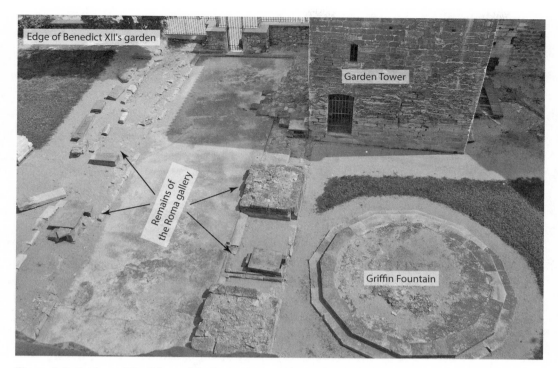

Figure 4–3: Gardens of the Palace of the Popes, Avignon (France), viewed from the vestiary in the pope's Study Tower.

Urban V, those views included what was evidently a spectacular fountain, the Griffin Fountain, the base of which is still visible beside the Roma (Figure 4–3).

Even at the great thirteenth-century castle-palaces of Caernarfon and Conwy (Wales), the records mention gardens—Conwy gardens associated with the queen's apartment (Creighton 2009, 72) and Caernarfon gardens outside the walls. Even in such a hostile environment, in the immediate aftermath of Edward I's brutal military conquest of Wales, palaces had to have gardens.

The cost involved could be very considerable. For example, Geoffrey I de Montbray, bishop of Coutances (1049–93), spent the enormous sum (for its day) of £300 to buy from Duke William of Normandy (the future King William I of England) "the better half of the city suburbs" of Coutances, where he not only built a hall and other buildings, but "planted a considerable garden (*virgultum*) and vineyard," In addition, he acquired a park, which he surrounded "with a double ditch and a palisade," growing in it "oaks and beeches and other forest trees, filling the park with deer from England" (quoted by J. Harvey 1981, 8).

At Windsor, around 1110, King Henry I bought land outside the castle, which became the King's Garden; and in 1195–96, he spent £30 to create the king's *herbarium*, a sort of garden perhaps linked to the royal apartments. In 1246, King Henry III spent more money on the King's Garden in order to move the gardener's house, repair the hedge, and lay out "a pretty garden" (virgultum) (J. Harvey 1981, 11).

MENAGERIES

If palaces had to have gardens and parks as part of their status, it seems that a frequent and important element of these was a menagerie of exotic animals. At the Palace of the Popes at Avignon, for example, although its urban situation did not leave space for very extensive gardens, there was nevertheless closely associated with the gardens the pope's menagerie. No traces of this have survived, but documents from the papal archive refer to one Michael Brown as "keeper of the wild animals" or "keeper of the woodland animals" as well as "keeper of the deer and master of the palace garden." Clearly, he had responsibility for the garden, the menagerie, and perhaps also for a deer park (although there seems to be no specific mention of that otherwise). The builder of the palace that immediately preceded the existing building, Pope John XXII (1316–34), is known to have had a collection of animals, including a bear, a lion, a camel, a bull, stags, and a wild cat, in the immediate area of the palace. Under Benedict XII (1334–42), it is not clear whether references are to a menagerie maintained at the Palace of the Popes or to one kept at the papal country-palace at nearby Pont-du-Sorgues, but under Clement VI (1342–52) the menagerie referred to in the records definitely seems to have been in the New Garden, where it was enriched by the addition of a lioness and a boar, and there are documentary references to the purchase of collars and cages for the lions. Documents also record food purchased "for the birds from foreign parts" belonging to the pope, so clearly there were also aviaries.

Menageries and, to a lesser extent, aviaries as characteristic features of palace gardens and parks go a long way back, and references thereto are found in many areas and periods. Menageries were already being established by much earlier rulers, as when the king of the Assyrians in what is now the Middle East in the ninth century BC, Ashurasirpal II, boasted that he had "organised herds of wild bulls, lions, ostriches and . . . monkeys and had them breed like flocks" (quoted by Littlewood 1997, 35).

Byzantine emperors also had menageries, for there is mention of an elephant and a giraffe kept by Emperor Constantine IX Monomachos in the eleventh century. Animals were evidently an important feature of the Philapation park, just outside Constantinople, for, when the western writer, Odo of Deuil, saw it in 1147, he noted that it contained "certain hollows and caves which, in lieu of forests, furnished lairs for the animals" (Maguire 2000, 252). As we shall see, the emperor Charlemagne had a menagerie at his palace at Aachen, and Henry I, king of England (1100–35), is recorded to have had a menagerie of exotic wild beasts at his palace at Woodstock in Oxfordshire. The contemporary historian William of Malmesbury mentions lions, leopards, lynx, camels, and a rare owl as forming part of this menagerie. In 1251, Henry III, king of England, received as a gift a polar bear, which was installed in the Tower of London. There are records of the chain and muzzle that were needed for it, especially when it swam in the River Thames. The Tower of London was also the place where lions belonging to the king were kept, cages for them being provided in the outer gateway, and at the royal palace of the Louvre in 1333 Philip VI, king of France, built a special structure, the House of the King's Lions, for his animals.

VIEWS

The artificially created landscape was also intended to offer satisfying views from the palace, and of the palace as it was approached. This aspect of a palace's surroundings is inevitably hard to reconstruct when so many landscape features have changed, but we can get a sense of it from the architectural features of a palace that were clearly intended to offer a view, as we have seen already in the case of the belvedere on top of the Tower of Isaac Angelos in the Blachernae Palace at Constantinople. The symbolism of gardens and views over and beyond into the surrounding landscape is arguably an important theme of the Alhambra at Granada (Spain). The Hall of the Two Sisters in the Palace of the Lions opens into a viewing chamber, known as a mirador, providing a view over the Lindajara Garden and, before the construction of Charles V's New Quarters in the sixteenth century blocked it, a view beyond the Alhambra over what was almost certainly an artificially created landscape outside the palace. The mirador is rich in inscriptions, of which the one by the court poet Ibn Zamrak around the entrance and windows observes that, from the vantage point of the mirador, the ruler "views the capital of his kingdom / each time he appears on the throne of the caliphate and shows himself" (Vílchez, Guarde, and Cuenca 2011, 231). We shall have to return later to the ideas in this poem that the garden has sacred qualities, embodied in the use of the word *rawda*, and that the caliph on his throne is being associated closely with the prophet Muhammad; but, here, we should take note of the poem's emphasis on the importance of the view from the mirador, from which the ruler looks out from his throne.

Elsewhere in Europe we find palaces built with attention to the importance of views, often from architectural features sometimes called gloriettes. This word meant airy rooms, often in a tower, and usually with a view; sometimes it referred to a separate range of rooms set in the midst of a park, or a chamber with a large window offering views, such as was built for King Richard II in 1377–78 at Corfe Castle in Dorset (England), looking out at the landscape around the castle.

In the case of Windsor Castle (England) in the early fifteenth century, there is an account of the view from the castle, written in verse by the imprisoned James Stewart and entitled *The Kingis Quair*. He was apparently looking out of a window set in one of the wall towers, and, according to his poem:

> Now was there made fast by the tower's wall
> A garden fair, and in the corner set
> A green herber, with wands long and small
> Railed about; and so with trees set
> Was all the place, and hawthorn hedges knit.

> (quoted by Creighton 2009, 169–70)

A contemporary text describing how Guillaume de Passavant, bishop of Le Mans, built his house in the mid-twelfth century emphasizes his attention to the view both from and to the hall of that house. According to this, he "had a garden (*viridarium*) planted with many sorts

Figure 4–4: View from the castle ridge, Stirling Castle, Stirling (Scotland), looking west showing the King's Knot and the Queen's Knot. Note the site of the King's Park, occupying the hill in the middle distance, now covered with a golf course. The steeply wooded slope below the viewpoint is the site of the Butt Well, where James IV's hanging gardens may have been laid out.

of trees for grafting foreign fruits," so that those looking out from the windows of the hall could "admire the beauty of the trees" (quoted by J. Harvey 1981, 10).

Often, all that remains of the artificially created landscape over which views were desired are the water features, especially lakes, around palaces. The magnificent lake created by James IV, king of Scotland, around his palace at Linlithgow (Scotland) was evidently intended to provide a vista from the palace, and also a view of the palace across the lake. The same must have been true of the lakes that can be shown to have formed a feature of the castles of Framlingham in Suffolk and Kenilworth in Warwickshire (England). The castles of Bodiam in Surrey and Leeds in Kent (England) still rise from their lakes, and Leeds has a free-standing gloriette in the lake, connected to the main part of the castle by a bridge (Creighton 2009, 78–80).

At Stirling (Scotland), some sense of what the view from the castle must have been can still be obtained (Figure 4–4). The modern golf course with scattered trees in the middle distance is where the King's Park was sited, probably from as early as the early twelfth century. The geometrically laid out earthworks on the near side of the road are known as the

King's Knot and the Queen's Knot. These were evidently garden features that were probably constructed in the early seventeenth century as part of a garden which was itself on the site of an earlier garden. For, there is a ditch on one side of the King's Knot and at an angle to it, which may have reflected the arrangement of that earlier garden; its purpose may have been to divide it from the King's Park beyond (Creighton 2009, 59). Moreover, on the steep slope below the castle perched on its ridge, there are traces of an extensive terraced—or "hanging" garden—which seems likely to have been created by King James IV (1488–1513).

MERGING INTERIOR AND EXTERIOR SPACE

Sometimes, gardens could be so much a part of a palace that the distinction between interior and exterior space was almost lost. Outside their principal city of Palermo in Sicily, the Norman kings built, in the twelfth century, a magnificent palace called the Zisa. In his chronicle, Romuald, archbishop of Salerno (1153–81), attributes this palace to William I (1140–66): "at that time, King William had a large and marvellously artificially created palace built near Palermo, which he called Zisa, surrounding it with beautiful fruit-trees and delightful pleasure-gardens, furnished with many streams and splendid fishponds" (Loud and Wiedemann 1998, 237). Much restored after its conversion to an early modern residence and a period of neglect in recent decades leading to partial collapse of the north side in 1971, the Zisa retains much of its original plan and elevation. The starkly rectangular building is arranged on three stories. On the west side, a long antechamber, parallel with the façade, opens through three arches on to the gardens beyond, with the central arch leading through the antechamber into the Fountain Hall, which rises through the lower two storys (Figure 4–5). This spectacular room is groin-vaulted, with three niches decorated with mqarnas (that is, Islamic pendant decoration) in stucco, as well as with mosaics above the fountain itself (Figure 4–6). The fountain evidently was modified in the Bourbon period, for there is an eagle painted immediately above it and there are eighteenth-century wall paintings on a level with it. But there is every reason to suppose that the basic structure is original.

The artificial waterfall onto which the fountain pours is decorated with raised, zig-zag patterning—or chevron—in the manner of Islamic decoration. Its purpose was to make the water gurgle as it flowed down to the series of mosaic-decorated basins in the floor of the Fountain Hall, and so through the antechamber to a rectangular basin out in the garden beyond. Between the Fountain Hall and the garden itself, the antechamber, which had several openings on to the gardens, formed an open belvedere offering views out across the garden beyond, while in the centere of the rectangular basin in the garden stood a pavilion offering a view back from outside into the Fountain Hall as well as away across the gardens. The intention must have been to create an artificial, indoor garden in the Fountain Hall, linked to the actual garden beyond both by the views and by means of the water course. This linkage between interior and exterior was heightened by the mosaics in the Fountain Hall, showing stylized garden scenes, and by the capitals of the columns around the room, which are decorated with birds—the only place in the palace where this is the case. On the second floor of the palace, which was originally unroofed, the space occupied by the Fountain

Figure 4–5: West façade, Zisa Palace, Palermo (Sicily), looking across the site of the former gardens. The large opening in the center leads to the Fountain Room, which appears in Figure 4–6.

Figure 4–6: Fountain Room, Zisa Palace, Palermo (Sicily). The fountain is in the arched recess on the right and the opening on to the gardens is off the picture to the left. The elaborate water course with two basins leads across the room from the fountain and its artificial waterfall. Note the Islamic-style mqarnas plaster decoration in the roof.

Court and the antechamber at ground-floor level is mirrored by a space focused on a water basin and with a belvedere offering views over the gardens beyond. This too was in effect a garden within the palace.

Another example of the same close integration between the palace and its surroundings is the Pope's Chamber in the Pope's Tower of the Palace of the Popes at Avignon. As we have seen, this was almost the most privileged and important room in the suite of papal chambers (above, p. 46). The original paintings on the walls of the room are still in existence from floor to ceiling, and they create a remarkable effect. At the bottom, a line of drapery has been painted, which is quite consistent with presenting the chamber as an interior room, and at the top there is a line of geometrical shapes with heraldic devices in them. But the space between them, which is the largest space, is filled with swirling series of leafy branches. The overall effect is not especially realistic for the branches swirl in circles, but the detail is highly naturalistic. The leaves are recognizable, as those of oak trees with accompanying acorns in part of the walls, for example; and the animals and birds, which include a squirrel, an owl, and a turtle dove, are convincing representations of reality even if the exact species of the birds is not always identifiable. The intention must surely have been to convey the idea that room was as much an outdoor space, part of the park or garden, as it was an interior space. This is all the more arresting because the windows of the room looked out westward over the pope's gardens, creating the impression that is was a continuation of the garden. This effect is increased by the fact that painted in the window openings are birdcages, and these are empty. It is as if the birds have been released and are flying in the garden, to return at any time to their cages in the room (Figure 4–7).

So powerful was the imagery of gardens and parks in the context of a palace that sometimes it was used in interior rooms without those rooms necessarily being connected to actual gardens outside. This seems to have been the case in the principal Norman palace of Palermo, the Palace of the Normans, which was inside the walls of the city. One of the main rooms, King Roger's Room, has windows facing out but was not directly connected with a garden so far as is known. Its walls and vaults are still covered with magnificent twelfth-century mosaics. The mosaics of the vaults, those that show lions, griffons, and an eagle, may be heraldic, but the mosaics covering the walls show scenes that likely were evocative of a garden or a park, just as were the paintings in the Pope's Chamber at Avignon. In the upper register of one of these is a hunting scene, in which two men with dogs take aim at stags, while below two lions stand on either side of a tree and two peacocks face each other. In another (Figure 4–8), the upper register is filled with two mythical centaurs (half men, half horses) aiming arrows at each other, while below there are leopards and peacocks between trees.

It is possible to interpret these scenes as purely symbolic. So the lions could have been no more than a symbol of kingship, the peacocks a symbol of eternal life, and the centaurs symbols of brute strength, like wild men in the later Middle Ages. But it seems more straightforward to interpret them as evoking gardens and parks in which, as we have been seeing, creatures such as peacocks, lions, and leopards might well have been; while the centaurs may have been primarily an evocation of hunting. Thus, King Roger's Room would have been a part of the palace intended to give the impression of a garden or park outside.

Figure 4–7: Wall paintings of empty birdcages, pope's chamber, Palace of the Popes, Avignon (France). The paintings are in the window embrasures.

Figure 4–8: Mosaic, King Roger's Room, Palace of the Normans, Palermo (Sicily). showing peacocks and leopards in a garden or parkland setting. The two centaurs may evoke hunting. (See insert for color version of this image.)

Something similar may be observable in the account by the western ambassador, Liud-prand of Cremona, of his visit to the Great Palace at Constantinople in the late tenth century and of his reception there by the emperor in the hall called the Magnaura. According to this account, "in front of the emperor's throne there stood a certain tree of gilt bronze, whose branches, similarly gilt bronze, were filled with birds of different sizes, which emitted the songs of the different birds corresponding to their species." Also, the throne itself was guarded by "lions of immense size" which were "coated with gold" and struck the ground with their tails, emitting "a roar with mouths open and tongues flickering." When Liud-prand approached the throne, "the lions emitted their roar and the birds called out, each according to its species" (Squatriti 2007, 198). Part of the grandeur of the throne was no doubt due to the fact that it could be made to rise into the air, a process that did not impress Liudprand himself. But the underlying idea seems to have been much the same as that of the mosaics in King Roger's Room in Palermo. The throne room was being presented as a sort of garden or park with birds, represented in a natural way by the automata on the throne and in the tree, and by the equally naturalistic lions.

LANDSCAPES AS PUBLIC AND PRIVATE SPACES

There was, however, a quite different way in which parks, and gardens in particular, could have been used to convey messages of power. That is when the park and garden were being used in much the same way as the interior rooms of the palace. They could be part of the design of the palace, and intended to function in the same way as the interior spaces. As we have seen, the design of palaces could encompass more public spaces, and also more private spaces (above chapter 2), and access to the latter could confer greater distinction on the ruler's closest followers or most favored guests. Thus their privacy and intimacy conveyed a message of power. We have already seen examples of gardens and parks where there seems to have been a distinction between large spaces on the one hand, and the much more inti-mate walled spaces on the other. This distinction may be what lay behind the creation of intimate dining spaces in gardens, as when in 1388–89 a second walled garden was created at the royal palace of Eltham in Surrey (England) where the king and queen could dine in summer (R. A. Brown, Colvin, and Taylor 1963, I, 934). We could interpret this as simply providing a convenient place for the monarchs to use; but we could equally see it as the creation of a private but outdoor space, access to which would confer political standing on ambassadors or guests who obtained it.

At Hadrian's Villa near Tivoli (Italy), there was at least one such dining space, the so-called Canopus. This was a long, rectangular water basin, lined with porticoes and statues, and set in a picturesque valley (Figure 4–9). At one end was a relatively small open-air tri-clinium or dining area arranged under a half-dome, with a splendid view across the water basin, lined with sculptures, and a shady artificial grotto behind it. The curved table against which the dining couches would have been set can still be seen in the triclinium (Figure 4–10). Here was all the magnificence and intimacy of an indoor triclinium, where the same messages of power through intimate access to the ruler could be conveyed.

Figure 4–9: The Canopus, Hadrian's Villa near Tivoli (Italy), looking down the water basin toward the outdoor triclinium at the far end.

Figure 4–10: Semicircular table in the open-air triclinium of the Canopus, Hadrian's Villa near Tivoli (Italy).

The architecture and associations of the Canopus may also have conveyed other messages about the ruler's power. The half-dome over the triclinium itself will have placed the ruler in the same grandiose context as domes over interior rooms, and may have associated him with religious ideas about power originating from the sun and the cosmos (above, pp. 80–85). But there may have been a further significance, for the Canopus was probably intended to evoke the temple of the goddess Serapis, which the emperor Hadrian had founded near Alexandria during a visit to Egypt in AD 130. It therefore may have conveyed the message that the emperor was a figure close to the gods, dining in a setting that resembled the temple of the goddess, which was situated above an arm of the River Nile just as Hadrian's triclinium looked out over the water basin of his garden.

GARDENS AS THRONE ROOMS AND COUNCIL CHAMBERS

One of the most interesting insights into the political message of gardens, however, comes from an epic poem in Old French, the *Song of Roland*. Written around the year 1100, this poem addresses the end of a campaign fought by the emperor Charlemagne in Spain, which was in his time largely in the hands of Muslim rulers. In the poem, Saragossa is ruled by a king, Marsilion, who offers gifts to Charlemagne, including lions, bears, hounds, seven hundred camels, and falcons (Duggan 2005, lines 182–86). These gifts helped to persuade Charlemagne to return to his own kingdom, placing his nephew Roland in charge of the rearguard of his army. But one of Charlemagne's knights, Ganelon, is treacherously working with King Marsilion to plot Roland's death, and the rearguard is attacked as it passes across the Pyrenees on its way back to France. Roland mounts an heroic resistance, but is eventually killed, blowing his horn, the Olifant, to alert Charlemagne with his last breath. Charlemagne duly turns his army round and returns to avenge his nephew.

The events narrated by the poem had some relationship to reality, insofar as Charlemagne really did conduct a campaign in Spain in the 780s, and his army really was attacked in the Pyrenees en route for home—or at least that is the account of the annals composed at his court at the beginning of the ninth century. But in the annals the attackers were not the Muslim king of Saragossa and his troops, as in the poem, but rather Christian Basques living in the area of the Pyrenees; and, although Roland does seem to have been an historical figure, there is no basis for the poem's account of his betrayal by Ganelon (Vance 1970, 96–99). Although the poem's account of events may therefore be almost as fictional as that of the Old English epic poem *Beowulf*, it is nevertheless entirely possible that the background detail given by the poet was authentic at least for his own time— around the year 1100. For the subject of the political meaning of gardens, a passage very near the beginning of the poem is striking. It concerns how King Marsilion of Saragossa was holding a council to discuss how to bring Charlemagne's campaign to an end:

> He went into a garden (*vergier*), in the shade;
> He laid himself down on a block (*perrun*) of grey marble (*marbre bloi*),
> With 20,000 of his men around him.
>
> (translated from Duggan 2005, lines 10–14)

Evidently, the poet of the *Song of Roland* envisaged that a garden could be an entirely appropriate place in which to hold a council. There even seems to have been something like a throne in this garden in the shape of the block or stone (*perron*) on which Marsilion lay. The translation of this word perron is in fact controversial. The word is related to modern French *pierre* "stone," so certainly something stone is intended, and that is confirmed by the poem with its reference to grey marble. But what exactly was the perron in Marsilion's garden?

The same word is used for something that stood in the courtyard of the Palais de la Cité in Paris. It is mentioned, for example, in a journal, contemporary with an insurrection of June 12, 1418, in the course of which the bodies of seven royal officers were shown "at the foot of the staircase of the palace on the perron." This suggests that the perron was not itself a staircase, as some scholars have thought, but rather a great stone. Like King Marsilion's perron, it was made of marble, because we have an account of how, in 1540, King Francis I of France received the Holy Roman Emperor, Charles V, "at the foot of the Great Staircase, near the perron of marble." So, at the Palais de la Cité, the perron was not part of the staircase but a separate feature. In another epic poem in Old French, *The Capture of the City of Orange*, written at the end of the twelfth century or the beginning of the thirteenth, one of the characters says that when he arrives in Paris, he will "dismount on the enamelled perron," which is presumably the perron in the courtyard of the Palais de la Cité (translated from Lachet 2010, line 1696). This passage suggests that it might have been merely a block to assist a person mounting or dismounting from a horse. But it is equally possible, perhaps more likely in view of the prominence given to it in the texts, that it was a stone of justice—a sort of platform from which announcements relating to the law could be made, and therefore a suitable place to display bodies of men killed in the revolt. There are records to the effect that the perron at the Palais de la Cité was one of the four places where the usher of the parliament announced decrees and where publications of peace were broadcast by the herald at arms. The perron would then have been symbolic of power, rather than a merely functional block of stone—something entirely appropriate to serve as a throne in a garden, or indeed in a palace.

This suggests that the poet of the *Song of Roland* was envisaging King Marsilion's garden as having a perron which was a formal feature, making the garden like a council chamber. He seems to have envisaged it as a sort of throne, in the form of a simple block of marble, or as a throne made of blocks of marble, or as a throne carved from a single block of marble. King Marsilion was lying on it, rather than sitting on it, because that was how Muslim rulers were envisaged as a behaving—lying in an exotic, Turkish manner.

Christian rulers, however, could equally be envisaged by poets as holding their councils in gardens. In *The Capture of the City of Orange*, the Christian count, William, receives a knight at his palace at Nîmes in Provence and, apparently in order to honor him, "sits beside him on a perron" (translated from Lachet 2010, line 213). This perron was presumably also serving as a throne in the garden, although Count William was not lying on it in the Turkish manner. Returning to the *Song of Roland*, a garden is where King Marsilion's emissaries find Charlemagne: "The emperor was in a great garden (*verger*)" (translated from Duggan 2005, line 103). This was a full-scale assembly, because Charlemagne was accompanied by his immediate councillors, including his nephew Roland, and also 15,000 of the French. The venue was evidently a courtly one, for the poet mentions white carpets to sit on, and describes the activities taking place as playing draughts and chess and excersing with "sword and spear" (translated from Duggan 2005, lines 110–13). So, courtly activities are taking place in the garden just as if it were the great hall of the palace. Charlemagne himself is formally seated on a golden *faldestoed* "under a pine-tree, near to a rose-tree" (translated from Duggan 2005, lines 114–16). The word faldestoed or faldstool means a folding throne, so this was presumably not envisaged as a permanent feature of the garden, but the pine tree, which of course was, was clearly also important in the formal arrangement of the ruler's reception of the envoys. The poet mentions it again later, when the king goes "beneath a pine-tree" to call "his barons to a council" (translated from Duggan 2005, lines 165–66). It is as if the poet envisages the garden as being as formally organized a space as the interior of the palace itself. That is further suggested by his account of how King Marsilion's envoys set up their tents in the garden while they pass the night and wait for Charlemagne's decision.

The poet seems to envisage the pine tree mentioned in the lines quoted above as equally part of the formal organization of the garden—as the place under which Charlemagne held his council. A similar image occurs in *The Capture of the City of Orange*, when the knight Gilbert comes to Count William in Nîmes:

> Under a branching pine-tree he finds William,
> In company with many renowned knights.
> Under the pine-tree, a minstrel sings
> An old song of great antiquity.

(translated from Lachet 2010, lines 136–39)

This was not a formal council, evidently, but it was nevertheless a meeting of the count and his knights, entertained by the minstrel, and it is represented as taking place under a pine tree. The pine tree seems to have been regarded as an especially important sort of tree, its evergreen foliage symbolizing majesty and greatness. So, when Roland is mortally wounded and dying, even though he was a hero rather than a ruler, the poet of the *Song of Roland* tells us that he withdrew to die underneath a pine tree (Duggan 2005, line 2357).

THE SYMBOLISM OF GARDENS AND PARKS

Gardens and parks, then, had as great a capability of conveying messages of power as did palaces themselves, in their design, in their furnishings, even in their vegetation and animals and birds. Sometimes, they were intimately linked with the palaces, so that the boundary between palace and garden or park was blurred. Sometimes, they were created artificially in the interior of palaces—such was their importance in conveying messages of power. What then were the messages of power the gardens and parks conveyed?

We have already seen one possible answer to that question, namely, that gardens and parks conveyed the same type of message of power based on the magnificence of the ruler as did palaces. They were as much vehicles of that message as richly decorated rooms or magnificent façades. But the messages of power conveyed by gardens in particular may have had deeper meanings. We can divide those meanings into three groups: religious, cultural, and political.

Religious Symbolism

The first book of the Old Testament, that is, the Book of Genesis, introduces a garden in the shape of the Garden of Eden, which it says that God created as a home for the first man, Adam:

> And the Lord God planted a garden eastward in Eden; and there he put the man whom he had formed. And out of the ground made the Lord God to grow every tree that is pleasant to the sight, and good for food; the tree of life also in the midst of the garden, and the tree of the knowledge of good and evil. And a river went out of Eden to water the garden; and from thence it parted, and became in four heads. (Genesis 2.8–10; Carroll and Prickett 1997, I, 1)

In the Vulgate, which is the Latin version of the Bible used in the Middle Ages, the word for garden in this passage is *paradisus*. This was originally a Greek word, which has become in modern English the word "paradise." In origin, a paradise was an "enclosed park, orchard, or pleasure ground," and the word was applied especially to the pleasure gardens and game reserves that were created by ancient rulers in the Near East. But, since it appeared in the Book of Genesis as the garden created by God, from which Adam and the first woman, Eve, were expelled after they had sinned, Christian writers soon began to transfer the word to mean the "abode of the blessed," or in other words "paradise" in our modern sense (Anon. 1991, s.n. paradise). So the garden, which the Book of Genesis describes as being both beautiful and productive and supplied with running water, became an equivalent of Paradise or Heaven. It is easy to see how this transference might have led to all gardens being regarded as reflections of the Garden of Eden, and so of Paradise itself. This could have a particular meaning for a ruler who wished his gardens to convey the message that he himself was associated with the deity. By creating a garden around his palace, or by making parts of his palace look like a garden, he was contriving to send a message of ideological power. Like God, he too was creating gardens like Paradise.

Another dimension to the religious interpretation of gardens appears at the very end of the Bible, in the Book of Revelation in the New Testament, in which the apostle John the Evangelist recounts his vision of the end of the world. According to him, he was shown, among other things, "a pure river of water of life, clear as crystal, proceeding out of the throne of God and of the Lamb" (Revelation 22.1; Carroll and Prickett 1997, II, 318). This is not specified as being in any way related to a garden, but the reference to a river proceeding out of the throne of God and the Lamb is reminiscent of the arrangement of the Fountain Hall at the Zisa in Palermo. There, as we saw, there is—if not a river—at any rate a rivulet, made to sound natural, flowing across the room and out into the garden beyond.

Fountains, in particular, were important elements of gardens and parks, because they too had religious significance. The Book of Psalms in the Old Testament addresses God with the words "with thee is the Fountain of Life" (Psalm 36.9; Carroll and Prickett 1997, I, 658). In the fifth century, a font for baptism was constructed at the papal palace of the Lateran in Rome. It consisted of a basin under a dome, with the inscription, "This is the Fountain of Life which purges the whole world" (quoted by Miller 1986, 139). Fountains then came to be associated with baptism and with the soul's salvation. Manuscripts from Charlemagne's court, such as the Godescalc Evangelistiary, include pictures of fountains where they are represented in garden or parkland settings with animals, birds, and plants around them (Figure 4–11). So it was an easy transition for fountains in actual gardens and parks to be regarded as evoking the religious connotations of the Fountain of Life, the source of God's goodness and salvation-giving grace, and this was the real subject of images like the one reproduced in Figure 4–11.

In the case of the Fountain Hall at the Zisa, it is not possible to tell how it was used, as it has been modified in modern times, and whether King William II sat on a throne in it to receive guests with the water flowing at his feet. At the palace city of Madīnat al-Zahrā, built in Andalusia in southern Spain by the caliph 'Abd al-Rahmān III (912–61), the room that looked out on to a garden that included water basins as garden features was, however, certainly a throne room. This was the Hall of 'Abd al-Rahmān III (*Salon Rico*), a magnificently decorated room, at the far end of which the caliph sat to receive his court, his guests, and ambassadors in state. According to the tenth-century writer, Al-Rāzī, the caliph sat "on the throne of the mihrab of the eastern hall overlooking the gardens" (Ruggles 2000, 101). The "eastern hall" was almost certainly the Hall of 'Abd al-Rahmān III, and the "mihrab" was a sort of niche at the far end of it, a feature also found in mosques, where it is the holiest part of the building. The view of the gardens referred to was a spectacular one. The caliph sat facing an open arcade at the opposite end of the hall, through which the so-called Upper Garden (Figure 4–12) was visible. Just as the view from the Fountain Hall at the Zisa embraced a stone pavilion rising from a pool, so there was, in the Upper Garden at Madīnat al-Zahrā, a pavilion which would have seemed to float on the water around it. Little is known of its form, or of that of the rest of the garden, but it was geometrically laid out, and beyond it was a view toward the Lower Garden, and the wider landscape of the Guadalquivir Valley.

That a garden could convey a message of the ideological power of the ruler—his closeness to the deity—is also suggested by the Arabic inscriptions in the Zisa's Fountain Hall. In one of these, the palace is referred to as "the earthly paradise" (Bresc 1994, 250–53), which reinforces the idea that the Fountain Court was intended to represent exactly that in the form of a garden in stone leading into the real garden beyond, and that this in itself conveyed the idea of a linkage between the lord's power and the earthly paradise. The idea of paradise as a garden occurs also in Islam, and surah 55 of the Koran reads:

> But for those who fear the majesty of the Lord there are two gardens . . . planted with shady trees . . . Each is watered with a flowing spring. . . . Each bears every kind of fruit in pairs . . . They shall recline on couches lined with thick brocade, and within their reach will hang the fruits of both gardens. (Dawood 1968, 20)

So, just as gardens could evoke paradise for Christian rulers, they could for Muslim rulers as well.

Figure 4–11: Fountain of Life represented in the Godescalc Evangelistary (Paris, Bibliothèque nationale de France, MS nouv. acqu. lat. 1203, fol. 3v). (See insert for color version of this image.)

The Bible, however, offered another dimension to the religious messages of power conveyed by gardens. This appears in the Old Testament again, this time in the Song of Solomon, or the Song of Songs, which is a love song of a lover for his spouse (also referred to as his sister), which was interpreted by medieval theologians as a foreshadowing of Jesus Christ's love for the Church. It too refers to a garden, here using the Latin word *hortus*, which it likens to the beloved herself:

> A garden enclosed is my sister, my spouse; a spring shut up, a fountain sealed. Thy plants are an orchard of pomegranates, with pleasant fruits; camphire and spikenard, spikenard and saffron, with all trees of frankincense, myrrh and aloes, with all the chief spices: a fountain of gardens, a well of living waters, and streams from Lebanon . . . Let my beloved come into his garden, and eat his pleasant fruits. (Song of Solomon, 4.12–16; Carroll and Prickett 1997, I, 762)

The image of the beloved as an enclosed garden (*hortus conclusus*) was taken by medieval theologians to relate to Christ's mother, the Virgin Mary, who conceived him without sexual intercourse and so she remained a virgin, her body "enclosed" like the enclosed garden of

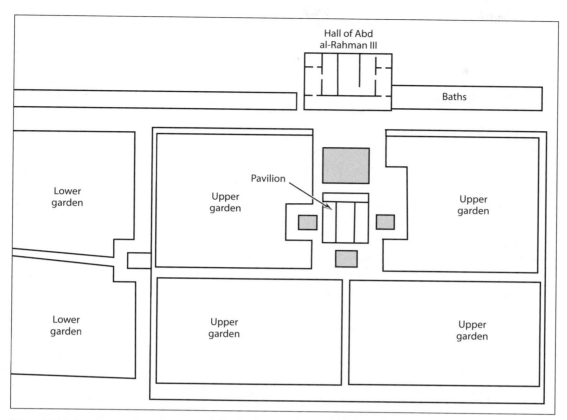

Figure 4–12: Diagrammatic plan of the Upper Garden, Madīnat al-Zahrā, near Córdoba (Spain), showing the Hall of 'Abd al-Rahmān III at the top, and the pavilion, itself surrounded by water basins (shaded grey) (after Ruggles 2000, 76, fig. 23, and Triano n.d., 113).

the Song of Solomon. There was nothing directly relevant to rulership about this, although it could explain why gardens were routinely enclosed. It does, however, underline the extent to which gardens could, at one level at least, be regarded as religious symbols. They consequently had further potential to convey a message relating to the ideological power of the Christian ruler.

Cultural Symbolism

This passage from the Song of Solomon, however, also carried the implication that gardens were related to love, and that the beloved coming into his garden and eating pleasant fruits related to the consummation of his love for his spouse. So gardens were seen as places associated with earthly love, even if that love was supposed to be of a sort that approached divine love in the Christian tradition. This brings us to the second sort of message that we could be conveyed by gardens, that is, those with a cultural meaning. One of the best-documented layouts of parks and gardens around a palace was that at Hesdin in the Pas-de-Calais area of northeast France. Virtually nothing of this layout remains after it was destroyed, together with the adjoining town and castle, in 1553. There is, however, a very full set of records relating to its construction, as well as accounts by writers such as the fourteenth-century poet, Gillaume de Machaut, making it possible to understand what it was like with some precision.

The records show that the park and gardens were the creation of Robert II, count of Artois (died 1302), although additions were made to them in the fifteenth century by Philip the Good, duke of Burgundy. They extended for more than two and half miles northward from the castle, and consisted broadly of three sections. The southernmost, around the castle itself, was an area of meadows, orchards of apples, cherries, plums, and pears, gardens of vines, roses and lilies, and a menagerie just inside the western boundary of the park. There was also a garden called "the little paradise" near a friary which was incorporated into the park. Beyond this southern section was a section consisting of woods and hills, and beyond that again lay the third and northernmost section, which was dominated by marsh. The River Ternoise flowed across it from east to west, and there were fountains, a fish pond, and a stud. A bridge led across the river to a building referred to in the sources as "the pavilion of the Marsh." This was more than what we would call a pavilion, for it had one or more galleries, with a residence nearby for the sergeant-in-charge, stables, and storehouses. Although it no doubt had practical purposes, it cannot have been primarily a functional building, because the bridge leading to it was lined with models of monkeys that moved mechanically; there were (at least until 1355) a number of devices in and around it that squirted water over guests by way of jollification; and it was surrounded by a meadow containing within it a fountain and several gardens, one of which was a walled rose garden, with shelters or bowers.

The sort of use to which this part of the park and gardens was put may be illustrated by a panel painting entitled the "Garden of Love" (Figure 4–13). This painting, which is now in the museum of the Palace of Versailles, is thought to be a sixteenth-century copy of a lost work, possibly a tapestry, which was probably made in 1431 at the court of Philip the Good, duke of Burgundy. The painting shows a gathering of people, all but one dressed in elegant white costumes, in the open air. At a table, set in the center beneath fruiting trees, sits Duke Philip the Good himself, identified as a duke by the herald standing with a drawn sword beside him, and as Philip the Good by his arms which appear on the building in the background, and also on the banner hanging from the trumpet of one of the musicians on the left of the picture. Servants are apparently clearing away gold vessels from the table, and other servants are washing other gold vessels at a fountain on the right. Clearly refreshments have been served. To the left of the table, a lady dressed in ermine, presumably the duchess, is persuading a couple to join the dance, which is being executed by four other couples in the bottom left-hand corner. In the right-hand corner, a lady and gentleman are mounted, with falcons on their wrists, and are presumably preparing to join in the falconry which is taking place in the background, beyond the stretch of water. Two servants seem to be engaged in driving waterfowl from the nearside of that water across to the falconers. Near the bottom of the picture, on the right-hand edge, a figure in red with a cane is probably the king's fool who can be recognized because a similar figure, with an annotation to the effect that he is the fool, appears on a contemporary playing card. At the bottom in the center, a woman carrying a carnation is strolling with a man—they are probably a newly wed couple,

Figure 4–13: "Garden of Love" panel, Palace of Versailles. (See insert for color version of this image.)

the duke's equerry, André de Toulongeon, and his bride. The carnation is a symbol of a bride (Buren-Hagopian 1985).

All this gives a sense of the sorts of activities for which a park like Hesdin might be used, and which might form part of an outdoor event such as is represented in the painting—music, dancing, eating and drinking, the entertainment provided by the fool, falconry, and also love—here represented by the newly wed couple, the love element underlined by the two dogs mating just in front of them. The known movements of Philip the Good and his court in 1431 suggest that this event took place in the park of Hesdin, and that it is that park which the artist was trying to evoke. If so, he did not do so very accurately, for there is no bridge, the building in the background is not the Pavilion of the Marsh, which was not on stilts as this building is, and a village appears just across the water—no such village existed in the park of Hesdin. Nonetheless, the painting may give us an impression of what a park like Hesdin was intended to be like—the ground smooth and suitable for an elegantly clad gathering of people to dance and eat and disport themselves, the landscape romantically attractive and adorned with fruit trees, the water picturesque and rich in wildfowl, the pavilion attractive with its ducal arms, its roofs decked out in gold, its peacocks, and its balcony offering a view over the park.

The title of the painting, the "Garden of Love," which was probably the title of the original from which it was copied, suggests that, just as the painting gives prominence to the newly wed couple, so the park and gardens was conceived as a place of love. In particular, they could be a scenario for re-enacting—or at least recalling the spirit of—the medieval romances in which gardens were an image of romantic love, a setting where lovers often met (Buren-Hagopian 1986, 131). The possibility that the Hesdin park and gardens were conceived as such a stage-setting is strengthened by the fact that one of their features was the number of mechanically operated models, or automata. The monkeys on the bridge leading to the Pavilion of the Marsh, and also the water-spouting devices there, have already been noted. The castle itself similarly contained a complex of galleries with water-spouting figures, which were probably counterweighted wooden statues. There was also an aviary with a fountain resembling a tree and, in the same spirit, there was nearby a "house of Daedalus," presumably a labyrinth since Daedalus was the hero of ancient literature who had penetrated the labyrinth of the monster called the Minotaur. Guillaume de Machaut was probably referring to Hesdin in 1335, when he described a visit to a place with "wonders, spouts, artifices, machinery, watercourses, entertainment and extraordinary things" (Buren-Hagopian 1986, 123). Such automata could evoke the romances and were sometimes actually a feature of them. In one called *Cleomadès*, which was dedicated to Robert II of Artois (d. 1302), there is a flying wooden horse, which assists the hero, together with a hen and chickens that are made of gold and sing, and a magical trumpet. In another, the *Romance of Troy*, there is a chamber with four automata, including a juggler who dances and plays instruments, and a maiden who dances, all made by "artifice, necromancy, and magic" (quoted by Buren-Hagopian 1986, 133).

One aspect of the cultural significance of parks and gardens could, then, have been their close association with this sort of romantic literature. But was this intended to convey a message of power, or was it just for the amusement of the ruler and his guests? There is no doubt that the association between gardens and love could be found at the very highest levels. At the English royal palace of Woodstock, for example, there was within the park a garden called Everswell, which was less than a hundred yards from the palace. Although it was destroyed in the eighteenth century, it was recorded by the seventeenth-century antiquary, John Aubrey. From the sixteenth century, this garden was known as Rosamond's Bower, after King Henry I's mistress, Rosamond Clifford. According to a legend recorded by Ranulph Higden in the fourteenth century, she had lived at the center of a labyrinth at this place, with the result that only the king could have access to her. Certainly, the royal records show that the garden was constructed in her lifetime, and that by the thirteenth century there was a chamber there called Rosamond's Chamber. Aubrey's sketch plan shows that the garden was enclosed, with what was apparently a gatehouse at one corner, and a pathway leading to a sequence of three pools, with water flowing from one into the next ("three baths in trayne" as Aubrey put it). The records show that there were also covered walkways around a cloister, gardens, and an orchard of pear trees.

In view of the quite early association between this garden and the king's mistress, it seems likely that love was the garden's theme. It may have had a particular connection with the twelfth-century romance *Tristan and Isolde*, in which the lovers met in an orchard near the royal castle. In this orchard was a marble pool, from which water flowed in a channel leading through Isolde's chamber, so that Tristan could contact her by dropping twigs into the stream. It does not seem impossible that the Everswell garden was intended to provide a stage set for a recreation of some such romance, or was at least intended to evoke the context of it.

As in the case of Hesdin, it is not obvious that this was associated with power, apart from the fact that the romantic literature in question was notably courtly in style, was indeed a sort of courtly literature, so that associating the park and gardens with it was the equivalent of building a palace in the most magnificent possible manner. You were, in other words, adding to the prestige of your palace by having a park and gardens which transported your guests into the world of romance. And the activities that took place around it, the games and pageants and receptions such as can be seen in the "Garden of Love," were a means by which the ruler could influence and impress both guests and his courtiers, and bind them into a relationship with him through sharing these activities with them. The activities could be seen as a form of court ritual that sought to reinforce the relationship between ruler and subject at the highest levels of the social scale. His garden was, in other words, conveying a message relating to his social power as well as to his magnificence.

The possible links between the power of rulers and literature are clear with regard to the stories of King Arthur, to which group the *Tristan and Isolde* romance belonged. From the time of Geoffrey of Monmouth's *History of the Kings of Britain*, completed in the late 1130s, certainly by 1139, Arthur as a great king of ancient Britain emerged as a very prominent image of courtly literature—and indeed of history, for Geoffrey's work purported to be history even if it was not. A whole series of romances about Arthur and his court were written across the ensuing centuries. These were widely read at the courts of rulers, and there are clear indications that the stories in question came to be re-enacted in a theatrical way at those courts. A Dutch chronicler called Lodwijk van Velthen, for example, gives an account of the marriage of Edward I, king of England, which is partly fictional, but probably reflects real practices. According to Lodwijk, this celebration included a play about King Arthur, and the knights present were named after Arthur's knights. The feast that was held in celebration of the wedding was punctuated by a series of play-acting interludes, as when a "loathly damsel," that is, an ugly girl, appeared with the ears of a donkey, a swollen throat, greasy hair, and a grotesque nose, demanding that two of King Arthur's knights, Sir Perceval and Sir Gawain, should go respectively to Leicester and to Cornwall, which those impersonating them at the celebration agreed to do (Barber 2007b, 92–94).

As with the love romances centered in the parks and gardens, it seems likely that this sort of play-acting was connected to the power of the ruler who orchestrated it—that it too conveyed a message of his social power, causing his military retainers to tie themselves to him through such play-acting, and showed him to be in the forefront of the courtly culture that these stories represented. At all events, considerable resources seem to have been put into creating the right ambience for these associations to be made. In 1344, when he was anxious to strengthen his military capabilities for impending war with France, Edward III, king of England (1330–77), ordered, according to the chronicler, Adam of Murimuth, a "most noble tournament or joust" to be organized at Windsor Castle, and to be publicized to potential participants overseas as well as in England. The event included an enormous feast in the great hall of the castle, as well as "in tents and other places." There was also "evening dancing and various entertainments . . . laid on in a magnificent fashion," and three days of jousting between the king with nineteen other knights and "all comers" (quoted by Barber 2007a, 38–39). Here then was a festival that was intended to be international and to attract knights from abroad, even if it was not very successful in this respect. And it was a festival, too, that must have spilled out of the castle into the park and gardens, where the outdoor eating, and also the jousts, took place.

But the festival was only a means to an end. At its close, Edward III announced that he was founding a very large knightly order, the Order of the Round Table. Already from around 1155, King Arthur had been credited with establishing a Round Table for his knights, and this aspect of the legends about him had been taken very seriously. An actual round table had been built for King Henry II to be installed in the great hall of the royal palace at Winchester (England), where it still is, and a series of tournaments called "Round Tables" had been held. Edward III was evidently capitalizing on all this to create a chivalric order which he no doubt hoped would attract knights from abroad to his court and to serve in his armies. His enemy, King Philip VI of France, certainly seems to have thought that this was the intention, because he promptly organized a rival Round Table of his own which was, according to the contemporary chronicler Thomas of Walsingham, "to attract the knights of Germany and Italy, in case they set out for the table of the king of England" (quoted by Barber 2007a, 41).

Edward III's order never really got going, and was soon superseded by his foundation of the Order of the Garter in 1348, but it is striking that it was intended to involve a structure that was probably not so different from a garden or park feature. This was the House of the Round Table, which Edward III ordered to be built at the end of the festival to accommodate

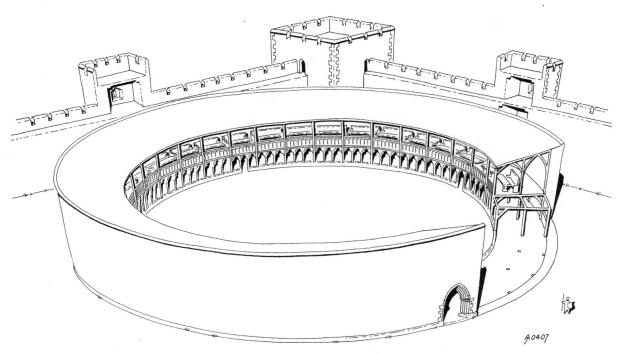

Figure 4–14: The House of the Round Table at Windsor reconstructed by Julian Munby.

the order of the Round Table, and on which the royal accounts show there was considerable expenditure down to November 1344, when the project was aborted. Archaeological excavations in 2006 showed that the house was a circular building, some 200 feet across, located in the Upper Ward of Windsor Castle (Munby 2007). This was not, of course, a location in the park or the gardens of the palace, but the building was probably unroofed and made at least in part of timber, so that it was effectively an open-air structure (Figure 4–14). Although there is no archaeological evidence for the function of the circular space in the center, it seems likely that it was intended for holding pageants and other festive events, with a covered walkway around the outside, and a first-floor gallery for the audience of them above.

Political Symbolism

If parks and gardens could be the setting for pageants and enactments of chivalry, romance, and love, then they also could have had political meaning in circumstances where cultural meaning shaded almost imperceptibly into political meaning. This may have been the case with Edward III's Round Table, where a cultural association with the romances of King Arthur could have had a clear political message in the context of recruitment for the king's French wars. Sometimes, however, the political meaning of the message being conveyed was entirely explicit. Writing of the park and gardens of Hesdin, Duke Philip the Good's chronicler, Georges Chastellain, described the reception in 1464 of a trade mission consisting of a hundred Englishmen. He tells us that they were led from the town into the park where they were so impressed by their surroundings that they declared themselves never to have seen such a fine wood, so full of deer, stags, and other animals. They were then brought to the river, where they were delighted by the fountains, and then to a magnificent open-air feast, with many servants. After this, they were conducted to the duke's apartment where they duly conceded everything he wished them to concede (Buren-Hagopian 1986, 123–24). The chronicler was, of course, prejudiced in the duke's favor, but he was no doubt right that the park was being used in this political way, even if the success of the effort was not quite as great as he maintained. Since the concessions were connected with trade and so with financing the machinery of power, here was a park being used to convey a message of the ruler's bureaucratic power.

This effect was produced by the grandeur and magnificence of the park and gardens. Statues of various sorts in the gardens could also convey a political message to ambassadors and others. When the Roman general Pompey the Great (d. 48 BC) established his gardens on the Field of Mars at Rome, these were not around a palace but rather around Pompey's new theater, and they were public gardens. They were nevertheless rather like palace gardens, for they had avenues of trees and fountains. They also had statues which represented the nations Pompey had defeated and brought under the dominance of Rome during his recent campaigns in the east, so that these statues were a message regarding his military success and therefore his suitability to rule Rome. There was also in the gardens a colonnade which sheltered paintings and cloth of gold from Pergamon, that is, booty from his conquests, which was presumably meant to convey a similar message. Impressing the populace with this public garden, and granting them access to it, were means of sending messages of social power.

English royal gardens from the Tudor age, at the other extremity of the period with which this book is concerned, offer another example of the use of statues to send political messages in the context of gardens. At his palace of Hampton Court (England), King Henry VIII (1509–47) had in his Privy Garden numerous wooden posts surmounted by carved and painted heraldic beasts, and long stretches of railing painted in the Tudor colors with white and green chevrons (Thurley 2003, 92). It is possible to catch a glimpse of such heraldic beasts, as well as of rails so painted, as they were in the Privy Garden at Whitehall Palace (England) in Henry VIII's time. They can be seen through the doors that open out on to the gardens on either side of a portrait scene of the king and his family that was painted around 1545 (Strong 1979, 34–36; Figure 4–15). The beasts were heraldic badges of the Tudor family, and they therefore expressed Henry VIII's legitimacy and his right to rule.

The plants and trees in parks and gardens also had the potential to convey such political messages to the ruler's subjects. According to the elder Pliny, when Pompey the Great had, in 61 BC, triumphed over a range of enemies, especially Mithridates of Pontos, he held a triumphal procession through Rome, which included (for the first time in Roman triumphal processions) living trees from areas in Asia and Africa conquered by Rome—balsam trees from Judea, palm trees from Ethiopia, and probably plane trees from Asia Minor

Figure 4–15: Detail of the right side of the painting *Family of Henry VIII*, unknown artist, *c.*1545, showing the view through an open door to the garden with heraldic beasts on poles. Note also the banners in Tudor colors lying on the ground. (See insert for color version of this image.)

(Östenberg 2009, 184–88). These trees from the far reaches of the Roman Empire were being treated as if they were captives in their own right. They constituted a sort of horticultural booty, and their presence may well have been intended to send the message that Pompey was a great conqueror who could gather such specimens from the wide area of his conquests.

Menageries could work in a similar way. The ruler's possession of a wide range of animals could convey a message about the range of his power, embracing those far-flung parts of the world from which the animals came, and also of his standing in the world if the animals had been given to him—as was often the case—as diplomatic gifts from other rulers. In 802, for example, the emperor Charlemagne received an elephant as a diplomatic gift from the caliph of Baghdad, Haroun 'al Rashid (Scholz and Rogers 1972, 82, s.a. 802). Just as with the park itself, the menagerie could be used to impress ambassadors, and the exotic animals in the park could be similarly deployed. The Byzantine emperor Nicephorus Phocas (963–69) seems to have tried to use such animals to impress an ambassador from the German empire, Liudprand of Cremona. According to the latter's account of his embassy, while they were dining, the emperor asked him whether the German emperor had game parks with wild donkeys and other animals. When Liudprand told him that the German emperor certainly had such parks, but not with wild donkeys in them, Nicephorus replied: "I will lead you to our game-park, whose enormity, as well as the wild, that is woodland, donkeys, you will marvel to see." When Liudprand saw these donkeys, he affirmed that he had not seen the like of them in Saxony, and was told by his Byzantine escort: "If your lord should be kind to the holy emperor, he will give him many of these animals, and it will be no small glory for Otto, when he shall possess what none of his predecessors in lordship even saw." Liudprand, however, was not impressed, since he could not distinguish the wild donkeys from tame donkeys in his native Italy, and his reaction displeased the emperor to the extent that Liudprand was given only two goats and no wild donkeys at all (Squatriti 2007, 260–61).

Particularly vivid evidence for the potentially political significance of collecting animals is provided by the mosaics of the long gallery which runs in front of the principal hall in the Villa Romana di Casale near Piazza Armerina (Sicily). These mosaics are all about the capture of animals, not for a menagerie as such, but rather for the display and killing of the animals in the Colosseum at Rome. The gallery is almost 60m long by 3m wide, with a semicircular space, or exhedra, at each end (see plan, Figure 6–18). The mosaic of the left-hand exhedra, as one faces the hall, shows a female figure with animals and the inscription "Mauretania"; a similar figure on the right has the inscription "India." Mauretania and India were the farthest-flung provinces of the Roman Empire, so that at once it appears that the mosaic of the gallery was making a political point about the extent of that empire. In between the left-hand exhedra and the center of the gallery, where the entrance to the hall is located, the mosaic represents a series of animals being captured from the provinces that made up the large administrative unit of the Diocese of Africa: panthers from Mauretania, antelopes from Numidia, wild horse from Tripolitana, the berber lion from Proconsolaris, and the wild boar from Bizacena. The mosaics show these animals being loaded on to a ship at the port of Carthage in north Africa, and in the middle they show them being unloaded at Ostia, the port of the city of Rome. In the right-hand section of the gallery, beginning with the exhedra representing India, the mosaics show the capture of tiger cubs, a griffon, a lion, and a wild donkey, together with dromedaries, tigers, hippopotamuses, elephants, emanating from India, and rhinoceroses, which are being loaded on to a ship at the port of Alexandria in Egypt (Figure 4–16).

This range of animals is thus intended to reflect the great extent of the Roman Empire, a message that is reinforced by the mosaicists' representation of the means of capturing these animals, which also corresponded to the particular creatures and to the parts of the Roman Empire from which they came. The methods illustrated were not always real ones—capturing tiger cubs by throwing a glass ball which distracted their parent, for example—but their

Figure 4–16: Detail of mosaics, long gallery, Villa Romana di Casale, near Piazza Armerina (Sicily), showing the capture of various animals. A rhinoceros is being led away on the left. The seated figure in the bottom right has sometimes been interpreted as representing the emperor who has been presumed to have been the villa's proprietor.

representation makes the message the mosaics were intended to convey clear enough (Figure 4–17).

As we noted, the animals represented in these mosaics were not intended for menageries, but rather for the Colosseum in Rome, where they would be killed in mock hunts called *venationes*, which might on occasions involve the emperor himself. Because of the difficulty and danger of killing it, an animal like a rhinoceros had a particular signficance for demonstrating the power of its assailant—in one instance, the emperor Commodus (177–92) had publicly killed a rhinoceros in the Colosseum in a carefully staged fight to demonstrate his power (Toner 2014). But the mosaics nevertheless suggest the role of animals as conveying a message about a ruler's far-flung political dominance, or at least political influence in the case of diplomatic gifts, and it seems likely that menageries shared in this meaning.

Figure 4–17: Detail of mosaics, long gallery, Villa Romana di Casale, near Piazza Armerina (Sicily), showing how an adult tiger is distracted by a glass ball in which an image of its young is reflected, thus preventing it from protecting that young from capture.

Animals in parks could also have conveyed a message of ideological power through their quasi-religious significance. The park at Charlemagne's palace at Aachen is described in a ninth-century Latin poem by Walafrid Strabo:

> A fine grove, murmuring streams
> playing in a green meadow and wild beasts and tame cattle playing.
> Wild oxen play with stags, wild roe with antelope;
> And should you wish it in future, lions too will leap, as is right.
> The bear, boar, panther, wolf, lynx, elephant
> Rhinoceros, tiger will come, and tame dragons too.
> They will share a common pasture with cattle and sheep.
>
> (Herren 1991, 118–39, at p. 135)

This is not, of course, a straightforward description of the park, but rather an evocation of heaven itself, where it was believed that discord between the creatures of the earth would be at an end. But it would have made sense only if there really had been a park with a variety of animals; and the Solomonic theme of Walafrid's verses points to another significance of parks, namely that they were part of the evocation of the king or emperor's Christ-like rulership. Just as his palace was like the kingdom of heaven, so his park created another image of that kingdom, in which wild animals played an important role.

CONCLUSION

The importance of gardens and parks as vehicles for messages of power seems clear from the attention the rulers devoted to them. A ruler's palace needed such artificial landscapes as part of its status. Gardens and parks were laid out, sometimes with great labor and at great expense, even in places, like the palace of Fishbourne, where the ruler in question was very newly established. Even where space was at a premium, as was the case with Stirling Castle, they were important enough to be developed in the most unpromising circumstances, in this case on the steep cliffs below the ridge on which the palace sits. Sometimes, they were intimately linked with the palaces to which they belonged, both physically and visually in terms of views from palace to garden and from garden to palace. Sometimes they were associated with menageries, which conveyed a message of power about the long reach of the ruler in obtaining the animals for them. Sometimes gardens were artificially created in the interior of palaces, or at least evoked by the decoration of those interiors. Sometimes they functioned as if they were the interior space of a palace transported to the outdoors, so that objects like stones and trees in them took on the same functions and the same capacity to convey messages of power as did the internal fittings and furnishings of palaces.

The messages of power that gardens and parks could send were not dissimilar to those that could be conveyed by the palaces themselves. First, there is ideological power. Just as palaces could represent the ruler as close to the divine, so too could gardens, because of the religious representation of the garden in sacred writings. Second, personal power, the association of gardens in particular with love-literature in the Middle Ages giving them the potential to serve as stage sets for the re-enactment of romances and chivalric events. The interaction between the ruler and his subjects or guests that such activities produced gave the gardens in which they occurred the capacity to convey messages of personal power. The ruler's position, or at least the position he claimed, was encapsulated in these activities. Third, bureaucratic power, with their animals and plants, gardens, parks, and their attendant menageries having the potential to convey messages of power about the reach of the ruler's authority through the world, either in terms of his conquests or his relationships with other rulers. The use of these places for impressing ambassadors and for providing diplomatic gifts, such as the wild donkeys that Liudprand was promised, was another aspect of the messages of bureaucratic power that they could send.

CHAPTER 5

The Power of Forests and the Hunt

If, as was argued in the previous chapter, gardens and parks could convey messages of power, to what extent could this also have been true of the much more extensive areas of the forests that often—although not always—lay close to, or indeed around, palaces and that were peculiarly subject to rulers? Could these forests too have been a mechanism for conveying messages of power, and, if so, to what type of power did those messages relate? We shall need to consider the ways in which rulers organized and administered their forests, for these may bear on messages of bureaucratic power. We shall need to consider also the associations the forests may have had in contemporary imagination, for messages of ideological power may have derived from them. And we shall need to consider the hunting that took place in forests, and sometimes in parks too, for the messages it may have sent not only about personal power, arising from the camaraderie of the hunt, but also about ideological power, if we consider the place of hunting in religious and other ideas.

DEFINING FORESTS

It is necessary first to define what is meant by "forest" in this discussion, for the word is not a straightforward one, and it has certainly had different meanings at different periods of time. Nowadays, a forest is usually envisioned as primarily an area of woodland, and the current *Oxford English Dictionary* definition is "an extensive tract of land covered with trees and undergrowth, sometimes intermingled with pasture" (Anon. 1991, s.n.). In this definition, it is the trees which occupy the lead position. In the Middle Ages, however, the word forest did not mean primarily an area covered with trees, but rather one that had a particular status under the law. The word, as it is found in early medieval Latin, Middle English, and Old French, seems to have derived from the classical Latin word *foris*, which means "outside." So the root meaning of forest was "an area outside something," and what it was outside was the law to which the rest of a ruler's territory was subject. This was, in England, the Common Law. When the twelfth-century bishop of London and royal treasurer, Richard Fitz Nigel, wrote an account of how the English royal exchequer, that is, the king's financial office, worked, he put this clearly:

> Indeed, the law of the forest, and the monetary or corporal punishment of those who transgress there, or their absolution, is separate from the rest of the kingdom's judicial system, and

is subject to the sole judgment of the king or his specially appointed deputy. (Amt and Church 2007, 91)

So, being outside the Common Law of the kingdom, forests were directly subject to the king, and could, in principle, only be royal forests. But this principle was not maintained, or at any rate not entirely. Forests did not remain exclusively royal, for they were granted away to followers of kings, and at certain times created by non-royal persons, although with the sanction of kings.

The word forest does not, however, go back to the beginning of the period this book is considering, that is, to the period of the Roman Empire. It is found for the first time only in the seventh century. The first reliable document in which its medieval Latin form, *foresta* or *forestis*, appears is a charter granted by Sigibert III, king of the Franks, in 648–50. From then on, it occurs routinely in documents. Before that, the equivalent word may have been the classical Latin *saltus* (plural *saltus*), which means an area that was uncultivated and lordless and was consequently directly subject to the Roman emperor. Imperial officials are said in the sources to have been in charge of saltus. So a saltus was much the same as a forest, and, although we cannot prove that royal forests developed out of Roman imperial saltus, there is a distinct possibility that this was the case. The sixth-century Frankish writer, Gregory of Tours, for example, mentioned the saltus of the Auvergne (Rubner 1963, 272).

Although it was their status that principally made forests and saltus what they were, they were nevertheless areas characterized by their landscape. As the Roman jurist, Aelius Gallus, wrote: "a saltus is a place where there are woods and pastures" (Glare 1990, s.v. saltus), and he could equally have been referring to medieval forests, which seem to have consisted of wooded areas interspersed with areas of pasture. Hatfield Forest in Essex (England), which still preserves the variety of landscape found in a medieval forest, is made up of woodland and pasture in just this way. The pasture is what is called "the plains," which are areas of open grassland or scrub, where cattle or other animals can be grazed. The rest consists of woodland, but this is also varied. Part is made up of coppiced trees, that is, trees pruned down almost to ground level and allowed to shoot again in order to create small sticks for firewood or for wattles; part is made up of trees allowed to grow much larger in order to provide substantial timber for building.

An important function of forests—and probably saltus too—was to provide opportunities for the ruler and his court to hunt. From the moment the word "forest" first occurs in a document, it is associated with wild animals and therefore presumably with hunting. The document of 648–50, mentioned above as the earliest document in which the word forest occurs, is a grant of land in the Ardennes "in places of great loneliness, in which great numbers of wild animals breed" (quoted by Zotz 1997, 95–96). A century later, the *Life of St Columbanus* records a complaint of a certain duke called Gunzo that, in the kingdom of the Franks, Christian hermits settling in the forest were disturbing the royal hunting (*venatio publica*) (Zotz 1997, 100). A similar picture is given for twelfth-century England by Richard Fitz Nigel: "The king's forest is the preserve of wild animals, not just any kind, but woodland creatures, and not everywhere, but in certain places are that are suitable for them" (Amt and Church 2007, 93). Although there are qualifications in this statement, the meaning is nevertheless that the forest was a sanctuary for woodland animals and therefore for hunting.

THE SCALE OF FORESTS

However important hunting may have been, kings and aristocrats could not have hunted in all the forests regularly, for forests were extensive and numerous. A fourteenth-century document shows that the forest of the Dreieich south of Frankfurt-am-Main (Germany), where there was an important royal palace, measured some 40km by 62km at its widest extent, and to the south it adjoined the forest of the Forehahi which stretched a further 45km or so to the south, reaching right to the banks of the River Neckar. If we count as a single area the several forests that were close to the palace of Aachen (Germany), we are dealing with an area stretching from northwest of Aachen to the River Warche in the south, and beyond the River Erft to beyond Brauweiler in the east. The extent of the forests in the Île de France, the area around Paris, was equally impressive, and so too were the scale and numerousness of English forests. Figure 5–1 shows the full extent of royal forests and also those belonging to the aristocracy, which are usually called chases, between *c.*1000 and *c.*1500. Not all the areas shown on this map were forests and chases at the same time, but it nevertheless gives an impression of the scale of the area involved.

It has been estimated that, around the time that Richard FitzNigel was writing his *Dialogue on the Exchequer* in the twelfth century, a third of England was forest (Semmler 1991, 131). Almost the whole of the county of Essex was a forest, and, when the Norman kings created the New Forest in the late eleventh century, the area of land involved was enormous. William I started it by designating some 75,000 acres, then added a further 15,000 or 20,000 acres, moving out some two thousand people in the process. Later, yet another area of between 20,000 and 30,000 acres was added (Petit-Dutaillis 1929, 169–70).

THE RELATIONSHIP OF PALACES TO FORESTS

Palaces and forests often, perhaps usually, seem to have gone together. A palace would generally have had around it a park and beyond that a forest. This is evident in a passage of *Sir Gawain and the Green Knight*, a poem of some 2,500 lines, written in Middle English in the late fourteenth century. The poem is, of course, a work of fiction, but the background in which it is set must have been recognizable to those who read it or heard it. The hero of the poem is Sir Gawain, one of King Arthur's knights. As a result of his meeting with a mysterious Green Knight at a feast in the king's hall, he is bound to set out a year after the feast to find that Green Knight at a certain Green Chapel. He does not know where that is, so the poet represents him traveling all over King Arthur's kingdom in search of it. On Christmas Eve, desperate to find somewhere to spend the night, he rides "into a dark forest, wonderfully wild" (K. Harrison 1998, line 741; Vantuono 1999, line 741). The poet here uses the Middle English word for forest, as he does later with reference to a deer hunt, and he de-

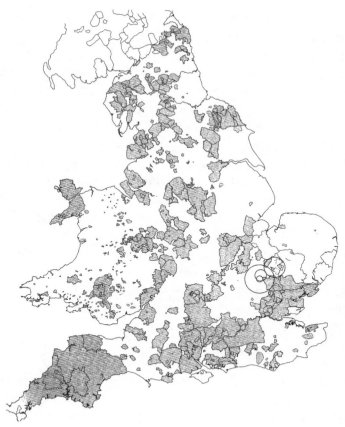

Figure 5–1: Map of forests and chases in England and Wales. Produced in the context of the Forests and Chases research project (St. John's College, Oxford), this shows the fullest extent of forests and chases, although the areas shown were not necessarily in existence as such at the same time. Royal forests in Scotland are shown in outline. Unshaded outlines in England mark ecclesiastical liberties such as the Palatinate of Durham. The circles show areas of eastern England designated as royal hunting reserves by the Stuart kings.

scribes the trees and moss growing in it. After entering this forest, Sir Gawain sees a castle surrounded by trees and "with a beautiful park all round." The latter had a "spiked palisade" and "ran two miles around" (K. Harrison 1998, lines 763–70). Here then was a castle—it turns out eventually to be the very castle of the Green Knight, Sir Bertilak, for whom Gawain is searching—set in a park of substantial size, enclosed by a palisade, itself set within a great area of what the poet here calls wood, but which he has previously called forest. Sir Gawain is hospitably received in this castle, and for three successive days Sir Bertilak's wife attempts to seduce him (as a test of his virtue and with her husband's permission), while Sir Bertilak and his court go out each day to hunt, first deer, then boar, and then fox in the park or in the forest around his castle.

Sir Bertilak's castle, with its park and forest, would have been typical of the residences of rulers and aristocrats in the Middle Ages. One of the grandest royal palaces of medieval England, which was almost as grand as the principal palace of Westminster, was the palace of Clarendon, lying three and a half miles from the city of Salisbury. The palace was extended and enriched on a considerable scale by King Henry III (1216–72), but it goes back to at least the time of King Henry I (1100–35), and it was substantially developed by King Henry II (1154–89), who held an important council there in 1164. Even in its present, almost completely ruined, state, it is an impressive complex, with the remains of its great hall,

Power of Forests & the Hunt   139

its chamber blocks, its chapel, its impressive wine cellar, its enormous stable-block, and its gardens lying below the queen's chamber and the great hall. Around it was an inner park, which—together with the palace itself—occupied an area of about 26 hectares (James and Gerrard 2007, 67). Since this was surrounded by a bank and outer ditch, apparently intended to prevent deer and other animals from entering, it was presumably not for hunting in, and may have had primarily the aesthetic and recreational roles of a park. Beyond it lay Clarendon Park proper, as it still does today, and still with its medieval outline and much of its medieval character. Just as the palace was magnificent, so was the park enormous. It occupied some 1,821 hectares, making it the largest such park known to have existed in England in the Middle Ages. Inside was the same mixture of coppices and pastureland found in Hatfield Forest. Its primary role as a hunting park, however, is suggested by the three "deer leaps," which are first shown on a mid-seventeenth-century map, but which were probably part of the medieval park (Richardson 2005, 116–17). These were places in the enclosing bank and ditch at which the bank was lower to allow deer to enter the park, but, because the ditch on the inside of the bank was deeper, they were prevented from getting out again. Beyond Clarendon Park is Clarendon Forest, approximately seven miles wide, just as it was in the twelfth century, and contiguous on its east side with Buckholt Forest, on its south side with Melchet Forest, the former contiguous with Chute Forest to the north, the latter with the New Forest to the south.

This close relationship between forests and palaces was typical. Some of these palaces, such as Writtle in the Forest of Writtle in Essex (England), were relatively modest affairs intended for occupation by the ruler or his guests when they were hunting, and nothing more. But Clarendon Palace was a top-of-the-range palace, particularly in the thirteenth century when Henry III added so much to it. So too was Woodstock Palace in Oxfordshire (England), where important councils were held in the twelfth century, but which, like Clarendon, was surrounded by park and forest. So too was Windsor Castle, with its magnificent chapel and great hall, which opened on to Windsor Great Park and the forest beyond.

The pattern was the same on the continent. As noted above, the palace at Aachen was situated at the heart of a complex of forests, which reached right to Aachen's gates. Although continuity cannot be proved, these forests were probably parts of the ancient forest of the Ardennes, in which the Roman emperors had hunted. From the eleventh century, they were granted away in periods when royal power was weak, and in the twelfth century they fell into the hands of a family of aristocrats who came to be known as the *Comites Nemoris*, the "counts of the wood." But the forests almost certainly had royal origins. In the case of one of them, the Monschauer Reichswald, the name Reichswald means "royal wood."

We can appreciate the importance of Aachen's relationship to these forests if we consider the palace's position in the landscape as a whole (Figure 5–2). For Aachen occupies a liminal, or borderline, position between settled, cultivated lands to the north and east, and the relatively raised and wilder land to the south, including the ridges called the Hautes Fagnes and the Hohes Venn, characterized by heathland, marsh, and woodland, and the long east-west block of high ground called the Rheinische Schiefergebirge, which includes the Ardennes and the Eifel. The distinction between this higher ground and the much more settled, agricultural land to the north is obvious even in the present-day landscape. The city of

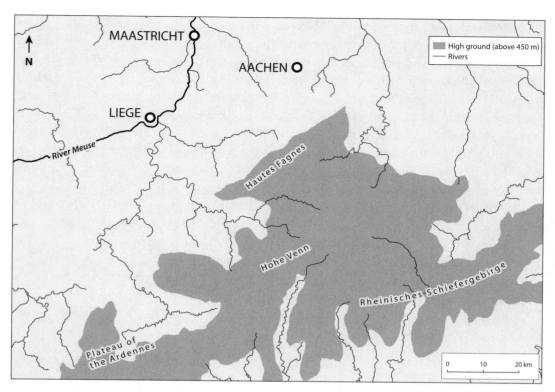

Figure 5–2: Sketchmap showing Aachen's borderline position in relation to the raised and wilder areas of the Hautes Fagnes, Hohes Venn, Rheinisches Schiefergebirge, and Plateau of the Ardennes.

Aachen, which has grown up around Charlemagne's palace, lies at the southern edge of a landscape of fields, and at the northern edge of a landscape of forest and rougher ground leading away into the high land to the south. This landscape is not, of course, exactly as it was in the Middle Ages. There has, for example, been extensive planting of conifer trees in the late nineteenth century and early twentieth; but as it no doubt was in the Middle Ages, it is still a very different landscape from that to the north of Aachen, and it must have been already in Charlemagne's time an area of woodland, forest-pasture, heath, and marsh—a forest landscape in other words. This liminal position must have been one of the principal reasons for Charlemagne's choice of the site for his palace, for it ensured that palace and forest would go together.

Aachen's position was not unique on the Continent, for the palace of Frankfurt-am-Main, which originated in Charlemagne's reign, appears to have been in a similarly liminal position, with the great forest of the Dreieich immediately adjacent to it and stretching, as previously noted, many miles to the south, the subsidiary palace of Tribur at its edge, and the forest of the Forehahi beyond it again, and the Wildbann of Lorsch beyond that. The eleventh-century palace of Goslar (Germany) lay close to the equally extensive forest of the Harz Mountains, the modern successor of which still broods over the palace from the rocky ridges that rise up within a mile or two of it.

The most thought-provoking site, however, is that of Lejre (Denmark), identified, as we have seen (above, p. 37), by later medieval written sources as a royal site of the Skjöldung kings of Denmark. There is no documentation whatsoever for the territorial organization around the palace in the time of the wooden halls there and in the time of the Skjöldung kings. But it is striking that Lejre, like Aachen, occupied a liminal site between the more cultivated land to the east and a landscape of glacial moraine deposits to the west. The latter was originally a wild area, dominated by boulder-clay forming hillocks and meres, suitable for hunting and fowling, and used for hunting in the modern period. It seems plausible that this "dead-ice" landscape, as it is called, represented an early Danish equivalent of a forest such as that around Aachen.

Evidence relating to County Durham (England) shows that temporary palaces could be constructed to facilitate the use of forests that had no palace adjacent to them. The bishops of Durham, who enjoyed many of the powers of the king, had, within their jurisdiction, the Palatinate, a great hunting forest in Weardale, a few miles west of Durham. In the late twelfth-century survey of their lands called Boldon Book, there is mention of the duties imposed on the villeins (or peasants) of part of those lands called Aucklandshire, which lay in a lower section of the Wear Valley, to build a temporary palace for the bishop in the forest:

> All the villeins of Aucklandshire . . . provide one rope at the Great Hunts (*magnas cazas*) of the bishop for each bovate and make the hall of the bishop in the forest 60 feet in length and in width within the posts 16 feet with butchering facilities and a store-house and a chamber and a privy. Moreover, they make a chapel 40 feet in length and 15 feet in width, and they have two shillings as a favour and they make their part of the enclosure around the lodges and on the bishop's departure a full barrel of ale or half if he should remain away. (Austin 1982, 41)

Evidently, the bishop had no permanent palace at the heart of the Forest of Weardale, and every year the villeins made a new one, or perhaps in reality they repaired and refurbished the previous year's construction. At all events, the account in Boldon Book makes it clear that this was a serious palace with a series of buildings and facilities. It also makes it clear that it was being built specifically for use by the bishop during the great hunts, for which the villeins also contributed rope, estimated according to the bovates (that is the units of land) that they held from the bishop. Here again, palaces and forests, and forests and hunting, went together, even if the palace in question had to be built anew—or rebuilt—every year.

Where later palaces were situated in large cities, their relationship to forests seems nevertheless to have been an important one. In the case of Nuremberg in southern Germany, the palace was also located right up against the city walls. Its site was no doubt partly chosen for its raised position, which added to its dominating character, and its defensibility; but it also provided access to the great forests of Sankt Lorenz and Sankt Sebaldus which surrounded the city, as appears graphically in a painting of 1516 (Figure 5–3).

The principal palace of the French kings in Paris, the Palais de la Cité, was located at the very heart of the city, so in that case there was no question of the palace having easy access to a forest. But the French kings developed the palace of Vincennes at only a short distance from Paris, with the great forest of the Bois de Vincennes around it. Similarly, Westminster

Figure 5–3: The forests of Sankt Lorenz and Sankt Sebaldus around the city of Nuremberg (Germany), as they appear in a painting of 1516. The palace is in the upper right-hand corner of the city as represented here.

Palace, on the edge of London, had no immediate access to a forest, or even a park, but this was compensated for by Windsor Castle, just a little way up the Thames Valley and thus easily accessible by water, with its Great Park and its forest around that. The lack of an extensive park or forest might also be compensated for by pageantry. When Henry VIII and Catherine of Aragon were crowned at Westminster in 1509, there was a "pagente like a park," which involved knights, foresters, various props to represent a forest, and deer that were hunted down by greyhounds in a staged hunt around the palace (Mileson 2009, 20).

This close relationship between palaces and forests may go back into the Roman period. In the case of the Villa Romana di Casale near Piazza Armerina, nothing is known of the landscape around it in the Roman period, but it seems likely that the remote and upland part of Sicily in which it lay was as much a forest, a saltus, as the forest around Clarendon Palace. At the Villa Romana di Casale, a large room, which probably served as a living room for guests, had a mosaic floor representing various forms of hunting—for deer (Figure 5–4), for fox, for boar, for hare, and for birds, in which falcons were used—as well as a scene of

Figure 5–4: Detail of mosaic *Room of the Small Hunt*, Villa Romana di Casale, Piazza Armerina (Sicily), showing stags being trapped in a net.

sacrifices being made at an altar to the goddess of hunting, Diana, and another scene of the lord and his guests feasting on game in the open air. With such a mosaic floor as this, it is hard to believe that the palace was not a center for hunting in a surrounding forest or its equivalent.

In the case of the emperor Nero's Golden House in Rome, it is known from the Roman historian Suetonius that it was surrounded not by a forest but by a garden on the scale of a park. This was evidently very extensive, for it contained "an enormous pool, more like a sea than a pool, . . . surrounded by buildings made to resemble cities, and by a landscape garden consisting of ploughed fields, vineyards, pastures, and woodlands—where every variety of domestic and wild animal roamed about" (Graves 1957, 224–25; cf. Rolfe 1998, II, 136–37). Evidently it was primarily for its aesthetic qualities and recreational opportunities, but it could also have been for hunting. It is known that a little later the emperor Domitian (AD 81–96) had a park for hunting around his palace, since we are told that he was watched by many people while he killed 100 beasts of different kinds in his park (Anderson 1985, 101). Not all types of hunting required an area as great as a forest; one type, for example, involved simply driving animals to a fixed point where the huntsman could kill them in full view of the spectators.

ORIGINS OF FORESTS

In the case of medieval England, scholars often assert that the forests we have been discussing only came into existence through the activities of the Norman kings after the Norman Conquest of 1066, which would mean that the relationship between forest and palace did not go any further back. It is almost certainly the case that the Norman kings did introduce into England the forest law under which royal forests were managed, so that in the technical judicial sense of "an area subject to forest law" forests did not exist before their time. But there are clear indications that pre-Conquest English palaces were already set in or near the sort of areas that would later be called forests, even if the judicial status of those areas had not reached the level of precision that the forest law of the Norman kings introduced. In the case of the palace of Cheddar in southwest England, the *Life of St Dunstan* reports that the king, Edmund (939–46), was there when he took the decision to strip Dunstan, the future archbishop of Canterbury, of his position and to exile him. Shortly afterward, however, the king was on horseback, engaged in hunting stags, when he was in danger of falling to his death down a steep cliff, and was only rescued when he repented for what he had done to Dunstan and resolved to restore him to his previous position (Stubbs 1874, 23–25, 91, 181, 269–70). Although this is hagiography, it seems clear that the cliff described was in the precipitous valley, the Cheddar Gorge, so the hunting must have been taking place in what would later be called Mendip Forest, in which Cheddar was situated. It looks fairly certain that, already in the tenth century, a palace like Cheddar was located close to or within a forest, in which the ruler could hunt, even if that forest was not subject to the same forest law as it would have been from the period of the Norman kings onward.

At an even earlier period, the Mercian palace of Tamworth (England), a favored residence of the great Mercian kings of the eighth century, such as Offa the Great (757–96), lay on the edge of Cannock Chase, a relatively high tract of land still characterized by woodland, scrub, and grazing—very much a forest landscape. Cannock Chase is documented as a royal forest in Domesday Book in 1086 (Dace 2001). Its proximity to Tamworth, however, suggests that its origins as a royal forest may have reached back to at least the eighth century, when it would have served the king's residence there. It was progressively alienated to the Bishop of Coventry after 1230, like the forests in the area of Aachen were granted away to the Counts of the Wood, so that it became a "chase," that is, a forest in the jurisdictional sense, but a forest subject to someone other than the king. In the seventh century, the Northumbrian royal palace of Yeavering (England) was located, just like Aachen is, at the edge of an area of farmland on the one side, and of wild upland on the other. In its case, the wild area is the Cheviot Hills, to the immediate west of the palace. Similarly, the Scottish royal center of Dunadd lay on the edge of an area of marshland, a situation that puzzled its excavators, but which may have been comparable to that of Lejre relative to the "dead-ice" landscape. The marshland would have provided opportunities for hunting wild fowl, so that it may well have had the status of a forest, even if it was not a wooded area.

The origins of forests connected with palaces may, however, have reached even further back. For there is a hint that the Forest of Weardale, as it was used by the Bishop of Durham, may have had its beginnings as a Roman saltus. Somewhere on the now heathery moorland

Figure 5–5: Roman altar from Bollihope Common preserved in the parish church, Stanhope (England). The first two words of the inscription read *Silvano invicto* "To Unconquerable Silvanus").

of Bollihope Common, in the heart of the forest, there was found in the nineteenth century a Roman altar, now preserved in the parish church of Stanhope (Figure 5–5). The inscription on its face reads in translation:

> To Unconquerable Silvanus, Gaius Tetius Veturius Micianus, prefect of the Sebosian Cavalry Regiment, on fulfilment of his vow willingly set this up for taking a wild boar of remarkable fineness, which many of his predecessors had been unable to bag. (Collingwood, Wright, and Tomlin 1995, no. 1041)

The army officer who names himself on this altar had evidently vowed to erect an altar if and when he killed the wild boar which was presumably famous for its ability to elude previous hunters. Dedicating the altar to Silvanus, a woodland god, would have been appropriate if Bollihope Common, and the area of what was to be the Forest of Weardale, were already the mixture of woodland and pasture (in the case of Bollihope Common, upland pasture) that characterized saltus and forests. If Weardale was already a forest renowned for its hunting, this would explain why Gaius Tetius Veturius Micianus made the journey to it—as he appears to have done—all the way from Lancaster in northwest England where his regiment was based at the time the altar was set up. It is tempting to think that this Roman saltus developed into the Forest of Weardale, and that the Bishop of Durham had a hunting palace in it because he was using an ancient forest going back to the Roman period.

The forest around the palace of Woodstock may have had even more ancient origins. Woodstock was already a royal residence in the time of King Æthelred II (978–1013/14), who held an assembly there. The palace was within the Forest of Wychwood, which reached its greatest extent under Henry III, when it stretched to the gates of Oxford and the steps of Beaumont Palace in that city. Even when it was reduced in size between 1219 and 1300, it still occupied a considerable area between the Rivers Windrush and Glyme. Its origins are unknown, but it is tempting to see it as originating in Iron Age sacred woodlands, even before the Roman invasion of Britain. It is striking that the Celtic woodland god, Cunomaglos, appears as an object of veneration in religious sanctuaries in the area of the Forest of Wychwood, so it is conceivable that in the pre-Roman period the area was regarded as a special and sacred place, one set aside from the normal rules of life just as later forests were. If it were such a special area—what would later be a *saltus* and then a forest—it would have had definite boundaries. So, it is striking that there survives a mysterious linear earthwork, consisting of a bank and outer ditch, and known today as the North Oxfordshire Grim's Ditch. The fragmentary remains of this can be interpreted as showing that it originally enclosed an area approximately seven miles across (nearly 5,700 hectares) of what is broadly the Forest of Wychwood, around and to the northwest of the palace of Woodstock. Although difficult to date, the earthwork is certainly very ancient, and may possibly be of the early first century AD. It could have been defensive, of course, designed to protect settlements within it from attack. But there is a problem with that interpretation, in that settlements that have been identified as contemporary with the North Oxfordshire Grim's Ditch that have been identified lie outside that dyke system and not within it. So it looks as if that earthwork may have been meant to preserve an area that was not settled or only settled to a limited extent—and it is an intriguing possibility that that enclosed area could have been an early equivalent of a forest, or maybe, because it was enclosed, an early equivalent of a park, albeit a very large one.

FORESTS AND BUREAUCRATIC POWER

If palaces were so closely associated with forests, perhaps over such a long period, did these forests convey messages of power as it has been argued that palaces did? If so, to what type of power did the messages pertain? What is clear for the Middle Ages is that forests could be the areas over which rulers exercised the most direct and most effective control. The ruler's power could be much more effective over a forest than over the rest of his kingdom or the area he ruled. This is well shown by the extraordinary powers English kings held over forests, especially in the twelfth and thirteenth centuries, as part and parcel of the forest law. So significant were these powers that opposition to them figured prominently in the demands of the English barons who rebelled against King John and forced him to agree to that document limiting his prerogatives, Magna Carta in 1215, and the Forest Charter in 1217. At the height of his powers, only the king could make a forest, or in principle, at least, only he could grant permission for a forest to be made; only he could hunt over the whole extent of the forest, regardless of private ownership within it, and he could exclude others from the forest; only he could hunt certain beasts there, notably deer; he could control the pasturing of pigs and cattle within the forest, as well as the feeding of hens and the collection of wood and honey that also took place in it; he had rights over the minerals extracted from the ground within the forest; and he could restrict or permit clearances of trees within the forest. As we saw, the forests in England, at any rate from the time of the Norman kings, were outside the Common Law, and subject rather to the forest law which gave the king these extensive powers. These he enforced through an impressive machinery of forest courts and forest officials. A forest warden, who was nominated by the king and directly responsible to him, was responsible for maintaining a single royal forest or a group of forests, and for the welfare of the deer population. The wardens in turn appointed foresters with the responsibility to patrol the forest, to preside over the forest courts that dealt with offenses against the forest law, and to oversee, for example, the removal of three claws from the forefoot of every dog living within the forest so that it could not harm the game—"lawing" it or "hambling," it as the process is sometimes called. Associated with the foresters, but directly answerable to the king, were: verderers, responsible for the "vert" (that is, the trees and the vegetation of the forest generally) and the deer living in the forest; and agisters, responsible for controlling the pasturing of pigs on acorns in the forest. Officials called regarders pursued those who had pastured animals in the forest unlawfully, which they investigated at the thrice-yearly inquests, ordered by the royal government. There was also a series of royal courts responsible for the forest: the Courts of Regard, responsible for the vert; and the Courts of Attachment, responsible for the venison. Inquests of the Venison were held whenever the carcass of a deer was found in the forest, and, strikingly, they functioned much like a coroner's court—so important was the protection of the deer. Set over the local courts were chief justices of the forest, one for the area north of the River Trent and one for the area south of it, and there was also a system of forest eyres—regular visits to the forests by itinerant justices to resolve cases in breach of the forest law. The Forest Charter of 1271 established assemblies called *swainmotes*, which met three times a year, to commit offenders to the courts held in the course of the eyres and to deal with other matters. For medieval English kings, the forest was arguably the most intensively governed and closely controlled component of their realm.

This English royal control of forests from the time of the Norman kings may have been particularly developed, but, as we have seen, it is argued to have been an introduction from the Continent, where control of this sort may have gone back much further in time. Indeed, the broad outlines of such a system are perceptible in very early written sources from the Continent. Already in the late sixth century, there is a hint of the existence of royal control of forests, and particularly the game in them, in the Gregory of Tours's *History of the Franks*. This tells how, in the year 590, King Guntram of the Franks was hunting in the forest of the Vosges mountains (Gregory uses the Latin word *silva* "wood" rather than saltus). According to Gregory, King Guntram

> came across the tracks of a wild ox which had been killed. He questioned the forester closely to discover who had dared to do this in the royal forest. The forester told him that it was Chundo, his own royal chamberlain. Relying upon what the man had said, Guntram ordered Chundo to be arrested, and to be loaded with chains. (Thorpe 1974, book 10, ch. 10)

The king decided to have Chundo judged on the basis of the result of an armed combat between his own champion and Chundo's but, when both champions were killed in this combat, Chundo tried to escape to a church to seek sanctuary. However, he was seized by the king's men, and the king had him stoned to death. Gregory weakens the impact of this story by asserting that the king later regretted this execution and therefore the loss of a servant he could ill afford to dispense with. But the underlying point of the story nevertheless was the importance of the royal forest, with at least one species of game under the king's especial protection, with a forester (Gregory's term is *custos silvalis*, "custodian of the forest") as an official to protect it or at least to report on who had harmed it, and with royal powers over transgressors of royal protection which extended to the death penalty.

Clearer evidence is given by a royal charter making a grant to the monastery of Stavelot-Malmèdy in the Ardennes (Belgium) in 670, which mentions royal officials called foresters (Müller-Kehlen 1973, 102). In 768, Pippin III, king of the Franks (751–68), granted to the monastery of Saint-Denis, just to the north of Paris, the royal forest of Yvelines, with defined boundaries, incorporating rights over serfs living in the forest, over water rights (for fishing), over pastures, and over wild beasts, and including also command of the foresters and their services (Petit-Dutaillis 1915, 126). It seems, then, that the king normally had these extensive rights, and the officials to enforce them, in his own hands. In the documents issued by later Carolingian kings, royal hunting rights in royal forests were firmly maintained, and fines were imposed on those catching and killing wild animals there. Clearance and settlement within the forest were strictly controlled, and charges were imposed for animals driven into the forest to feed on acorns and beech-mast, except when this was completely prohibited. No one was allowed to release his dogs from their leashes in the forest. To enforce all these regulations, the Carolingian kings had the services of royal officials called foresters, as appears in Pippin III's charter of 768. A document of around the year 874 introduces us to a "servant of the king" called Wito, who was the "superintendent of all the forests" (*princeps super omnes forestas*) (quoted by Zotz 1997, 104).

There were other ways in which forests, and parks too, could convey messages about the ruler's bureaucratic power through the material resources which they offered. Even when the ruler was not hunting in a park or forest, he could still benefit from the venison that could be obtained there, and we have records of the large quantities of venison the medieval English kings ordered from their parks and forests to supply their feasts. Other game could be treated in the same way. The timber of all sorts from forests could also benefit the ruler, either directly or because he could tax others who extracted it. Pasture rights within the forest were another resource for the ruler. He could have his own animals pastured in the forest. Or he could make others pay for the privilege of pasturing their animals, whether they were members of forest communities within the forest, or of communities living outside it who drove their animals into it to feed. The animals in question were sometimes pigs, who were driven into the forest to feed on acorns. In medieval England, this was subject to a special tax called pannage, payable to the king; but it is clear from Charlemagne's *Capitulare de Villis* that, already in the eighth and ninth centuries, controlling the feeding of pigs in forests was an important issue for a ruler. In England, some of the earliest documents for the great forest area of the Weald in southeast England relate to permission granted to the monastery of Minster-in-Thanet on the eastern tip of Kent to pasture pigs there—the permission exonerated the monastery from paying dues to the king, but such payment was evidently the norm. Sheep and cattle were also pastured in forests, to the ruler's profit, and large upland pastures for cows in the forests of northern England were known as vaccaries. The collection of honey from the hives of wild bees was also subject to dues payable to the king both in England and on the Continent, so it too was another resource. The same was true of the king's rights over minerals extracted within the forests. The king's rights over forests gave him, potentially at least, total control of these. Mineral extraction was important in many forests, coal and iron for example in the Forest of Dean (England), various metals in the Cotswolds (England), iron in the Ardennes (Belgium), but perhaps nowhere more strikingly than at Goslar (Germany), where the forest immediately adjacent to the palace contained the great silver mines on which so much of the power and wealth of the kings of Germany was based.

The proximity of forests to palaces, then, may have been because the forests were important tools for conveying messages, and were indeed a clear source of power for a ruler. Because the king had such control over a forest, such rights over activities within it, and such potential for deriving resources from it, it obviously made sense for it to be under the direct and immediate supervision of his palace. In his absence, his representative—his constable, his warden, or his castellan—could continue to guard his rights using the palace as his headquarters. So forests and palaces went together, but not always the other way round—many forests, Hatfield Forest for example, were not centered on a palace, although in the case of this example there was a small hunting lodge in the nearby Writtle Forest. The message of bureaucratic power conveyed by forests could thus derive from the scale of the ruler's power over forests, and the abundant evidence throughout them of the exercise of that power. Just as the courts and offices in and around the great hall in the Palace of Westminster conveyed a message of bureaucratic power, so the forests themselves could do the same through the omnipresence of ruler's officials, the holding of ruler's courts, the harvesting of game for the ruler's feasts, and so on.

FORESTS, HUNTING, AND PERSONAL POWER

Could forests also convey a message of power pertaining to the personal power of rulers, that is, the power arising from their personal relationships with their subjects and with others? It was argued previously that the intimate chambers of rulers within palaces could be an instrument of personal power, because they enabled the ruler to give distinction to his most important subjects and guests by admitting only them to these most private spaces (above, pp. 44–49). Much the same thing may have been true of intimate gardens created around a palace (above, p. 115). In the light of this, it is striking to read another passage that Richard Fitz Nigel wrote about the royal forests of twelfth-century England:

> In the forests are the kings' retreats (*penetralia*), and their greatest delights. For they go there to hunt, leaving their cares behind, to refresh themselves with a little rest. There, setting aside

the turmoil of serious matters intrinsic to the court, they breathe fresh air freely for a little while; and that is why people who violate the forest are punished solely at the king's will. (Amt and Church 2007, 91)

This could be read quite straightforwardly to mean that the forests offered the king a sort of getaway from his responsibilities. But, since we know that major councils were held at palaces in the forests, as at Clarendon and Woodstock, this straightforward reading does not seem particularly convincing. As with private chambers in palaces, it is equally likely that the away-from-it-all character of the forest, which Fitz Nigel refers to, similarly offered the king the opportunity to distinguish and honor particularly important people. They alone would be invited to accompany the king into the forest itself. Fitz Nigel's use of the Latin word *penetralia* may be significant here, for it occurs in other texts referring to the innermost, most intimate parts of palaces—the parts that it was a privilege to penetrate—hence the word penetralia attached to them. In Virgil's first-century AD epic poem, the *Aeneid*, for example, the king of the defeated city of Troy, Priam, was killed by the city's attackers after he had taken refuge in the penetralia, the innermost part, of his palace (Durand and Bellessort 1948–57, book 2, line 484).

The guests that a ruler might especially want to impress by taking them into his forests were visiting rulers of other states and kingdoms, or ambassadors sent by them to negotiate with the ruler in question. We have already seen this in the case of the Holy Roman Emperor's ambassador, Liudprand, whom the Byzantine emperor sought to impress by showing him the wild donkeys in his park at Constantinople (above, p. 132). Perhaps that was the reason for holding great councils at palaces in forests, as at Clarendon and Woodstock. To pursue this further, however, it is necessary to turn to the question of rulers hunting in forests, and the potential of hunting for conveying messages of personal power.

Hunting could be a means not only of creating but also of displaying social relationships between the ruler and the subjects or visitors who accompanied him. Certainly by the fourteenth century, and probably much earlier, hunting was a formal, courtly activity, just like the processions and ceremonies that took place in the palace or in its gardens. This is clear from manuals of hunting, such as that by Edward, duke of York (d. 1415), which describe the very formal ways not only of killing the game, but also of butchering it (unmaking it, that is) after the kill, and then of sharing the parts of the animal. The fifteenth-century Devonshire Hunting Tapestries, now in the Victoria and Albert Museum in London, give an impression of the extent to which hunting was regarded as a formal, courtly activity (Figure 5–6). The figure shows a detail of a boar hunt in progress, with a lady and gentleman standing in magnificent garments around the kill. It is unlikely that this was a realistic representation, and that it was feasible for such garments to have been worn in such a situation, but the tapestry emphasizes the way in which hunting could be thought of as a courtly activity.

The role of such courtly hunting in conveying a message of power to visiting ambassadors or visiting fellow-monarchs is vividly shown by a much earlier source, the ninth-century *Poem on Louis the Pious* by Ermold the Black. This contains a quite detailed account of a hunt that took place in the course of a visit by a king of the Danes, Harald, to Louis the Pious's palace at Ingelheim in Germany. Although Danish history in this period is poorly

Figure 5–6: Hunting boar, Devonshire Hunting Tapestries, Victoria and Albert Museum, London (England), detail showing the rich apparel of the participants. (See insert for color version of this image.)

documented and much about it is obscure, it seems clear that Harald's authority in his own country was anything but unchallenged. He was making this visit to Ingelheim, in company with his queen, with a view to securing Louis the Pious's support for his throne, while Louis the Pious on his side was anxious to secure him as an ally, and to seal their relationship by getting the pagan Dane and his queen to accept Christianity. The visit did indeed culminate in the baptism of Harald and his queen, with Louis the Pious and his queen Judith as godparents, so that the desired alliance was successfully secured. The visit then turned to matters of power, and the way in which the Danes were received and the way in which they responded to their reception mattered. It is therefore all the more striking to find a hunt given such prominence in Ermold the Black's account of the visit.

Ermold's description of the hunt (Faral 1932, lines 2362–447) begins with Louis the Pious preparing for the hunt soon after dawn, and inviting Harald to join him. The hunt, Ermold then goes on to explain, was to take place on a nearby "island in the River Rhine, covered with cool meadows and shaded by woods," where there "abound wild animals of all sorts, which take cover throughout the woods." This island, which was no doubt larger than any of the islands now in the River Rhine at Ingelheim, was presumably as much a park as a forest, for it was enclosed by water just as a park was enclosed by a wall or bank. Also, the wild animals were there because the island had been deliberately stocked with them. It is otherwise hard to believe that an island in the river would naturally have supported large populations of them. The contention that the island was deliberately stocked is further supported by the fact that among the animals found there were bears, which were not native to the Rhineland in the ninth century, and so must have been imported specifically for hunting (Hauck 1963b, 43–44).

Ermold then describes how Louis the Pious, his queen Judith, "magnificently arrayed," his eldest son Lothar, and the royal guest Harald came to the hunt accompanied by courtiers and a crowd of lords. All this must have emphasized the ceremonial character of the event. Ermold then describes the hunt, in which Louis the Pious and Lothar played distinguished parts, and then the après-hunt ceremonial meal in the open air, which—as Ermold makes clear—was a grand occasion:

> Now the venerable emperor and his suite, laden with venison, prepare to go home. But, in the middle of the woods, Judith has cleverly arranged a bower of greenery: branches of willow and broom, stripped of their leaves, have been used to form the enclosure; fabrics have been hung around and above. The queen herself prepares on the grass a seat for the pious king and orders the meal to be served. Soon, with hands washed, Caesar and his beautiful wife rest themselves side by side on gilded armchairs. The handsome Lothar and Harald, the guest of the king, take their places at the table where the king invites them. The rest of the hunters sit on the grass and all rest their weary bodies in the shade of the forest. Soon the servants bring the roasted flesh of the beasts killed in the hunt: venison covers the emperor's table. Hunger is overcome; they raise cups to their lips, and thirst in its turn is chased away by the sweet beverage. The generous wine makes happy the bold hearts, and all return to the palace with spirit. (translated from Faral 1932, lines 2415–34)

Even when they return to the palace after this meal, the ceremonies of the hunt have not yet been completed, for Louis the Pious must still see to the ceremonial distribution of the game among his servants.

Harald the Dane seems to have been the principal intended audience of the message of power conveyed by the hunt, and Ermold the Black emphasizes in the next lines the impact that it, and other events that have taken place at Ingelheim, have had on him:

> At the sight of all these things, Louis the Pious's guest Harald is agitated with numerous thoughts. He is amazed by the power of the king, his authority, his religion, the devotion he offers to God. Chasing all hesitation from his heart, he says at last what God inspires him to. Penetrated by the faith, he addresses the king, before whom he has spontaneously prostrated

himself: "Powerful Caesar, pious adorer of God, who excel in directing the subjects of the master of the world who have been entrusted to you! I recognize the glory and the moderation, the valour and the piety, the power and the indulgence which God has granted to you." (translated from Faral 1932, lines 2448–59)

Harald duly paid homage to Louis the Pious and became his vassal and his ally. Ermold the Black's poem is, of course, a work of literature intended to flatter the emperor, rather than a piece of straight reportage; but the role of the hunt as conveying a message of the ruler's personal power, and also in creating and reinforcing relationships between the ruler and fellow rulers, could hardly be more clearly presented.

Another ninth-century writer was Notker the Stammerer, who wrote a biography of the emperor Charlemagne, which is more a collection of anecdotes than a factual record. These anecdotes, however, are likely to reflect the realities of Notker's time, even if their details are more fiction than fact. It is therefore striking to find among them an account of a hunt that is briefer than Ermold the Black's account of Louis the Pious's hunt, but is clearly based on the same ideas about the hunt's importance in impressing visitors to the royal or imperial court. Notker the Stammerer recounts how Charlemagne received at his court at Aachen some ambassadors whom Notker calls "Persians," but who were in fact from the Muslim caliphate of Baghdad. Notker tells of how impressed they were by the Aachen palace church, and by a sumptuous feast which the emperor invited them to, but also by a hunt. He writes:

Charlemagne . . . prepared to go off into the forest grove to hunt bison and wild oxen. He took the Persian envoys with him; but when they set eyes on these immense animals, they were filled with mighty dread, and they turned and ran. Our hero Charlemagne, on the contrary, knew no fear: sitting astride his spirited horse, he rode up to one of the beasts, drew his sword and tried to cut off its head. (Thorpe 1969, 144–45, sec. 8)

Notker's account of this incident continues with a story of how Charlemagne was slightly injured by this beast, and how it was then killed by a courtier who was in disgrace but was re-instated as a result of this. But what is notable for the present is the impression the hunt was supposed to have made on the Persians—the message of power, in other words, that it conveyed to them.

The extent to which the hunt sent a message of personal power with reference to the relationships between the king and his allies, his faithful men, and his vassals stands out in the cycle of Welsh stories called the *Mabinogion*. One of these, which involves a hunting expedition engaged in by the emperor Maxen Wledig, contains the following:

With him were two-and-thirty crowned kings that were his vassals; not for the delight of hunting went the emperor with them, but to put himself on equal terms with them. (quoted by G. Jones 2010, 36)

The text is late and the narrative fictional, but the underlying idea suggests the way in which hunting contributed to a ruler's personal power. Hunting in this story is a means for the ruler to form relationships with his vassals by fraternizing with them in the hunt—to convey, in other words, a message of the ruler's personal power.

Participation in the royal hunt was no doubt a sought-after privilege defining the level of intimacy and the importance of the relationship between the king and his allies, faithful men, and vassals. To have a share in the pursuit, killing, and butchering of the beast, and in the distribution of the game might well have been the same type of sought-after privilege as was attending the *levée* of Louis XIV at Versailles. The message of personal power conveyed by the ruler's admitting his favored subject to his hunt may not have been very different.

FORESTS, HUNTING, AND IDEOLOGICAL POWER

Hunting could also convey a message pertaining to the ideological power of rulers, in terms of their courage and strength in the hunt. Modern studies of Roman and medieval rulers often attribute to them a love of hunting, as if this were part of their individual characters and enthusiasms. No doubt some rulers were genuine hunting enthusiasts—King William I of England, for example, was reputed to have "loved the stags so very much, as if he were their father" (Swanton 1996, 221), and the German emperor Frederick II himself wrote a major treatise on hunting with falcons, which leaves no doubt of his personal involvement in it (Willemsen 1973). But to treat hunting as no more than an enthusiasm of rulers does no justice to its prominence in the written sources, and to its persistence as an activity of rulers throughout the period this book is concerned with, as well as long after it and long before it.

Hunting as an Essential Part of Rulership

Hunting may have been an essential part of rulership in the ancient world. King Ashburnipal of the Assyrians left inscriptions describing his hunting exploits in close relationship to his kingship, as for example:

> I, Ashburnipal, king of the Universe, king of Ashur, in my recreation on foot seized a raging lion of the plain by its ears, and with the help of Ashur and Ishtar, lady of battle, I pierced its body with my own lance. (quoted by Anderson 1985, 6–10, esp. p. 7)

The palace of Tiryns was decorated in the thirteenth century BC with hunting scenes, as was the palace of Pilos, destroyed in around 1200 BC. Hunting was developed by the Persian kings, for whom "this display of royal prowess before the people's eyes was part of the kingly function, not merely a sport," and they even used a hunting scene on their royal seal (Anderson 1985, 12–15, 63–67). For these ancient kings, it seems that hunting was conveying a message of ideological power. The message was that hunting and rulership went together; to be a ruler you needed to be successful in hunting, and your power in the hunt reflected your power as a ruler.

A similar message is evident in Ermold the Black's account of the hunt at Ingelheim, in which he particularly emphasizes the ability of Louis the Pious and his son, Lothar, in killing animals, an ability that presumably set them apart as an emperor and a future emperor:

Caesar, ardent, himself kills a host of animals, striking them with his own hand. The agile Lothar, glowing with youth, kills through his prowess a number of bears. (translated from Faral 1932, lines 2388–91)

In his fourteenth-century French hunting manual, Gaston Phoebus particularly emphasized how dangerous was bear hunting (Bise 1984, 76), so this passage was evidently intended to underline the courage of Lothar. Also present at the hunt was Lothar's half-brother, Charles. A child at the time of the hunt, Charles was the son of Louis the Pious and the empress Judith, his second wife. He was to become future king of the western part of the Frankish kingdom, but his claims to this would be disputed by his half-brothers from the moment that Louis the Pious first intimated his intention to make him a co-heir. In the hands of Ermold the Black, the hunt offered an opportunity to present him as a potential king, even as a child, because of his courage in hunting. According to Ermold, Charles longed to kill a hind disturbed by the dogs, but his mother would not let him go after it. Finally, it was brought to him, Ermold writes, and, seizing appropriately sized weapons, he killed the animal while, the poet asserts, "the virtue of his father and the name of his ancestor enhanced his prestige" (translated from Faral 1932, lines 2410–13).

The attribution to the Roman emperor Domitian of the credit for killing a hundred wild animals in his park at any one time (above, p. 144) no doubt served the same purpose of conveying a message of fitness to rule, and of the ideological power that stemmed from hunting. Similarly, the German chronicler Widukind of Corvey emphasized how many animals the German ruler Henry I killed in the hunt: "He was so skillful in the hunt that one time he killed more than forty wild beasts" (Bachrach and Bachrach 2014, bk 1, ch. 39).

Another of Notker the Stammerer's stories is based on the same idea. According to Notker, Pippin III, king of the Franks (d. 768), discovered that "the leaders of his army were in the habit of speaking contemptuously of him in private." So he had a bull "of fantastic size and ferocious temper" released and then a lion set on it. He then commanded his courtiers to drag it off the bull or to kill it and, when they were too afraid to do so, he "rose without hesitation from his throne, drew his sword, and cut through the lion's neck and severed the bull's head from its shoulders." The result of this feat was that the courtiers acknowledged his "right to rule over the whole of mankind" (Thorpe 1969, bk 2, ch. 13). This was, of course, just a story, but the underlying idea is clear—the ruler's power was linked to his ability to kill animals.

This is probably how the accounts in the sources should be understood, of rulers continuing to hunt even when they were very old. When Charlemagne's other biographer, Einhard, asserts that the emperor was still hunting "although enfeebled by old age" (Thorpe 1969, 83), at the very end of his life, this was surely intended to convey the message that the old man was still the ruler, that he still had the power to govern, because he had the power to hunt. Something similar probably lies behind the claim that Henry VIII, king of England, continued to hunt even when ravaged by age, obesity, and illness (Thurley 2003, 71).

There may be an echo of this in the epic poem, *Perceval*, written by Chrétien de Troyes in the 1180s and concerning the quest of King Arthur's knight, Sir Perceval, for the Holy Grail. In the course of the quest, Perceval comes to a river, on which is a boat with two men, one of whom is fishing. This man offers him lodging, and is probably the king—the Fisher King—who later receives him in his castle, but who cannot rise to welcome him because of his disability. When Perceval leaves the castle next day, he meets a weeping woman who explains the king's disability:

> Good sir, he is king, I can well tell you, but he was wounded and truly maimed in a battle so that he cannot manage alone. He was wounded by a javelin between the two thighs, and is still in pain so that he cannot mount a horse. But when he wishes to distract himself or to have some pleasing diversion, he has himself carried into a small boat and goes fishing with a hook, for this he is called the Fisher King. (quoted by K. G. Tracy 2010, 106–07)

Although hunting is here presented as a relaxation for the king, the fact that he is characterized as the Fisher King because he cannot himself hunt except by fishing underlines how intrinsic a part of rulership hunting was regarded. The maimed king—in this case a king maimed in the genitals—cannot hunt.

The epic Latin poem, *Charlemagne and Pope Leo*, written around the year 800, also carries the clear implication that undertaking hunting was an essential part of rulership. It begins by representing Charlemagne in all his glory, shining like the sun, and it sets out his characteristic activities: promoting learning, building the city of Aachen like Rome, and taking an active part in a great and evidently ceremonial hunt in the forest around Aachen (Brockmann et al. 1966, lines 1–326). The poem is fragmentary, but the hunting section must nevertheless have been a very substantial part of it, dwarfing the account, for example, of the feast at which the pope was entertained at Paderborn (lines 524–39).

The importance of hunting in the office of kingship is similarly suggested by Asser, the contemporary biographer of King Alfred of the West Saxons. He gives an account of that ruler's kingly duties, which he continued to discharge even when faced by Viking attacks and his own illness. Prominent among these is "pursuing all manner of hunting" as well as giving instructions to his "falconers, hawk-trainers and dog-keepers" (Keynes and Lapidge 1983, sec. 76). Also, Asser makes clear that even in his youth Alfred had been marked out as a king in the making by his hunting:

> An enthusiastic huntsman, he strives continually in every branch of hunting, and not in vain; for no one else could approach him in skill and success in that activity, just as in all the other gifts of God. (Keynes and Lapidge 1983, sec. 22)

Political and Military Symbolism of Hunting

That the success of the ruler in hunting could have quite explicit political symbolism is suggested by lines from a poem of the ninth-century Walafrid Strabo, addressed to Emperor Louis the Pious:

> Just as the bear, boar, timid hare and swift stags
> Antelope, wolf, and huge herd of wild cattle
> Fear your bow in the lovely glades,
> So the Bulgar and the cur of Sarah, bad guest of the Spaniards,

The brutish Britton, shrewd Dane and dreadful Moor
Bow their necks in terror before your venerable hands.

(Herren 1991, 138–39, lines 250–55)

Hunting was clearly equated with military victory. Walafrid Strabo's lines echo a more down-to-earth comment by the Greek historian Xenophon that Cyrus, the great Persian ruler in the sixth century BC, was distinguished from his brother who "could neither keep his seat in the hunting field nor his throne in a crisis" (quoted by Anderson 1985, 62).

The theme of rulership and hunting is taken further on a well-known monument in Rome. After the emperor Constantine (306–37) defeated his rival Maxentius at the Battle of the Milvian Bridge outside Rome in 312, and became sole ruler of the western Roman Empire, the Senate erected the Arch of Constantine, a triumphal arch that still stands close to the Colosseum in the center of the ancient city. A prominent part of the decorative scheme consists of a series of eight sculptured scenes of hunting on circular panels known as tondi. These are placed above the smaller, side openings of the arch, four of them on each side. They were not made for the Arch of Constantine, since the style of their carving is quite different from scenes specially carved for it, and it is clear that the faces of some of the characters represented have been re-carved to convert them into likenesses of Constantine and possibly his co-emperor Licinius. So these tondi must have been taken from an earlier monument which, to judge from the style of the sculpture, was probably erected by or for the emperor Hadrian. There is no way of knowing what sort of a monument that was, but it was presumably a public one on a considerable scale.

The tondi show, first, the scene of the emperor's departure for the hunt (Figure 5–7). The emperor stands on the right, while one attendant holds his spear, and another his horse. The scene appears to be taking place at the gate of the city, for a masonry arch appears behind the emperor, with the forest indicated by the tree on the left-hand margin of the tondo. The scene resembles in its form scenes on triumphal arches showing the departure of the emperor to pursue a military campaign, so the message being conveyed may be that, for the emperor, hunting was on the same scale of importance as warfare as a test of his courage and strength.

Three of the other tondi show hunting in progress: hunting of the bear, the lion, and the boar, respectively. In the scene of the boar hunt (Figure 5–8), the emperor is mounted and followed by two mounted companions who ride behind him. The emperor has his arm raised and—although the sculpture has broken away—he was clearly about to plunge his spear into the boar which runs at the feet of his horse. Just as the departure for the hunt scene resembled a scene showing departure for a military campaign, so this scene is strongly reminiscent of scenes of an emperor defeating and riding down hostile barbarians who fall beneath the feet of his horse. It seems the parallel between hunting and warfare is again being emphasized. The same can be said of the scene of the bear hunt (Figure 5–9). In this too, the emperor is accompanied by mounted companions, and in this too he is evidently raising his arm to plunge his spear into the bear, which is trying to run away to the right. The similarity with scenes of emperors crushing barbarian enemies is equally marked here, and the message being conveyed about the emperor's strength and courage is all the clearer

Figure 5–7: Tondo showing the departure of the emperor for the hunt, Arch of Constantine, Rome (Italy).

if bears were regarded, as Gaston Phoebus later regarded them, as especially dangerous game to hunt.

There are four more tondi showing scenes of the emperor making sacrifices in thanks for the game he has killed, respectively, to: the god of the sun, Apollo; the woodland god, Silvanus; the goddess of hunting, Diana; and the hero, Hercules. These mirror scenes of sacrifices being offered at altars after military victories, so they too underline the link between hunting and warfare. This link is particularly clear in the case of the tondo showing the sacrifice to Hercules (Figure 5–10).

In this scene, the emperor stands on the right. He is about to place the sacrifice on the altar that stands between him and his three companions, one of whom holds what is presumably the emperor's spear. Above appears an image of Hercules, identified by the lion-skin garment appearing just above the emperor's head. This image seems to make a clear allusion to warfare, for Hercules is sitting on a bench supported by two cuirasses. A cuirass

Figure 5–8: Tondo showing the emperor hunting boar, Arch of Constantine, Rome (Italy).

Figure 5–9: Tondo showing the emperor hunting bear, Arch of Constantine, Rome (Italy).

Figure 5–10: Tondo showing the emperor making a sacrifice to Hercules in thanksgiving for the hunt, Arch of Constantine, Rome (Italy).

is a sort of body armor, which would have been worn in battle, but not in a hunt. Also, he holds in his left hand a statuette of a winged figure, certainly a figure of a Victory, and so also a symbol of military victory. Here, then, hunting appears clearly as an activity comparable to warfare. Just as rulers could have messages of ideological power conveyed by their triumphs in battle, so similar messages could be conveyed by their success in hunting. This may have been the message of whatever monument it was for which the emperor Hadrian commissioned the tondi; and it may also have been the message conveyed by placing them on the Arch of Constantine almost two centuries later.

The same idea recurs in a contemporary poem celebrating the victorious capture of a city by the Byzantine emperor John II Comnenos in 1133:

> I know, O divine emperor, the laws of the hunt. He who takes a boar, may achieve this after a long time, and with many toils; likewise he may catch a pard after a long time and with much lying in wait. But this prey of yours, your hunting, is the work of a few days, though it is verily a great work. A mighty city is captured, the fortifications are overcome, . . . such a hunter has our Comnenian master [the emperor] learned to be. (quoted by Maguire 1994, 197)

Here, the military activity of capturing the city is equated with hunting.

Hunting could also play a part in conveying a message of ideological power arising from perceptions of the social hierarchy. As we have already seen, forests were royal in origin, and *saltus* equally were imperial in origin. Even when the royal monopoly of forests ceased, they nevertheless remained a preserve of royalty and the aristocracy. Particular forms of hunting, especially hunting deer with hounds, were reserved for the kings, and later for their aristocracy. The fact that some types of hunting could be socially superior to others offered the possibility of using hunting as a means of conveying messages pertaining to the social hierarchy, at the pinnacle of which sat the ruler. This is graphically demonstrated in the wall paintings that survive in the Stag Chamber at the Palace of the Popes at Avignon (see plan, above, Figure 2–30). This chamber, which was the work of Pope Clement VI (1342–52), was apparently built as a particularly private space, a sort of study, to which only the most favored guests and colleagues of the pope would have been admitted. The paintings on the walls are entirely of various hunting scenes, which seem to be arranged in a hierarchy, according to the status of the types of hunting represented. The stag hunt is painted on the wall opposite the entrance from the Pope's Chamber. On the wall opposite to that, to the left of the entrance, is the hunt with the falcon. The next hunt in order is that of the boar, appearing twice on ceiling beams; then the hunt with cross-bow and bow, a less prestigious form of hunting, represented on the wall plate farthest from the principal entrance; then rabbit hunting and trapping, on the upper friezes of the other two walls. The hunt with the ferret appears on the left-hand wall, and various types of fishing on the right-hand wall. These various types of hunting were significant for their relationship to the social hierarchy. That involving the stag was at the pinnacle and it was that scene which anyone entering the Stag Chamber saw first. In less prominent positions in the room were the hunts appropriate to lesser social orders, such as the hunt with the ferret. The message conveyed was one of the ideological power of the ruler, who was at the apex of a hierarchy symbolized by different types of hunting.

Religious Symbolism of Hunting

The capacity of hunting to convey a message of ideological power may at times have gone even further. It could even be imbued with religious significance, and nowhere is this more obvious than in the series of seven fifteenth-century tapestries now preserved in the Cloisters Museum in New York, where they are known as the Unicorn Tapestries. They were first recorded in the modern period as being in the château of Verteuil, an aristocratic country palace in western France, but there is no evidence to show for whom or for what residence they were actually made. Since the subject of all the tapestries is the hunt for the unicorn, a mythical beast, there is no question of these tapestries representing actual events. Nevertheless, they may provide a guide to the ideas associated with hunting and the significance with which it could be imbued. The seven tapestries fall into three groups which are differentiated by their style and by the details of their subject matter.

The first group, which now consists of two tapestries, begins with a scene of three splendidly dressed hunters setting out through the forest, accompanied by two dog handlers or "lymerers" with their dogs. The second scene shows the unicorn, which has evidently been the object of the hunt, enclosed in a fence, in which is a pomegranate tree to which it has been chained. Comparison with other works of art on the same subject suggests that scenes are missing here, which would have shown the unicorn tamed by a maiden, in whose lap it lays its head. It might then have been shown attacked by the hunters, but their weapons did it no harm, and the scene of it enclosed and chained would have been the final scene in the sequence. For, this hunt for the unicorn was an allegory of love. The unicorn stood for the lover, who was subdued by the maiden, and then was wounded by the hunters, who themselves represented the pangs of love. Finally, the unicorn was chained and fenced in the indissoluble bond of marriage.

The second group of tapestries consists of two fragments, one showing a hunter blowing a horn, the other showing a unicorn, the neck of which is being fondled by a woman (only her right hand is visible) while hounds wound it. These scenes are fragments from another sequence of scenes showing the hunt for the unicorn, which symbolizes the story of Christ entering the womb of the Virgin Mary to be born as a man, and eventually to be crucified. In this sequence, the unicorn is Christ, the woman who caresses it is the Virgin Mary enticing it into her womb as it lays its head on her lap, and the huntsman with the horn is the angel Gabriel who announces to the Virgin Mary that she will give birth to Christ.

The third group consists of four tapestries, and is probably a complete series of scenes. In the first, the unicorn is discovered by the hunters drinking from a fountain in company with wild animals, including lions and a stag. In the second scene, the unicorn tries to escape across a stream but is intercepted by the hunters and attacked by the hounds (Figure 5–11). In the third scene, the unicorn is at bay, surrounded by the hounds and the hunters with their spears. And, in the fourth scene, the unicorn is killed by spear thrusts and then carried across the back of a horse to the palace, where the lord and lady are coming out to receive it.

Comparison with other representations of the subject suggests that here the unicorn again represents Christ, but the hunt is an allegory of his passion and Crucifixion, so that

Figure 5–11: Unicorn leaping into a stream to escape the pursuit of the hunters, Unicorn Tapestries, Cloisters Museum, New York (USA). (See insert for color version of this image.)

the dead unicorn brought to the palace represents Christ taken down from the cross after his Crucifixion. The iconography of these tapestries thus raises the possibility that the message of power conveyed by hunting could be one pertaining to the ruler's close relationship to the deity. Just as it has been argued that domed halls could have sent a message of the cosmic power of the ruler, so his role in hunting could have associated him with Christ or with the gods.

That there could have been religious symbolism in hunting which enabled it to convey such a message of power is further suggested by a scene represented on a sarcophagus carved in the eighth century, perhaps at St. Andrews (Scotland), where it is still preserved in the cathedral museum (Figure 5–12). It was probably made for a king, possibly Oengus, son of Fergus (d. 761), an ambitious ruler of what was then the British kingdom of eastern Scotland, who was later regarded as the founder of St. Andrews. The carving on one of the long sides of the sarcophagus shows, on the right, David, king of Israel, identifiable because he is forcing open the jaws of a lion (Henderson 1998, 119–21). This representation, with its emphasis on his imposing costume and the rich sword at his side, may have been intended

Figure 5–12: Replica, conserved in the Custom House, Leith (Scotland), of the St. Andrews sarcophagus, St Andrews Cathedral Museum, St. Andrews (Scotland). The hunting scene represented on the side of the sarcophagus with the representation of King David killing a lion on the right.

to equate Oengus with David, and thus to convey the message that the ruler was as close to God as David had been.

On the rest of the carved side, a hunt is taking place, clearly in a forest as indicated by the foliage. In the lower part, a man on foot with dogs seems to be flushing out the game; in the upper part, a mounted huntsman—perhaps another representation of the king—prepares to kill a lion, just as the ancient kings of Assyria were represented on carved reliefs taking part in the royal lion hunt. In this scene, the hunt is presumably a religious symbol, connected with the representation of David and his place in the Bible, and also a symbol of power because the king is killing the greatest beast of all, the lion. The message of ideological power being conveyed was that of the god-like character of the ruler.

Forests and Nationhood

Hunting was not, however, the only way in which forests could convey messages of ideological power. It is arguable that, in the later Middle Ages at least, the forest, in the sense here rather of a wooded area than an area subject to forest jurisdiction, had a particularly potent charge as a symbol of German nationhood. Since Roman writers had described the early German barbarians as living in forests, such as the great Hercynian Forest which appears in the writings of Julius Caesar, so in the later Middle Ages German scholars and artists who read these authors used their writings to fashion German nationhood as associated with

Figure 5–13: *St. George and the Dragon*, 1510 (oil on parchment on limewood), by Albrecht Altdorfer (*c*.1480–1538) 28.2 x 22.5 cm, Alte Pinakothek, Munich (Germany). (See insert for color version of this image.)

forests. It is arguably in this symbolic role that forests appear in the paintings of Albrecht Altdorfer, for example in his *St. George and the Dragon* (Figure 5–13).

As in other of his paintings, the forest itself is the dominant element in the scene, dwarfing the saint and his antagonist in a sea of greenery. Very possibly, the forest's role here was to represent German nationhood, to be itself the focus of attention for that reason. If forests in paintings could have such connotations, so could real forests around palaces. Just as the forest in Altdorfer's painting may have symbolized German nationhood, so the forest around a palace may have done the same. But it may not only have been in late medieval Germany that the symbolism of the forest had such importance. Although it is not easy to see what the importance of its symbolic presence may have been for the power of rulers, it is certainly the case that forests occupied an important position in a series of literary works, from Shakespeare's Forest of Arden around 1600 through the series of Arthurian romances to the *Tristan* romances and other literary texts of the twelfth century in which the forest was the "forest of courtly romance." Just as was argued in the previous chapter with regard to gardens, this world of courtly romance may have been connected with the symbolism of power, and forests may equally have played their part, in their real existence as well as in their appearances in literature. Just as a garden could provide a stage set for a ruler who rooted his power in idealized perceptions of King Arthur and similar literary figures, so the forest may have provided a stage set beyond the garden.

The messages of power conveyed by that stage set may then have been charged with an imaginative apparatus deriving from such bodies of literature as the stories of King Arthur's knights, or indeed the earlier stories such as those of Beowulf. If, as seems possible, the stories of Beowulf were known, perhaps even originally created, at Lejre, then the glacial moraine hunting landscape adjacent to the great halls there may have had the same imaginative charge in the early Middle Ages as the forests of Arthurian knights did in the later Middle Ages. That would have been the landscape from which the monster Grendel emerged, and through which the hero (and future king) Beowulf pursued him to his death. So any ruler hunting in it may well have been conveying a message of power through the association with the former hero which his hunting there gave him.

CONCLUSION

It is then the contention of this chapter that forests were an important tool in the hands of rulers. They could convey messages of bureaucratic power through the sheer administrative control that the ruler was capable of exhibiting with regard to them, and from the resources, in venison and other materials and produce, that he was able to derive from them. They could convey messages of personal power through the hunting that took place in them, and that itself provided a rich opportunity for bonding between the ruler and certain of his subjects, as well as for the assertion and representation of hierarchical relationships. But it is argued here that they could also convey messages of ideological power. This was partly through hunting itself, with its potential for the ritualized presentation of power, as well as with its conceptual associations as an essential part of rulership and its religious significance in Christianity arising from its association with the passages in the Bible. It is, of course, possible to be skeptical of the line of argument advanced here. It is equally feasible to regard forests as no more than areas of a particular type of production, and to see them as no more important than any other of the ruler's lands. It is possible too to accept literally what is said by writers like Richard Fitz Nigel—that forests were simply places of relaxation for rulers, and that they indulged in hunting for the same reason—and to fall back on the idea that rulers, and their aristocrats, hunted simply because they were enthusiastic about it, and had forests because they wanted suitable spaces to exercise their favorite hobby. But it is hard to see how any of this explains the prominence of forests and hunting, not least in public monuments and displays, across such a long period of time, or the scale of forests and the complexity of the administration involved in running and controlling them, or the effort and resource that went into the creation of game parks from the time of the ancient Assyrians onward. Something more must have been at stake, and the contention of this chapter is that that something was power—perhaps chiefly ideological power, but also to a not inconsiderable extent bureaucratic and personal power.

PART III

Cities

Where a ruler's palace was sited within a city, or closely attached to a city, there must have been the potential for the city to convey messages of power to reinforce those of the palace itself. Even a city without a ruler's palace within it or attached to it could equally have been the vehicle of such messages, especially where its political profile was high, and perhaps especially where the ruler was a frequent visitor, or a builder or patron of buildings or quarters within it, even if he was not a resident.

The messages in question could have been conveyed in a variety of ways. In quite down-to-earth terms, the layout of the streets of the city, or the relative heights of buildings in it, or the emphasis given to its fortifications or particular quarters within it could have served this function. The siting of a palace at the highest point of a city, for example, may have been a potent symbol to convey a message of power, as in another way may the existence of a particularly regular layout of streets, where the regularity could be credited to the ruler and seen as a symbol of the regularity of his power. Such layouts could also have had a deeper significance for power, if, for example, they were intended to make the city resemble the heavenly Jerusalem, in much the same way as we shall see rulers' palace-churches being constructed and decorated to mirror it. It is these ways in which cities may have conveyed messages of power that form the subject of chapter 6.

Just as palaces could have formed stage sets for the ruler to convey messages of power through the processions and rituals that took place in them, so the same may have been true of cities. Elaborately formal ceremonies for a ruler to enter his city, either in a victory procession, a triumph, or in an entry procession, an *adventus*, were evidently in existence and in widespread use at various periods. They have the potential to cast light on how the city was developed as a stage set for conveying messages of power through these ceremonies—in its layout, in its buildings, and in the associations with which different quarters of it were imbued. The messages conveyed could have been of various types—pertaining to bureaucratic power when they were concerned with the ruler's ability to dominate his city, but also pertaining to social power where the ruler's entry into the city was a process of social bonding, and also pertaining to ideological power where the ruler was entering the city in a way that personified a divine figure and so associated him with that figure. It is these aspects of the use of cities by rulers for conveying messages of power that is the subject of chapter 7.

CHAPTER ~6

Cities, Planning, and Power

For a city to have been planned in a consistent, regular way, perhaps with a rectangular grid layout of streets, must always have been a means of conveying a message relating to the power of the individual responsible for the planning. Where that was the ruler, then the message pertained to his efficacy in achieving the planning in question and the power that had made it possible for him to secure its execution. Regularity of plan, however, may not have been the only means by which cities could convey messages of power. The relative heights of the different elements in them—where, for example, the ruler's palace was at the highest point of the city—could equally have conveyed a message of power, relating to the ruler's hierarchical dominance over his subjects in the lower part of the city. The choice of site for the city could then have been of particular importance when it came to siting its various elements in relation to one another.

PROMINENT SITES OF CITIES AND PALACES WITHIN THEM

In ancient Rome, as has been seen (above, pp. 12–13; Figure 2–1), the palaces built on the Palatine Hill rose above and dominated the Roman Forum, where important temples were located, as was the Senate House itself. The Forum was the real focus of power in the period of Roman Republic, and remained a powerful place, in principle if not in fact, under the emperors. The height of the Palatine Hill was only partly a result of the natural lie of the land. Its sides had been artificially extended by a series of massive building works, creating under-crofts and substructures to support the hill above, and the buildings on the edge of it. The artificiality of the hill is especially apparent on its southern side, facing the Circus Maximus, where the buildings on its sides were supported on huge structures, extending out beyond the rock of the hill itself. So enormous was the work involved that the hill's present shape is effectively man-made, and it rises as much as 15m above the natural rock.

In other places across Europe, the natural relief of the land provided the opportunity for citing the rulers' palace in a dominant position above the city. The tenth-century city of Madīnat al-Zahrā (Spain), built by, or at least for, the caliph, 'Abd al-Rahmān III, and very much his own city, shows clearly how the site for a city could be chosen with a view to conveying a message about the caliph's dominance at the apex of the social scale. To be sure, the site in question had various advantages from a constructional point of view, in that it was well placed for the principal routes from the neighboring city of Córdoba, and it was close to quarries from which the vast majority of the materials for the construction came. But it had one feature that must have struck its architect as daunting from a practical point of view: it lay not on the broad plain of the valley, but on the steep slope at the foot of the Sierra Morena, so that much of the city had to be built on what was a steep and rocky cliff. Archaeological excavations have shown the scale of earth- and rock-moving that were required to render the site suitable for building, as the steepness of the slopes involved was considerable. The complex of buildings forming the alcázar, the palace-quarter, was laid out in the highest part, up against the slope of the Sierra Morena. Within that was the caliph's residence, the Dar el-Mulk, which has been identified as such by virtue of being the richest and grandest residence, its ruins still preserving remains of rich wall- and floor decorations. Since it stood at the very highest point of the city, the caliph was at the peak of city, which was laid out below, just as he claimed to be at the peak of the social hierarchy.

The same message of power may have been conveyed by the layout of the city of Palermo, which the Norman kings of Sicily adopted as their principal city in the twelfth century. There, the palace of that period, the Palace of the Normans, occupies the highest site in the city, as is apparent in the view of it from outside the medieval city (Figure 6–1).

Similarly, the royal and imperial palace of Nuremberg loomed over the north side of its city, dominating it and offering the ruler who stayed in it stunning views down over the city which lay—actually and symbolically—below him. The site was otherwise not ideal, for the palace was built on a hard sandstone ridge, rising steeply with a slope of between 75° and 90°, the bedrock visible in great layers beneath the palace's walls. Its position is represented graphically in an illustration in the late fifteenth-century Nuremberg Chronicle (Figure 6–2), which shows the palace in the background, with its great two-storied hall and chapel on the left, and the various fortified towers belonging to it and to the adjacent residence of the constable, who was in charge of it, rising on the right. Below it stretches the city, with its numerous churches and residences, and with its double line of fortified walls, built in the first half of the fourteenth century.

The builders of the Nuremberg palace obviously were concerned also with the defensive potential of its site, so that the approach to it was punctuated by great fortified towers, such as the Simwell Tower (Figure 6–3) at the entrance to the inner bailey. Nevertheless, the priority of creating a dominating, imposing palace complex seems even greater here than the priority of creating a fortification. The tower, like the others in the palace such as the Heathen's Tower, is much higher than could possibly have been needed for defense. It was rather intended to produce exactly the effect that is so evident in the Nuremberg Chronicle's view of Nuremberg, that is, of a palace rising up above the city that it dominated, visually and—at least in the hopes of the ruler—politically.

Away in the east of Europe, the Kingdom of Bohemia offers an even more dramatic example of a palace in a high and dominating position. This is the royal palace at Prague (Czech Republic), located on the ridge called the Hrad. This palace probably had its origins in the ninth century, although it reached its apogee with the development of the site by Charles IV (1346–78). He heightened his predecessors' palace by an entire story, additionally constructing a magnificent hall with windows and a belvedere balcony looking down

Figure 6–1: View of the Palace of the Normans, Palermo (Sicily) from the Colonna Rossa outside the medieval walls, showing its dominant position at the highest point of the city.

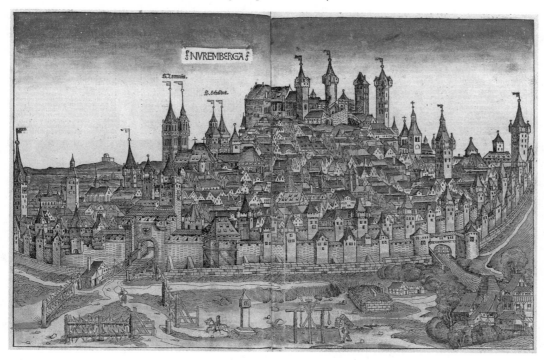

Figure 6–2: Illustration of the city of Nuremberg, Nuremberg Chronicle, showing the city walls in the foreground and the imperial palace at the furthest and highest point.

Cities, Planning & Power   173

Figure 6–3: The Simwell Tower, royal and imperial palace, Nuremberg (Germany), guarding the approach to the palace.

on the city below. Just across the courtyard from the palace, he rebuilt St. Vitus's Cathedral, almost as his palace church, in the latest style of soaring Gothic architecture, so that the palace and the cathedral tower above the district of the city called the Mala Straná immediately below, and—across the River Moldau—the old town of Prague and the new town which the king himself had had laid out around it (Figure 6–4; see also Figure 6–17).

At about the same time, at the opposite corner of Europe, in Andalusia, then ruled by a series of Muslim rulers, comparable developments were taking place at the ancient palace complex of the Alhambra (Spain), perched on a precipitous ridge of land looking down on the city of Granada (Figure 6–5). This site had already been a center of power for earlier Muslim rulers, but the fourteenth-century Nasrid sultans developed it further, constructing on it a series of palaces, looking down on and dominating the city below. The process was completed by the emperor Charles V's construction of his neoclassical palace (above, pp. 63–65), which in its turn dominated the other palaces.

A final example of palaces situated on sites dominating their cities is Stirling Castle (Scotland), set on an equally precipitous ridge of rock, looking down over the city of Stirling and the Scottish lowlands around it (Figure 6–6). This ridge had been the site of a fortified palace of the Kings of Scots from at least the twelfth century, but it reached the peak of its importance under the Stewart kings, James III (1451–88) and James IV (1488–1513), who built a palace-complex on it. This was visible from the city below it, and also separated from it by a natural cleft in the ridge, which must have had symbolic significance in underlining the ruler's superiority to the people.

Figure 6–4: Royal palace and St. Vitus's Cathedral on the Hrad, Prague (Czech Republic), viewed from the Old Town, with the Charles Bridge on the left and the Mala Straná between the far bank of the River Moldau and the palace. See also Figure 6–17.

Figure 6–5: View of the Alhambra, Granada (Spain) from the quarter called the Albaicin. The large, square, tower-like building in the foreground is the Palace of Comares, with the Palace of the Lions to the left of it, and another palace (of which little remains) called the Palace of the Partal on the same side. The palace of Charles V is the large rectangular building on the right.

Figure 6–6: View of Stirling Castle, Stirling (Scotland), looking southwest, with the River Teith in the foreground and the castle on the partly tree-covered hill in the center. The restored gold paint of James IV's great hall gives it a gleaming appearance in the sunlight. The old city straggles along the ridge to the left.

Conveying a message of power relating to the social hierarchy need not have been the only reason for choosing such sites, and their defensibility was no doubt also a factor. Nor was there any fixed law for the design of cities, which required palaces to be at a high point, and clearly some sites were totally inappropriate for such planning on the basis of their relief—London, for example, where the principal palace, Westminster, was on the level of the river; and Paris too where the principal palace, the Palais de la Cité, was on the Île de la Cité, an island in the River Seine. It is notable in both cities, however, that further palaces, the Tower of London and the Louvre, which occupied sites at the entrance to London and Paris respectively along their rivers, were made to look as high as possible through aspects of their construction, as if to compensate for the low-lying sites of the principal palaces.

In the case of the Tower of London, so great was the builders' desire to create a structure of imposing height that its keep, the White Tower, was made to seem taller than it really was. Recent studies of the second story have shown that the present roofing and vaulting are secondary to the rest of the structure, and that the building was originally unroofed at that level (Figure 6–7).

All the accommodation was below, on the ground and first floors, and the second storey was an open space with the original roofs of the first floor level hidden behind its high walls. Traces of the eaves of those roofs can still be seen on the interior faces of the walls of the

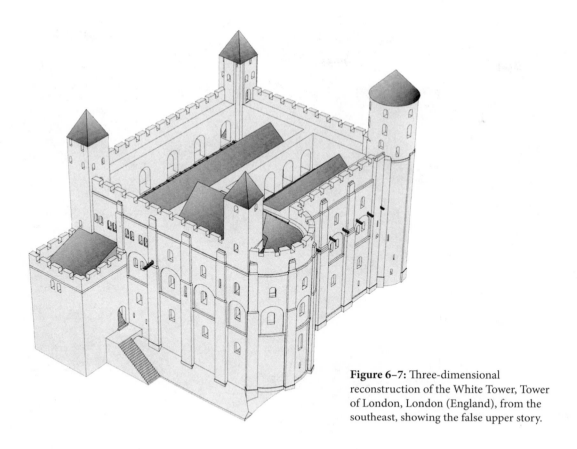

Figure 6–7: Three-dimensional reconstruction of the White Tower, Tower of London, London (England), from the southeast, showing the false upper story.

second story. This open second story naturally had the function of providing a series of battlements and a wall walk for sentries at a higher level than would otherwise have been possible; but the primary purpose must surely have been to maximize the impressiveness of the height of the White Tower as seen from the river or from the city—an impressiveness that must have been heightened by the tower being covered with the white lime wash from which it takes its name.

In the case of Paris, the Louvre was provided by King Philip Augustus (1180–1223) with an enormous tower or *donjon*, rising to a height of no less than 31m. It no doubt had an important military function guarding the approaches to Paris from the west, for it not only had very thick walls (2.3m) but it also came to be integrated with the city walls. But the donjon must equally have had a symbolic significance, its height being a symbol for the power of the king over his city and over his kingdom. In the thirteenth-century French troubadour poems, known as *Chansons de Geste*, it appears in the two called *Ralph of Cambrai* and the *Pilgrimage of Charlemagne* as "the highest tower in the city of Paris" (Bove 2003, 60), and it is possible that it was one of the places where the king's vassals swore homage to him. Certainly, the donjon was carefully preserved in the fourteenth century when the king of France, Charles V (1364–80), rebuilt the palace not as a fortification but as a magnificent residence. It has long since been destroyed to make way for the early modern

Figure 6–8: Palace of the Louvre (Très Riches Heures of the Duke of Berry, Musée de Condé, Chantilly (France), fol. 10v. October, detail). The keep (*donjon*), originally built by King Philip Augustus (1180–1223), is the high tower at the center of the later palace. (See insert for color version of this image.)

palace of the Louvre, the present-day museum; but excavations in the courtyard of that museum have recovered enough of the plan of the donjon to show what an imposing building it must have been, and the effect of it in its pristine state can be gauged from the painting of it in the Très Riches Heures of the Duke of Berry, which shows the late medieval palace with donjon at its center (Figure 6–8).

THE SYMBOLISM OF CITIES

The positions of dominance over cities given to palaces had an intellectual justification, based on the idea that the ruler was the head of the body politic. For example, in twelfth-century Palermo, that is, in the period when the Palace of the Normans was built, Hugo Falcandus wrote: "Just as the head rises above the rest of the body, so the palace, arranged and adorned in this way, anointed by the grace of every kind of delight, overlooks the whole city" (Loud and Wiedemann 1998, 260). In tenth-century Andalusia, when the city of Madīnat al-Zahrā was being built, the Arabic scholar al-Farabi represented a city as a body arranged hierarchically with a head, which was the ruler directing society from the top, and a heart, which was the society of the city itself, supporting the ruler and being directed by him (Acién Almansa 1987, 14; Triano 2010, 135–36, 503). Behind al-Farabi's writing lay the philosophical writings of ancient Greek scholars such as Plato, whose work, the *Timaeus*, was widely known in eleventh- and twelfth-century Europe through the Latin translation of Calcidius. Plato equated human society, and the city in particular, with the human body, having three levels: the highest in which men issued commands; the middle, in which men acted on those commands; and the lowest, in which men were governed and ruled by the levels above them. Thus, in describing the creation of cities, Plato—as translated by Calcidius—recounted that the quasi-divine founder

> ordered the chief men of this city as the most prudent and wise to dwell in the highest places of the city; under them were to live the young soldiers outfitted with arms, to whom he subjected the tradesmen and masses, so that the chief men as ones full of wisdom might give orders, the soldiers might act and carry them out, and the masses might furnish appropriate and useful service. (quoted by Lilley 2009, 9)

Educated men in the Christian world involved in the development of cities might well have been familiar with Plato's description, as those involved in the development of Madīnat al-Zahrā in the Muslim world no doubt were with the writings of al-Farabi. For them, the eminence of palaces thus had the potential to convey a sophisticated message of power, even if for the uneducated that message was more simply based on the high position of the palace or, in the case of palaces like the Tower of London and the Louvre, the semblance at least of the palace dominating them by their sheer scale. In the case of the educated at any rate, the message was one of ideological power, to the effect that the ruler occupied his natural position in human society.

That message of ideological power could also have had another dimension. For cities could be envisaged as an image not only of human society but of the whole cosmos. Roman writers described the cities of the Etruscans in pre-Roman Italy, for example, as laid out with two axes intersecting each other at right angles, the north-south axis or *cardo* in Latin, and the east-west axis or *decumanus*. The four quarters, into which the city was consequently divided, were seen as reflections of the way the cosmos itself was organized, and the way that ancient people looked to the four quarters of the sky for auguries to predict the future— the northeast quarter was the most favorable for the future if auguries appeared there, the northwest the least favorable, and the southeast and southwest respectively each less favorable. Since the other streets of the city followed the orientation of the cardo and the decumanus, the result, even when the border of the city was in the form of a circle, was a gridiron layout, which thus had a cosmic significance. The ruler who dominated such a city was dominating the cosmos itself which the city represented.

The idea of laying out a city in this way was taken over by the Romans, who succeeded the Etruscans as rulers of Italy. The Roman historian Plutarch shows that he knew about cosmic rituals of city foundation when he describes how the founders of Rome dug a round trench into which they placed ritual deposits, and the city was laid out in a circle around it.

Other references describe how, inside the circle, there were laid out the north-south cardo and the east-west decumanus, and at the point where they crossed was a shaft, closed by a stone, which was believed to lead down to the underworld (Gutkind and Gutkind 1965–72, IV, 18–19).

This account was obviously mythical, not least because it seems unlikely on the basis of archaeological evidence that Rome was really planned in anything like this way. Nevertheless, new Roman cities were indeed laid out with the principal streets intersecting at right angles in the center of the city, where the main square (the forum) was located. Although most cities actually had rectangular (playing-card) boundaries, like Roman forts, the Roman writer on architecture, Vitruvius, does envision a circular city such as Plutarch described (Gutkind and Gutkind 1965–72, IV, 54).

The idea that the layout of a city could reflect the cosmos was deep in the geometry that was used, for geometry in ancient science was regarded as nothing less than the language of the cosmos (above, pp. 86–96). Thus proportions and geometrical forms, as used in the layout and the buildings of the city, were simply representations of the architecture of the supreme Creator. This idea was carried over into the Christian period when scribes, from the early ninth century at the court of the emperor Charlemagne, copied an ancient text called the "Land-Surveyors" (*Agrimensores*) and from this and other texts Christian Europe acquired a knowledge of ancient geometry and of its practical application. In the Christian view, however, God was equated with the supreme Creator, and he could be viewed as a creator who used a pair of compasses in his work of creation just as did a land surveyor. In the early fourteenth-century Holkham Bible Picture Book (London, British Library, MS Additional 47682, fol. 2), for example, He is represented sitting on the disk of the Earth with just such compasses in His hand (M. P. Brown 2007, 31–32). So, just as God measured out the earth, so the ruler measured out cities, and those cities were seen as symbolizing the harmony that God wished to see on earth, as it was present in heaven.

Classical geometry may have been applied to the laying out of cities in the Middle Ages. Certainly, some of the new towns of the twelfth century and later, such as Bury-St-Edmunds (England), Grenade-sur-Garonne (France), or Terranuova (Italy), were laid out using the forms and proportions of classical geometry, just as the ancient philosophers imagined. In early Ireland, where there were no cities as such, classical geometry may still have been applied, perhaps with an even stronger symbolism, to great monasteries, such as Armagh, Clonmacnoise, and Nendrum, which were laid out in such an extensive and complex way that they were almost cities in their own right, monastery-cities, in effect. In these, the monastery's church and the buildings for the monks were located in a circular enclosure at the center, with one or more zones in a circular form around it. Archaeological excavation at Nendrum has shown three such zones, defined by walls. Zone 1, the inner enclosure, was presumably for the fully professed monks; zone 2, the middle enclosure, was for those engaged in sacred studies; and zone 3, the outer enclosure, was occupied by craft workshops and buildings for those whose role was to serve and supply the monastery (Figure 6–9). The complex was thus rather like the sort of hierarchically arranged city examined above, while the use of circles for the enclosures suggests the sort of symbolic geometry which Plutarch described. The inner—and most important—enclosure was naturally the highest point of

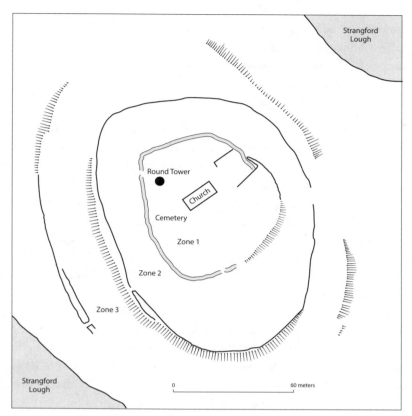

Figure 6–9: Diagrammatic plan of the site of the monastery Nendrum (Ireland). Zone 1 can be interpreted as the inner enclosure for fully professed monks; zone 2 as the middle enclosure for sacred studies; and zone 3 as the outer enclosure for craft workshops and service- and supply buildings (after Edwards 1990, 108, fig. 50).

the site. In these ways, cities were reflections of the cosmos at a deep level, so that whoever ruled the city, whoever had their residence at the highest or most dominant point of it, was equated with the ruler of the cosmos, with God—or at any rate Christ—in the Christian period.

In the Christian period, however, the idea of the city as a symbol of power in the cosmos reached a climax in connection with the city that was central to the Christian religion itself, Jerusalem. In historical terms, Jerusalem was of course where Jesus was crucified, where his tomb was to be found and venerated in the church of the Holy Sepulchre, and where he was believed to have risen from the dead. It was regarded as the center of the world, and is so represented on medieval world maps such as the thirteenth-century example preserved in Hereford Cathedral (P.D.A. Harvey 2006). But Jerusalem had an even greater significance in terms of what Christians believed would happen at the end of the world. In the Book of Revelation, John the Evangelist, in describing his vision of the end of the world, wrote that he saw "the holy city, New Jerusalem, coming down from God out of heaven, prepared as a bride adorned for her husband" (Revelation, 21.2; Carroll and Prickett 1997, II, 317). This New Jerusalem, or Heavenly Jerusalem, was to play a crucial part in the Last Days, and John described what he had seen in some detail, for an angel carried me away in spirit to a great and high mountain, and showed me that great city, the holy Jerusalem, descending out of heaven from God, having the glory of God: and her light was like unto a stone most precious, even jasper stone, clear as crystal; and had a wall great and high, and had twelve gates, and at the gates twelve angels, and names written thereon, which are the names of the twelve tribes of the children of Israel.

John went on to explain that these twelve gates were arranged symmetrically with four to the north, four to the south, four to east, and four to the west, and that the city itself was symmetrical, for he emphasizes that it "lies foursquare, and the length is as large as the breadth" (Revelations 21.10–16; Carroll and Prickett 1997, II, 317–18).

The idea that a city was an image of this Heavenly Jerusalem is represented on some German city seals, which were used to authenticate documents issued by the city councils. This suggests that the city councillors who had designed or commissioned them saw their city as holy, mirroring of the Heavenly Jerusalem on earth. An example is the first seal of the city of Trier (Germany) (Figure 6–10). This shows the walls of Trier with the inscription *Sancta Treveris* ("Holy Trier"), while around the edge of the seal the inscription reads *Trevericam plebem Dominus benedicat et urbem* ("May the Lord bless the people and city of Trier"). In the center of the city stands Christ (designated by his cruciform halo) presenting a key to the city's patron saints, Peter and Eucharius, both labeled on the seal. Below, the citizens of Trier reach up toward these persons. The alpha and omega (the first and last letters of the Greek alphabet) on either side of Christ's head were an explicit reference to John's Revelation, when he writes that, as the New Jerusalem descended from above, Christ on his throne said "I am the Alpha and the Omega, the beginning and the end" (Revelation 21.6; Carroll and Prickett 1997, II, 317). Trier was being presented here as the Heavenly Jerusalem on earth.

This may also have been the theme of the seals of the city of Cologne (Germany). On both the earliest (twelfth-century) seal and the second "Gothic" seal (Figure 6–11), there is represented a walled city with gates reminiscent of medieval representations of the Heavenly Jerusalem.In the center of the "Gothic" seal sits the figure not of Christ but of St. Peter. His presence is explained by the fact that he was the city's patron; but it was also through him alone that access could be gained to the Kingdom of Heaven, the New Jerusalem that is, and the keys that he had been given for this purpose are represented in his hand. As Christ says to him in the New Testament, "I will give unto thee the keys of the kingdom of heaven" (Matthew 16.19; Carroll and Prickett 1997, II, 24). So his presence on the seal is just as consistent with the idea that the city was the Heavenly Jerusalem as was the presence of Christ on the seal of Trier.

In the case of Cologne, it was not just the seals that represented the city as the Heavenly Jerusalem, but also the layout of the city's walls. These were semicircular in shape, which, given the limitations imposed by the fact that the city was on the banks of the River Rhine, seems to have been intended to make them resemble as far as possible the walls of Jerusalem, which were envisaged as being circular. The Cologne walls had twelve gates—the same number as the Heavenly Jerusalem in John's Revelation. Moreover, several of these gates did not have any roads leading to them, so it seems to have been the symbolic significance of their number that controlled the planning of the layout.

Figure 6–10: First seal of the city of Trier (Germany). Although the earliest record of the existence of this seal is provided by an impression of it attached to a document of 1227, the seal is believed to date from the twelfth century. The matrix illustrated in reversed form here (note the handle at the top) is somewhat later in date (Markus Spaeth, pers. comm., citing Diederich 1984).

Figure 6–11: Second (Gothic) town seal of Cologne, *c.*1169, Kölnisches Stadtmuseum, Cologne (Germany), matrix illustrated in reversed form.

Cities then had the potential to convey powerful messages of ideological power, representing in their layout the position of the ruler at the head of the social hierarchy, and even, in Christian countries, as a parallel to Christ, ruling over the Heavenly Jerusalem. This potent symbolism may have been one reason why rulers were so concerned to play a part in the development of cities, sometimes laying out new features or new quarters in them, sometimes building them from scratch. The symbolism of the city could then be applied to the ruler.

RULERS AS CIVIC FOUNDERS

The role of rulers in the development or foundation of cities is evident in the actions of ancient rulers, and nowhere more so than in Rome. In ancient Rome, between the Roman Forum and the Field of Mars, there was a sequence of fora, each with its temple, which succeeding rulers of Rome constructed at enormous expense. First, the forum of the dictator, Julius Caesar (d. 44 BC); then the forum of the emperor Augustus (27 BC–AD 14), with that of the emperor Nerva (AD 96–98) squeezed in beside it; and finally the greatest forum of all, that of the Emperor Trajan (AD 98–117), the conqueror of the area of Dacia, north of River Danube. A forum was an important place in any city. Intended first and foremost as a marketplace, it was also a place for meetings, discussions, and a range of public and private activities, including judicial functions (Hornblower and Spawforth 2003, 586). Fora were therefore very appropriate places for the emperors to patronize with a view to enhancing their status with the citizens.

The scale of Trajan's Forum was daunting. It consisted of a great colonnaded piazza, beside which was the Basilica Ulpia, an enormous hall, of which only a fragment is now visible, the rest buried under the modern Via dei Fori Imperiali. Beside the basilica was the Column of Trajan, around which spiraled carvings of the events of Trajan's wars against the Dacians. Next to this again was the Temple of the Emperor Trajan, built by his successor Hadrian so that Trajan could be venerated as a god. And, along the side of the great square lay the most remarkable of all the elements of Trajan's Forum, the multi-story indoor shopping complex known as Trajan's Markets, which curves around the great semicircular feature (the *exhedra*) opening off the square (Figure 6–12). Although this has sometimes been regarded as a development separate from the forum, it does look from the way in which it follows the forum's shape to have been an integral part of the great urbanization project which was Trajan's Forum.

The imperial fora are testimony to the impetus, indeed the necessity, for Roman rulers to celebrate and consolidate their positions through urban development. Being emperors—or in Julius Caesar's case would-be emperor—meant that they built or expanded cities. It would appear from the developments that the emperors undertook such building and expansion of cities because this was simply part of the job. The rulers of Rome contributed other architectural elements to their capital city, including: the Theatre and Porticus of Pompey, built as Rome's first theater by Caesar's rival Pompey the Great (d. 48 BC) as a victory monument; and the Pantheon, the great temple with its enormous dome, erected by the emperor Hadrian in 118–25, which has justly been called "one of the most magnificent architectural monuments of antiquity" (Claridge 1998, 201).

Rome is a classic example of rulers' involvement in the development of cities, but equally striking are the cities of Sirmium and Thessaloniki in the Balkans expanded by the emperor Diocletian, or the city of Trier (Germany) with its imperial expansion as a palace city in the fourth century, or the city of Constantinople (Istanbul, Turkey), developed not from scratch but from the much smaller city of Byzantium by the emperor Constantine in the early fourth century. The latter, which had a history stretching back to the seventh century BC, had already been laid out anew by one of Constantine's predecessors, the emperor Septimius Severus (AD 193–211), with great monuments like the Hippodrome (or race course) and the Baths of Zeuxippus probably planned if not completed, and a regular layout of streets in the Roman manner. Figure 6–13 shows the probable location of these streets, which were not all at right angles to each other because of the slope of the site, but were nonetheless regular and generally straight. Here was a city intended to proclaim that it was laid out by the firm hand of an emperor. The emperor Constantine (306–37) extended the city further, beginning the construction of the Great Palace to the south and east of the Hippodrome, building the Forum of Constantine along the principal way through the city, and developing new districts on the west side of the original city—also with a regular layout of streets—within a new enclosure of walls, the land-walls of Constantine.

Figure 6–12: Trajan's Forum, Rome (Italy), looking across the *exhedra* toward Trajan's Column with the Markets of Trajan on the right.

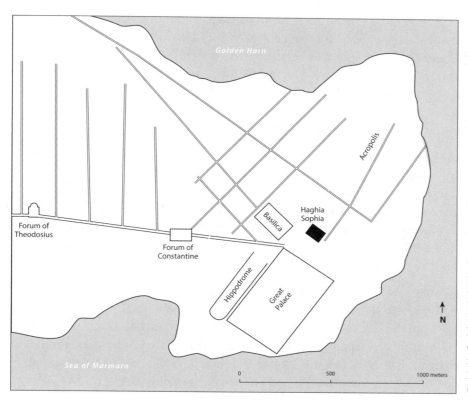

Figure 6–13: Diagrammatic plan of the layout of the eastern part of Constantinople (Istanbul, Turkey). The acropolis, which was at the core of the ancient city of Byzantium, is marked, and the area outside this quarter is that laid out, evidently on a regular plan, by the emperor Septimius Severus. Note the Hippodrome, the construction of which he is supposed to have initiated. The development of the city was taken further by Constantine. Note his Great Palace and the Forum of Constantine (after Berger 2000, fig. 1).

Both phases of urban development had clear political implications. When Septimius Severus gave the city its new layout, he had just defeated his rival to the imperial throne, Pescennius Niger, and had largely destroyed Constantinople in the process. So his restoration of the city was certainly intended to signify his domination of that part at least of the Roman Empire. When Constantine expanded the city and named it after himself, he too had just defeated a rival, Licinius, in 323, and was refounding Byzantium as Constantinople—as a new imperial capital to replace the ancient capital of Rome, and as a monument to himself. Written sources for the early history of this new capital make clear its political significance for the emperor and his office. It was, according to them, Constantine himself who marked out its site with his lance, the symbol of his authority. In 330, when the city was dedicated, the ceremony involved a great procession which intoned religious chants while a statue of the sun god Apollo, the head of which was made to look like the head of Constantine himself to emphasize the emperor's proximity to the god, was placed at the top of a great column. Then a priest announced the name of the city, Constantinople, the city of Constantine. The link between the city and the emperor could not have been made clearer.

In the Muslim world, the link between the city and the caliph, the Muslim ruler, was also striking, and the caliph's role in the development or foundation of cities seems there too to have been an intrinsic part of his office (Safran 2000, 53). Already, the second of the Abbasid caliphs, al-Mansur (d. 775), had founded the city of Madīnat al-Salām (the "City of Peace"), the first Baghdad, on the River Tigris in 762. A little later, the caliph Harun al-Rashid (786–809) had expanded the city of Raqqa. The caliph Al-Mamun (813–33) had built al-Rahba on the banks of the River Euphrates, and al-Mutasim (833–42) had moved to the new city of Samarra in 836. Later, the first of the Fatimid caliphs, al-Mahdi (909–34), had founded his new capital outside Qayrawan and named it, after himself, al-Mahdiyya. A particularly clear case of a new city being founded by a caliph as one of the credentials of his rule is Madīnat al-Zahrā itself. Its foundation four miles outside Córdoba by the caliph ʿAbd al-Rahmān III is described by Ibn Hawkal, who came to the area in the course of a visit to Spain in 947–51:

> He laid out markets there, ordered baths, caravanserais [accommodation for caravans], palaces and parks to be built; he invited people to come and live there and ordered the following proclamation to be announced throughout Al-Andalus: "Whoever wishes to build a house or choose a residence near the sovereign will receive a sum of 400 dirhams." A flood of people rushed to build there, the buildings became so dense and the city became so popular that it acquired such proportions that the houses formed a continuous line between Córdoba and [Madīnat al-]Zahrā. The prince transported there his treasure, his offices, his prison, and his supplies. (quoted by Triano n.d., 173)

So Madīnat al-Zahrā was a city founded and built by the caliph, who was also responsible for encouraging people to settle there. Different writers give dates of either 936 or 940–41 for its foundation, but the latter seems more likely on the grounds that ʿAbd al-Rahmān III was involved in military campaigns up until 936. The significance of the foundation date, however approximate, lies in the fact that ʿAbd al-Rahmān III had taken the title of caliph in 929, after a series of military victories. He had previously been only an emir.

In Islam, the office of caliph was an important one, because the caliph was regarded as the successor of the prophet Muhammad, and as such responsible for all the Muslim faithful. In principle, at least, there could only be one caliph in the Muslim world. Yet, in practice, when 'Abd al-Rahmān III made himself caliph, he was setting himself up against the caliphs of the Abbasid family who had been established since the mid-eighth century in Baghdad, and against the Fatimid caliphs who were based in North Africa and who had assumed the title of caliph in opposition to the Abbasids in 909. So 'Abd al-Rahmān III had to prove that he was the legitimate caliph rather than his Abbasid and Fatimid rivals, and to achieve this he needed to do things that identified him as a caliph. Founding Madīnat al-Zahrā was surely one of those things. It underlines how essential to a Muslim ruler were the messages of power conveyed by his city or cities.

In England in the late ninth and tenth centuries, the kings of the southern English kingdom of Wessex, Alfred (871–99) and his successors, especially his son, Edward the Elder (899–924), initiated and presided over a spectacular process of urban foundation, which created most of what were to become the county towns of southern and midland England. The fact that these new towns (or *burhs*) were fortified, either by re-using old Roman walls, as at Winchester, or by making new ditches and earthen banks, as at Wallingford, has encouraged scholars to think that they were all built as a defense against the Vikings, who had threatened the very existence of the kingdom of Wessex during Alfred's reign, and continued to pose a grave military threat to his successors into the tenth century. It can be argued, however, that they had as much to do with the message of power they were capable of conveying as with the practical needs of defense.

The archaeological excavations conducted in Winchester in the 1970s showed that, when King Alfred had developed the city as a burh, and as his capital with its palace and royal monastery quarter, its streets were arranged in a rectangular, grid layout (Figure 6–14). Winchester had originally been founded by the Romans, and it would be natural to assume that this grid street plan was merely the ancient Roman layout that the king was adopting; but the excavations showed that this was not the case. Between the end of the Roman Empire and King Alfred's time, Winchester had become a much smaller city, and the Roman streets had become overlain with soil and their courses lost to view. When King Alfred came to develop the city in the late ninth century, he therefore began from scratch, creating a completely new street layout. This nevertheless formed a grid plan similar to a Roman layout, even if it did not follow the actual Roman layout buried under the Winchester of his day. King Alfred clearly used his newly developed city to present himself as a ruler every bit as powerful as a Roman emperor, with a city just as sophisticated in the message of power it could convey. It was no doubt for the same reason that he rebuilt the Roman walls to serve as the defenses of his burh, for the excavations showed equally clearly that these walls were ruined before Alfred's time. How much easier—but how much less Roman—it would have been to have fortified the city with timber palisades rather than stone walls.

Winchester was not the only city that King Alfred and his successors built with a grid layout of streets in the Roman manner, for many of their newly founded burhs still show such a layout in their streets, although only at Winchester has the date of the grid been proved by archaeologists. At Wallingford, however, the fact that the grid of the streets has

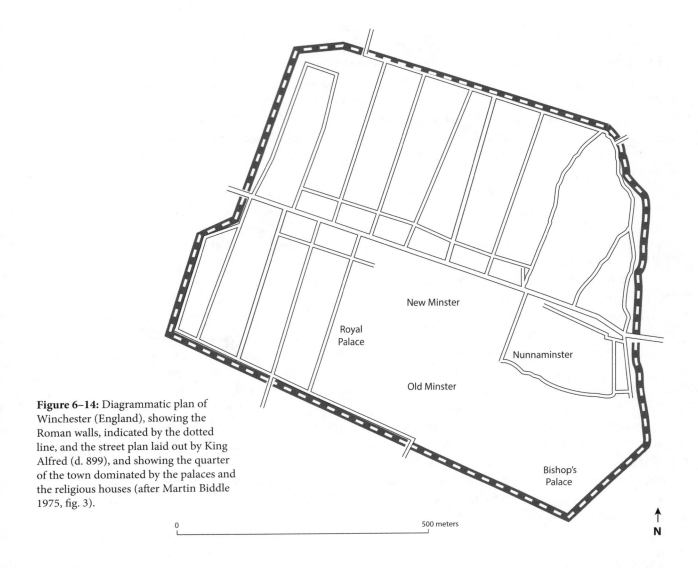

New Minster

Royal
Palace

Nunnaminster

Old Minster

Figure 6–14: Diagrammatic plan of Winchester (England), showing the Roman walls, indicated by the dotted line, and the street plan laid out by King Alfred (d. 899), and showing the quarter of the town dominated by the palaces and the religious houses (after Martin Biddle 1975, fig. 3).

Bishop's
Palace

0   500 meters

N

evidently been partly destroyed by the Norman castle (Figure 6–15) suggests that it must have originated before the Norman Conquest, very likely in King Alfred's time, or shortly afterward. So the burhs need not have been merely practical, military creations. Like the other cities we have been looking at, they too could be deliberately planned to convey a message of power about the greatness, and perhaps the similarity to Roman emperors, of the rulers who founded and developed them. And also to underline ideas of the new city's association with the cosmos and with the Heavenly Jerusalem which, as we have seen, was also envisaged as having a rectangular grid layout of streets (above, p. 182).

The idea that the cities founded by pre-Conquest English kings were, like Madīnat al-Zahrā, a necessary part of their legitimacy as rulers, appears in the *Life of King Alfred* by Asser, who knew the king well. In this, he enthused about the king's various activities:

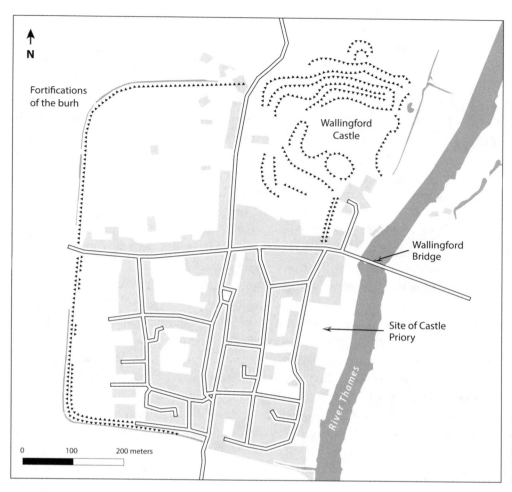

Figure 6–15: Diagrammatic plan of Wallingford (England), showing the interruption of the grid pattern of streets by the Norman castle.

What shall I say of his [King Alfred's] frequent expeditions and battles against the Vikings and of the unceasing responsibilities of government? What of his daily involvement with the nations which lie from the Mediterranean to the farthest limit of Ireland? . . . And what of the cities and towns ordered to be rebuilt and others ordered to be constructed where previously there were none? (Keynes and Lapidge 1983, 101, ch. 91)

We could of course interpret what Asser says here as no more than a description of one of the ways in which Alfred, as a resourceful king, tried to rebuild his kingdom ravaged by the Vikings, and to ensure that it could be defended in the future. The building or rebuilding of cities and towns, with their defensive walls and ramparts, would then have been no more than a practical step taken to attempt to meet a particular external threat. But it is more likely that the building and rebuilding of "cities and towns" was being treated as one of the "responsibilities of government," just as important as waging war against the Vikings. It was an action of principle as much as of practicality. We know from the writings he has left us that Alfred was a philosophically sophisticated king, who might indeed have thought about cities in the way that is suggested here.

In his *New Towns of the Middle Ages*, Maurice Beresford (1967) examined the enormous activity of kings of England, especially in the twelfth and thirteenth centuries, in building new towns in England, in their lordship of Aquitaine in southern France, and in the conquered territory of Wales. One of the most impressive of them as a civic founder was Edward I, king of England (1272–1307), who built a series of new towns in Wales (above, pp. 66–67). The most spectacular of these can be seen at Conwy on the north coast, Beaumaris on the tip of the island of Angelsey, Flint on the estuary of the River Dee, and above all the great fortress and town of Caernarfon, guarding the Menai Straits. But there were others that have left fewer remains, including Criccieth on the Lleyn Peninsula, and Rhuddlan. Great scholar as he was, Maurice Beresford was much more interested in the economic and social results of the foundation of new towns than he was in the ideas that may have provided at least additional motives for the many foundations. His whole aim was to show that new towns were the work of practical, pragmatic men, interested in rents, tolls, and defense, and were certainly not conveying messages of ideological power.

Now, Edward I certainly was concerned with such practical functions of his new towns. Their formidable walls, and the great castles constructed within them, leave no doubt that defense was a primary consideration. Moreover, the king encouraged people —through granting financial and economic inducements—to come and settle within the walls, just as 'Abd al-Raḥmān III had done at Madīnat al-Zahrā. These new inhabitants were to be English, for another of the practical purposes of the towns was to establish English colonies to overawe the defeated and hostile Welsh, as well as, with their markets and trading privileges, to make the towns a source of royal revenue.

Yet, such down-to-earth practical ideas cannot have been the whole story. The scale of building undertaken was much greater than was necessary for defense in circumstances where the defeated Welsh were leaderless and broken. And, as regards revenue, Edward I spent far more on his Welsh towns—£3,500 on the walls of Caernarfon alone—than he could conceivably have hoped to recoup, given that the taxes imposed on a town like Caernarfon were very modest (Beresford 1967, 44, 257–70). Rather, Edward I must surely have been building towns on this scale because that was what a ruler was expected to do, an activity which through its ambition and scale proved that he was a real king and a great one at that.

In common with other new towns of the thirteenth century, Caernarfon's streets were laid out in a rectangular, gridiron fashion. Beresford thought that such a layout was merely practical, because it made the surveying necessary to plan it out easier, and because it simplified the calculations of the area of plots within it. But grid layouts were also characteristic of Roman cities, as at Constantinople, and what Edward I really may have been doing at Caernarfon was, like King Alfred at Winchester, building a town that would put him on an equal footing with the Roman emperors of the past.

CAPITAL CITIES

The activity of rulers in the development of cities was even more apparent in urban centers that they developed as their capital cities. There was, for example, a long history of royal intervention in the development of Paris, which was emerging as the capital of the Kingdom of France. It was the king of France, Philip Augustus, who built the first walls around Paris in *c*.1189–1211 (Figure 6–16).

These walls were not just defensive in purpose, but were intended to expand the area occupied by the city, since they enclosed previously undeveloped land, especially on the left bank of the River Seine. The king was active in seeking to encourage urban development on this land, for he issued decrees that required landowners to permit building on vineyards within the walls. It is likely too that his walls were intended also to accelerate the development of the right bank of the River Seine, for the king's biographer, Rigord, noted that the king "was anxious to have the city full of houses to the foot of the walls" (quoted by Lorentz and Sandron 2006, 40). Indeed, the walls seem also to have been associated with the development of Les Halles as a great market quarter of Paris, which was also largely the work of the kings. Already in 1137, King Louis VI the Fat (1108–37) had founded the market of the Champeaux on the site of what was to become Les Halles. Land in that quarter of the city was parcelled out in a rectangular pattern of streets shortly after the construction of the walls of Philip Augustus, and so was very likely an integral part of the project of building Les Halles. Already in 1184, the king had had the main streets of the city paved, and he was almost certainly involved in the opening up of new streets and the regular parceling out of building plots.

In 1358, the provost (or leader) of the merchants of Paris began building new walls that took in even more land on the right bank of the River Seine. These were evidently military in function, not least because of the threat posed to Paris at that time by English armies campaigning in France in the course of the Hundred Years War. But two aspects suggest that these walls too, whatever their military significance, were equally seen as symbolic of the king of France's power. First, the responsibility for their construction was taken over by the king, Charles V (1364–80), in 1365, which is why they are called the Walls of Charles V. So they became a monument to the king more than to the merchants who had initiated them. Second, they enclosed a large area of undeveloped land in the flat, marshy area known as the Marais (Figure 6–16). It is possible that a major element in the king's involvement in them was therefore the desire to make Paris the largest city in Europe in terms at least of the extent of its walls. The walls were intended, in other words, to distinguish him as the greatest ruler in Europe.

Furthermore, the message of power intended to be conveyed by Charles V's walls may have been in direct response to the building work of Charles IV, who constructed new walls in Prague between 1348 and 1350. Those new walls in Prague took in the area west of the Hrad (Figure 6–17), which was green field then and to a large extent still is now. The effect of building them, however, was to make the area of ground occupied by Prague, or at least the area enclosed by its walls, much larger than the area of ground enclosed by the walls of Paris, which had been built by Philip Augustus, at the end of the twelfth century. Paris was

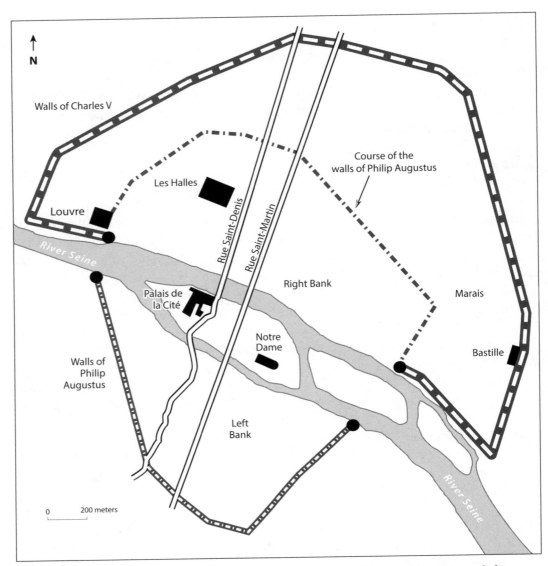

Figure 6–16: Diagrammatic plan of Paris (France), showing the city in the fourteenth century, including, on the right bank, the walls of Charles V with the course of the superseded walls of Philip Augustus within them; and, on the left bank, the walls of Philip Augustus (1180–1223) as refurbished and provided with a ditch by Charles V (1364–80). Note also the location of the Palais de la Cité, the Louvre, and Les Halles, around which a grid layout of streets was created (after Lorentz and Sandron 2006, 50).

one of the greatest cities of Europe, and Charles IV was clearly trying to put Prague in a position to rival it or surpass it. The point seems to have been taken in Paris for, when the French king, Charles V, took over the building of new walls in 1365, they added to Paris the same area that Charles IV's walls had added to Prague (P. Johanek, pers. comm.). At both Prague and at Paris, the walls were much more than just a defense for the city. They were part of the city's claim to greatness, and so of the claim to greatness of the king who had built them. Their purpose seems to have been as much to convey a message of ideological power as to defend their cities by military means.

That Charles IV of Bohemia's foundation of the New Town at Prague was an essential part of developing and promoting the grandeur of his rule is suggested by its context. The year of the foundation, 1348, was the same year in which Charles IV founded the University of Prague, and the same year too in which he had the law of Bohemia re-codified. These actions were intended par excellence to demonstrate that he was in the first league of rulers, in promoting the culture of his kingdom, and in attending to its laws, just as Roman emperors like Theodosius and Byzantine emperors like Justinian had attended to the laws of their empire. The foundation of the New Town was no doubt an action of the same sort, conveying a message of power to justify his position as a great ruler. In the year following the foundation, he was ceremonially crowned King of the Romans (that is, king of Germany and Holy Roman Emperor in waiting) at Aachen. The message must have been that a crowned king revised the laws of his kingdom, founded a university to allow his capital city to compete in cultural terms with its rivals such as Paris, and he founded or expanded cities, just as the Roman emperors had done before them.

Charles IV's political ambitions appear clearly in the detailed planning of the New Town (Figure 6–17). It included the provision of enormous squares, notably the Great Market (*Forum Magnum*), now Charles Square, the enormous scale of which clearly showed that it was intended for great gatherings of people in the context of ceremonies and festivals. Other elements seem to have been intended to make the New Town resemble the contemporary vision of the Heavenly Jeursalem (above, pp. 181–82). It had, for example, a rectangular disposition of the streets, which was oriented to the four points of the compass as the Heavenly Jerusalem was expected to be. The main east-west axis was formed by Pig-Market leading westward from St. John's Gate, while the north-south axis led from the ancient Bohemian royal shrine on the eminence called the Vyšehrad right across the New Town and through to the main square of the Old Town. The two axes crossed each other in the Charles Square, in the middle of which was the Corpus Christi Chapel, no doubt deliberately intended to be reminiscent of Jerusalem as it is represented in medieval maps, with intersecting streets focused on the Holy Sepulchre where Christ's body had lain before the resurrection.

Moreover, Charles IV devoted immense resources to the establishment of approximately forty churches, including religious foundations, in the New Town, and his aim must have been to make a sort of holy city, no doubt with intentional allusions to Jerusalem and also perhaps to Rome. These included the monastery of Our Lady and Slavonic Patrons (later known as the Emmaeus), in which the wall paintings emphasized the importance of the Holy Lance used at the Crucifixion of Jesus in Jerusalem, and the rotunda dedicated to St. Longinus whose lance it was. There was also a church of Saints Peter and Paul, staffed by a religious order called the Custodians of the Holy Sepulchre. Not only was this order closely connected with Jerusalem, but its church in Prague contained a replica of the church of the Holy Sepulchre in Jerusalem, which was believed to stand over the tomb from which Jesus Christ had risen from the dead. The New Town was evidently considered a reflection of Jerusalem itself and of the Heavenly Jerusalem. The message clearly was that the founder and ruler of such a city was in some sense a Christ-like figure in his own right.

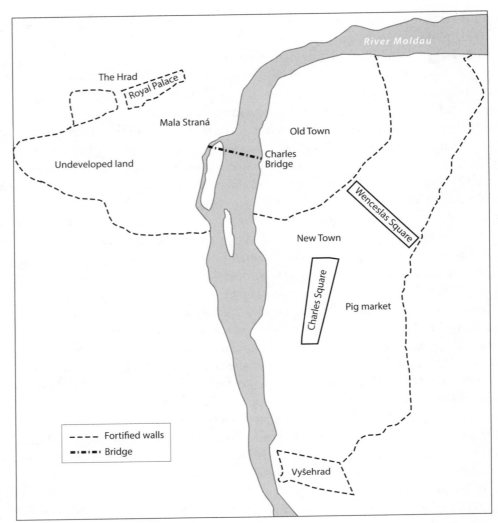

Figure 6–17: Diagrammatic plan of Prague (Czech Republic) around 1400 (after Boehm and Fajt 2005, map 2).

PALACES AS CITIES AND CITIES AS COMPONENTS OF PALACES

A further indication of the importance of cities to the ideological power of rulers is the extent to which those rulers seem to have built their palaces to resemble cities or at least to be organic parts of cities. In his book on architecture, Alberti (1404–72) wrote: "A palace (*domus*) is a little city"; and, writing of Federico of Montefeltro's palace of Urbino, the schoolmaster Mabilio da Novate observed: "this is not a palace but a city" (*non domus ista sed urbs*). This sentiment was echoed soon afterward by the courtier and author Castigilione (1478–1529) describing the same building as "a city in the form of a palace" (all quoted by Boucheron 2004). In the case of the Urbino palace, these writers were presumably referring to its extensive character, with its courtyards, apartments, and gardens, which would have made it seem like a city. But the idea that palaces were like cities seems to have reached much farther back in time.

The Villa Romana di Casale near Piazza Armerina (Sicily), for example, is a complex of buildings, which looks as if it was conceived to resemble a city rather than a residence (Figure 6–18). For its architect applied to it the motifs and elements of city planning. These included an entrance like a monumental gateway in the wall of a Roman city, consisting of three arches, and beyond it a large entrance court, with arcades of columns, looking much like a city square. Beyond this again was a large and elaborate Roman bath complex, just like the baths in Roman cities, such as the Imperial Baths at Trier, or the Baths of Caracalla in Rome itself. The public latrines located off the entrance courtyard were another urban touch, as were spaces that archaeologists have interpreted as shops, and that are reminiscent of the shopping complex of Trajan's Forum in Rome. Walkways like those around the main peristyle-courtyard, looking like streets in the monumental heart of a Roman city, led away to a row of halls or basilicas, such as would have lined the the forum of a Roman city, and been the meetingplaces for the principal citizens or for the city senate, and the places where legal cases were held. Aqueducts supplied the villa with water, just as in a city, and, if there was no circus for gladiatorial combats and other public displays, there was at least a sigma-courtyard shaped like a circus which evoked this aspect of a city.

Much the same can be said of earlier villas, such as the second-century Hadrian's Villa near Tivoli (Italy). This consisted of a sequence of imperial residences, with sports grounds, baths, and racetracks (hippodromes), which create a clear impression of a city and not merely a palace. But the urban character of a palace reaches a new level in the Palace of Diocletian at Split. The reconstruction of the site as a whole (Figure 6–19) shows that the emperor's residence itself only occupied one side of what was a miniature city. It was surrounded by walls with flanking towers looking very much like those erected around cities, with three gates leading through the walls to wide streets; and the approach to the residential rooms through the peristyle-courtyard (above, pp. 12–14) was the sort of feature that might have been expected in a Roman city.

This tendency for palaces to resemble cities can be found in later periods, and not only with respect to stone palaces. At the northern heart of the ancient kingdom of Northumbria as it existed in the seventh century, the royal palace of Yeavering, made not of stone but of earthen banks and great baulks of timber, also had one feature suggestive of a city. At the point of its fullest development (Figure 6–20), the palace consisted of a large enclosure surrounded by an earthen bank with a palisade on top of it, beside which were two timber halls, connected by an enclosure. To the left of these is a wedge-shaped structure, the only structure of its kind ever discovered on a site of this date. The remains have been interpreted as tiered seating for spectators to witness or participate in whatever was being done at the point of focus of their view, where the king's throne may have been. The most likely function would have been for the king to promulgate edicts, or to pronounce judgments—for which the post behind his throne may have had some symbolic significance (Barnwell 2005, 181). It is, however, also possible to interpret it as a segment of an amphitheater such as the Romans used for gladiatorial combats; or as a theater, for that is what it most looks like if it is compared with Roman theaters in stone—perhaps a theater where great barbarian epics such as *Beowulf* might have been acted out or at least recited. Whichever it was, it looks like the sort of feature we should expect to find in a Roman city, reinterpreted here in the north

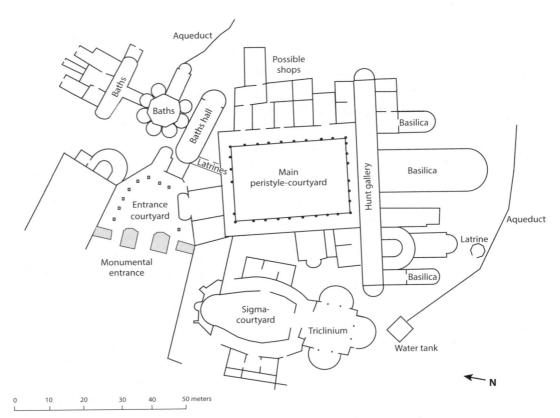

Figure 6–18: Diagrammatic plan, Villa Romana di Casale, near Piazza Armerina (Sicily), showing the principal excavated and partially surviving buildings (after MacDonald 1982–6, II, 205, fig. 207).

Aqueduct

Possible shops

Baths

Baths

Baths hall

Basilica

Latrines

Main peristyle-courtyard

Hunt gallery

Basilica

Aqueduct

Entrance courtyard

Latrine

Basilica

Monumental entrance

Sigma-courtyard

Triclinium

Water tank

N

0 10 20 30 40 50 meters

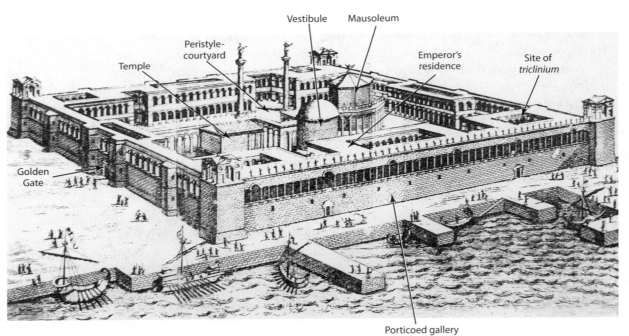

Vestibule

Mausoleum

Peristyle-courtyard

Temple

Emperor's residence

Site of *triclinium*

Golden Gate

Porticoed gallery

Figure 6–19: Reconstruction by Farlati et al. (1751) of the Palace of Diocletian, Split (Croatia), showing the regular layout and quasi-urban characteristics of the complex.

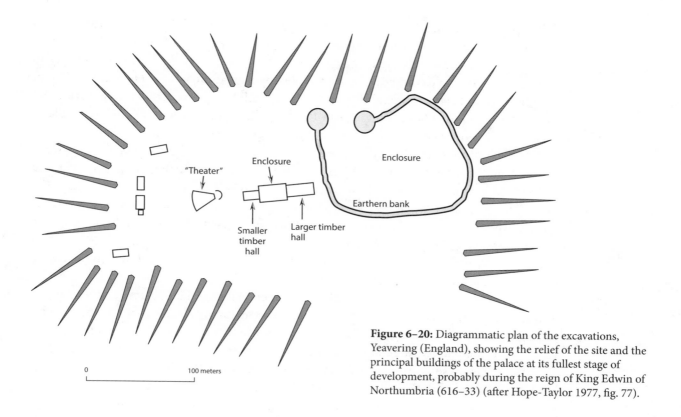

Figure 6–20: Diagrammatic plan of the excavations, Yeavering (England), showing the relief of the site and the principal buildings of the palace at its fullest stage of development, probably during the reign of King Edwin of Northumbria (616–33) (after Hope-Taylor 1977, fig. 77).

of Britain in timber, while the spread of other structures discovered at the site gives Yeavering the feel of a complex site in some ways resembling a city. There were, of course, no cities worthy of the name in seventh-century Northumbria, but that kingdom was not cut off from knowledge of Rome and its former empire, for the missionary, Paulinus, who (according to Bede) baptized Northumbrian converts at Yeavering had himself come from Rome (Colgrave and Mynors 1991, bk 2, ch. 14).

Building palaces with some resemblance to cities seems to have continued. The palace of Ingelheim (Germany) of around 800 had a monumental gateway like the triumphal entrance to a city, and it had circuit walls with flanking towers along them, very like the palace of Split and much like Roman cities. Like the Villa Romana di Casale, there was a basilica, where meetings and feasts would have taken place. And there was a semicircular courtyard lined with columned porticoes, reminiscent of Trajan's Forum at Rome (above, p. 184, Figure 2–13, and Figure 6–12).

A fourteenth-century example of a palace resembling a city is that of Vincennes (France), developed most fully by King Charles V (1364–80). Although this palace was significantly modified in the sixteenth century and has been much degraded over subsequent centuries, not least through its use as a modern army headquarters, the medieval palace is still an impressive monument, now restored in the course of a major research project devoted to it. One of its most striking features is the wall with flanking towers that surrounded it, just as the palaces of Split and Ingelheim were surrounded by walls. As in the case of those much earlier palaces, the effect is to make Vincennes resemble a city with its walls and towers. This was all the more so at Vincennes because the wall encloses such a large area, and because the towers were immensely high. They were originally built to a height of approximately 40 meters, and the whole complex was surrounded by a great moat 4.5 meters deep. Most of the towers have been considerably lowered as they fell into ruins across the centuries, but they still give an idea of how impressive they must have been, while the Tour du Village, over the main entrance to the palace, retains its original height (Figure 6–21).

The effect of these towers must have been to give a stunning city-like view of it from a distance, and this can be appreciated in a miniature in the Très Riches Heures of the Duke of Berry (Figure 6–22), which shows the palace of Vincennes rising above the forest. The highest tower, that in the center, was Charles V's private residence in the form of a keep or *donjon*, while the towers on either side of it, shown of course to their original height, are the flanking towers of the walls of the palace and the Tour du Village itself. The illusion that the palace is really a city is striking, even though it was really nothing of the kind. So close were cities to the idea of rulership.

If cities were so important to kings that they often modeled their palaces on them, it was also the case that parts of cities were sometimes restructured to make them in effect outlying parts of the palaces themselves, creating the sense that the city functioned as an antechamber to the palace. At Federico II di Montefeltro's palace of Urbino (Italy) the palace closed in the main square of the city on two sides. The third side of the square was occupied by the cathedral which the duke had also built, or at least rebuilt, and the fourth was occupied by the buildings that had been the communal palace, that is, the center of the civic government of the city of Urbino before the duke had taken control of it. The square must have appeared as a part of the palace, leading to it, acting as an antechamber to it. And this effect was probably heightened from the 1470s, when porticoes were built running round it, linking it physically to the palace buildings themselves, and continuing the palace architecture into the city.

Another example of this sort of absorption of a city by a palace is the city of Mantua, also in northern Italy (Figure 6–23). In 1472, the duke, Ludovico Gonzaga, had the monastery of Sant' Andrea, in the northern part of Mantua, suppressed and converted into a college of priests under his own patronage; and its church was rebuilt for the duke as the church of Sant' Andrea by the architect Alberti, whose book we quoted from earlier, making it almost an extension of the palace. The duke was also responsible for creating, or at least for formalizing, the processional way, the Asse Gonzaghesco, which led from the southern gate northward across the city, past the church of Sant'Andrea, to his palace. The duke's New Palace (*Domus Nova*) looked down on the city which the duke dominated, and which had been effectively converted into an approach to, and an outer part of, his palace.

As at Mantua so too at other places, the processional ways created for the ruler to enter his palace by passing ceremonially through the city made the city an integral part of the palace. According to the twelfth-century writer Hugo Falcandus, at Palermo, a paved street, the Marble Way, led from the Palace of the Normans, the royal palace, in the upper part of the city, to the port, while a second route, the Covered Way, led from the royal palace to the archbishop's palace and so to the area of the cathedral (Loud and Wiedemann 1998, 260).

Figure 6–21: Tour du Village, Palace of Vincennes (France), guarding the main entrance to the palace's courtyard. This is the only tower to have retained its original height, and the ditch in front of it has been restored to its original depth (Chapelot 2011, fig. 6 caption)

Figure 6–22: Palace of Vincennes (Très Riches Heures of the Duke of Berry, Musée de Condé, Chantilly (France), fol. 12v, December, detail). The higher, central tower is the keep; the other towers are those of the wall surrounding the palace. (See insert for color version of this image.)

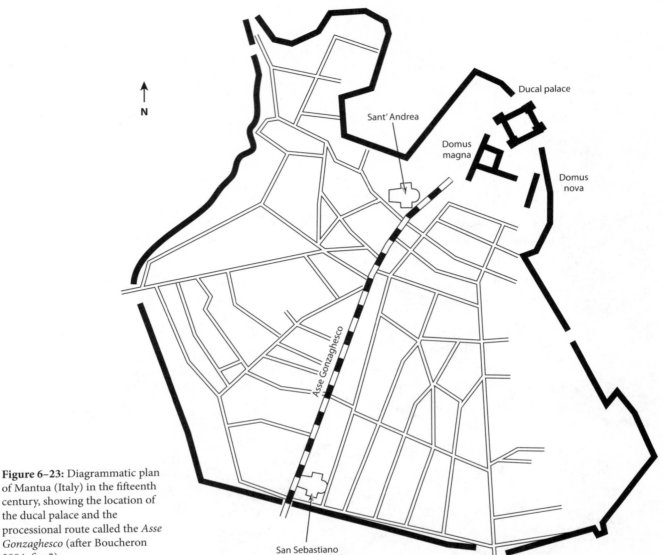

Figure 6–23: Diagrammatic plan of Mantua (Italy) in the fifteenth century, showing the location of the ducal palace and the processional route called the *Asse Gonzaghesco* (after Boucheron 2004, fig. 2).

In Paris, such processional ways led from the Palais de la Cité in the center of the city to the nearby cathedral of Notre Dame, and so across the River Seine and through the north gate in the city walls to the great burial church of Saint-Denis beyond, the route marked by a series of elaborately carved crosses called Mountjoys (J. Bennert 1992, 54). In London, a great processional route led from the Tower of London, where the king-elect spent the day before his coronation at Westminster Abbey, to the Palace of Westminster, where he was to spend the night before the ceremony. At the time of the coronation, the route was lined with citizens and subjects who had come to witness this royal event (below, pp. 216–17). Another such route was the ramped street at Madīnat al-Zahrā (below, p. 215).

CONCLUSION

The proposition of this chapter is that cities, and the planning of cities, can be seen as comparable to palaces in their importance to rulers and their potential for conveying messages of power. Those messages could have been, at a basic level, that the regular and imposing layouts of cities created or sponsored by the ruler were a sign of his power and effectiveness. At an equally basic level, the fact of the ruler's palace occupying a site dominating the city—or being built in such a way that it appeared to dominate the city through its artificially enhanced height—conveyed a message about the ruler's position at the pinnacle of a hierarchy mirrored by the physical form of the city.

There could, however, be deeper messages. In the case of the dominating height of the palace, the message could have drawn on philosophical constructs of the ruler as the head of a human body, with the lesser parts—his subjects—below him. In this case, the city would have been perceived as an image of the body, with the ruler's palace as the head of it. In the case of the regular planning of the city, the message conveyed could have been deeper still, with the geometrical layout of the city making it an image of the cosmos over which the ruler had power. So, in his palace dominating the city, he was presenting himself as a cosmic ruler. Where, moreover, the layout of the city could be conceived of as a reflection of the Heavenly Jerusalem, so the ruler could be associated with Christ.

Whatever the messages of power which cities could convey in these ways, it is clear that they had the potential also to convey a quite fundamental message about the legitimacy of the ruler—that the foundation or development of a city, especially a capital city, was to be seen as an essential part of rulership. It could be quite simply something that rulers had to do to prove that they were what they claimed to be. This seems very obviously to have been the case with the cities founded by caliphs, which were often called after them as if to underline the point; but it seems entirely possible that it was an important element in urban foundation and expansion in Christendom too. In cases such as that of Paris and Prague, we seem to be seeing rulers competing to show their status through the development of their capital cities.

It is a striking demonstration of the importance of cities to rulers that their palaces, or complexes of palaces, could in some cases resemble cities in various ways. They were built to contain features that were really urban features, so that the ruler's residence itself resembled a city. In this microcosm of a city, the same messages of power that the city itself conveyed could be conveyed by the palace—its regular layout like the cosmos, its complexity of buildings permitting processions through it to equate it with a city, its resemblance to images of the Heavenly Jerusalem to underline the ruler's position.

Finally, it was not necessary for a city founded or developed by a ruler to have a palace within it or attached to it. But, where this was the case, it was possible for the city to be absorbed as an integral part of the palace, so that the city—or parts of the city—functioned as an antechamber to the palace. The architecture, as in the case of the square at Urbino, could be modified to show that the city was fulfilling this role. The message of power conveyed must have been that the ruler's palace and the city merged into one, which could all the more effectively convey messages of power about the ruler's efficacy or about the cosmos or about the Christ-like relationship of the ruler to the Heavenly Jerusalem.

CHAPTER ~ 7

Triumphs and Entries

The City as Stage Set

One of the most important ways in which cities offered rulers the possibility of conveying messages of power was through the various ceremonies, especially the triumphs and entries, that took place in them. A triumph was a triumphal procession by means of which the ruler entered a city following a military victory. There had been triumphs, chiefly in the city of Rome itself, from a very early period in Rome's history, but, in origin, rulers were not the only recipients of triumphs. The triumphs held in 80/81 BC and 61 BC, for example, were in honor not of a ruler but of the Roman general Pompey the Great (d. 48 BC). From the time of the first of the emperors, Augustus (27 BC–AD 14), however, triumphs were in practice granted only to emperors or members of their families, and not to victorious generals. So they became exclusively for the glorification of the emperor. As we shall see, they continued to be a part of the ceremonial involving rulers and cities long after the end of the Roman Empire.

If a triumph was one way in which a ruler ceremonially entered a city, the other was by means of an entry (*adventus*). In principle at least, an entry occurred as a normal part of the process of a ruler traveling across his empire, and, like a triumph, it was a ceremony with a series of formal rituals attached to it. In the Roman period, entries differed formally from triumphs, since triumphs had to be granted by the Senate whereas entries did not. In practice, however, triumphs and entries were often indistinguishable. This was true also of the Middle Ages, when entries as well as triumphs continued to be of considerable importance to rulers and cities and, as in the Roman period, they were often hard to distinguish from each other. As mechanisms for conveying messages of power, triumphs and entries offered considerable potential because of the inherently theatrical character of the processions they involved.

THE DEVELOPMENT OF TRIUMPHS AND ENTRIES

Roman triumphs were quintessentially theatrical celebrations of victory within a formalised framework of procession and ritual. This is evident in the first reasonably reliable and detailed account of a triumph, that written by the contemporary historian Josephus near the end of his book, *The Jewish War* (G. A. Williamson 1981, 370–73). The triumph in question took place in AD 71, to celebrate the victories of the emperor Vespasian, whose son, the future emperor Titus, had just returned from putting down a Jewish revolt in Palestine. During the course of that campaign, he had largely destroyed the city of Jerusalem and its temple. Titus had arrived back in Rome, having sent on ahead of him the leaders of the Jewish revolt, together with 700 ordinary prisoners, whom he had "picked out for their exceptional stature and physique . . . intending to display them in his triumphal procession" (G. A. Williamson 1981, 370). At Rome, the senate decreed that both Vespasian and Titus should have separate triumphs, but they opted for a joint celebration.

Josephus describes the triumph, and it is also depicted on the triumphal arch which was erected in the Roman Forum some time after the death of Titus in AD 81. The first stage involved the army and the senior figures of the city. The night before the triumph the two emperors slept outside the sacred core of the city, at (or near) the Temple of Isis in the part of ancient Rome called the Field of Mars. This part of the city lay beyond the line of its sacred enclosure, the *pomerium*, although the temple itself straddled that line (Figure 7–1). According to Josephus, "all the soldiers had marched out under their commanders" and had established themselves near the temple. At dawn, Titus and Vespasian came out "wreathed with bay and wearing the traditional crimson robes" and proceeded to a dais, where they sat on ivory chairs, while the soldiers acclaimed them. Titus and Vespasian then offered prayers to the gods and the latter made a speech to the senate, the senior magistrates, and the leading citizens, who were also gathered.

The time had now come for the emperors to pass across the pomerium, into the sacred core of the city. After breakfasting, they proceeded to what Josephus calls "the gate which took its name from the triumphal processions that always pass through it" (the Triumphal Gate as it is known to modern scholars, although it is not possible to identify it with any surviving or known gate). There they "sacrificed to the gods that stand on either side of it," which presumably were statues, and then the second phase of the triumph, the procession, began. The Arch of Titus has carved on it a scene of Titus in the procession, standing upright in a *quadriga*, that is, a chariot drawn by four horses (Figure 7–2).

Josephus gives no further information about the route of the triumph except that it ended at the Temple of Jupiter on the Capitol; but the evidence available for other triumphs suggests (although the details are disputable) that it passed, or perhaps visited, the Theatres of Balbus, Marcellus, and Pompey, and then led through the Circus Maximus, normally used for chariot-racing, and so past the Palatine Hill; that it turned left at the amphitheater of the Colosseum, passed across the site of the future Arch of Titus, and so along the Sacred Way across the Roman Forum (Figure 7–3). The procession bore left under the place where the Campidoglio now stands to the Temple of Jupiter. There, the *triumphatores*, Titus and Vespasian, offered sacrifices and said prayers. After this, Josephus wrote, there was feasting.

Roman entries, like Roman triumphs, involved ceremonial processions of comparable theatricality. Certain of the scenes on the Arch of Constantine in Rome, for example, provide one of the most vivid accounts of that emperor's ceremonial entry into Rome. The arch has three openings, with above the largest and central opening an inscription, which appears on both sides of the arch, and which states that it was dedicated by the senate and

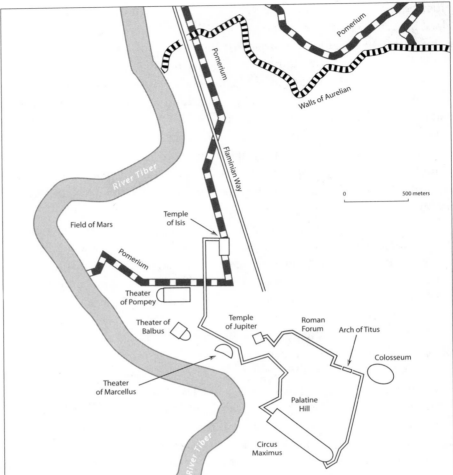

Figure 7–1: Diagrammatic map of the probable route of the triumph of Emperor Vespasian and future Emperor Titus, Rome (Italy). Beginning from the Temple of Isis, the triumph proceeded via the Circus Maximus, around the Palatine Hill, to turn left at the Colosseum, and so, by way of the site of the future Arch of Titus, across the Roman Forum to the Temple of Jupiter. Notice the sites of the Theatre of Balbus and the Theatre of Marcellus, which the triumph probably visited, and the site of the Theatre of Pompeii, which it is less likely to have done (after Anon. 1997, 33).

people of Rome to the emperor Constantine (306–37), because he had freed the Roman republic (by this time it was really an empire rather than a republic) from tyranny and faction by the just force of arms. This is a reference to the military campaign which Constantine fought in 312 to oust the rival emperor Maxentius, whom he defeated at the Battle of the Milvian Bridge, a few miles to the north of Rome.

The arch was erected to commemorate this victory and the emperor's entry into Rome that followed. This was an entry and not a triumph because it had not been granted to him by the senate as a mark of distinction, but it was nevertheless closely bound up with a military victory, and the representation of Constantine's entry in a sculptured frieze beginning on the west side of the arch starts with images of his military success (Figure 7–4) and runs on around the arch to show his entry into Rome. In this, the emperor appears (headless now following damage across the centuries) seated on a chariot drawn by four horses, while his cavalry and infantry move ahead of him, their dragon banners floating in the wind, to the gate of the city.

Figure 7–2: Sculptured relief panel, Arch of Titus Rome (Italy), showing the future emperor Titus riding in a quadriga (a four-horse chariot) in the course of his triumph. Note the winged figure of victory, at the top right of the panel, sitting behind the emperor and guiding him. The arch was situated on the approach to the Roman Forum.

Panel-reliefs of Marcus Aurelius

Inscription

Panel-reliefs of Marcus Aurelius

Dacian

Dacian

Hunting tondi

Great Trajanic Frieze

Frieze showing Constantine's victories and entry into Rome

Figure 7–3: South side, Arch of Constantine, Rome (Italy). Most of the decoration is reused from earlier monuments: the panel reliefs of Marcus Aurelius are reused from a monument of the time of Marcus Aurelius, emperor (161–80); the panels from the Great Trajanic Frieze probably come from an imperial monument of the time of Trajan (98–117), or perhaps more likely of the time of his successor, Hadrian (117–38); and the figures of Dacians at the top level are of the same date. However, the frieze showing Constantine's victories and entry into Rome was carved specially for the arch.

Figure 7–4: The emperor riding in his quadriga, frieze showing Constantine's victories and entry into Rome, Arch of Constantine, Rome (Italy).

After the fall of the Western Roman Empire in the mid-fifth century, triumphs continued to be staged for the Byzantine emperors in Constantinople in the Eastern Roman Empire. By the time of the emperor Justinian (527–65), however, the emperors did not lead their own armies as earlier Roman emperors had done. The emphasis of the triumph consequently changed, so that its real focus was on the appearance of the emperor in the great Hippodrome of Constantinople, where he was hailed by the citizens, rather than on a triumphal entry into the city. Nevertheless, the essence of the ceremony still remained as it always had been. In 956, for example, the armies of the emperor Constantine VII Porphyrogenitus (913–20, 945–59) had won a victory over the Muslim emir of Aleppo in Syria and had captured his cousin. In this case, the emperor's triumph involved a service of thanksgiving in the church of Haghia Sophia alongside the Great Palace in Constantinople, and then a triumphal procession not to the Hippodrome but to the Forum of Constantine (see above, Figure 6–13). There, the Muslim prisoners were lined up facing the emperor, who personally trampled on the neck of the emir's cousin—such a trampling was a tradition of Byzantine triumphs (McCormick 1986, 159–63).

In Western Europe, triumphs continued to be held in the barbarian kingdoms that succeeded the Roman Empire. In Italy, the barbarian king Theoderic (471–526), held a triumph in Rome to celebrate twenty years of rule, and this involved a procession to the Roman Forum, where the king addressed a speech to the senate and the people, followed by a parade into the imperial palace, circus games, and the distribution of royal gifts (McCormick 1986, 273). This was very much as the Roman emperors had organized such events. In the Kingdom of the Visigoths in Spain, the writer Julian of Toledo gives an account of a triumph for King Wamba (672–80) in 673 after his victory over a usurper who had tried to seize his throne. This triumph, like its Roman predecessors, involved captives (McCormick 1986, 306–307). But the most graphic account of an early medieval triumph is that given by the sixth-century writer, Gregory of Tours, in his *History of the Franks*. This concerns the triumph of the king of the Franks, Clovis, in the city of Tours after his victory in 507 over the Visigoths in southwest Gaul. According to Gregory, Clovis was received at the church of St. Martin in Tours, and

> he stood clad in a purple tunic and the military mantle, and he crowned himself with a diadem. He then rode out on his horse and with his own hand showered gold and silver coins among the people all the way from the doorway of St Martin's Church to Tours Cathedral. From that day he was called consul or augustus. (Thorpe 1974, book 2, ch. 38)

There is nothing like so much detail here as for the Roman triumphs, but the reference to the wearing of the purple tunic and the diadem are reminiscent of them, and, as we shall see, so too was the distribution of coins.

Mirroring Roman triumphs in an equally striking way at a much later period was the triumph of the German emperor, Frederick II (1194–1250), which took place in 1237 at the city of Cremona (Italy). This, like Roman triumphs, involved the display of the enemy leader, in this case Pietro Tiepolo, son of the doge of Venice and the chief magistrate (or *podestà*) of Milan (Bertelli 2001, 62). Likewise, in 1325, a triumph was celebrated at the city of Lucca in Italy for the lord of that city, Castruccio Castracani, to celebrate his victory over the city of Florence. According to the chronicler:

> Castruccio, in a seat on the chariot, open on all sides, drawn by four white horses, dressed richly in purple and gold, with a garland of laurel on his head, showed with a serene expression, in Caesarean majesty, the dignity of a king. (Bertelli 2001, 62)

In this case, the triumph made its way from the battlefield of Altopaisco to Lucca, with bareheaded prisoners marching before the chariot, and citizens of Lucca dragging the spoils of war behind it.

More than a century later, on February 26, 1443, the city of Naples was entered in triumphal procession by its new ruler, Alfonso the Magnanimous, king of Aragon (1416–58). The city was at that time the capital of the Kingdom of Naples, which Alfonso had conquered in the previous year from the then ruling French dynasty, and his triumph was to commemorate this event. A series of contemporary writers describe it in some detail. The night before, Alfonso stayed outside the city in the monastery of San Antonio, just as Titus and Vespasian had lodged outside Rome in the Temple of Isis. Whereas they had entered Rome through the Triumphal Gate, Alfonso entered Naples through a specially made breach in the walls, emphasizing that he was the conqueror of the city. At the breach, he was awaited by the leading citizens of Naples with a triumphal chariot for him. Alfonso, wearing a laurel crown, seated himself in this chariot on a golden throne decorated with purple, and he was drawn through the city by four white horses with golden bridles, just as the chariot of Titus and Vespasian was a quadriga, drawn by four horses (see Figure 7–2). Alphonso is shown seated in his chariot on a sculptured panel above the triumphal arch erected some years later as the entrance to the royal palace of the Castel Nuovo in Naples (Figure 7–5). Accompanied by

Figure 7–5: Triumphal arch at the entrance to the Castel Nuovo, Naples (Italy). The sculptured panel showing King Alfonso the Magnanimous's triumphal entry into Naples in 1443. The king is seated on a gold throne on the triumphal chariot, drawn by four horses, and he is holding an orb to represent how widely his power extended over the world. Musicians walk in front of his chariot, and the citizens of Naples follow.

trumpeters and clerics carrying relics of saints, the triumphal procession took a circuitous route through Naples, just as the Roman triumphs had taken a circuitous route through Rome. Passing through the Piazza del Mercato, where a temporary triumphal arch had been erected, and into each of the four quarters of the city, the triumphal procession finally entered the cathedral to offer prayers, just as the triumph of Titus and Vespasian culminated in prayers and sacrifice offered in the Temple of Jupiter in Rome. Alphonso's triumph then proceeded to the royal palace, where—just as in the Roman triumph—there was feasting (Helas 2009).

THE THEATRICALITY OF TRIUMPHS AND ENTRIES

The potential of entries and triumphs to convey messages of power lay not only in the ceremonial procession itself, but also in the theatrical events that accompanied it. Josephus described, as part of the triumph of Titus and Vespasian, theatrical performances on "travelling stages," many of which were "three or even four storeys high" and "hung with curtains interwoven with gold," while all were "framed in wrought ivory and gold." On these were presented as a series of tableaux scenes from the recent Jewish war and, he writes:

> Here was to be seen a smiling countryside laid waste, there the whole formations of the enemy put to the sword; men in flight and men led off to captivity; walls of enormous size thrown down by siege engines, great strongholds stormed, cities whose battlements were lined with defenders utterly overwhelmed, an army streaming inside the ramparts, the whole place reeking of slaughter, those unable to resist raising their hands in supplication, temples set on fire and houses torn down over the heads of their occupants, and after utter desolation and misery rivers flowing, not over tilled fields, supplying drink to men and animals but through countryside still blazing on every hand. (G. A. Williamson 1981, 372)

The "innumerable spectacles, so magnificent in every way one could think of," included displays of "priceless marvels of many different peoples . . . brought together on that day, showing forth the greatness of the Roman Empire." Among them were "masses of silver and gold and ivory in every shape known to the craftsman's art," carried along "like a flowing river." There were also "hangings borne along, some in the rarest shades of crimson, others embroidered with life-like portraits by Babylonian artists; transparent stones, some set in golden crowns." And there were statues of Roman gods, "animals of many kinds," men "arrayed in garments of true scarlet dye interwoven with gold," and of course the "host of captives." No expense was spared, evidently, to magnify the theatrical aspects of the triumph. Dramatic shows were equally part of Alfonso the Magnanimous's triumph in Naples, including a mock battle between knights and men dressed as Turks. A message of power based on the ruler's efficacy as a military leader was clearly being conveyed by these triumphs.

Entries offered similar potential for conveying messages of power through their attendant theatrical shows. The near-contemporary account in the "Chronicle of Flanders 580–1467" of a ceremonial entry made by Duke Philip the Good (1419–67) into the city of Ghent in modern Belgium in 1458 provides an excellent illustration. The whole setting of this entry was theatrical in its magnificence. The streets were hung with cloths of different colors, bearing short texts from the Bible as well as the badges and mottoes of the duke, while numerous torches blazed above the gate and walls. Trumpeters and minstrels played from the top of the gate, and all the priests, deans, and beguines (holy women) of the city had assembled by the gate, "each in their most precious copes, habits, and chasubles . . . in the manner of a fine procession." But the most theatrical aspect of the entry was provided by the tableaux presented on a series of stages set up along the duke's route from the city gate to his palace in the city. The first pair of stages was occupied by two prophets carrying scrolls. Others, set up farther on, had scenes from the Bible, such as the story of the Prodigal Son who (in the parable told by Jesus Christ) wasted his money but was received back by his father; others had more secular scenes, such as that of Julius Caesar, who was supposed to have been the founder of Ghent, or of a black lion with its white lioness and lion cubs—the black lion roared and was "masterfully crafted and lifelike." Another showed the Roman general, Pompey, accompanied by four "knights splendidly armed with wonderfully emblazoned shields in the Roman style," and, kneeling before him, the king of the Armenians.

Pompey was supposed to have imprisoned this king for rebelling against him, and the scene on the stage showed the general generously granting him mercy. Still more stages had scenes involving a fearsome giant and a series of wild animals, King Solomon and the Queen of Sheba from the Old Testament of the Bible, and "a great grey elephant" from whose trunk "wine spouted forth." In this case, however, it is known from the chronicle that the entry was "organized by the aldermen and others of the same city of Ghent," so that the messages of power were as much ones they wished to convey to the ruler—that he should be generously merciful like Pompey, for example—as ones emanating from the ruler himself (A. Brown and Small 2007, 176–78; see also 167–76). They must nevertheless have been conceived of as being acceptable to him.

THE CITY AS STAGE SET: CITY GATES

The importance of cities as stage sets for these events is underlined by the architectural provision made for them. Considerable resources were devoted to building and planning cities so that they would be suitable to host entries and processions. First, there were the city gates through which triumphs and entries passed. Although Alfonso of Aragon's triumph in Naples in 1443 did not use a city gate but rather a breach created in the wall, in most triumphs and entries the city gate by which the ruler entered the city featured prominently, and was an important structure. This is apparent in Josephus's account of the triumph in Rome with his reference to the procession passing under the Triumphal Gate. It is evident too in the prominence of the city gate in Roman sculpture showing the entry of emperors to cities. The panel reliefs of Marcus Aurelius on the long faces of the upper level the Arch of Constantine (above, Figure 7–3) are sculptures originally from a monument erected by or for the emperor Marcus Aurelius (161–80), perhaps some sort of funerary monument. One panel shows, symbolically at least, the emperor making his entry into Rome (Figure 7–6).

The emperor in the center of the panel, with a laurel wreath on his head and with a flying figure of victory holding more laurels over him, is received by an armed woman wearing a helmet. This scene is clearly meant to be taking place at the gates of Rome, for the buildings of the city appear in the background, and the armed woman is a personification of the city.

The same emphasis on the importance of the city gates is evident in the contemporary panegyric on the emperor Constantine's entry into the city of Autun in 311:

> Immortal gods, what a day shone upon us . . . when you [Constantine] entered the gates of this
> city, which was the first token of our salvation, and when the gates, curved inwards and flanked
> by twin towers, seemed to receive you in a kind of embrace. (MacCormack 1981, 28)

It is apparent also in the ceremony of the handing over of the keys at the city gate in medieval triumphs and entries (Figure 7–9). It was often at the city gate that the medieval ruler would confirm the rights and privileges of the city, and where he sometimes performed ceremonies such as the knighting of young men. The city gate through which he entered could have an historical significance, for example the Royal Gate of Seville in southern

Figure 7–6: Entry of Marcus Aurelius into Rome, Arch of Constantine, Rome (Italy). The Colosseum is represented on the right, the Roman Forum on the left.

Spain. It was through this gate that Ferdinand III, king of Aragon (1199/1201–1252), made a triumphal entry into the city in 1248 after he had conquered the city from the Muslims. When in 1410 the heir to the throne, Ferdinand of Antequera, likewise made a triumphal entry into Seville after his victory over the Muslims at the Battle of Antequera, the earlier triumph of Ferdinand III was explicitly recalled—Ferdinand of Antequera was given his predecessor's sword outside the city, and in the procession he took it into the cathedral and placed it on Ferdinand III's tomb. When King Philip II (1556–98) made an entry into Seville in 1570, he too passed through the Royal Gate, just as Ferdinand III had done before him, by which time it was decorated with a sculpture of Ferdinand III with the inscription, "Ferdinand broke the locks and the name of Ferdinand shines as the stars in the sky" (Ruiz 2012, 91, and passim).

Resources were often lavished on the gates through which rulers habitually entered the city, in order to make them sufficiently grand but also to adapt them in specific ways for the ceremonies involved. A classic example is the Porta Nigra at Trier (Germany) (Figure 7–7).

Figure 7–7: Porta Nigra, Trier (Germany), viewed from outside the city.

This now looks like a free-standing structure, but that is because the Roman wall that joined it on either side has been destroyed, and its present appearance is further confused by the fact that a medieval church was built in the remains of the gate (its apsidal east end is visible still, protruding from the tower on the left). In origin, the Porta Nigra was a gate leading through the Roman walls of Trier to the imperial palace and the forum beyond, and it was certainly the gate by which the emperor would have entered the city. Even in its present much-damaged state, it is clear that it was a grand structure. It is equally clear that it was built to maximize its usefulness as a stage set for entries or triumphs, rather than its capability for defending the city against attack. The rows of large windows, with galleries behind them, suggest that its function was primarily for spectators standing in the galleries to watch the entry or triumph, or for actors to present a theatrical performance. The low priority given to defense in designing it is shown by the attached stone columns that decorate the façade, and the lack of indications of places protected from enemy arrows or bolts where soldiers could have stood on the gate and fired at the enemy in their turn.

In the Middle Ages too, the grandest city gates could be those through which triumphs and entries passed. In the city of Cologne (Germany), there were two such gates, one that was used by the Archbishop of Cologne, a powerful ruler in the context of medieval Germany, when he was entering the city from his residence near Bonn, and one that was used

Figure 7–8: Severinstor gateway in the medieval walls of Cologne (Germany), viewed from outside the city (after the painting by Jakob Scheiner, 1877). Tohma; http://www.kunstbilder-galerie.de/app ?service=external/Painting&sp=l793194; public domain

by the newly crowned King of the Romans (King of Germany) when he entered the city after his coronation at Aachen. The two gates were the Severinstor and the Weyertor, both of which were more elaborate than the other gates of the city, embodying architectural features which suggest that they were designed, just like the Porta Nigra, as much to provide a suitable stage setting for the triumphs and entries than for defense against possible enemies. The Severinstor, used by the Archbishop of Cologne, is still standing, although much restored (Figure 7–8). The height and imposing character of the tower above the gate itself are striking. It is not clear, however, what defensive function it could have had, and it seems likely that its function was to distinguish the gate as an important entry point to the city, and perhaps also to provide a viewpoint for those wishing to watch the ceremonial entries of the archbishop. Also striking are the remains of a balcony above the arch, accessible from the stair towers on either side. It seems likely that the purpose of this balcony was to accommodate the audience, perhaps dignitaries, perhaps ladies, who were there to observe those parts of the ceremonial entries that took place outside the gate, or perhaps to participate in

Figure 7–9: Weyertor, Cologne (Germany), illustration from *Die Cronica van der hilliger stat van Coellen*, fol. 223, showing the king witnessing a tournament in front of the city gates.

them. It is also possible that the balcony was intended to accommodate musicians and actors presenting the theatrical tableaux to mark a ceremonial entry.

The Weyertor, which the king used for his entries, is no longer standing, but a seventeenth-century drawing of it shows that it too had a balcony. A woodcut of 1499 actually shows this being used, in this case by the king and others, including ladies, watching a tournament or a military display outside the gate (Figure 7–9).

THE CITY AS A STAGE SET: THOROUGHFARES

Once within the city gate, the ruler making his triumph or entry ideally needed a wide and imposing route through the city, leading to the forum or the palace or the principal religious building, and providing space for the audience of the triumph or entry to line up along it, and for the theatrical shows and ceremonies that were part of the triumph or entry. Such routes—they might appropriately be called "thoroughfares"—were especially striking in Roman cities. In these, a wide thoroughfare often led from a grand city gate, through one or more triumphal arches, down to the forum, which was the governmental and commercial heart of the city. Such thoroughfares, as for example at the city of Djemila in Roman North Africa (modern Algeria), were often lined with elegant stone arcades or porticoes. Often too, they had way stations, that is, places where people could pause to watch the traffic moving along the thoroughfare. These were equipped with benches or places to lean, and they offered a good view of the thoroughfare through wide openings. They could be designed as *exhedrae*, that is, semicircular spaces, opening off the thoroughfare, or fountains with seating space attached to them. They were no doubt used on an everyday basis as places for the inhabitants of the city to rest and talk; but they must also have had a specific function as places where spectators could watch the triumphs and entries of rulers passing down the thoroughfare.

Figure 7–10: Ramped street, Madīnat al-Zahrā near Córdoba (Spain), looking south, with the arches of the Great Portico, the entrance gate for the road leading from Córdoba, appearing on the left. Note the benches on either side of the ramped street, and, in the center, the stubs of the doorways that could be closed across it.

In the tenth-century caliphal city of Madīnat al-Zahrā, a thoroughfare has been excavated leading from the gate by which the city would have been entered from the principal road, that from Córdoba, which would have been used by the caliph making a ceremonial entry into the city (Figure 7–10). This thoroughfare, the so-called ramped street, was wide and superbly paved, and it had along it stone benches, presumably for the use of the spectators who were watching the ceremonial entries as they processed across the city to the great reception hall beyond, the Hall of ʿAbd al-Rahmān III (*Salon Rico*), or perhaps for the courtiers and officials who lined the street to make the processions all the more impressive. The figure shows that the street was divided into sections by doors, although all that is left now are the stone stubs of their frames. The function of these doors seems likely to have been part of the ceremony accompanying the entries. Presumably, the procession would have been greeted at each of these doors, and maybe ceremonially admitted. The thoroughfare at Madīnat al-Zahrā probably extended a considerable distance beyond the city, for the road from Córdoba clearly was a very grand road, along which several tenth-century bridges were built, and which was actually metaled. No doubt there were ceremonial meetings with escorts for the approaching caliph and approaching ambassadors all along it.

The New Town of Prague offers a comparable example from the fourteenth century of a new city designed and built to incorporate a thoroughfare for processions, no doubt including entries and triumphs, but most clearly seen in what is known of the royal coronation procession. According to the *Order for the Coronation of the Kings of Bohemia* and the chronicle of Přibík Pulkava z Radenína of the late fourteenth century (Rosario 2000, 85; Fajt et al. 2006, 214–15), the coronation ceremony began on the day before the actual coronation, when the king went on foot from the palace on the ridge called the Hrad at the western extremity of Prague (see above, Figure 6–17), across the River Moldau, to the church of Saints Peter and Paul on the eminence of the Vyšehrad, which was at the southern end of the city, farthest from the Hrad. There he was shown the shoe of Přemysl the Ploughman, supposedly the ancestor of his dynasty, the Přemyslids; and what was believed to be that ploughman's satchel was hung from his shoulders. Then in the evening the king returned to St. Vitus's Cathedral on the Hrad to hear the service of vespers, along a thoroughfare that led from the Vyšehrad to the monastery Na Slovanech, then across the enormous Charles Square (originally the Great Market) that Charles IV had created, and that must have been a very imposing space for this procession. From there, the ruler who was to be crowned passed under the elaborately decorated Powder Tower, complete with heraldic shields, and marking the entrance to the Old Town (Figure 7–11). Passing on through the Old Town, he crossed the imposing square with the town hall, over the Charles Bridge with its splendid view up to the palace and St. Vitus's Cathedral (see above, Figure 6–4), and so across the area of the city called the Mala Straná to the cathedral itself. There, the archbishop of Prague greeted him in the south porch of the cathedral. The same processional route was also used for funeral processions. On December 11, 1378, Charles IV's body was borne along the same route from the Hrad to Vyšehrad and so back for burial in St. Vitus's Cathedral.

In the medieval City of London, a comparable thoroughfare was the street known then and now as Cheapside, although it was then much wider than it is now (Figure 7–12). This too was used for entries and triumphs, but it was also the central part of the processional route the king followed in state from the Tower of London to Westminster Abbey on the day before his coronation (below, p. 328). The figure shows how wide and straight Cheapside was in the Middle Ages, and how it had along it a series of conduits, the purpose of which was to supply drinking water; but they may well have been much more elaborate fountains, the areas around which are likely to have served as way stations along the route, where the procession would have paused against the imposing backdrop of the fountains. Indeed, the descriptions of royal entries into London show that one of these conduits, the Great Conduit, was grand enough for pageants to be mounted on top of it, while it ran with wine rather than water (Kipling 1998, 13). Cheapside led into St. Paul's Cathedral, where the procession halted for a service, before it went on down what is now the modern Strand, past the cross at Charing Cross, which commemorated Edward I's queen, Eleanor of Castile, but which also no doubt formed a way station for the procession. Then again along King Street, which led to the great gate of the precinct of Westminster Abbey, and so on to the palace where the king was to spend the night before his coronation in the abbey church.

Figure 7–11: Powder Tower, Prague (Czech Republic), viewed from outside the Old Town.

Figure 7–12: Diagrammatic plan of the City of London in the Middle Ages, showing Cheapside and its conduits and cross (after Lobel and Johns 1989, map 3).

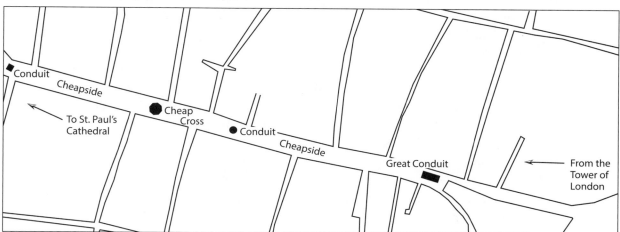

THE CITY AS STAGE SET: TRIUMPHAL ARCHES

Thoroughfares could be lined with triumphal arches, especially in Roman cities, and these often magnificent structures were another way in which the architecture of the city was adapted to the needs of triumphs and entries. One of their main functions was to serve as memorials to the triumphs or entries of particular emperors, but they were much more than just commemorative monuments. They were an imposing addition to a city's thoroughfare, capable of making triumphs and entries passing along it more dramatic and powerful through the stage setting they provided for them. In Roman cities, they could be built in the heart of the city, as the Arch of Constantine was erected by the Roman Forum almost at the centre of ancient Rome, and they could also be built immediately inside city gates, as was the case at Reims (France), where a triumphal arch called the Porte de Mars, which still stands just outside what is now the railway station, was originally situated immediately inside the actual city gate (Figure 7–13). Building an arch in this position enhanced not only the grandeur of the thoroughfare that led through it but also the city gate that stood opposite it.

The building of triumphal arches may well have continued after the end of the Roman Empire in western Europe, although the only surviving example is an arch at the monastery of Lorsch (Germany), rather than in a city (Figure 7–14). This arch is dated to the eighth or ninth century on the basis of the style of its decoration, although there are no written sources referring to it or explaining what it was used for. It was always a free-standing arch with a tower for a spiral staircase at each of the short ends. Like the Arch of Constantine, it had three openings, and they had Roman-style columns attached to the wall between them. The uppermost part had no inscription or sculpture such as we see on the Arch of Constantine, but it did have a chamber at that level (the windows lighting it are visible in the figure), which is a feature it shares with the Arch of Constantine. (The roof of the Lorsch arch, which is its least Roman element, is a modern feature, added by the architect who restored the arch.) The gate into the monastery precinct from outside was—before its demolition—beyond the arch as it appears in the figure, approximately where the white-painted building stands, and the monastery church is behind the spectator. The arch must have functioned much as Roman triumphal arches did, that is, to increase the grandeur of a procession through it, in the case of Lorsch a procession from the gate of the monastic precinct to the church.

At the city of Madinat-al-Zahra in the tenth century, however, the thoroughfare known as the ramped street (above, p. 215) entered the city through the Great Portico, an impressive arch with a series of subsidiary arches on either side of it, which, although it had less depth than its Roman equivalents, was for all intents and purposes a triumphal arch (Figure 7–15). In front of the Great Portico was what seems to have been a sort of parade ground for military displays, or perhaps for exactly the sort of ceremonies outside the gate that appear in medieval manuscript illuminations of such ceremonies in Christian contexts, such as tournaments or military displays (Figure 7–9), or the handing-over of the keys of the city to the ruler as he arrived in front of the gate (Figure 7–19). That the purpose of the Great Portico was to create an impression and to enhance whatever ceremonial took place in front

Figure 7–13: Porte de Mars, Reims (France).

Figure 7–14: Triumphal arch, monastery of Lorsch (Germany), seen from inside the monastery precinct.

City as Stage Set   219

Figure 7–15: The Great Portico, Madīnat al-Zahrā near Córdoba (Spain), seen from outside the city.

of it, and whatever processions passed through it, is shown by the fact that the two openings on the right in Figure 7–15 were not really openings at all. There was no way through them; they were there simply to impress. Also, there are indications in the surviving masonry that there was a platform above the largest arch of the portico, from which spectators could have watched entries arriving at the portico, just as was the case with the balconies that were part of the Severinstor and the Weyertor in Cologne.

Between 1234 and 1240, the Holy Roman Emperor, Frederick II (1220–50), built the Porta di Capua, which was both a triumphal arch and a fortified gateway, situated where the great highway from Rome crossed the River Volturno into the city of Capua (Italy). Although only the lower courses of the Porta di Capua survive, together with the sadly damaged sculpture now in the city museum, later drawings and descriptions make it possible to reconstruct Frederick II's gate as consisting of two massive towers with a wall between them. Through this wall opened the entrance arch which led into an unroofed courtyard between the two towers, and beyond that on to the bridge itself (Figure 7–16). The Porta di Capua was unquestionably a defensive structure for it had underneath it a system of underground stairways and rooms, reaching down some 12m below ground level, and intended to allow the garrison not only to take refuge from attackers, but also to obtain water from the River Volturno—for one of the underground corridors led out to the river under shelter of the towers. But the structure was much more a triumphal arch than a fortification, as evidenced by the fact that the multangular parts of the towers were built of enormous blocks of a fine white stone called travertine. This is rather like white marble in appearance, and it con-

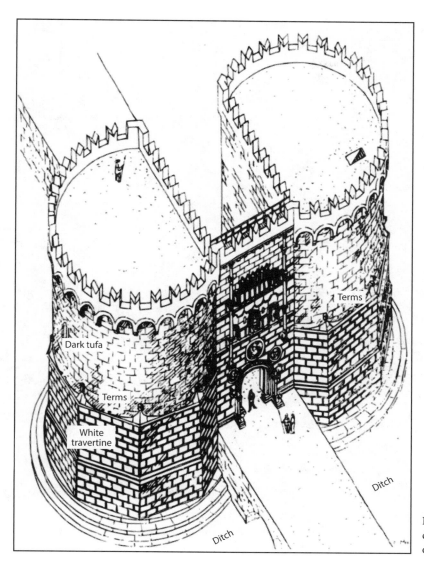

Labels in figure: Terms, Dark tufa, Terms, White travertine, Ditch, Ditch, Ditch

Figure 7–16: Reconstruction of the Porta di Capua, Capua (Italy), as viewed from outside the city (after Willemsen 1953).

trasted in a decorative way with the towers above, which were made of a much darker stone called tufa. The junction between the two types of stone was decorated with terms, that is, carved heads on pinnacle-like bodies, while the façade above the entrance arch was adorned with a series of sculptures, including one of the emperor himself (below, pp. 231–32, and Figure 7–26).

Another triumphal arch was built at the entrance to the courtyard of the royal palace, the Castel Nuovo in Naples, between 1450 and 1471 (Figure 7–17). The style of this shows clearly the influence of the Italian Renaissance, for it is self-consciously imitative of classical models. Its function as a triumphal arch, however, is clear from the sculptured scene of the triumphal entry of Alfonso the Magnanimous above the entrance arch, as well as from the bronze doors, which have on them a remarkable series of battle scenes (Figure 7–18).

Figure 7–17: Triumphal arch, Castel Nuovo, Naples (Italy). This formed the main entrance to the palace.

Figure 7–18: Detail of the bronze doors of the entrance, Castel Nuovo, Naples (Italy), showing one of the several battle scenes represented on them.

MESSAGES OF POWER

If triumphs and entries were such theatrical events, with so much attention devoted to making cities into stage sets for them, what messages of power could they have conveyed? For one, they may have been messages relating to the power that derived from rulers' relationship with their subjects, personal power, that is. For triumphs and entries were a means by which the ruler could appear directly to many classes of his subjects in the city. In the triumph of Titus and Vespasian, for example, there were three phases, each of which involved different groups in the city. The first phase, which consisted of Vespasian saying prayers and making a speech outside the city by the Temple of Isis, involved the army and the high officials and senators of Rome. The third phase, which consisted of the prayers and sacrifices at the Temple of Jupiter and then the feast hosted by the emperor, was naturally directed at a select audience of those who were present in the temple and could be guests at the emperor's feast. But the second phase, which consisted of the procession through Rome, brought Titus and Vespasian into contact with the population of Rome on a large scale. For, in his account of the triumph, Josephus emphasized the efforts that had been made to give the procession a mass audience of the city at large:

> Notice was given in advance of the day appointed for the victory procession, and not one person stayed at home out of the immense population of the city: everyone came out and, although there was only standing-room, found a place somewhere, so that there was barely enough room for the procession itself to pass. (G. A. Williamson 1981, 370)

The procession passed, Josephus wrote, "through the theatres to give the crowds a better view." By AD 71 there were three theaters in ancient Rome. That built by the Roman general Pompey before 55 BC has not survived. The contemporary Roman writer Pliny says that it could accommodate 40,000 people, but the figure of 18,000 is probably more accurate. Nevertheless, it was absolutely enormous. The second, the Theatre of Balbus, was quite close to the Theatre of Pompey. The third, the Theatre of Marcellus, is visible as ruins looking down over the River Tiber. It too was enormous, even bigger than the Theatre of Pompey, and capable of holding 20,500 people. The triumph may not have visited the Theatre of Pompey, given its position relative to the Temple of Isis and the procession's route, but it must have passed close to it, and it presumably did visit the Theatre of Marcellus and the Theatre of Balbus. These two alone offered a vast amount of seating for the triumph's audience (see above, Figure 7–1).

Messages of personal power seem also to have been inherent in the opening act of medieval entries, which often began outside the city, where the ruler would be met by a delegation of the inhabitants of the city in question. When the exarch of Ravenna, who was the Byzantine emperor's representative in Italy, visited the city of Rome, judges and officials from the city met him as far away as 30 miles from the walls, while the city militias, together with schoolchildren waving palm leaves and olive branches, and the less senior members of the clergy of Rome, met him one mile from the walls (Kantorowicz 1944, 211). This sort of entry is found again when the Frankish ruler Charlemagne approached Rome in 800 just before his coronation as emperor by the pope:

> Pope Leo came to meet him with the Romans to Mentana, twelve miles from the city, and welcomed him with the greatest humility and respect. (Scholz and Rogers 1972, 80, s.a. 800)

When Duke Philip the Good (1419–67) made his entry into Ghent in 1458, its first phase took place about three miles from the center of the city, where the officials and magistrates of the city rode out to meet the duke, "accompanied by various notables, and noble citizens . . . all mounted on horseback and dressed in black," a procession that involved 400 horses (A. Brown and Small 2007, 176).

Such a rendezvous outside the city clearly had the potential to convey a message of power about the ruler's superior relationship to his subjects and their deference to him. It was a message that could perhaps have been calibrated by the distance outside the city at which the rendezvous took place. The rendezvous would be followed by a ceremony just outside the city gate. In the case of Philip the Good's entry into Ghent, the party that had met him three miles from the city then escorted him to the area outside the northwest gate of Ghent, the Walpoort. There,

> the deacons and all the sworn members of the guilds and the sworn members of the weavers were spread out as far as possible, each finely dressed in his long cloak of office down to the ground and as many as 500 in number, each bearing a lit torch in his hand. When they became aware of the approach of my redoubted lord, they fell to their knees and removed their hats in fine and graceful order. (A. Brown and Small 2007, 177)

Another aspect of the reception of the ruler at the gate of the city could be the offer to him of the keys of the city. This is represented in manuscript illustrations, for example one showing the entry of the German ruler Henry VII into the city of Turin in Italy in 1310 (Lampen 2009, 3, 4, and n. 8). The emperor is there shown approaching the city gate. He is wearing a crown, with his queen also crowned behind him and his knights in armor with heraldic pennants. The citizens of Turin are shown riding out through the city gate, and the city keys are being offered to the emperor by the first rider. The citizens too have their heraldic pennants, and the scene that was depicted must have been an impressively bright and ceremonial one.

Rather later, a similar scene is shown in a miniature in the Lucerne Chronicle of Deibold Schillings the Younger, published in 1513 (Lampen 2009, 7). It illustrates the entry of the German emperor Sigismund into Lucerne in 1417 with contemporary historical detail (Figure 7–19). The miniature shows the north gate of Lucerne, recognizable by the shrine known as the Grosse Heiland which is represented on the right. Out of the gate, which is adorned with an heraldic shield, stream soldiers, clerics (with their distinctive headgear), and townsmen, led by musicians. The town leader, with a woman, perhaps his wife, behind him, kneels before the mounted Sigismund, and has evidently just given him the key to the city which the emperor holds in his hand.

In this part of the entry too, the message of power was first and foremost about the allegiance and subservience of the subjects to the ruler. That message, however, could be modulated by the ceremonies outside or at the city gate. In medieval entries, the ruler could be asked to accept certain conditions before he actually entered the city. He might, for example, be required to swear again his oaths to protect the interests of his subjects, or to endorse an agreement with the city in question. In 1127, for example, the King of France with the newly elected Count of Flanders, William, arrived outside the city of Bruges in the Low Countries and, according to the chronicler Galbert of Bruges:

> [t]he king and the count assembled with their knights and ours, with the citizens and many Flemings in the usual field where the reliquaries and relics of the saints had been collected. And when silence had been called for, the charter of liberty of the church and of the privileges of St Donatian was read aloud before all. . . . There was also read the little charter of agreement between the count and our citizens . . . Binding themselves to accept this condition, the king and the count took an oath on the relics of saints in the hearing of the clergy and people. (J. M. Murray 1994, 137)

Figure 7-19: The entry of Emperor Sigismund into Lucerne in 1417, as illustrated in the 1513 Lucerne Chronicle of Diebold Schillings the Younger.

Meetings like this, which evidently took place in a field designated for the purpose outside the city, could be important for the power of rulers that derived from their relationship with their subjects, for here were opportunities for direct contact and dialogue between the two, even if the result was the constraint—at least in a formal way—of the ruler's power. Triumphs and entries were potentially all the more powerful a mechanism for conveying a message of personal power, because they allowed rulers to communicate with their subjects, including subjects of lower as well as upper classes.

The most obvious message that triumphs had to send, however, was concerned with the military successes of rulers. The long lines of chained captives which formed part of a triumph, the piles of booty, enemy weapons in disorganized piles, the scenes of conquest represented or re-enacted, models of the captured cities—all represented in graphic and accessible form the emperor's success in war. The triumph of Vespasian and Titus after the Jewish Wars, for example, displayed the spoils from the Temple of Jerusalem, which Titus's army had destroyed when it had captured the city—the golden seven-branched candlestick, the golden table, the Jewish Law, and the trumpets of the Temple—as is shown by the sculptured scenes on the Arch of Titus, the triumphal arch erected to commemorate this triumph.

As Josephus explains, the theatrical shows, which were part of a triumph, could recreate the emperor's military campaigns for public view. This must also have been done on the occasion of the emperor Constantine's entry into Rome, for on the Arch of Constantine the events of the campaign which led up to his victory over his rival Maxentius at the Battle of the Milvian Bridge in 312 appear in a sculptured frieze just below the roundels of sculpture on the arch. This frieze may well be a reflection in stone of the theatrical re-enactments accompanying the entry. It begins on the short west end of the arch with Constantine's army on its way to Rome. On the south side of the arch, the story continues with this army besieging the city of Verona (Figure 7–20). Constantine's army is shown attacking from the left, with the defenders hurling rocks from the walls of the city, and one of them falling head-first to the ground. The emperor himself is the much larger figure on the left, with a winged "victory" flying near his head. There then follows the Battle of the Milvian Bridge, and the frieze shows the soldiers of the defeated emperor Maxentius being drowned in the River Tiber. Celebrating Constantine's military success was tantamount to celebrating his legitimacy as emperor in a period when military victory was regarded as a qualification for that office. The arch offered the opportunity to commemorate this in stone, as the entry had no doubt offered the opportunity to represent it in dramatic form.

The decoration of the Arch of Constantine is an amalgam of newly carved elements and earlier sculptures deriving from monuments erected to Constantine's predecessors (above, p. 205), which showed similar military success. On either side of the central passage are panels showing warfare between the Romans and the people called the Dacians, who lived north of the River Danube. One panel shows an emperor mounted and trampling on a fallen Dacian, while a Roman soldier prepares to kill another (Figure 7–21). That these enemies of Rome were Dacians is shown by their costumes and especially their distinctive hats. The principal wars against them were fought by the Romans under the emperor Trajan (98–117), so it seems likely that this panel was carved to commemorate the victories of Trajan. The reason for re-using it in the Arch of Constantine may have been to save the bother of making new sculptures, but more likely it was to associate Constantine with his great military predecessor, Trajan. The implication was that Constantine was as great a military leader as Trajan had been. The point was underlined by placing two additional scenes of the Dacian wars at the short ends of the arch at the uppermost level, and standing large statues of Dacians on pedestals at the same level, all taken from earlier monuments carved during the reigns of Trajan or Hadrian (Figure 7–3).

The messages of power that triumphs and entries had the potential to send were not only about the military achievements of the ruler. Some scenes on the Arch of Constantine rep-

Winged victory   Emperor Constantine   Constantine's soldiers   Defenders of Verona

Figure 7–20: Constantine's army besieging Verona, detail of the frieze showing Constantine's victories and entry into Rome, Arch of Constantine, Rome (Italy).

Figure 7–21: The emperor attacking his Dacian enemies, panel from the Great Trajanic Frieze inside the central opening, west side, Arch of Constantine, Rome (Italy).

resent the emperor's actions once he was inside the city. These relate to his exercise of power in the interests of his subjects. For the frieze represents the emperor speaking directly to his subjects from the platform (the *rostra*) in the Roman Forum (Figure 7–22). The emperor (his head broken off) stands in the center, with the stone screen that bounded the rostra on either side of him. Senators surround him there, and the people of Rome stand below on either side, evidently listening with rapt attention.

Another scene in the frieze shows a different stage of the emperor's entry, and shows Constantine giving money to the poor in a rather formal and institutionalized way (Figure 7–23). The headless figure of the emperor is seated on a throne in the center of the scene with a coin holder in his right hand. The sculptor has carved the depressions in it for holding the coins, some of which are dropping down to those who reach up toward the emperor and are waiting to receive the coins as alms. On either side of the emperor appear officials who are apparently keeping records of what is distributed, and who (in other parts of this scene not pictured) are also helping with the distribution. Clearly, the generosity displayed in this scene had more to do with bureaucratic power, in the way it was organized, than with personal power in the form of relationships between the emperor and his subjects.

A notably military emperor was Marcus Aurelius (121–80), who fought successful campaigns against various barbarian peoples, including those called the Marcomanni and the Quadi. The sculptured panels from a monument of his, which were also incorporated into the Arch of Constantine, naturally celebrate his success in warfare, but there are also scenes showing his efficacy as a ruler in practical terms. In one of these, Marcus Aurelius is represented showing generosity to his subjects (Figure 7–24). The emperor sits on a throne-stool and hands money to an official for distribution to the people who appear below him, including a child and a father with another child on his shoulders. In the second scene (Figure 7–25), a bearded prisoner has to be supported by a boy as he appears before the enthroned emperor to appeal for mercy, while the emperor sits in judgment on him, with Roman military standards appearing behind him.

It is not easy to define what types of power were the subject of the messages being conveyed by representations of military victories and of generosity in alms-giving. On the one hand, it is possible to see these activities as relating to bureaucratic power. The representations of officials on the scenes of alms-giving on the Arch of Constantine seem to emphasize that the exercise was made possible by bureauratic power and the organization that underpinned it. On the other hand, generosity and liberality were qualities of rulers just like magnificence, so that the display of them was much more intended to convey a message of ideological power. Generosity, in other words, was an essential part of rulership itself, and served also to associate the ruler with God or the gods, from whom all things flowed. The same ambiguity surrounds the message of power being conveyed by the celebration of military victories. On the one hand, they too were made possible, at any rate in the Roman Empire, by bureaucratic structures which permitted the raising, deployment, and supply of armies. On the other, military victories could be seen as pertaining to the essence of a ruler's ideological power. The fact that emperors won—or presided over the winning of—victories was one of their principal qualifications for power. It was as much part of their ideological power as was their relationship to the divine.

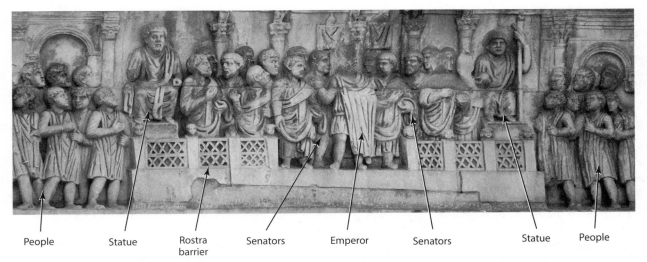

People   Statue   Rostra barrier   Senators   Emperor   Senators   Statue   People

Figure 7–22: The emperor speaking from the rostra, detail of the frieze showing Constantine's victories and entry into Rome, Arch of Constantine, Rome (Italy).

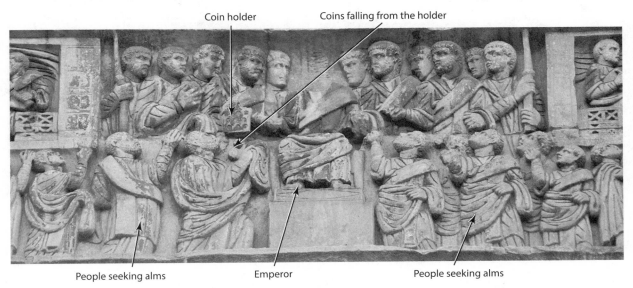

Coin holder   Coins falling from the holder

People seeking alms   Emperor   People seeking alms

Figure 7–23: The emperor giving money to the poor during his entry into Rome, detail of the frieze showing Constantine's victories and entry into Rome, Arch of Constantine, Rome (Italy).

In the case of later rulers, a message more clearly concerned with ideological power was that of the extent to which their power was cast in the mold of the Roman emperors of the past, so that they could be seen as the legitimate heirs of those rulers. Such a message was no doubt conveyed by the emperor Frederick II's entries and triumphs, but it is clearly perceptible in the form and decoration of the Porta di Capua that he built (above, pp. 220–21). Its overall form was Roman, parallelling the Roman triumphal arch of Rimini (Italy) which, like the Porta di Capua, stood at the entrance to the bridge leading into that city. The Rimini

Figure 7–24: Emperor Marcus Aurelius distributing gifts of money to his subjects, Arch of Constantine, Rome (Italy).

Figure 7–25: Emperor Marcus Aurelius giving mercy to prisoners, Arch of Constantine, Rome (Italy).

arch also was built between two towers, just like the Capua arch, and both were a sort of hybrid between a triumphal arch and a gate. The surviving Roman gates of Rome, for example, the Porta Appia and the Porta Ostiensis, are both in just this form—an arch between two towers. The decoration of the Capua arch also incorporated Roman elements, no doubt to convey the same message (Figure 7–26).

The use in the Capua arch of white travertine blocks taken from the Roman amphitheater in Capua was not haphazard. They were cut by Frederick II's masons in a particular way, with their edges chamfered (this is what has produced the effect of very prominent joints between each block). This type of masonry effect had been used in the Roman period, but not very widely, and it was used in Frederick II's time exceptionally, one notable example being the great Crusader castle of Crac-des-Chevaliers in the Holy Land. It was not used

Figure 7–26: Porta di Capua, Capua (Italy), viewed from outside the city, showing the white travertine blocks in the lower parts of the towers, with the darker tufa blocks above. The carved heads, or terms, now in the Capua Museum, were originally at the apices of the upward-pointing triangular projections of travertine. Notice the joints between the travertine blocks, emphasized by chamfering.

again widely until the Renaissance period, when chamfered stonework of this sort is a common feature of the lower stages of palaces and great houses. So Frederick II's use of these chamfered travertine blocks was a remarkable thing in his time (Shearer 1935, 51–56). Here was a ruler who not only made his arch look Roman, but also gave it the grandeur of a striking masonry technique that was innovative and was not to be seen again for centuries. At the junction between the travertine and the tufa, the former was carried up at each angle into a sort of pyramid shape. Each of these shapes was then capped with a sculptured "term," that is, a figure without arms but with a body absorbed in the architectural form below it. Although these terms were newly carved by Frederick II's sculptors, they were a distinctively Roman type of decoration.

The message of the arch and towers was furthered by the figures on the façade which faced anyone approaching from outside the town. The seated figure under the arch in the center of the second stage of the façade was evidently of Frederick II himself, as is described by a sixteenth-century Capuan document (Shearer 1935, 24, 71–74). The sculpture, much damaged, is preserved in the Capua Museum. Enough of it remains, however, to show, first, that the statue was (on grounds of its technique) newly made by Frederick II's craftsmen rather than being taken from a ruined Roman site and re-used, and that it represents the emperor wearing a very classical, Roman, toga-like costume. Also the placing of a statue of the emperor in this position over the arch was another feature of Roman triumphal arches, for example the arch of Rimini in Italy.

Immediately below the figure of the emperor was a large female bust, almost three times life-size, which also survives in the Capua Museum, but in a rather less damaged state. It is clear that this too was carved specially by Frederick II's craftsmen, and it too is markedly Roman in type, resembling in particular a bust of Diana still in place in the Roman amphitheater in Capua. The head on the arch represented the goddess Juno, and was probably intended as a personification of the emperor's recently issued code of laws (Shearer 1935, 74–78). On either side of the female head were two even more striking busts, this time of bearded men. Now destroyed inscriptions identified them as Frederick II's key ministers, Pietro della Vigna on the left and Taddeo da Sessa on the right (Shearer 1935, 75–98). These busts were certainly specially carved for the arch, since they fit neatly into their places in round niches. Yet, they too are very Roman and classical in appearance. Here then was an emperor whose government was considered to be so much on a par with the Roman emperors that his ministers could appear as if they were toga-clad senators of antiquity, that his triumphal gate could be built in imitation of similar Roman monuments, that the travertine blocks used in it could be tooled in a very distinctive Roman style, and that it could be decorated not only with Roman-type terms, but also with a statue of the emperor himself in Roman dress.

A ruler's relationship to the Roman past was not, however, the most radical message of ideological power the entries and triumphs had the potential to convey. For, a more radical message could have been simply about the ruler's relationship to the divinity, or, more radical still, the way in which he represented the divinity. Not the least important aspect of Roman triumphs was that they were religious events. In the triumphs before Constantine's conversion to Christianity in the early fourth century, the *triumphator* seems to have been closely associated with the god Jupiter, for his dress on the occasion, and what he carried, suggested such an association. A religious significance of this sort continued to be attached to triumphs, and also to entries, across the centuries. Although the emperor Constantine (306–37) was the first Christian emperor of Rome, the Arch of Constantine was the work of the Roman Senate, which was at the time largely pagan. So the senators naturally continued to see the emperor in pagan terms, although they associated him not so much with Jupiter as with the cult of the Unconquered Sun. Indeed, Constantine himself was devoted to this cult, which seems to have become associated in his mind with Christianity. At any rate, as we have seen, the Arch of Constantine includes a frieze showing Constantine's victories and entry into Rome. Immediately above this on the short faces of the arch, at the same level as the hunting tondi on the long faces, are two large roundels, specially carved for the arch rather than re-used from another monument. That on the west side shows the moon, that on the east the sun (Figure 7–27). The sun is represented driving his four-horse chariot (a quadriga) rising from the ocean, represented by the sea god lying on the waves at the bottom of the roundel. Since this roundel is immediately above the scene in the frieze of Constantine's victories and entries into Rome which shows the emperor driving his quadriga (Figure 7–4), it seems that the designer of the arch wanted those who saw it to associate

Figure 7–27: The sun driving his chariot and rising from the ocean, tondo on the short east side, Arch of Constantine, Rome (Italy). The tondo is directly above the scene of Constantine in his quadriga, which is part of the frieze showing his victories and entry.

Figure 7–28: Medallion of the emperor Constantius entering London after his reconquest of the province of Britain in 296. The emperor is mounted, and a figure personifying the city kneels before the gate. The inscription around the edge reads *Redditor lucis aeternae* ("Restorer of Eternal Light").

Constantine in his chariot making his entry into Rome with the sun rising into the sky in his chariot. Thus, his entry into the city was likened to the rising of the sun and he himself was being identified with the sun. Clearly a message of ideological power was being conveyed.

When the inhabitants of a city met the emperor at the city gates or farther out from the city, this reception could also convey a message about the god-like status he was believed to have, as much as a message about his relationship to his subjects. In Roman entries, the emperor's subjects, dressed in white with wreaths, carried torches; incense was burned and flowers were scattered in the path of the ruler; images of gods were carried; sacrifices were made; and the ruler was greeted as "benefactor and saviour." In short, the ruler was being treated as a god, as is underlined by some of the coins and medallions struck to mark such occasions. For example, when Constantine's father, the emperor Constantius, reconquered the Roman province of Britain in 296, a gold medallion was struck to commemorate what was no doubt his triumph (Figure 7–28). At the base of the design, a Roman galley is presumably a reference to the reconquest of Britain involving a naval campaign. The emperor, however, is depicted on horseback approaching the gate of London, which is shown on the right with the figure personifying the city kneeling before it and holding up her arms to the emperor. The message relating to the power of the emperor can only have been one relating to the religious aspects of ideological power, since the inscription around the medallion designates Constantius as "Restorer of Eternal Light," presumably a reference to the divine power of the sun (Kantorowicz 1944, 214).

Messages about the proximity of the ruler to the divine could also be conveyed by medieval triumphs and entries. Such a message seems to be implied by the sculpture on the tower arch spanning the new bridge built by Charles IV, the Charles Bridge in Prague. As we have seen, this bridge was on the ceremonial thoroughfare from the Old Town to the palace on the Hrad (above, p. 216). On the Old Town side, the tower arch was decorated with a series of carvings, which are largely still in place (although much restored) (Figure 7–29). These included, just above the tower arch, a line of heraldic shields that have on them the arms of the various kingdoms and duchies which Charles IV ruled. Above these, and between the figures, are carved the shields of the Holy Roman Empire (the eagle) and of the Kingdom of Bohemia (the lion). The message being broadcast here was the wide extent of Charles IV's power, and also of the power of the crown of Bohemia. Above the line of shields are seated the figures of Charles IV himself on the left, and his son, the future King Wenceslas IV, on the right. They both sit in majesty, holding in their left hands the orb of royal power, topped with a cross, and wearing crowns on their heads. They are associated with the divine in that between them stands the figure of St. Vitus, patron of Prague and Bohemia. He was an early Christian martyr in Italy, whose arm had been presented as a holy relic (according to his legend) to the first Duke Wenceslas of Bohemia in the early tenth century. It was enshrined in St. Vitus's Cathedral of, of which he was the patron saint and to which the bridge leads. Charles IV himself had rebuilt the cathedral in spectacular Gothic style, and had raised it to be an archbishopric. The message was clearly that Charles IV had contributed all this to Bohemia and had consequently associated himself closely with that kingdom's patron saint.

Above St. Vitus are two more statues, one of which represents Sigismund, the saint-king of Burgundy, a Christian king, murdered by being drowned in a well in 523/4 and subsequently venerated as a saint and martyr. Charles IV had been responsible for bringing his relics to Prague in 1354, and in 1365 he had acquired more of them when he was crowned King of Burgundy at Arles in southern France (Rosario 2000, 63; Klaniczay 2002, 330). In 1366, King Sigismund was declared to be a Bohemian patron saint, like St. Vitus. Since it was Charles IV who had brought this martyr's relics to Bohemia, he could take credit for whatever benefits they were thought to have bestowed. The potential message of power of the tower arch was that the ruler had safeguarded the welfare of the realm by endowing it in this way and giving it a new patron saint.

But the message may have gone further, for the sculpture of Charles IV on the tower arch associated him with St. Wenceslas, the saintly Duke of Bohemia (921–29), and his own ancestor, in a very direct way. The statue of Charles IV shows him wearing draped around his shoulders a sort of scaly armor (Figure 7–30). This looks like the armor worn in the Byzantine Empire at earlier periods, and it was certainly not the armor of Bohemia or Germany in Charles IV's day. This sort of armor, however, was the normal costume that St. Wenceslas was shown wearing in pictures of him.

Wenceslas was supposed to have been responsible for advancing the conversion of Bohemia to Christianity and to have been martyred by his brother in a political killing in 929. He

Figure 7–29: The tower arch, Charles Bridge, Prague (Czech Republic), viewed from town with the Hrad and the palace beyond.

Figure 7–30: Charles IV wearing scaly armor, town-side of the tower arch, Charles Bridge, Prague (Czech Republic).

was a very important saint in the Kingdom of Bohemia, and especially to Charles IV who had built a magnificent chapel for him in St. Vitus's Cathedral, and who had also written in his own hand an account of his life and death. He also treasured a sword which was supposed to be the Sword of St. Wenceslas, and was regarded as a holy relic in its own right. In addition, in Charles IV's time, a fragment of the saint's relics was inserted into its blade. The king had a magnificent sheath made for the sword, and it was used in the coronation ceremony that he devised, particularly for the swearing of the king's oath. The naked sword in the right hand of Charles IV's statue on the Charles Bridge must surely represent this sword.

So the tower arch was associating Charles IV with the divine, by presenting him as a "new Wenceslas," the embodiment of the kingdom, and the guarantor of its religious faith.

Although the Prague tower arch no doubt reflected the image being projected by entries and triumphs, there was an even more direct way to send a message about the ruler's proximity to the divine. According to the Bible, when Jesus Christ entered the city of Jerusalem just before his arrest and Crucifixion, he did so as King of the Jews, although he rode a donkey rather than a horse to show his humility (John 12.12–15; Carroll and Prickett 1997, II, 133). Nevertheless, his entry into Jerusalem had the potential to be a model for the entry into their cities of Christian rulers, who could be seen as representing Jesus Christ, or perhaps even to be identified with Jesus Christ, when a clear message of ideological power would be conveyed on behalf of the ruler. Such a paralleling between Jesus Christ's entry and the entries of later rulers took an extreme form when Frederick II entered the city of Jerusalem itself in 1229 in the course of his crusade, an event commemorated by the contemporary poet Marquard de Ried in the clearest possible terms:

> When the servant of God, Frederick the Great, comes
> The sun shines, the wind is gentle, the water boils, the earth turns green . . .
> Jerusalem rejoices . . .
> Before it was the magnificent king Jesus, now it is Frederick,
> Both ready to suffer, they are glorified in you.
>
> (quoted by Kantorowicz 1944, p. 210, n. 19)

The idea that the king's entry into a city was like the entry of Jesus Christ into Jerusalem was equally clear in other, less superficially obviously Christ-like entries. The entry of the exarch of Ravenna into Rome (see above, p. 223) involved children waving palm leaves and olive branches, and when the exarch finally arrived at St. Peter's in the city of Rome, everyone cried, "Blessed is he who comes in the name of the Lord." The parallels between this and the account of Jesus Christ's entry which appears in the Gospel of St. John in the Bible are striking:

> On the next day many people that were come to the feast, when they heard that Jesus was coming to Jerusalem, took branches of palm trees and went forth to meet him, and cried: "Hosanna: Blessed is the King of Israel that comes in the name of the Lord." (John 12.12–13; Carroll and Prickett 1997, II, 133)

The passage in John's gospel would seem to be the source of the carrying of palm leaves in the entry of the exarch of Ravenna and of the chant with which he was greeted. His entry to Rome was presented like Jesus Christ's into Jerusalem, and by implication the message of power was that he was a Christ-like ruler.

This idea of representing the king as Jesus Christ and the city he was entering as Jerusalem, even when it was a quite different city as it usually was, reached great heights in the later Middle Ages, by which time it had developed in quite sophisticated ways. Jesus Christ's entry into Jerusalem itself could be seen in two ways: It was either his actual entry in historical terms as it is described in the Bible; or it was his entry into the Heavenly Jerusalem, so that the city he was entering was not a city of this world but of Heaven, the city that would appear at the end of the world. It could equally have been seen as an image of his ascending into Heaven after he had risen from the dead, which fits with the idea that the city he was entering was the Heavenly Jerusalem. And his entry into Jerusalem could be seen as well as an image of the Last Judgment, when he would come again to judge mankind, and the faithful would themselves enter the Heavenly Jerusalem. But, in addition, Jesus Christ's coming had for long been closely connected with the idea of his coming into the world at Christmastime, that is literally with his "coming," which is what Advent—the period immediately before Christmas—means. So his entry into Jerusalem could have been seen as an image of his coming into the world as he did at his birth.

Such messages relating to the Christ-like ideological power of the ruler seem particularly apparent in a triumphal entry that took place in 1440 (Kipling 1998, 48–60). In that year, the citizens of Bruges in modern Belgium had made peace with their ruler, Philip the Good, after they had revolted against him and expelled him from the city. No doubt as part of the process of reconciliation, they organized for him a triumphal entry into the city on the third Sunday of Advent, that is, December 11. The level of theatrical design and business devoted to this event is remarkable, and it is clear that Philip the Good's entry was being treated as nothing less than the entry of Jesus Christ. In the morning, the priests read out the words of John the Baptist from the Gospel of St. John, which pertained to Jesus Christ's coming: "I am the voice of one crying in the wilderness, Make straight the way of the Lord" (John 1. 23; Carroll and Prickett 1997, II, 114). According to the Bible, John the Baptist was literally preparing the way for Jesus Christ's appearance by preaching and making known his future appearance, and it was he who identified Jesus Christ as the son of God. In this case, however, it was the duke who was coming, so the implied identification with Jesus Christ seems clear. At the gate of Bruges, the entry even involved the appearance of John the Baptist himself at the gate of the city in the afternoon. Standing amid a green wilderness mounted on a cart, John the Baptist was taken to meet Duke Philip and led him through the city, underlining the idea that he was to be thought of in some way as Jesus Christ come into the world. Along the route the duke followed through the city, prophets from the Old Testament of the Bible recognized him as the Messiah, as Jesus Christ. Each prophet stood on a stage with a banner fixed to it that read: "This is the day which the Lord hath made: we will be glad and rejoice therein" (Psalms 117 (118).24; Carroll and Prickett 1997, I, 706). The day of Duke Philip's entry was then to be regarded as on a par with the day of Jesus Christ's coming.

About halfway along the processional route, there was on a platform a tableau of the shepherds adoring the baby Jesus with Mary and Joseph, as the Bible describes them doing in the Christmas story, while above it a throne of God, with God represented as a bright light, appeared with angels around it. Significantly, as the duke passed by, one of the angels said to the shepherds, "I proclaim to you with great joy that today you will know that God comes," just as in the Bible's Christmas story the angels announced the birth of Jesus to the shepherds. Near the end of the processional way, Duke Philip crossed a bridge which had been made to look like a model of the city of Bruges itself. In front of it sat a figure representing the biblical King David, the ancestor of Jesus Christ and founder of Jerusalem, with a banner reading, "Let the city rejoice that seeks the Lord." The underlying idea of the entry was that Duke Philip was entering Bruges as Jesus Christ entered Jerusalem, but equally as Jesus Christ entered the world at Christmastime, which was the point of the allusions to the Christmas story.

Sometimes entries of rulers could be organized to associate the theme of Jesus Christ's ascension into heaven with what Christians envisaged as the triumph over death. After Henry V, king of England (1413–22), had won his great victory over the French at the Battle of Agincourt in 1415, London organized a triumph to celebrate his return (Kipling 1998, 201–209). The pageants along the king's processional way into the city made it seem as if he was quite literally entering heaven, as did Jesus Christ after he had risen from the dead. At London Bridge, the gate had been made to look like the gates of heaven, with two giant warders guarding what a notice declared to be the "City of the King of Justice," that is, of Jesus Christ. The wooden turrets that had been erected on the bridge were covered with cloth painted white and jasper green, the latter color being that of the Heavenly Jerusalem. A great wooden castle was built across Cheapside, also featuring the green color of the Heavenly Jerusalem, and with a banner over the gates through it reading, "Glorious things are spoken of thee, O city of God" (Psalms 87(86).3; Carroll and Prickett 1997, I, 688). Along the way, the king met St. George, the patron saint of England, and then angels singing an anthem based on the text from the Bible referring to Jesus Christ, "Blessed is he who comes in the name of the Lord." The king then met white-bearded prophets, who released a great flock of birds, some of which settled on the king. There followed other inhabitants of the Heavenly Jerusalem: apostles, martyrs, virgins, and angels, and archangels. The king was entering his city as a triumphant ruler, but he was also entering the Heavenly Jerusalem as a subject only of God Almighty, whose appearance marked the climax of the pageants.

In this case too, the message of the ruler's ideological power could be moderated by other elements, which may well have been introduced by the city authorities in organizing the triumph. Part of the intended message seems to have been that the king's military success at Agincourt was due to God rather than to himself, and a contemporary writer records the humble manner in which he took part in the procession, "pondering the matter in his heart, . . . rendering thanks and glory to God alone, not to man" (Kipling 1998, 206).

CONCLUSION

Triumphs and entries, then, were important elements in the messages of power that cities had the potential to convey. Both rituals had a long history from the Roman period across the Middle Ages, although the distinction between them was not clearly maintained. Their immense theatricality and the fact that they were played out before large audiences of all classes greatly enhanced their potential to convey messages of power, especially where gateways, thoroughfares, and triumphal arches, or—in the cases of Prague—bridges, were constructed or modified to enhance cities as stage sets for them.

The messages of power they had the potential to convey could have related to personal power, where the exchanges between ruler and subjects formed part of the ceremonies involved. These activities were admittedly formal and ritualized, but they brought the ruler and his subjects in the city together. The potential was considerable, at least so far as triumphs and entries involved the upper levels of urban society, who might be involved in the ceremonial agreements between ruler and subjects which often marked them in the later Middle Ages. Especially in medieval entries and triumphs, such messages could be subtly modified to accord with the attitudes of the subjects themselves in cases where the ceremonies were organized by the city rather than by the ruler.

Other messages were also conveyed, most obviously, in the case of triumphs, pertaining to the ruler's efficacy in military victories, since these were naturally the focus of the triumph. But messages could also be conveyed about other aspects of the ruler's power, as is evident in the scenes of his institutionalized distribution of alms to the poor. Whether military efficacy and generosity to the poor should be regarded as conveying messages of bureaucratic power or ideological power is, as we have seen (above, p. 228), open to discussion.

Finally, triumphs and entries had the potential to convey messages of ideological power. They could, in the case of medieval entries and triumphs, convey a message about the power of the ruler being rooted in the Roman past and the power of emperors of antiquity. But there could also be more radical ideological messages about the ruler's power stemming from his close relationship to the divine. In the Roman context, such messages concerned the identification of the ruler with a god come to the temple of his city. It is striking that there equally developed in medieval entries the potential to convey a message about the ruler as Christ-like, almost as Christ himself, come to the Heavenly Jerusalem as the city he was entering was imagined to be. Triumphs and entries offered the opportunity to make these ideas explicit through the dramatic performances and tableaux that formed an important part of them.

In another way too, triumphs and entries offered the potential for images of the ruler's power to be communicated in a permanent way, through the carvings on triumphal arches which formed an important part of the city's street furniture, and marked the course of subsequent triumphs and entries. So the architecture of the city as a stage set for entries and triumphs was capable of transmitting a message of power even when those entries and triumphs were not actually taking place. The message of power made in stone was an enduring one.

PART IV

Holy Places

The importance of ideological power to rulership has been a frequent theme of previous chapters. The notion that rulers could be closely associated with the supernatural or the divine, from which their power might be seen to flow, and could even be identified with divine figures, was clearly very important in the construction not only of palaces, but also of artificial landscapes, and even of cities insofar as they were organized for the staging of entries and triumphs. To pursue the notion further, however, it is necessary to examine the holy places that rulers either patronized or created, and these are the subject of this part of the book.

There were naturally pagan as well as Christian and Muslim holy places. The Roman emperors were closely associated with temples, such as that of Jupiter on the Capitol in Rome. The emperor Hadrian (117–38), for example, constructed on the Field of Mars in Rome the enormous Pantheon which, although its function is unknown, must in some way have been a temple to the sun, regarded as a deity with whom the emperors were closely associated or even identified (below, pp. 357–58). But this part of the book will nevertheless concentrate on Christian holy places, with one excursion into the Muslim world, because the richness of the monuments, combined with the level of documentation which provides evidence for the ideas and purposes underlying them, makes them an especially rewarding study. Chapter 8 will examine the importance for power of the relics of saints, or of Christ. These objects were generally portable, so that it was not essential for them to have been connected with particular places. Nevertheless, if rulers were to exploit them as sources of power or conveyors of messages of power, they needed to find or construct for them buildings in which they could be enshrined and displayed and, sometimes, make less permanent arrangements for them to be displayed in public. Chapter 8 focuses on these aspects, although it begins with the relationship between relics and cities, forming a bridge with the previous part of the book. Chapter 9 then examines the religious buildings, which were either churches integral to palaces, palace churches in other words, or were great cathedrals and abbeys—or in the case of Córdoba a mosque—that had been adopted and modified to serve the needs of rulers.

CHAPTER 8

Power, Place, and Relics

The aim of this chapter is to explore the ways in which the presence in a ruler's palace or in his city of the relics of saints or of Jesus Christ himself could convey messages of power relating to the ruler as it were by proxy—or, in other words, the ways in which the power of the relics could be transferred to the ruler who possessed them and had them enshrined in his palace or his city. To enable us to appreciate the full potential of this process, we need to consider first the nature of relics themselves and the perceived nature of their power.

The Christian martyrs were those who had died for their faith, usually in the time of the persecutions of Christians in the Roman Empire, before the first Christian emperor Constantine (306–37) put an end to those persecutions. From as early as the second century, the martyrs had been regarded by Christians as a special category of the dead, deserving to have great attention paid to their mortal remains. Following the accession of Constantine to the imperial throne and the cessation of the persecutions, however, Christians ceased to be martyred for their religion, aside from the occasional missionary martyred by being put to death by the heathens he was trying to convert. So, in the course of the fourth century, saints—particularly holy Christians who had not been martyred, but who had led especially saintly lives as bishops, abbots, monks, hermits, or virgins—came to be regarded as equivalent to martyrs. By the end of the fourth century, Christianity was characterized by the practice of praying to these saints and martyrs for their aid, the practice of holding special services for them, and by the practice of making pilgrimages to their graves.

The underlying belief was that the martyr or saint received special treatment from God in recognition of his or her sufferings or virtues or pious works. This special treatment meant that the soul of the saint or martyr was taken to heaven immediately after death, and was already with God, even before the Last Judgment, when the souls of other Christians would be judged. But the saint or martyr was also present in his or her mortal remains on earth, which meant that there was, to express it crudely, a sort of hotline between those remains and the soul of the saint in Heaven. So the saint could be contacted in heaven by the believer's prayers when said in close contact with the saint's remains (or bodily relics), and the saint would then intercede with God to grant those prayers. Moreover, this power could be spread, for the bodily relics could be fragmented and distributed, with each fragment providing the same direct line as the undivided bodily relics had done; further, the power of the bodily relics could be transferred to non-corporeal or secondary relics, that is, objects or materials that had merely been in contact with the saint's remains, and could then be used in the same way as the bodily relics.

Powerful as were the relics of saints and martyrs, however, still more powerful were the relics of Jesus Christ himself. These were chiefly from his Passion, and especially from the events surrounding his Crucifixion. According to the Bible, Christ was arrested in Jerusalem because the high priests of the Jews claimed that he was presenting himself as King of the Jews. Brought before the Roman governor, Pontius Pilate, he was condemned to be crucified. First, however, he was whipped (the flagellation as it is called). Then:

> when [the Roman soldiers] had plaited a Crown of Thorns, they put it upon his head, and a reed in his right hand: and they bowed the knee before him, and mocked him, saying, "Hail, King of the Jews." (Matthew 27.29; Carroll and Prickett 1997, II, 42)

This mocking of Christ thus involved a Crown of Thorns being placed on his head instead of a real crown, and a reed in his hand in place of a royal scepter. He was then nailed to the cross and, during this Crucifixion, someone "took a sponge, and filled it with vinegar, and put it on a reed, and gave him to drink" (Matthew 27.48; Carroll and Prickett 1997, II, 42). To speed his death, the Roman soldiers supervising the execution came to break his legs; but when they found that he was dead already:

> one of the soldiers with a spear pierced his side, and forthwith came there out blood and water. (John 19.34; Carroll and Prickett 1997, II, 143)

Aprocyphal versions of the gospels and later texts came to name this soldier Longinus (Livingstone and Cross 1997, 994).

Of course, there could be no question of Christ's body being a relic, because after the Crucifixion he was believed to have risen from the dead and to have ascended directly and bodily into heaven. Nothing of his body was left on earth except the foreskin which had been removed from his penis when he was circumcised according to Jewish custom, and also the blood that had flowed from his side during his Crucifixion. It was believed, however, that Christ's Passion had created a number of secondary relics, which owed their power to having been in contact with his body, or even to having been soaked with his blood. These included the Crown of Thorns, the reed, the sponge, the spear or lance which was used to pierce his side (the Holy Lance as it was called), the wood of the actual cross (the True Cross), and the nails used in the Crucifixion. There were also secondary relics from the earlier period of his life, including his swaddling clothes in which he had been wrapped as a baby.

Nothing seems to have been known of these secondary relics of Christ in the first centuries after his Crucifixion. But writers of the end of the fourth and beginning of the fifth century, for example the church historian Rufinus of Aquileia and the Bishop of Milan, Ambrose, recorded a tradition that Helen, mother of the first Christian emperor Constantine, had discovered the True Cross on the site of Christ's Crucifixion (Mount Calvary) just outside Jerusalem. According to Rufinus, "part of it she presented to her son, and part she put in silver reliquaries and left in the place where it is still kept," which is in the Church of the Holy Sepulchre in Jerusalem (quoted by H. A. Klein 2004, 33). She was also supposed to have discovered at the same time the Holy Lance, and two of the nails used to nail him to the cross. She left the Holy Lance in Jerusalem, where it was enshrined in the church of St. Simon, but the two nails she sent to her son Constantine.

Whatever the truth about Helen's discovery of these relics—and it is certain that she did visit the Holy Land in 326 and founded churches at the Mount of Olives in Jerusalem and at Bethlehem—the True Cross was being venerated at Jerusalem, in the church of the Holy Sepulchre built over the supposed site of Christ's grave, from the mid-fourth century, for the contemporary writer Cyril of Jerusalem (d. 387) mentions it. In 455, there is mention of the office of "guardian of the True Cross" at the church of the Holy Sepulchre, and there is mention of a procession around 570 that culminated in oil being blessed by contact with the True Cross in one of the chapels of the church of the Holy Sepulchre, where it was kept along with other relics of Christ's passion, including the notice naming him as King of the Jews that was placed over his cross, the sponge, and the reed that was placed in his hand when he was mocked by the soldiers (Frolow 1961, 58, nos. 18, 35).

In 614, however, Jerusalem was conquered by the Persians, who were not Christians, with important consequences for the relics of Christ. The Holy Lance is supposed to have been taken to Constantinople at this time, and it appears subsequently in the church of St. Mary of the Lighthouse in the Great Palace of the emperors there. As for the relic of the True Cross, attempts were made to conceal it in a vegetable garden, but in the end it had to be given up to the conquerors, who took it back with them to be reviled by their priests. In 622, the Byzantine emperor, Heraclius (610–41), went to war with the Persians to regain the territory they had captured from his empire, including the Holy Land, and—according to some sources—specifically to recover the True Cross. In 630, he defeated the King of Kings of Persia, Chosroes II, and restored the True Cross to Jerusalem. Its presence there was short-lived, however, for in the face of the Arab conquest of the Holy Land in 635 it was removed to Constantinople.

The True Cross was eminently suited as a relic to being distributed as small fragments. Although the portion of it that purportedly was left in Jerusalem by Helen was evidently not large, for it could be fitted into a "small box" (a *loculus* in Latin), from an early date fragments of it were distributed. Sometimes they were given to pilgrims, as in the case of one given by the Patriarch of Jerusalem to a lady-pilgrim, Melania, in 402. Evidently a portion was given the king of Georgia, Wachtang Gourgoslan, during his pilgrimage to the Holy Land around 460, for afterward he gave it to the cathedral at Nikoz. Sometimes, too, portions were stolen by pilgrims and visitors. There was a portion at Apamaea near Antioch, and the churches of Rome also had portions. A reliquary containing one in the Sessorian Church in that city was supposed to have been given by the emperor Constantine himself, and another was given to Pope Leo I by the Patriarch of Jerusalem in 454. So the True Cross was a very widely distributed relic of Christ, even though its principal portions were those in Jerusalem and Constantinople. As we shall see, those in Constantinople remained there only until the thirteenth century, when they were taken to France (below, p. 247).

Relics, however, had the particular characteristic that, unlike palaces, cities, gardens, forests, and so on, they were portable, and could easily be moved from place to place. Using them to send a message of power on behalf of a ruler therefore required them to be anchored in some way in his palace or city, or at least to be made regularly available in such places. For a ruler to be sure of exploiting the potential of relics, they needed to be given a permanent and imposing home, and they needed to be integrated solidly in the perceptions of his subjects or of others, such as ambassadors or fellow rulers, whom he needed to impress. Ownership had to be visible. Hence occurred the construction of new buildings or the modification of existing buildings to accommodate them, and hence also occurred the creation of religious feasts, during which the relics could be publicly displayed and venerated. It is to the ways in which this exploitation of the power of relics was achieved that this chapter now turns.

ENTRIES OF RELICS INTO CITIES

Since relics, of saints and martyrs, but especially those of Christ, were believed to be a source of power, it was believed that their presence in a city would transfer that power to the city itself. From the fourth century onward, relics were often moved (or "translated") into cities. And, just as rulers were received into a city with a ceremonial entry or a triumph as a tribute to their power, their government, or their military success (above, chapter 7), so relics could be received into a city in a similar way. Just as the ruler was powerful, so too were the relics. And because it was believed that the saint in question, or, in the case of the relics of the Passion, Christ himself, continued to live in the relics, treating them as if they were on the same level as a powerful ruler was especially appropriate. The most vivid illustration of the ceremony with which relics were received is provided by a small ivory plaque, now preserved in the cathedral of Trier (Germany), but probably originally from Constantinople, the capital of the Byzantine Empire (Figure 8–1). This shows a chariot drawn by horses or mules. The chariot is grandly decorated with carving, and is strongly reminiscent of the chariots used by emperors for their entries into cities (above p. 206). This chariot is not carrying an emperor, but rather two bishops (identified as such by the vestments they are wearing), who hold between them a reliquary, that is, a casket containing relics. Just as the emperor processed through the city in the course of his entry or his triumph, so here the chariot with the bishops and the reliquary is similarly passing through the city, with the heads of men appearing at the upper level of the building in the background to watch the procession pass, and with other men at the level below this swinging censers to fill the air with incense and increase the holiness of the occasion.

In front of the chariot walk four men carrying candles in their hands. The second one from the right is clearly represented as wearing on his head a crown or diadem, with pendants hanging down on either side of his face. This identifies it as the imperial diadem, and this figure must therefore represent the Byzantine emperor actually taking part in the entry of the relics. So it was not just that the entry of the relics into a city was treated like the entry of a ruler; the ruler himself could take part in it, and in this case clearly quite a humble part, for the emperor is not riding in the chariot but walking.

The connection of this scene with the emperor was probably closer still, for other elements of the scene depicted make it possible to be fairly sure of identifying the actual event

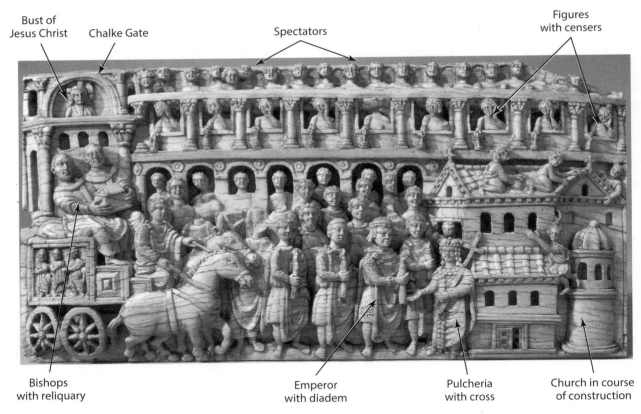

Bust of Jesus Christ — Chalke Gate — Spectators — Figures with censers

Bishops with reliquary — Emperor with diadem — Pulcheria with cross — Church in course of construction

Figure 8–1: Entry of relics into Constantinople, ivory plaque, Trier Cathedral, Trier (Germany), ninth or tenth century.

being represented. According to a ninth-century Byzantine writer called Theophanes the Confessor, the emperor Theodosius II (402–50) was persuaded by his sister Pulcheria to send gifts to Jerusalem: first, a donation for the poor and, second, a golden, jeweled cross to be erected at the place where Jesus Christ had been crucified. In return the Patriarch (or Archbishop) of Jerusalem sent him relics of St. Stephen, the first Christian to have been martyred—in his case by stoning—as is described in the New Testament Acts of the Apostles (Livingstone and Cross 1997, 1540). The emperor's sister, Pulcheria, is supposed to have seen in a vision that these relics were being brought to Constantinople, and

she arose taking her brother with her and went to greet the relics. Receiving them into the palace, she founded a splendid chapel for the holy Protomartyr [St Stephen], and in it she deposited the relics. (quoted by Vikan and Holum 1979, 127)

The Trier ivory panel seems to be a representation of these events, or at least of the ceremonial entry of the relics into Constantinople, with, on the right, the workmen still engaged in finishing the church in which the relics are to be enshrined, so it is likely that this is the church that Pulcheria founded in the palace at Constantinople, while the female figure with the cross standing in front of it to receive the relics is surely Pulcheria herself.

The arrival of the relics of St. Stephen at Constantinople is supposed to have taken place in 421, but Theophanes was writing, as noted above, in the ninth century and the ivory itself, although very difficult to date, may be no earlier than the ninth or even the tenth centuries. So it is possible that the whole story is not factually true and that the entry of the relics of St. Stephen never happened like this. But, even so, the carver of the panel must have been representing an entry of relics into a city that would have been familiar to—or at least convincing to—those who saw his carving. Whatever the details, however, we have a clear image of an entry of relics looking like a ruler entry and being closely associated with the emperor and, in this case, a close family member.

The entry of the relics into a city was a complex and elaborate ceremony, and the Trier ivory panel probably depicts only a part of it. If the church shown being built is indeed the chapel of St. Stephen, then the scene is taking place within the Great Palace of Constantinople, and the gate represented on the left-hand side is the Chalke Gate to that palace, which is known to have had an image of Christ over it at certain periods, as it appears on the ivory panel. So what we are seeing is the end of the procession of the relics, which has passed through the city and is now passing through the palace precinct, before the final stage of the entry in which the relics would be deposited in the church. The first phase, just as with a ruler entry, would have seen the relics met at the gates of the city, just as a ruler was. According to the account in the Life of St. Symeon Stylites the Elder, when his relics arrived at the city of Antioch in Asia Minor in 459,

> the entire city went out to greet the incredible sight, everyone clad in white, with candles, lamps, and hymns, all shouting and saying: "Our shepherd has come bringing to us a heavenly treasure which is beyond price. Make open the gates of the city, while men rejoice and the earth is made glad." (Vikan and Holum 1979, 117)

If relics of saints were important enough to be treated with entries in this ruler-like way, the entries of those directly connected with Jesus Christ himself were treated with even more elaborate ceremony, as, for example, when King Louis IX of France (1226–70) obtained from the Latin emperor of Constantinople, Baldwin II (1228–61), relics of Christ's Passion. The relic of the Crown of Thorns arrived outside the city of Sens, near Paris, on August 9, 1239. According to the Archbishop of Sens, Gautier Cornut, the king himself, came to meet it, just as the Emperor Theodosius had evidently done prior to the scene represented in the Trier ivory. But Louis IX went a step further, for in deference to the power of the relic he came barefoot, dressed only in a tunic rather than in his royal robes. Just as Theodosius's sister Pulcheria was involved in the entry of the relics of St. Stephen, so at Sens the king's brother, Robert of Artois, was also present—and he too was simply dressed, and accompanied by knights, all barefoot as a sign of their humility toward the relic. The king and his brother took the reliquary containing the Crown of Thorns on their shoulders and carried it to the cathedral of Sens where it was displayed to the people, before the king took it in the same humble manner into Paris. Other relics of Christ's Passion, including fragments of the True Cross, the sponge, and the Holy Lance, were received in 1241 with similar ceremony.

Figure 8–2: King Henry III carrying the Holy Blood in procession to Westminster (Cambridge, Corpus Christi College, MS 16, fol. 216r), an illustration from Matthew Paris, *Chronica Majora*.

Across the Channel, the contemporary chronicler, Matthew Paris, described how the king of England, Henry III, received from various senior churchmen in the Holy Land, including the Patriarch of Jerusalem, a portion of the Holy Blood, which had flowed from Christ's side at his Crucifixion. The reception of this relic consisted of the king leading a procession on foot all the way from St. Paul's Cathedral in the east of London to Westminster Abbey and the Palace of Westminster in the west. He carried the Holy Blood in a crystal vase in his own hands, the relic sheltered under a canopy (or palanquin) carried by four men, just as a ruler himself would have been sheltered during a procession (Figure 8–2). Accompanied by the monks of Westminster, he then carried the relic around Westminster Abbey and the apartments of the Palace of Westminster before presenting it to the monks to be enshrined in the abbey.

Not all translations of relics into cities were as vividly documented as these, but it is likely that many had the same sort of elements, making the arrival of the relics resemble the arrival of a ruler. When, for example, the relics of the great military saint, Mercurius, were translated into the city of Benevento in southern Italy by its ambitious duke, Arechis (758–87), there was a ceremony of handing over the keys of the city to the saint, just as living rulers might accept the keys of the city at its gate in the course of their entries (above, pp. 224, 225).

RELICS AS GUARDIANS

Relics were believed to guarantee a city's safety, just as a ruler was expected to do, because they were believed to represent the special protecton of the city by the saint or by Christ.

When in 386 Ambrose, bishop of Milan, discovered in his city the relics of two early Christian martyrs, Gervasius and Protasius, he preached a sermon, declaring that he had been looking for defenders for his flock, and that he had found them in these martyrs:

> These are the sort of defenders which I wish for, these are the sort of soldiers which I have; these are not earthly soldiers, but soldiers of Christ. (quoted by Bozóky 2006, 35)

According to the *Church History* of Sokrates, written between 438 and 443, when Helen sent a portion of the True Cross to her son Constantine in Constantinople:

> He, being persuaded that the city would be perfectly secure where that relic should be preserved, privately enclosed it in his own statue, which stands on a large column of porphyry in the forum called Constantine's at Constantinople (quoted by H. A. Klein 2004, 36).

The story may not be true, and Sokrates appeals to the accounts given by the citizens of Constantinople as his only authority, but it clearly shows the belief in his time that relics defended cities.

Similarly, the city of Apamea in Asia Minor possessed a portion of the cross. According to the sixth-century writer Procopius of Caesarea, the citizens believed that this would be "a great protection for themselves and for the city" (quoted by H. A. Klein 2004, 37). When Constantinople was besieged in 626 by the people from the steppes called the Avars, and again in 717–18 by the Arabs, relic processions formed part of the arrangements for the defense of the city. In the first siege, the relic of the True Cross was taken in procession around the city walls, together with the robe of the Blessed Virgin Mary. In the second siege, the procession also involved the True Cross. In the time of the emperor Michael II (820–29), while the Slavs were attacking Constantinople, it is recorded that his son Theophilos and the patriarch Antonios led a similar procession around the walls of Constantinople, carrying the "lifegiving wood of the cross and the robe of the most holy Mother of God," while the emperor himself led his army against the enemy (Baynes 1949, 258–59; H. A. Klein 2004, 56).

Such practices can be found right across the Middle Ages. In 1204, for example, the city of Bruges in modern Belgium had acquired some of the Holy Blood of Christ. From at least 1291 when the first reference to this occurs in our sources, this holy relic was taken every year on a procession organized by the craft guilds of the city. From at least 1303, this procession made a circuit of the city's walls which had been built in 1297 (A. Brown 2011, 8–10). The holy relic was evidently expected to reinforce the protection of the walls against enemies, and perhaps also to strengthen the unity of the urban community living within them.

Relics, however, were not just about defending cities from attack; they were also—or so it appears from the texts that have come down to us—about protecting the people who lived in the city, and also in the wider territories or kingdom around it. In the sixth century, the Frankish queen Radegund, who was living in a nunnery in Poitiers (France), asked King Sigibert of the Franks for permission to approach the Byzantine emperor for a portion of the True Cross, giving as a reason that this was "for the salvation of the whole country and the stability of the kingdom" (Bozóky 2006, 53). The first of these expressions was entirely religious in character, but the second surely embodied a political dimension. The relics really were believed to guarantee, through their power, the rule of the king.

There are many other examples of such statements. When the code of laws of the Franks called the Salic Law was revised in 763–64, the preface stated that the people of the Franks would receive "bounty, peace, joy, and happiness" from Jesus Christ, because, whereas the pagan Romans had burned the bodies of martyrs, mutilated them, and thrown them to the beasts, the Franks had adorned them with gold and precious stones. Even more clearly, when the Breton potentate Solomon made grants to a priory at a place called Plélan in 869, he gave it the relics of a saint called Maixent "to increase the happiness and peace of all Brittany." And, according to a twelfth-century account, the king of Asturias in northern Spain, Alfonso III the Great (d. 910), brought the holy ark (a container or reliquary containing many important relics) from Toledo to his new capital city of Oviedo "for the stability of the kingdom and for his salvation and that of all the people" (quoted by Bozóky 2006, 58–62, 68). Aside from their purely religious function of giving direct access to God, relics were evidently expected to promote peace and to repress rebellion. So the close association of rulers and relics enhanced the power of the former—in this case, the power deriving from their proximity to the divine—in ways that were explicitly political.

RELICS AND CAPITAL CITIES

In view of all this, it seems natural that, when rulers established capital cities, they wanted to concentrate in them as much of the power of relics as possible. The belief that relics promoted stability, and were powerful in the defense of cities, made collections of them especially appropriate for capital cities. If they were to be the main centers of power, they should have the most extensive and potent collections of relics. So it is no surprise to find that Constantinople, the principal city of the Byzantine Empire, had one of the richest relic collections in Europe, including a relic of the True Cross, the Holy Lance, relics of Christ's apostles, the head of St. John the Baptist, the relics of the Old Testament prophet Samuel, the relics of the first martyr, Stephen, and the robe of the Blessed Virgin Mary, and her shroud and girdle as well as Jesus's swaddling clothes with the marks of drops of her milk on them. To these were added in the tenth century the Mandylion, a cloth on which was believed to be imprinted a reflection of Christ's face, and the sandals he had worn. In the eleventh century was added the letter that Christ himself was believed to have written to Abgar, king of Edessa, and in the twelfth century the stone on which Christ's body was supposed to have been laid out after the Crucifixion.

Most of these relics were kept in the Great Palace, which was the real power hub of Constantinople and of the Byzantine Empire. Although at least one fragment of the True Cross seems to have been in the great church of Haghia Sophia, which lay just outside the palace, most of the relics were in the church of St. Mary of the Lighthouse, which had been rebuilt by the emperor Michael III in 864, and lay at the heart of the inner palace, called the "sacred palace" or the Boukoléon. This church was the palace church par excellence, close to the public and private centers of the palace, its services conducted by the emperor's own clergy.

It was the principal focus for the veneration of the True Cross and the Holy Lance, and it was there that visiting rulers, such as Amaury, the Crusader king of Jerusalem, were shown the relic collection.

The belief that the presence of a relic enhanced the standing of a city was made stronger by the fact that, at least since the ninth century, relics had been believed to have a mind of their own, or at least to be able to make choices by mediating the wishes of the saint to whom they belonged or, in the case of Passion relics, of Christ. So, when the relics of St. Benedict, sixth-century author of the Rule of St. Benedict, were stolen from Monte Cassino in southern Italy and brought to the abbey of Fleury (Saint-Benoît-sur-Loire) in France, this theft was considered to have been permitted by the saint. He wished to be moved, so his relics allowed themselves to be stolen. Thus, the fact that relics allowed themselves to be brought into a city was itself a sign of the favor in which the saint held that city. It is clear enough how their presence could have been translated into a message of power on the ruler's behalf.

The importance of such a relic collection to the making of a capital city was consequently all the greater. It appears clearly in what happened subsequently to Constantinople's relic collection. After the capture of the city by the army of the Fourth Crusade in 1204, a Latin (that is a western European), Baldwin I of Flanders (1204–5), was installed there as emperor. When one of his successors, Baldwin II (1228–61), was chronically short of money, Louis IX, king of France, managed to obtain from him the relic of the Crown of Thorns for his own capital of Paris, by paying a large sum of money, the amount he was prepared to pay underlining the relic's importance to Louis. The Archbishop of Sens, Gautier Cornut, regarded Louis IX's obtaining of the Crown of Thorns as a sign of God's favorable attitude to the Kingdom of France: "God chose our France especially so that the Lord's name might be praised from East to West" (quoted by Bozóky 2007, 29). The service book called the Antiphonary of Sens treated the Crown of Thorns as having been sent to the king of France to seal an alliance with God that would last until the Last Judgment. The service book for devotion to the Crown of Thorns in Paris addressed the city itself in this way:

> To you, O famous city,
> endowed with every praise, mother
> of learning, the Crown [of Thorns] was
> entrusted; in you it was placed, city of Paris.
>
> (quoted by M. Cohen 2010, 96)

The Passion relics' importance was therefore political—as a symbol showing how close the king was to the divine—and they were important for the standing of his capital city.

The belief that the ability of a ruler to create a relic collection was a sign of the favor he enjoyed with God, Jesus Christ, and the saints was all the more reason for rulers with ambitions to create capital cities for their realms to build up such collections. When the eighth-century Duke of Benevento in southern Italy, Arechis, was establishing the city of Benevento as his capital, he obtained for it the relics of the Twelve Martyrs who had been killed in the time of the persecutions of Christians in southern Italy, and he ordered his realm to be dedicated to them. A little later, in 763, his officer brought from Constantinople the relics of St. Helianus, one of the forty martyrs who were supposed to have died at a city called Sebasteia.

In 768, Duke Arechis had the relics of Mercurius, who was in fact a local saint but was identified with the great Byzantine military saint of that name, translated to Benevento. St. Mercurius was one of the great military saints of the neighboring Byzantine Empire, and the martyr was made patron of Arechis's duchy of Benevento and was called the protector of the city and of the people. Like the saints mentioned above, he was believed to have organized his own translation to Benevento, by declaring in a dream vision that this was his wish, by giving the location of his grave also in a dream, and by showing exactly where his relics were during the excavation, also by means of a dream. Finally, after Duke Arechis's time, between 821 and 836, the relics of St. Januarius were stolen from Naples and brought to Benevento by two counts, Sico and Sicardus, leaving the inhabitants lamenting (according to the account of the translation) that "the city's protection is now removed, for our father Januarius, who has protected us for so long, has been taken away from us." Benevento was the gainer, Naples the loser.

Relics then could convey the message that a capital city, and the realm it dominated, were especially favored, and that the ruler who ruled them was correspondingly favored by the saints, or the martyrs, or Christ himself. In the case of the church of St. Mary of the Lighthouse in Constantinople, the relics enshrined there also symbolized the military expansion of the Byzantine Empire, especially between 944 and 1032 when the emperors were pushing back their frontiers in the Middle East, including the Holy Land, and the lands south of the River Danube. It was, for example, from Edessa—not outside the empire but close to where the emperor was campaigning—that there were brought to Constantinople the Mandylion and the letter of Christ to King Abgar, and from Syria, and other areas of Byzantine military campaigning, that there were brought the sandals of Christ.

The relics also reinforced the idea that Constantinople was a sort of Heavenly Jerusalem, so that the emperor's proximity to God was underlined by the resemblance of his city to God's city. In 1200, when there was a revolt in Constantinople, the guardian of the relics, Nicolas Mesarites, dissuaded rebellious workmen from doing damage by declaring that, because Constantinople possessed Christ's swaddling clothes and shroud, as well as the True Cross, the Crown of Thorns, the Lance, and the Reed, it was in effect Jerusalem and the other places of the Holy Land, including Nazareth and Bethlehem. The city should therefore not be molested or damaged (Magdalino 2004, 27).

Nothing shows more clearly that the same ideas were at work in Paris in the thirteenth century than that the church which King Louis IX built to hold the relics of the Passion, that is the Sainte-Chapelle, was in the Palais de la Cité in the heart of Paris. Just as the church of St. Mary of the Lighthouse was at the heart of the Great Palace of Constantinople, so the Sainte-Chapelle was at the heart of the royal palace. In his first and second document establishing the Sainte-Chapelle's foundation, Louis IX was explicit that it was designed and built specifically to hold the relics of the Passion:

> That venerable and holy chapel, in which the most sacred crown of the Lord, the True Cross, and many other precious relics are located, which should be honoured with perpetual praise to God, so that this place should benefit for all time from frequent devotions of divine service. (quoted by Sauerländer 2007, 117)

Figure 8–3: East end of the Sainte-Chapelle, Paris (France) (Paris, Musée du Moyen Âge, Bénédictionnaire-Missel du Duc, fol. 83v), an illustration from the Benedictional of the Duke of Bedford, showing the high altar and the reliquaries under the ciborium (canopy), and the Duke of Bedford (who was then the ruler of Paris) praying before the altar. (See insert for color version of this image.)

That the chapel was designed for this purpose is shown by the arrangements at the east end, which can be seen in its original condition in an illustration in the fifteenth-century Benedictional of the Duke of Bedford (Figure 8–3). This shows behind the high altar a gallery, which still exists in reduced form, with spiral staircases on either side of the high altar giving access to it. The gallery, open at the front, gave access to the reliquaries containing the relics of Christ's Passion with over them an elaborate ciborium or canopy. The reliquaries would have been seen against the painted glass in the windows of the chapel, so that the effect would have been spectacular and mysterious. If the illustration in the Benedictional of the Duke of Bedford gives a realistic impression, the reliquaries were in a position high enough to dominate the whole chapel and to be seen by anyone entering it (Sauerländer 2007, 119).

The décor of the chapel was focused on the relics. The surviving painted glass in the windows contains scenes of Christ's Passion, with the window showing Christ wearing the Crown of Thorns forming a backdrop to the shrine. The twelve statues of the apostles in niches against the walls carry in their hands crosses, which can be interpreted as consecration crosses of the chapel but must surely also be allusions to the True Cross in the shrine on the gallery. The martyrs, who are represented in the quadrilobed painted panels on the walls, were surely being presented as the successors of Christ, receiving their crowns just as he received the Crown of Thorns. In a classic book, Robert Branner (1965, 57) argued that, in the Sainte-Chapelle, "the extensive gilding of the masonry, the backgrounds of the frescoes, which resemble enamels and chased gold, the angels in the dado spandrels and the statues of the Apostles affixed to the sides of the building strongly suggest a contemporary gold and enamel reliquary turned outside-in." The chapel was itself a reliquary designed and built to hold the relics of Christ's Passion.

The Sainte-Chapelle was a two-story chapel, with the principal chapel in which the Passion relics were held at first-floor level, and a rather lower—but also quite magnificent—chapel at ground-floor level. This may have been intended to reflect the design of the chapel at Golgotha on Mount Calvary, where the Crucifixion was believed to have taken place, and perhaps also the Church of the Holy Sepulchre at Jerusalem, which was also two-storied, and the contemporary dimensions of which seem to have influenced those of the Sainte-Chapelle (Gasser 2007). In the upper chapel of the Sainte-Chapelle, the reliquaries themselves may have been intended to call to mind the sacred shrine of the temple in Jerusalem as described in the Old Testament of the Bible, that is, the Ark of the Covenant as it was conceived in the Middle Ages in western Europe—mounted on supports of which the supports of the tribune in the Sainte-Chapelle were reminiscent (Bozóky 2007, 31). The message being conveyed would have been that the French king was as much favored by God in the possession of the relics of Christ, as biblical kings such as Solomon had been in the possession of the Ark of the Covenant.

RELICS OF CHRIST AND ROYAL ASSOCIATION WITH THE DIVINE

In other ways too the relics of Christ's Passion were ideal objects to be associated with kings and their capitals. Christ himself was regarded as a king, albeit not the sort of earthly king of the Jews that his persecutors envisaged, but a king nonetheless, which is why his entry into Jerusalem before his Crucifixion was seen as the entry of a ruler (above, pp. 236–38). When the Crown of Thorns was placed on Christ's head by the Roman soldiers, the intention was to mock him, but it was nonetheless a crown. In Christian eyes, his humility as the Son of God in enduring this mockery flowed from his power as a heavenly king. So, in the Christian world, kings wanted to be associated with him, to prove that they ruled by his authority, and nothing could show this better than the fact that they possessed and venerated the Crown of Thorns that had been placed on his head. It was par excellence a royal, Christian symbol, and for it to be at the heart of a capital city, as it was at the Sainte-Chapelle, was exactly what a medieval king wished for. Because of their association with Christ the heavenly king, the True Cross and the other relics of Christ's Passion had similar importance for medieval kings.

Also, the divisibility of both the Crown of Thorns and the True Cross made them very suitable relics for kings to possess, because parts of them—fragments of the True Cross and thorns from the Crown of Thorns—could be distributed as royal gifts, especially to allies and favored fellow rulers. A great many fragments of the True Cross were distributed in this way from Constantinople. In 872, for example, ambassadors of the Byzantine emperor, Basil I (867–86), gave a reliquary of the True Cross to the east Frankish ruler Louis the German (806–76) at Regensburg in Germany; and at the beginning of the eleventh century another was given to the son of the king of Hungary (Frolow 1961, 85–86, no. 203). Such relics were also distributed from Paris: between 1364 and 1380 the king of France, Charles V, sent a fragment of the True Cross from the Sainte-Chapelle to the Grand Master of the Teutonic Order, a military order engaged in campaigns against heathens in eastern Europe (Frolow 1961, no. 745); and around 1370 the same king sent to his brother, Louis of Anjou, a "polyptych" to place at the back of an altar, richly decorated, and containing relics of the True Cross, the Crown of Thorns, the Holy Lance, the reed that Christ had in his hand while he was mocked by the soldiers, the sponge, the garment he was wearing just before his Crucifixion, together with other Passion relics (Frolow 1961, no. 753). Even when relics were not presented to foreign rulers in this way, they could still be distributed to monasteries and churches in foreign lands as symbols of the ruler's dominance over, or association with, them.

The ruler could also have the role of mediator between his subjects and relics, especially relics of Christ's Passion. He could, for example, be closely involved in the religious services that took place around those relics. In Constantinople in the tenth century, for example, the emperor had a prominent part in "adoring" the True Cross at the church of St. Mokios, while a fragment of it was being taken on procession through the city (Frolow 1961, no. 129), and for the same period we hear of the emperors coming to kiss that relic during the festival of its "adoration," on the third Sunday of Lent (Frolow 1961, no. 143).

At the Sainte-Chapelle in Paris, the connection between the relics of Christ's Passion and the ruler was even more strongly underlined. The king was presenting himself as the mediator between God and his people. It was he who was responsible for the relics; he had the keys to the shrine (although the treasurer had another set); and it was he who personally undertook the "display" (*ostensio*) of the relics on Good Friday (Figure 8–4).

As we have seen in the case of King Louis IX's obtaining relics of Christ's Passion for Paris, a ruler could play an important, and sometimes very personal, role in obtaining relics for his capital city. In the case we are about to look at, that of Karlštejn in the kingdom of Bohemia, the relics obtained by the ruler were kept not in the capital city of Prague itself but in a fortified palace some twenty miles away, from which they were regularly taken into the city to be displayed to the faithful. Charles IV, king of Bohemia, had begun to build this fortified palace in 1348, and, whatever may have been his original plan for it, by 1357 (for which date we have a foundation charter creating a college of priests to say services in the

Figure 8–4: Louis IX undertaking the "display" (*ostensio*) of the True Cross (Cambridge, Corpus Christi College, MS 16, fol. 141v), an illustration from Matthew Paris, *Chronica Majora*. Note the apparently specially constructed wooden stage on which this is taking place. The king, who is labeled and wears his crown, holds the True Cross in his draped hands, and the words coming out of his mouth read, *Ecce crucem Domini* ("Here is the cross of the Lord"). Below him, another figure holds up the Crown of Thorns.

various chapels at Karlštejn) it was dominated by chapels, of which there were no less than five, with the most important of them in the highest and most commanding position.

The layout of Karlštejn is best appreciated by following the sequence of buildings and spaces that anyone entering the palace would have passed through, as seen in an oblique aerial view (Figure 8–5). The castle is nowadays entered by the gate, of which the defensive tower is visible in the lower right-hand corner of the image. In the fourteenth century, however, it would have been entered by the Vorsilka Gate on the left side of the image. Crossing the bailey through another imposing gate, the residential part of the castle known as the "imperial palace" was reached. In addition to chambers and halls for living, this contained two chapels, dedicated respectively to St. Nicholas and St. Palmatius (the latter later re-dedicated to St. Wenceslas), although little remains of them. Beyond the "imperial palace," and rising up the slope, stood the tower known as the Lesser Tower. When first built, this too may have contained chambers and halls for living, but by 1357 it had been rebuilt so that its principal feature was two chapels on the first floor, that of the Blessed Virgin Mary with the much smaller chapel of St. Catherine opening from it. These chapels were extremely impressive chiefly because of their wall paintings and wall decorations. But neither was the most impressive chapel in the palace. From the chapel of the Blessed Virgin Mary, a bridge (rebuilt in the nineteenth century but probably on the site of the original) leads to the first floor of the Great Tower, occupying the highest part of the site. From the end of the bridge, a staircase winds upward to the second floor of the Great Tower. There, it opens into one of the most lavishly decorated spaces to survive from anywhere in medieval Europe, and perhaps one of the most lavishly decorated spaces ever built: the chapel of the Signs of the Passion. This was where the relics of Christ's Passion that Charles IV had acquired were kept, at least from 1357, when the foundation charter referred to it as being dedicated to "the Signs of the Passion" (Figure 8–6).

The chapel was intended to represent the Heavenly Jerusalem so that it would be the most appropriate place for relics that related to Christ's Passion in the earthly Jerusalem. The staircase that provided access to the chapel was itself treated as a religious space, for it was painted with scenes from the life of St. Wenceslas going up, and scenes from the life of St. Ludmila coming down. The intention may have been to associate it with the ladder, which—according to the Old Testament of the Bible—Jacob saw in a vision, admittedly with angels rather than saints going up and down between Heaven and the place where he was sleeping. If this association was indeed intended, the chapel to which the staircase led would have been the Heavenly Jerusalem, to which Jacob's Ladder similarly led (Studničková 2009).

The chapel itself is stunning, for its walls are lavishly clad with semi-precious stones. The use of these jewels further contributed to making this chapel an image of the Heavenly Jerusalem (Plumpe 1943; Möseneder 1981). In the Old Testament, the prophet Isaiah was thought to have been referring to Jerusalem, when he made God say to the Jews:

I will lay thy stones with fair colours, and lay thy foundations with sapphires. And I will make thy windows of agates, and thy gates of carbuncles, and thy borders of pleasant stones. (Isaiah 54.11–12; Carroll and Prickett 1997, II, 816)

Figure 8–5: Oblique aerial view of Karlštejn Castle (Czech Republic). The castle is sited on the hillside above the village which lies to the right.

Figure 8–6: Interior of the Chapel of the Signs of the Passion, Karlštejn Castle (Czech Republic), with the altar on the right. Notice the plates of semi-precious stone covering the lower part of the walls, the paintings of saints by Master Theodoricus above them, and the golden vaults decorated with stars to represent the heavens. The metal altar screen is original. (See insert for color version of this image.)

More explicitly, in the New Testament the Book of Revelation describes a vision of the Heavenly Jerusalem which will appear at the end of the world as shining with and being built of semi-precious stones:

> Her light was like unto a stone most precious, even like a jasper stone, clear as crystal . . . And the building of the wall [of the city] was of jasper; and the city was pure gold, like unto clear glass. And the foundations of the wall of the city were garnished with all manner of precious stones. The first foundation was jasper, the second, sapphire; the third, a chalcedony; the fourth, an emerald; the fifth, sardonyx; the sixth, sardius; the seventh, chrysolite; the eighth, beryl; the ninth, a topaz; the tenth, chrysoprasus; the eleventh, a jacinth; the twelfth, an amethyst. And the twelve gates were twelve pearls; every several gate was of one pearl: and the street of the city was pure gold, as it were transparent glass. (Revelation 21.11–20; Carroll and Prickett 1997, II, 318)

In the Chapel of the Signs of the Passion, the semi-precious stones of various types set into a background of gold in the lower part of the walls must have been intended to bring to mind these visions (Figure 8–6). Especially striking is the use of jasper, which corresponds to John the Evangelist's vision in the Book of Revelation, as is the use of translucent semi-precious stones in the windows, which corresponds directly to Isaiah's prophecy, "I will make thy windows of agates" (Isaiah, 54.12; Carroll and Prickett 1997, I, 816).

The image of the Chapel of the Signs of the Passion as the Heavenly Jerusalem is reinforced by the panel paintings with which the upper parts of the walls are covered. These are the work of a great fourteenth-century painter, Master Theodoricus, and they represent Christ's Crucifixion, above the high altar, and a Man of Sorrows (that is Jesus Christ as he was mocked), together with numerous portraits of saints. These are arranged around the painting of the Crucifixion, with the angels and archangels alongside them, so as to represent the most holy figures arranged around Christ in heaven, the "court of heaven" on the walls of the Karlštejn chapel, just as they were no doubt envisaged in the Heavenly Jerusalem. But these paintings also take us back to the relics, not just of Christ's Passion, but also of the saints themselves who are represented. For each painting has in the bottom of its frame a compartment in which there has been placed a relic of the saint whose portrait it is. Even more than the Sainte-Chapelle, this chapel is like a great reliquary, not just for the relics of Christ's Passion, but also for the relics of a multitude of saints.

The Chapel of the Signs of the Passion housed the relics of Christ's Passion, but it is a remarkable series of wall paintings in the chapel of the Blessed Virgin Mary in the Lesser Tower that graphically represents the extent of Charles IV's personal involvement in obtaining these and in enshrining them. The first of these paintings is believed to show him receiving a thorn from the Crown of Thorns from the French dauphin, the future King Charles V (Figure 8–7).The second shows a green-clad ruler also handing a relic to Charles IV. This ruler is not identified but may be Peter of Lusignan, king of Cyprus, or Louis the Great, king of Hungary, or Aloysius Gonzaga, duke of Mantua, from whom Charles IV received a relic of the sponge (Rosario 2000, ch. 2). At all events, the two paintings clearly show Charles IV receiving relics from other rulers. Especially notable is the emphasis the painter has placed on his crown, which is the crown not of the kingdom of Bohemia, but of the Holy Roman

Empire, clearly recognizable by its shape with the arch across the top of it. Since Charles IV is shown receiving relics from rulers who are wearing royal or ducal—but not imperial—crowns, perhaps their exact identity is less important than the idea being projected that Charles IV is receiving relics as an emperor from subject kings.

The third scene shows Charles IV with what is apparently a small wooden cross between his finger and thumb, which he is inserting into a large, golden cross on the altar (Figure 8–8).This golden cross is almost certainly the one preserved in the treasury of St. Vitus's Cathedral in Prague as the Reliquary Cross of Bohemia, and referred to in Charles IV's letter to the pope on December 21, 1357 as the newly made "solemn cross of pure gold and the most precious pearls," in which he has had placed "part of the wood of the True Cross, a thorn from the Crown of Thorns, Christ's sponge, and a relic of St John the Baptist, as well as many other relics" (Homolka 1998, p. 96).

The wall paintings in the Chapel of the Blessed Virgin Mary seem to lead the viewer toward the entrance to the passage which itself leads into St. Catherine's Chapel (on the right of Figure 8–7). This little chapel is another richly decorated space, with the same use of semi-precious stones to cover the walls as we have seen in the Chapel of the Signs of the Passion. Its function is uncertain, but perhaps the relics of Christ's Passion were kept in it while the Chapel of the Signs of the Passion was being built.

Karlštejn, in short, was nothing less than a palace for relics. Although it had been built before Charles IV's time, and the Greater Tower was certainly defensive in character as originally built, Charles IV modified it to make relics its raison d'être. It was a palace that had the potential to convey the message of power that the ruler was entrusted with relics of the very holiest character, and that his power was such that he could create for them buildings that were both secure and incomparably rich in their decoration. Clearly, Karlštejn's message must have been that Charles IV was a ruler close to God.

Two of the relics of Christ in particular, the True Cross and the Lance, also had more specific connotations for rulers, because they came to be closely associated with rulers' military campaigns, and above all with their victories. The True Cross indeed became quite simply a symbol of victory, as is apparent already in the case of the first Christian emperor, Constantine (306–37). According to his biographer, Eusebius of Caesarea, Constantine won his decisive victory over his pagan rival Maxentius at the Battle of the Milvian Bridge following a vision of the cross in the sky, in response to which he placed that symbol on the shields of his soldiers. In the later fourth century, in the imperial cities of Milan and then Ravenna (Italy), the Roman emperors who succeeded Constantine abandoned the traditional symbols of imperial power in favor of the cross, which became the Cross of Victory. It was only a short step from this to using a relic of the True Cross as a victory-bringing object to carry in warfare. The contemporary writer Theophylact Simokatta relates that, when the Byzantine emperor Maurice (582–602) went to war, "the wood of Christ's cross was raised aloft on a golden pole," and carried before the emperor as he led his army on campaign (quoted by H. A. Klein 2004, 40). In the tenth century, in the reign of the Byzantine emperor Constantine VII Porphyrogenitus (913–59), a treatise on warfare, closely associated with the emperor himself, explains that when the emperor and his army go on campaign a relic of the True Cross is carried to bring victory, and a jeweled representation

Figure 8–7: Emperor Charles IV receiving relics from fellow rulers and placing them in a reliquary cross, painting on the west wall of the Chapel of the Blessed Virgin Mary, Karlštejn Castle (Czech Republic). (See insert for color version of this image.)

of the Cross was used as a standard. The chamberlain, according to this text, marched in the middle of the vanguard of military officers "carrying the holy and life-giving wood of the Cross with the case about his neck," while in front of the officers there marched the standard-bearer carrying "a golden, jewelled cross" (quoted by H. A. Klein 2004, 57). The cross was used as the ruler's standard in battle in the period of the Carolingian kings in the eighth and ninth centuries, for the early ninth-century tract called the *Libri Carolini* states: "The cross is the ensign of our king . . . our host follows the cross into battle" (quoted by Rosario 2000, 44). After the armies of the First Crusade had conquered Jerusalem from the Saracens in 1099, it was believed—or at any rate claimed—that they had found the True Cross, or at least a portion of it, in the city. According to the historian Albert of Aix, it had not come to light at the point that the Crusader army marched to attack the port of Ascalon. But, as soon as it was discovered, the patriarch of Jerusalem, Arnulf, and Peter the Hermit rushed to take it to reinforce the army. At the capture of the city of Caesarea in 1101, it was carried with the

Figure 8–8: Emperor
Charles IV placing relics in
a reliquary cross, detail of
paintings on the west wall,
Chapel of the Blessed Virgin
Mary, Karlštejn Castle
(Czech Republic). (See
insert for color version of
this image.)

army by the patriarch Daimbert. Other Crusade-period writers, such as Fulcher of Chartres
and William of Tyre, confirm that the True Cross and other relics routinely accompanied
the Crusader armies.

There survives in the imperial treasury in Vienna a gold and jeweled reliquary cross,
known as the Imperial Cross. It was almost certainly used as a battle standard by medieval
rulers, for it bears the following inscription:

> Before this cross of the Lord may the followers of the evil enemy flee; and therefore may all
> opponents retreat also from before you, Conrad. (quoted by Anon. 1987, 155)

The dating of this Imperial Cross, which is based on the style of its decoration, shows that
the Conrad in question was the German king, Conrad II (1024–39), who was Holy Roman
Emperor from 1034, although the cross was certainly also used by his successors even
though it had his name on it. The inscription suggests that the cross was intended to be car-

Figure 3–1: Dado tiling, Patio de las Donacellas, Palace of Pedro the Cruel, Alcázar, Seville (Spain).

Figure 3–2: Studiolo, Palace of Federico of Montefeltro, Urbino (Italy).

Figure 3–18: Miniature showing throne of Emperor Theodosius the Great (379–95).

Figure 3–29: Sanctuary pavement, Westminster Abbey, Westminster (England).

Figure II–1: Château of Dourdan and its garden and park (Très Riches Heures of the Duke of Berry, April).

Figure 4–2: Palais de la Cité, Paris (France) and its gardens (Très Riches Heures of the Duke of Berry, June, detail).

Figure 4–8: Mosaic, King Roger's Room, Palace of the Normans, Palermo (Sicily).

Figure 4–11: Fountain of Life represented in the Godescalc Evangelistary.

Figure 4–13: "Garden of Love" panel, Palace of Versailles.

Figure 4–15: Detail of the right side of the painting *Family of Henry VIII*, unknown artist, *c.*1545.

Figure 5–6: Hunting boar, Devonshire Hunting Tapestries, Victoria and Albert Museum, London (England).

Figure 5–11: Unicorn leaping into a stream to escape the pursuit of the hunters, Unicorn Tapestries, Cloisters Museum, New York (USA).

Figure 5–13: *St. George and the Dragon* by Albrecht Altdorfer.

Figure 6–8: Palace of the Louvre (Très Riches Heures of the Duke of Berry, October, detail).

Figure 6–22: Palace of Vincennes (Très Riches Heures of the Duke of Berry, December, detail).

Figure 8–3: East end of the Sainte-Chapelle, Paris (France), an illustration from the Benedictional of the Duke of Bedford.

Figure 8–6: Interior, Chapel of the Signs of the Passion, Karlštejn Castle (Czech Republic).

Figure 8–7: Emperor Charles IV receiving relics, painting on the west wall of the Chapel of the Blessed Virgin Mary, Karlštejn Castle (Czech Republic).

Figure 8–8: Detail of Figure 8–7.

Figure 8–9: The Imperial Cross, Schatzkammer, Kunsthistorisches Museum, Vienna (Austria).

Figure 8–11: Henry II of Germany receiving the imperial regalia, an illustration from the Sacramentary of Henry II.

Figure 9–7: Nave of St, St. Mary's Church, the former palace church, Aachen (Germany), looking up to the cupola.

Figure 9–10: Emperor Justinian and his court, mosaic on the north wall of the choir, church of San Vitale, Ravenna (Italy).

Figure 9–15: View westward down the nave, Cappella Palatina, Palace of the Normans, Palermo (Sicily).

Figure 9–16: Gold tesserae cladding the walls, Cappella Palatina, Palace of the Normans, Palermo (Sicily).

Throne

Figure 9–25: View toward the sanctuary, Monreale Cathedral (Italy).

Figure 11–17: St. Wenceslas's Chapel, St. Vitus's Cathedral, Prague (Czech Republic).

Figure 11–19: Wilton Diptych, National Gallery, London (England).

ried in battle to ensure victory over the ruler's enemies. Charles IV of Bohemia had the present foot made for it in the fourteenth century, as a further inscription on it makes this clear. Originally, however, the cross no doubt was fitted on to a shaft to enable it to be held aloft by a standard-bearer as the ruler's army marched along or advanced into battle. This cross was not, however, just a symbol, for it was made to contain two important relics. Between the arms and the square section just above the fourteenth-century foot, the jeweled plate can be opened to reveal a space within the stem. This was occupied by some of what was believed to be the actual wood of the True Cross, which was only removed some time after 1350 when Charles IV made a separate reliquary for it. Up until that time, the Imperial Cross's ability to drive away enemies was evidently believed to derive from the wood of the True Cross within it.

The second relic contained in the Imperial Cross was the Holy Lance with which Christ's side was pierced at the Crucifixion. This relic is still contained within the Imperial Cross, seated below the jeweled plate covering the cross's arms. When that plate is removed, the Holy Lance is visible, neatly fitted into the space under the plate (Figure 8–9). This relic has had a long history of physical change and modification, as recent investigations have shown. Around the spearhead is a "cuff" made of gold, clearly visible in Figure 8–9. On this cuff are inscribed in fourteenth-century script the words, "lance and nail of the Lord." This cuff and inscription, which are probably (based on their date) the work of Charles IV, show that at that time the spearhead was believed to be (or perhaps to have had incorporated into it) the lance or spear that had wounded Christ's side during his Crucifixion. This means that the Holy Lance in the Imperial Cross was being claimed to be the same relic as King Louis IX believed himself to have obtained from Constantinople in the thirteenth century. Perhaps—in the way of the cult of relics—both objects were small parts of the original Holy Lance used at the Crucifixion. In Charles IV's time, it was clearly also believed that one of the nails used to fix Christ to the cross was also somehow embedded in the Holy Lance, perhaps underneath the golden crosses that appear on the iron core.

However, if the fourteenth-century gold cuff is removed, there appears below it another cuff, this one made of silver, and bearing the inscription:

> Henry, by the grace of God the third emperor of the Romans, ordered this silver cuff to be made for the confirmation of the nail of the Lord and the lance of St Maurice. (quoted by Anon. 1987)

This Henry was Henry IV, king of Germany (1056–1105), who was from 1084 the third Holy Roman Emperor of the name of Henry. In his time, the spearhead was evidently believed to have belonged to St. Maurice, who was a Roman soldier martyred in the persecutions of Christians by the Roman emperors, and buried at the monastery of Saint-Maurice in Switzerland. (Presumably, it was believed that he had somehow acquired the spear used to wound Jesus Christ's side in the course of his Crucifixion.) Underneath the silver cuff is yet another cuff, this one made of iron and bearing no inscription; and under that is the spearhead itself, which reveals that the reason for making the first and iron cuff was that the spearhead had a break in it, probably caused by the center of its blade being hollowed out, as is evident in Figure 8–10, so that the cuff was designed to protect it from coming apart.

Figure 8–9: The Imperial Cross, Schatzkammer, Kunsthistorisches Museum, Vienna (Austria). View with the arm plate removed to show the Holy Lance within. Note the gold cuff wrapped around it. (See insert for color version of this image.)

Figure 8–10: The Holy Lance, Schatzkammer, Kunsthistorisches Museum, Vienna (Austria), drawing of the spearhead with the cuffs removed to show the innermost parts (after Kirchweger 2005, 211, fig. III.1).

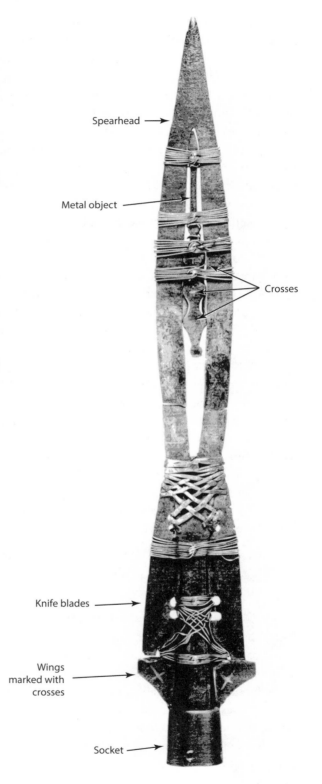

The spearhead itself is made of iron. Beginning at the base, there is visible the socket into which the shaft would have fitted. Immediately above that, the spearhead opens out into two "brackets" or wings, each marked with crosses, and these wings identify the spearhead as belonging to a so-called wing-spear type, known from the Carolingian realms of western Europe in the eighth century. So the spearhead itself certainly cannot be the weapon used to wound Christ's side, nor can it have belonged to the Roman martyr, Maurice, who lived and died in the time of the persecutions of Christians, much earlier than the Carolingian period. Above the wings are two plates, apparently the blades of knives, bound to the spearhead by metal wire and by leather thongs. Their significance is quite unknown. Equally mysterious is the fact that above them the spearhead has been hollowed out to create a space approximately 24cm x 1.5cm. This contains a metal object, pointed at the top, and with three round areas along its length, each marked by a cross laid on in bronze. This object might have been believed to be a nail used in the Crucifixion, although it does not look much like a nail. Possibly the crosses marked in gold on the round areas indicate where tiny fragments of what was believed to be such a nail have been inserted.

Whatever this spearhead originally was, it is possible to trace its history back to the ninth century, when it was already believed to be the Holy Lance used to wound Christ's side, and was kept in a chapel in Modena (Italy). From there, however, it was obtained by a minor king, Rudolf II of Upper Burgundy (880/5–937), who sold it to the German king, Henry I (919–36). That this lance really was the one later inserted into the Imperial Cross is shown by a description of it given by the writer at the German court, Liudprand of Cremona, in 958/62, who describes the knife blades on either side of the center, the opening chiseled in the middle, and the central metal object—he says that the crosses (presumably those on the round parts) mark the position of nails of the Lord (Wolf 2005, 29).

Like the True Cross, the Holy Lance was believed to bring victory to the ruler who possessed it. According to the written sources, Henry I carried this "victory-bringing lance" at the crucial battle he fought against the Magyars on the River Unstrut in 933. When Henry I's successor, Otto I (936–73), fought an even more crucial battle against the Magyars at the Lechfeld, the contemporary writer Widukind of Corvey refers to him fighting the battle after having taken in his hands his shield and the Holy Lance (Wolf 2005, 27–28). To have such a relic in the royal collection of a ruler's capital city or private chapel must have conveyed a message of ideological power relating to his proximity to God.

RELICS AND REGALIA

The importance of relics to rulers lay also in the way in which they came to be merged with regalia, that is, with crowns, scepters, and other objects that singled out the ruler from his subjects. A royal Lombard crown preserved in the treasury at Monza had incorporated into it a nail of Christ's Crucifixion, while the crown of the Kingdom of Bohemia has an inscription explaining that a thorn from the Crown of Thorns forms part of it. These objects were regalia in that kings wore them and were crowned with them, but they were also relics. In addition, the Imperial Crown, now in Vienna, with a bow over it naming Conrad II, by the later Middle Ages came to be regarded as having been the crown of the great Frankish king and first Holy Roman Emperor Charlemagne (768–814), and so as being a holy relic through its association with that saint-ruler.

Just as the Holy Lance could convey a message of power relating to the ruler's ability and success in battle, it could also convey a message relating to the legitimacy of the ruler's power. This derived from its character as a lance, irrespective of its Christian connotations. A lance had been a symbol of rulership from at least the time of ancient Greece. In the Roman world, it was the symbol of the ruler's authority from the earliest times. According to the Roman writer Trogus Pompeius, the early kings of Rome had lances as tokens of their power instead of diadems (Alföldi 1959, 3). A coin, probably of 209 BC, shows the Roman king Latinus, dressed only in a loincloth as was traditional, but carrying a lance which he holds as a symbol rather than as a weapon, and which is much more prominent than that held by the figure facing him (Alföldi 1959, 5, pl. 6.1–5). That the lance was an important symbol of power also for the Germanic barbarians who came to dominate Europe after the collapse of the Roman Empire in the fifth century is indicated by the account of Gregory of Tours which describes how, in the course of the civil wars between the various kings of the Franks that racked their kingdom in the late sixth century, King Guntram resolved to hand over his share of the kingdom to his nephew, King Childebert. According to the contemporary writer, Gregory of Tours:

> King Guntram placed his lance in King Childebert's hand and then he said: "This is a sign that I have handed the whole of my realm over to you. Go now, and by this token take under your own rule all my cities, just as if they were yours." (Thorpe 1974, book 7, ch. 33)

At the beginning of the eleventh century, a lance was represented as a piece of divinely given regalia in the service book called the Sacramentary of Henry II of Germany. This shows the coronation of Henry II as Holy Roman Emperor, as is indicated by the representation of the imperial crown with its arch over the circlet. Henry is shown receiving this crown from Christ, together with a sword, perhaps the Sword of Charlemagne, from an angel, and the lance, perhaps the Holy Lance itself now in Vienna, from another angel (Figure 8–11). In the fifteenth-century work, *The Travels of Sir John Mandeville*, the Holy Lance—or at least its head—is shown in a series of miniatures being held as a sort of scepter not only by the King of France, but also by the Byzantine emperor and the German Holy Roman Emperor (Gastgeber 2005, 64–65). Each of them evidently claimed to possess a Holy Lance, which was used a royal or imperial scepter.

Other items of royal and imperial regalia with which a ruler was invested at his coronation came to be seen as relics. The sword the German king received at his coronation at Aachen (and that perhaps appears in Figure 8–11) was believed to have been the sword of Charlemagne, which was believed by the fourteenth century to be particularly holy because it had been miraculously given to him by an angel (Kühne 2000, 116). The regalia of the English kings likewise included a sword supposed to have been the sword of the eleventh-century saint-king, Edward the Confessor, whose relics were enshrined in Westminster Abbey, the English coronation church (below, pp. 371–74).

Figure 8–11: Henry II of Germany receiving the imperial regalia (Munich, Bayerische Staatsbibliothek, Clm 4456, fol. 11r), an illustration from the Sacramentary of Henry II, Regensburg, after 1002. Henry II's arms are supported by churchmen as he receives from Christ above his crown, and from angels on either side a lance, perhaps the Holy Lance (left), and a sword, perhaps the Sword of Charlemagne (right). (See insert for color version of this image.)

Such relics which also served as regalia, must have conveyed a message of the ruler's ideological power as it derived from beliefs about his proximity to the divine. The wide diffusion of that message was made possible by the ceremonies and rituals that were developed to enable these relics to be displayed to those subjects on regular occasions and in very public places. The first such display is recorded as having taken place in the city of Basel, Switzerland in 1315 on the initiative of the German ruler, Frederick the Fair (1314–30), who was faced with a rival emperor Ludwig IV (1282–1347). It was a great event, which included games and tournaments. According to a chronicler, Matthias of Neunberg, there was also a display of objects that were in part relics, and in part imperial regalia, including the Holy Lance, a nail of Christ's Crucifixion, a relic of the True Cross, and the crown and sword of Charlemagne (Kühne 2000, 85). The message of power that could be conveyed to the benefit of Frederick the Fair from such a display was made absolutely clear by the Archbishop of Cologne preaching a sermon to the effect that whoever had possession of the imperial regalia-cum-relics was the legitimate ruler, and whoever did not have possession of them was not (Kühne 2000, 86). Thus, it really mattered for Frederick the Fair to show that it was he who had them. In 1322, however, Ludwig IV's party captured him, and his brother sent the imperial relics to Ludwig in the city of Nuremberg (Germany). Ludwig duly held a display there, and then another in the city of Regensburg, where he stood on the wooden structure built for the purpose and personally held the relics up to view.

Early in the reign of Charles IV of Bohemia, the regalia-cum-relics were transferred from the castle of Trifels (Germany), where they traditionally had been kept when not being used or displayed, to Prague, into which city they were brought with an entry such as the one we have seen represented on the Trier ivory, and they were then taken for safe-keeping to Karlštejn (above, pp. 245–47). The regalia-cum-relics were, however, brought regularly from Karlštejn to Prague for public display. There they were put on show on Palm Sunday, 1350, on a wooden stage in Charles Square (the Great Market) in Charles IV's New Town at Prague. From 1356, they were displayed there annually at the newly established Feast of the Lance and the Holy Nails (Kühne 2000, 112–13). For the display of 1365, there survives a detailed order of ceremonies, which consisted of four phases, in each of which different groups of relics were displayed. In the first phase were displayed no doubt richly decorated bust-reliquaries of saints, including those of the Bohemian patron saints, Wenceslas, Vitus, Sigismund, and Adalbert, which belonged to St. Vitus's Cathedral in Prague; in the second, there were a series of relics of Christ's Passion and the relics of St. Clement, which also belonged to the cathedral; in the third, the crowds were shown the relics from Karlštejn, including the reliquary cross that Charles IV had had made; and in the fourth stage, there were held aloft the imperial regalia-cum-relics—the sword of Charlemagne, the sword of St. Maurice, the crown of Charlemagne, together with other relics—a tooth of St. John the Baptist and the arm of St. Anne, as well as Passion relics—the True Cross, the Holy Lance, and the nails of Christ's Crucifixion.

That this feast was a major public event is clear from the statement of the Bohemian writer Beneš Krabice of Weitmile that "there came to Prague such a multitude of people from all parts of the world that no one would believe it unless he had seen it with his own eyes" (quoted by Kühne 2000, 114). Those coming on pilgrimage at the time of the feast were entitled to an indulgence, that is, a remission for the time their souls would suffer in purgatory after their deaths, and this no doubt contributed to the feast's success as the focus of a pilgrimage, which may have been one of the largest north of the Alps. With an area of 553m x 146m, Charles Square offered scope for enormous gatherings of people, for its size has since been rivaled only by such spaces as the Place de la Concorde in Paris.

Corroboration of the popularity of the feast and relic display in Prague with pilgrims is provided by a pilgrim badge that was found in an excavation in Prague and was presumably one of many produced for pilgrims to take away with them as a memorial of the feast. This shows Charles IV himself kneeling with the Holy Lance in his hands before the pope, who is distinguished by the tiara he is wearing and the key he is carrying as a symbol of his succession to St. Peter. The heraldic shield of St. Peter below the figure of the pope in the lower register of the badge is a further allusion to the papacy which had authorized the feast. The shields of the Kingdom of Bohemia and of the Holy Roman Empire, which occupy the rest of the register, associate Charles IV closely with the feast. Evidently, the message of the ruler's involvement with the relics of Christ's Passion was spread among a wider public, in the city of Prague, but also those coming from far away to Prague, and to those seeing the pilgrim badge taken home by pilgrims and visitors to the feast.

In 1361, a similar display of relics had been held by Charles IV in the city of Nuremberg to mark the birth of his son and heir, Wenceslas. Here the relationship between the display and the ruler's power was underlined by the place where it was held. The display took place from the western gallery of the Church of the Blessed Virgin Mary, in the New Market, which had been created on the site of the Jewish ghetto, destroyed in the pogrom of 1349 for which Charles IV had given his approval and support. Just as at Prague, the display was a focus for visitors and pilgrims, and the papacy granted an indulgence for those attending (Kühne 2000, 130). The message of power—unsavory as it may have been—must have related to Charles IV's promotion of Christianity through his support for the destruction of the Jewish community, and so to his favorable relationship with God, from whom his power ultimately derived.

When civil war broke out in Bohemia in the reign of Charles IV's son and successor, Wenceslas IV (1378–1419), and Karlštejn ceased to be a safe repository for the imperial regalia and relics, they were transferred first to Hungary, and then in 1422 to Nuremberg indefinitely, where they were kept from 1438 onward in a suspended shrine in the chapel of the Neue Spital (New Hospital). Their display in Nuremberg continued to be an annual festival, associated with an important trade fair. The display took place in the New Market on a specially built display booth rather than on the western gallery of the church of the Blessed Virgin Mary. A woodcut dating from some time after 1487 shows what the display from the platform looked like (Figure 8–12). It shows the display booth rising to two stories. It had a bell to call the attention of the crowds to the display, and from its roof there flew flags that depicted on them the Holy Lance and the Crown of Thorns, as well as the emperor's coat of arms. In the top story, five bishops wearing mitres are depicted holding reliquaries in their hands to display them to the crowds below. Between them are assistants holding candles. On the extreme left is a man whose beard and dress suggest that he is a civic official, for the city of Nuremberg was closely involved in the display, not least because of the importance of the trade fair that went with it. Immediately to the right of him is another layman holding a list and a pointer—he is probably responsible for checking which relics are being shown, and perhaps for calling out what they were. Below is hung a rich fabric, with candles in front of it. Below this again is the second story of the structure, a sort of gallery in which there are armed men. Indeed, the display must have posed a considerable security risk, and their role was no doubt to act as security personnel. Below them again, at ground level, is the audience—members of the laity, including a woman with a child and a peasant identified by the tool he is carrying and by his attire, and a pilgrim with a pilgrim's badges on his hat and a pilgrim's staff in his hand (Kühne 2000, 2–4).

Displays of relics were not limited to the imperial regalia-cum-relics, nor to cities closely associated with rulers. But, where they were, the potential they offered for disseminating to a wide public a message of the ruler's power deriving from his closeness to God were considerable. In the later Middle Ages, Charlemagne's palace city of Aachen claimed that its

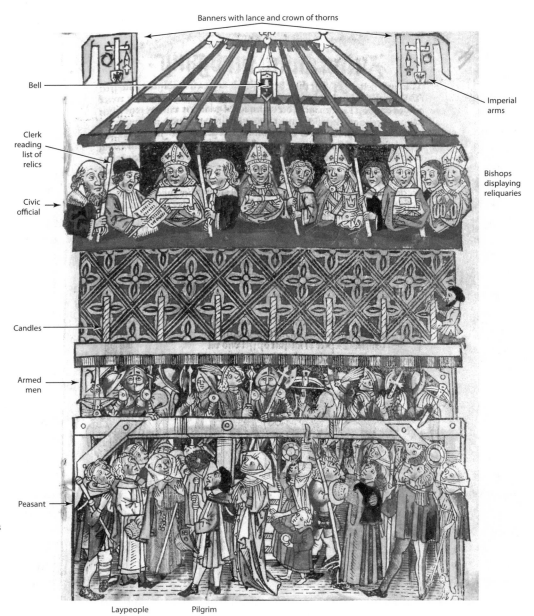

Banners with lance and crown of thorns

Bell

Imperial arms

Clerk reading list of relics

Bishops displaying reliquaries

Civic official

Candles

Armed men

Peasant

Figure 8–12: The "display" of imperial regalia and relics in Nuremberg (Nuremberg, City Archives, Rep 52 a, Rst Nbg, Handschriften, Nr 399 a, fol 4, an illustration from Peter Vischer, Nuremberg relic book, after 1487).

Laypeople   Pilgrim

collection of relics, which included important relics of the Blessed Virgin Mary herself, had been given to it by Charlemagne in person. The church also had custody of two items of the imperial regalia-cum-relics, the Purse of St. Stephen and another crown believed to have been that of Charlemagne, together with the gospels on which the ruler being crowned would swear his oath of office. From the late thirteenth century, the church seems also to have had a full set of regalia made for it by Richard, earl of Cornwall, who was briefly king of the Romans. At Aachen, displays of relics are documented from 1312, and from 1349 a

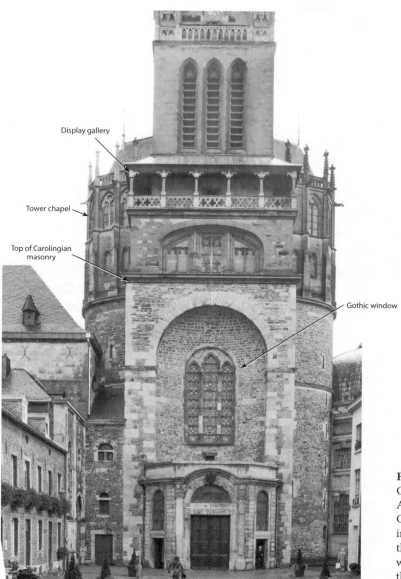

Display gallery

Tower chapel

Top of Carolingian
masonry

Gothic window

Figure 8–13: West front, St. Mary's Church, the former palace church, Aachen (Germany), showing the Carolingian and later components, including the relic-display gallery. Note the modern porch protruding westward from the original west front; the Carolingian bronze doors are now hung in the opening of this porch.

display was held regularly every seven years. By 1350, the west front of the church at Aachen had been reshaped to facilitate these displays (Figure 8–13). As is evident from the different colors of the masonry in the building, the original towers of the westwork, with their spiral staircases, have been extended upward to form tower chapels. Between them has been constructed a gallery from which the relics, including no doubt the imperial regalia-cum-relics, were displayed. (The tower rising above the gallery is modern, but it is a replacement for a previously existing tower.)

CONCLUSION

The power believed to be inherent in relics made them potent vehicles for conveying messages of power. Because they offered direct access to the power of the saints or of Jesus Christ himself, their presence in a city or at a royal or imperial center was an important matter. Where a ruler had been responsible for locating them there, perceptions of his power could be enhanced by the fact that he had been able to do this, especially as relics were believed to have the capacity to choose where they were to be enshrined. So their presence consituted an endorsement of the ruler's authority, as well as a source of power in its own right.

The entries of relics into cities underlined these ideas by treating the relics as if they were the equivalent of rulers, entitled to the same ceremonial as the ruler himself. The place subordinate to the relics which rulers sometimes adopted on the occasion of relic entries served to further emphasize the power of the relics and the ruler's relationship to them. The belief that relics could act as guardians, against military aggression and other troubles, made them especially suitable as focal points of cities and royal and imperial centers, as of kingdoms more widely. Hence, rulers' relic-collecting activties were sometimes closely linked with the creation of capital cities. It was no accident that the greatest collections of the relics of Christ, the most potent of all, were located in the capital cities of Byzantium and France, two of the most powerful—or at least most ambitious—states of Europe.

Possession of relics also had an importance for the ruler himself. The relics of Christ, as sought-after as they were, underlined the ruler's efficacy in obtaining them; but they could also associate him with Christ. A ruler who possessed them and handled them was evidently a great enough ruler to be permitted to do these things, and also was a ruler who could be associated with Christ himself through the intimacy with the relics which he enjoyed. This was all the more true where relics and the royal and imperial regalia merged, so that relics were part of the regalia, and the regalia were themselves treated as if they were relics.

The messages of power conveyed by relics in all these circumstances must have been primarily about ideological power—the ruler's proximity to, and even identification with—the divine as the source of his power. But, paradoxically, relics could also convey a message of personal power, because of their capacity to attract to them large numbers of people in search of the spiritual benefits they were thought to bring. So the presence of relics in capital cities and at other royal sites could convey a message of the ruler's care for his subjects in making available to them such holy and beneficial objects. So, too, relic displays involved a mass audience gathered to witness the relics and to have impressed on it the ruler's worthiness to be associated with such holy objects.

CHAPTER 9

Churches, Mosques, and Power

The aim of this chapter is to explore the potential for conveying messages of power of the great religious buildings that were often either a part of palace complexes or near neighbors of palaces by considering a small group of significant buildings. It will consider their setting, their relationship to other buildings and features of the palace sites in question, and the way they were built and decorated. The buildings to be considered are mainly great Christian churches, with one important mosque, that of Córdoba (Spain). By their nature, these buildings were potentially powerful tools for conveying messages of ideological power. Yet, they were first and foremost seen as the houses of God, so that their role with respect to the ruler could be one of tension. So, this chapter will consider how far they were intended unequivocally to convey a message about the ruler's ideological power deriving from God, and how far were they intended instead to convey messages about the restriction of that power resulting from the ruler's position subordinate to God and therefore to the clergy. For, the Church was both a very powerful institution and a spiritual organization claiming to be more closely in touch with God than even a ruler could be. In this connection, much depended on the status of the religious buildings relative to the palaces. Churches that were palace churches, for example, could be unequivocally powerful vehicles for conveying messages of ideological power on behalf of rulers, since those rulers were their principal patrons and their most important users, and since the churches themselves were integral parts of their palaces. Where a palace church was the responsibility of a religious community of some importance in its own right, the messages of power it conveyed relative to the ruler could be qualified by reference to the ruler's perceived subordination to God. Such qualification might be expected to be greater in the case of churches which, although they were closely adjacent to palaces, and were extensively patronized and used by rulers, were not palace churches at all, but rather the cathedrals of bishops, archbishops, and patriarchs, or the churches of independent and powerful monastic communities and their abbots.

AACHEN

The palace church at Aachen (Germany), which was built by the emperor Charlemagne (768–814) as part of his palace complex, is in some respects a very straightforward example of a building intended to convey a message of power on behalf of the ruler. First, the dominance over the site accorded to the palace church is plainly evident even from a diagrammatic plan of the buildings of the palace that survive in part or are known to have existed from archaeological excavation (Figure 9–1). This shows the palace church, the nave and westwork of which still stands to its full height. Its original sanctuary was replaced by a larger Gothic choir in the fourteenth century; while the north and south basilicas are known only from foundations (although the northern wall of the former was still standing in the nineteenth century). The atrium (or entrance courtyard) survives fragmentarily in its northeast corner; otherwise, it is known only from excavations, although its broad shape is still reflected in the frontages of the canons' houses which have been built over its side walls, on either side of what is now the Domhof. At the far end of the corridor, which ran northward from the church, stood the great hall, probably the secular focus of the palace. The tower, known as the Tower of Granus, against the southern part of its east wall stands to what is probably almost its full height, but the rest of the great hall as originally built survives only as foundations. It was reconstructed in the later Middle Ages, especially in the fourteenth century.

The layout of the Carolingian palace, despite being incomplete, gives the clear impression that the palace church was the dominant part of the palace. Taken together with its atrium, and its attached north and south basilicas, it must have been a much more elaborate and imposing structure than the great hall. Indeed, it was longer than the great hall, and it must surely have been the more impressive element of the two. The message of power can only have been to the effect that here was a ruler whose authority depended on God. The prominence accorded to the palace church was also reflected in the sequence of building. Recent archaeological excavation under the nave floor of the church has recovered wooden piles giving a dendrochronological date of 793 at the earliest for the beginning of construction, while restoration of the dome has produced a dendrochronological date of 813 at the latest (Kraus 2013, 143–48). That the church may have been completed earlier than 813 is suggested by a letter of Alcuin in 798 referring to the upper columns of the nave as being in position (Bayer, Kerner, and Müller 2014, 118–21, no. 3). The church, in other words, was certainly completed in less than twenty years, and probably much more quickly even than that. Enormous resources must have been deployed to achieve such a building timetable for what was, for the period, a very ambitious structure. By contrast, structural investigation of the Tower of Granus has shown that it had not been completed by 815. Since this tower had openings into the great hall and was evidently all part of the same construction, that dating must apply equally to the great hall as a whole. So the palace church was built first, and the great hall was built, or at least finished, subsequently, perhaps several years subsequently.

It also seems that it was the building of the church that controlled the alignment of the palace. For the church was precisely orientated—that is, laid out in an east-west direction with its choir and high altar on the east—as a church was by this period supposed to be aligned and built, and the great hall lay exactly parallel to it, with the corridor running perpendicular to both. So the orientation of the palace church controlled the layout of the palace as a whole. The efforts that were made in order to achieve this are evident in the relationship between the palace and the layout of the streets of Aachen (Figure 9–2).

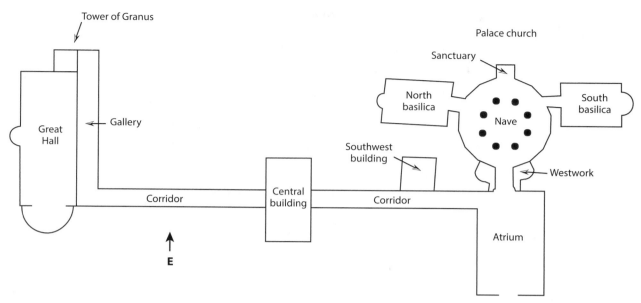

Figure 9–1: Diagrammatic plan of the palace of Aachen (Germany), as built by Charlemagne (after Sebastian Ristow et al., in Kraus 2013, 120).

Aachen had in origin been a Roman city, which had very likely grown up around a series of hot springs, serving at least three sets of baths. There has not been enough archaeological excavation to be certain how many of the Roman buildings were still standing when Charlemagne built his palace, although the fact that the medieval street plan follows so much of its Roman predecessor, a characteristic grid plan, suggests that many still were standing, or were at least still substantial ruins. That Roman grid plan, unlike the palace, was not aligned east-west. Rather, it was aligned north-west to south-east, as is shown by excavated Roman buildings, such as a bathhouse to the east of the palace, and the line of Roman streets that have been reconstructed on the basis of excavations and existing streets which fit the presumed Roman grid plan. The mismatch between the orientation of the palace and that of the Roman street plan is very considerable. The palace, in other words, was simply smashed through the Roman grid plan. The result is the awkward bend of Schmiedstrasse running round the southwest corner of the church's atrium, still apparent in present-day Aachen, and the development of the medieval marketplace north of the great hall on a triangular site—sandwiched between the east-west alignment of the great hall and the north-west to south-east alignment along its north side of the Jakobstrasse, which followed the line of the earlier Roman street. Another Roman street had run diagonally across the site of the atrium of the church. When the atrium was excavated, the drainage gutters of this street were discovered, and it was clear that major work must have been done to cover them over, level the street, and build the atrium of the church on its site. Indeed, excavations have also shown that the church itself was built over substantial Roman baths, laid out, like the others, north-west to south-east (Schaub 2014). So creating a palace on the scale of Charlemagne's which

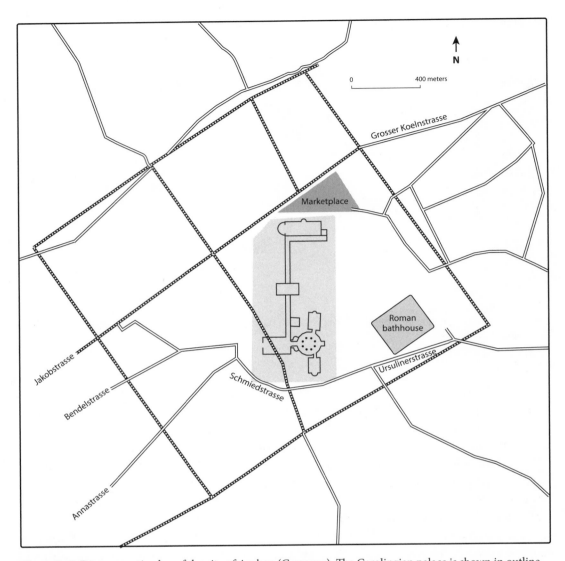

Figure 9–2: Diagrammatic plan of the city of Aachen (Germany). The Carolingian palace is shown in outline with its presumed "palace area" shaded in light grey. The reconstructed Roman grid of streets is shown with dotted lines, the medieval streets, which sometimes coincided with them, are shown in double lines. Note the orientation of the Roman bathhouse, thought to have been re-used in the Carolingian period. Note too the triangular shape of the marketplace and the awkward curve of Schmiedstrasse, both features produced by the mismatch between the orientation of the Roman streets and buildings and the strictly west-east layout of the palace (after Hugot 1965, fig. 1).

followed a quite different grain from the preceding city layout was a major undertaking and, if the Roman buildings were still occupied, a major disruption. One of the priorities of the design of Charlemagne's palace clearly was to give the church a dominant position in it, by laying the whole complex out in a precisely east-west direction—to make it conform to the orientation of the palace church.

The importance of the church also appears from the way in which it was umbilically linked to the great hall. As noted above, a corridor led from the great hall to the northeast corner of the atrium of the church. Its foundations were excavated in the early twentieth century, and much of its southern end still survives. It was built on two stories, with the route from the great hall to the church passing along the upper story. (The central building, which is of unknown function, has now been shown to be subsequent, possibly of the mid-ninth century.) This upper-story arrangement is probably reflected in an account in the contemporary court annals, the Royal Frankish Annals, of an accident that happened in 817 to Louis the Pious, Charlemagne's successor:

> When the emperor left church on Maundy Thursday after the holy office was over, the wooden arcade through which he was walking collapsed on top of him and knocked him to the ground, with more than twenty of his companions. This happened because the arcade was made of shoddy material. The worn-out and rotten cross-beams could no longer hold up the weight of the framework and wainscoting above them. (Scholz and Rogers 1972, 102, s.a. 817)

Although its meaning is not absolutely clear, it looks as if this annal was referring to the corridor from the church to the great hall at Aachen. So, the "wooden arcade" referred to the first-floor passage. The excavated remains did not make it possible to establish for certain how the corridor connected with the church, but it is likely that it led into the first-floor gallery, at its western end—the part of the church, as we shall see, where the emperor's throne stands now, and may well have stood in Charlemagne's time.

The idea that priority was given to the church in the planning of the palace is reinforced by its grandeur as a building. The church was approached from the west and the atrium, which led to the west door of the church, was originally the first element of that grandeur. The only visible traces of the original walls are in the northeast corner of the Domhof, where it is possible to see the original window, which would have lit the passage leading to the corridor to the great hall (Figure 9–3). Nevertheless, archaeological excavations and study of surviving fragments of the original atrium make a reconstruction feasible. The side walls of the atrium were punctuated by four projecting exhedrae, that is, features opening into semicircular niches. These were subsequently—perhaps very soon after their construction—provided with an arcade of arches to separate them from the atrium (Figure 9–4).

The effect must have been very grand. The exhedrae, in particular, may have been intended to imitate a similar feature in Trajan's Forum in Rome (above, Figure 6–12) and to give the palace a status similar to that enormous monument. Certainly, they reflected the tall, semicircular niche on the west wall of the church, creating a balanced and monumental courtyard. The reconstruction includes at the center of the atrium a bronze fountain in the form of a pinecone, which survives and is presently stored in the entrance passage to the church, although it is not certain that it has been associated with the church since it was built. If it has been, however, it is significant that this pinecone had, at its base, representations of the four rivers of paradise, so that it conveyed a message not just of grandeur, but also of the ruler's claim to have power over the world through contact with God.

The eastern end of the atrium was closed by the almost self-contained western part of the building (above, Figure 8–13). This consisted, on the ground floor, of the west entrance to

Figure 9–3: Northeast corner of the Domhof, St. Mary's Church, the former palace church, Aachen (Germany). The Domhof is on the site of the Carolingian atrium. The large arched entrance to the right of the bicycle has behind it the lower story of the two-story corridor which led to the great hall in the Carolingian palace. For a general view of the Domhof, see above, Figure 8–13.

the church leading to the interior of the nave through a vaulted passage. (The entrance was originally under an arched niche as is shown in Figure 9–4; this has now been filled with a modern porch, as appears in Figure 8–13, and the entrance itself has been moved westward.) On either side of the entrance was a round tower containing a spiral staircase. Above the passage, on the first floor, was an area lit by a western window, later enlarged to form the present Gothic window. This area communicated with the first-floor gallery around the nave.

One of the grandest aspects of this western part is the set of massive bronze doors with their lion-head knockers which originally closed the west door, but are now postitioned as

Figure 9–4:
Reconstruction of the atrium on the site of the present Domhof, St. Mary's Church, the former palace church, Aachen (Germany), looking toward the church.

the entrance doors of the later porch (Figure 9–5). The knockers that the lion heads once held are missing, but it is still possible to appreciate the quality of the bronze casting involved in producing both these and the decorative molding of the doors. The investment of materials, time, and expertise in producing these doors was immense. Each door, apart from the lion head, was cast in a single piece, 3.95m high and 1.35m wide, and weighing 2.5 metric tons. Archaeological excavations in the Katzhof, the square between the palace church and the great hall, have brought to light a worksite specially constructed for casting metal, so the casting appears to have been done there. It was presumably done by specialist craftsmen brought to Aachen for the purpose. Their achievement was all the greater because these were the first doors of their kind made in Western Europe since the Roman period (Kramp 2000b, I, 242). And they are only one of no less than five sets of doors made for the palace church. The north- and south-side entrances, both at ground-floor and at gallery level, were equipped with somewhat smaller but equally grand bronze doors. Four sets survive, two at the side entrances to the gallery, and one on the ground floor, at the side entrance called the Merchants' Door which today opens onto the Katzhof to the north. Together with the grilles around the gallery, the segments with their complicated patterns cast in one piece, the scale of bronzework undertaken to glorify the church was enormous.

The most ambitious part of the palace church, however, was the present nave (Figure 9–6). It is octagonal and surrounded at ground level by an aisle, and above by first-floor

Figure 9–5: Bronze doors at the west entrance, St. Mary's Church, the former palace church, Aachen (Germany). The doors now open into a modern porch.

galleries, separated from it by the bronze grilles mentioned above. It rises as an uninterrupted space to the dome at its apex (Figure 9–7). To those who visited the church when it was first built, the effect must have been awe-inspiring. Indeed, Notker the Stammerer, writing in the later ninth century, describes its effect on some Muslim ambassadors:

> They climbed up to the gallery which runs round the nave of the church and from there they gazed down upon the clergy and military leaders. Then they returned to the emperor and were not able to refrain from laughing aloud because of the greatness of their joy. They clapped their hands and kept on saying: "Until now we have seen only men of clay: now we see golden men." (Thorpe 1969, 144; cf. Ganz 2008)

The effect was evidently produced partly by Charlemagne's courtiers assembled in the church, but the building itself and view from the first-floor gallery were clearly also important elements. Notker's narrative is probably nothing more than a fanciful story, but it nevertheless gives an impression of the effect the church made and the strength of the message of power it consequently conveyed.

What precisely that message was can be appreciated by considering earlier buildings that were "centrally planned," meaning that, like the Aachen palace church, they had octago-

Figure 9–6: View across the nave, looking west, St. Mary's Church, the former palace church, Aachen (Germany), with the throne appearing in the western gallery. Note, in the foreground, the candelabra given by the emperor Frederick Barbarossa in the twelfth century.

Figure 9–7: Nave of St, St. Mary's Church, the former palace church, Aachen (Germany), looking up to the dome. The mosaics and the marble cladding are modern, but they are thought to reflect the original decoration. (See insert for color version of this image.)

Figure 9–8: Exterior from the southeast, church of San Vitale, Ravenna (Italy).

nal—or sometimes circular—rather than rectangular naves. It may be, indeed, that the message of power conveyed by the Aachen palace church depended on evoking these earlier buildings. Such a possibility is strengthened by the fact that these buildings were, on the one hand, uncommon and, on the other, closely associated with renowned earlier rulers. The most obvious model for the plan adopted by the architect of Aachen is the church of San Vitale at Ravenna, which was the Byzantine emperor's principal city in Italy between 526 and 548. This church has many similarities to the Aachen palace church. It too has an octagonal nave (Figure 9–8). It also has a western narthex not unlike the westwork at the Aachen palace church, and it has a first-floor gallery (Figure 9–9, and compare Figure 9–6).

In the sixth century, the church of San Vitale, although it was not a palace church, had been a symbol of Byzantine imperial power in Italy. It appears to have been built by the archbishop of Ravenna, Maximian, in partnership with a banker, Julius Argentarius, but it is very likely that they were acting on behalf of the emperor Justinian (527–65), who successfully (for a time at least) reconquered Italy from the barbarian kings who had ruled it since the end of the western Roman Empire in 475. The surviving mosaics in the choir make clear its close association with the emperor. On the north wall is a mosaic of Justinian with his court seen making offerings for the mass that would have been taking place at the high

Figure 9–9: Interior looking east toward the choir, church of San Vitale, Ravenna (Italy), with the first-floor gallery to either side of the choir.

altar below (Figure 9–10), while on the south wall is an equally prominent mosaic of his queen, Theodora, and her court. By Charlemagne's time, the Byzantine emperors had been expelled from Ravenna, and materials were removed from the city for the purpose of building Charlemagne's palace at Aachen. For Charlemagne's palace church to have evoked, by conscious reminiscence, a church so closely associated with one of the greatest of Byzantine emperors would therefore have sent a clear message of Charlemagne's power.

The Aachen palace church, however, was not merely an imitation of San Vitale. In some respects it was a more ambitious construction. Whereas the gallery at San Vitale did not cross the east end, that at Aachen did, so that the east end had a complete upper story, and there were in effect two churches, one set above the other (Ley 2014, 109; see below, Figure 9–13). Also, the dome at Aachen was not like that at San Vitale. It was proportionately higher and more ambitious not only than the dome of San Vitale but also than that of any earlier centrally planned buildings, going back even to the Roman Pantheon of the first century (Heckner 2012, 51–52). In these respects, Aachen was in advance not only of San Vitale, but also of Haghia Sophia, the church built by the emperor Justinian's church adjacent to his palace at Constantinople. The message being conveyed was that of the superiority

Figure 9–10: Emperor Justinian and his court, mosaic on the north wall of the choir, church of San Vitale, Ravenna (Italy). (See insert for color version of this image.)

of Charlemagne to the earlier Roman and Byzantine emperors, whose churches were in these respects less ambitious and less spectacular. Here was a church, at the heart of his palace, that was even greater than theirs.

San Vitale and Haghia Sophia, however, were themselves following in a line of centrally planned churches, which included the church of the Holy Sepulchre at Jerusalem, built by the emperor Constantine, as well as his Golden Octagon in Antioch, which is today known only from written texts. In these cases, too, there was a clear association between a great emperor and centrally planned churches. Emulating such an association may explain why the early kings of the Franks adopted as their palace church in Cologne (Germany) the centrally planned church of St. Gereo, which had been built in the fourth century. It may explain also the construction of centrally planned churches at Salerno and Pertica (Italy) by the kings of the Lombards who had expelled the Byzantine emperors from much of Italy; and the construction by the ambitious and quasi-independent Lombard dukes of Benevento of a centrally planned church at their principal city of Benevento (Italy). This church, which has been preserved, was dedicated to the Holy Wisdom like the emperor Justinian's church at Constantinople (Haghia Sophia means "Holy Wisdom"). By building a centrally planned palace church, therefore, Charlemagne may have been intending that the message of power it should convey would be that of his authority as being in succession to, and greater than, that of rulers stretching back to Constantine himself.

There may, however, have been a further dimension to his palace church's message of power. For the question of whether or not it imitated San Vitale or Haghia Sophia, or any of the other centrally planned churches which had been built before it, may be less important than the ultimate inspiration of all these churches. That may have been nothing less than the temple at Jerusalem, not so much the first temple built by King Solomon, but rather the New Temple, as originally envisaged in the vision of the prophet Ezekiel in the Old Testament, and then actually constructed in Jerusalem as a centrally planned building. If the centrally planned character of the Aachen palace church was intended to evoke this, then the message it conveyed was clearly that its builder, Charlemagne, was comparable to a king of the Old Testament, responsible for building the temple in Jerusalem. Although the model for Aachen was not the original temple built by King Solomon, an association nevertheless was created between Charlemagne as a builder and this greatest of the God-inspired rulers of the Old Testament, and there are references in contemporary texts to Aachen as the "temple of Solomon." In the hands of Christian writers, beginning with the Revelation of St. John the Evangelist in the New Testament, the image of the New Temple in the vision of Ezekiel was merged with the image of the Heavenly Jerusalem, so that the Aachen palace church could equally have conveyed the message that it was a representation of that celestial city. So its ruler was in the image of Christ himself who was the ruler of the Heavenly Jerusalem (Ley 2014).

This was certainly the implication of the mosaic that decorated the inside of the dome when the church was first built. Although it has been destroyed, what it showed is known from early modern drawings and engravings, especially one by Ciampini (Figure 9–11), and the modern mosaic in the dome shows the same subject (above, Figure 9–7). That subject was Christ as the king of the Heavenly Jerusalem. The mosaic represented him enthroned with the twenty-four elders below him, as are described in the vision of the Heavenly Jerusalem in the Revelation of St. John the Evangelist:

> And immediately I was in the spirit: and, behold, a throne was set in heaven, and one sat on the throne. . . . And round about the throne were four and twenty seats: and upon the seats I saw four and twenty elders sitting, clothed in white raiment; and they had on their heads crowns of gold. The four and twenty elders fall down before him that sat on the throne, and worship him that liveth for ever and ever, and cast their crowns before the throne. (Revelation, 4.2–10; Carroll and Prickett 1997, II, 303)

Ciampini's engraving shows the elders rising from their seats and holding their crowns in their hands in preparation for falling down before the throne and casting them before it. It is hard to escape the conclusion that the palace church was first and foremost intended to represent the Heavenly Jerusalem, and to convey a message about the ideological character of Charlemagne's power. So great a ruler was he, so close to God, that his palace church was an evocation of the Heavenly Jerusalem.

Figure 9–11: Engraving by Ciampini of the original dome mosaic, St. Mary's Church, the former palace church, Aachen (Germany) (Ciampini 1690–99, plate XLI).

This message may have been underlined by the position of the ruler's throne, which stands today at the west end of the first-floor gallery, clearly visible through one of the openings in the gallery arcade. It is at the top of a flight of steps, which raise it above the level of the bronze grilles around the gallery. It is made of four great sheets of white marble, held together by iron fixings (Figure 9–12). There was no seat; the central space was filled with a wooden stool, on which the throne's occupant sat. The throne was almost certainly in the gallery in 936, when the contemporary chronicler Widukind of Corvey describes the coronation of Otto III in 936 in Aachen, and how he was "led to the throne, to which he ascended by means of a spiral staircase," that is one of the staircases in the towers of the western part of the church (Hill 1972, 115). The case for thinking that the throne had been in its present position since the church was built, however, rests chiefly on the arrangement of the bronze grille across the opening in the gallery in front of it. This is the only place in the gallery where the bronze grille has a hinged gate in it. Since the opening provided by this gate led on to the empty space of the nave below, it cannot have been intended for anyone actually to pass through it, but rather to give a clear view down from the throne to the present site of the altar of St. Peter in the sanctuary, which is where the original high altar was probably located, and also to the pulpit (or ambo). This sight line from the throne is marked in Figure 9–13.

Figure 9–12: Side view of the throne in the western part of the gallery, St. Mary's Church, the former palace church, Aachen (Germany).

All the bronze grilles around the gallery have been removed and replaced at least once in past restorations of the church, so it is not absolutely certain that the grille with the gate is in its original position, but it is hard to see what its function could have been in any other part of the gallery. It seems likely, then, that the current position of the throne was part of the original design of the church. The message of power conveyed was that this was a church dominated by the ruler's throne. The throne's position, however, offered the ruler seated in it another view. This was upwards and across the dome, so that the ruler was directly facing the figure of Christ enthroned represented in the mosaic. Just as the ruler looked down on the church below him, so he looked up—eyeball to eyeball as it were—to the heavenly king enthroned, from whom—so the message being conveyed evidently was—his power derived.

That message, however, would not have been an unqualified one. Although the throne's position gave it these views of the high altar and pulpit and Christ in Majesty, it also underlined the limitations of the ruler's relationship to God. For it made clear that he was just a layman and, even when seated on his throne, he had no place in the most sacred part of the

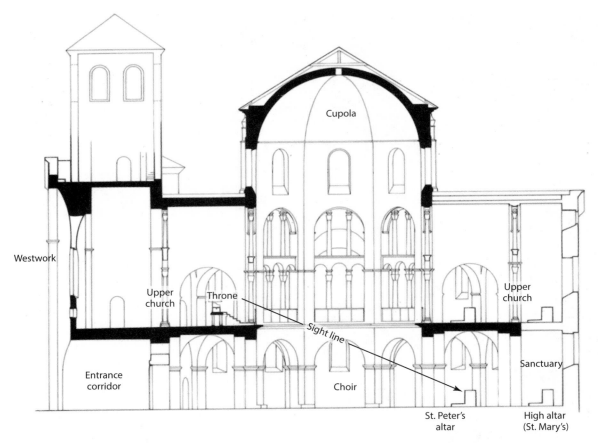

Figure 9–13: Diagrammatic cross-section of St. Mary's Church, the former palace church, Aachen (Germany), showing the upper church occupying the gallery, the first floor of the westwork, and the first floor of the sanctuary. The throne is in the western part of the gallery, and the sight line of its occupant to St. Peter's altar is marked. By the thirteenth century, when the church was used both as a parish church and a church for a community of canons, St. Peter's was not the high altar, which lay further east (as marked in the figure). But excavations in the area of St. Peter's altar revealed remains of a relic chamber, suggesting that the original high altar was on or near its site (after Kreusch 1958, fig. 38, and Bayer 2009).

church. This is reinforced by the functions the various parts of the church seem to have had. For, although we have been referring to the church as the "palace church," it was evidently much more than just a chapel for the palace. It is known that a religious community of canons providing services for the church under an abbot was expanded between 972 and 1003, when the abbot became known as a provost, and was reformed in 987. Since the documents recording these changes make no mention of the community's origins, it is likely that those origins went back to an earlier period, probably to the time when the church was built. By the thirteenth century, it is clear that the present octagonal nave served as the community's choir, and that the choir stalls were placed there. They were subsequently moved into the new Gothic choir, and in 1414 the octagonal nave was known as the "old choir" (Bayer 2014, 206). However, not only was the church that of a community of canons, but it also functioned as a parish church, as was documented in the Middle Ages, but is also evident from the modern archaeological excavation around it of a mixed eighth-century cemetery, suggesting that a church that preceded Charlemagne's construction of the present building had burial rights appropriate for a parish church that presumably would have been transferred to its successor (H. Müller 2014). In the new church, it seems likely that the upper church, including the gallery, functioned as a parish church, with its altar in the first floor of the sanctuary (Figure 9–13), and its baptismal font in the western part of the upper church. Even when a free-standing baptistery was constructed in the Domhof in the twelfth century, the font in the upper church continued to be used for baptisms on special festivals, and it was only removed in 1803. If this division between the parish church on the first floor and the canons' church on the ground floor went back to the time of Charlemagne, as seems plausible, then it follows that his throne was firmly in the lay part of the church, and not in the more sacred part devoted to the canons. The message being conveyed was that, however close to God, the ruler was nevertheless just a layman.

At Aachen, then, the grandeur of the palace church, in conjunction with its prominence in the palace as a whole, and in whatever might have been left of the Roman city, was surely intended to convey a message of the importance of Christianity in Charlemagne's rulership, and the centrality of ideological power to his position. The church balanced the great hall, or perhaps over-balanced it—for it was surely the more spectacular of the two buildings; the resources devoted to its construction and decoration had been immense. Its centrally planned character conveyed a message that set the ruler in a favorable relationship to earlier rulers who had built such churches, and in relationship too to Christ, king of the Heavenly Jerusalem. In the views it offered, notably of Christ enthroned in the dome-mosaic, the position of the ruler's throne reinforced this, while at the same time qualifying it. For its position in what was probably the lay part of the church left no doubt that the ruler was a layman and his place was with the laity and not in the more sacred part of the church with the canons.

CAPPELLA PALATINA, PALERMO (SICILY)

There were no such complications of status in the case of a palace church of comparable grandeur to that of Aachen, the Cappella Palatina in Palermo (Sicily), built by King Roger II (1130–54) in the principal palace of the rulers of Sicily, the Palace of the Normans. Conveying messages of power in this building was no doubt an important priority for him. This was especially so because he owed the title of king to Pope Anacletus II, who was at the time one of two rival claimants to the papacy, the other being Innocent II who eventually triumphed over Anacletus, so Roger II's position and status were far from being secure. He was also threatened by the hostility of the Byzantine Empire, which his grandfather, Robert Guiscard (d. 1085), had dispossessed of Apulia and Calabria; and of the German empire, which regarded southern Italy as one of its territories. He therefore had a great incentive to present himself as clearly as possible as legitimately a king, and as a grand and powerful king at that. This may account for the enormous investment he made in the construction of his palace church.

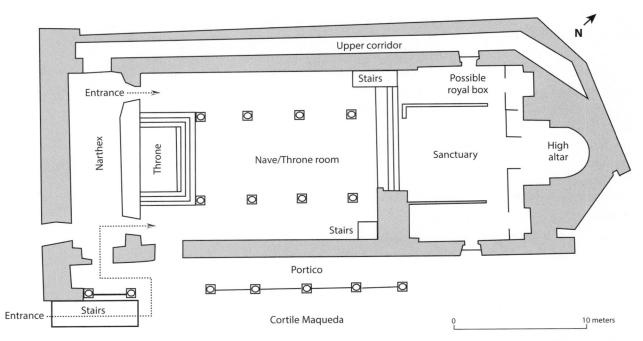

Figure 9–14: Diagrammatic plan of the Cappella Palatina, Palace of the Normans, Palermo (Sicily) (after Tronzo 1997, fig. 6, and Dittelbach and Sack 2005, 63).

There is a document showing that the Cappella Palatina was probably begun in 1132 as a church to be dedicated to St. Peter, and there is a further record of its being consecrated in 1140. It is possible, however, that it was finally completed a little later, for there is an inscription in mosaic around its cupola, which dates it to 1143. There is, at first glance, nothing unusual about the design of the Cappella Palatina, which survives much as Roger II built it, and with a great deal of its original decoration, especially its mosaics. Its plan is that of a basilica (Figure 9–14), with an aisled nave with two lines of columns and arches, and a sanctuary with three apses or quasi-apses. The sanctuary is covered with a dome. As the plan shows, stairs lead up from the courtyard to the chapel at first-floor level via a portico. A door near the west end of the south side led directly into the nave, and another to the west of it led into the narthex, that is the wide room at the west end. From this, two doors led into the north and south aisles of the nave respectively. At the eastern ends of these aisles there are stairs leading down to the crypt, which was created out of part of the earlier ground-floor Norman chapel, modified with massive transverse walls to permit the building of the Cappella Palatina above it.

One of the most striking aspects of the chapel's plan is the throne platform against the west wall of the nave. The throne no longer exists, and the platform was modified substantially in the eighteenth century, but there is no doubt that a throne was positioned here from the beginning (Figure 9–15). The figure shows the west wall of the nave dominated by an enormous mosaic figure of Christ in Majesty, seated on his throne, with the cherubim above. The figure of St. Peter, the dedicatee of the chapel, is on his right, and that of St. Paul is on

Figure 9–15: View westward down the nave, Cappella Palatina, Palace of the Normans, Palermo (Sicily), showing the throne platform, with its marble backdrop immediately below the mosaics on the west wall. (See insert for color version of this image.)

his left. The lower part of the wall is covered with six panels over a dado decorated with blank arches, and topped with a gable surmounted by a cross. In the center of the upper row of panels is a large octagonal piece of porphyry, a rare purple marble that especially designated a ruler, both because it was rare and because (like the cloaks of the Roman and Byzantine emperors) it was purple.

There is no doubt that the decoration of the lower part of the wall was modified by the eighteenth-century Bourbon rulers of Palermo, for their heraldic arms are below the porphyry roundel. But, equally, it seems certain that the throne of the kings of Sicily did occupy this site in the church. The lions, which are part of the original mosaic decoration, were probably intended to allude to the lions around the throne of King Solomon, and were often used as attributes of a throne. Also, the westernmost bay of the nave is wider than the other bays, suggesting that it was built to accommodate the throne and its platform. And, most tellingly, the church does not have—and apparently never had, for there is no sign of it in the masonry—a central west door, as would have been expected. Instead, there were the two doors leading from the narthex into the nave. The only explanation can be that the space where a central west door would have been was occupied by the throne.

The situation of this throne must have conveyed a much less equivocal message about the power of the king than did the throne in the west gallery at Aachen. As he sat on his throne against the west wall, the Sicilian ruler would have looked along a veritable axis of images expressing the ideological power of rulers in relation to Christ's power. This axis ran west-east along the Cappella Palatina, beginning with the earthly ruler on his throne on the platform against the west wall, at the feet of Christ represented in the mosaic above, looking down the nave to a mosaic of the biblical king and lawmaker, Solomon, on the west side of the dome, paired with the biblical king, David (a late replacement, but probably an authentic one). In the dome above the sanctuary, there is another enormous mosaic of Christ as a ruler, surrounded by an inscription in mosaic of the Old Testament text applied to God by the prophet Isaiah, but used by Christ of himself in the New Testament Acts of the Apostles: "Heaven is my throne and the earth is my footstool" (Isaiah, 66.1, Acts 7.49; Carroll and Prickett 1997, I, 825, II, 157). In the central apse, there is yet another mosaic of Christ, in the act of blessing with his right hand. Seated under the mosaic of Christ in Majesty, and looking down the length of the church toward these other mosaics of Christ, the ruler was intended to be regarded as a figure in close association with Christ. His church was his own throne room as well as that of Christ, the King of Kings.

The effect created by the decoration of the chapel was not, however, just a matter of the choice of the subjects of the mosaics, but also their richness, and above all the use of gold tesserae (Figure 9–16).Like other buildings considered in this book, the church was surely intended to represent the Heavenly Jerusalem on earth, which a contemporary writer Bruno of Segni described as "a city of pure gold, which is like clear glass . . . everywhere gold shines, everywhere all things shine with the light of wisdom" (Borsook 1990, 38). The spectacular golden glow of the recently restored mosaics in the Cappella Palatina leaves no doubt that this was the sort of effect that was intended.

With the completeness of the decorative ensemble in the Cappella Palatina and the clear message it projects of royal power, it is difficult to imagine that it might have been differently conceived, as first built. But one aspect of the decoration does suggest this possibility—the ceiling of the nave and its aisles (above, Figure 9–15). Whereas the sanctuary and its apses are vaulted in stone and decorated with mosaics, the ceilings of the nave and aisles are made of wood, and the wood is carved in the Islamic form of decoration called *mqarnas*. These ceilings are lavishly decorated with paintings, executed in characteristically Islamic style, and representing secular subjects, such as dancers, girls, and kings. The Sicilian royal court was heavily influenced by Muslim culture, as witnessed by the construction of the extramu-

Figure 9–16: Gold tesserae cladding the walls, Cappella Palatina, Palace of the Normans, Palermo (Sicily). (See insert for color version of this image.)

ral of the Zisa palace in Muslim style (above, pp. 111–13), so it is not surpising that its crafts-men drew on such Muslim decoration. What is surprising, however, is that they should have applied it to the nave and aisles of a church, decorating it with secular scenes. The contrast between these ceilings and the religious mosaics covering the inside of the dome and the vaults of the sanctuary raises the possibility that the nave as originally built was not really part of the church at all, but was a throne room, with the sanctuary to the east originally being the totality of the chapel. The position of the royal throne in that chapel would then have been the royal box, which it has been suggested was located at first-floor level in the north wall of what is now the sanctuary (Figure 9–14).

If this was the form of the original Cappella Palatina—and the interpretation of it as being like that is disputed—changes were soon made. The mosaics that cover the walls and vaults of the sanctuary now extend westward along the walls of the nave and of the aisles, and they seem to form a continuous sequence from west to east down the church. In the nave, there are scenes from the Old Testament's Book of Genesis, showing, for example, the story of Adam and Eve, including their sinning and expulsion from the Garden of Eden; in the aisles, there are scenes showing the preaching of Saints Peter and Paul; both sequences lead up to the images of Christ, the prophets, the apostles, and the saints in the sanctuary. The scenes in the nave thus depict man's creation and fall, the scenes in the aisles show Christ's apostles working for the salvation of mankind, and the scenes in the sanctuary show the Heavenly Jerusalem. When these mosaics were completed, therefore, there can be no doubt that the present nave and sanctuary were both parts of the church as they are now. But it is possible that nave and aisle mosaics were completed somewhat later than the sanctuary mosaics—the result of a change in plan, perhaps under King Roger II's successor, William I (1154–66). It is the case too that the mosaic of Christ Enthroned over the throne on the west wall was an afterthought, because it blocks an original window. So the possibility remains open that, as originally designed, the Cappella Palatina was an adjoining throne room and chapel rather than just a chapel. Whatever the truth of this, there is no doubt that, throughout its history, it was a building intended to emphasize, every bit as much as the Aachen palace church did, how close the ruler was to God, and that the nave did indeed accommodate the ruler's throne, even if it was always part of the chapel rather than a self-contained throne room.

SAINTE-CHAPELLE, PARIS (FRANCE)

An equally grand religious building, evidently intended to represent the Heavenly Jerusalem, was the Sainte-Chapelle, the principal addition made by Louis IX, king of France (1214–70), to the Palais de la Cité in Paris. Like the Cappella Palatina, this was simply a chapel for the palace, although it was served by a community of canons. As appears in contemporary images, such as the view of the Palais de la Cité in the Très Riches Heures of the Duke of Berry, executed by the Limburg brothers around 1400, this chapel was as dominating a building as was the palace church at Aachen, and must have been widely visible across Paris (above, Figure 4–2).

Its significance derived not only from its dominating aspect, but also from the style of its architecture, known to modern scholars as the Rayonnant Style. This style was especially associated with the royal court—hence its alternative name, the Court Style. It was characterized by a picturesque exterior with gables and finials, by enormous windows with intricate tracery, and by fine detailing of the interior, and it was particularly used at the royal abbeys of Royaumont and Saint-Denis, as well as in the Sainte-Chapelle. If it was indeed a style especially associated with the royal court, then it may well have sent a message of power represented by the innovative sophistication of the French king in patronizing the development of this latest, highest, most ethereal version of Gothic.

Moreover, that message was sent very widely, for the style was imitated after about 1260 across France, for example, at the churches of Saint-Germer de Fly and Chambly, and the cathedrals of Beauvais and Clermont-Ferrand. It was particularly carried by the Mendicant Friars in the construction of their churches, which gave it a further diffusion. Nor was its influence limited to France, for it was especially striking at the cathedral of Leon in northern

Spain, begun in 1255 by the then bishop who was a cousin of King Louis IX of France. And its use was equally prominent at the cathedral of Old St. Paul's in London, and at the German cathedrals of Freiburg, Strasbourg, and above all Cologne. Here it displaced earlier styles of German architecture, as it displaced earlier English styles of architecture when it was used for the great abbey church of Westminster, as rebuilt by Henry III, king of England (1207–72). In this way, the style of the Sainte-Chapelle conveyed a message of power on behalf of the French king. It spread across Europe, and represented a general subservience to French culture, which was made possible by the wealth and political power of Paris, and the artistic patronage of the French king. Wherever this Court Style appeared, the message of power it conveyed would have been that of the cultural dominance of the French monarchy (see also below, p. 304).

HAGHIA SOPHIA, CONSTANTINOPLE (ISTANBUL, TURKEY)

The Great Palace of the Byzantine emperors at Constantinople was an enormous complex of buildings, embracing a whole series of palace churches, which included the church of St. Mary of the Lighthouse where the emperor's principal relic collection was kept (above, p. 250). But just beyond the palace's gate, the Chalke Gate, stood Haghia Sophia. This was not a palace church like those studied so far, but rather the cathedral of the Patriarch of Constantinople. It was a church so enormous and so grand that, as the Aachen church must have dominated the other buildings of Charlemagne's palace, it must have dominated the Great Palace of the Byzantine emperors (Figure 9–17). Its size and grandeur, reflecting the fact that it was the metropolitan church of the leading patriarch of the Byzantine Church, were the result of rulers' patronage. An earlier cathedral had been rebuilt by the emperor Theodosius the Great after a fire in 404; but after sustaining damage resulting from riots in 532, it was the emperor Justinian who rebuilt it from scratch, and it was completed and dedicated at Christmas 537. Like the church at Aachen, it was a "centrally planned" church, although it was based on a square exterior, whereas the church at Aachen had a sixteen-sided exterior with an octagonal nave; and it was covered with a dome. Whereas Aachen's dome was the highest of its time in proportional terms, that of Haghia Sophia was the largest ever to have been built—a truly imperial structure. Like Aachen's dome, it too may have been intended to convey a message of power connecting the ruler to the Heavenly Jerusalem.

The message of power it conveyed, however, seems qualified in the light of the way in which the emperors used the church. There exists an account of just this in the tenth-century *Book of the Ceremonies*, which, for major Christian festivals, including Easter, Whitsun, Christmas, Epiphany, and so on, sets out the form of an elaborate procession, and so gives an impression of how the emperor was involved with the ceremonial of the cathedral at the great festivals of the Christian year. According to this text, the emperor's ceremonial procession from the Great Palace to Haghia Sophia began with an elaborate series of events within the palace itself. The emperor first prayed in the apse of his throne room, the Golden Triclinium (above, pp. 31, 33), under a mosaic showing Christ enthroned. He then visited the

Figure 9–17: Former church of Haghia Sophia by the Great Palace at Constantinople (Istanbul, Turkey). The minarets date from the conversion of the church into a mosque.

various palace churches themselves, and venerated the relics that they contained. After all this, there was placed on his head the imperial crown, and on his shoulders the imperial mantle or *chlamydis*, and he received his arms as symbols of his military leadership. In the hall of the palace called the Great Consistory, he took into his hands the relic which was believed to be the rod carried by the biblical figure, Moses, when he led the Israelites; and he took also the Cross of Constantine, associated with the ruler who had been the first Christian emperor in the fourth century. There could scarcely have been a clearer series of messages concerning the emperor's ideological power. He then passed through the military part of the palace, the *scholae*, where he collected a ceremonial escort of soldiers carrying standards. Then, making his way to the part of the palace near the Chalke Gate, he was received by representatives of the popular factions of the city, the Greens and the Blues, and the Reds and the Whites. Present there too were members of corporations, medical doctors, civil servants, ambassadors, and others. Here then was a message partly of personal power, partly of bureaucratic power.

These messages of power, however, came to be qualified as soon as the emperor and his escort passed through the Chalke Gate, across the courtyard outside, and so to the vestibule of the narthex (i.e., the west part) of Haghia Sophia (Figure 9–18). There the emperor was received by the patriarch, whose church this was, and his clergy. At the Beautiful Door, the patriarch took the emperor's crown from him, and then accompanied the emperor across the narthex to the Imperial Doors, where the latter prostrated himself three times as a gesture of humility. The emperor then walked with the patriarch across the nave to the Holy Gates, which were the entrance through the sanctuary barrier into the most holy part of the church around the high altar. There, the emperor stood on a disk of the imperial stone, porphyry, let into the floor, while the patriarch passed through the Holy Gates to the high altar. Then, after again prostrating himself three times, the emperor too passed through the Holy Gates, prostrated himself in front of the patriarch, and laid his gifts on the altar. He then left the sanctuary, and proceeded to the emperor's lodge, the *metatorion*, which was constructed as a private space for the emperor at the southern end of the south transept. During the celebration of the Eucharist that followed, the emperor returned to the Holy Gates but did not enter the sanctuary again. After the Eucharist, he moved to the room called the Holy Well, where he distributed alms and had his crown restored to him. Then, he returned to the Great Palace, with further ceremony, but by a simpler route than the one he had followed on his way to the church (*Book of the Ceremonies*, summarized in Dagron 1996, ch. 3).

In this account, the contrast between the rituals in Haghia Sophia relative to those in the Great Palace for the status of the emperor stands out clearly. The message conveyed by the palace rituals was evidently about the closeness of the emperor to God and the importance to his rule of his relationship to the divine. But, equally clearly, the church rituals qualified that message by showing the emperor's inferior position to the patriarch's. To be sure, carrying the Rod of Moses, the emperor presented himself as a ruler modeled on the figures of the Old Testament, empowered by God to lead his people (like Moses) or to rule over them (like David and Solomon). In Haghia Sophia, however, in the patriarch's church, the emperor was subject to the priests, and the power he derived from God was mediated by them. The emperor's crown was taken from him by the patriarch on entering the church; hence, he was excluded from the sanctuary during the mass. However much Haghia Sophia had been built by emperors, however closely connected it was to their Great Palace, however much it represented the Heavenly Jerusalem, within it the patriarch was the ruler and the emperor was subject to him.

This limitation of the emperor's power was emphasized by the mosaic, which dates probably from the late ninth or tenth century, over the central one of the Imperial Doors, which the emperor would have passed under as he entered the nave of the church (Figure 9–19). It shows Christ enthroned in majesty, with the emperor prostrate before him. The emperor extends his hands and raises his head as if begging for forgiveness. He is, in other words, represented as a penitent before Christ. In the roundels on either side of the throne appear the Virgin Mary, presumably interceding with her son for the emperor's pardon, and the Archangel Michael, who weighs souls at the Last Judgment, and is presumably represented as deferring judgement on the penitent ruler.

The evidence surveyed above makes it possible to understand the relationship between the Great Palace and Haghia Sophia as one that conveyed a qualified, even an ambiguous,

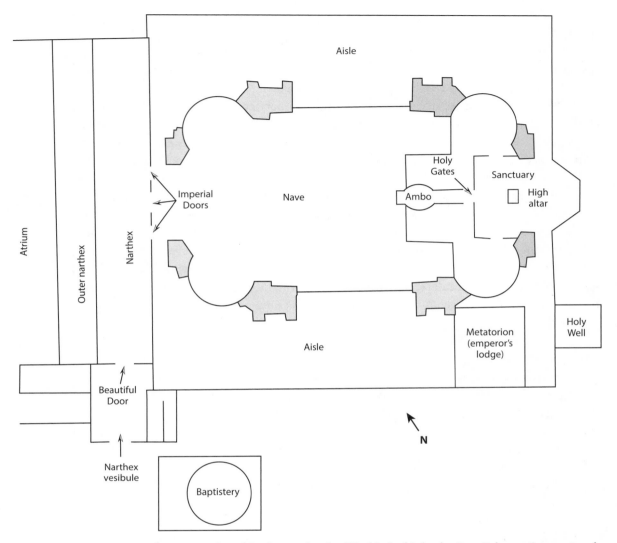

Figure 9–18: Diagrammatic plan of the former church of Haghia Sophia by the Great Palace at Constantinople (Istanbul, Turkey) (after Dagron 2003, fig. 5).

message of power. The scale of the church, its proximity to the palace, and its importance in the emperor's ceremonial life leave no doubt that that message underlined the ruler's close relationship with God. At Constantinople, however, the form of the ceremony examined above equally underlines the role of Haghia Sophia in conveying a subtler message of power. Close as the emperor may have been to God, his power was secondary within the church to that of the patriarch, and his rule depended on his humility and penitence before God. A similar message may have been conveyed by the position of the ruler's throne in the Aachen palace church, but at Haghia Sophia this may have been more pronounced. However much the patriarch may have been dependent on the emperor's patronage, he was the leader of the

Figure 9–19: Mosaic above the central Imperial Door in the former church of Haghia Sophia by the Great Palace at Constantinople (Istanbul, Turkey).

Christian community, which gave him a claim to be the emperor's superior. And Haghia Sophia was first and foremost the patriarch's church.

ST. VITUS'S CATHEDRAL, PRAGUE (CZECH REPUBLIC)

A parallel relationship between cathedral and palace can be observed in Prague (Czech Republic), capital of the Kingdom of Bohemia. Since the ninth century there had been a church next to the royal palace on the ridge called the Hrad, which rises above the city on the opposite bank of the River Moldau (above, Figure 6–17). This had been rebuilt in the eleventh and twelfth centuries to create a substantial Romanesque church that was the seat of the Bishop of Prague. The king and emperor Charles IV (1346–78), however, had still more ambitious plans for the cathedral. He first had the pope create Prague as an archbishopric, and at the same time he had the Romanesque church demolished and began the new cathedral of St. Vitus. According to an inscription below his portrait-bust in the triforium, this church was built "at his own expense" (Crossley and Opačić 2005, 62). Like the Aachen palace church and like Haghia Sophia at Constantinople, this new cathedral was both very grand, and an architectural triumph. It was built in the most up-to-date Gothic style, begun by an architect brought in from Avignon, Matthew of Arras, and after his death in 1356 continued by the Rhineland architect Peter Parler. And it rose up just across the courtyard from the palace, which it dominated in height and in grandeur (Figure 9–20). The close relationship to the palace is shown by the elaborate south entrance to the St. Vitus's Cathedral of, the portal of the south transept, which directly faced the palace across the square, and was the emperor's way into the church. It is a very striking piece of architecture, topped by a gallery accessible by a stone spiral staircase decorated with heraldic motifs. The gallery was probably intended for the display of relics and the royal regalia, which were kept in the adjacent Wenceslas chapel or in the treasure chamber above it, from which it was accessible. The façade of the portal is decorated with a contemporary mosaic, the only one of its kind north of the Alps, which shows the Last Judgment (Figure 9–21).

Christ is depicted in the center of the mosaic, supported by angels in a mandorla, and judging between the blessed and the damned. On his right kneels his mother, the Virgin Mary, on his left is St. John the Evangelist, also kneeling. On the left are martyrs, with below them the blessed dead being raised from their graves by angels; on the right are saints, and below them the damned being handed over by the archangel Michael to devils who are leading them to Hell. Below Christ are the Bohemian patron saints, Procopius, Sigismund, Vitus, Wenceslas, Ludmila, and Adalbert, who seem to make the Last Judgment a particularly Bohemian matter. Below them—in the spandrels of the central doorway—Charles IV himself and his queen are represented kneeling in veneration of Christ. The mosaic certainly contributed to the grandeur of the church; but the message of power it sent was an equivocal one. On the one hand, it emphasized the ruler's ideological power. Its subject of the Second Coming, when Christ would return to the earth to pass judgment on the living and the dead, could be equated with the arrival of a new emperor, as was done by the writer Honorius of Autun (1080–1154) (Rosario 2000, 86). Moreover, the angels supporting the mandorla of Christ are represented holding the instruments of the Passion—the pillar to which Christ was tied when he was flogged, the Crown of Thorns, the cross itself on which he was crucified, and the lance with which his side was pierced while he hung on the cross. As noted above (pp. 265–71), these were closely related to the imperial regalia, one item of which was believed to be the Holy Lance itself. So the mosaic was making the point that the emperor's power derived from Christ. As Honorius of Autun put it, "As an emperor on the day of his solemn entry has his standard, scepter and crown carried before him, even so on the great day when the Son of God shall show Himself to the world for the second time, shall the cross, the lance, and the Crown of Thorns be borne in triumph by the angels" (quoted by Mâle 1913, 370). On the other hand, like the mosaic about the Imperial Doors in Haghia Sophia, the Prague mosaic emphasized the ruler's subjection to Christ, before whom he and his queen knelt, placed in the spandrels of the central doorway, separated from the Bohemian saints and the figure of Christ. For St. Vitus, like Haghia Sophia, was not a palace church, even if it almost functioned as one. It was an archbishop's cathedral, and qualifying the message of the ruler's power deriving from God may have been as important to the Archbishop of Prague as the Patriarch of Constantinople.

Figure 9–20: View looking north from the entrance to the palace to the Cathedral of St. Vitus, Prague (Czech Republic), showing the south transept, marked by the large window on the right, and the three openings of its portal below it.

Figure 9–21: Mosaic of the Last Judgment, portal of the south transept, Cathedral of St. Vitus, Prague (Czech Republic).

WESTMINSTER ABBEY (ENGLAND)

Whereas Haghia Sophia was a cathedral, an example of a great monastic church adjacent to a palace was the church of Westminster Abbey in its close proximity to Westminster Palace (England). Westminster Abbey had been founded in the tenth century, but it was King Edward the Confessor (1042–66) who both established a palace next to it and rebuilt it on a scale exceeding any other church in England at the time, and on a par with the greatest churches on the Continent. Edward's church was 98.2m long, surpassed only by the imperial church of Speyer (Germany) at 109m long, and possibly also by the cathedral of Mainz (Gem and Ball 1980, 44–46). Little is now visible of this eleventh-century phase of the church's construction, but some of its masonry still survives in the west towers, and it seems clear that, when the church was rebuilt by King Henry III (1216–72), the dimensions of its nave were preserved in the subsequent rebuilding.

Henry's rebuilding began with a new Lady Chapel, begun in 1220. It is not clear whether this marked the beginning of a campaign to rebuild the whole church, and whether the king was involved substantially at this stage; but there is no doubt that from 1245 there was a concerted effort at complete rebuilding, and that the king was its principal patron. Indeed, he contributed more to the rebuilding than any other patron of his period in Western Europe contributed to such a project. The monies and materials he supplied ultimately amounted to between £40,000 and £50,000, equivalent to the whole of the royal revenues for two years. The king established a special exchequer for the building, his own mason Henry de Reyns was in charge of the construction, and Odo the goldsmith, closely associated with the king as adviser and agent, was a keeper of the works. Expensive too was the new shrine of the canonized King Edward the Confessor, Henry III's special patron. This was begun in 1241 and continued in the making for more than twenty years; the treasures adorning it were so rich that they were pawned in 1267 for no less than £2,500 (R. A. Brown, Colvin, and Taylor 1963, I, 148).

Like the churches examined earlier in this chapter, the new church of Westminster Abbey was a grand building. Its architecture was grand in scale and detailing, and its decoration was magnificent, for its architect made extensive use of polished marble in the lower stories, as well as carved diaper work, with plain surfaces additionally painted to look as if they were carved with rosettes, the ribs and bosses of the vaults gilded, and sculptured leaves and figures everywhere. The church seems to have been deliberately intended to convey the message that the Kings of England were every bit as great as the Kings of France, the greatest rivals in power and prestige of English thirteenth-century monarchs. For the architecture of the new church, which stands outside the development of English styles, seems to have been designed to imitate the churches patronized by, or closely associated with, the French monarchs. Although it is not clear how far the new church adopted the style of the great cathedral of Reims which was, as we shall see (below, pp. 329–31), the church where the kings of France were crowned, it certainly must have reminded those who saw it of that church. The relationship is best seen in the elevation of the nave, and in the tracery of the windows, which consists of two pointed arches below with a roundel between them (Figure 9–22),

0   10m

Figure 9–22: Left: Nave elevation Reims cathedral (France), after G. G. Dehio and G. von Bezold, *Die kirchliche Baukunst des Abendlandes*, 2 vols. (Stuttgart 1884–1901), plate 384 (2), detail; right: east elevation, south transept, church of Westminster Abbey (England) after J. P. Neale, *The History and Antiquities of Westminster Abbey* (London, 1856), plate XXXIII, detail (images juxtaposed by C. Wilson 2008, fig. 16).

although the tracery at Westminster is in some respects more advanced than that of Reims— the roundel is better integrated with the arches below.

Reims Cathedral was not the only French church of which the new church of Westminster Abbey was reminiscent, however, for it also had features recalling those of the equally great cathedral of Amiens, also in northern France, including the height of the nave arcade openings, and the tall clerestory windows. But the architecture of the new church of Westminster Abbey may chiefly have reminded those who saw it of churches patronized directly by the French kings, especially the Sainte-Chapelle in the Palais de la Cité in Paris, which had the same curving triangular windows found in the new church of Westminster Abbey. The cathedral of Notre Dame in Paris, adjacent to the Palais de la Cité and much patronized by the kings, may also have been influential. There was, for example, a close similarity between the chapter-house windows at Westminster Abbey and those of one of the south nave chapels of Notre Dame in Paris. So Henry III was adopting for his new church the Rayonnant style, so closely associated—or so it can be argued—with royal power in the Kingdom of France (above, pp. 294–95). That adoption, however, was not total. It is impossible to pin down the exact influences of French churches, and the Rayonnant style in particular, on Westminster Abbey. For its architect adopted a series of up-to-date French features, including the plan of its east end, the rose windows, the north portals, the bar tracery, the tall clerestory, and the internal height and elongated proportions. But several aspects of his work derived from English rather than French architecture, especially the greater emphasis placed on the triforium, the lack of architectural sculpture and column figures on the north façade, and the use of Purbeck marble—the particularly English pseudo-marble from the Isle of Purbeck in Dorset. The message being conveyed by the church was that it was a work of the English king, and that it was every bit as royal and grand as the churches patronized in and around Paris by the French kings.

Further, it was adapted to the king's requirements. An example of this may be the provision of a royal pew on the west side of the south transept. There, the east cloister walk of the monastery was incorporated into the transept, with high masonry screens used to mask this as seen from inside the church. Above those masonry screens, on the first floor or the triforium level, there was created a room approximately 8.2m high. If this was a royal pew, the views it offered, especially from its north end, toward the crossing of the church and the sanctuary, with their altars, would have made it a very suitable location for such a pew, comparable as it would have been in this respect to the western gallery of Aachen, and to the *metatorion* in Haghia Sophia (above, pp. 286–89, 297, 298). Two features of the abbey's construction and layout favor this idea. First, the supposed royal pew has a lobby in its south end, decorated with rib-vaulting and high-quality sculpture, including the heads of a king and queen, which suggests that the room itself had originally had a much grander function than its later use in the seventeenth century as a muniment room. Second, it seems that there existed a route giving direct access from the palace to the supposed royal pew (Figure 9–23). Following this, when the king left the Privy Palace, or perhaps the high table end of Westminster Hall, to go to the church, he would have passed through the postern in the boundary wall of the abbey to approach the church from the east. The importance of the route at this point is shown by the fact that a buttress is missing on the northwest side of the chapter house, its omission presumably being to allow the route past the chapter house to a door leading via spiral stairs up to the lobby of the royal pew in the west gallery of the transept. So, both the architecture of the church and aspects of the layout surrounding it have been specially designed to provide the king with a privileged pew and access to it.

Equally indicative that Westminster Abbey was a royal abbey was the new thirteenth-century chapter house. According to the contemporary historian, Matthew Paris, "the lord king built this incomparable chapter house" (Carpenter 2010, 32). In addition to the grandeur of the interior, it had a splendidly vaulted entrance lobby with wall-arcading and other lavish decoration, taking in the cloister bay opening out from the lobby. Close royal involvement in its creation is indicated by its tiled floor, which had two strategically placed bands

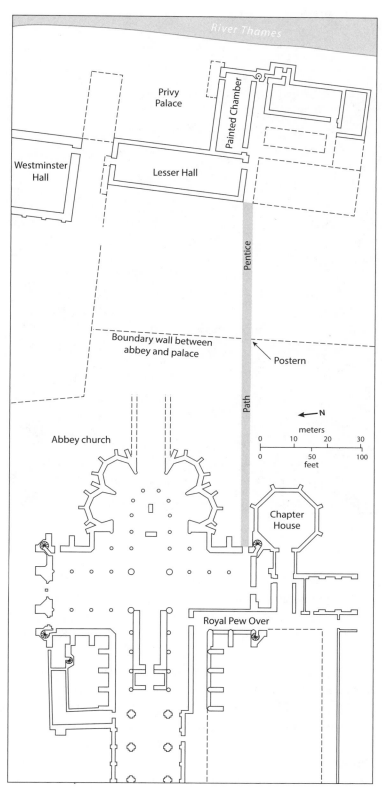

Figure 9–23: Route from the Privy Palace to the supposed royal pew, Westminster Abbey (England) (after C. Wilson 2008, fig. 9, detail, with added captions).

Figure 9–24: Floor tile in the chapter house, Westminster Abbey (England), decorated partly with centaurs and mythical beasts around the edges, but principally with a shield bearing the royal arms of England.

of tiles running to left and right of the entrance eastward across the floor, showing thirty-one shields bearing the royal arms of England, each one made up of four tiles (Figure 9–24). In addition, the inscription in the tiled floor made clear Henry III's patronage and also, perhaps, his use of the building. It read: "Henry, friend of the Holy Trinity" (Keen 2010, 230–31).

Royal involvement with the chapter house is underlined by the fact that the king went to great trouble to provide a second lectern for it, based on one he had seen at St. Albans Abbey (England). Known as the *letrinium regis*, this was commissioned from John of Gloucester in 1259 and was to be ready for the next time the king arrived at Westminster. Clearly it was a grand affair, and its purpose may well have been for the king himself to address meetings in the chapter house. For, the resources lavished on the chapter house may in part have been intended to make it a grand enough space for meetings to be held which dealt with the king's business, as well as the daily meetings of the monastic chapter. Certainly, it was from the outset used as a place for meetings of the realm, as when in 1265, during the parliament convened by rebel, Simon de Montfort, it was where the king's oath not to take revenge on his opponents and his confirmation of Magna Carta were announced. Later, it was a meetingplace for the commons in Parliament, first in 1352 and then three times in the 1370s and 1380s.

The royal character of the chapter house must have been further strengthened by the use of its undercroft as a place for storage of part at least of the royal treasure. The first documentary evidence for this comes from the reign of Edward I, when a burglary occurred in 1303, but there had apparently been previous burglaries in 1299 and during or before 1296. But there are indications that the undercroft functioned as a royal strong room from the time of its construction. This is suggested by: the heavily barred windows; the tightly restricted access through a narrow and inconspicous door inside the church itself; and the fact that its central pillar has small cavities apparently for concealing valuables. These have no sign of ever having had doors to close them, they were presumably covered with plates of marble to make them secret and concealed storage places (Ashbee 2010, 113–14). It is known that an additional room, known as the Pyx Chamber, in the abbey was also used as a storage space for treasure, from 1303, along with the Tower of London.

Although there was a palace chapel in Westminster Palace, St. Stephen's Chapel, and although Westminster Abbey was in principle a monastery under the leadership of an abbot, the church nevertheless seems in outward appearance at least as much a palace church as was Aachen. The king's patronage was enormous, and he clearly had a controlling influence on the rebuilding project. The church and the chapter house were adorned with his heraldry, and the chapter house was used for his meetings. As we have seen, the south transept may have provided a royal pew with private access to the palace. Although, aside from the sanctuary pavement considered above (pp. 91–96), the church does not seem to convey messages of power taking in the Heavenly Jerusalem, it equally shows none of the qualifications of the messages of power it conveys as does Haghia Sophia.

MONREALE

A final case, however, underlines how significant a factor could be the tension between the ruler and the leaders of a church that had the status of a cathedral. Early in his reign, Roger II had been developing Cefalù (Italy), along the coast from Palermo, to be a cathedral and a royal necropolis (Borsook 1990, 13). It in fact never fulfilled these functions, and Palermo became the principal center of the kings of Sicily. In 1130, Roger II was crowned in Palermo Cathedral close to his palace, the Palace of the Normans, and so too in 1166 was William II (1166–89) as a minor. Soon after he came of age in 1171, however, William II, probably because of discord with the archbishop of Palermo, Walter Ophamil, built the abbey of Monreale, in a royal park in the mountains above Palermo, beginning in 1174. Although Palermo Cathedral was by then a very grand building constructed by Ophamil on the site of the former mosque, it seems that William II felt he needed a church on that scale but one

Throne

Figure 9–25: View toward the sanctuary, Monreale Cathedral (Italy), with the image of Christ the Ruler of the World in the apse. Note the position of the throne. (See insert for color version of this image.)

that was independent of the archbishop. Monreale was to be a very grand affair, closely connected with the monarchy, subject only to the pope, and with the abbot entitled to wear the insignia of a bishop, and from 1183 having the rank of an archbishop. It was like a counterblast to Archbishop William, who had built the cathedral of Palermo. The church of Monreale was not a palace church, although there was a modest royal palace as part of the abbey (Meier 1994, 90–91). It was a cathedral, but outside the control of the Church of Sicily and the Archbishop of Palermo, and therefore much closer to the ruler.

As in the other churches considered in this chapter, the magnificence of the building, its mosaics, and its bronze doors at the western entrance, must have been intended to convey a message of the ruler's power. As with the mosaics in the Cappella Palatina, the theme at Monreale of the scenes on the bronze doors and the scenes of the mosaics was the progress of sacred history toward the Heavenly Jerusalem which reached its climax in the sanctuary. In the church of Monreale, however, the emphasis on the relationship of the king to God was even stronger. For, the sanctuary had an enormous mosaic of Christ the Ruler of the World (*Pantocrator*) on its east wall, and the most prominent feature on the north side was the royal throne (Figure 9–25).

Although restored in modern times, the throne platform appears much as it was originally constructed (Figure 9–26). A flight of steps leads up from the sanctuary floor to the platform, with stone screens on either side. The platform would no doubt originally have supported a folding throne (a *faldistorium*), like the modern replica shown. Two carved lions are found where the stone screens meet the wall, and there are lions in the mosaics in the gable above the throne. These were intended, as with the lions decorating the throne in the Cappella Palatina, to make the throne resemble the throne of King Solomon (above, p. 292). Between the platform and gable are two dark panels of the rare marble porphyry, especially associated with rulers. The mosaics around the throne underline how much Monreale was a church designed to send a message about the king's closeness to God. Above the throne, a mosaic shows Christ crowning William II, who is named in an inscription and is wearing court dress of the Byzantine emperors (Figure 9–27). From above, angels fly down with the orb and scepter, that is the regalia used in the coronation ceremony. The inscription is from Psalm 89 (88).21: "Mine arm also shall strengthen him," from the full text (verses 18–21), addressing the Lord God:

> For the Lord is our defence; and the Holy One of Israel is our king. Then thou spoke in vision to thy holy one, and said, I have laid help upon one that is mighty; I have exalted one chosen out of the people. I have found David my servant; with my holy oil I have anointed him: with whom my hand shall be established; mine arm also shall strengthen him. (Carroll and Prickett 1997, I, 689)

Facing the throne on the south side is a mosaic of the Old Testament figure, Jacob, with the inscription, "The sceptre shall not depart from Judah, nor the ruler's staff from between his feet until he comes to whom it belongs." Standing below Jacob is an Old Testament prophet, Malachi, carrying a scroll with part of the text used in ceremonies of acclamation of kings. William II was evidently being presented as a ruler on a par with Old Testament rulers, especially with King David, and close to God.

William II's throne itself was part of a sequence of thrones represented in the mosaics. Christ is seated on his throne in the mosaic above the royal throne showing the coronation of William II. The mosaics in the aisle-apses show the Virgin Mary and the apostles Peter and Paul enthroned. And, in the vault of the presbytery, the mosaic shows the *Hetiomasia*, that is, the empty throne. This object, which had been represented in much earlier Christian art, for example in the mosaics in the sixth-century Arian Baptistery in Ravenna (Italy), illustrated the passage in Psalms 9.7: "But the Lord shall endure for ever: he hath prepared his throne in judgement." So, the Hetiomasia was the throne prepared for the Second Coming of Christ, when he would appear on earth to conduct the Last Judgment, as is described in the New Testament Book of Revelation. In art, this throne can have on it a cross on a cushion, the Gospels, the scroll with the seven seals, the lamb frequently with a dove, a veil, and sometimes with a footstool, which is sometimes replaced below the throne by the mountain from which flow the seven rivers of paradise. In the Arian Baptistery in Ravenna, the Hetiomasia has on it a purple cushion adorned with gold strips. On this is a gem-bedecked cross, with a purple cloth draped round it. The color was important to a ruler, the purple being an imperial color (Figure 9–28). In a representation of the Hetiomasia in a fifth-century stone-

Figure 9–26: Royal throne on the north side of the sanctuary, Monreale Cathedral (Sicily).

Figure 9–27: Mosaic above the royal throne, Monreale Cathedral, Palermo (Sicily), showing Christ crowning King William II.

carving from Constantinople, it even has on it the imperial cloak, the chlamydis (Bezzi 2007, 80, and fig. 33), as if to emphasize that this is not only the throne prepared for Christ, but also the throne of the secular ruler, in this case the Byzantine emperor.

Monreale then was a cathedral founded by the ruler and decorated with scenes relating to kingship. The prominence of the royal throne and the mosaics and inscriptions around it suggest that it was intended by William II as a coronation church, although the disruption that overtook the Kingdom of Sicily even in the course of his own reign, and which culminated in the absorption of the kingdom into the wider Kingdom of Italy, meant that it had no real future as such. It was intended too to be a royal necropolis, and a number of tombs of members of William II's family, including his father and predecessor William I, were in fact located in it. So the church was a cathedral, created by the king, intended to be a coronation church and a royal mausoleum, which was—through its mosaics and their inscriptions—presented as an image of the Heavenly Jerusalem. It is an example of the lengths to which rulers would go to use churches as instruments of power.

Figure 9–28: *Hetiomasia* mosaic, Arian Baptistery, Ravenna (Italy), one of the many representations in this building showing the empty throne prepared for the Second Coming.

CÓRDOBA (SPAIN)

As in Christianity and in paganism, so in Islam, holy buildings were potentially important in conveying messages of power. One of the clearest cases of this is the Great Mosque of Córdoba (Spain). The Christian kingdom of the barbarian people called the Visigoths in Spain had been destroyed by Muslim invaders from North Africa in the early eighth century, with the result that Spain, apart from the small kingdom of Asturias in the north, fell under the rule of a series of Muslim emirs, and so became part of the Muslim world. That world had taken shape when the Arabs, newly converted to Islam, expanded militarily from the Arabian peninsula to conquer, in the course of the seventh and early eighth centuries, the provinces of the Byzantine Empire in the Middle East, together with the former kingdom of Persia, and the whole of North Africa, which had since the fifth century been the kingdom of a barbarian people called the Vandals. At the beginning of this remarkable expansion, the Arabs had been led by the prophet Mohammed himself, and then by a series of caliphs closely connected with him and known as the Rightly Guided Caliphs. Subsequently, the office of caliph was taken over by members of a family called the Umayyads, who established the center of their power in Damascus. These caliphs ruled the Arab world, at least in principle, until 750, when the ruling caliph and most of his family were killed in a bloody coup. They were succeeded by a long line of caliphs from the Abbasid family who established their center of power in Baghdad. But one of the Umayyads, 'Abd al-Rahmān, escaped the massacre of 750 and, after wandering as a refugee across the Muslim world for five years, arrived in Spain. Capturing Córdoba, he made it the center of his power in the peninsula, and became the first Umayyad emir of Córdoba (756–88), the most powerful ruler in the fragmented political situation of Muslim Spain. He and his successors ruled as emirs of Córdoba, until in 929 'Abd al-Rahmān III declared himself to be caliph. This was an important step, as we have already seen in the context of the founding of the city of Madīnat al-Zahrā (above, pp. 186–87). In principle, there could be only one caliph in the Muslim world, because the caliph was regarded as the successor of the prophet Mohammed and the Commander of the Faithful. So 'Abd al-Rahmān III was challenging the position of the Abbasid caliphs in Baghdad, and also the power of the Fatimid caliphs in North Africa who had also claimed the caliphate in opposition to the Abbasids twenty years earlier. After 'Abd al-Rahmān III's assumption of the title, all subsequent Umayyad rulers of Córdoba were styled caliph, until their power foundered at the beginning of the eleventh century.

The Great Mosque of Córdoba, which the Umayyads built, largely survives because it was converted into the cathedral of Córdoba after the Christian reconquest in 1236. Its situation was intended to convey a message of power for the ruler of Córdoba. For, it occupied a focal position within the Muslim city, near the Roman bridge as restored by the Muslim emirs, probably close to the principal gate, the Bab al-Sudda, and just across the street from the palace of the emirs and later of the caliphs (the building is now the bishop's palace). The emir 'Abdullāh (888–912), great-grandson of 'Abd al-Rahmān II (822–52), constructed a covered passageway (a *sabat*) to link the palace directly to the Great Mosque, and a replacement for this was made by al-Hakam II (961–76) when he had extended the mosque. The sabat was an architectural feature indicative of how closely the mosque was associated with the emirs and then the caliphs.

Moreover, the Great Mosque was built in a series of stages that reflected the growing power of the Muslim rulers of Córdoba (Figure 9–29). The first phase was built, between 785/8 and 786/7, by the first emir, 'Abd al-Rahmān I, he who had fled from Damascus. It consisted of a courtyard with a minaret, on the south side of which opened a prayer hall consisting of eleven parallel naves, ending in the *qibla*—that is, the wall of the mosque that faced, at least in theory, toward the holy Muslim city of Mecca. In the following century, the emir, 'Abd al-Rahmān II (822–52), may have widened the prayer hall by two naves, and he certainly extended it by eight bays. Then, 'Abd al-Rahmān III (912–61), the emir who declared himself caliph in 929, replaced the minaret with a larger one, and constructed a series of porticoes around three sides of the courtyard, probably in 951. His son and successor, al-Hakam II, lengthened the mosque by twelve bays toward the south, building an elaborate *mihrab* (that is a sacred space) in the form of a domed room, with chambers set into the

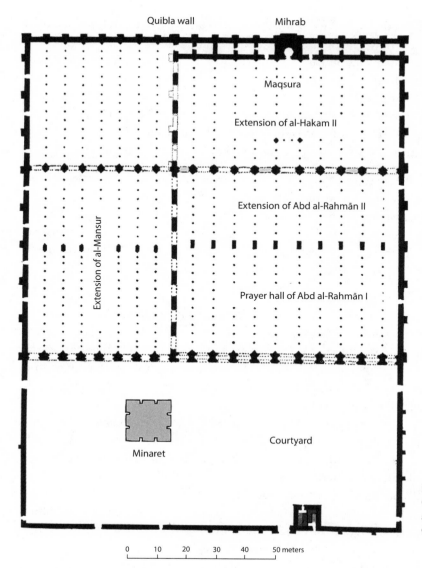

Quibla wall   Mihrab

Maqsura

Extension of al-Hakam II

Extension of Abd al-Rahmān II

Extension of al-Mansur

Prayer hall of Abd al-Rahmān I

Courtyard

Minaret

0 10 20 30 40 50 meters

Figure 9–29: Diagrammatic plan of the Great Mosque of Córdoba (Spain), showing the phases of building (after O. Grabar 1987, fig. 27).

quibla on either side of it, and three domed bays in the cross-nave immediately to the north. In 987, the *hayib* (chief minister) of Caliph Hisham II, al-Mansur, who held the reins of power rather than the caliph himself, made the last modification to the building before the Christian reconquest by adding another eight naves to the east side of the prayer hall.

The original building and progressive enlargements reflected the political and military progress of the Muslim rulers, and their need to express and demonstrate the legitimacy of their power. Even before they claimed the caliphate in 929, ʿAbd al-Rahmān I and his successors needed to assert their legitimacy as rulers against the hostility of the Abbasids, the family that had tried to kill all their family and that now held the caliphate of Baghdad. This may be why the plan of the first phase of the Great Mosque, with aisles perpendicular to the qibla wall, recalled the plan of the Aqsa mosque in Jerusalem, while its height recalled the Great Mosque of Damascus. Both these were built by the Umayyad caliph al-Walid (705–15).

The mosaics on the qibla wall and in the mihrab and its side chambers in al-Hakam's extension to the Great Mosque (Figure 9–29) are very unusual, both in Islamic art and in Muslim Spanish art. Their use recalls al-Walid's mosques at Jerusalem, Damascus, and Medinah. Indeed, just as al-Walid had "commanded" the Byzantine emperor to supply mosaics and mosaicists for the Great Mosque of Damascus, so al-Hakam is said to have obtained mosaicists from Byzantium. Indeed, the contemporary writer, Ibn Idhari, is quite explicit:

> In the year 956, they began to cover the edifice with mosaics. Al-Hakam had written to the king of the *Roum* [the Byzantine emperor] on this subject, and had ordered him to send a capable worker, in imitation of that which al-Walid had done at the time of the construction of the Great Mosque of Damascus. The caliph's ambassadors brought him the mosaicist as well as thirty-two *quintaux* of mosaic cubes that the king of the *Roum* had had sent to him as a present. (quoted by Dodds 1992, 22; Sezgin, Ehrig-Eggert, and Neubauer 2008, II, 303; French translation by Marçais)

Although the mosaics in the Great Mosque of Córdoba are quite different in subject matter and in style from the mosaics of the Great Mosque of Damascus, for the former are abstract patterns while the latter represent cityscapes, it nevertheless seems clear that part of their point was to underline that the Great Mosque of Córdoba was a suitable successor to the Great Mosque at Damascus, thus demonstrating that the Umayyads were the legitimate rulers in Spain as they had been in Syria.

The point was made also by a relic that was preserved in the Great Mosque of Córdoba. This was supposed to have been the copy of the Koran, which the Rightly Guided caliph Uthmān (644–56) had been reading at the time of his murder—which is why spots of his blood were on it. Not only was there in the Great Mosque this sign of Uthman's quasi-sanctity, but it may also have served as a reminder of his murder. That crime had nothing to do with the Abbasids, but it may nevertheless have evoked the other murders of ʿAbd al-Rahmān III's relations at the hands of the Abbasids in 750. This Koran, preserved in the mosque they had built, could thus have symbolized the legitimacy of the Umayyad caliphs as successors to the Rightly Guided caliphs, as well as indirectly bringing to mind the illegitimacy, resulting from their crime, of the Abbasid caliphs. It was also being used, much as Christian relics were, to convey a message about the ideological power of the caliph. For, the writer al-Idrisi describes a ceremony in the Great Mosque in which this book was taken from the room to the left of the mihrab every Friday morning in a candle-lit procession and placed on a pulpit while the imam read from it (Dodds 1990, 100–101). This resembles a procession in the Christian, Mozarabic liturgy described by Isidore of Seville and Beatus of Liebana, which involved the reading of the gospel preceded by a procession. The Koran of Uthman was being used as a relic in much the same way as Christian relics were used (above, pp. 242–72), even though such relics were not really a part of Islam. The desire of the caliphs to enhance their legitimacy and power may have lain at the root of this apparent adoption of a Christian usage.

The Great Mosque may have served a similar purpose in the Umayyad caliph's rivalry with the Fatimid caliph after 929, when 'Abd al-Rahmān III assumed the title of caliph. For, his rebuilding of the courtyard of the Great Mosque introduced a minaret as a prominent feature of it, and minarets were considered by the Fatimids to be unacceptable additions to buildings. The inclusion of such a prominent one at Córdoba can only have been intended to send a message of hostility and superiority to the Fatimids.

The extension of the Great Mosque by al-Hakam II seems still more clearly to have been intended to enhance the position of the caliph and to develop his authority, in this case in ways that were influenced by Christian, especially Byzantine, treatment of rulers. For, an important aspect of al-Hakam II's extension was the construction of a maqsura, that is a space reserved for the caliph in front of the mihrab. This had stone screens around it and an elaborate vaulted dome over it (Figure 9–30, Figure 9–31). This was surrounded by richly decorated intertwining arches, which give it an air of opulence and grandeur (Figure 9–32).

Just as kings and emperors did in the Christian churches we have been examining, the caliph would have made his appearance in the Great Mosque surrounded by architecture decorated as richly as possible, emphasizing his greatness, and also his relationship to God. This was an even more important part of the legitimacy of Muslim caliphs than it was of Christian rulers, for the caliph, as the successor to Mohammed, was by virtue of his office Commander of the Faithful. So the care and promotion of Islam was a key part of his duties, and he had to appear as a person worthy and capable of guaranteeing this. Not only did his position in the most decorated and holiest part of the Great Mosque underline his position, but so too did the inscriptions on the qibla, in the mihrab, and in the maqsura. These include, for example, texts from the Koran such as:

Those who say "our Lord is God", and further stand straight and steadfast, the angels descend on them, "fear ye not nor grieve, but receive glad tidings of the garden which you were promised. We are your protectors in this life and the hereafter, therein shall you have all that your souls desire, therein shall you have what you ask for; a gift from the One Oft-Forgiving, Most Merciful." (Koran 41:30–32; quoted by Khoury 1996, 86)

On the face of it, this is not a political text, until it is remembered that the caliph was the Commander of the Faithful, and that it was he above all who was charged with saying "our Lord is God" and standing "straight and steadfast." Another inscription from the Koran reads:

He created all things and he has full knowledge of all things. That is God your Lord, there is no God but He, the Creator of all things; then worship Him, He has power to dispose of all affairs. (Koran 6:101–2; quoted by Khoury 1996, 86)

Here too, by inference, the caliph should derive from God "the power to dispose of all affairs." As a final example, we can take an inscription that is not from the Koran: "The dominion is God's upon guidance, God's praises upon Muhammad the seal of the Prophets" (quoted by Khoury 1996, 86). The implication was clearly that God was guiding the caliph.

Figure 9–30: Maqsura in the extension of al-Hakam II, Great Mosque of Córdoba (Spain), viewed across the bay in front of the mihrab, with the edge of the sabat door on the right.

Figure 9–31: Dome over the space in front of the mihrab in the extension of al-Hakam II Great Mosque of Córdoba (Spain).

Figure 9–32: Arch in front of the mihrab in the extension of al-Hakam II, Great Mosque of Córdoba (Spain).

CONCLUSION

Messages of ideological power could thus be conveyed by religious buildings in a number of ways. The sheer scale of those buildings relative to the other palace- or city buildings around them could give a graphic image of the importance of the divine to the ruler, all the more so when, as at Aachen, there had been substantial modification of the cityscape for them to be constructed. Grandeur, richness, and innovation in architecture were other elements that could contibute to the messages being conveyed. In the case of the Great Mosque of Córdoba, the growth of the rulers' power was reflected quite precisely in the expansion and enrichment of the building. The particular elements introduced into religious buildings to make them more suitable for the use of rulers and for conveying messages about their power are also striking, from the throne in its western gallery at the Aachen palace church to the maqsura at Córdoba, and the throne platforms at the Cappella Palatina and Monreale Cathedral in Palermo. The messages of power conveyed by religious buildings, however, were not always unequivocally in the rulers' favor. As we have seen, there was tension inherent in the relationship between the ruler and the religious authorities—bishops, patriarchs, and so on—responsible for the buildings the rulers were using. In the case of Christianity, that responsibility was not merely a practical arrangement; it derived from the role of churchmen as the mediators and interpreters of God's word, and the belief that the religious buildings were God's. Such tension could be reflected in the way in which the buildings were arranged and the ways in which they were used, or—in the case of Monreale—the lengths to which rulers would go to ensure that even a cathedral was independent of the church hierarchy of their kingdom.

PART V

Inauguration Places and Burial Places

This part of the book explores the messages of power that could be conveyed by places connected with the beginnings and ends of reigns: the places where rulers were inaugurated in their offices, and the places where their bodies were buried or otherwise disposed of. In the case of the former, it will concentrate to a large extent on Christian churches which fulfilled the function of being places of inauguration. But it will also look at inauguration in pre-Christian contexts, both in the Roman world and in Ireland and Scotland, to consider what similarities might have existed between Christian and non-Christian practices, and therefore in the messages of power that places of inauguration could convey. In the case of burial places, it will examine the possible messages of power that could be conveyed by burial mounds with their origins in prehistory, by stone mauseolea emerging as a type of burial place for rulers in the Roman period, and by Christian churches which became the requisite necropolises for lines of rulers and their families. As with palaces and cities, the emphasis will be on examining the architecture, decoration, and design of the places in question, but also on what can be known of the practices involved in both inauguration and disposal of the body, for these too could convey messages of power.

CHAPTER 10

The Inauguration of Rulers

Places and Rituals

The aim of this chapter is to explore the importance of the places where rulers were inaugurated. What was the significance of the development of particular places as the only places where rulers of particular states could be inaugurated? Why had they been chosen as, or at least had emerged as, the principal places for this function? What spiritual or traditional importance did they embody that might account for their predominance in inaugurations? How had they been planned and designed to provide suitable stage sets for the rituals of inauguration that took place in them? Where buildings were involved, how did their architecture and decoration fit them for the inauguration rituals that took place in them? Above all, how did those rituals interact with the places and their various buildings or features to convey messages of power?

ROMAN AND BYZANTINE INAUGURATIONS

Of course, rulers did not have to be inaugurated at particular sites or in particular buildings. The Roman Empire had, in principle at least, an elective rulership, so that the elevation of an emperor involved two processes: his formal election by the senate and his acclamation by the army as a gesture of their accepting him as the ruler. In 275, Tacitus—a rather improbable candidate for rulership because of his advanced age—was first elected by the Senate and then acclaimed by the army on the Field of Mars just outside Rome. At a previous election, that of the emperor Pertinax in 192, the order of these two processes had been reversed. Pertinax was first acclaimed in the camp of that unit of the army called the Praetorian Guard, and he was then elected by the senate as an affirmation of his selection by the army.

In these cases, the inauguration was tied to Rome, since the senate was based in Rome, and the acclamation by the army in the case of both Tacitus and Pertinax also took place at sites in Rome. But when Julian was made emperor in 360, he was acclaimed by the army while he was on a military campaign and, although the senate was called on to ratify his elevation, there was no sense that that elevation had to take place in Rome. The same was true in 364 for the elevation of Valentinian, who was also on a military campaign when, in his case, he was elected by a conclave of generals. Earlier, in 305, Constantine had been made emperor by the army in York, where he was based as its commander, although he did not become emperor of the whole western empire until after his victory at the Milvian Bridge in 312.

Even if the inauguration of emperors was not fixed to a particular place or places, however, it was, early on in the history of the Roman Empire, acquiring elements of ritual that made it more than an impromptu process. The new emperor had to be clothed in an imperial tunic and a toga of purple fabric. Purple was the badge of a general who had been involved in a battle, but it became the fundamental symbol of emperorship. The new emperor had to be shod in red shoes; he had to be accompanied by twelve *lictors*, that is, torchbearers; and he had to be seated on the *sella curculis*, which was for all intents and purposes a throne. When Julian was acclaimed by the army in 360, he took a gold torc as a symbol of his office in a rather impromptu way; but later he was described as wearing a diadem. Already at the beginning of the fourth century, Constantine is represented wearing a diadem; this was evidently a mark of his office as emperor, and it seems likely that he assumed it at the point of his inauguration to that office.

After the end of the Roman Empire in the West, the surviving Eastern Roman Empire had its principal center, as we have seen, in Constantinople. The emperors were increasingly fixed there, and it was natural that it should emerge as the place of their inauguration. In the fifth and sixth centuries, certain places within the city came to be of critical importance to the ceremonies. This is well shown by the inauguration of the emperor Anastasius in 491. The inauguration began in the Hippodrome, the chariot-racing stadium adjacent to, and connected by a corridor to, the Great Palace. The emperor had a *kathisma*, that is, a box or gallery, in the Hippodrome, from which he could make appearances to the assembled people. On the advice of the magistrates, the senators, and the patriarch, and presumably because there were fears of disorder, the empress Ariadne, the previous emperor Zeno's widow, appeared in state in this kathisma, and announced that she had ordered the election of a new emperor, which was to be done by "the most glorious magistrates and the sacred Senate, with the concurrence of the vote of the most noble armies" and "with the holy gospels exposed in the midst" (Brightman 1901, 370). In fact, the senate proceeded to ask Ariadne herself to choose the next emperor, and it was she who chose Anastasius. The next day Anastasius went to the portico outside the Great Triclinium of the Great Palace. There he swore two oaths, one to the magistrates and senators to the effect that he would not bear grievances against anyone and that he would govern the empire well, and another to the patriarch that he would uphold Christian orthodoxy. He then went to the kathisma in the Hippodrome. There were the people in the tiered seating and the soldiers in the area below the kathisma. After the people had acclaimed him, the soldiers raised him on a shield, and a torc was placed on his head. The soldiers then raised the military standards, which they had been holding lowered, and people and army acclaimed the new emperor again. Anastasius then withdrew to a room off the Hippodrome, where the patriarch said a prayer and placed on him the purple imperial cloak and the diadem. After this, Anastasius returned to the kathisma for a further acclamation as "augustus," and to engage in a series of exchanges of formal words with those assembled. This part of the ceremony ended with the new emperor promising everyone a gift of five gold pieces and a pound of silver. He then proceeded to the church of Haghia Sophia to offer gifts, and then to a coronation feast with the city magistrates.

Anastasius's inauguration embodied the older elements of acclamation by people and army and election by the senate. The ritual of raising the new emperor on a shield was also older, appearing in the middle of the fourth century, when it was apparently adopted from barbarian custom. But the importance of particular places—the Hippodrome, the Great Triclinium, the church of Haghia Sophia—seems to be much more sharply focused than in earlier inaugurations. Although Haghia Sophia appears rather as an appendix to the process, it is also striking that there was a greater Christian element in the proceedings. It was explicit that during Anastasius's election the gospels were displayed. The patriarch was involved in the election process and in investing the new emperor with the cloak and diadem in the room off the Hippodrome, as well as with that part of the inauguration that took place in Haghia Sophia.

A further stage in the development of these religious elements was reached in 602, when Phocas became the first Byzantine emperor actually to be crowned in a church. Admittedly, his successor, Heraclius, was crowned in the Great Palace. But, in 641, Constans II became the first emperor to be crowned in the ambo, or pulpit, of Haghia Sophia. From then on the ceremony of inauguration came to be focused on that church. According to formulations of it, such as are found in the tenth-century *Book of the Ceremonies*, the ceremony consisted of a procession from the Great Palace to Haghia Sophia, where the patriarch invested the emperor with the purple cloak and other symbols, and placed the diadem on his head. The emperor was then acclaimed by the people in the church itself rather than in the Hippodrome. Since these formulations had by their nature a particularly ecclesiastical emphasis, they make no mention of the more secular aspects found in earlier inaugurations, which may nevertheless have persisted. It does not follow, in particular, that the new emperor was not raised on the shield in the Hippodrome because these sources do not mention it, nor that he did not make a gift to all those present. In the latter case in particular, it is unlikely that he did not do so. Nevertheless, it seems clear that the inauguration had become a much more religious process than it had been, and that its real focus had become the church of Haghia Sophia. When Constantinople and the Byzantine Empire were conquered by western crusaders in 1204 and a Latin (or western) emperor, Baldwin I, was inaugurated, the religious element in the process was further enhanced by the anointing of the emperor with holy oil by the patriarch. This was a borrowing from inaugurations in western Europe, where it had been introduced into Frankish royal inaugurations in the mid-eighth century.

The message of power conveyed by the inauguration of Roman and Byzantine emperors thus changed across the centuries. In the Roman world, the election by the senate was evidently intended to send the message that the emperor ruled only by consent in a state that was still notionally a republic. The agreement of the army, together with the elevation of the emperor on the shield, and the raising of the standards when the torc was placed on him, was intended to send the message that the emperor was at least notionally a military leader, whose tenure of office would benefit the military fortunes of the empire. Even bearing in mind the character of the source materials for later inaugurations, however, it appears that the religious elements in the inauguration came to predominate over these democratic and military elements. From 641, the Byzantine emperor had to be crowned in a church, and particularly in the church of Haghia Sophia. The message of power now being sent was the dependence of the emperor's power on God, and, within the empire he was to rule, the central importance of Constantinople, in which city of course stood Haghia Sophia.

EARLY MEDIEVAL INAUGURATIONS IN WESTERN EUROPE

That Constantinople should have emerged as the place where inaugurations of emperors had to take place is not surprising. It was, after all, the greatest city of the eastern Roman Empire, and later of the Byzantine Empire, and it was increasingly the city in which the emperors were settled, and where they had their greatest palace. In western Europe, however, developments in the processes of inauguration of rulers could produce surprising results when it came to the places that were fixed on as the venues where inaugurations had to take place. In the barbarian successor-kingdoms to the Roman Empire in the West, there seem to have been no fixed places where inaugurations of rulers took place, any more than there were in the early Roman Empire. Sometimes, there is simply no record of the place where inaugurations happened, which must suggest that the places themselves were not important. In the Carolingian Empire, for which the sources make it possible to construct a comprehensive list of inauguration places, there was clearly no question of a single site for royal inaugurations, although it was normal for kings to be promoted to the rank of emperor by the pope in St. Peter's, Rome, as Charlemagne had been in 800.

The inauguration of Frankish kings could happen in a range of places—at Soissons (France) for Pippin III's inauguration in 751, at Saint-Denis (France) for his subsequent inauguration by the pope in 754, at Noyon (France) and Soissons respectively for his successors Carloman and Charlemagne in 768. In 813, Charlemagne's son Louis the Pious was inaugurated in the newly built palace church at Aachen, but in 816 the same ruler was inaugurated again by the pope in Reims rather than in Aachen. Aachen was used again in 817 for the inauguration of Louis the Pious's eldest son, Lothar, but it had evidently not become the fixed place of inauguration. This was partly the result of the disintegration of the Carolingian Empire following the death of Louis the Pious in 840. In 855, for example, Charles the Bald was inaugurated at Limoges in western France, as ruler of what had become the kingdom of West Francia. In 869, he was inaugurated at Metz, when he became king of Lorraine, the kingdom of which Metz was at the heart. Even within the individual kingdoms into which the Carolingian Empire had been split, however, there was little sign that inauguration of rulers became tied to any specific place for its ceremonies to be performed.

AACHEN AS AN INAUGURATION PLACE

In the early eleventh century, however, in the kingdom of Germany that had evolved out of the eastern kingdom of the former Carolingian Empire, inaugurations of rulers were fixed to take place at the palace constructed by the emperor Charlemagne at Aachen. It was there that Henry III was inaugurated as king of the Germans in 1028, and from then on until 1531 almost all German kings were inaugurated there. The only exceptions were the claimants to the throne that was then occupied by Henry IV, that is Rudolf von Rheinfelden in 1077 and Hermann von Salm in 1081, who were crowned at Mainz and Goslar respectively. From 1028 onward, to be a legitimate king of Germany you had to be crowned in Aachen. This was so important that the rival kings of the Romans, Otto IV (1198–1218) and Philip von Schwaben (1198–1208), elected by different factions, vied for access to Aachen to be crowned, and Frederick II twice besieged the city in 1214 and 1215 to achieve it. Even when, after his own coronation and anointing in Aachen in 1531, Ferdinand I arranged for his son to be crowned and anointed in Frankfurt-am-Main (Germany), thus bringing to an end the role of Aachen in this respect, he nevertheless sent assurances to the city that it still in principle retained its role, as did his successors. As Haghia Sophia was for the Byzantine Emperors after 641, so after 1028 was Aachen the obligatory place of coronation for German rulers. This was set out formally in the emperor Charles IV's Golden Bull of 1356/7, although by then other places were linked with Aachen as obligatory sites in an extended process of inauguration. By the fourteenth century, to become king of Germany, a candidate had to be elected at Frankfurt-am-Main, and then crowned and anointed at Aachen, before (as he generally hoped) being inaugurated as emperor in St. Peter's Church in Rome by the pope.

What seems to have given Aachen its status as a place for inaugurations was not its political importance in the kingdom of Germany. With the breakup of the Carolingian Empire, it had ceased to be a central place in any of the successor kingdoms. As those coalesced into the kingdoms of France and Germany, Aachen occupied a position peripheral to both these states, as it does today. So, although it lay within the kingdom of Germany, the heartland of that kingdom had moved to the east, particularly to Saxony and the great imperial city of Magdeburg, or to the middle Rhineland and cities such as Mainz and Speyer. Aachen was a city of the past, but it seems to have been precisely this fact which gave it the power to assume the monopoly of royal inaugurations in Germany.

For its importance lay in its association with the traditions concerning the Frankish emperor, Charlemagne (768–814). These traditions are evident in the rituals and ceremonies of consecration and anointing of the ruler, which are known in detail only from the coronation and anointing of Sigismund in 1414, but which were clearly elaborate and impressive already by the mid-thirteenth century, when Richard of Cornwall, brother of King Henry III of England, was crowned king of Germany at Aachen and was moved to send a series of letters about this coronation back to England. The picture that emerges from the sources for 1414 and later is an impressive one, showing in some detail how the rituals of coronation and anointing had developed by the later Middle Ages. After his election at Frankfurt-am-Main, the king elect made a slow journey to take him the 250 kilometers to his coronation at Aachen. On his arrival at the city, he camped outside the city walls for a period of at least three days, and then presented himself at the Cologne Gate. There, he was met by the dean and canons of St. Mary's, the former palace church of Charlemagne's palace, with a processional cross, probably the Lothar Cross still preserved in the Aachen cathedral treasury, and a reliquary of Charlemagne made in the form of the emperor's bust, containing part of his skull and topped with a magnificent crown. Led by this bust-reliquary, the procession made its way to the former palace church. The king elect would have approached the church from the north and then would have passed through the atrium at its west side (above, Figure 8–13), through the eighth-century bronze doors, and so into the octagonal nave. Above this was hanging the magnificent candelabra given by the emperor Frederick Barbarossa in the twelfth century, inscribed with words invoking Aachen as the Heavenly Jerusalem (above, Figure 9–6). In the choir was the shrine of Charlemagne, adorned with figures of the line of rulers who were his successors, and of course the predecessors of the new emperor. Before the shrine, the king elect prostrated himself with his arms outstretched like a cross while a *Te Deum* was sung. After this, he went to his lodging, to return the next day for the actual coronation and enthronement itself.

On the day of his coronation, the king elect was taken to the high altar, where he swore an oath on the Coronation Gospels, received oaths of obedience from the lay and ecclesiastical lords, and was anointed with holy oil. He was then washed, dressed in the appropriate garments, and crowned by the Archbishop of Cologne. He was girded with the sword believed to be that of Charlemagne, which he used to dub knights. Taken then up into the gallery, the newly crowned king was enthroned by the Archbishop of Mainz and the Bishop of Trier on the throne (above, Figure 9–12) which was believed to have been the throne of Charlemagne. From the church, the king then proceeded along the upper stage of the two-storied corridor leading across to the great hall of Charlemagne's palace, the building converted into the town hall in the fourteenth century (above, Figure 9–1). Here, he gave a great feast, at which the principal nobles acted as his servants, and an ox-roast was held outside for the citizens of Aachen.

The earlier coronation of Otto I at Aachen in 936 did not establish Aachen as the requisite place of coronation as Henry III's inauguration did in 1028. But, as described by the contemporary writer, Widukind of Corvey, it was as impressive as the later medieval inaugurations and broadly similar to them. According to Widukind, the king was first enthroned in "the portico of the basilica," a place now not certainly identified. He then went in a great procession into the church, where he was received by the Archbishop of Mainz. The latter asked the people present to raise their right hands to elect the king. He was then escorted behind the altar "on which lay the royal insignia—sword with sword-belt, cloak with bracelets, staff with sceptre and diadem." The archbishop gave these to the king with various exhortations, which were much the same as the oaths sworn by the king in the later ceremony; and then:

> Having been sprinkled with holy oil and crowned with a golden diadem by the bishops . . . the king was led to the throne, to which he ascended by means of a spiral staircase. The throne of marvellous beauty had been constructed between two marble pillars, and from there the king could see and be seen by all. After the divine praise was intoned and the mass was solemnly celebrated, the king descended from the throne and walked to the palace. Going up to a marble table decorated with royal utensils, he sat down with the bishops and all the people while the dukes waited on them. (Hill 1972, 114–15)

After the initial enthronement in the "porticus," the pattern was broadly the same as that of later medieval ceremonies, except that in those the king had already been elected at

Frankfurt-am-Main so it was not necessary to repeat this at Aachen, and his oaths which were sworn in the church were more formal than in the tenth-century account. Although in both the 936 inauguration and in the later medieval inaugurations, the church was the most important focus of the ceremonies, also important was Charlemagne's great hall where a feast was held after the events in the church, just as the Byzantine emperors went from their inauguration in Haghia Sophia to a feast with the magistrates of Constantinople.

In the fourteenth century, the Aachen great hall was rebuilt by the city's burghers, probably in close association with the emperor Charles IV. Its importance as the place where coronation-feasts were held is clear from the fact that that rebuilding followed exactly the plan of Charlemagne's great hall, with the new building using the foundations of the old one. That those feasts were themselves an early and formal part of the process of inauguration is shown by the account given by Widukind of the 936 ceremony where at the feast the king was served by the dukes of the various duchies of the kingdom, as in the later account the king was served by the various nobles. Clearly, the feast was capable of taking the form of a ritual acceptance of the new king's status and right through the ritual of the dukes serving at the feast.

The primary message of power in these rituals must surely have been that of how the king's legitimacy depended on his succession to Charlemagne. As a site, Aachen's importance depended on Charlemagne. It was his city. At its center stood his palace and his palace church, in which the inauguration primarily took place. The regalia used were believed to be his. From the twelfth century, he was present in his golden reliquary in the nave of the church. In the fourteenth century, his bust-reliquary presided over the inauguration. So the king's inauguration was an exercise in connecting him with the past and with a particular ruler of the past.

Why should the desire to make these connections have become so strong by 1028 that Aachen was established as the requisite inauguration site for the German kings? Charlemagne had evidently been a ruler much admired and looked up to in his lifetime and after his death. Einhard's *Life of Charlemagne*, written in the reign of his son, Louis the Pious (814–70), and widely read in the ninth century, eulogized him. In a more colorful way, so too did the fanciful stories contained in Notker the Stammerer's later ninth-century *Life*. Although they were not factually accurate, they presented Charlemagne as a great ruler, wise and shrewd. Yet it cannot have been that ruler's reputation as it was promoted by these works that led directly to the choice of Aachen as the obligatory inauguration site from 1028. The reason for the choice may have been less Charlemagne's reputation as a great ruler *tout court*, but rather the increasing veneration offered to him as a saint.

It is striking that it was in the year 1000, not so many years before the inauguration of Henry III at Aachen in 1028, that there occurred the first event indicating that Charlemagne was by then regarded as a saint, even if he had not been formally canonized. In that year, the emperor Otto III staged an opening of Charlemagne's tomb in the palace church. It is now impossible to reconstruct what this opening really amounted to; but the very fact that it took place is a clear indication that Charlemagne was being treated as a saint. The opening was, in other words, the equivalent of what was done to saints when their remains or relics were translated to new shrines perhaps in another church, or elevated to more raised shrines in the same church, except that in this case Charlemagne's body was not actually moved from its original resting place. Otto III's opening of the tomb was described shortly afterward in picturesque detail by Adhemar of Chabannes, writing in southwest France. According to this account, Otto III found Charlemagne in his tomb not lying but rather seated, clad in his full regalia which were, like his body, as undecayed as when he had been buried. Only a portion of his nose, Adhemar explained, had suffered damage in the nearly two centuries since his interment, and this was repaired with a gold plate. Whatever the truth of this account, and it seems unlikely that Charlemagne was in fact buried seated upright in the way described, such failure to decay was a definitive sign of sanctity, following from the biblical text to the effect that God would not allow "his saint to see corruption" (Psalms 15(16).10; Carroll and Prickett 1997, II, 646), that is, in the sense of bodily decay. So there is no doubt that in the early eleventh century, Adhemar of Chabannes's source believed that there were clear signs of Charlemagne's sainthood revealed in the opening of his tomb in 1000. It is disputed what that source was, but it seems likely that it was someone close to the circle of Otto III. The story further underlines the belief in Charlemagne's sainthood by describing how Otto III took one of Charlemagne's teeth to keep, clearly regarding it as a holy relic. So it seems likely that the choice of Aachen as an obligatory inauguration place was closely related to, if not the direct result of, Charlemagne's rise to sainthood, a rise confirmed by his formal canonization by the pope in 1166, itself sponsored by the emperor Frederick Barbarossa (Kemp 1979, 109)). Rulership had become so religious in character that the inauguration site needed a powerful religious charge, which was at Aachen provided by the vivid traditions—not to mention the palace buildings and the regalia—of a ruler who was not only looked up to as a great ruler, but was venerated as a saint.

WESTMINSTER ABBEY AS AN INAUGURATION PLACE

As Aachen became the obligatory inauguration place of the German kings in 1028, so only relatively few years later Westminster Abbey became the obligatory inauguration place of the English kings. With the coronation of Harold Godwinsson at Westminster Abbey on January 6, 1066, there was initiated in the abbey church, which had only just been completed in its late eleventh-century form, the continuing series of coronations of English monarchs. After Harold's coronation, the only coronation not to have taken place there was the first coronation of Henry III, which took place at Gloucester because of the circumstances of the civil war after the death of King John; and even that was followed by a second coronation in Westminster Abbey on May 17, 1220. Just as it is arguable that Aachen was the obligatory inauguration site of the German kings because of its close connection with Charlemagne as a saint, so Westminster Abbey's monopoly on the coronation of the English kings was bound up with a saint-king of England, Edward the Confessor (1042–66). Shortly after his death, this ruler came to be venerated as a saint because of his supposedly virtuous and chaste life—he was formally made a saint by the pope in 1161, although his body had already been translated to a shrine in 1102 and *Lives* of him as a saint had been written in the early twelfth century. When Harold Godwinsson was crowned at Westminster Abbey immediately after King Edward's death, however, this was presumably less to do with the latter's supposed status as a saint than with Harold's claim to be Edward's declared heir. That claim was disputed by William the Conqueror, whose reasons for being crowned at Westminster Abbey shortly after his successful invasion of England in 1066 were no doubt the same as Harold's had been. But from then on Westminster Abbey's position as a coronation church was tied up with Edward's sainthood. Certainly, the crown used in the coronation was supposed to be Edward's crown, as was the ring, just as at Aachen where the crown used was supposed to have been Charlemagne's, even if quite erroneously, as was the sword used in the coronation, and—of course—the throne in the gallery. In the course of his coronation in the church, a new king of England was invested with the crown and ring of Edward the Confessor. He wore these during a sung mass, after which he processed to the shrine of Edward the Confessor, where he gave the saint back his regalia and was given a substitute crown. As with Charlemagne at Aachen, Edward the Confessor's importance to Westminster Abbey as an inauguration place was very considerable.

The role of Westminster Abbey as the coronation place was emphasized by its function of holding in its treasury the royal regalia, including the crown—indeed, these objects were only loaned to kings for their coronations, and had to be returned to the abbey at the end of the day, to be replaced by alternative regalia. The Fourth Recension of the order of the English coronation, which was certainly in use by 1308, shows that, when a coronation was to take place, a platform was erected in the crossing of the church of Westminster Abbey with steps to the choir and the high altar, and a throne on top of it (Binski 1995, 130; Strong 2005, 80–90). On the eve of the coronation, the prince was to ride from the Tower of London to the Palace of Westminster, allowing himself to be seen by the people, and then to undertake a vigil of prayer. At an assembly of prelates and nobles in the palace on the day of the coronation, the king was to be bathed and installed on a raised throne in Westminster Hall. He was to be greeted by the officiating clergy, and then to return with them in procession to the church of Westminster Abbey, together with the sacred vessels, the regalia, three state swords, and the royal spurs. The procession would pass through the choir and the king would be installed on the throne on the platform. The king was to be led to the high altar where he prostrated himself, pronounced the royal oaths, and was anointed under a processional canopy.

The church of Westminster Abbey was to such an extent a coronation church that, when it was rebuilt in the thirteenth century (above, pp. 302, 304, 305), it was in important respects designed as such. In particular, it could accommodate the temporary stage in the crossing. This was clearly a substantial affair, high enough for nobles on horseback to ride beneath it, as is recorded in a memorandum for the works of 1307–11 (Binski 1995, 131). The crossing was also the focus for the more publicly visible aspects of the coronation ceremony. This is presumably why, despite the construction of a lantern tower, the crossing was designed in a particularly spacious way with relatively slight crossing piers. Another aspect of the design of the church as a coronation church was the treatment of the tribune as a proper gallery, even though this had not been done in any other contemporary major church. This gallery was quite richly decorated, although it had no provision for altars. Probably, its purpose was to allow more people to be present at the coronation ceremony to listen to it, and, crucially, to acclaim the king when, after he had been installed on the throne on the platform, the archbishop asked the people from each of the four sides in succession whether they would accept the king. Later versions of the order of the coronation ceremony give the people's response as "so be it! so be it!" and "long live the king."

At both Aachen and Westminster, then, the primary message of power conveyed by the inauguration site seems likely to have been the dependence of the ruler on God, as was underlined by the anointing with holy oil which formed part of the inauguration, together with his status as a ruler imitating and reflecting a saint-king who was a predecessor. As will be discussed in the next chapter, the distinction between saints and rulers could be blurred; and for the new ruler to be closely associated with a saint-ruler of the past could only have underlined his ideological power. The importance at Aachen and Westminster of a close connection between the inauguration and a royal saint is paralleled in fourteenth-century Prague, where there was a close connection between the inauguration ceremony in the St. Vitus's cathedral and the relics of Wenceslas, saint-duke and ancestor of the kings of Bohemia. In the case of the kings of France, however, the relationship to a saint of the church that emerged as their obligatory inauguration place did not involve a saint-king, but rather a saint-archbishop. The church in question was Reims Cathedral.

REIMS AS AN INAUGURATION PLACE

Whereas Aachen became the requisite inauguration place for the German kings in 1028, and Westminster Abbey for the English kings in 1066, the emergence of Reims Cathedral for the French kings was later. Although King Henry I of France was inaugurated at Reims in 1027, this ceremony did not make it the obligatory inauguration place for his successors. This only occurred following the inauguration there of Louis VII in 1131, for from that date the inaugurations of all French kings, with only two exceptions, were held in Reims Cathedral, right down to the very last inauguration of a French king, that of Charles X in 1825. The two kings who were not inaugurated there are the exceptions that prove the rule. Louis VI (1108–37) was hurriedly crowned in Orleans after the murder of King Philip I, when holding the inauguration at Reims was not really feasible. And, much later, Henry IV (1589–1610) was inaugurated at Chartres during a period of religious warfare, when Reims was held by his enemies (Brühl 1950, 13).

The reasons for the choice of Reims for this role seem to parallel those that brought about the respective choices of Aachen and Westminster, but in its case the association with a saint that it claimed was even more intimately associated with the ceremony of inauguration. Reims had been the place where, in the early sixth century, the first Christian king of the Franks, Clovis (d. 511), had been baptized by the saint-archbishop of Reims, Rémi. The baptism evidently had no connection with Clovis's inauguration as a ruler, for he had become king of the Franks long before it took place. The connection between that baptism and ruler-inaugurations began to be established, however, when in the later ninth century the archbishop of Reims, Hincmar, wrote a *Life* of King Clovis. This included a legendary incident in which, as Archbishop Rémi was preparing to baptize Clovis, he had no access to the chrism (i.e., the mixture of holy oil and balsam) which he needed to carry this out. At this crucial point in the proceedings, a dove miraculously descended from above bearing in its beak an ampulla, that is a flask, of chrism, and it was this God-given chrism which Rémi used to baptize the king. The miraculous ampulla that the dove had brought was believed to have been preserved at the abbey of Saint-Rémi in Reims, an abbey founded by St. Rémi and which was his burial place. The ampulla appears in an order for a coronation compiled in 1231, and at that point it is clear that the chrism it contained was believed to be being miraculously replenished in perpetuity. On the day of the coronation in Reims Cathedral, the ampulla was brought in ceremonial procession under a canopy from Saint-Rémi to be used in the king's anointing.

Although this use of the ampulla can only be clearly documented in 1231, it is possible that its importance goes back much farther in the case of those royal inauguration ceremonies that took place at Reims even before the city became the obligatory inauguration place of the French kings. It is striking that already in the late tenth century, the chronicler Flodoard of Reims gives what appears to be a fictional account of Clovis's baptism that quite closely reflects the Reims inauguration ceremony as it was carried out in the later Middle Ages. At that time, the practice was for the king to be summoned to his coronation in the cathedral from his bedchamber in the Palace of Tau, the archbishop's palace where he stayed during the inauguration. Flodoard's description of Clovis's baptism does not exactly match this, but he does emphasize the king's chamber. To that chamber, according to him, Archbishop Rémi went to teach the king about Christianity, and it was from there that he led the king to his baptism in the cathedral, just as in the inauguration ceremony the king was led from his chamber to the cathedral. The link this account seems to establish between Clovis's baptism and the inaugurations of later kings at least opens the possibility that already in Flodoard's time such inaugurations were being modeled on what was believed to have taken place at Clovis's baptism. So, when Flodoard gave an account of that baptism, he was describing it in terms of the way he knew that kings were inaugurated at Reims.

In the twelfth century, Reims's claim to be the obligatory inauguration place of the French kings began to be challenged by the abbey of Saint-Denis which, under the leadership of Abbot Suger (1122–51), had aspirations to assume that role. In 1180 or 1181, King Philip Augustus had himself crowned there even after his inauguration at Reims in the previous year. Although Saint-Denis did not succeed in usurping Reims's position, Philip Augustus did designate it as the place where the regalia used in the inauguration at Reims should be kept. Thus that inauguration came to involve two churches in addition to Reims Cathedral itself. At the inauguration, the holy ampulla had to arrive from the abbey of Saint-Rémi, escorted by its abbot, while the regalia arrived from the abbey of Saint-Denis, equally escorted by its abbot. In many ways, this multiple participation in the inauguration, especially that of the high-status royal abbey of Saint-Denis, can only have confirmed Reims's status as the obligatory inauguration place. The layout of the Palace of Tau further underlined it, for from the later Middle Ages, it was permanently linked by a corridor to the south transept of the cathedral to facilitate the procession from the king's chamber to his inauguration. When it was rebuilt in the thirteenth century, the cathedral was decorated apparently with the inaugurations in mind. Its west façade was dominated by a line of statues of kings. This was typical of many churches of the period, but what was special about Reims was the sculpture in the center of the row of kings showing Clovis being baptized. His naked body is represented emerging from the baptismal font. By linking Clovis's baptism to his successor kings in this way, the decoration of the cathedral was surely intended to establish it as an inauguration place.

Association with saints, especially saints who were past rulers or—in the case of Reims a saint-bishop who had baptized the first Christian among them—was clearly an important element in establishing an obligatory inauguration place. Alongside the markedly religious aspects of the ceremony, this association made the inauguration even more a vehicle for expressing the ideological power attributed to the ruler.

THE HILL OF TARA

The emergence of churches as obligatory inauguration places is the pattern clearly observable in most of Christian Europe. In Ireland and Scotland, however, there was a quite different tradition of inauguration places. There, outdoor inaugurations were a feature of kingship. One of the most spectacular and complex of such sites was the Hill of Tara about twenty miles north of Dublin (Ireland), a grass-grown hill, running north to south, approximately a mile in length. Apart from a small church, which was first mentioned in about 1191–92, there are no buildings on the hill—just a series of earthworks (Figure 10–1). The first of these, called Tech Midchúarta (Banqueting Hall), consists of two parallel earthen banks running from the north up toward the summit of the hill. It seems likely that this was the type of prehistoric monument termed a cursus, which was probably built for use by processions moving along it. It could equally have functioned in that way in later periods. To the west of it are a series of burial mounds or barrows, some with ditches and banks around them—so-called ring-barrows or saucer-barrows, while just beyond the south end of it is a more or less circular earthwork, the so-called Ráith na Senad (Fort of the Synods), on the summit of the hill. Excavations have shown that this feature has been much modified over time. It began as an enclosure with a large bank and ditch around it, probably of Iron Age date, and perhaps ceremonial in character because the ditch was inside the bank. It was then modified as a series of circular enclosures of rather later Iron Age date, but similarly with ceremonial functions. It was then used as a cemetery, with burials that should probably be dated to approximately the first to the second century AD. Finally, excavations have recovered structures and finds which may indicate that, in its last period, down to perhaps the fourth century AD, it was either a residence for someone quite wealthy and powerful, or it continued to be a site for religious rituals. A recent geomagnetic survey of the summit of the Hill of Tara has shown that there was around this monument a much larger enclosure, measuring 210m north-south by 175m east-west, which appears to be centered on it, and perhaps more specifically on its first phase of development. Nothing of this enclosure is visible on the ground, and there is no dating, but this was clearly another impressive monument. Yet another enclosure, known as Ráith na Ríg (Fort of the Kings), overlapped this large enclosure and stretched southward. It was oval-shaped, with a circumference of more than a half mile, and it too had an outer bank and an inner ditch. Excavations and radiocarbon dating suggest that this monument and the Ráith na Senad date to sometime between *c.*370 BC to *c.*AD 406. Within the south edge of the Ráith na Senad and equally within the north edge of Ráith na Ríg is Duma na nGiall (Mound of the Hostages). This consists of a stone-lined chamber and passage leading to it through an earthen mound heaped over the top, and is dated to 3500–3100 BC, when it was a focus for many burials. To the south, in the center of Ráith na Ríg, are two earthworks, joined together in a figure- eight shape. These earthworks, which have never been excavated, are known as the Forrad (the Mound) and Tech Cormaic (Cormac's House). The Forrad consists of a central mound (presumably a burial mound), with two banks around it separated by a ditch. There is no dating evidence, apart from the possibility that a Bronze axe recovered from a modern grave came from the Forrad. Tech Cormaic consists of two banks with a ditch between them, and it was probably a fort. There are, in addition, other monuments within Ráith na Ríg. At the summit of Forrad's mound is a phallic standing stone, called Lia Fáil, which is known to have been moved from a position near Duma na nGiall in 1824 (and may therefore have been part of that tomb) (Figure 10–2). To the south of Ráith na Ríg there survives the southwest part of what was another enclosure, this one called Ráith Lóegaire (Lóegaire's Fort). It seems to have had two banks. It has never been excavated and nothing is known of its date. If all this sounds complicated, the recent geophysical survey of the Hill of Tara has shown that the monuments referred to above are only the best preserved of a series of mounds, ring-barrows, and enclosures, none excavated or dated.

Mysterious as the monuments on the Hill of Tara remain, their existence leaves no doubt that the hill was a place of considerable importance in the prehistoric period. The scale of interment in Dum na nGiall, perhaps the oldest surviving monument on the hill, already suggests this importance, and the complex of burial mounds and enclosures, now known to be far more numerous than previously suspected, underlines this. Moreover, there seems to have been a continuing awareness of the importance of the monuments on the hill. Thus Dum na nGiall was not destroyed when Ráith na Ríg was constructed many centuries later, but rather it was incorporated into that ringwork. With a similar level of respect for its venerability, it had been used for Bronze Age interments without disturbing its core. With similar respect for earlier monuments, Ráith na Senad was built in the exact center of the earlier ditched pit circle.

None of this proves that the Hill of Tara was a center for kings or whatever other sorts of ruler there may have been in the prehistoric period. Given how few finds there have been from the hill, and given the relative scarcity of distinctive royal regalia from any period of Irish history, it is perhaps not surprising that nothing distinctively royal has been found on the hill. But neither is there any clear evidence for a royal residence there. As we have seen, the Forrad is probably a burial mound. Ráith Lóegaire, as a bivallate ringwork, is a possible contender to be regarded as a royal residence, but it has never been excavated and nothing is known of what may have lain within it. As for Ráith na Ríg, the location of the ditch *inside* the bank makes it look much less like the sort of defensive enclosure that might have surrounded a royal residence, and much more like the perimeter of a sacred space. The last phase of Ráith na Senad can be interpreted as a royal residence, but it is just as likely to have

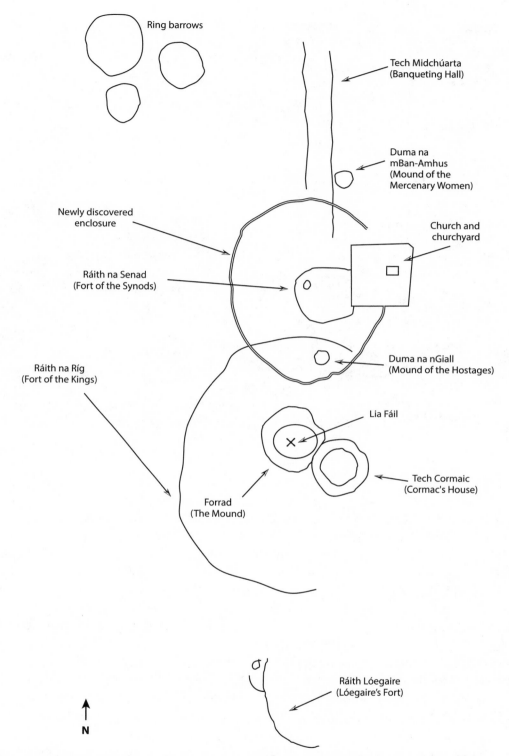

Ring barrows

Tech Midchúarta
(Banqueting Hall)

Duma na
mBan-Amhus
(Mound of the
Mercenary Women)

Newly discovered
enclosure

Church and
churchyard

Ráith na Senad
(Fort of the Synods)

Duma na nGiall
(Mound of the Hostages)

Ráith na Ríg
(Fort of the Kings)

Lia Fáil

Tech Cormaic
(Cormac's House)

Forrad
(The Mound)

N

Ráith Lóegaire
(Lóegaire's Fort)

Figure 10–1: Diagrammatic plan of the Hill of Tara (Ireland), showing the summit of the hill with the principal earthworks and other features (after Fenwick and Newman 2002, fig. 3, and Grogan 2008, fig. 1.1).

Figure 10–2: View north from the Forrad, Hill of Tara (Ireland).

been a ritual site. As for Tech Midchúarta, if it is correctly interpreted as a cursus, then it too probably belonged to a religious rather than a royal site. Of course, it might have been used by kings in approaching Tara, but it could equally easily have been for the use of religious processions that had no particular connection with kings and their inaugurations.

What is clear about the Hill of Tara, however, is that there is no firm dating later than the early fifth century for any of the monuments on it, and most are much more ancient than that. The only possible exception is Tech Midchúarta, the eastern bank of which encroaches on one of the—presumably prehistoric—barrows north of the Ráith na Senad, the barrow called Duma na mBan-Amhus (Mound of the Mercenary Women). This means that Tech Midchúarta was built later than this barrow, and so need not be part of the prehistoric complex on the Hill of Tara (Newman 2007, 421). Excavations at a similar earthwork called Knockans in the nearby township of Teltown have shown that it had two relatively late phases of construction, dated to some time between AD 640 and 780, and between AD 770 and 990. So it is not impossible that Tech Midchúarta is also of that sort of date, and is therefore evidence for activity on the Hill of Tara at a similar time. But, until the monument is excavated, this remains conjectural. Aside from this, the fact is that, for the period after the beginning of the fifth century, there is no archaeological evidence from the Hill of Tara.

There is, however, written evidence for its association with kingship, the earliest of which is Muirchú's Life of St Patrick, written in the seventh century about the fifth-century missionary of Ireland. This begins with Lóegaire, "a certain great king, a fierce and pagan ruler (*imperator*) of the barbarians, ruling in Tara, which was the chief place of the Irish (*caput Scottorum*)" (Byrne 1973, 254). This designation of the Hill of Tara suggests its importance not just for local kingship, but for the claims of certain kings to be rulers of all Ireland. Early annals confirm its importance by recording, albeit very succinctly, that the hill was the focus of military activity by various kings, who presumably wanted to take control of it because having control over it would have validated the claims they may have had to be kings of all Ireland. An annal for 840, for example, records that Feidlimid mac Crimthainn, king of Munster, halted at Tara and captured a certain, Gormlaith, styled queen of Tara. Another, for 1000, notes that Brian Bóruma, king of Munster, led his army toward Tara but in his case failed to reach it (Bhreathnach 2011, 144). Moreover, rulers who were certainly historical figures were styled "king of Tara," and are named in lists of kings of Tara such as *Baile Chuinn Chétchathaig* ("Vision of Conn of the Hundred Battles"). One of them, Máel Sechnaill II (980–1002, 1014–22) had a court poet, Cúán úa Lochcháin (d. 1024), who was probably the author of a *dindschenchas* poem, that is, a poem concerned with monuments and the traditions relating to them—in this case a poem focused on the Hill of Tara. It is preserved in the Book of Leinster, along with a prose list of the monuments there, probably also by Cúán úa Lochcháin. Now, it is these texts that supply the names of the monuments on the Hill of Tara, and also point to some of the traditions about them. It is possible literally to conduct a tour of the Hill of Tara with the dindschenchas in hand and, although there is some confusion, it is clear that the author took very seriously what must in his day have been simply grass-covered earthworks much as we see them now. There was even a seating plan for Tech Midchúarta, which the dindschenchas treated as a feasting hall (Macalister 1931, 18–19, 60; Bhreathnach 1995, no. 32).

The text that presents the Hill of Tara as a center of royal inauguration, albeit in its own mythical world, is *De Shíl Chonairi Móir* ("Of the Race of Conaire Mór"), which may have been written in the eighth century, and describes the inauguration as king of Conaire Mór. This describes a series of magical tests that a candiate for the kingship of Tara had to pass. It relates how there was a royal chariot at Tara, which could only be used by one destined to receive the kingship; how the chariot contained a mantle that would fit that person and no other; how there were two stones that would only part to allow the chariot through when it was driven by a man deemed acceptable to hold the "sovereignty of Tara"; and how the stone called Fál, the "stone penis," would screech against the chariot axle, when the man driving it was worthy to have the kingship of Tara. According to this text, Conaire Mór went to Tara and, having successfully shown his fitness to rule by passing the magical tests, he was duly inaugurated as king (Gwynn 1912, 138–39). The ruler is legendary and the account is mythical, but it embodies the idea that a site like the Hill of Tara was one where kings were inaugurated.

Such a mythical account of inauguration on the Hill of Tara, however, may reflect the essence of Irish inaugurations that were real enough and that involved outdoor sites. The fact that the names of such sites often included the Irish word *leac* (stone) suggests that they were often furnished with stones, or perhaps outcrops of rock (Fitzpatrick 2004a, ch. 3). These cannot, of course, have performed the magical actions described in *De Shíl Chonairi Móir*, but they could nevertheless have fulfilled a function similar to that of thrones. That is to say that the ruler sat or stood on them as part of his inauguration. Some known inauguration sites have incised footprints on outcrops of rock, suggesting the possibility that the ruler stood with his feet in them during his inauguration. An example is the footprint incised on rock at the early Scottish royal center of Dunadd, although it is not known whether the rock in question was an inauguration stone (Lane and Campbell 2000, 247–49). And there were even stone inauguration thrones, one of which may have been the rough stone throne now in the Ulster Museum. This formerly stood on Castelreagh Hill in Ulster, which may have emerged as an inauguration site of rulers who became important in the fifteenth century, the Clann Aodha Buildhe (Fitzpatrick 2004a, 156–61).

There survive documents down to the end of the sixteenth century describing the ceremonies that took place at some of these sites in Ireland. In the course of these, the king was vested with robes, he proceeded in a clockwise direction around the inauguration site, and the royal rod was bestowed on him. There was then a proclamation of his kingship and the people present acclaimed him. He then surrendered his horse and his garments, and was ritually bathed. There followed ceremonial alcoholic drinking, the chanting of the king's genealogy, the singing of an inaugural ode, and a rite involving the throwing of a single shoe (Fitzpatrick 2004a, 1–12). Although the influence of the Church on these ceremonies is clear enough, for they also involved the use of reliquaries containing the remains of Christian saints or martyrs, it is difficult to escape the idea that they really derive from a preChristian past. Just like the Christian coronation ceremonies, however, they seem to have a powerful religious element, and may in some way have been connected with pre-Christian paganism.

It is an intriguing idea that inauguration ceremonies involving stones, or stone objects, may have happened widely, outside Ireland and Scotland. Many of the tenth-century kings of England, for example, were inaugurated at Kingston-on-Thames. Although the early form of the name meant "the king's vill" rather than "the king's stone," and although the stone displayed in the town today as the coronation stone only came to light in the eighteenth century and its interpretation is certainly based on no more than the imagination of antiquaries of that period, the inaugurations at Kingston-on-Thames were not at all connected with a monastery or with a royal palace (Keynes 2014). It seems likely that they were outdoor inaugurations like those known from Ireland, even though it cannot be shown that they had ancient, let alone pagan, associations.

Indeed, it is tempting to think that the apparent contrast between Irish and Scottish inaugurations and those at the heart of Europe, at Aachen, and Reims, and Westminster, is exaggerated by the differing character of the sources from the two areas. What is known of

Constantinople, Aachen, Reims, and Westminster as inauguration places comes largely from handbooks of inauguration ceremonies written by churchmen, or from the writings of chroniclers who were themselves churchmen; while what we know of Irish inaugurations often comes from vernacular fictional texts, heroic and romantic in character, or from the writings of unsympathetic authors like Gerald of Wales, or the sixteenth-century English who observed the Irish ceremonies in the last days of their existence. That Christian churches as inauguration places may have had more in common with inauguration places like Tara than is immediately apparent is suggested by the survival of one of the most remarkable objects associated with royal inauguration, the Stone of Scone.

This object is only clearly documented after its seizure by the English invaders of Scotland in the late thirteenth century. After he defeated the king of Scots, John Balliol, in 1296, King Edward I of England (1272–1307) made a triumphal procession through the newly conquered kingdom, in the course of which he removed various Scottish treasures and had them taken to Westminster Abbey, where they were placed by the shrine of Edward the Confessor. They included: the Scottish regalia, which Edward I seized at Edinburgh; the Black Rood of St. Margaret of Scotland, a reliquary believed to contain a fragment of the True Cross; and the Stone of Scone. Edward I took this from the abbey of Scone in eastern Scotland—hence its name—and placed it in Westminster Abbey. It is an oblong block of sandstone, measuring 670 x 420 x 265mm, and weighing 152 kg. It is a rather rough block, with a number of chisel-marks on it, and it has two iron rings set into it, presumably to make it possible to carry it.

There is no evidence that the Stone of Scone was a holy relic, like the Black Rood of Scotland, for the legend that it was in origin the stone on which the Old Testament figure Jacob had slept while he dreamed of a ladder ascending to heaven only appears after the stone had arrived at Westminster Abbey (Aitchison 2003, 116). Even though it was not a relic, it was considered by Edward I to be important. Not only did he take the trouble to have it transported from Scotland to Westminster, but he also ordered his goldsmith to make an expensive bronze throne in which to mount it. In any event, money seems to have run out (Edward I's wars were expensive), and there was made instead a decorated wooden throne, the so-called Coronation Chair, which is still preserved in the abbey, and which held the Stone in a space underneath its seat, until its return to Edinburgh in 1996 (Figure 10–3). It cannot be proved that the Coronation Chair was used in inaugurations of English kings thereafter. It is, however, quite possible that it was, for—as we have seen—a throne was mounted for the ceremony on the platform in the crossing of Westminster Abbey, and the Coronation Chair could have been moved to serve that purpose. It is in fact hard to see why Edward should have installed the Stone in such a throne at all unless using it in inaugurations was his intention. He would thus have been associating the stone with an English royal throne, just as he was claiming to be lord over the Kingdom of Scotland.

Edward I's treatment of the Stone of Scone indicates that he believed it to be an important object for Scottish kings, and it was probably used in their inaugurations. Scone was certainly a place where those inaugurations took place. In 1292, for example, Edward I had issued a document authorizing the inauguration of John Balliol at Scone. There was an important abbey there, founded by King Alexander I of Scots in 1114. So it seems likely that

Figure 10–3: Coronation Chair after restoration, Westminster Abbey (England), with a computer simulation of the Stone of Scone in its original position below the seat.

Scone was developed to resemble places like Westminster Abbey, with Scone Abbey functioning as an inauguration church for Scotland, as Westminster Abbey was an inauguration church for England.

For the inauguration of King Alexander III at Scone in 1249, however, there are detailed, and apparently independent, accounts in the late medieval chronicles of John Fordun and the *Scotichronicon* of Bower, the latter of which even has a picture of the event (Aitchison 2000, fig. 16). According to these sources, the inauguration ceremony differed from those at Westminster Abbey and comparable inauguration places in that it consisted of two parts. The first part resembled inaugurations at places like Westminster. It involved the king swearing an oath, and being blessed and ordained by the Bishop of St. Andrews. But the second part took place out of doors. The bishops and the nobles present led Alexander to a point "in front of the cross that stands in the graveyard at the east end of the church," and there installed him on a royal throne "in accordance with the custom which had grown up in the kingdom from antiquity," while his genealogy was read out to those assembled. Fordun identified this throne with the Stone of Scone, for he commented that to be a properly inaugurated king, one had to have sat on the Stone of Scone (Aitchison 2000, 94).

Once the stone was in Westminster, some other arrangement would have to have been made for the inaugurations of Scottish kings, but Scone nevertheless remained the place of inauguration, beginning with that of the rebel against Edward I, Robert Bruce, in 1306, at least until the coronation there of James I in 1424. Although it seems therefore that the importance of Scone for inaugurations did not entirely depend on the Stone being there, this does not detract from the significance of the trouble that Edward I went to in order to obtain the Stone and to mount it in the Coronation Chair. If the Stone was a sort of inauguration throne in its own right, and if part of the ceremony of inauguration was outdoors, this may provide a glimpse of a quite different tradition of inaugurating kings than the one we have seen at Westminster, Reims, and Aachen. And, more importantly, Edward I was evidently in a position to grasp its significance.

That should give us pause before we dismiss an object such as the Stone of Scone as characteristic only of the peripheries of Europe, areas outside the mainstream of European Christendom. It is admittedly tempting to see it like that. For, in addition to the Irish inauguration-stones and possible Scottish inauguration-stones such as that at Dunadd, another possible parallel for the Stone of Scone is in an equally peripheral situation, but on the eastern edge of Europe. This was Karnburg, the inauguration site of the Dukes of Carinthia, located in the far eastern extremities of the Austrian Alps, at the edge of the central stage of European politics, as represented by the great empire of Charlemagne and, later, the Holy Roman Empire and the Kingdom of France. There, at Karnburg, the so-called Prince's Stone, an upturned Roman column, and the Duke's Throne, constructed of plates of stone with a stone seat, were used, according to fourteenth-century sources, in the inauguration of Duke Meinhard II in 1286, when the practice may well have been already ancient—for there is what appears to be an account of their use for the inauguration of Duke Hermann of Carinthia in 1161.

On the other hand, the presence of stones that were either used as thrones or had throne-like functions has already been noted at the very heart of the Kingdom of France, in the Palais de la Cité in Paris, as has the appearance of such stones (perrons) in the *Chansons de Geste* which lay at the heart of French courtly culture (above, pp. 117–18). There was an outdoor stone throne closely associated with the German kings, above the River Rhine at Rhens, just upstream from Koblenz, with commanding views over the valley. It was on this throne that the newly inaugurated king of Germany was required to sit, at any rate in the fourteenth century (Gussone 2000, 40). It formed a compulsory stopping point on the journey around his kingdom which he made after his election at Frankfurt-am-Main and his inauguration at Aachen. As it appears from comparing a painting of 1785 with the extant remains, it has been very heavily restored, no doubt in the period of high German romantic nationalism; but nonetheless it seems clear that it was indeed a stone throne in an outdoor situation, and as such not so far removed from the Irish examples of such thrones, and perhaps too from the Stone of Scone.

It may be indeed that a stone throne at the very heart of the Carolingian and later German Empire should be thought about in the same terms—the throne of Charlemagne in the western gallery of the Aachen palace church, no less. If this throne is in its original position (above, pp. 286–89), it is of course an indoor rather than an outdoor throne (above, Figure

9–12). But three aspects of its construction suggest the possibility that it is more like objects such as the Stone of Scone than might be thought: first, its rough, almost makeshift, character. The base plate, for example, has had its mouldings cut away at some point where it joins the steps. Moreover, it is in two parts, so that it was necessary to use metal brackets to fix them together as well as a rough hollowing out to accommodate wooden pegging—possibly to fix some other structure into the throne. Second, the slabs of marble that form the sides and back of the throne are not only spolia, reused from some Roman structure, but they have not been properly finished for their incorporation in the throne. They have been shaped to form the arms and back, although only crudely and without decoration, and they still have on them Roman graffiti, including a gaming board. Third, there are clear indications that the throne was used as a relic in its own right, for the passage created underneath the base-plate by its elevation on four pillars shows polishing on the stones created by pilgrims crawling along it, a practice documented in the later Middle Ages, and moldings have been cut away to give more space for this crawling, which was of course a penitential activity.

The first two of these aspects can be interpreted as showing that the throne must have been made later than the church itself, for it is surely too rough to have been designed for Charlemagne's magnificent building. It is, however, hard to avoid the conclusion that the throne was contemporary with the church, for—as has been seen—the bronze grille below it has a gate that opens to facilitate the view of the throne's occupant down to what was formerly the site of the high altar. Since the grilles are certainly original to the church, the throne must itself have been part and parcel of its design (above, p. 287). If the throne is original, or even if it belongs rather to the tenth century—for the account by Widukind of Corvey of the coronation of Otto I in 936 strongly suggests that it was by then in its present position—then its makeshift character raises the possibility that it was the stones of which it was made that gave it its significance. It consisted in other words of stones to be venerated.

Such a contention may find some support in the throne's unusual character. Thrones from medieval Europe were not generally like it, not constructed in other words of great plates of marble. In the churches of the twelfth-century kings of Sicily, at Palermo and Monreale, for example, what we find is throne platforms, handsomely decorated, with magnificent backdrops—and on these throne platforms it was clearly intended that a metal folding throne should stand, as has been reconstructed in Monreale (above, pp. 308–10). A Carolingian example of such a folding throne is the so-called Throne of Dagobert, which was at Saint-Denis in the twelfth century, when the abbot Suger considered it as the throne on which the king of France sat after his coronation to receive homage (Charles-Gaffiot et al. 2011, 276–77). That is not to say that there are no parallels to the Aachen throne, but they seem to be connected to it in very specific ways. The throne in the eleventh-century German palace at Goslar, for example, resembles the Aachen throne. But that was probably because Goslar was a palace in many ways built in imitation of Aachen, so that the similarities between this throne and the one at Aachen rather underline the latter's distinctiveness.

The Aachen throne was eminently unsuitable as a throne in the materials it used and the way it was designed. It was not even possible to sit in it without the support of a rather basic arrangement of three wooden boards installed inside it, because the use of the marble slabs did not allow the creation of a stone seat. Those marble slabs had to be held together with unsightly metal straps. There must surely have been some compelling reason to use them as the basis of the throne, or at least to construct a throne which must have given the overwhelming impression that they were of some great significance. The use of these slabs of marble remains thought-provoking, for the throne was certainly treated as a relic and an object of pilgrimage in its own right. Maybe this was simply because Charlemagne was believed to have sat on it, so that the throne had the status of a secondary relic. But, if there was something special about the marble slabs forming the throne, there was more to it than that; and we are faced with the intriguing possibility that here, in the gallery of the church of Aachen, at the heart of the Carolingian empire, at the site that became the obligatory inauguration place of the German kings, at the center stage of European politics, we may have something that is not so far from the world of the Stone of Scone.

MARRYING THE KINGDOM

Apparently pre-Christian inauguration ceremonies may have had more in common with their Christian counterparts in other ways too. In the twelfth century (when Ireland had long been Christian), Gerald of Wales described the inauguration of a king in the district of Kenelcunill (Tír Conaill) in northern Ireland. This involved the king-to-be having "bestial intercourse" with a white mare before all his people while "professing himself to be a beast also." The mare was then killed, butchered, and boiled. The broth from this boiling was used as a bath for the king, who sat in it "surrounded by all his people," eating the meat and drinking the broth. "When this unrighteous rite has been carried out," Gerald notes, "his kingship and dominion have been conferred" (O'Meara 1982, 109–10, part 3, sec. 102). Although Gerald was intent on presenting the Irish as a barbarous and uncivilized people and so was no doubt presenting them in the worst possible light, it remains the case that this all sounds genuinely derivative from pagan practices. For, the king was engaging in a rite of marriage with the mare, who may have represented a goddess; and the ritual seems to have involved a horse sacrifice and the sympathetic fusing of the king and his people through the flesh of the animal. The ceremony thus emphasized the ideological power of the king by presenting him as close—intimately close in this case—not to the Christian God but to a pagan goddess.

Pre-Christian as the idea of sexual intercourse with the beast representing the kingdom may be, it may give pause for thought that the notion of the king marrying the kingdom appears in the French inauguration rituals in an entirely Christian context. This is only clearly articulated in the sixteenth century. At Henry II's inauguration in 1547, the king received from the Archbishop of Reims a beautiful ring which he had blessed and, according to a contemporary description, with this "the king married the kingdom" (Jackson 1984, 85). Although the significance of the ring had not previously been expressed in this way, the placing of a ring on the king's finger had been part of his inauguration since the thirteenth century. There was nothing intrinsically pagan about this. Bishops were envisaged as marrying their churches when they were consecrated, also symbolized by a ring. In the sixteenth century the king's marriage to the kingdom was clearly bound up with legal ideas about the inalienability of the kingdom. For the jurists, its implication was that he could not alienate—or give away—any of it, just as a husband could not alienate his wife's dowry. Nevertheless, the fact that the idea should occur in the French inauguration ritual as well as in the ritual described by Gerald of Wales does raise the possibility that the Irish inaugurations were not so dissimilar from those elsewhere as appears at first sight.

Another aspect of the French inauguration ritual may lead to a similar line of thought. Already in a German *ordo* of Mainz from around 961, the procedure was that the king should come to the church from his bedchamber (Jackson 1984, 133). At the inauguration of Charles V in 1364, it was the bishops who went to that bedchamber in the Palais de Tau at Reims to fetch the king, whom they found lying on a bed. Although it was only in connection with the coronation of Charles IX in 1561 that it was explicitly stated that the king was asleep and had to be wakened before he could be taken to the church to be inaugurated, the idea of the sleeping king may nevertheless have been present in earlier inaugurations. Already by 1100 the king is said to have endured a night vigil before his inauguration, been given a purificatory bath, and been put back to bed before being fetched to be taken to the church. The image of the sleeping king can be interpreted in various ways. It can be seen as a symbol of the continuity of the monarchy. The new king was merely sleeping, so there had really been no interval in the occupancy of the throne. It can also be seen in terms of the solar symbolism which was so dominant at the court of Louis XIV (1643–1715). Just as the rising (*lever*) of that ruler was explicitly related to the rising of the sun, so the wakening of the sleeping king before his coronation can equally be thought of as symbolizing the rising of a new sun. It is striking that the image of the sleeping king recurs in legends about kings, notably the mythical King Arthur, whose sleep was merely an interval before his resumption of the kingship. Those legends take us back to the Celtic world and to what was—perhaps only superficially—a different set of ideas about kingship. But how different really were they?

CONCLUSION

The messages of power that inauguration sites could send were evidently of varying types and of varying degrees of complexity. When a Roman emperor was acclaimed by the army on the Field of Mars, or in the course of a military campaign, the message was clearly enough focused on the emperor's role as a military leader, and on the army's acceptance of him as such. When the Senate elected him, the message was that his power conformed to the democratic aspirations of the Roman republic, even if in fact he was to be the autocratic ruler of a republic that was no more than notional. The Christian impact on inauguration sites was also in some senses straightforward enough. The ruler came to be regarded as receiving his power from God, so that it was natural enough for the inauguration, wherever it took place, to involve religious leaders, such as the Patriarch of Constantinople in the case of Byzantine imperial inaugurations. Equally, it was obvious enough in this context why churches gained greater importance as inauguration sites, as Haghia Sophia did in Constantinople from the mid-seventh century onward. If the ruler derived his power from God, it was natural enough for the essential elements of his inauguration to be transferred to a church.

More complex, however, were the processes by which obligatory inauguration places were chosen or developed as such. Often, they were part of important palaces, as was the case at Aachen, Westminster, and Prague—and indeed Constantinople, where the Hippodrome and the church of Haghia Sophia were immediately adjacent to the Great Palace. But evidently this was not the only reason for their status as obligatory inauguration places. In the case of Aachen, that status only emerged long after the palace had lost its political significance. Holding inaugurations in a place closely associated with a saint-ruler of the past was in at least some cases the key. At Aachen, it was Charlemagne who dominated the inaugurations, at Westminster it was Edward the Confessor, and at Prague, Wenceslas—all saint-rulers of the past. At Reims, although Clovis was not regarded as a saint, the bishop who baptized him was, and the later use in inaugurations of the miraculous chrism brought to Archbishop Rémi by the dove fully associated Reims with a saintly past, even if the king who was at the heart of this, Clovis, was not himself a saint.

Inauguration places such as the Hill of Tara, however, and objects used in inauguration such as the Stone of Scone, show that there were different, perhaps pre-Christian, beliefs involved in the choice of some inauguration places. But in these cases, as has been argued, there was perhaps more resonance between the beliefs they represented and those represented by sites such as Aachen than is immediately obvious. The use of stones as thrones, and of stone thrones, may be one indication of this. But there may be others too. As set out above, Gerald of Wales's undoubtedly extravagant account of the mating between the king-to-be and the mare suggests the notion that the king was, at his inauguration, entering into a marriage with his kingdom.

This chapter then has discussed various types of inauguration of rulers and the messages of power they could send—from the elections and acclamations of the Roman rulers, to the inaugurations in churches in close association with saintly relics of the past, to the ritual of bestial intercourse described by Gerald of Wales. It may be, however, that, once allowance has been made for the differing character of the sources for these inaugurations, it is the similarities between them that are most arresting. Certainly, the inauguration rituals differed in different states, and changed across the centuries, but it is perhaps their fundamental similarities and continuities that should strike us most forcibly.

CHAPTER 11

Death and Power

The Burial Places of Rulers

The aim of this chapter is to explore the ways in which the places where rulers were buried could send messages of power, either on behalf of the rulers in question, or of their successors. For burial places could be planned and constructed by rulers during their lifetimes, so that whatever messages of power they were designed to send would have had the potential to benefit them in life. Equally, they could be, and perhaps more naturally were, the concern of the rulers' successors. So the messages of power the burial places could send were as much for their benefit as for that of the deceased. To emphasize the power or the grandeur or the piety or the legitimacy of deceased rulers could only have been to the good of their successors. How then could burial places send messages of power? Did the sites of those burial places contribute to the messages of power, either because of the importance of their position, or because they caused the burial places to be accessible to greater numbers of visitors? How did the design of tombs bear on the messages of power conveyed? What was the importance of the development of fixed places for the burial of whole lines of rulers, and how was it possible to organize their tombs in ways that made their messages of power explicit? What was the role of funeral ceremonies and beliefs about rulers' bodies?

BURIAL MOUNDS

Scale

Choice of site and grandeur of design as means of sending messages of power are clearly evident in the spectacular tombs of Roman emperors of the first century AD. With these, one of the primary messages was simple and direct in asserting the magnificence of the rulers who either had been, or were to be, buried within them. Already in his lifetime, the first Roman emperor, Augustus (27 BC–AD 14), began the construction of his mausoleum in Rome. It was one of the earliest building projects of his reign, apparently finished as early as 23 BC, more than twenty years before his death. It was in the form of a burial mound but, today, its ruined state makes it difficult to resolve exactly what was its original design (Figure 11–1). But what is not in doubt is that it was absolutely enormous, its outer wall 89m in

Figure 11–1: Mausoleum of Augustus, Rome (Italy), view of the entrance side.

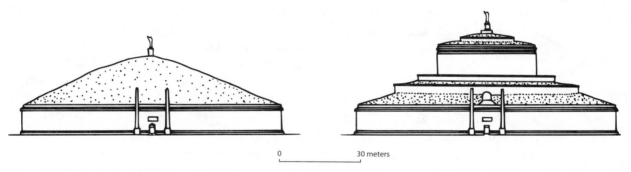

0   30 meters

Figure 11–2: Alternative reconstructions of the Mausoleum of Augustus, Rome (Italy), proposed by Johnson (2009), fig. 8.

diameter, and the structure as a whole rising to a height of around 50m, possibly more—it is not possible to tell exactly how high it originally was because the top no longer exists. It remains impressive because of its scale even in its ruined state, and it must have been stunning indeed when it was still intact. The Greek geographer, Strabo (64/63 BC–*c.*AD 24), describes it as a "great mound near the river on a lofty foundation of white marble" (Johnson 2009, 21–22). This suggests that the mausoleum was basically an earthen burial mound, with a marble retaining wall (the low outer wall is now largely stripped of its marble) around it. This is what is shown in the left-hand reconstruction in Figure 11–2.

As appears in the view shown in Figure 11–1, the mausoleum has a series of three circular walls, one within the other. Beyond the outer wall just mentioned, the second wall can be seen rising, and within that the third wall. These walls may have been intended merely to stabilize an enormous mound of earth which entirely covered them (as in the left-hand reconstruction); but it is equally possible that they formed great monumental steps that divided the mound into sections, as is shown in the right-hand reconstruction. Either way, this was a very impressive structure indeed, and was probably the largest of its time in the city of Rome. An emperor who could build his mausoleum on such a scale, runs the message it clearly sent, was a very great ruler indeed, who intended to be remembered across the ages. The message, in other words, was first and foremost that of the majesty and grandeur of the emperor—and also of his family, members of which were also to be buried there, beginning with his nephew Marcellus in 23 BC.

A century later, another Roman emperor built an equally impressive mausoleum, also basically in the form of a burial mound, on the other bank of the River Tiber. The emperor was Hadrian (AD 117–38), and the mausoleum he built is what is now the Castel Sant'Angelo. It was so massive that it was absorbed into the city's defenses as early as the sixth century, and it eventually became a great fortress of the popes, with a fortified corridor built in 1277 to link it to the nearby papal palace of the Vatican. Like the Mausoleum of Augustus, the Mausoleum of Hadrian was begun during the emperor's lifetime, probably in AD 123, fifteen years before his death, although it was not dedicated until AD 139, after he had died. And like the Mausoleum of Augustus, it was enormous, and it remains a dominating structure even in modern Rome (Figure 11–3). Much of the stonework visible on the outside dates from the medieval and Renaissance periods when the mausoleum was modified for its new role as a fortification, but the basic shape remains as Hadrian had it built. The outermost component is a square base, its sides measuring 88.9m, and its outer wall rising some 12m (the fortified corner towers in the figure belong to an additional outer wall of the medieval period). Within the Roman outer wall, there is another wall, and then a great stone cylinder, 74m in diameter at its lowest stage, and rising to a height of 21m above the base. At the top of the cylinder, in its center, there rose a further tower, which is now obscured by later masonry but which contains within it two spaces built by Hadrian, and now known as the Sala del Tesoro and the Sala delle Bandiere (both within the central block rising from the cylinder in Figure 11–3).

The original form of the mausoleum is not easy to establish, but a possible reconstruction of it is shown in Figure 11–4. The outer wall is here reconstructed with corner piers, one of which survives, while the drum is reconstructed with pilasters around it, this part of the reconstruction being based on fragments of the Roman pilasters that have been recovered from the site. Archaeological evidence suggests that above the cylinder rose an earthen mound, shown planted with trees, comparable with that of the Mausoleum of Augustus. Through that mound rose the central tower. The whole was, in this reconstruction, crowned with a bronze statue of the emperor driving a four-horse chariot, a quadriga, in triumph—plausible enough, even if lacking evidence to support it. Whatever the difficulties of reconstruction, however, it is beyond doubt that the Mausoleum of Hadrian was also a very grand structure indeed, and that it was intended to reflect the power of Hadrian himself, and of his successors who were also buried there until the early third century.

In spite of their masonry walls, the Mausoleum of Augustus and the Mausoleum of Hadrian were essentially great burial mounds, with the chambers to hold the remains of the

Figure 11–3: Mausoleum of Hadrian (Castel Sant'Angelo), Rome (Italy), viewed from across the River Tiber.

emperors inside them. They show how impressive such mounds could be, and this goes for other cultures as well as that of Rome. Great burial mounds were built in many parts of Europe back into the prehistoric period, and some of the greatest belong to the centuries after the end of the Roman Empire in the West. However impressive they may be, it is not always possible to be sure whether or not they were built for rulers, because there are often no written sources or inscriptions to explain for whom they were intended or to illuminate the status of their occupants; but in the case of two of the greatest, those at Jelling in southern Denmark, there is really no doubt that they were royal mounds. Even in their present eroded and damaged condition, they are enormous. The northerly of the two needed a staggering 1288m^2 of stones and earth to construct it; it measures 62m across and it still stands to a height of 8m (Figure 11–5). The mound immediately to the south of it is even larger, measuring 78m across. These mounds dwarf the modern buildings around them and must always have been stunningly impressive. But they were not the only impressive aspects of Jelling. Recent excavations have shown that the North Mound stood in the center of a ship-setting, that is a series of large stones laid out to make the shape of a Viking ship with pointed bows and a pointed stern. Such ship-settings were not uncommon in early Scandinavian burial sites, but this one was colossal, some 350m long. Recent excavations have also

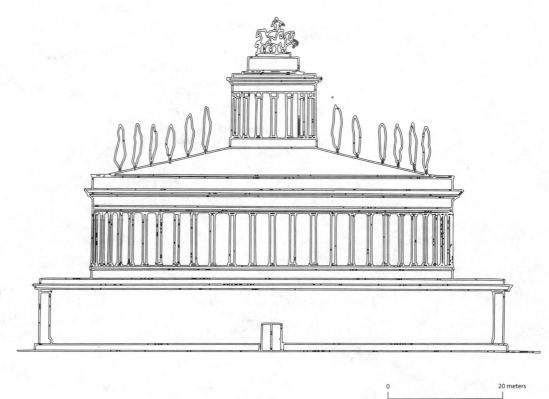

Figure 11-4:
Reconstruction of the Mausoleum of Hadrian (Castel Sant'Angelo), Rome (Italy), proposed by Johnson (2009), fig. 18.

0   20 meters

shown that it fitted neatly into a great palisade, which enclosed both it and the two mounds in the form of a parallelogram (Figure 11–6).

No dating evidence has been recovered from the ship-setting, but there are some clues as to when it was constructed. The fact that the South Mound has been built over the top of it suggests that it was made earlier than that mound, but equally the North Mound is so neatly central to it that it must have been conceived of as an integral part of the burial place of which that mound formed a part. The fact, too, that the ship-setting fits so neatly into the palisade suggests that the latter was planned in conjunction with it. So the assumption must be that both mounds, the ship-setting, and the palisade are broadly contemporary with each other. For the mounds, this has been confirmed by samples of wood that have been dendro-chronologically dated to around the 960s (Hvass 2011, 82–83).

The North Mound had within it a burial chamber, which was found during excavation to contain traces of a rich burial. So the idea may have been that the deceased was interred in the middle of a great ship represented by the ship-setting. The South Mound was almost completely excavated in the 1940s, but no trace of a burial was found in it, so it remains a mystery. To add to the mystery, there was another burial found by archaeologists on the site, this one under the medieval church between the two mounds, and consisting of a burial chamber with fragments of human bone and fragments of textile and metalwork resembling, and so perhaps broadly contemporary with, that found in the burial under the North Mound.

Figure 11–5: North Mound, Jelling (Denmark), with the church on the extreme right. Compare Figure 11–6.

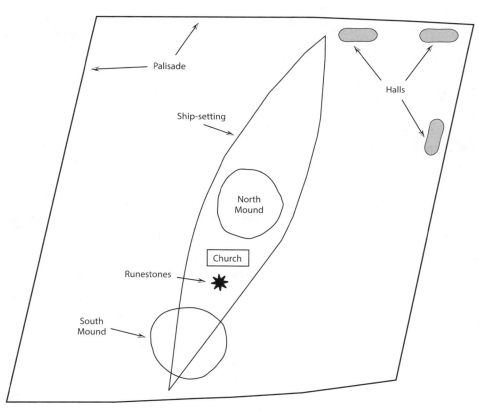

Figure 11–6: Diagrammatic plan of Jelling (Denmark), showing the two mounds with the ship setting, the enclosing palisade in the form of a parallelogram, the church, and the site of the runestones (after Hvass 2011, figs. 39 and 65).

Burial Places of Rulers   349

Difficult to understand as all this is, there is no doubt that Jelling was a royal burial place. This is because between the two mounds and just to the south of the church are three rune-stones. The largest of these is clearly shown in the same position as it is at present on a drawing of Jelling made in 1591, and excavations in 1981 provided proof that it is indeed in its original position, apart from some subsidence that has taken place since its erection. The smaller runestone alongside it was recorded in its present position on drawings of the site made from the 1630s onward, so it too may be where it was originally erected. An inscription on the smaller stone reads, in translation:

> King Gorm made this monument in memory of Thyre, his wife, Denmark's adornment. (Sawyer and Sawyer 2003, 692, 703)

There are complications in translating this inscription, especially as to whether "Denmark's adornment" refers to Gorm or to his wife. But none of this undermines the force of the inscription in showing that Jelling was a site connected with the royal family of Denmark in the tenth century. King Gorm probably died around 958, to be succeeded by his son, Harald Bluetooth (d. 985/6), who was responsible for erecting the larger runestone. The inscription on this reads, in translation:

> King Harald commanded this monument to be made in memory of Gorm, his father, and in memory of Thyre, his mother—that Harald who won the whole of Denmark for himself, and Norway, and made the Danes Christian. (Sawyer and Sawyer 2003, 692, 703)

"This monument" is presumably a reference to the runestone, which is a grand one with a figure of Christ represented on it (below, Figure 11–7). If these successive kings of Denmark were active in raising inscribed runestones at Jelling, it seems likely that the mounds too were royal constructions. The dendrochronological dates of around the 960s from both of them further suggests that they were the work of Harald Bluetooth.

Beyond this, the interpretation of the site is fraught with problems. It may be speculated that the grave in the North Mound was that of Thyre, and the grave under the church that of Gorm; or perhaps Gorm was originally buried in the North Mound but transferred to the grave under the church after Harald had converted the Danes to Christianity. Perhaps only Gorm was buried at Jelling and the South Mound was a sort of sham, designed to suggest that both king and queen were buried at Jelling, one in the North Mound, one in the South Mound, when in fact the queen was not. These difficulties, however, should not be allowed to obscure the basic fact that here was a mausoleum that was every bit as impressive in scale as those of Augustus and Hadrian, and was, beyond reasonable doubt, a royal mausoleum even if its detailed interpretation remains problematic.

Position

The impressiveness of all these monuments, however, was not dependent only on their scale but also on their position. The Mausoleum of Augustus was situated on the Field of Mars (Jacobs and Conlin 2014). This area, which was immediately outside the walls and the sacred enclosure (the pomerium) of Rome, was a very important one for the city. Military exercises took place on it (hence the name); triumphal processions began there (above, p. 203); the great Republican leader Pompey had built his monumental theatre there. As one of the principal routes into the city, the Via Flaminia, passed across it, so travelers approaching Rome from the north could not fail to have had a view of the Mausoleum of Augustus as they arrived. Also, part of Augustus's scheme for his mausoleum was the laying out of public gardens around it, so that residents of the city and others would have opportunities to be impressed by it, in addition to the times when their journeys along the Flaminian Way, or their attendance at ceremonies and other activities, brought them into proximity with it. The Mausoleum of Hadrian was in an equally dominant position on the opposite bank of the River Tiber to the Mausoleum of Augustus. With its own bridge, the Pons Aelius, constructed by Hadrian specially to provide access to it, it was the focus of urban development in that part of the city, and it must have been an even more dominating monument when it was built than it is today, surrounded as it is by newer buildings.

The dearth of written evidence for early Scandinavian history makes it impossible to be definite about whether the mounds at Jelling enjoyed a similarly dominant position, but there are clear signs that they did on the basis of what has been discovered from archaeological excavation and surveying about the communications system that existed at the time they were built. For it is clear that Jelling occupied a central position in the Denmark of its time, near to the Haervej, the great road (the name means "army-road") running north-south down the Jutland peninsula. The original course of this road is still visible in the deeply incised trackways preserved in the woods near Jelling where the road was on its way to nearby Skovdal Kro. That Harald Bluetooth was intent on developing access to Jelling is suggested further by the archeological excavation of a great bridge at Ravning Enge, 10km southwest of Jelling. This bridge, which was probably on the Haervej and so would have facilitated access to Jelling from the south, was an enormous structure. With a width of 5.5m, it had two carriageways, and it was no less than 700–760m in length, being built of 1500 large oak timbers. It cannot be proved that the bridge was built by Harald Bluetooth or in connection with the Jelling mounds. But dendrochronological dating of timbers from it shows that the trees used were felled around the year 979, which is during his reign, so it is very likely that it was his work. Just as the mounds and the ship-setting could have conveyed a message of power relating to the dominance and control of King Harald and his family, so too could the approach route to it, passing as it seems to have done over a bridge every bit as impressive as Hadrian's Pons Aelius.

The Jelling mounds are the only great burial mounds outside the Roman Empire for which we have such clear evidence as the runic inscription provides as to their builder and perhaps their occupant or occupants. In other cases, we have no such helpful evidence, and the dearth of written sources for the periods to which archaeologists assign them means that there is doubt as to the degree of political development achieved by the states in which they were built. So, it is possible that they were not so much the burial mounds of rulers as those of members of a broad, aristocratic class. We do, however, have an account of a royal burial mound in a work of fiction, which may nevertheless reflect the real circumstances of actual mounds that are extant even if this one may never have existed. The work of fiction in question is the Old English epic poem, *Beowulf* (above, pp. 37–38). This work ends with the death of the hero, Beowulf. He had reigned for thirty years as king of the Geats in the area that is now southern Sweden. The poet recounts how the Geats made him a splendid pyre, on which they cremated his body (Fulk, Bjork, and Niles 2008, lines 3137–38). Then, around the pyre, they made for him a burial mound "on the headland, so high and broad that seafarers might see it from afar." They then placed in the burial mound rings and jewels. The poet's account is not always clear, but the emphasis on the scale of the burial mound and its prominence as seen from the sea stand out as aspects of it (Fulk, Bjork, and Niles 2008, lines 3156–62).

In a similar vein is the supposedly factual account of a chieftain's funeral given by the Arab writer, Ibn Fadlān, as part of an account of an embassy that he undertook in 921–22 from the Caliph of Baghdad to the king of the Bulgars who lived along the River Volga. On his journey, he came across the people he called the Rus (*Rusiya*), and was a witness to the funeral of their king. This involved hauling a ship on to the shore and making it into a funeral pyre for the deceased, then building over it "something like a rounded mound. In the middle of this, they erected a great of beam of birch-wood, and wrote upon it the name of the man and the name of the king of the Rus" (Frye 2005, 70).

These fictional and factual accounts may well illuminate the significance of the position of extant burial mounds. At Borre (Norway), beside the Oslo Fjord, for example, there still stand—much eroded—a group of seven large mounds, some more than 45m across and still 5–6m high. This group, which archaeological investigation has shown to have been in origin even larger, is today close to the shore of the fjord, and it must have been even closer when it was built, since the sea level was at that time higher than it is now. Also, the Oslo Fjord is narrow in the area of Borre, so that the mounds would have been a dominant feature for ships that would necessarily have passed close to them. Nothing is known for certain of who the occupants of these mounds were. But excavation has shown that they were buried with rich objects, and in at least one case in association with a ship; and a recent survey has shown that timber halls were erected close to them, which was also the case with the mounds at Jelling. So, it seems likely that these were the graves of rulers. Indeed, the Old Norse poem *Ynglingatal*, probably written around 900, refers to two early kings as having been buried "on the point of the ridge by the Vadla stream," which the thirteenth-century Icelandic writer, Snorri Sturlusson, identified with Borre (Skre 2007a).

It was not only the landscape that such mounds could dominate. Just as the Mausoleum of Augustus and the Mausoleum of Hadrian dominated Rome, so the great mounds immediately outside the early medieval trading settlement of Kaupang (Norway) dominated not only the settlement itself, but also the road that led from it to what appears to have been the political center at Huseby just inland (Skre 2007c, 363). Equally, the great mound of Gokstad a little way to the south of Kaupang has been shown by recent archaeological research to have dominated a trading settlement comparable to Kaupang and situated along the shores of the fjord near the modern settlement of Sandfjord.

If the scale and dominating position of a mound or mausoleum could carry a message as to the power of the ruler, or of his successor who constructed the monument for him after his death, more sophisticated messages could also be conveyed. These might have to do with the achievements of the ruler, which could themselves underpin his personal power. Where the monument existed already during his lifetime, those messages could benefit him while he lived; where it was the creation of his successor, the messages' import could (or so the latter might hope) be transferred to him, assigning to him power by virtue of being the dead ruler's successor.

In the case of the Mausoleum of Augustus, the message was a written one, for an account of the deeds of the emperor was inscribed on tablets on the doors of the mausoleum and updated during his lifetime. The mausoleum thus embodied a record of his deeds, including his military achievements. The effect of this must have been increased by the location of the mausoleum on the Field of Mars, with its military associations. Indeed, the funeral of Augustus was more than anything like the triumphal processions which normally started from that part of Rome. According to contemporary chroniclers, his coffin was accompanied by a wax effigy wearing triumphal dress, while there was another image of gold, and a third carried on a triumphal chariot just like an emperor taking part in a triumphal procession. Images of the peoples that Augustus had added to the empire were part of the procession, just as images of the defeated peoples accompanied a living emperor in a triumph. And it was proposed that the procession be led by the image of Victory and should be routed through the Triumphal Gate, as triumphs were (Versnel 1970, 122–23; Davies 2000, 66–67). The mausoleum was clearly viewed as a symbol of victory in its own right, as a monument to the emperor's deeds during his life and after his death.

As we have seen, Augustus had his mausoleum built early in his reign, so that this message about the triumphs of his career was broadcast both during his lifetime and after his death. At Jelling, the runic inscription quoted above not only assigned the credit for the runestone's erection to Harald Bluetooth, but also declared his principal successes as a ruler in his own right. He was, according to the inscription, "that Harald who won the whole of Denmark for himself, and Norway, and made the Danes Christian." The Scandinavian kingdoms were at an embryonic stage of development in the tenth century, and Harald is here credited with creating a joint kingdom of Denmark and Norway, as well as with bringing about the conversion of the Danes to Christianity. The runestone was a magnificent affair, much grander than most such inscribed stones, and with a magnificent image of Christ sculpted on one side, a lion on the other, and the runic inscription boldly executed on the third (Figure 11–7). Together with the two great mounds, if he was indeed their builder, the runestone must have sent a clear message about the achievements and status of Harald Bluetooth.

Similar messages could be conveyed by the more transient but no less powerful medium of oral performance in connection with the funeral. According to *Beowulf*, after Beowulf's ashes had been placed in the mound,

Figure 11–7: Reconstruction of the runestone erected by King Harald Bluetooth, Jelling (Denmark). The representation of the Crucifixion of Jesus Christ, with part of the runic inscription just visible at the bottom.

Then the warriors rode around the burial-mound,
twelve of them in all, æthelings' sons.
They recited a dirge to declare their grief,
spoke of the man, mourned their king.
They praised his acts of heroism and his deeds of valour,
they praised highly his glory.

(Alexander 2003, lines 3169–74, modified)

Just as with the inscribed deeds of Augustus, or the briefer inscription for Harald Bluetooth, here were the deeds—including the military success, if that is what is meant by his heroism, valor, and glory—of the dead ruler being publicly celebrated.

The *Beowulf* poet tells us that on the hero's pyre, which was later incorporated into his burial mound, there were hung "shining mail-coats and shields of war" (Alexander 2003, lines 3139–40), presumably symbolizing the ruler as a military leader. These lines find a parallel in another Roman funeral monument for an emperor, which was not a burial

Figure 11–8: Detail of the base of Trajan's Column, Rome (Italy), showing sculptured shields and mail-coats.

mound but a column—Trajan's Column. That this monument, which was planned by Trajan as part of the development of his forum in Rome (above, pp. 184, 185), was to be the place for the deposition of the emperor's ashes is affirmed by contemporary writers such as Cassius Dio, and confirmed by the existence in its base of a vestibule and a chamber, the latter inexplicable unless it was intended as the emperor's last resting place. What is striking in light of the *Beowulf* poet's account of its hero's pyre is that the base of the column is sculpted with shields and mail-coats just as Beowulf's pyre was adorned with the real things (Figure 11–8). As the dirge at Beowulf's funeral had celebrated his valor, so the sculpture on Trajan's Column celebrated the emperor's military victories.

Another military aspect of Beowulf's funeral was the practice of the warriors riding around the barrow. The poet explains nothing about this, but it is striking that a feature of pagan Roman imperial funerals was the *decursio*, that is the circling round the pyre of priests, but also of soldiers and chariots. Of course, it is possible that the *Beowulf* poet knew the Roman sources, and drew from them his description of what was in effect a decursio for Beowulf as an imaginative embellishment of the account of his hero's funeral; but it is equally possible that he was drawing on genuine traditions relating to the funerals of rulers in barbarian society. When the Gothic historian, Jordanes, described the funeral of the great ruler of the Huns, Attila, in the mid-fifth century, he described how his body was placed in the midst of a plain and lay in state in a silken tent as a sight for men's admiration. The best horsemen rode around in circles after the manner of circus games, in the place to which he had been brought, and told of his deeds in a funeral dirge. (Mierow 1915, 124, with modifications)

In this case too, it is possible that Jordanes was adapting stock descriptions of Roman imperial funerals, but the resemblance is not precise, and the fact that he goes on to summarize the dirge and mentions a funeral feast which he calls by the presumably Hunnic word, *strava*, suggests that his account genuinely reflected what had happened at this funeral. In Attila's funeral too, the display of weapons was an important element: The mourners placed over his grave "the arms of foemen won in the fight."

The role of ships in connection with the burial mounds of barbarian rulers seems clearly to pertain to barbarian culture, since ships were not a feature of Roman imperial funerals; but equally it parallels Roman imperial funerals in that ships were par excellence tools of war. So the use of a ship may have made the barbarian funeral just as much a military triumph as the Roman imperial funerals were. Near the beginning of the poem, the *Beowulf* poet describes an earlier funeral than Beowulf's own, that of the Danish king, Scyld Scefing. This took the form of burial in a ship, in which the king's body was laid together with "the weapons of a warrior, war accoutrement, swords and body-armour" (Alexander 2003, lines 39–40). The *Beowulf* poet envisaged this burial ship as being launched on to the sea as the culmination of the funeral. Whether or not that ever happened in reality, ships were an important element in some of the most spectacular burial mounds in Scandinavia, the Gokstad mound for example, and in England, where ships were incorporated into burials in at least two of the great mounds at Sutton Hoo in Suffolk. And, although there seems not to have been a ship in the Jelling mounds, they were closely associated with a ship-setting.

Ships can be interpreted in religious terms, as the vehicles by which the dead man was to be conveyed to whatever afterlife was envisaged in pagan religion. But they can also be seen as elements in the celebration of the warlike character and military achievements of the deceased. For a seagoing people, ships—or at least warships—were the greatest of military tools. Just as the Roman emperor was represented driving a quadriga, so the Germanic ruler was buried in a ship. Of course, it is unlikely that ships were always signifiers of military prowess—the ship found in the mound of Oseberg (Norway), for example, held the remains of women and so is unlikely to have been involved with military prowess. But, where the burials of kings were concerned, the military dimension of the ship burial may very likely have been uppermost in the minds of those who saw the ship installed in the mound. Presumably its installation involved a triumphal procession with the ship as its center point, a procession comparable to the triumphal processions of Roman imperial funerals. The ship may well have conveyed a message about the ruler's achievements in war as much as it may have been intended as his vehicle to convey him to the world of the afterlife.

This role of burial mounds in celebrating the achievements of rulers was primarily about personal power—about the reputation of the ruler among his subjects, and about their consequent willingness to render him their obedience in the context of a relationship with him which, if it was not personal in the sense that they had face-to-face contact with him, was nevertheless personal in the sense that their relationship to him was created by his magnificence or his achievements, especially as a successful warrior or a leader in warfare. Burial mounds, however, could also carry messages of ideological power, and this is most clearly evident in the Mausoleum of Augustus and the Mausoleum of Hadrian. For, these monuments provide evidence that the ruler was being presented as a figure who derived his power from the divine, and above all from the sun as a god.

DIVINE AND COSMIC RULERSHIP

Roman emperors were believed to become gods after their deaths in a procedure known as an apotheosis. At the beginning of the empire's history, this involved the Roman Senate, which decided whether the deceased emperor was worthy to become a god, and, where the decision was in the affirmative, issued a decree to that effect. But very soon, certainly by the second century, this had become a formality, and the emperor was generally elevated to divine status as an automatic right. The apotheosis could be symbolized in the funeral, as when an eagle was released from the top of the funeral pyre to represent the emperor's soul rising to the heavens to join the ranks of the gods. This was illustrated in sculpture, for example on the column of Antoninus Pius in Rome, on the base of which the emperor is shown rising with the wings of an eagle sprouting from his body, with two eagles escorting him on his journey to heaven (Davies 2000, 43, fig. 33). The ideological power of the emperor as a god thus related mostly to his posthumous existence; but the beliefs involved in it must have strengthened his power during his lifetime as well, when he was presumably viewed as a candidate for the status of a god, and also the power of his successors, who were similarly candidates for that honor.

Burial mounds, however, could and did convey more specific messages and, in the case of the Mausoleum of Augustus, the message seems to have been concerned very much with power accruing to the emperor through his association with the sun. The sun was an object of worship in the Roman Empire, as the sun-god Apollo, and especially in the later empire as the Unconquered Sun. Cicero referred to the sun as "the leader, prince, and governor of the stars" (Davies 2000, 86), so that it was natural enough to identify the emperor with such an all-powerful ruler. It has already been noted that allusions in the architecture and decoration of palaces in various periods tended to identify the ruler with the cosmos (above, pp. 83–96). Such an identification is clear in the Mausoleum of Augustus. For, in 9 BC, the emperor Augustus brought to Rome an obelisk from the Egyptian City of the Sun (*Heliopolis*) and had it erected near his mausoleum as the gnomon (the shadow-pointer) of a giant sundial. This sundial, which has been partially excavated under the Field of Mars, gave the time of day and also the position of the sun in the zodiac of constellations.

The proximity of the Mausoleum of Augustus to this sundial must have carried the message that the emperor's power was closely connected with that of the sun and that, through his god-head, his power would be eternally reborn (at any rate in his successors) just as the sun passed ceaselessly through the zodiac. That message was reinforced when, in AD 118, the emperor Hadrian began building the great temple of the Pantheon a short distance from the Mausoleum of Augustus and in direct line of sight from its entrance. Although the function of this building is not fully understood, it has an enormous dome which, like the domed halls in palaces (above, pp. 80–85), was surely intended to represent the heavens—indeed, this was explicitly stated by Cassius Dio, who wrote, "because of its vaulted roof, it resembles the heavens" (Davies 2000, 82). At the apex of the dome is a round opening, an *oculus*, through which a shaft of sunlight penetrates, causing a disc of light to move around the walls of the building, as the sun moves across the sky. This must have created the impression that the sun was actually moving through the building, which Hadrian used both as a reception hall and a temple. The construction of the Pantheon meant that there was even more cosmic symbolism in the vicinity of the Mausoleum of Augustus, reinforcing the idea that the emperor had been—and was—a ruler like the sun, indeed perhaps was the sun itself.

This notion of cosmic kingship may have been embodied also in the Mausoleum of Hadrian. A corridor runs around and through the interior of the central cylinder of the monument. It is a wide one, and it has ventilation shafts to enhance the comfort of being in it. It was clearly not a service corridor, but rather one intended to accommodate substantial processions. The key point, however, is that it would have led those processions in a counterclockwise circulation around the burial chamber at the core of the monument. This counterclockwise direction was regarded in Roman times as representing the movement of the sun, so that it was like making the mausoleum itself a symbol of the sun, with the processions mounting the corridor moving like the heavens themselves. That the emperor Hadrian was preoccupied with the relationship between his power and the sun is shown by his adoption of the name "Aelius," meaning "the sun." Indeed, the bridge that he built across the River Tiber to the mausoleum was called the Pons Aelius ("the Bridge of the Sun"). There is therefore no doubt that he was serious about identifying himself with the sun, and although his mausoleum contains no helpful inscriptions to this effect, it seems likely that it presented an image of the deceased emperor as the sun.

Such messages about the ideological power of rulers deriving from association with divinities may also have been carried by burial mounds outside the Roman Empire, but the lack of written sources for the periods and areas in question, and the consequent lack of understanding of the nature of paganism outside the Roman Empire, make it impossible to know. Occasionally, grave-goods recovered from the mounds suggest that they may have embodied ideas of divine kingship, as in the case of the carved and decorated whetstone from the ship burial in Mound 1, at Sutton Hoo (England) (Figure 11–9). The fact that the base has a convex cup, which would have fitted over a seated person's knee, has led it to be interpreted as a scepter, which the ruler could have had in his hand—resting on his knee—as he sat on his throne. The carved heads may represent severed heads, and so may be related to the cult of the head which appears in prehistoric Irish art, and also among the peoples of Gaul at the time of their conquest by the Romans in the first century BC. The ring at the top of the whetstone is capable of being turned, and may be a symbol of the sun as may the stag atop it, for Celtic material from the Val Camonica in northern Italy associates stags with the sun (Enright 2006, 49). Whereas all this can be no more than conjecture, there are nevertheless strong indications of the worship of the sun in paganism outside the Roman Empire. A clear example is the model, now in the National Museum in Copenha-

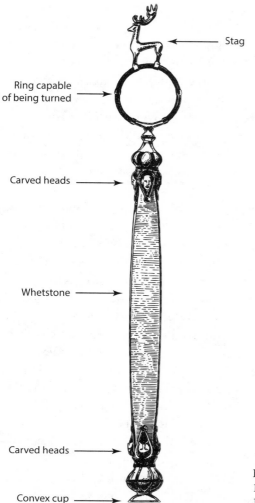

Stag

Ring capable
of being turned

Carved heads

Whetstone

Carved heads

Convex cup

Figure 11–9: Whetstone scepter from Mound 1, Sutton Hoo (England) (after Bruce-Mitford 1975–83, II, fig. 237).

gen, which comes from a deposit in a bog, Trundholm Moss in West Zealand. This model, which is of a chariot of the sun, the sun represented by a great golden disk, indicates that sun worship was current among the pagan barbarians. So it is possible that their rulers were identified with the sun.

DOMED MAUSOLEA

In the Roman Empire, burial mounds did not have a future. A long-standing tradition of burial in domed buildings increasingly came to the fore, and from the third century emperors were usually interred in such domed mausolea, which often had two stories. Like the burial mounds, these domed mausolea also offered scope for sending messages of power, and that in quite similar ways. One of the central features of the palace city of Split (Croatia) was that it included a mausoleum for its builder, the emperor Diocletian (d. 311) (Figure 11–10). This mausoleum is the octagonal structure, with its colonnade of columns around it, and a grand opening to the entrance courtyard which is just visible at the far right side of the image. The mausoleum had two stories: a crypt below the base of the colonnade; and a high hall capped by a dome above it. It was a very grand and imposing structure, large enough indeed to be converted into the cathedral of Split when the city had long ceased to be an imperial residence. The medieval tower of the cathedral, the building of which destroyed the vestibule of the mausoleum, is visible to the right of the octagonal center of the mausoleum, and the choir of the cathedral, which was attached to the mausoleum by breaking through the wall, is visible on the left. As for the magnificence of the original building, the colonnade was a considerable contribution to this, and so was the scale and opulence of the interior decoration, including a sculpted frieze running round the building below the roof, as well as the imposing character of the dome.

Whereas burial mounds were exclusively for pagan burials, domed mausolea, such as that of Diocletian, were preferred for burials of Christian rulers, and these could be just as imposing and grand, if not more so. According to his biographer, Eusebius, the first Christian emperor, Constantine (306–37), for example, built for himself in Constantinople a mausoleum of "incredible height," covered inside with marble, while the ceiling was covered with gold, and the roof with gilded bronze tiles which "dazzled the distant beholder" (quoted by Johnson 2009, 121–22). This mausoleum was later converted as the whole or part of the church of the Holy Apostles. That church was demolished following the Turkish conquest in 1453, so that nothing remains of it. An impression of its imposing character may, however, be gained from the mausoleum of the emperor's daughter, Constantina, attached to the church of Santa Agnese in Rome. This building, which is now the church of Santa Costanza, still exists, much in its original form (Figure 11–11). It is a single-story building, with an imposing central space, rising to a considerable height, lit by clerestory windows, and with a dome. Around it runs an aisle with niches in the outside wall. There is a magnificent entrance portico, and there was originally a colonnade running around the outside, although virtually nothing of this survives. The magnificence of the mausoleum was further enhanced by a rich decoration of mosaics, a considerable proportion of which survives in the encircling aisle, and in the niches, but not in the main central space.

To illustrate the grandeur and imposing character of these domed mausolea, a final example is the two-storied structure built by the Christian king of the Ostrogoths, Theoderic, who ruled Italy in the late sixth century, in Ravenna (Italy), his principal city (Figure 11–12). This is octagonal, with the entrance to the lower story at ground level, and a series of niches running round the other seven sides. Above this is a gallery, which would once have had a colonnade, remains of which can be seen in the masonry of this level, running round on either side of the upper entrance door. The whole is capped with the most grandiose feature of all, a single block of stone which forms the dome, and has a series of "brackets" radiating out from it. The resources required to procure this massive block, to shape it, and to place it on top of the mausoleum, must have marked Theoderic out as a really great ruler in the eyes of contemporaries. The contemporary writer known as the *Anonymus Valesianus*, for example, refers to the mausoleum as "a work of marvellous size," built by the ruler during his lifetime, and for which he "sought out a huge rock to place on the top" (quoted by Deliyannis 2009, 124).

Figure 11–10: Mausoleum of Diocletian, Split (Croatia). View from the east gate of the Palace of Diocletian, showing the octagonal mausoleum and its colonnade, with the later belfry and choir attached when it was converted into a Christian church.

Figure 11–11: Interior, church of Santa Costanza, Rome (Italy), showing the central dome of this former imperial mausoleum.

As with burial mounds, so with domed mausolea, in that their situation could contribute as much to their imposing character as their architecture and decoration. The Mausoleum of Diocletian, for example, stood more or less at the center of the palace city of Split, adjacent to the tetrapylon, a monument which marked that point. So the mausoleum was a focal point, clearly visible from the east gate and from the main processional street which led across the city from the Golden Gate on the west. The Mausoleum of Constantine had an equally prominent if less central position, in Constantinople, for it stood on one of the highest hills of the city. Mausolea were often outside the walls of cities, as was customary for cemeteries in general, but in such situations they could still have a dominating position. The Mausoleum of Constantina stands beside the Nomentanan Way, a great artery leading into Rome, and it occupies a raised position above the surrounding areas. As for the Mausoleum of Theoderic, it too was extramural, and, while the contemporary context of its position is difficult to reconstruct, it seems unlikely that such an imposing structure occupied anything but a prominent and dominating position.

Domed mausolea do not seem to have been about the military and other achievements of the rulers buried in them as some burial mounds were, although no doubt the funeral ceremonies and processions that took place around them offered scope for conveying such martial messages of power. But, like the burial mounds, they had clear potential to send messages about the ideological power of rulers. Just as in the case of domed halls in palaces (above, pp. 80–85), and just as in the case of the Pantheon, domed chambers in mausolea could create an architectural context in which the cosmic power of the deceased ruler—and by inference that of his successors—could be reflected. The dome, in other words, symbolized the heavens in which the ruler's power was embedded and from which it derived.

Such messages relating to cosmic power could equally be projected by other parts of the site in which the mausoleum stood, as was the case with the sundial that Augustus built near his mausoleum. This seems to have been the case also with the mausoleum of the emperor Maxentius (306–12), which he built as part of a palace complex (the so-called Villa of Maxentius) on the Appian Way, another route leading into Rome. This mausoleum was a round, domed structure in a large enclosure, and, while the dome may well have evoked the cosmic power of the emperor, such power was also reflected in the full-size circus—comparable with the Circus Maximus in Rome itself—which was laid out immediately adjacent to it (Figure 11–13). The racing charioteers would have begun at the starting gates on the left of the image, when the barriers had been raised by mechanical devices in the flanking towers, one of which survives to almost its full height. They would then have raced along the left-hand chariot track, around the central feature (the *spina*), and back along the right-hand chariot track. They would thus have moved in an anti-clockwise direction, just as the heavens were believed to be moving above the earth. The cosmic association of the circus is made explicit (in a tone disapproving of the pagan associations of chariot racing) by the Christian writer Tertullian (*c.* AD 193–220), according to whom the Romans "consecrated the four-horse chariot to the sun, the two-horse to the moon" (quoted by Davies 2000, 83–84). They are also carved on the frieze around the interior of the Mausoleum of Diocletian.

The circus was, in other words, an image of the cosmos. The circus at the Villa of Maxentius was not, of course, entirely—or perhaps even primarily—connected with the mauso-

Figure 11–12: Mausoleum of Theoderic, Ravenna (Italy).

Figure 11–13: Circus of the Villa of Maxentius on the Appian Way, Rome (Italy). View toward the starting gates and the mausoleum.

leum of the emperor, for it was also connected directly to the adjacent palace, and there was the usual imperial box from which the emperor watched the races. But it is striking that there was also such a close proximity between the circus and the mausoleum, with the starting gates a few meters from the latter's enclosure. Indeed, that enclosure, which has deep, rectangular niches around the inside, may have been where the chariot teams prepared themselves before moving to the starting gates. There may, in other words, have been a direct connection between circus and mausoleum. The anti-clockwise rotation of the chariots around the circus symbolized the turning of the heavens and so evoked the cosmic power of the emperor, in life and in death. This connection between burial places and circuses may also be reflected in other contexts, notably in the carvings of circuses on sarcophagi, and on mausolea—chariot races appear, for example, in the third-fourth century carvings on a sarcophagus from *Aquinum* and another now in the Vatican Museum (Vespignani 2010, 87, and figs. 14–15), and on the doorway into the late Roman mausoleum which is the chapel of S. Aquilino at the church of San Lorenzo in Milan (Johnson 2009, 162).

As to the function of the two stories of domed mausolea, there are few clues. It is possible that one story was used for the actual burial of the ruler, while religious rituals took place in the other, presumably in commemoration or celebration of the deceased. This seems to fit the Mausoleum of Diocletian. It is likely that the lower story—the crypt—of that monument was where the ruler was buried, because it was built in rough stone without decoration, and access to it was by a right-angle passage. All this seems more appropriate to the burial place itself, where the remains would have been placed and access to them would not normally have been required. On the other hand the lavishness of the decoration of the upper story, and the imposing vestibule to it, now destroyed to make way for the cathedral bell tower, suggest that it was used for religious rituals.

In the case of Christian domed mausolea, there are the fullest clues to the use of the two chambers in the mausoleum of Theoderic in Ravenna. There, the discovery of socket-holes in the walls of the lower chamber suggests that there were originally screens dividing the space so that it could have functioned as a chapel. There, no doubt, memorial services for the ruler would have taken place. If that was so, the upper story would have been where the ruler was actually buried, and it contains at the present an enormous porphyry bath, which may have been used as a coffin. This is recorded as having been at various places in Ravenna in past years so there is no certainty that it acted as Theoderic's coffin; but the theory that it did is not wholly implausible, and, if it did, the ruler's corpse would have lain in it, in the center perhaps of the upper story of his mausoleum where it now stands. Above it would have been the colossal block of stone which was the roof, painted with an enormous jeweled cross of victory, traces of which are still visible.

NECROPOLISES

The domed mausoleum was essentially a free-standing structure, although it could be attached to a church in the case of Christian mausolea, as with the Mausoleum of Constantina in Rome, attached to the church of Santa Agnese. Sometimes, too, a mausoleum was so grandiose that it could become a church in its own right, which may have been the case with the emperor Constantine's mausoleum of the Holy Apostles in Constantinople, perhaps converted into a church in the later fourth century. It was possible, however, for Christian churches to be constructed and developed primarily as mausolea for rulers, so that the churches fulfilled other functions but had a predominant focus on the burial places of rulers within them. If those burial places were to convey messages of power in the interests of the successors of the dead, it was potentially important for emerging states to create fixed necropolises where their rulers could rest together, be commemorated and venerated, and symbolize in various ways the legitimacy and strength of their successors.

The process of creating such necropolises could be very tentative, and even ineffective. The first Christian king of the Franks, Clovis (d. 511), seems to have founded in his capital city, Paris, the church of the Holy Apostles as a necropolis for himself and his family in imitation of Constantine's mausoleum, also dedicated to the Holy Apostles, in Constantinople. But, although Clovis himself and various members of his family were buried there, the church had no long-term future as a royal necropolis. That there was no recognized necropolis for the Carolingian kings is shown by the fact that, when the emperor Charlemagne died in 814, his biographer, Einhard, reported that there was uncertainty as to where he wanted to be buried, and a site was found inside the church of his palace at Aachen (Bayer 2014). But this did not result in the church becoming a necropolis for subsequent rulers, and the only other ruler ever to have been buried in it was Otto III (996–1002). Where a church did become the necropolis for the rulers of a state, however, it could become an important tool for conveying messages relating to the power of living rulers. Early examples of such royal necropolises are found in Spain. Silo, king of Asturias (774–83), for example, established that for his dynasty in the church of St. John of Pravia, where the royal tombs were placed along a passage leading into the nave. Similarly, in 1063, Alfonso V, king of the emerging Spanish kingdom of Leon, founded a necropolis for the kings of Leon in the church of St. Isidore in the city of Leon.

One of the clearest examples of such a necropolis, however, is the great abbey of Saint-Denis near Paris. In the Roman period, there was on the site an extramural cemetery, where there was supposed to have been buried St. Denis, a Bishop of Paris martyred during the persecutions of Christians of the late Roman period. A Frankish royal church had been built here by the second half of the sixth century, for the Frankish queen Arnegund (d. 565 x 570) was buried in it, as were two sons of King Chilperic in 580. Saint-Denis was also used for royal burials in the seventh century, when King Dagobert was buried there in 539 and King Clovis II in 654. It was later favored as a burial place by two of the Carolingian rulers, Pippin III (d. 768) and Charles the Bald (d. 870). But it still did not become an established royal necropolis, for Carolingian and French rulers were buried at a number of different places as late as the eleventh and twelfth centuries. King Philip I (1060–1108), for example, was buried at the abbey of Saint-Benoît-sur-Loire (France) rather than at Saint-Denis, and King Louis VII (1137–80) was buried at the abbey of Barbeau (France). But, from then on, Saint-Denis became an established royal necropolis, and all the kings of France were buried there until Louis XV (1715–74), with the sole exception of Louis XI (1461–83). Burial at Saint-

Denis was, for that long period, part and parcel of being king of France. Just as the kings were crowned at Reims, so they were buried at Saint-Denis. As the kingdom of France became more established and more powerful, so Saint-Denis as a necropolis developed in parallel.

The most closely comparable emergence of a royal necropolis to that of Saint-Denis is that of Westminster Abbey (England). The church built by King Edward the Confessor (d. 1066) was its founder's burial place, but there is no sign that it was planned as a necropolis, or that it emerged as one at an early date. Before 1272, only Edward himself, his queen Edith, and King William I's queen Matilda had been buried there. But when, in 1272, King Henry III, who had been responsible for the rebuilding of the church (above, pp. 302, 304, 305), was buried in the choir, he began a trend and, following his example, a long succession of English kings was destined to find their resting places in the abbey. The only exceptions were to be Edward II (1307–27), whose tomb was at Gloucester Cathedral, Henry IV (1399–1413), who was buried in Canterbury Cathedral, Edward IV (1461–70, 1471–83), whose tomb and chantry was in the Chapel of St. George in Windsor Castle, and Richard III (1483–85), who was buried in the Franciscan Friary in Leicester..

As a royal necropolis, Westminster Abbey was closely linked to the development of the English state, for it was also an inauguration site, umbilically connected with the Palace of Westminster and with the meeting places of parliament in the palace and in the abbey itself (above, p. 307). The deceased kings of the past watched together over the activities of the living king. Their presence in the kingdom's necropolis could send a message that helped to guarantee his legitimacy and to confirm his rights; and this message could be articulated by the tombs themselves within the church.

The development of royal monuments within a church was not necessarily the work of the ruler or his family. In the the case of the treatment of royal tombs in the abbey of Saint-Denis, the initiative came partly from the kings themselves, but partly—and perhaps as importantly—from the monks of Saint-Denis, who had ambitions in their own right to make their church the royal necropolis of France. Regardless of whose initiative the process of building and arranging tombs was, however, the implications for the consolidation and presentation of royal power were the same. In the time of Suger, abbot of Saint-Denis (1122–51), although there were royal burials in the abbey, little attention seems to have been devoted to the tombs themselves. This situation changed, however, for we hear of magnificent tombs in gold and silver having been erected in front of the high altar for King Philip Augustus (1180–1223) and King Louis VIII (1223–26), and what was probably an equally imposing tomb in bronze was created for the Carolingian ruler, Charles the Bald (d. 870), at the entry to the monks' choir, while a monument to the seventh-century king, Dagobert, and his queen, Nanthild, had been erected near the high altar. This was, so far as is known, all the initiative of the monks of Saint-Denis (E. A. R. Brown 1985, 244). If they were trying to promote their church as a royal necropolis, they succeeded spectacularly in the reign of Louis IX (1226–70), during which there took place, presumably with the king's approval if not encouragement, a search in the abbey church for all the royal remains interred there. Once found, those remains that had not previously been honored with tombs were translated to brand-new ones, with effigies in thirteenth-century costume sculpted for them in

Figure 11–14: Tomb of Clovis II and Charles Martel, former abbey church of Saint-Denis (France). The tomb was carved in the mid-thirteenth century.

stone. These tombs still exist, although their current arrangement bears no relationship to how they were disposed after this thirteenth-century translation process. Figure 11–14 shows the tomb made at that time for a Frankish king of the sixth century, Clovis II, and the mid-eighth century Carolingian mayor of the palace, Charles Martel.

In addition to housing royal burials, it is clear that the monks of Saint-Denis made efforts to present the royal tombs in ways that enhanced the standing of the royal dynasty. At the time that the translation process mentioned above took place, the reigning kings of France belonged to the Capetian dynasty, which had been initiated as a royal line when, in 987, Hugh Capet had become king by displacing a claimant to the throne from the much weakened line of the Carolingians, who were descended from the emperor Charlemagne (above, p. 77). Given the reputation of that emperor, this left the Capetian kings perennially open to the accusation that they were not the legitimate kings of France, but usurpers. King Philip Augustus had countered this by asserting that his family had inaugurated a "return of the Kingdom of France to the stock of Charlemagne," specifically by virtue of the fact that his mother, Adela of Champagne, and his wife, Isabel of Hainaut, were both descended from Charlemagne. As has been discussed in the case of King Philip the Fair's statues of kings in the great hall of the Palais de la Cité in the early fourteenth century demonstrating royal descent, this issue was a live one (above, pp. 77–78). It would seem that the translation of the royal remains to new tombs in the abbey of Saint-Denis was a similar response a generation earlier. For, the arrangement of those tombs, as it is reconstructed in Figure 11–15, must have been designed to emphasize the seamless succession to the kingship from the Carolingians to the Capetian kings.Parts of this arrangement had been created before the translation of the 1260s: the tomb of the Merovingian king Dagobert and his queen Nanthild, to the southwest of the altar of St. Denis; the tombs of Philip Augustus and Louis VIII in the middle of the choir, with the tomb of the Carolingian Charles the Bald at its entrance. The new tombs of the 1260s were those arranged in lines on either side of the choir. Those on the left of Figure 11–15 (the south side) were the tombs created for the rulers of what was to become France before the beginning of the Capetian royal dynasty in 987. At the west end was the joint tomb of the Merovingian king, Clovis II, and the Carolingian mayor of the palace, Charles Martel. Immediately east of this was the joint tomb of the latter's son, the first Carolingian king, Pippin III, and his queen Bertha. Then came more Carolingians: the joint tomb of King Carloman (d. 771), son of Pippin III, and Ermentrude, queen of King Charles the Bald; and that of Carloman (d. 884) and Louis III (d. 884). On the other side of the choir were a series of Capetian (or at least post-Carolingian) tombs. They began at the western end of the sequence with Hugh the Great (d. 956), the ancestor of Hugh Capet, whose tomb was a joint tomb with that of King Odo (888–98). The latter ruler was not a Capetian but equally was not a Carolingian, belonging as he did to a family that interrupted the Carolingian dynasty and prepared the way for the accession of Hugh Capet (987–96). East of this was the joint tomb of the Capetian King Robert the Pious (972–1031) and his queen, Constance of Arles, then the joint tomb of his descendants Louis VI (1108–1137) and Henry I (1031–60), and, finally, the tomb of the son of Louis, Philip (d. 1131), and his wife, Constance of Castille.

Here was an arrangement of tombs designed to send a clear political message: the seamless transition from the Merovingian and Carolingian rulers of what was to become France to the Capetian kings of France as they continued to rule in the thirteenth century. Soon after this arrangement of tombs had been made, the remains of King Louis IX were interred next to those of Louis VIII and Philip Augustus. When Louis IX was canonized in 1298, however, the then king, Philip the Fair (1285–1314), wanted to have the new saint's remains translated to the Sainte-Chapelle in the Palais de la Cité. This was successfully resisted by the monks of Saint-Denis, however, and Philip the Fair had them translated to a position beside the graves of Philip Augustus and Louis VIII at Saint-Denis. In 1306, he ordered a further re-arrangement of the royal tombs in the choir so that the tombs of the Capetians were intermingled with those of their predecessors. This may have been another effort to repulse attacks on the legitimacy of the Capetians. In tandem with it, the monks of Saint-Denis rewrote the history of France, removing any mention of Hugh Capet's usurpation. The tombs, like the history, and like the statues in the great hall of the Palais de la Cité, were evidently intended to send a message of the continuity of royal power from the earliest times, and the legitimacy of the present holders of it. In this way, the burial places of kings were being used to convey messages of power about the legitimacy of their successors' rule.

Saint-Denis and Westminster were very long-lived necropolises. The necropolis of the dukes and kings of Bohemia, which Charles IV established in the St. Vitus's Cathedral next

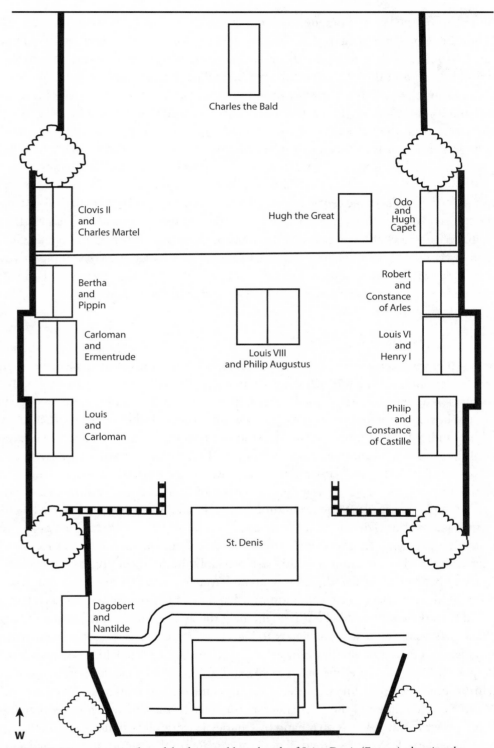

Figure 11–15: Diagrammatic plan of the former abbey church of Saint-Denis (France), showing the arrangement of royal tombs in the choir, as made in the 1260s, under King Louis IX. Based on an eighteenth-century plan (after E.A.R. Brown 1985, fig. 3).

to his palace on the Hrad at Prague, proved to be more transient but just as ambitious. Just as Hugh Capet had displaced the Carolingian rulers, so Charles IV's father, John of Luxembourg (1310–46), had come to the throne of Bohemia when the long and ancient line of Přemyslid dukes and then kings of Bohemia had failed. His accession was not an usurpation, but he and his son after him were open to the accusation that they were not real Bohemians, but foreigners from the western part of Europe, and that they could not participate in the glories that the native Přemyslid line had enjoyed. Just as in Saint-Denis the thirteenth- and early fourteenth-century arrangements of tombs asserted the legitimacy of the Capetian dynasty, so in St. Vitus's Cathedral new tombs were created and arranged to emphasize the legitimate succession of Charles IV's dynasty, that of the Luxembourgs, to the line of the Přemyslids. In the center of the cathedral's choir was a "lesser choir" with the altar of the Blessed Virgin Mary established in the 1360s and served by a college of priests. This constituted a royal chantry to pray for the souls of those buried there, principally Charles IV and his family. From 1373, however, the relationship between the Luxembourg dynasty and the Přemyslids was emphasized when new tombs for the latter were sculpted in stone and placed in the chapels radiating from the east end of the cathedral.

RULER-SAINTS AND NECROPOLISES

As a burial place and a source of power for rulers, St. Vitus's cathedral had another significance, for it contained the tomb of the early Přemyslid duke, Wenceslas. According to the Lives written about him, he succeeded his father, Vratislav I, as duke in 921 while still a child, and he reigned at first under the regency of his mother Drahomir, his brother Boleslav, and his grandmother Ludmila—it was she who was responsible for his Christian education and she herself was murdered, apparently by anti-Christian elements in Bohemia, and Wenceslas had her remains translated to Prague, where she was venerated as a saint. Wenceslas was responsible for advancing the conversion of Bohemia to Christianity by sending out priests after the murder of his grandmother, and he was also a military leader, defending Bohemia against the German duke, Arnulf of Bavaria. In 929, however, he was forced to offer tribute payments (the so-called "tribute of peace") to the German king Henry I the Fowler who invaded Bohemia, and this was probably the political pretext for his brother Boleslav to have him murdered. Boleslav invited Wenceslas to Stará Boleslav to attend the baptism of his son, and there he had him murdered outside the sanctuary of the church, it was said with the connivance of a priest who held the door of the church shut against him.

Wenceslas seems almost immediately to have been regarded as a martyr. Miracles were reported at his grave, and Boleslav himself arranged the translation of his body to the church of Prague on March 4, sometime between 932 and 938. A series of passions of him was written, including one in Bohemia in the tenth century and another written by Bishop Gumpold of Mantua at the request of the German emperor, Otto II. In the fourteenth century, a passion of him was written in his own hand by Charles IV himself (Klaniczay 2002, 101–108).

The presence in St. Vitus's Cathedral of of the remains of this saintly ancestor had a major impact on the plan and construction of the new cathedral, which Charles IV had built from scratch. According to the eleventh-century chronicler Cosmas of Prague, Wenceslas constructed in his lifetime a church at Prague in honor of the holy martyr Vitus, whose relics he had obtained, and this church was a rotunda (Wolverton 2009, 82). It is generally identified with the remains excavated under the south transept of St. Vitus's Cathedral in the early twentieth century, and consisting of a rotunda with four apses. After his murder came to be regarded as a martyrdom, Wenceslas's own remains were translated to the southern apse of this chapel, as Figure 11–16 shows. So important was the tomb of the saint that, rather than the relics being translated, its original site was respected when the much larger Romanesque basilica was built, and it was respected too by the architects of Charles IV's new cathedral, who left it undisturbed and built over it their chapel of St. Wenceslas with its magnificent decoration (Figure 11–17). In this chapel the shrine of St. Wenceslas was located over his original grave, and here too were kept the royal regalia which the ruler used at his coronation. The saint's remains were evidently an important element in the power of St. Vitus's Cathedral as a necropolis.

At Westminster Abbey too, the church's saint, King Edward the Confessor (1042–66), was focal to the royal necropolis as it developed. In the choir of the church, from the mid-thirteenth century onward, the tombs of the kings of England were grouped around that of Edward, so that, as a king who had been so virtuous that he had been canonized, he was sanctifying—and in a sense endorsing—the succession of the English kings. The details of Edward's canonization show how the early initiative for it came as much from the religious community of the church as from the reigning king. Although Edward's body had been ceremonially translated to a new tomb in the church in 1102, he was evidently not regarded at that time as having been formally canonized. That was only achieved in 1161 after a long campaign by the monks, admittedly supported in the later stages by the reigning king, Henry II. From the 1220s and 1230s, however, there developed a close relationship between the cult of Edward the Confessor and the English kings, beginning with Henry III's special devotion to him, as is emphasized by the St Albans historian, Matthew Paris, who says that in his plan to rebuild the east end of Westminster Abbey the king was "inspired by his devotion to St Edward" (quoted by Binski 1995, 1, 3). It was almost certainly the king who had the magnificent new shrine made with its Cosmati marble base, and the Cosmati marble floor of the chapel on which it stood. The king's devotion was further emphasized by his initial burial in the former grave of Edward the Confessor, after he had decided in 1246 to be buried at Westminster rather than at the Temple Church in the City of London "on account of reverence for the most glorious King Edward whose body lies at Westminster" (Wander 1978, 153, quoting a royal charter). There is a clear relationship between Edward's shrine and Henry III's equally expensive tomb standing to the south of it, which seems to have been designed to have been the same height as the shrine and to have been made of the same Cosmati marble, as if to emphasise the close relationship between king and saint (Figure 11–18).

At the ceremony of the translation of the saint's body to the new shrine, the saint's body was carried on the shoulders of King Henry III himself, aided by the very highest-ranking of porters—his brother Richard of Cornwall, the princes Edmund and Edward, the Earl of

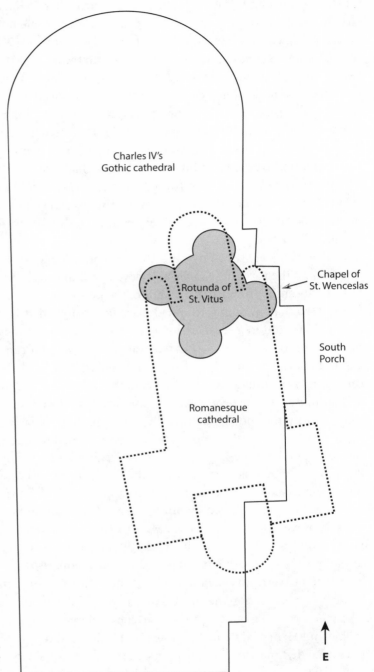

Charles IV's
Gothic cathedral

Chapel of
St. Wenceslas

Rotunda of
St. Vitus

South
Porch

Romanesque
cathedral

E

Figure 11–16: Simplified diagram of excavations under the cathedral of St. Vitus, Prague (Czech Republic) (after Rosario 2000, ch. 5, fig. 4).

Figure 11–17: St. Wenceslas Chapel, St. Vitus Cathedral, Prague (Czech Republic), seen through the west door. (See insert for color version of this image.)

Figure 11–18: Shrine of King Edward the Confessor, Westminster Abbey (England), showing its relationship to the tomb of King Henry III, which appears to the left of it.

Surrey, and Philip Basset, the justiciar. Indeed, there are indications that the frantic activity in completing the east end of the church, involving enormous expenditure even in years when the royal finances were very bad, was aimed at making it possible to translate the saint's body in 1269, this being the first year since 1258, and the last year until 1353, when the translation could fall on Easter Sunday on the same day of the year as the initial translation of 1163, also on Easter Sunday, had done, which is a measure of the saint's importance to the king in the context of his new church (Carpenter 2002, 42).

Later, Richard II's close association with Edward the Confessor is shown equally vividly by the representation of the saint as one of the king's patrons on the painted diptych called the Wilton Diptych (Figure 11–19). On the left-hand panel of the diptych, the king kneels in adoration of the Blessed Virgin Mary who is represented on the right-hand panel. The king is supported by: St. John the Baptist, represented in the clothes he wore in his desert abode and with the lamb (representing Jesus Christ) in his arms; St. Edmund, the English king martyred by the Vikings in the late ninth century (the arrow he carries symbolizes the nature his martyrdom); and—in the middle and most prominent—Edward the Confessor, crowned and dressed in white to symbolize his virginity and purity, which were the principal grounds for his canonization. In his hand, he holds a ring which, according to the *Lives* of him as a saint, he had once given to St. John the Evangelist who appeared to him in disguise, only to receive it back miraculously from pilgrims returning from the Holy Land.

The concern of Henry III and most of his successors to be buried close to Edward the Confessor's shrine was no doubt in part motivated by their desire for personal salvation. Being buried close to a saint or saints was a key means of ensuring one's successful passage through the Last Judgment, for when the dead were raised you would be raised in company with—and hopefully under the protection of—the saint near whose shrine you had been buried. But the proximity of royal tombs to a saint's shrine could also contribute to the message of power which the necropolis was sending. This is clear in the case of Westminster Abbey, for, at least in the later Middle Ages, Edward the Confessor was a centrally important saint to the English kings. Not only was he the founder and principal saint of their necropolis church; but he was also regarded as the king who had issued the Laws of Edward the Confessor, which were apocryphal but regarded as a defense against tyrannical rule. Indeed, the text entitled *La estoire de Seint Aedward le Rei*, compiled before *c.*1260, presented Edward the Confessor as a king replete with virtues as a lawgiver, a conciliator, and an equanimitous ruler who showed no irrational anger toward his subjects (Binski 1995, 62). The ruling king's emphasis on his attachment to the saint can only have been intended to send the message that he too had the virtues of his saintly predecessor, thus giving him the potential of increasing his personal power through the trust of his subjects.

The importance of royal or ducal saints like Wenceslas and Edward the Confessor was not limited to the sort of dynastic necropolis which Westminster Abbey and St. Vitus's Cathedral became. Already in the middle of the seventh century, only a couple of generations after the conversion of England to Christianity, there were a series of sites associated with the English martyr-king, Oswald of Northumbria, in ways that strikingly resemble the later medieval examples. According to Bede in his *Ecclesiastical History of the English People*,

Figure 11–19: Wilton Diptych, National Gallery, London (England). The principal subject is King Richard II (left-hand panel) kneeling in veneration of the Blessed Virgin Mary who appears in the right-hand panel, holding the Christ child. In the middle of the line of three saints standing behind Richard II is Edward the Confessor, who holds the ring he was supposed to have given to the disguised John the Evangelist. (See insert for color version of this image.)

when Oswald was killed on the battlefield of *Maserfelth* in 642, his enemy, the pagan king Penda of Mercia, "ordered his head and his hands to be severed from his body and hung on stakes" (Colgrave and Mynors 1991, book 3, chap. 12), perhaps as a means of humiliating the fallen king, perhaps as some sort of sacrifice to pagan gods. Whatever the truth of that, it is striking that it was his successor as king of Northumbria who was responsible for moving Oswald's head and arms to be venerated as saintly relics. "A year afterwards," wrote Bede, "his successor [King] Oswiu came thither with an army and took them away. He buried the head in a burial place in the church of Lindisfarne, but the hands and arms he buried in the royal city of Bamburgh" (Colgrave and Mynors 1991, book 3, chap. 12). As for the body, Bede explains that it was discovered by Osthryth, queen of Mercia, the daughter of Oswald's brother and successor Oswiu. She took the body to Bardney, "a famous monastery in the kingdom of Lindsey, . . . which was greatly loved, venerated and enriched by the queen and her husband Æthelred." Within a few years of Oswald's death then, there were no less than three places which had bodily remains, relics that is, of him, and in each case through the agency of a king or a queen.

Moreover, the places themselves were strikingly royal in character. Lindisfarne, a monastery and a bishop's see, had been founded by King Oswald himself, and there are clear indications in Bede that the kings of Northumbria remained very closely associated with that church, one of them—Ceolwulf—even retiring to it as a monk. Bamburgh was of course a royal fortress—perhaps we should call it a royal palace. The details we have about the enshrinement of Oswald's arms there are very slight, but they are interesting. Bede gives what was clearly a legend attaching at any rate to the saint's right arm when he recounts a story of how, when the king was sitting down to a feast, a royal officer responsible for relief of the poor came to tell him that many poor people were nearby asking for alms. When the king duly ordered the food that was set before him to be given to them, as well as the silver dish which he ordered to be broken into pieces, Bishop Aidan, who was by him, took his right hand, saying, "May this hand never decay." Bede explains that this prayer was granted. After Oswald's hand and arm had been cut off, they remained undecayed and kept "in a silver shrine" in St. Peter's church at the palace of Bamburgh where they "are venerated with fitting respect by all" (Colgrave and Mynors 1991, book 3, ch. 6).

In the early twelfth century, Symeon of Durham inserted into his *History of the Kings of the English and the Danes* a passage that may have been written much earlier, and which confirms the installation of at any rate the right hand of Oswald at Bamburgh:

> There is at the top of the mount [i.e. the rock on which what was in Symeon's day the castle of Bamburgh stood] a beautiful church, in which is a fine and precious shrine. In this, wrapped in silk, is the right hand of St Oswald the king, which remains undecayed. (translated from Arnold 1882–5, II, 45)

The failure of the hand to decay was a sure sign of Oswald's sanctity, and Alcuin in his *Bishops, Kings and Saints of York* adds further that the saint's nails continued to grow (Godman 1982, line 308). One of the functions of this relic of Oswald was no doubt to convey a message about the closeness to the divine of the palace of Bamburgh, and by extension the royal house of Northumbria. Association with the royal saint would have helped to confirm its authority, just as Edward the Confessor did for the later medieval kings of England.

From what Bede says, Bardney, where Oswald's headless and dismembered body was enshrined, was also a royal monastery. Although there are no remains today of the early church, it is clear that the tomb was handled in a royal way. Over it, according to Bede, was placed the saint's "banner of gold and purple"; and, in the late eighth century, according to Alcuin, King Offa of Mercia:

> adorned the tomb
> with silver, gold, gems, and much finery,
> making of it a splendid and enduring monument.
>
> (Godman 1982, lines 388–91)

There is no evidence for what the political motive of Osthryth—and perhaps also of her husband King Æthelred of Mercia—may have been in creating this cult site. But the basic point that we are dealing with a royal cult in close association with the aspirations of living royalty seems clear enough. Indeed, it is underlined by what subsequently happened to Oswald's body. The Viking invasions of the ninth century were unquestionably damaging to monasteries in northern and eastern England, and it appears that Bardney was either destroyed or declined drastically in that period. At all events, in 909 the Anglo-Saxon Chronicle (Swanton 1996, sub anno) relates that the lord of the Mercians, Æthelred, and his wife Æthelflæd, daughter of King Alfred of Wessex, known as the "lady of the Mercians," removed the body from Bardney to the church of St. Peter (later dedicated to St. Oswald) which they had founded at Gloucester (England). There are fragmentary remains of this church just to the northwest of Gloucester Cathedral, and excavations have shown that a really substantial eastern chapel was added to it at an early date, presumably to house the relics of the royal saint. As Mercia was merged into the kingdom of England in the course of the tenth century, Gloucester remained a royal place. It had been fortified and probably provided with a grid layout street plan by Æthelred and Æthelflaed, it had a royal palace called Kingsholm which was closely associated with St. Oswald's Church, and it was to become one of the places, alongside Winchester and Westminster, where the king of England would regularly wear his crown (Biddle 1986).

The connection between the resting places of the relics of royal saints and the power of living rulers can be even more evident in the case of the funeral of a ruler who was himself regarded as a saint immediately on his death. When the emperor Constantine planned the church of the Holy Apostles in Constantinople as his mausoleum, he arranged to have, on either side of his tomb, twelve *thekai* (a difficult word possibly to be translated as "cenotaphs," "pillars," or "plaques") dedicated to the twelve apostles. In 336, the year before his death, he had the relics of the apostles Andrew and Luke translated into the church, and he presumably intended relics of the other ten apostles to follow them. At any rate, according to his biographer, Eusebius, he and the apostles "were honoured with the performance of the sacred ordinances and mystic services" (quoted by Johnson 2009, 120). He was, evidently, to be regarded as the thirteenth apostle, responsible for the conversion of the Roman Empire to Christianity as the apostles had been responsible for preaching Christ's message after his crucifixion. Eusebius represents Constantine as being accepted into heaven directly after his death, like a saint, rather than having to wait for the Last Judgment.

But Eusebius went further. Constantine was to remain "the greatest emperor of all things," continuing to rule, in other words, after his death. This was apparently more than just the biographer's idea, for, although Constantine had died on May 22, a document of August 13 in the same year was still dated by the years of his reign, as if he were still alive. The emperor's corpse, in other words, continued to rule. This can be interpreted as resulting from a period of inter-regnum after Constantine's death, when his sons were all proclaimed emperor simultaneously—a sort of ruse, in other words, to gloss over this political dislocation in the empire. Equally, however, it may point to the idea that deceased rulers could come to be viewed as saints simply in their capacity as rulers, and that their bodies could be treated in ways not dissimilar to those in which saints bodies were treated.

As has been seen in the case of S. Oswald, individual parts of the bodies of saints could be venerated as relics. In Oswald's case, the division of the body was attributed to the malicious action of an enemy, which may reflect a contemporary current of disapproval in some parts of the Christian church for such dismemberment carried out by Christians even for the purpose of obtaining relics. But, in fact, the breaking-up of saints' bodies to create a multitude of bodily relics of them became a normal part of their cult, and major churches increasingly had collections of such relics. In the light of this, it is striking that from the twelfth century onward there began the practice of dividing the bodies of high-ranking persons, especially rulers, even when there was no question of their being canonized. Their body parts were then interred or enshrined in different churches—they were treated, in other words, much like saints would have been. This practice was evidently disapproved of by some sections of the Church, and especially by scholars of the University of Paris, so that in 1299 the pope condemned it in a bull, *Detestandae feritatis* (E. A. R. Brown 1981, 221). But, despite the efforts of the pope and the scholars of Paris, the desire to divide the bodies of deceased persons remained strong; and the chief effect of the pope's bull was to restrict the practice to rulers, for only they could successfully obtain the necessary papal dispensations to release them from the prohibition embodied in the bull.

The reasons for wanting to divide a body could have been practical. Where someone died at a distance from their chosen or customary place of burial, the body might need to have its organs removed so that it could be transported without decaying unacceptably during the course of the inevitably slow journey from the place of death. In such circumstances, the body could be disemboweled and the organs could be buried in a separate grave at the place where the person had died. Thus, for example, the German emperor, Otto I (962–73), died at Merseburg in Germany and was disemboweled before his body was taken to the city of Magdeburg for burial, the entrails being buried at Memleben (E. A. R. Brown 1981, 226). In the case of Henry I, king of England (1100–35), who died in Normandy, his body was disemboweled and embalmed, with his entrails being buried at Bec (France), before being transported to England for burial at the abbey he had founded for this purpose at Reading in Berkshire (Hollister 2004).

Important as the practical reason for division of the body no doubt was, however, there was clearly a strong motivation arising from the piety which the ruler had and which he no doubt wished to demonstrate to his subjects. When the German emperor, Frederick Barbarossa, died in 1190 while he was on a crusade to the Holy Land, his body was disemboweled and then boiled to remove the flesh, so that his bones could be taken on with the crusade to the city of Tyre, which was its objective, and there buried (E. A. R. Brown 1981, 227). In Spain, Alfonso X, king of Castile (1252–84), stipulated in his will that his body should be buried in either Santa Maria de Murcia, which he called the capital of his kingdom, or in Seville, but that his heart should be taken to Jerusalem and buried on Calvary, where Christ was crucified (E. A. R. Brown 1981, 234). In addition to wishing parts of their bodies to be buried at especially holy places, rulers could have another motive for having their bodies divided. This was a wish to associate their remains with those of members of their family. In

France, Philip V (1316–22) arranged for his body to be buried at Saint-Denis, while his heart was to be buried where his wife's body and that of his only son were to lie, that is at the convent of the Cordeliers in Paris. His entrails were to be buried where lay the heart of his grandfather, at the convent of the Dominican Friars in the same city (E. A. R. Brown 1980; Bande 2009, 92–93). Dividing the body between religious houses like this also meant that the deceased ruler had a very particular claim to benefit from the prayers of more than one religious community, which he no doubt hoped would facilitate the passage of his soul through purgatory.

For all these pious motives, however, the division of the body was clearly capable of sending a message of ideological power in the interests of the ruler's successors. If his body was being treated much like that of a saint, his relationship to God must have been a favorable one, suggesting the legitimacy and God-given character, not only of his own power but also by association with him that of his successors. And more than one place was being established for him to be commemorated and his virtues rehearsed, thus widening the audience of the message of power relating to the legitimacy of a dynasty which could produce such rulers.

THE RULER AND HIS BODY

There may, however, have been another dimension to the attitudes to the ruler's body which these practices reveal. Despite the views of Christian thinkers such as Augustine of Hippo about the complete separation of the soul from the body after death, there was clearly in the Middle Ages a belief that saints continued to have an existence in their physical remains. This is especially obvious in miracle-stories in which the saint miraculously leaves his shrine to effect the miracle in question, as is illustrated, for example, in one of the windows representing such a miracle of St. Thomas Becket in Canterbury Cathedral (Caviness 1981, 187, fig. 124). But it underlies many aspects of the cult of saints in general. It was precisely because saints were believed to be simultaneously in heaven and present in their earthly remains that it was so desirable to make pilgrimages to their shrines and to be buried close to those shrines.

So it could be also with rulers. Just as Eusebius regarded Constantine as continuing to rule as an emperor, and just as that document issued three and a half months after his death continued to treat him as a living man (above, p. 377), so other rulers too could be regarded as still having an existence in their corpses. It has been seen already how Otto III is supposed to have found the body of the emperor Charlemagne in 1000, seated and completely undecayed in his tomb in the palace church of Aachen (above, pp. 326–27). Now, not until the late twelfth century was Charlemagne formally made a saint, but this account makes clear that he was regarded as the equivalent of a saint already in 1000, since his body was believed to be undecayed like that of a saint. Charlemagne's continued existence in his body was evidently believed to be an existence that would end only with the Day of Judgement. There seems, however, to have been another belief that could develop around the body of a ruler, which was that the deceased continued to live in his body until the point of the funeral—which takes us back to Eusebius's account of the aftermath of Constantine's death.

When Philip V, king of France, died, for example, his corpse was clad in royal robes and a crown was on his head, just as was the case with Charlemagne's corpse as discovered by Otto III. Philip's corpse also held in its hands the symbols of royal power, the scepter and the hand of justice (that is, the rod with a hand at the top of it). In Philip's case, and in that of other rulers, accounts and other documents were only transferred to the name of his successor after his funeral. Until then, he was still king, still living and ruling in his dead body.

These ideas are most graphically illustrated by the funeral of Francis I, king of France (1515–47), who died at the château of Rambouillet on 31 March. His body was disemboweled, and his heart and entrails were enshrined in silver caskets close to the relics of the saints in the church of Haultbrière. His body was then transferred to the château of Saint-Cloud. On April 24, more than three weeks after the king's death, a lifelike effigy of him, which had been made in Paris in the intervening period, was placed on a bed of state in the great hall of the château. Sitting upright, dressed in full royal robes, wearing the crown, and with the scepter and the hand of justice next to it, the effigy was treated for eleven days just as the living king would have been, including meals being served to it with all the customary etiquette of a king's dining table. The effigy was then removed and the coffin itself replaced it as the object of mourning. Then, on May 21, seven weeks after the king's death, the body was taken in procession to Notre-Dame-des-Champs in Paris. On May 22, it was joined by the effigy—and the effigies of Francis I's two sons who had predeceased him—and these and the body were taken on in procession to the cathedral of Notre Dame. In that procession, the coffin was borne on a "chariot of arms" and surrounded by mourning; but the effigy of the king was treated, as it had been at Saint-Cloud, as if it were the living king. At Notre Dame, the effigy was placed on top of the coffin in a structure with candles burning called a *chapelle ardente*; and then coffin and effigy were taken in procession to Saint-Denis. There the effigies were removed, and the body was placed in the grave along with the symbols of sovereignty. They were, however, almost immediately removed since the sovereign power itself clearly could not be buried; and the herald cried out, "The king is dead! Long live the king!"—the second part of this cry being a reference to Francis I's son, Henry II, who only formally succeeded to the kingship at this point.

It is not easy to interpret the meaning of practices such as these. Perhaps they derive from the concept that the ruler in effect had two bodies, one a living and dying body, the other the office of rulership itself, regarded as an undying body. This concept could have had a basis in the belief that kingship somehow had a spiritual existence in its own right; or in legal ideas regarding kingship as an undying office. The funeral of Francis I would have been the moment at which the king's living and dying body was placed in the earth, while the king's other body—the undying essence of kingship—passed on to his successor. The same sort of idea may have underlain the use of an effigy. Its progress in the funeral procession was treated as the triumph of a living ruler, so it represented the body which was the undying essence of rulership; while the coffin itself held the living and dying body of the king and was treated with mourning. Whatever the truth behind all these beliefs and practices—and there is no certainty as to what it was or even if it was always the same truth—what is clear is that they must have contributed considerably to the messages of power conveyed by the ruler's necropolis. If rulers continued to live in their bodies in some way, so much the greater must the power of such places have been considered. If the funeral was the real point of transmission of power from the deceased to his successor, so much the more crucial was the role of the necropolis.

TOMBS

Just as the beliefs and practices focused on the body and the funeral of the ruler could enhance the messages of power conveyed by a necropolis, so too could the design and style of the tombs that covered the rulers' remains. Two of the greatest tombs in the church of Saint-Denis are those of King Francis I and his queen, and of King Louis XII (1462–1515) and his queen. Both of these are double tombs, representing the kings' and queens' bodies in two contrasting ways. On the tomb of Louis XII and his queen, the lower level represents their corpses, sculpted naked and in graphic detail—even the incisions and stitches made during their disemboweling and embalming are represented. Above are sculptures of the king and queen alive, kneeling in prayer (Figure 11–20, Figure 11–21). The tomb of Francis I and his queen follows a similar pattern.

It is tempting to think that tombs such as these represent the concept of the king having two bodies, and that they should be seen as a permanent record of a royal funeral, with its coffin and its lifelike effigy of the deceased. But the praying figures of Louis XII and Francis I on their tombs cannot be the stone equivalent of effigies, because the figures have no regalia, not even crowns. It is documented that the effigies used in the funerals were equipped with regalia, for in the case of Francis I's effigy there are records of two pairs of hands being made for it, one pair in an attitude of prayer, the other shaped so as to be able to hold the scepter and the hand of justice. This, however, does show that the effigy had two roles—symbolizing the majesty of the king with his regalia, and symbolizing his piety as expressed in his prayers. It may be that the praying figures on the tombs of Louis XII and Francis I were intended to represent this pious aspect of the kings. Nevertheless, tombs like this did convey the idea that the king continued in some way to live after his death—that he was, like a saint, present in his tomb—and, in the case of the tombs of Louis XII and Francis I, continuing to pray with his queen, no doubt for their own salvation, but no doubt also for the well-being of their successors.

Tombs like these could also send a simpler message of power. Just like the Mausoleum of Augustus and other monuments, they could perpetuate in the memory of the rulers' subjects the achievements of the deceased rulers, and thus contribute by association to the power of their successors. Francis I's tomb, for example, with its large central opening, smaller side openings, and its attached classical columns, had the form of a Roman triumphal arch (Figure 11–22). Its purpose must have been to evoke the king's—admittedly unfulfilled—aspirations to be Holy Roman Emperor, and also his famous victories. These latter are represented in sculptured reliefs around the base of the tomb, just as Trajan's victories were represented on his column in Rome. Just as the king's funeral had elements of a triumphal procession, so the tomb resembled a triumphal arch. Indeed, one of the sculptured scenes on Louis XII's tomb shows the king as the focus of a classical triumph at Milan, with the figures in it actually dressed in Roman costume.

Figure 11–20: Tomb of King Louis XII and his queen, former abbey church of Saint-Denis (France).

Although the inspiration behind these tombs was the particular military ambitions of the kingdom of France in the late fifteenth and early sixteenth centuries, and in Francis I's case with his ambition to become Holy Roman Emperor, tombs in general could convey messages as to the greatness and achievements of their occupants, which could by inference be of benefit to their successors as rulers. The founder of the Norman kingdom of Sicily, Roger II (1130–54), evidently intended his tomb to convey a message of power. For, he established for his dynasty a church some miles along the coast of Sicily from Palermo, his capital city, to act as a necropolis. This was the church of Cefalù, to which he presented two sarcophagi. In one of these, he evidently intended himself to be buried.

These sarcophagi carried a particular message, because they were made of porphyry, the purple color of which stone made it particularly appropriate for emperors, since purple was a color indicative, at least in the Byzantine Empire, of imperial power. (Porphyry was also used by the popes, who also had claims to imperial dignity in their own right.) Moreover,

Figure 11–21: Detail of the carved cadavers of King Louis XII and his queen at the lower level of their tomb, former abbey church of Saint-Denis (France).

Figure 11–22: Tomb of King Francis I and his queen, former abbey church of Saint-Denis (France). Note the figures praying at the top and the carved cadavers below.

porphyry was always a rare and exclusive stone, quarried at only one place, Djebel Dukah, known in antiquity as Mount Porphyry; and, to make the stone still more exclusive, after the Arab conquests of the southern and eastern Mediterranean basin in the seventh century, access to the quarries was cut off. So from then on porphyry could only be obtained by reusing the stone, which naturally had to be obtained from the most high-level places in the former Roman Empire, chiefly from Rome itself. Roger II's choice of porphyry therefore carried a clear message of his aspirations as a ruler.

Roger II was buried not at Cefalù, but at Palermo, in the cathedral, where his body occupied another porphyry tomb. The mid-twelfth century saw a tussle between Cefalù and Palermo Cathedral as to which would be the necropolis of the kings of Sicily, a struggle which Palermo won—it also fought off the claims of the nearby cathedral of Monreale, which was established by King William II of Sicily as a rival necropolis (above, pp. 307–8). When Frederick II, king of Sicily (1198–1250) and Holy Roman Emperor (1220–50), built up his kingdom and Palermo as his capital, he had the two sarcophagi which Roger II had given to Cefalù transferred to Palermo Cathedral. In one of them, he himself was buried, and to the other he transferred the remains of his father Henry VI, king of Sicily (1194–97). The cathedral had also another porphyry sarcophagus, in which were placed the remains of Henry VI's queen, Constance. It is not certain where in the cathedral the porphyry sarcophagi were located (they are currently in the south aisle), but wherever they were they must have created a considerable impression, and conveyed a clear message of the imperial aspirations of Frederick II, his father, and his predecessor, Roger II.

In addition to the use of porphyry for the sarcophagi, the tombs conveyed a further message of power in that the sarcophagi were placed under canopies of stone—all of which seem to have been creations of Frederick II (Figure 11–23). These canopies, the columns supporting them also made of porphyry in the case of Frederick II's tomb, were surely intended to be reminiscent of the thrones of the emperors of antiquity, as they appear, for example, on ivory diptychs. The message being sent was that the rulers interred in them were every bit as great as the Roman emperors. But the canopies also resembled the canopies usually made of fabric and wood which were erected over altars (although those were admittedly usually square rather than rectangular). Viewed in this light, the tombs also conveyed a message of the closeness of the rulers to God, represented by the resemblance of their tombs to the altars where Christ's body was present at the mass. Frederick II was presenting himself and his predecessors as great rulers, comparable to emperors if not actually emperors, as was his own case, who also had a close relationship to the divine. In this way, the tombs of his necropolis sent a message of ideological power relating both to himself during his lifetime, and to his successors after his death.

For the use of tombs as instruments of power, one final example is too spectacular to be passed over. It is the tomb of Ladislas, king of Naples (1414–28), which dominates the church of San Giovanni a Carbonara in the city of Naples. It is so enormous that it forms the arch between the nave of the church and the choir (Figure 11–24). Immediately above the opening to the choir, the king and his queen are sculpted seated and facing out into the nave of the church. The fact that they are dressed as deacons, while at the same time holding orbs and wearing crowns, underlines the message of ideological power that this monument was

Figure 11-23: Tomb of Frederick II, Palermo Cathedral, Palermo (Sicily).

Figure 11-24: Tomb of King Ladislas and his queen, church of San Giovanni a Carbonara, Naples (Italy).

intended to convey. The monarchs were here being represented as having the status of deacons. They were not priest-rulers, but they were, according to their monument, verging on this. Above these sculptures, the king's corpse is sculpted, lying on a tomb under a canopy, crowned and robed and being blessed by a priest, with angels drawing back the curtains to give a view of it. Here, we meet again the representation of the two bodies of the ruler—in this case with the living body below, the corpse above. In this tomb, however, there was a third representation of the ruler: the magnificent, mounted figure at its summit, armed and wielding his sword in triumph. Here was a message about the military achievements, or at least military capabilities, of King Ladislas, as clear and as dramatic as anything that adorned the mausoleum of Augustus or the column of Trajan.

Burial Places of Rulers   385

CONCLUSION

Burial places could convey various messages of power. Certain of these were simple. They underlined the grandeur and the efficacy of the ruler in question, through the grandeur of their design, or more explicitly through inscriptions or texts associated with them. They could serve to underline the military achievements of the ruler, through the representation of his military activity or through their form as related to the arches of military triumphs. Other messages of power could relate to the legitimacy of the deceased ruler and, by implication, that of his successors. This could extend to whole lines of kings, where a burial place had been developed as a necropolis for a kingdom. Indeed it seems clear that such necropolises in themselves sent a message of power, over and above the deliberate arrangement of rulers' tombs within them.

Messages of ideological power could be more subtle but nonetheless clear in emphasizing the relationship of the deceased ruler to the divine. In the context of the pagan Roman Empire, there could be an emphasis on the parallelism between the ruler and the sun, or on his apotheosis as a god in his own right. In Christian contexts, the message conveyed was no doubt first and foremost about the ruler's piety. Indeed, it is not easy to distinguish the extent to which the ruler's burial place was intended to promote the welfare of his soul and its passage to heaven, as much as to send a message of power in the interests of his successors. But perhaps the distinction is an unreal one. The ruler naturally wished for the welfare of his soul; but his piety was an element of his power in that it showed his closeness to God from whom power was believed to flow.

The cult of saints also had a role to play in the messages of power sent by rulers' burial places. This was partly because of the importance in rulers' necropolises of former rulers regarded as saints. But it was also because of the blurring between saints and rulers, so that a ruler came to be regarded as not dissimilar to a saint in his own right. This was not just in the treatment of his body, but also in a belief that the ruler was still present in his body after his death, just as was a saint.

CHAPTER 12

Conclusion

The preceding chapters have made the case that the various types of site created by, or associated with, rulers were capable of, and in many cases designed for the purpose of, conveying messages of power. Making that case has involved considering the design of palaces and their individual components. Palaces, it has been argued, functioned as stage sets for displays of rulership. Aspects of their design and decoration conveyed messages of ideological power where, for example, they were intended to represent palaces as heavenly locations—the Heavenly Jerusalem, for example. Other aspects of their design were intended to convey messages of power relating to rulers' relationship with their subjects, whether these were seen as placing subjects and rulers on a relatively equal footing, as in the case of great halls, or whether they were intended to convey a message relating to rulers as segregated from all but their most favored subjects, as in the case of private apartments, with their innermost cores separated from the outside world by an *enfilade* of rooms.

Making the case has also involved considering the functions of designed landscapes—gardens, parks, forests—as conveyors of messages of power. Gardens and parks could be designed in much the same way as the palaces they often surrounded. They were intended, it is argued, to provide stage sets for the presentation of messages of power in the same way as palaces, and sometimes gardens in particular, could function as outdoor palaces. Forests too could be landscapes similarly designed, in part at least, to convey messages of power, whether about the ruler's bureaucratic power in the hold he had over them from a governmental point of view, or about his personal power in the relationships that were shaped and displayed in the practice of hunting in the forests, or about his ideological power where that hunting was symbolic of his quasi-divine character, or the forests of the nationhood of his kingdom.

As for cities, the case has been made in the preceding chapters that they could equally be symbolic of rulers' power, and that indeed the very act of founding a city was itself intended to convey a message of power. Where cities contained palaces, the cityscape might be absorbed into the palace, just as a palace could be designed to resemble a city. Like the palaces and the landscapes, the cities too could be designed to provide stage sets for the display of rulers' power, in their processions, their public appearances, their entries, and their military triumphs.

The holy places that rulers built or patronized, it is argued, were equally vehicles for messages of power, which were naturally concerned principally with ideological power—the relationship between the ruler and the gods or God and their representatives. Because of the lack of evidence of how pagan temples were used and the ceremonies involved, the book's discussion has been focused on Christian holy places, with the single addition of the Great Mosque of Córdoba. The case has been made that messages of ideological power, and in some cases messages of the restriction of that power, were intended to be conveyed by these places, although in certain circumstances the power of the ruler was mediated by the rival power of the clergy controlling the church.

Finally, the places marking the beginnings and ends of the reigns of rulers have also formed part of the book's case. Inauguration places, with the rituals of inauguration that took place in them, were—it has been argued—effective conveyors of messages of power, as were burial places of rulers, especially where these were established for whole dynasties or sequences of rulers. Then in particular, they were capable of conveying messages of power on behalf of current rulers long after the deceased rulers of the past had been interred in them.

To all this, as was noted at the outset, a counter-case can be made. The various aspects of the design and decoration of palaces, the creation of artificial landscapes, the foundation and shaping of cities, the patronage of holy places, and the development of places for inauguration and burial can all be interpreted as nothing more than the perquisites that went with the job of being a ruler. Their principal purpose, viewed in this way, was to give rulers the comfort, luxury, and self-importance they craved; or, in the case of holy places and burial places, to give them the very best chance of enjoying good relations with the divinity, and so of promoting the happiness of their souls after death. Readers must judge whether this counter-case is preferable to the case advanced in this book, although the two need not, of course, be mutually exclusive. What was designed to convey a message of power could equally have had the effect of contributing to the ruler's well-being.

As was also noted at the outset, the book has pursued its discussions around a series of examples chosen for the wealth of material and interpretative potential that they offer. So the book has not sought to provide an account of overall chronological development or geographical variation. Nevertheless, it is possible to chart some changes, such as the development in medieval palaces of suites of apartments in preference to great halls as the most important element, and the increasing sophistication of bureaucratic arrangements as can be seen at the Palace of Westminster or the Palace of the Popes at Avignon.

For this author, however, the most striking feature of the sites examined is the similarity in the messages of power which, if the book's case is accepted, they were designed to convey, even when they were separated by great extents of space and time. For example, the message that the ruler was a cosmic figure, in direct contact with the universe at large, likened to the sun and the celestial bodies, seems to appear in palaces as widely separated as Nero's Golden House in Rome of the first century AD, and the sanctuary mosaic of Westminster Abbey in England of the thirteenth, or from the sixth-century cosmic dome of Haghia Sophia in Constantinople, to the fourteenth-century domes of the Muslim palaces of the Alhambra. Although, as noted above, the development of the apartment as a more important element of palaces than the great hall is found in medieval palaces such as the Louvre, it is nevertheless the case that developed apartments, sometimes with *enfilades* of rooms, are found much more widely, for example in the Palace of Domitian of first-century AD Rome. Likewise, the design of gardens and parks seems to show a remarkable similarity between sites as widely separated as the Palace of Domitian again and the park of Hesdin from the twelfth century and later, while the treatment of hunting as an almost ceremonial activity designed to convey messages of power is prominent across the whole extent of space and time considered by this book.

In the case of cities too, there are striking elements of similarity. Their layout, for example, in geometrical ways is a striking common element of many of them; maybe it was for convenience, maybe—as this book argues—it was an expression of the ruler's control of the universe. Likewise, the practice of holding entries and triumphs occurs in much the same ways in widely separated contexts. In some respects, no doubt, this was no more than superficial imitation of the past on behalf of the later rulers who followed these practices; but it is hard to escape the conclusion that there was more to it than this, and that underlying this sort of use of cities was a consistent desire to create mechanisms for sending messages of power which had persisted across many centuries and in many parts of Europe.

For holy places, the similarity between Christian Europe on the one hand and Roman pagan Europe and Muslim Europe on the other is less immediately obvious because of the different religions involved. But, as has been noted, there are also striking similarities, for example in the use of domes as representations of the heavens, and indeed in the use of relics, the importance of which is a striking aspect of Christian holy places. Although the use of these was unusual in the Muslim world, they had a place in the Great Mosque of Córdoba. For inauguration places, there was of course change resulting from the introduction of Christianity, notably the emergence of anointing the ruler with holy oil from the eighth century; but it has nonetheless been seen how smooth at least in the Roman world was the transition from non-Christian to Christian inauguration, so that the similarities seem to loom larger than the discontinuities.

Finally, in the case of burial places, the apparent similarities between such superficially different sites as the mounds and ship-setting of Jelling on the one hand and the mausolea of the first-century AD Roman emperors on the other seems particularly arresting, as does the appearance in very different contexts of the notion that the ruler lived on after his earthly decease.

There can be no firm conclusions, of course, given the book's selective approach; but nonetheless the far-flung examples that have been considered create a presumption that rulership had many startling similarities across wide extents of space and time. Those extents could probably be made even wider with comparable results. As has been noted, the significance of hunting as a ceremonial activity is as striking in the world of the Assyrian rulers as it was in that of late medieval and early modern rulers of Europe. The messages of power conveyed by elements of palace design, as discussed in this book, could equally be discussed in comparable ways of much later palaces, for example those of the Baroque period—indeed the book has made one small excursion in this direction in summing up its conclusions about the style of palaces (above, p. 97). Similarly, there may have been little difference between the intentions of the emperors who founded the Imperial Fora in Rome, and King Christian IV of Norway (1588–1648) who laid out his new city of Christiania after the destruction of the original city of Oslo by fire in 1624.

Readers may, of course, conclude that there is nothing suprising about these sort of similarities, because there were limits to how rulership could be presented, and that consequently we should see no great significance in parallelisms in the development of sites associated with it. For this author, however, this seems an inadequate interpretation. The common themes and common elements explored in this book must surely point to underlying similarities in the nature of the power that rulers were wielding, or at least claiming, and the messages about it that they wished to be conveyed through the sites they founded, patronized, or were associated with.

What sort of power was chiefly involved? The messages of personal power that could be conveyed by great halls, aspects of city design, or sites prepared for hunting have been noted. So too have the messages of bureaucratic power apparently conveyed by the complexes of administrative offices found in some palaces. But the most persistent messages of power that the sites considered here were conveying were those of ideological power, concerning the close relationship of the ruler to the divine. This book is not claiming, of course, that ideological power was necessarily the most important type of power the rulers had. Just as the Roman emperor was represented as a god, so too his government had formidable bureaucratic resources. Just as the King of Sicily's Cappella Palatina represented him as dwelling in the Heavenly Jerusalem, so he was crucially dependent on the personal power he derived from his relationship to his vassals. It is, however, the contention of this book that the persistence of messages of ideological power conveyed by the sites it has considered should be taken seriously. In answer to the question of why, across so many centuries and in so many parts of Europe, people were willing to accept the authority of rulers, and to glorify them in religious and quasi-religious ways, the material examined in this book seems to create a presumption at least that the ideological power that rulers could represent themselves as holding was centrally, perhaps crucially, important to their authority.

THEMES AND TOPICS

Chapter 1: Introduction

THE COURSE OF HISTORY

This book requires its readers to keep track of the **outline of European history** across a broad time range. The easiest way to do this is by using historical atlases, which give an immediate impression of the rise and fall of empires and kingdoms. Especially useful are, for the whole period covered by this book, M. Almond et al. (1994), Scarre (1995), Anon. (1997), and Mackay and Ditchburn (1997); for the Roman Empire, Konstam (2003); and for the Middle Ages, Jotischky and Hull (2005). For accounts of **particular kingdoms, empires, or reigns**, it is easiest to consult dictionaries and encyclopaedias, either online or in printed form—for example: Strayer (1982–2004), Schulman (2002), Hornblower and Spawforth (2003), Bjork (2010). Useful narrative summaries, together with analytical essays, can be found in Fouracre (2005), McKitterick (1995), Reuter (2000), Luscombe (2003a), Luscombe (2003b), Abulafia (1999), M. E. Jones (2000), and Allmand (1998).

DIFFERENT APPROACHES

Kantorowicz (1957) is a very important treatment of **approaches to rulership**, using artistic sources to a certain extent, but chiefly drawing on written ones, including legal texts and commentaries. Ullmann (1966, 1970, 1975) focuses chiefly on works of political philosophy, as does Nelson (1977b), in her case especially on Hincmar of Reims. Tout (1920–33) is a classic treatment of rulership, in this case in the kingdom of England, treated on the basis of administrative documents. For the study of narrative sources, see, for example, Given-Wilson (2004).

THE NATURE OF POWER

The **types of power** presented here are adapted from the highly influential formulation of models of power (or authority as he called it) by the German sociologist, Max Weber (1947, 297–333), or in another translation Weber (1968, I, 215–45). For further discussion of these, see Rollason (2012a, 69–71), chapters 4–6 of which examine the evidence for respectively ideological, bureaucratic, and personal power, with bibliography and critical commentary, although only in the period 300–1050. For an example of **bureaucratic power**, the classic treatment of the Roman Empire's bureaucracy is A. H. M. Jones (1964). The thesis that law chiefly controlled the nature of power was most influentially developed by Kantorowicz (1957). The importance of **personal power** is examined by Bloch

(1961) and Ganshof (1964). These books are principally concerned with the personal relations known in the context of medieval society as feudal relations, in which the man taking an oath of loyalty to his lord or ruler receives land to support himself and agrees to perform military service for his lord. Many discussions of this have been published, notably by S. Reynolds (1994). For the use of personal power in early modern courts such as Versailles, the classic study is Elias (1983), translated from Elias (1975). For commentary on this, see Duindam (1994). Also valuable is Adamson (2000). For **ideological power**, see, for example, the discussion of the god-like character of the Roman emperors in Price (1984); and, for the possibly sacral character of the barbarian kings, see Erkens (2005, 2006) and Enright (1983). There is an excellent summary of the evidence for this sort of kingship in Scandinavia in McTurk (1975–76, 1994), and a thought-provoking, if rather wild, account of the evidence for the sacral character of Anglo-Saxon kingship in Chaney (1970). For discussion of the Christian impact on kingship, see, for example, Ullmann (1969) and, especially for anointing, the various papers by Nelson (1967, 1971, 1977a, 1987). The boldest statement of the idea that there was a long-term continuity in ideological power is that by Oakley (2006).

Part III: Palaces: Introduction

The work dealing most directly with the theme of **palaces as instruments of power** is Steane (2001, especially chs. 2–4), although its attempt to present a discussion based broadly on an historical narrative makes it sketchier than it need be. Nonetheless, the approach adopted in it has been an important source of inspiration for this book; and the author's analysis of the architectural design of the headmaster's study in the school he taught in as a "seat of power" is especially illuminating (Steane 2001, 11). The book's scope is Europe-wide, but a work limited to England, which is nevertheless illuminating for palace design in general, is Thurley (1993). Despite its title, this provides an insightful commentary on medieval palaces (chs. 1–2) as well as detailed consideration of their early modern successors. Another highly illuminating work, this one focusing on Byzantine palaces, is Carile (2012). A more general discussion, which addresses the general theme of this section as regards the early Middle Ages, is Bandmann (2005). For discussions of the **meaning of the word "palace"** and the complexities of using it, see, for example, Duval (1978), Staab (1990), Zotz (1990), and Renoux (2001). See also Lalou (1996) and Viarre (1961). Moulinier-Brogi (2003) provides a detailed analysis of the use of the word *palais* (palace), especially in Old and Modern French.

Chapter 2: The Power of Design

The most insightful **general works** are Thurley (1993, especially ch. 5) and Steane (2001, chs. 2–4). A classic study is Girouard (1978), although it does not focus on rulers' palaces primarily, and it ranges from the Middle Ages to the twentieth century. An important collection of papers dealing with elite residences of the late Middle Ages and the Renaissance is Guillaume (1994). Burroughs (2002) is a discussion of **façades** in Renaissance palaces. For the development of **staircases** as an aspect of palace design, see Anon. (1985), and especially the contribution of Whiteley (1985). For **peristyle courtyards**, the most interesting discussion is Swoboda (1969). **Triclinia** and their function are the subject of an exciting paper by Lavin (1962). The significance of **domes** is the subject of E. B. Smith (1950) and Lehmann (1945). Manzano Martos (1994) examines the cosmic significance of Muslim domes, relating them to Arabic poetry, and tracing them back to the Sassanid kingdom and beyond. Early medieval **timber halls** are discussed by Laing (1969), N. Reynolds (1980), Cramp (1993), and Hamerow et al. (2011, with further bibliography). On the hall and the "treasure-throne" in *Beowulf*, see Rollason (2009). There is further discussion of halls in the context of *Beowulf* in Niles (2007, 171–77, 83–200). For notes on the poem, see Fulk, Bjork, and Niles (2008) and Orchard (2004). On the change from great halls to **apartments**, see the classic discussion, for English examples, of Girouard (1978). There is a more recent discussion, not focusing on royal palaces but nonetheless useful, by J. Blair (1993). On the **enfilade** in early modern apartments, there is a classic paper by Baillie (1967). Germane to the theme of **controlling access** to the lord in a palace is Dixon (1996). The **private and public spaces** in palaces are discussed in the context of late medieval France by Whiteley (1996). The ways in which palace design was intended to facilitate **ceremonial functions** is the subject of Kerscher (2000), which deals with the palaces of the Kingdom of Majorca and of the popes in the thirteenth and fourteenth centuries. Also germane to this is Paravicini (1997) and Zotz (1991).

Chapter 3: The Power of Style

Magnificence as a necessary characteristic of a ruler's life is explained for the Renaissance period by Thurley (1993, 11–13, 18). Strong (1984) principally concerns magnificence in seventeenth-century monarchy, but the approach is illuminating for other periods, and Part I, Chapter 1 reviews the Middle Ages. Fraser Jenkins (1970) is a discussion of magnificence in the context of Cosimo de' Medici. A lucid work on the Hunting of the Unicorn Tapestries is Cavallo (1998). The **Court Style** in France is discussed in a classic work by Branner (1965), who extended his discussion to Westminster Abbey in Branner (1964). His ideas were critically reviewed for England by Colvin (1983), and for France by M. Cohen (2010), who argues for a bottom-up genesis of the style. The spiritual significance of **geometry** in ancient and medieval architecture is controversial. The views set out in this chapter are drawn from Götze (1998). Leistikov (2008, 151–52), however, dismisses this writer's views on the importance of the eight-pointed star as "fantasy," but without providing counter-arguments. Musca (2002, 1–9) emphasizes the range of geometrically rigorous buildings, including the castle of Conisborough (Yorkshire); frequent occurrence of a form, however, does not necessarily militate against its significance. See also Hiscock (2000), the focus of which is chiefly on ecclesiastical buildings.

Chapter 4: Gardens, Parks, and Power

Littlewood (1997, 18–21) gives an account of ancient **Near Eastern parks and gardens**, as well as those of the Arabs. He notes that, already in the ninth century BC, the Assyrian king Ashurnasirpal II (883–59 BC) claims in an inscription that in his royal garden are "trees [and plants raised from] seeds from wherever I discovered [them] . . . in the countries through which I marched and the mountains which I crossed." The political importance of gardens to rulers is shown by the claim of an earlier Assyrian king, Shalmaneser III (858–24 BC), that he attacked the royal residence of an enemy and "I cut down his gardens." Farrar (1998) gives a straightforward account of **Roman gardens**, dealing with architectural features in them, ornamental pools, fountains, and so on. However, the principal contribution to understanding of Roman gardens in recent years has been made by Jashemski and Jashemski (1979), focusing on excavation and research at Pompeii. A much older study, which is still useful for its discussion of representations of gardens in mosaics and paintings, is Grimal (1943). Von Stackelberg (2009) gives a much more thoughtful and insightful discussion; chapter 3 deals particularly with aspects of "the politicization of the Roman garden," and how "ownership of a large garden could be used as a political tool," including the use of gardens by Pompey, Caesar, and Hadrian at Hadrian's Villa. Particularly interesting about the emperor Nero's Golden House and its parkland setting is Champlin (1998). More focused on the philosophy of gardens than on their significance for power is Giesecke (2007).

Littlewood (1997) gives a wide-ranging account of **Byzantine palace gardens**, including their menageries, and relating them to earlier and later gardens. In particular (pp. 33–35), he documents rooms in the Great Palace of Constantinople and other Byzantine buildings, which were made to look like gardens. Thus the emperor Constantine VII turned the throne room called the Golden Triclinium (*Chrysotriklinos*) "into a blooming and odoriferous rose garden, as tiny, variegated mosaic cubes imitated the colours of freshly opened flowers" (quoting Theophilos, *Continuation*). Equally thoughtful is Maguire (1994), which discusses the ideology of Byzantine gardens. See also Maguire

(2000). Littlewood, Maguire, and Wolschke-Bulmahn (2002) offer a collection of rather specialist papers, which are less concerned with the issues raised in this chapter.

The fullest study of **Andalusian gardens and parks** is Ruggles (2000), but there is also a thoughtful discussion by Dickie (1968). For **medieval and later gardens and parks**, J. Harvey (1981) offers a wide-ranging treatment, focused principally on medieval gardens but also ranging more widely, with rich illustrative material. The book shows its age, however, since its author feels impelled to argue for the existence of medieval pleasure gardens created for their aesthetic quality, as distinct from their productivity as vegetable and fruit gardens. Also useful is C. Thacker (1979, 81–93). Gesbert (2003) gives an excellent discussion of the range of **terms for gardens** used by medieval writers. She shows how variable was their use, but she also shows clearly that the pleasure garden was a major concern for them. The Old French *vergier* (cf. modern French *verger* "orchard") has the Latin form *viridarium* or *virgultum*, both of which can be translated as "garden." So *vergier*, as it occurs in the *Song of Roland*, should probably be translated "garden," although it may mean a grassy, green garden, rather than a formal one. A lucid discussion of **English royal gardens**, including those of Windsor, Caernarfon, Conwy, Westminster, and Eltham, based on an intimate knowledge of the royal records, is Colvin (1986). Creighton (2009) examines **landscapes around English castles and palaces**, arguing that they are artificially created to a much greater extent than has been previously recognized. On the importance of views from castles, see Ashbee (2004). With regard to **literary and religious associations**, the garden and its importance for human and divine love is imaginatively discussed by McLean (1981, ch. 4). The significance of fountains in gardens and elsewhere is the subject of Miller (1986), and the Fountain of Life is the subject of Underwood (1950). On Arthurian traditions, see Barber (2007a); for the Round Table project and the Order of the Garter, see H. E. L. Collins (2000, ch. 1), and Barber (2007b). For the Winchester round table, see Biddle (2000). The significance of the gardens in the *Song of Roland* and *The Capture of the City of Orange* is the subject of a remarkable book by Labbé (1987). **Sixteenth-century gardens** are the subject of a classic study by Strong (1979). The fullest work on **menageries** remains Loisel (1912), but there is an important discussion of Carolingian examples by Hauck (1963a), and thoughtful comments on Byzantine examples by Littlewood (1997, 35–38) and on British examples by Creighton (2009, ch. 4). For menageries at Avignon, see Gagnière (1988). See also Pastoureau (2008).

Chapter 5: Forests, Parks, and the Power of the Hunt

FORESTS AND PARKS

There is a detailed entry for forests in Anon. (1977–98, s.v. Forst). The **linguistic origins** of the word forest are discussed by Meineke (1995), the historical origins and development by Wenskus (1995). See also Zotz (1997), particularly for evidence that forests were controlled by royal officials and were important as hunting grounds from an early date. These publications discuss the alternative derivation of the word "forest" from the Old High German word *First/Forst* "boundary-fence." This has not been generally accepted by scholars; it would, in any case, have little effect on the interpretation of a forest as a defined area. There are illuminating discussions of **forest law** by Kaeuper (1985) and of forests in Europe by C. R. Young (1985). The best discussion of the origins and administration of forests, however, is Lorenz (1996). Works discussing English forests, and forest law in particular, are Cox (1905), C. R. Young (1979), and R. Grant (1991). Richardson (2005, 11–13, 155–58) provides a helpful glossary of the technical terms used for forest officers and aspects of forest administration in England, as well as a discussion of these. For the Continental situation, see Semmler (1991). Rubner (1963) remains the principal discussion of the relationship between Roman saltus and medieval forests. The arguments he presents do not definitely prove the existence of such a connection, but they are very suggestive of its existence. Devroey and Schroeder (February 2012), however, argue that at least in some areas the saltus was more varied than Rubner and others envisaged. The **economic**

role of forests in supplying the ruler with food, materials, and food, as well as with income from forest renders, is discussed by G. Jones (2010, especially pp. 39–41 on mineral extraction) and, with arguments specific to vaccaries, by Winchester (2010). That economic production was the principal role of forests rather than hunting is the argument of Rackham (1993). For the Continent in this respect, there is an excellent treatment by Devèze (1966). A parallel controversy as to whether economic functions were paramount revolves around parks, and is extensively discussed in the case of English parks by Mileson (2009). See also the papers in Liddiard (2007). Cummins (2002) presents a stimulating argument for seeing medieval parks as managed landscapes, like those of the eighteenth century. See also Fletcher (2011). The **relationship between palaces, forests, and parks** is discussed, largely with reference to Germany, by Bosl (1963). His conclusions that forests were administered from palaces is disputed by Gauert (1965), who maintains that they were in fact administered from "royal courts" (*Konigshöfe*)—a distinction that is not easy to grasp. Lorenz (1996), however, sets out a series of texts that show that, in the early medieval period at least, there is clear evidence of the management of forests from palaces, as for example the palaces of the Merovingian kings of the Franks at Clichy and Crécy-en-Ponthieu (France). For the relationship between English medieval castles and their forests and parks, see Creighton (2002, 185–93). For the **symbolism** of forests in late medieval Germany and the painting of Altdorfer, see Wood (1999, 128–76), and Schama (2004, 81–100). The role of forests in **English literature** is the subject of Saunders (1993). For forests in **England**, there is a general discussion by Langton (2010). Bond (1994) provides a clear and illuminating essay on the nature and origin of parks and, especially, forests—including the **Mendip Forest**—with reference to those in the area of Wessex in southern England. Rackham (1993) examines in detail **Hatfield Forest** and is disinclined to accept that forests had an important function as royal hunting grounds. Forests in early medieval Britain, including **Cannock Chase**, are discussed by G. Jones (2010). The **Weald** is the subject of Witney (1976), although his principal focus is on the pasturing of pigs there. See also Everitt (1986, 35–38). On the forests of the **Ile de France** around Paris and their use by kings for hunting, see Le Jan-Hennebicque (1980).

HUNTING

Ancient hunting is brilliantly discussed by Anderson (1985), and there is a classic discussion of Roman hunting by Aymard (1951). **Medieval hunting** is the subject of Cummins (1988) and R. Almond (2003), both of whom give accounts of its aristocratic context. Hunting is, however, also examined with considerable insight by Marvin (2006), by Mileson (2009, ch. 1), and by MacKenzie (1988). The last of these is principally concerned with the role of hunting in European imperial expansion in Africa and Asia in the nineteenth and twentieth centuries, but also surveys earlier hunting back to the ancient period. His discussion of more modern hunting is thought-provoking with regard to the issues raised in this chapter. An important work on Scottish hunting and forests is Gilbert (1979). **Early medieval hunting** and its significance is discussed with great insight by Nelson (1987, 166–70, 177). See also the detailed treatment by Jarnut (1985). Lavelle (2007, 73–76) sets out the evidence for the importance of hunting for pre-Conquest English kings, especially the reference in the Anglo-Saxon Chronicle to Earl Harold Godwinsson intending to invite King Edward the Confessor to hunt at Porteskewett in Wales, and Gautier (2006) comments interestingly on the origins of hunting parks, and the possible location of the parks of Earl Harold's family in Sussex, especially around Bosham, which is represented in the Bayeux Tapestry. For **Frederick II's hunting**, and, for the images in his manual of hunting, see Willemsen (1988) and Fried (1997). The **hunting manual of Edward, duke of York**, is lucidly discussed by Marvin (2006, 111–31). The **Devonshire Hunting Tapestries** are reproduced and discussed by Woolley (2002), the **Unicorn Tapestries** by Cavallo (1998), from which the interpretation of the three series of tapestries and their meanings is taken. Cavallo's book is extremely clear and thought-provoking with excellent use of illustrations.

Chapter 6: The City as a Statement of Power

The **symbolism** of medieval cities, in terms of hierarchy and harmony, the application of geometry, and ideas of the Heavenly Jerusalem, is most fully and stimulatingly discussed by Lilley (2009). He also summarises discussions about knowledge of Calcidius's translation of Plato in Western Europe, which is discussed at greater length by Dutton (1983). **Etruscan and Roman towns** in this connection are discussed by Gutkind and Gutkind (1965–72), who provide a useful survey of European cities, discussed country by country, from antiquity to the modern period. The writings of **al-Farabi** are discussed by Triano (2010, 134–37). **Prague New Town** as a holy city and a reflection of the Heavenly Jerusalem is discussed by Crossley and Opačić (2005). The **seal of Trier** and the idea that this and other cities of the Rhineland could have been regarded as holy cities and representations of the Heavenly Jerusalem is discussed by Haverkamp (1987). The **seals of the Rhineland cities** in general are discussed, and well illustrated with commentary, by Diederich (1984). For the **image of Cologne and Trier** as holy cities in early modern sources, see Schmid (2012).

The significance of urban architecture in Rome as an **aspect of the rule of the emperors** is perceptively discussed by Chaisemartin (2003). The broad context of **caliphs founding cities** from the eighth century onward is surveyed by O. Grabar (1987, 165–79) and by Acién Almansa (1987, 13–14). The cities of the Fatimid caliphs are discussed, with regard especially to Cairo, by Sanders (1994). For the limits of the caliphs' role in the foundation of cities, which relied on attracting others to form their population and to create economic viability, see Kennedy (2010). The **Roman and Byzantine emperors** founding and building cities in the Balkans are discussed and illustrated by Ćurčić (2010, 15–32).

The political and military circumstances of **King Alfred's reign** have often been discussed, for example by Wormald (2004) and Abels (1997). That Alfred was a philosophically sophisticated king, who might indeed have thought about cities in the way that is suggested here, is argued by Pratt (2005). The towns themselves are discussed from this point of view by Lilley (2009). Their archaeology is summarized by Biddle (1976b), and the arguments for seeing these places as planned towns rather than simply fortresses is made by Biddle and Hill (1971) and by Biddle (1976a). A fine discussion of the **new towns of Edward I** remains Beresford (1967, 35–51), although reference must now be made to Lilley (2009). More detail on the costs of these towns and the sequence of their construction is presented in R. A. Brown, Colvin, and Taylor (1963), where the point about Caernarfon's apparent imitation of the land-walls of Constantinople is made.

For discussion of **palaces as cities and cities as palaces**, see Boucheron (2004), where the quotations from the Italian authors noted here are given and discussed. There is a useful discussion in Italian of palaces and cities in late Roman and early medieval Italy by Augenti (2004). The general point about the relationship between villa architecture (or palace architecture) and the architecture of cities is made by MacDonald (1982–86, 277–79, and passim) and, in the context of Balkan cities and palaces, by Ćurčić (2010, passim). For the context of palaces and cities in the Kingdom of Sicily, see Martin (2004).

Chapter 7: The Ruler Enters His City

The clearest account of **Roman triumphs and entries,** based so far as possible on reliable written sources and on scenes from triumphs represented in Roman sculpture, especially that on triumphal arches, is Östenberg (2009), which is also very well illustrated. Payne (1962) is an entertaining summary of what Roman writers said of triumphs, but it is completely uncritical, and takes what the early first-century AD writer Livy says about ancient triumphs in the period of the Roman kings entirely seriously, when it is generally considered by scholars to be fictional. Beard (2007) gives serious and perceptive consideration to the extent to which the written sources were not describing triumphs as they actually took place, but were instead using an imaginary image of the triumph to increase the glory of the general or emperor to whom it was granted. She also provides a discussion of what is known of the route of triumphal processions through Rome, and of the role of the Theatre of Pompey (pp. 22–29, 92–105). Versnel (1970) considers the origins of the triumph in an Etruscan New Year festival. He lays emphasis on the close relationship between triumphs and entries, and on the role of the *triumphator* as representing the god Jupiter. Itgenshorst (2005) is the most authoritative treatment of triumphs in the period of the Roman republic, which she also catalogues. Elsner (1998, 33–35) gives an insightful account of an entry described by the fourth-century writer, Ammianus Marcellinus, that of the emperor Constantius into Rome in 357. In a book principally devoted to **entries and triumphs in the Byzantine Empire**, MacCormack (1981) devotes a chapter to the classical tradition of entries. McCormick (1986) is primarily concerned with the continuation of the entry, and especially of the cult of victory associated with triumphal entries, after the end of the Roman Empire in the West (mid-fifth century) in Byzantium but chiefly in Western Europe. He does, however, give a useful and insightful account of triumphs and entries under Roman emperors, and the analysis of the phases of the triumph of Titus and Vespasian given here is his (pp. 14–16). An exhaustive discussion of entries in Latin histories and literary texts, as well as in the Bible and the works of early Christian writers is Dufraigne (1994), who provides a detailed foundation for considering the relationship between rulers and Christ in the context of entries.

With regard to **medieval entries and triumphs**, vivid and insightful accounts and discussions of the **triumph of King Alfonso the Magnanimous at Naples** are Bertelli (2001, ch. 4) and Helas (2009). Bertelli provides a wide-ranging survey of medieval triumphs and entries, including those of **Frederick II** and of **Castruccio Castracani**. There is a general discussion of the relationship between entries and the space provided by the city in Schweers (2009). For **Byzantine triumphs and entries**, see MacCormack (1981, 17–89). See, for example, her account of the triumph of the emperor Justinian, involving also his general, Belisarius, represented on the Chalke Gate in Constantinople, and described by the contemporary writer Procopius (pp. 74–76). She also gives a very illuminating discussion of the **Missorium of Theodosius** as evidence for the increasingly static role of the emperor in ceremonies (pp. 214–20). For **post-Roman triumphs in the West**, including those of Theodoric and Clovis, see McCormick (1986), who discusses also the entry of the exarch of Ravenna into Rome. The classic discussion of entries and their relationship to **Christ's entry into Jerusalem** is a stimulating paper by Kantorowicz (1944). This provided the starting-point for a book that is deservedly a classic by Kipling (1998). It deals with a number of entries in England, France, and the Low Countries in the later Middle Ages. In opposition to Strong (1984), Kipling argues that these medieval entries were not just random series of theatrical and other events, but were systematically constructed to convey a religious message, which was principally to equate the king with Christ, and to see his entry as an advent, like Christ's entry into Jerusalem. Kipling further maintains that it is possible to discern four types of advent in the range of entries for which we have descriptions: the historical entry of Christ into Jerusalem; the advent of Christ into human hearts; the advent of Christ into the Heavenly Jerusalem; and the advent of Christ into heaven. This may seem a little over-elaborate, however, and it is not always easy to see how these types of advent really relate to medieval entries and the theatrical pageants which often accompanied them. Kantorowicz's simpler distinction between Christ's historical entry into Jerusalem and his apocalyptic entry into the Heavenly Jerusalem seems more sustainable and is followed in this chapter.

Entries in the **Low Countries** from the twelfth century to the fifteenth century are surveyed and discussed by J. M. Murray (1994), and Hurlbut (2001) considers them alongside Burgundian entries, drawing interestingly on anthropological work to interpret them. A. Brown (2011, especially 234–47) sets entries in the context of wider civic ceremony; see also A. Brown (2006). The importance of **city gates** as the place where keys were handed to the ruler and other ceremonies performed, as well as their importance as symbols of the city, receives a perceptive and stimulating discussion by Lampen (2009). A full account of entries into cities in the **later medieval German empire**, with a very useful schematized map of their phases, is Schenk (2003). The political context of **late medieval English entries**—the desire of York for example to make good its position with a new dynasty—is treated clearly and effectively by Attreed (1994), but it does not seem to have much bearing on the shape and broad meaning of entries. More insightful in general terms is the discussion of **Parisian royal entries** by Bryant (1986), which emphasizes the progress of the *parlement* to have itself fully represented in entry processions. Lavéant (2006) provides the text of a play presented at a royal entry into **Abbeville** in 1531, with commentary on the significance of the representation of the king in such plays. For **French entries** more generally, see Bryant (2007). Entries in late medieval and early modern **Spain**, notably that of Ferdinand III and Ferdinand of Antequera into Seville, are discussed by Ruiz (2012, 76–84).

The most useful account of the sculptured scenes on **Roman triumphal arches** is Kleiner (1992), which is clear, detailed, and well-illustrated. MacDonald (1982–6, II, 75–86) provides a discussion of triumphal arches from the point of view of their architecture and their position in the city-scape. Very illuminating from the latter perspective is Richmond (1933), who argues that triumphal arches were often built in front of city gates, and often merged with city gates. MacDonald (1982–6, II, ch. 4) presents evidence for the importance of arches, thoroughfares, and way-stations in Roman cities, but he does not see them in the context of rulers' processions but rather as—in the case of thoroughfares–facilities for the day-to-day use of the citizens. No doubt they served that function too, but it is hard to agree with the exclusiveness of this interpretation, or to understand why MacDonald thought that more ancient cities were primarily built for the ceremonial purposes of their rulers whereas Roman cities were not. Elsner (1998, 126–30) offers a thoughtful discussion of processions and their architectural context.

The importance of **medieval city gates** and the ceremonies performed by them is Lampen (2009), who also discusses the representation of gates and walls on city-seals. The architecture of gates is not widely discussed, but for England see Turner (1970, 67–72), who favours the defensive function of gates over any other, and Creighton and Higham (2005), who emphasise rather the symbolism of walls (pp. 166–68). J. D. Tracy (2000) is a collection of essays ranging globally, showing inter alia "the association between royal power or sovereigny and the enclosure of towns" (p. 6).

Chapter 8: Power and Relics

The classic study of the **cult of saints and relics** in western Europe is P. Brown (1981). There is, however, a more extended summary-account than the one given in this chapter in Rollason (2012a, 382–87). The most stimulating treatment of the political importance of relics and relic-cults, which also contains a history of their development, is Bozóky (2006). A classic study is Delehaye (1933), which remains illuminating. The principal study of thefts of relics, which develops the idea that relics had a mind of their own, is Geary (2011). The role of relics in relation to royal power in early medieval England is the subject of Rollason (1986) and is further discussed by Rollason (1989, chs. 5–6).

There is a useful summary of the history of the **Passion relics** in Bozóky (2006, 21–22). The most important study of the relics of the **True Cross** is Frolow (1961), where the legends of its finding by Helen are discussed, as well as the history of the subsequent dispersal of fragments of it. The book is remarkable for the extensive catalogue of documentation which it presents. The finding of the True Cross, its development as a symbol of victory, and the later development of legends about it are set out by Bozóky (2006, 75–82). On **Constantine** and his vision of the cross, see also A. H. M. Jones (1962) and, more recently, Stephenson (2009, 182–87).

The relationship between entries of rulers and **entries of relics** is examined by Kantorowicz (1944) and by Bozóky (2006, 206–08). The significance of the **Trier ivory** in this respect has been much discussed. Vikan and Holum (1979) is the most useful treatment, and the interpretation set out here is based on it. Brubaker (1999) argues that the gate represented is the Chalke Gate of the Great Palace, and Wortley (1980) argues convincingly that the ivory, which is dated to the ninth or tenth centuries, is a fictional picture of the entry of the relics of St Stephen in 421, even though it no doubt reflects genuine relic-entries of a later date. The view of Spain (1977) that the ivory belongs to the sixth century is neither convincing nor generally accepted. A pioneering paper on the **use of relics in the defense of cities** in the Byzantine Empire is Baynes (1949). The subject has been developed by H. A. Klein (2004) and Frolow (1961), and, for western Europe, by Bozóky (2006, 50–73), which is also the best discussion of the relics as promoting the stability of the people. The use of relics for the defense of Constantinople in the early sixth century is documented by Frolow (1961, no. 54) and H. A. Klein (2004, 57). In the west, the practice of taking relics around the walls of cities for purposes of defense is examined by McCormick (1986) for the early Middle Ages. The procession of the **Holy Blood in Bruges**, including its relationship to the walls of the city, is the subject of A. Brown (2011), and of earlier papers by the same author (A. Brown 1997, 2006). With regard to the Holy Blood procession, he notes that "the encircling of the civic space by the Holy Blood relic reinforced at a spiritual level the protection offered by the walls and gates" (2011, 9). The use of the **True Cross in battle** by the Byzantine Emperors is illuminatingly treated by Frolow (1961), and discussed further by Bozóky (2006, 114–15). Its use by the Crusaders in the Holy Land is the subject of A. V. Murray (1998). The argument that a **capital city**, or at least a principal focus of power in a kingdom or empire, could be marked by a collection of relics, as at Saint-Denis (for Paris), Aachen (for the Holy Roman Empire), Monza (for the kingdom of the Lombards), and Arles (for the kingdom of Provence), are presented by Kühne (2000, 668–69), and developed further by Bozóky (2006, ch. 3).

As regards **relics and regalia**, the use of the **spear** as a symbol of authority in the Roman period and earlier is the subject of a classic study by Alföldi (1959), where references to coins and carvings and the writings of Trogus Pompeius (p. 3) can be found. Alföldi argues for the existence of continuity between the significance of the spear from very ancient times, right across the Roman period. Pasquini (2005) discusses the spear's importance as a symbol of power in the Roman period. The **Holy Lance**, as a relic and symbol of authority, and the Vienna Holy Lance of the German emperors in particular, are the subject of a series of illuminating papers edited by Kirchweger (2005). Especially useful are the papers by Wolf (2005) and Gastgeber (2005), while Mehofer, Leusch, and Bühler (2005) and Schreiner, Desnica, and Jembrih-Simbürger (2005) report on modern scientific investigations of the Vienna Holy Lance. The classic study of this object, however, is Schramm (1954–6, II, 492–537). The images from *The Travels of Sir John Mandeville* are discussed by Gastgeber (2005), and the image of Henry II's coronation from the Sacramentary of Henry II by Wolf (2005). There are illuminating comments on the symbolic importance to royal power of the Holy Lance in Kühne (2000, 95). On **crowns and relics**, see Schramm (1954–6, III, 869–83). The **Monza crown** is extensively discussed by Buccellati and Snapp (1995–1999), the **German imperial crown** by Schulze-Dörrlamm (1991) and more briefly in guide-books to the Imperial Treasure Chamber at Vienna by Anon. (1987) and Leithe-Jasper and Distelberger (1998). The **Bohemian crown** is illustrated and discussed by Dubská (2003, 173–77). There is an illuminating discussion of the history of the **German imperial relics**, and especially the tendency from around 1300 to treat the regalia as relics in their own right, in Kühne (2000, 92–104). The pioneering and effective discussion of **displays of the imperial relics and regalia** is Kühne (2000). The Feast of the Lance and the Nails at Prague is treated by Boehm and Fajt (2005, 205), Fajt et al. (2006, Cat. 57), and Kühne (2000, 106–24). The latter author discusses the "displays" at Nuremberg (pp. 130–52), and at Aachen (pp. 153–84).

Chapter 9: Churches, Mosques, and Power

On the **relationship between ruler and church**, see Dagron (1996), English translation Dagron (2003), Ullmann (1969), and Nelson (1987). The significance of **centrally planned churches** in relation to possible models and to the Heavenly Jerusalem is lucidly discussed, with a particular focus on Aachen, by Ley (2013, 2014). A similar theme is pursued for Byzantine examples by Carile (2012). There is a more **general discussion and a catalogue** by Untermann (1989).

Chapter 10: The Inauguration of Rulers: Places and Rituals

The most useful discussion of **Roman and Byzantine inaugurations**, solidly based on the sources it quotes at length or paraphrases in detail, is Brightman (1901). There is discussion of the role of the patriarch and its significance by Charanis (1941). Critical of this is the rather cursory commentary on Byzantine coronations by McCormick (1991). For the introduction of anointing into Byzantine inaugurations, see Nicol (1976). For **medieval and early modern inaugurations**, an important collection of papers is Bak (1990). Boumann (1957) is devoted to the development of *ordines* (written instructions) for coronations. Brühl (1962) provides a trenchant discussion of Carolingian and Ottonian inaugurations, with an invaluable list of where both they and crown-wearings took place. The nature of Carolingian anointing as an element of royal inauguration is discussed in a series of articles by Nelson (1971, 1976, 1977a, 1987). On the origins and nature of royal anointing, there is a thought-provoking discussion by Enright (1985). The most penetrating discussion of the **French inauguration** is Jackson (1984). He is especially illuminating on the idea of the king's marriage to the kingdom, and on the sleeping king (pp. 85–90, 131–54). There is a classic discussion of **Reims** as an inauguration city by Le Goff (1996–98). See also the impeccably scholarly and source-focused dissertation by Brühl (1950). On the Carolingian and traditions about St. Rémi, see Depreux (1991). For **late medieval German inaugurations**, there is useful discussion by Erkens (2009 [for 2008]). There are important papers on the **Aachen inaugurations** in Kramp (2000b). See especially Gussone (2000), Kramp (2000a), S. Müller (2000), and Rotthoff-Kraus (2000). Important articles published elsewhere include Boshof (1991), Heidenreich and Kroll (2006), and Schulte (1924). For the conflict between Otto IV and Philip von Schwaben, see Schaller (2000). On the king's approach to Aachen for his inauguration, see Volk (1999). There is a summary of this material to the extent that it relates to the inauguration of Richard of Cornwall by Rollason (2012b). The classic history of **English inaugurations** is Schramm (1937), but there is a more recent, lavishly illustrated, summary by Strong (2005). Sixteenth-century English inaugurations are perceptively analysed by Hunt (2008). **Irish inaugurations** are the subject of Fitzpatrick (2004a), who provides a penetrating discussion of the inauguration sites and the rituals that took place at them. See also Fitzpatrick (2003, 2004b). An important discussion emphasising the pagan, otherworldly aspect of inaugurations is by Gleeson (2012).

Carlen (1992) provides a useful summary and discussion of **coronation-churches** throughout the period under consideration here, but looking back also to Assyrian and Judaic coronation places. His analysis of what such churches had in common (pp. 72–78) is especially thought-provoking. The classic study and cataloguing of medieval **regalia** across Europe is by Schramm (1954–56). The fullest treatment of the English regalia, of which very little survives, is C. Blair (1998), and there is a summary by Strong (2005). For an up-to-date summary of the evidence for the regalia which Richard of Cornwall is supposed to have had made for Aachen, see Rollason (2012b). For the French regalia, see Gaborit-Chopin (1987), although this is almost wholly modern.

Chapter 11: Death and Power: The Burial Places of Rulers

In terms of **general ideas**, funerals and burial places functioning for the benefit of the survivors is explored, for example, by Lucy (2000). Davies (2000) provides a penetrating discussion of the imperial burials in Rome, and pursues in a stimulating and lucid way the themes of monuments as an "image of things achieved" (chapter 2) and as "an imperial cosmos" (chapter 3), as well as examining their design (chapter 5) and the significance of their situation (chapter 6). The significance of royal corpses and the treatment of them is illuminatingly dealt with by reference to pre-Conquest England by Marafioti (2014). The clearest and best-illustrated general survey of the **development of the architecture of tombs, mausolea, burial chapels**, and burial in churches generally is Colvin (1991), which ranges from the prehistoric to the modern period with many insights. It does not, however, deal with burial mounds that do not have architectural features in stone, so monuments such as Jelling do not feature in it. Curl (2002, chs 2–3) provides a somewhat more up-to-date discussion of architecturally developed burial places than does Colvin. Johnson (2009) provides a comprehensive survey and discussion of **Roman mausolea**; Davies (2000) examines the imperial funerary monuments of the city of Rome. Mackie (2003) examines Roman and immediately **post-Roman rulers' mausolea** in the context of an exploration of the development of chapels. The treatment of the ruler as a "hero" and the location of mausolea in **central positions in cities** are discussed by A. Grabar (1946, I, 227–34), in the context of Constantinople. There is a survey of earthern **burial mounds** of the early Middle Ages by Müller-Wille (1983), and a discussion of the possible significance of the situation of such monuments by Williams (1999). The **significance of the ship** in early Scandinavia is the subject of Crumlin-Pedersen and Thye (1995); the Oseberg ship-burial is discussed by Ingstad (1995) and more recently by Holck (2006). For Frankish and later French **royal necropolises**, there is an excellent catalogue, a chronological account, and perceptive ideas in Erlande-Brandenburg (1975). For a catalogue of the location of royal graves in Frankish, English, and Lombard territories, see K. H. Krüger (1971). For **England**, there is an unilluminating survey of royal tombs by Duffy (2003), which at least provides some references. For **Spain**, there is a recent survey and analysis by Dectot (2009). K. Krüger (2006b) discusses and documents the early medieval Spanish pantheons. Bertelli (2001, 214–30) offers a survey of the development of tombs, concentrating chiefly on **Italy**, notably with a very illuminating commentary on the tomb of Robert the Wise in Santa Chiara, Naples. This was comparable to the tomb of Ladislas in San Giovanni a Carbonara, but it scarcely survived bombardment in the Second World War. For the **porphyry tombs of Palermo**, and the importance of porphyry, the classic work is Deér (1959).

Johnson (2009, 11–13) summarizes what is known of **Roman imperial funerals**, including the *decursio*; and characteristically illuminating is Davies (2000, 8–11). Arce (2000) offers a penetrating discussion of late Roman funerals, and he also comments on the significance, and potential factual accuracy, of Jordanes's account of the funeral of Attila the Hun. However, the clearest and fullest account of Roman imperial funerals is provided in a book primarily devoted to later centuries, that by Giesey (1960, 147–53). Regarding **medieval and renaissance funerals**, Nelson (2000) gives what is little more than a documented catalogue of Carolingian funerals; much more useful is Erlande-Brandenburg (1975, chs 1–3, dealing with the period from the Merovingians to the thirteenth century with many insights). The most brilliantly perceptive discussion, however, is that of Giesey (1960), beginning with the funeral of Francis I, and working back into earlier centuries, not only in France, but also in England and Germany. A critical aspect of medieval practice was that of the **division of the body** and the burial of the parts in different places. A key discussion of this subject in the context of French practice is by E. A. R. Brown (1981), who analyses the effect of Boniface VIII's bull, *Detestande feritatis*, arguing that it made division of the body more of a royal prerogative than it had previously been. The practice of heart burial in France receives a more detailed treatment, but with similar conclusions, in Bande (2009). E. A. R. Brown (1980) explores the funeral arrangements of Philip V himself, the first king of France to have had three graves with different parts of his body, and is illuminating about the motives for such division. Hallam (1982) provides a survey of royal burial, with emphasis on the division of bodies and the cult of kingship.

The fullest monograph on **royal saints** is Klaniczay (2002). This considers central European saints in depth, but it also ranges more widely, including discussions of early English royal sanctity, and the relationship between sanctity and sacral kingship. English royal saints are discussed by Rollason (1989, 113–29) and also by Ridyard (1988). For the **canonization of saints**, including Charlemagne and Edward the Confessor, the most useful book remains Kemp (1979). For a general account of the cult of saints and relics, see Bartlett (2013). For the cult of **Oswald, king and martyr**, see A. T. Thacker (1995) and Cambridge (1995). For Oswald's cult at Gloucester, and for the development of the city, see Heighway (1984). The **blurring between rulers and saints** is discussed by E. A. R. Brown (1981) and by Marafioti (2014), who argues that rulers, however much they were superficially treated in the same way as saints after their deaths, were nevertheless quite distinct.

The concept that the king had **two bodies**, one physical and mortal, the other one the embodiment of his kingship as it passed to his successor, is developed and explored in a classic study by Kantorowicz (1957), the section on funerals specifically being pp. 409–12. This book has deservedly had a considerable influence. The idea that Roman imperial funerals embody the idea of the ruler's two bodies appears in Arce (2000), and it is at the heart of the study of French Renaissance funerals by Giesey (1960). It has also had a considerable influence on E. A. R. Brown (1978), who argues, however, that the double funeral of Louis X was not so much the result of ideology as of the particular difficulties of his successor, Philip V, in gaining the throne, and that the second funeral of this monarch was politically necessary since the funeral was the time when the transfer of power really took place—and Philip V had been prevented from attending the first funeral. For a critique of Kantorwicz and Giesey in connection with the tomb of Louis XII in Saint-Denis, see Blunk (2007, summarized above, p. 381). An important element in this discussion of the king's two bodies is the use of the **effigy** in place of the corpse. A recent publication of the effigies preserved at Westminster Abbey (A. Harvey and Mortimer 2003) provides stunning illustrations of these objects, although for a detailed assessment of them the work of Hope and Robinson (1907) is still essential. For brief commentary on the scholarship on **Beowulf's burial mound** with further references, see Fulk, Bjork, and Niles (2008, 270–71). The fullest treatment of the poet's image of the burial mound, and of the other funerals in the poem, is Owen-Crocker (2000).

SITES

Aachen (Germany)

On the **palace**, three recent works, which derive from ongoing research projects and from a major restoration-programme devoted to the palace church, have taken publication on Aachen a considerable step forward. They are: H. Müller et al. (2013), Heckner and Beckmann (2012), and H. Müller, Bayer, and Kerner (2014). Rollason (2015) provides a critical summary. Among the numerous earlier publications, still worthwhile are: the collection of papers edited by Bayer, Jülich, and Kuhl (1986); Falkenstein (1966), on the functions of the palace, especially the problem of why part of it was referred to as the "Lateran"; and Falkenstein (1981) on the constitutional status of the church. The historical significance of Aachen as palace and city is illuminatingly discussed by Nelson (2001). There is an excellent short account by McClendon (2005), 105–23, although readers need also to refer to more recent publications.

Bayer (2014) discusses the functions of the **palace church (St. Mary's)**, and the accommodation of the canons and laity in it. See also H. Müller et al. (2013, 193–209). The most effective discussion of the relationship of the church to earlier models, and to the New Temple and the Heavenly Jerusalem, is Ley (2013, 2014). There is further discussion in relation to the geometry of the church by Heckner (2012). The construction of the dome has been definitively established by research published by Kempen (2012). Its original decoration is the subject of Wehling (1995), and there is an up-to-date summary in Anon. (2014, Orte der Macht, Katalog, nos. 284–85). Imitations of the church are discussed by Verbeek (1965). On the bronze grilles around the gallery, the principal work is Pawelec (1990). The **throne** and the evidence for its date and original position have been discussed in unprecedented detail by Lobbedey (2014), who is sceptical of the idea that the marble plates were relics from Jerusalem put forward by Schütte (2000). It is still worth consulting Beumann (1965). For the church as an **inauguration place**, still useful are the papers in Kramp (2000b), especially S. Müller (2000) and Kramp (2000a). See also Rollason (2012b), which summarizes earlier literature. For the relic-"displays", see Kühne (2000, 153–84). On the **great hall** and the **Tower of Granus**, see Müller et al. (2013, 133–38, 61); see also Ley (2010), Ley and Wietheger (2010), Ley (2012).

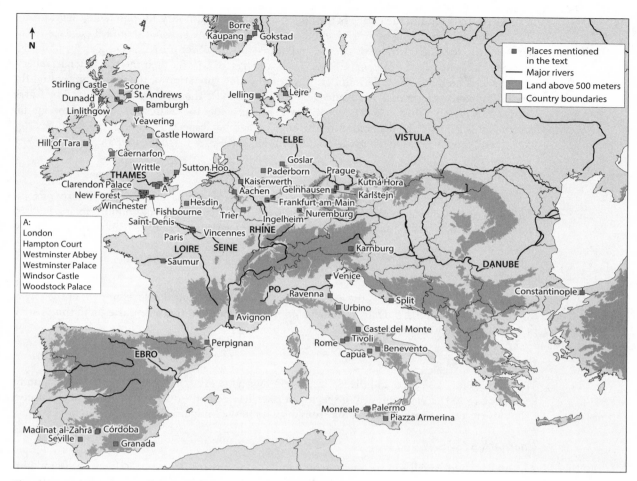

Sketch map of sites discussed. (See insert for color version of this image.)

For **urban archaeology**, there is a summary by Andreas Schaub of the results of recent excavations in Kraus (2013, 318–57). For the Roman period, see Andreas Schaub's contribution to Kraus (2011) and, for the Roman remains under the palace church, see Tanja Schaub (2014). For the **forests** around Aachen, including the Ardennes, and especially the "county of the wood", the classic studies are by Kaspers (1957) and Ewig (1976–9). For a summary see Rollason (2012c). There is a critique of Kaspers in Müller-Kehlen (1973); for the argument that the pattern of land ownership and land use in the Ardennes was complex, see Devroey and Schroeder (February 2012). For the **park** and **menagerie**, see Hauck (1963b, 39–42).

Avignon (France), Palace of the Popes

The best treatment of the **plan and the functions** of the rooms is Schimmelpfennig (1994); there is also a scholarly and lavishly illustrated account by Vingtain (1998). A discussion emphasising the relationship between architecture and ritual is offered by Kerscher (2000, 169–224, 2002). Lentsch (1990) discusses the arrangement of **bureaucratic offices**. On the bureaucratic offices which were located in the city around the Palace of the Popes, including the almonry, the penitential services, the office responsible for fixing bulls to documents (the office of the *bullatores*), and the Palace of the Marshall, who was a magistrate with police and justice functions, see Carru (2004). For the paintings in the **Stag Chamber**, see Vingtain (1998, 257–60, and figs 39–55); for their interpretation as reflecting the social hierarchy, see Mérindol (1993). Another interpretation of them as representing the pope's dominance over nature is advanced by Anheim (2008). The **gardens** are discussed by Carru (2004) and Vingtain (1998, 176–77, 243–47), who also provides the clearest treatment of the significance for this topic of the decoration of the Pope's Chamber, especially the empty bird-cages (pp. 107–21, and figs 23–36). On the gardens and the **menageries**, see Gagnière (1988).

Bamburgh (England)

G. Young (2003) provides a summary of recent excavations, which have revealed structures of some sort under the medieval chapel. The best treatment of the historical background remains Bateson (1893). Cambridge (1995, 134–39) gives a stimulating interpretation of the site in relation to St. Oswald's cult.

Benevento (Italy)

Belting (1962, 156–80) presents the evidence for the role of relics in the development of the city as the capital of the Lombard duchy of Benevento in the eighth and ninth centuries, and this is summarized by Bozóky (2006, 59–60, 131–33).

Borre (Norway)

The mounds are described and placed in context by Myhre (1992). An ongoing project, including excavation in 2007 and geophysical surveying in 2008, has led to the discovery of traces of two timber halls close to the mounds (information from displays in the Midgard Historisk Senter, Borre).

Caernarfon (Wales)

An authoritative overall account, although in guide-book form, is Taylor (1989). For the foundation of the town and its monuments, see R. A. Brown, Colvin, and Taylor (1963, II, 369–95). For the gardens, see R. A. Brown, Colvin, and Taylor (1963, I, 381 n. 3, and fig. 39). R. A. Brown, Colvin, and Taylor (1963, I, 370) identify the resemblance of the walls to those of Constantinople. For a discussion of Caernarfon as designed to provide "a consciously royal spectacle of power," see Fradley (2006).

Capua (Italy), the Porta di Capua

The most stimulating and illuminating discussion remains Shearer (1935), with some correction to Shearer's interpretation proposed by Willemsen (1953). On the symbolism of the arch, see Enderlein (2001). On spolia and antique references in the monument, including its relationship to other triumphal arches and its sculptures, see Meredith (1986, 1994). See also Wagner (2005).

Castel del Monte (Italy)

The fullest treatment of this monument's geometry is Götze (1998). Zara (2011) takes a more extreme view, arguing that the monument's geometry was intended to evoke musical proportions and symbolism. Krönig (1994) provides a more conventional account, and, for more recent research, there is a collection of papers edited by Licinio (2002b). In particular, Götze (1998, 117, 29–40, 44–46) argues for the geometry of the Castel del Monte being based on an eight-pointed star. Leistikov (2008, 151–52) dismisses this as fantasy. Reports on research conducted in the 1990s are provided by Schirmer and Zick (1998) and Schirmer (2009). See also Wagner (2005). The function of the spaces in the building is discussed by Musca (2002), who argues that they were practicable, despite the shape imposed on them by the building's octagonal layout.

Castle Howard (England)

A lucid and stimulating discussion of Vanbrugh's work at Castle Howard is Hart (2008). On the significance of the classical orders as used in the Renaissance, see Guillaume (1991, passim).

Clarendon Palace (England)

The forest and park are discussed in illuminating detail by Richardson (2005), and there are more general chapters on the same subject in James and Gerrard (2007), who also discuss the palace itself. For more detail on the latter, however, see A. B. Robinson and James (1988).

Constantinople (Istanbul, Turkey)

General accounts of the **city** include those of Sherrard (1965), Maclagan (1968), Magdalino (2007), and Harris (2007). Müller-Wiener (1977) provides a detailed reference book to the monuments. See also Ćurčić (2010, 77–100, 85–202, 67–77, 350–69, 528–45). The account of Constantine's foundation and dedication is given in English in Sherrard (1965, 8–11), drawing on the work in French of Lathoud (1924, 1925). For the planning of the city and its adaptation for processions, see Berger (2000, 2001) and Mango (2000). For **Haghia Sophia**, see Mark and Ahmet (1993). Recent archaeological research is presented by Dark and Kostenec (2009). Dagron (1996, 109–29, and passim) gives an illuminating analysis of the church in relation to ceremonial. For the **Great Palace**, see Bardill (2006) and Kostenec (1999, 2004); for reference, Müller-Wiener (1977). On its likeness to the Heavenly Jerusalem, see Carile (2012, 157–78). Featherstone (2005, 2006, 50–56) provides the most illuminating commentary and reconstruction plan of the Golden Triclinium (*Chrysotriklinos*). For its treatment as an artificial garden, see Maguire (2000, 33–35). For the palace church of the Blessed Virgin Mary at the Lighthouse, note particularly Magdalino (2004) and H. A. Klein (2004). Bozóky (2006, 85–92) sets out the evidence for the relics which were brought to Constantinople, as does Magdalino (2004). Maguire (2000) gives a full and well-illustrated survey of the two **parks**, the Philopation and the Aretai, and he also discusses the emperor Basil I's **garden** of the Mesokepion.

Córdoba (Spain), Great Mosque

Christys (2010) discusses the **focal position** of the mosque in the city. For the *sabat* linking the palace and the mosque, see Dodds (1992, 15–16). For the **extensions** of the mosque and their inspiration, see Ettinghausen and Grabar (1987, 128) and Dodds (1990, 94–107, 1992). For further **historical interpretations**, see Khoury (1996, 83) and Safran (2000, 62–68, 104–05, 74–75). For **textual sources**, see, for reference, Sezgin, Ehrig-Eggert, and Neubauer (2008). For the use of the Koran of Uthman as a **relic**, see Dodds (1990, 106–09). Ewert (2009) discusses the systematic use of **spolia** in the two principal prayer halls to imitate earlier mosques.

Dunadd (Scotland)

For publication of the excavations and discussion of the significance and context, see Lane and Campbell (2000).

Fishbourne (England)

Cunliffe (1971, ch. 7), the excavator of the site, gives an accessible account of the archaeological results relating to the reconstruction of the **garden** in the peristyle-courtyard. Littlewood (1997, 18) argues that this and the southern garden show the imitation by native rulers of "the assertion of imperial might demonstrated by the complex of buildings and gardens on the Palatine."

Frankfurt-am-Main (Germany)

The **palace** and the **forests** around it are the subject of Schalles-Fischer (1969). For the palace, see also Zotz, Heinemeyer, and Orth (1985–, 131–456) and Picard (2004); for the forests, see also Gockel (1970).

Gelnhausen (Germany)

For the **buildings and sculpture** of the palace, and the function of its rooms, see Binding (1965, 1996, 262–92); for a discussion of its **portico façade**, see Swoboda (1969, 220–21). In general, see also and Zotz, Heinemeyer, and Orth (1985–, 613–24) and Zettler (2001). I have not been able to consult U. Klein (2010).

Gokstad, Norway

For the most up-to-date accounts of ongoing archaeological research on the burial mound and the settlement now known to have been near to it, see http://www.khm.uio.no/prosjekter/gokstad/.

Goslar (Germany)

Binding (1996, 223–34) gives a detailed summary of the **palace remains**. See also Meckseper (1991). For the position of Goslar relative to other royal palaces, see Zotz (1996). On the area around and its **forests**, see Berges (1963). See also, Römisch-Germanischen Zentralmuseum Mainz (1978, 169–80, especially fig. 2).

Granada (Spain), Alhambra

For a general guide and illustrations, see see also the perceptive discussion of O. Grabar (1992) and Bermúdez López (2010, 110–27). On the **Palace of Comares** within it, Dickie (1992, 135) argues that the entrance façade was intended as a backdrop for the enthroned ruler; and Dickie (1981) argues also that the palace reflected a normal Grenadine house, arranged around a courtyard with apartments for the various wives of the owner. On the representation of the Seven Heavens in the **Hall of the Ambassadors**, see O. Grabar (1992, 142–44). For the **inscriptions**, see the extremely useful Vílchez, Guarde, and Cuenca (2011), which gives the inscriptions in the original and in English translation, together with a photographic atlas of the buildings for locating them. On the **Palace of Lions**, Ruiz Souza (2001) argues that it was a scholarly centre (*madrasa-zawīya*), with the Hall of the Kings as its library, on the grounds that the palace is related to similar structures in the Maghreb; his view, which is controversial, has been accepted by C. Robinson (December 2008) and Echevarria (December 2008). Rosenthal (1985) provides the fullest discussion of the **Palace of Charles V**, including the parallels to it in Roman architecture. The **gardens** are lucidly discussed by O. Grabar (1992, 115–32); see also Ruggles (2000, 163–208).

Hampton Court (England)

Much the most useful and incisive treatment is by Thurley (2003). On the **great hall**, see pp. 51–52. The **gardens** are discussed by Strong (1979, 25–34).

Hesdin (France)

The discussion of the park and gardens is based on the work of Buren-Hagopian (1986), who follows Charageat (1950) in assigning the design of most of the park to Robert II, but takes the view that the automata in the park and in the palace were not inspired by Islamic culture. The view that they were is presented, without any evidence beyond that disputed by Buren-Hagopian, by Miller (1986, 143–44, and n. 22). The **Garden of Love painting** is discussed in detail by Buren-Hagopian (1985). Creighton (2009, 148–49) discusses the **park** with a somewhat updated plan of it, as does Duceppe-Lamarre (2008). Dowling (2012) shows from the written records that the park was not only for aesthetic value and pleasure, but was also highly productive, not only of timber but also of luxury food-stuffs such as venison and fresh fish. I have been unable to consult Salamagne (2008).

Ingelheim (Germany)

Grewe (1998, 1999, 2001, 2014) reports on the excavations he directed, and provides an up-to-date account of the monument, superseding previous publications. On the paintings in the basilica, the fullest account remains Lammers (1971–72). I have been unable to consult Stella (2015).

Jelling (Denmark)

Stammwitz (2010) provides an excellent recent survey of the site. Brief reports on the on-going archaeological research at the site can be found at http://jelling.natmus.dk/what-is-the-jelling-project/. For the **North Mound**, see Andersen (1995), Staecker (2004, 78–82) and Pedersen (2006, 295–304); for its date, Dyggve (1948, 193–94), Stammwitz (2010, 425), and compare Randsborg (2008, 7), referring to an unpublished dendrochronological date. Regarding the removal of the burial, Krogh (1983) pursued the hypothesis that Harald Bluetooth had transferred the remains of King Gorm, his father, to the church between the Jelling mounds at the time of his conversion. Incautiously accepted by Roesdahl (1987, 162–65), this was attacked by Andersen (1995), who interpreted the removal as grave robbery. Stammwitz (2010, 429), however, argued that the grave was in fact that of a woman rather than of King Gorm. To add to the difficulty of accepting Krogh's hypothesis, there is doubt as to whether the burial excavated under the church (Krogh 1983, 198–201) antedated the church's construction, and was therefore unconnected with Denmark's conversion to Christianity. Indeed, Staecker (2004, 94) doubts even that the timber buildings excavated under the present medieval stone church were churches at all. For the excavations of the **South Mound**, see Dyggve (1948, 195), and Hvass (2011, 33–41). An authoritative discussion of the **runestones**, with English translations of their inscriptions, is Sawyer and Sawyer (2003). Hvass (2011, 61–65, 85–86) reports on recent excavations confirming that the larger runestone is in its original position. Stammwitz (2010, 426) and Randsborg (2008, 2) refer to the recent discovery of the very large **ship-setting**, and plans and photographs of the new discoveries are published by Hvass (2011, figs 20, 35, 41, 65). Excavations at the bridge at **Ravning Enge** are briefly reported on by Jørgensen (1997) and Moestrup (2011).

Kaiserwerth (Germany)

See Binding (1996, 318–26).

Karlštejn (Czech Republic)

A useful and authoritative guide is Fajt, Royt, and Gottfried (1998). On the **structure** of the palace and the arrangement of its elements, see Durdík (1998). For the **painting decoration**, see Homolka (1998); on that of St Catherine's Chapel, see Petrů (2003); on that of the Great Tower, see Fajt and Royt (1998b), Fajt and Hlaváčová (2003), and Royt (2003). For the representation of the Luxemburg family tree in the "Palace," see Stejskal (1978). On the use of **semi-precious stones** on the walls of the Chapel of the Signs of the Passion, see Möseneder (1981) and compare Plumpe (1943). On the palace's **function**, see Dvořáková (1964), Kavka (1998, 16–17), Fajt and Royt (1998a, 94–99), Studničková (2009), and Bartlová (2003). I have been unable to consult Bareš and Národní Památkový (2010).

Karnburg (Austria)

The principal study of the inauguration site is by Dopsch (1995). There is a summary by Airlie (2003).

Kaupang (Norway)

The publication of the excavations and authoritative discussion is Skre (2007b), Skre and Hines (2007), and Skre (2011).

Kutná Hora (Czech Republic)

There is a good account in Knox (1962, 65–71). I have been unable to consult the summary by Velímský (2013).

Lejre (Denmark)

Pending the publication of the report on the recent excavations, the most useful collection of material for the halls and for the surrounding topography is Niles, Christensen, and Osborne (2007).

Linlithgow (Scotland)

There is an authoritative guidebook by Pringle (1989). Background information about the palace and its landscape can be found in Caldwell and Lewis (1996). See also Dunbar (1999, 5–21 and passim).

London (England), Tower of London

On the residential and palatial functions of this complex, see Thurley (1995), and Ashbee (2006). On the White Tower, the fullest study is Impey (2008). For the false upper story, see pp. 81–85 and fig. 60. Loisel (1912, 155) documents the polar bear, and the arrangements for the lions are discussed in Keevill (2004, 106–08).

London (England), Westminster Abbey; see Westminster Abbey

London (England), Westminster Palace; see Westminster Palace

Lorsch (Germany)

For an excellent and well-illustrated discussion of the Lorsch arch, see McClendon (2005, 92–102), which also considers sympathetically but critically the hypothesis of Krautheimer (1942) that it was modeled on the Arch of Constantine. For recent research at Lorsch, see Ericsson and Sanke (2004).

Madīnat al-Zahrā (Spain)

For the **political and ideological context**, see Safran (2000, 56–60); for al-Mansur's foundation of his own city, Madīnat al-Zahīrā, see pp. 101–2. For the **monuments and their landscape-setting** Triano (2010) is indispensable; an authoritative English summary is to be found in Triano (n.d.). A thought-provoking analysis of the relationship between the architecture and that of the **late Roman period** in Spain is made by K. Krüger (2006a). For the **relationship to Córdoba**, see Acién Almansa and Triano (1998) and Mazzoli-Guintard (1997). On the **gardens** in conjunction with the buildings, see Ruggles (2000, 52–85).

Monreale (Italy)

In general, see Dittelbach (1999, 2003) which focus on the symbolism of the church. For the mosaics, see also Borsook (1990, ch. 4).

New Forest (England)

The acreages involved in the creation of forest and the number of people deported are the estimated by Petit-Dutaillis (1929, 169–70). On the forest generally, see Tubbs (1986, 67–79). On the Domesday Book record of it, see also Mew (2001 for 2000), who makes pertinent comments on the level of control the forest status gave to the king.

Nuremberg

An authoritative account of the **palace**, with reports on recent excavations, is Friedel(2007). The **Church of the Blessed Virgin Mary** is excellently discussed by Nussbaum (2000, 123–24). Kühne (2000, 130–52) discusses the **relic "displays."** The **forests** around the city are described by Schama (2004, 94–95).

Paderborn (Germany), palace

The most important publication of the modern excavations is Fenske, Jarnut, and Wemhhoff (2001), but there are summaries in Stiegemann and Wemhoff (1999, 175–221).

Palermo (Italy)

Meier (1994) is a brilliant and incisive treatment of the city and its Norman palaces, including less well-known ones such as Favara. For the **Palace of the Normans**, see pp. 37–54 and passim. Kitzinger (2001) discusses the **Pisan Tower**. For the **Cappella Palatina**, see the remarkable photographic atlas, with introductory papers, edited by Brenk, Agnello, and Chiaromonte (2010) and the collection of papers edited by Dittelbach (2011a). There is an authoritative guide to the **lower church**, dealing also with aspects of the upper church, by Dittelbach and Sack (2005); see also Sack et al. (2007). The thesis that the Cappella Palatina, before it was modified, incorporated a chapel east of the chancel steps, and a royal hall to the west of them was developed by Tronzo (1997), although prefigured by Ćurčić (1987). Despite criticism, Tronzo (2010) broadly adhered to it. Anzelmo (2011) emphasizes the secular character of the **ceiling paintings** in the nave and its aisles, which may support it. Borsook (1990, ch. 3, especially pp. 39–40) and Johns (2011, 560) oppose Tronzo's thesis, arguing that the **mosaic programme** throughout the Cappella Palatina was a unity from the beginning. Brenk (2010, 37), however, favors a somewhat later dating for the nave-mosaics, suggesting the possibility of a later modification of the design, but still within the reign of Roger II. For the possible significance of changes in the **floor decoration**, see Longo (2011, 491). On the **throne platform**, see Dittelbach (2011b, 537) and Bloom (2011). Grube and Johns (2005) offer technical and iconographic studies of the **ceiling paintings**. For the **royal box**, see Kitzinger (1949, 283–86), Tronzo (1997), and Meier (1994, 98–99). Brenk (2011, 598, fig. 28), however, reports that the exterior wall of the north chancel aisle shows no sign of a formerly existing opening. Borsook (1990, 20, 22–24) concludes from the evidence of the mosaics that the king was expected to be in the north chancel aisle, although she believes that the king had a folding throne there, rather than using a royal box. For the tombs in **Palermo Cathedral**, the essential work remains Deér (1959). For the **Zisa**, see Meier (1994, 68–79). Caronia (1982, 47–68) provides a description of the Zisa and an account of its restoration (pp. 169–275), with lavish illustration. The inscriptions are clearly set out and the general significance of the Zisa and related sites are discussed by Bresc (1994).

Paris (France)

An excellent summary of the history of Paris and illuminating maps are provided by Lorentz and Sandron (2006). The fullest work on the **Palais de la Cité** remains Guérout (1949–51), but there is a useful summary in Lorentz and Sandron (2006, 80–87). See also Bove (2003). On the Great Spiral Staircase, see Whiteley (1989, 133–42), who discusses the **Parliament Altarpiece**, and Whiteley (1985). On the **functions of the great hall**, see J. Bennert (1992, 47) and Bove (2003, 54). The **statues of kings** are the principal subject of J. Bennert (1992); see also U. Bennert (2004). An important collection of papers on the **Sainte Chapelle** is Hediger (2007). For the **windows** and their iconography, see Jordan (2002). On the chapel's **style**, the classic discussion interpreting the Rayonnant style as a royal one is by Branner (1965, 56–84). On the style's diffusion and importance, see Branner (1965, 93–122), and, for its effect on Westminster Abbey, Branner (1964). As regards France, however, Branner's interpretation has been questioned by M. Cohen (2010). She argued that although the royal works, such as Royaumont and the Sainte-Chapelle are the principal survivals of buildings in the Rayonnant style, they represented only a small proportion of the buildings under construction at the same time. In Paris, these included no less than fifty-five new churches and similar buildings, which may have been just as involved in the creation of the Rayonnant style as was the king himself, even though the surviving remains from them are much more fragmentary. For example, capitals from the church of St. Symphorien on the Île de la Cité are in the Rayonnant style, as is a portal embrasure from the church of Saint-Pierre-aux-Boeufs, while on the left bank of the River Seine the surviving refectory of the Franciscan Friars suggests that their friary too was in the Rayonnant style, as does the bar-tracery in the church of the Jacobin Friars. So it may be that the Rayonnant style was not so much associated specifically with the royal court as with the city of Paris. In that case, the development of that style was not so much a top-down process emanating from the court, rather than a much wider one drawing in a much wider spectrum of society. See now also M. Cohen (2015), a formidable study of the Rayonnant Style and the Sainte-Chapelle with a particular focus on sacral kingship in France. For the **Passion relics**, see Bozóky (2007) and illuminating papers by Billot (1991, 2004). Note also that Sauerländer (2007, 117) has taken issue with the view of Branner (1965, 57) that the Sainte-Chapelle was as a building designed as a reliquary. For the **Louvre** as built by Charles V, the disposition and function of the spaces is here taken from Salamagne (2010); note, however, the somewhat different views of Whiteley (1992). On the staircase, see Whiteley (1989, 142–44).

Perpignan (France), Palace of the Kings of Majorca

The fullest up-to-date studies are the papers edited by Catafu and Passarrius (2014). Especially helpful for the elements and their functions is Posthoumis (2014); for the staircases, see p. 83. Also useful and drawing more on written evidence is Español (2014).

Piazza Armerina (Sicily), Villa Romana di Casale

There is a classic discussion of the palace in English by R. J. A. Wilson (1983), who is skeptical that it was built for an emperor, as is Duval (1978); a more recent publication, containing short, technical reports, is Pensabene (2010). For the **interpretation of the Hercules mosaics**, see Lavin (1962, 7–8).

Prague (Czech Republic)

Useful for the background and development of the city is Demetz (1997). See also Dragoun (2009). For an interpretation of its significance in the fourteenth century, see Rosario (2000). The **New Town** as a holy city and a reflection of the Heavenly Jerusalem is discussed by Crossley and Opačić (2005). The **Charles Bridge** is the subject of Rosario (2000, ch. 7); see also, for the identification of the saints, Fajt et al. (2006, catalogue); and for the bridge and coronation processions, Gajdošova (2012). **St. Vitus's Cathedral**, the south portal and its mosaic are discussed by Rosario (2000, ch. 5). The **coro-**

nation ritual is examined by Crossley (2000, 167–68). For the cathedral's **burial functions**, see Crossley and Opačić (2005), and, for the Luxembourg mausoleum in particular, Crossley (2000). There is perceptive commentary on all this, with an illuminating treatment of **St. Wenceslas's chapel**, in Rosario (2000, ch. 5); see also Dubská (2003, 93). For the identification of the **rotunda** excavated under the cathedral with that built by St. Wenceslas, see Rosario (2000, ch. 5). For the cult and hagiography of **St. Wenceslas**, see Klaniczay (2002, 100–08, 329–30, and passim). On the **palace (Prague Castle)**, see Dubská (2003).

Ravenna (Italy)

On the city's early history, see Augenti (2008); on its early buildings, see Deliyannis (2009) and Verhoeven (2011). The argument that **San Vitale**, and contemporary churches in the city, were built to convey a message of power for the emperor Justinian is cogently advanced by Von Simson (1987), which remains a classic work; for the explicitly imperial character of the **mosaics**, see especially p. 30. On all aspects of the church, see Deliyannis (2009, 222–50). The representations of the *crux gemmata* and the *crux hastata* in the **mosaics at Ravenna** are discussed and illustrated by Pasquini (2005). See also Carile (2012, 129–55) on **Sant' Appollinare Nuovo**. Mackie (2003, 168–72) gives a detailed account of the **Mausoleum of Theodoric**, including recently discovered evidence for the division of the lower space by screens to form a chapel. There is also an account of the mausoleum's architecture in Deliyannis (2009, 124–36).

Reims (France)

On the development of the cathedral, see Demouy (2005). For Reims as an inauguration place, see above, p. 400.

Rome (Italy)

A useful and authoritative reference guide to the monuments in general is provided by Claridge (1998). The sculpture on the **Arch of Constantine** is discussed by Kleiner (1992, 444–55); for the views of the arch and the significance of its solar iconography, see Marlowe (2006). M. W. Jones (2000) focuses largely on the proportions of the arch. For the **Arch of Titus**, see Kleiner (1992, 185–91). Summaries of what is known of the **Golden House (*Domus Aurea*)** are given by Claridge (1998, 290–92) and MacDonald (1982–6, I, 31–41). There are also more detailed studies by Boëthius (1960), Hemsoll (1990), Warden (1981), and J. B. Ward-Perkins (1956). The interpretation advanced here is based on Swoboda (1969, 50–52). For the park, see Champlin (1998). The classic study of the **Lateran** remains Lauer (1911) but, for a more recent summary, see Luchterhandt (1999b). On the apse mosaic of Leo III's triclinium, see Luchterhandt (1999a). Davies (2000, ch. 2, and pp. 137–42), provides commentary on the **Mausoleum of Augustus** and the **Mausoleum of Hadrian**. She also explains and maps the setting of the Mausoleum of Augustus on the Field of Mars, and reports on excavations of the Sundial, commenting on the implications for cosmic kingship (Davies 2000, 124–5, ch. 3). There is more up-to-date material and reconstructions in Johnson (2009, ch. 2), who disagrees (p. 21) with Davies regarding her interpretation of the Mausoleum of Augustus as a conscious imitation of Egyptian monuments. Hesberg and Panciera (1994) provide a technical account of the building and inscriptions of the Mausoleum of Augustus. For the **Mausoleum of Constantina (Santa Costanza)**, there is a useful discussion, with reconstruction drawings, in Johnson (2009, 139–56). See also Claridge (1998, 375–76). Johnson (2009, 86–93) gives a detailed account of the **Mausoleum of Maxentius**, with reconstructions and critical commentary on them. See also Claridge (1998, 339–40). A practical introduction to the **Palace of Domitian** is given by Claridge (1998, 134–41). For more detailed discussion, see MacDonald (1982–6, I, 49–74) and Royo (1999, 304–68). See also Augenti (2004). **Pompey's Gardens** are excellently treated by Kuttner (1999). For the **Theatre of**

Pompey, see Beard (2007, 22–31). The function of **Trajan's Forum** as propaganda and its wider significance as a statement of imperial power are discussed by Packer (1997, 259–83, 2001, 187–91). On the **Pantheon,** see now Todd and Jones (2015).

St. Andrews (Scotland)

The representation of hunting on the St. Andrews Sarcophagus is emphasized by Henderson (1998, 155–56). For further studies of this object, see the papers edited by S. Foster (1998).

Saint-Denis (France), former abbey church

Erlande-Brandenburg (1975) remains fundamental for the period down to Louis IX; chapter 3 is devoted to an illuminating exposition of the development of Saint-Denis as a **necropolis** from the Merovingian period to the time of Louis IX, including detailed discussion of the arrangement and rearrangement of the royal graves under that monarch. There is a more recent, and equally illuminating, discussion by E. A. R. Brown (1985), carrying the history of the Saint-Denis necropolis into the Revolutionary and post-Revolutionary periods. Brown advances the case that the **rearrangement of the tombs in 1306** was intended to emphasize the supposed unity of the Carolingian and Capetian families, and mirrored the arrangement of figures in the Palais de la Cité. Leistenschneider (2008) offers a detailed and scholarly discussion of Saint-Denis as a "royal cemetery." The particular strength of her book is its discussion of the development of **royal burials at Saint-Denis from 1306**, including the Valois graves, although she offers an illuminating discussion of the political implications of the 1164/67 scheme (pp. 53–60). She is unconvinced by Brown's interpretation of the 1306 changes, believing that they were rather to do with giving appropriate prominence to the grave of Louis IX, and creating space for future graves. Wright (1974) argues the case that the **initiative for the development** of Saint-Denis as a necropolis came chiefly from the monks, and that it was stimulated from the later twelfth century by the burial of Louis VII at Barbeau and the monks' desire for their church to become the principal royal necropolis. On the **early burials** of members of the ruling Merovingian family, there is full discussion and illustration in Fleury, France-Lanord, and Blanc (1998), and a critical commentary on this publication by Neumayer (2000). For the **archaeological investigations** at Saint-Denis, see Bernardi, Wyss, and Meyer-Rodrigues (1996). The **tombs of Louis XII and Francis I** are richly illustrated and perceptively discussed by K. Cohen (1973, ch. 6). In discussing Louis XII's tomb, Blunk (2007) opposes the view of Kantorowicz (1957, 426–30) and Giesey (1960) that the double-decker tombs found in Saint-Denis from the time of Charles VIII (died 1498) represented the idea of the king's two bodies (above, p. 402) and aspects of the royal funeral ritual. Rather, he argues, they were the product of French military and diplomatic activity in Italy, which gave the French access to Italian models, especially the tomb of Gian Galeazzo Visconti in Pavia.

Saumur (France)

For a full account of the architecture and archaeology, see the papers edited by Litoux and Cron (2010); on the **Great Spiral Staircase**, see Litoux, Hunot, and Prigent (2010, 62–65).

Scone (Scotland)

On the **Stone of Scone**, there is a semi-popular account by Aitchison (2003), and a more weighty collection of papers edited by Breeze, Clancy, and Welander (2003). See also Driscoll (2004).

Seville (Spain), Alcázar

The fullest archaeological treatment of the complex, including the **Gothic Palace** and the **Palace of Pedro the Cruel**, is by Tabales Rodríguez (2010, 287–331). Important for analyzing the elements of these is Almagro (2009) but there is a useful introduction, now somewhat outdated, by Hernández-Núñez and Morales (1999, 40–71). For the Palace of Pedro the Cruel, the **dome of the Hall of the Ambassadors** is the subject of Manzano Martos (1994, 32–38). On the **façade**, see Cómez (2006, 81–90). Ruggles (2004, 91–92) discusses the relationship between this and the Cuarto Dorado at the Alhambra. Ruggles (2004, 94–96) considers possible reasons why Pedro the Cruel should have adopted **Mudéjar architecture** whereas Alfonso X had been content to construct the Gothic Palace which was at least superficially Gothic in style. She favors the idea that Pedro the Cruel's use of Mudéjar style was intended to distance himself from the Gothic culture of the north, creating a particularly Andalusian identity rather than a Muslim one. On the **gardens**, see Ruggles (2000, 141–47).

Split (Croatia), Palace of Diocletian

The most useful recent treatment is Ćurčić (2010, 32–42), but there is a helpful account by Wilkes (1993). The view that the **peristyle-courtyard** and the **vestibule** were designed merely for convenience of access to different parts of the palace is proposed by Wilkes (1993, 56–59), whereas the view that these were intended to facilitate expressions of the emperor's power is that of Ćurčić. On the **Missorium of Theodosius**, see Cormack (2000, 63, 64, and references); Ćurčić (2010, 98) compares the architecture represented on it to the fifth-century portico of Haghia Sophia in Constantinople, but the argument is equally applicable to the Palace of Diocletian. For the portico arrangement of the **residential block**, see Swoboda (1969, 148–53). Johnson (2009, 59–70) discusses the **Mausoleum of Diocletian** and reconstructions of it, and assesses the scholarship to date; and there is further commentary in Ćurčić (2010, 26–29, 32–38).

Stirling Castle (Scotland)

A recent popular account, nevertheless based on up-to-date scholarship, is J. G. Harrison (2011). See also Fawcett and Tabraham (1999) and, on the **great hall**, Fawcett (2001). There is a perceptive discussion in Dunbar (1999, 39–55, and passim). The artificial **landscape** of Stirling Castle is discussed briefly by Creighton (2009, 59), and some aspects of it are discussed in more detail by J. G. Harrison (n.d.). See also Royal Commission on the Ancient Historical Monuments of Scotland (1963, I, 179–223).

Sutton Hoo, Suffolk, England

The major excavation of **Mound 1** is comprehensively reported on by Bruce-Mitford (1975–83), and the more recent excavations of other mounds are summarized by Carver and Evans (2005). The fullest commentary on the **whetstone** from Mound 1 is that of Enright (2006); this book, although some of its method is controversial, starts some stimulating lines of thought about the whetstone as a symbol of royal power. The **site** of Sutton Hoo is examined in the papers published by Carver (1992) and Kendall and Wells (1992); the **landscape context** by T. Williamson (2008).

Tara, Hill of (Ireland)

For a detailed account of the monuments and excavations down to the late 1990s, see Newman (1997); for subsequent archaeological research, especially the discovery of the **new enclosure**, see Fenwick and Newman (2002). The excavations of **Duma na nGiall** are reported by O'Sullivan (2005), those of **Ráith na Senad** by Grogan (2008), and those of **Ráith na Ríg** by Roche (2002). For **Tech Midchúarta**, see also Newman(2007) and Waddell (2011, 197–199). The **landscape context** of the hill is analyzed by Newman (2011). An extraordinarily useful reference tool is Bhreathnach (1995); this is focused chiefly on written sources, although it does contain some archaeological and place-name discussion. Bhreathnach, Dowling, and Schot (2011) is primarily devoted to the context of Tara rather than to the monument itself. Still useful, especially for the **dindschenchas** poem, is Macalister (1931).

Tivoli (Italy), Hadrian's Villa

For a general introduction, see MacDonald and Pinto (1995). For recent discussions, see Ricotti (2001), Adembri and Cinque (2006), Ragni (2010). A full catalogue and description of the site is provided by Marina De Franceschini (1991). For the **canopus**, see pp. 214–314; for the **Maritime Theatre**, pp. 185–98; and for the **Piazza d'Oro**, pp. 147–59. Note that this book is rather technical, giving measurements rather than analysis. The significance of the **Piazza d'Oro** as a peristyle courtyard is raised by Swoboda (1969, 64–65). See also M. De Franceschini and Veneziano (2011). The **gardens** are lucidly discussed by Farrar (1998, 52–54, and passim).

Trier (Germany)

The most useful account of the **monuments** remains Römisch-Germanischen Zentralmuseum Mainz (1980). For a more recent summary, see Kuhnen (2003). The earliest **seal** of Trier is discussed by Haverkamp (1987, 121–23).

Urbino (Italy)

Osborne and Cornish (2003) provide a general, illustrated account. The development of the palace and of the city is the subject of Benevolo and Boninsegna (2000) and of the introductory essays to the exhibition catalogue edited by Marchi and Valazzi (2012). On the **studiolo**, see Fenucci and Simonetta (2007). On this type of room in general, see Liebenwein (1977). The discussion of the **relationship between town and palace** derives from Boucheron (2004, passim).

Venice (Italy), Palace of the Doge

For descriptions with illustrations, see Wolters (2010) and Delorenzi (2011). For analysis of the ritual functions of the palace in relation to St. Mark's, see Crouzet-Pavan (2004).

Villa Romana di Casale

See **Piazza Armerina**.

Vincennes (France)

A useful collection of papers in popular style is edited by Chapelot (2004). More scholarly, but less focused on the palace, is the collection edited by Chapelot and Lalou (1996). On the **towers and walls**, see Chapelot (2011). For the **Bois de Vincennes**, see Derex (1997) and Foucher (1996).

Westminster Abbey, London (England)

For **architectural history and royal patronage**, see Gem and Ball (1980), Binski (1995), Lewis (1995), and C. Wilson (2008). For Henry VII's chapel in particular, see Tatton-Brown (2003). For the **documentary evidence** for the abbey, see R. A. Brown, Colvin, and Taylor (1963, I, 130–57). Branner (1964) argued for the influence on Westminster Abbey of the **"French court style"** or Rayonnant style, as represented especially by the Sainte-Chapelle; Lewis (1995) for the influence of Reims Cathedral. Binski dismissed Branner's concept of a "court style," and C. Wilson (2008) argued that the style of Westminster Abbey was principally English rather than French. On the **tombs**, Binski (1995, 90–93) regarded the burial of Henry III in 1272 as the point of inception of Westminster as a royal mausoleum. The space around the tomb of Edward the Confesssor was consequently cramped, and

Henry V's chantry had to be built on a bridge at first-floor level (Hope 1913–14). For the **effigies of monarchs** preserved at Westminster, see S. Harvey (2003) and, for more detailed documentation and commentary, Hope and Robinson (1907). For the inscription on the **sanctuary mosaic**, see Wander (1978, 139–41), Binski (1990, 10), and R. Foster (1991, 87–88). A rather ill-informed discussion, concentrating on perceived metrical forms, is provided by Howlett (2002, 106–07). The interpretation of the mosaic as a cosmological diagram presented here is drawn from R. Foster (1991), who developed the work of Wander (1978). Neglected in the papers edited by L. Grant and Mortimer (2002), it is sufficiently convincing to merit close attention. See also Carpenter (1996). For the **royal pew**, see the convincing discussion by C. Wilson (2008, 64–69); Binski (pers. comm.), however, criticizes the idea, arguing that the creation of the gallery in the south transept was a matter of practicality arising from the retention of the Lady Chapel, which necessitated the incorporation of the east cloister walk into the transept; and that the king is more likely to have attended mass sitting in the sanctuary itself, as the King of Sicily did at Monreale. Vincent (2001) provides a thoughtful discussion of the **Holy Blood**, and especially the theological doubts about the validity of such a relic. The definitive treatment of the **Coronation Chair** is by Rodwell et al. (2013). The **chapter house** is dealt with in an excellent collection of papers edited by Rodwell and Mortimer (2010). For the burglaries there in 1296, 1299, and 1303, see Ashbee (2010).

Westminster Palace, London (England)

For the overall plan and situation, see R. A. Brown, Colvin, and Taylor (1963, 491–552) and, for recent excavations, see Thomas, Cowie, and Sidell (2006). On **Westminster Hall**, see M. Collins et al. (2012, 203) and C. Wilson (1997, 43). C. Wilson (1997, 280, n. 46) makes the case that it was of a single span, rather than three-aisled. On heating and accessibility, see Wilson (1997, 34). On the **marble table** and its functions, see Collins (2012, 210) and R. A. Brown, Colvin, and Taylor (1963, 544). On the location of the law **courts**, see Wilson (1997, 37). On the religious character of the hall and its relationship to Winchester Cathedral, see C. Wilson (1997, 43). The rebuilding by Richard II is the overall subject of this last paper. On the **throne**, see M. Collins et al. (2012, 207–08). Binski (1986) is the fullest treatment of the **Painted Chamber**; for the interpretation of the paintings of biblical kings as connected with Edward I's relationship to the crusades, see Reeve (2006). For the **Exchequer**, see R. A. Brown, Colvin, and Taylor (1963, I, 492, 538–42).

Winchester (England)

See Biddle (1973), Biddle (1975), Biddle and Keene (1976), and Biddle (1983). Publication of full reports on the excavations on which these papers are based is still awaited.

Windsor Castle (England)

Still useful as a general guide is Hope (1913). An excellent discussion of Edward III's **royal lodgings** is C. Wilson (2002). On the **Round Table** and its use, see Munby, Barber, and Brown (2007). On the **park and forest**, see Astill (2002, 10–12); there is disappointingly little on the pre-modern landscape of the palace in Roberts (1997).

Woodstock Palace (England)

On **Everswell garden** in the park of Woodstock, see Colvin (1986, 18–20), and Meier (1994, 160–62), Bond and Tiller (1997, 46–47), and Creighton (2009, 141–42). There is an excellent discussion of the **park** by Bond (1997). For the antecedents of **Woodstock Forest** in the Forest of Wychwood, and the possible antiquity of that forest as a hunting reserve, see Yeates (2008) and Copeland (2002). For the **North Oxfordshire Grim's Ditch**, see Copeland (1988, 2002, ch. 6). For the Forest of Wychwood's relationship to Oxford and Beaumont Palace, see G. Jones (2010, 49, and plate 24 and fig. 9).

Writtle (England)

The hunting lodge was excavated and published by Rahtz (1969).

Yeavering (England)

Hope-Taylor (1977) remains the most important account, written by the excavator; for critical reinterpretations of the site, see Frodsham and O'Brien (2005). On the **theater**, see Barnwell (2005). For the situation of Yeavering relative to the **Cheviot Hills**, see Hope-Taylor (1977, 2, fig. 1).

References

Abels, Richard. 1997. *Alfred the Great*. London and New York: Longmans.

Abulafia, David, ed. 1999. *New Cambridge Medieval History: Volume 5, c. 1198--c. 1300*. Cambridge: Cambridge University Press.

Acién Almansa, M. 1987. "Madīnat al-Zahrā' en el urbanismo musulmán." *Cuadernos de Madīnat al-Zahrā'* 1: 11–26.

Acién Almansa, M., and Antonio Vallejo Triano. 1998. "Urbanismo y estado islámico: de *Corduba* a *Qurtuba*-Madīnat al-Zahrā'." In *Genèse de la ville islamique en al-Andalus et au Maghreb occidental: [tables rondes, Madrid, 24–25 mars 1994 et 16–17 novembre 1995]*, edited by Patrice Cressier, Mercedes García-Arenal and Mohamed Meouak, 107–36. Madrid: Casa de Velázquez.

Adam, Robert. 1764. *Ruins of the Palace of the Emperor Diocletian at Spalatro in Dalmatia*. [London]: Printed for the author.

Adamson, John, ed. 2000. *The Princely Courts of Europe: Ritual, Politics and Culture under the Ancien Régime, 1500–1750*. London: Seven Dials.

Adembri, Benedetta, and Giuseppina Enrica Cinque. 2006. *Villa Adriana: la pianta del centenario: 1906–2006*. Firenze: Centro Di.

Airlie, Stuart. 2003. "Thrones, Dominions, Powers: Some European Points of Comparison for the Stone of Destiny." In *The Stone of Destiny: Artefact and Icon*, edited by David J. Breeze, Thomas Owen Clancy and Richard Welander, 123–38, Monograph series / Society of Antiquaries of Scotland, 22. Edinburgh: Society of Antiquaries of Scotland.

Aitchison, Nick. 2000. *Scotland's Stone of Destiny: Myth, History and Nationhood*. Stroud: Tempus.

———. 2003. *Scotland's Stone of Destiny*. Stroud: Tempus.

Alexander, Michael, trans.. 2003. *Beowulf: A Verse Translation*. Rev. ed, Penguin Classics. Harmondsworth: Penguin.

Alföldi, A. 1959. "Hasta-Summa Imperii: The Spear as Embodiment of Sovereignty in Rome." *American Journal of Archaeology* 63 (1): 1–27.

Allmand, Christopher, ed. 1998. *New Cambridge Medieval History: Volume 7, c. 1415–c. 1500*. Cambridge: Cambridge University Press.

Almagro, Antonio. 2009. "El Alcázar de Sevilla: un palacio musulmán para un rey cristiano." In *Cristianos y Musulmanes en la Peninsula Ibérica: la guerra, la frontera y la convivencia: XI Congreso de Estudios Medievales 2007*, edited by Ladero Quesada and Miguel Ángel, 331–66. Avila: Fundación Sánchez Albornoz.

Almond, Mark, Jeremy Black, Felipe Fernandez-Armesto, et al. 1994. *The Times Atlas of European History*. London: Times Books.

Almond, Richard. 2003. *Medieval Hunting*. Stroud: Sutton.

Amt, Emilie, and S. D. Church, eds. and trans. 2007. *Richard fitzNigel, Dialogus de Scaccario: the Dialogue of the Exchequer; Constitutio Domus Regis: Disposition of the King's Household*, Oxford Medieval Texts. Oxford: Clarendon Press.

Andersen, Harald. 1995. "The Graves of the Jelling Dynasty." *Acta Archaeologica* 66: 281–300.

Anderson, J. K. 1985. *Hunting in the Ancient World*. Berkeley: University of California Press.

Anheim, Étienne. 2008. "La 'Chambre du Cerf': Image, savoir et nature à Avignon au milieu du XlVe siècle." In *I saperi nelle corti: Knowledge at the Courts*, edited by Clelia Arcelli, 57–124, Micrologus, 16. Florence: SISMEL—Edizioni del Galluzzo.

Anon. 1977–98. *Lexikon des Mittelalters*. 9 vols. Munich: Artemis.

———. 1985. *L'escalier dans l'architecture de la Renaissance*, De architectura, Colloques, 2. Paris: Picard Paris: Picard.

———. 1987. *Weltliche und Geistliche Schatzkammer: Bildführer*. Vienna.

———. 1991. *The Oxford English Dictionary*. 20 vols. Oxford: Clarendon Press.

———. 1997. *Großer Atlas zur Weltgeschichte*. 2nd ed. Braunschweig: Westermann.

———. 2014. *Karl der Große / Charlemagne*. 3 vols. Dresden: Sandstein Verlag.

Anzelmo, Francesca Manuela. 2011. "Classification of the Decorated Garments and Headdresses in the Ceiling Paintings of the Cappella Palatina." In *Die Cappella Palatina in Palermo: Geschichte, Kunst, Funktionen. Forschungsergebnisse der Restaurierung*, edited by Thomas Dittelbach, 499–506. Künzelsau: Swiridoff.

Arce, Javier. 2000. "Imperial Funerals in the Later Roman Empire." In *Rituals of Power: From Late Antiquity to the Early Middle Ages*, edited by Janet L. Nelson and Frans Theuws, 115–29, The Transformation of the Roman World, 8. Leiden: Brill.

Arnold, Thomas, ed. 1882–5. *Symeonis monachi Opera omnia*. 2 vols., Rolls Series, 75. London: Longman.

Ashbee, Jeremy A. 2004. "The Chamber Called Gloriette: Living at Leisure in Thirteenth- and Fourteenth-Century Castles." *Journal of the British Archaelogical Association* 157: 17–40.

———. 2006. "The Tower of London as a Royal Residence 1066–1400." PhD diss., University of London.

———. 2010. "The Royal Wardrobe and the Chapter House of Westminster Abbey." In *Westminster Abbey Chapter House: the History, Art and Architecture of a 'Chapter House beyond Compare,'* edited by Warwick Rodwell and Richard Mortimer, 112–23. London: Society of Antiquaries.

Astill, Grenville. 2002. "Windsor in the Context of Medieval Berkshire." In *Windsor: Medieval Archaeology, Art and Architecture of the Thames Valley*, edited by Laurence Keen and Eileen Scarff, 1–14, British Archaeological Association Conference Transactions, 25. Leeds: Maney Publishing.

Attreed, Lorraine. 1994. "The Politics of Welcome: Ceremonies and Constitutional Development in Later Medieval English Towns." In *City and Spectacle in Medieval Europe*, edited by Barbara A. Hanawalt and Kathryn L. Reyerson, 208–31. Minneapolis: University of Minnesota Press.

Augenti, Andrea. 2004. "Luoghi e non luoghi: Palazzi e città nell'Italia tardoantica e altomedievale." In *Les palais dans la ville: Espaces urbains et lieux de la puissance publique dans la Méditerranée médiévale*, edited by Patrick Boucheron, Jacques Chiffoleau, Theis Valérie, et al., 15–38, Collection d'histoire et d'archéologie médiévales, 13. Lyon: Presses Universitaires de Lyon.

———. 2008. "Ravenna, die Hauptstadt der Ostgoten." In *Rome and the Barbarians: The Birth of a New World*, edited by Jean-Jacques Aillagon, 261–64, Arte antica. Venice: Skira.

Austin, David, ed. and trans. 1982. *Boldon Book: Northumberland and Durham*, History from the Sources. Chichester: Phillimore.

Aymard, Jacques. 1951. *Les chasses romaines, des origines à la fin du siècle des Antonins*, Bibliothèque des Écoles françaises d'Athènes et de Rome, 171. Paris: Boccard.

Bachrach, Bernard S., and David Stewart Bachrach, trans. 2014. *Widukind of Corvey, Deeds of the Saxons*. Washington, DC: Catholic University of America Press.

Baillie, Hugh Murray 1967. "Etiquette and the Planning of the State Apartments in Baroque Palaces." *Archaeologia* 101: 169–99.

Bak, János M., ed. 1990. *Coronations: Medieval and Early Modern Monarchic Ritual*. Berkeley: University of California Press.

Bande, Alexandre. 2009. *Le coeur du roi: les Capétiens et les sépultures multiples, XIIIe–XVe siècles*. Paris: Tallandier.

Bandmann, Günter. 2005. *Early Medieval Architecture as Bearer of Meaning*. Translated by Kendall Wallis. New York and Chichester: Columbia University Press.

Barber, Richard. 2007a. "The Round Table Feast of 1344." In *Edward III's Round Table at Windsor: The House of the Round Table and the Windsor Festival of 1344*, edited by Julian Munby, Richard Barber, and Richard Brown, 38–43. Woodbridge: Boydell and Brewer.

———. 2007b. "Why did Edward III Hold the Round Table? The Chivalric Background." In *Edward III's Round Table at Windsor: The House of the Round Table and the Windsor Festival of 1344*, edited by Julian Munby, Richard Barber, and Richard Brown, 84–99. Woodbridge: Boydell and Brewer.

Bardill, Jonathan. 2006. "Visualizing the Great Palace of the Byzantine Emperors at Constantinople." In *Visualisierungen von Herrschaft: frühmittelalterliche Residenzen: Gestalt und Zeremoniell: internationales Kolloquium 3./4. Juni 2004 in Istanbul*, edited by Franz Alto Bauer, 5–45, Byzas, 5. Istanbul: Ege Yayınları.

Bareš, Petr, and Ústav Národní Památkový. 2010. *Karlštejn a jeho význam v dějinách a kultuře*. Prague: Národní památkový ústav, Ústřední pracoviště.

Barnwell, P. S. 2005. "Anglian Yeavering: A Continental Perspective." In *Yeavering: People, Power and Place*, edited by Paul Frodsham and Colm O'Brien, 174–84. Stroud: Tempus.

Bartlett, Robert. 2013. *Why Can the Dead Do Such Great Things? Saints and Worshippers from the Martyrs to the Reformation*. Princeton: Princeton University Press.

Bartlová, Milena. 2003. "Karlštejn: A Sacred Place and Castle of the Holy Grail: Critical Comments." In *Court Chapels of the High and Late Middle Ages and Their Artistic Decoration = Dvorské kaple vrcholného a pozdního středověku a jejich umělecká výzdoba*, edited by Jiří Fajt and Klášter Anežský, 28–31. [Prague]: National Gallery in Prague = Národní galerie v Praze.

Bateson, Edward. 1893. *A History of Northumberland: Volume 1: The Parish of Bamburgh with the Chapelry of Belford*, Northumberland County History. Newcastle-upon-Tyne: A. Reid.

Bayer, Clemens M. M. 2009. "Die Aachener Marienkirche in der Diözese Lüttich: zu Funktionen, zur rechtlichen Stellung und zur Stiftsverfassung: eine Skizze." In *Dombaumeistertagung: Europäische Vereinigung der Dombaumeister, Münsterbaumeister und Hüttenmeister: Aachen 2009*, edited by Helmut Maintz, 55–74. Aachen: Dombauleitung Aachen.

———. 2014. "Das Grab Karls des Grossen." In *Die Aachener Marienkirche: Aspekte ihrer Archäologie und frühen Geschichte*, edited by Harald Müller, Clemens M. M. Bayer, and Max Kerner, 225–35, Der Aachener Dom in seiner Geschichte. Quellen und Forschungen, 1. Regensburg: Schnell and Steiner.

Bayer, Clemens M. M., Theo Jülich, and Manfred Kuhl, eds. 1986. *Celica Iherusalem: Festschrift für Erich Stephany*. Cologne and Siegburg: Respublica-Verlag F. Schmitt.

Bayer, Clemens M. M., Max Kerner, and Harald Müller. 2014. "Schriftquellen zur Geschichte der Marienkirche bis ca. 1000." In *Die Aachener Marienkirche: Aspekte ihrer Archäologie und frühen Geschichte*, edited by Harald Müller, Clemens M. M. Bayer, and Max Kerner, 113–90, Der Aachener Dom in seiner Geschichte. Quellen und Forschungen, 1. Regensburg: Schnell and Steiner.

Baynes, Norman Hepburn. 1949. "The Supernatural Defenders of Constantinople." *Analecta Bollandiana* 67: 165–77. Reprinted: Norman Hepburn Baynes, 1955. *Byzantine Studies and Other Essays*, 248–60. London: Athlone Press.

Beard, Mary. 2007. *The Roman Triumph*. Cambridge, MA: Belknap Press of Harvard University Press.

Belting, Hans. 1962. "Studien zum beneventanischen Hof im 8. Jahrhundert." *Dumbarton Oaks Papers* 16: 141–93.

Benevolo, Leonardo, and Paolo Boninsegna. 2000. *Urbino*. 3rd ed. Rome: Laterza.

Bennert, J. 1992. "Art et propagande politique sous Philippe IV le Bel: le cycle des rois de France dans la Grand'salle du Palais de la Cité." *Revue de l'Art* 97: 46–59.

Bennert, Uwe. 2004. "Ideologie in Stein: zur Darstellung französischer Königsmacht im Paris des 14. Jahrhunderts." In *Opus Tesselatum, Modi und Grenzgänge der Kunstwissenschaft, Festschrift für Peter Cornelius Claussen*, edited by Katharina Corsepius, Daniela Mondini, Darko Senekovic, et al., 153–63, Studien zur Kunstgeschichte, 157. Hildesheim: Olms.

Beresford, Maurice W. 1967. *New Towns of the Middle Ages*. London: Lutterworth Press.

Berger, Albrecht. 2000. "Streets and Public Spaces in Constantinople." *Dumbarton Oaks Papers* 54: 161–72.

———. 2001. "Imperial and Ecclesiastical Processions in Constantinople." In *Byzantine Constantinople: Monuments, Topography, and Everyday Life*, edited by Nevra Necipoğlu, 74–87, Medieval Mediterranean, 33. Leiden: Brill.

Berges, Wilhelm. 1963. "Zur Geschichte des Werla-Goslarer Reichsbezirks vom neunten bis zum elften Jarhrhundert." In *Deutsche Königspfalzen, Band 1*, edited by Karl Hauck, 113–57. Göttingen: Vandenhoeck and Ruprecht.

Bermúdez López, Jesús. 2010. *The Alhambra and the Generalife: Official Guide*. Madrid: Patronato de la Alhambra y Generalife.

Bernardi, Philippe, Michael Wyss, and Nicole Meyer-Rodrigues, eds. 1996. *Atlas historique de Saint-Denis: des origines au XVIIIe siècle*, Documents d'archéologie française, 59. Paris: Éditions de la Maison des Sciences de l'Homme.

Bertelli, Sergio. 2001. *The King's Body: Sacred Rituals of Power in Medieval and Early Modern Europe*. University Park: Pennsylvania State University Press.

Beumann, Helmut. 1965. "Grab und Thron Karls des Grossen zu Aachen." In *Karl der Grosse: Lebenswerk und Nachleben*, edited by Wolfgang Braunfels. 4 vols. Düsseldorf: Schwann.

Bezzi, Matteo. 2007. *Iconologia della sacralità del potere: il tondo Angaran et l'etimasia*. Spoleto: Centro Italiano sull'Alto Medioevo.

Bhreathnach, Edel. 1995. *Tara: A Select Bibliography*, Discovery Programme Monographs, 1. Dublin: Royal Irish Academy.

———. 2011. "Transforming Kingship and Cult: The Provincial Ceremonial Capitals in Early Medieval Ireland." In *Landscapes of Cult and Kingship: Archaeology and Text*, edited by Edel Bhreathnach, Ger Dowling, and Roseanne Schot, 126–48. Dublin: Four Courts Press.

Bhreathnach, Edel, Ger Dowling, and Roseanne Schot, eds. 2011. *Landscapes of Cult and Kingship: Archaeology and Text*. Dublin: Four Courts Press.

Biddle, Martin. 1973. "Winchester: The Development of an Early Medieval Capital." In *Vor- und frühformen der europäischen Stadt im Mittelalter: Bericht über ein Symposium in Reinhausen bei Göttingen in der Zeit vom 18.–24. April 1972*, edited by Herbert Jankuhn, Walter Schlesinger, and Heiko Steuer, 229–61. 2 vols. Göttingen: Vandenhoeck and Ruprecht.

———. 1975. "*Felix Urbs Wintonia*: Winchester in the Age of Monastic Reform." In *Tenth-Century Studies: Essays in Commemoration of the Millennium of the Council of Winchester and Regularis Concordia*, edited by David Parsons, 123–40. London and Chichester: Phillimore.

———. 1976a. "The Evolution of Towns: Planned Towns before 1066." In *The Plans and Topography of Medieval Towns in England and Wales*, edited by Maurice W. Barley, CBA Research Report, 14. London: Council for British Archaeology.

———. 1976b. "Towns." In *The Archaeology of Anglo-Saxon England*, edited by David M. Wilson, 99–150. Cambridge: Cambridge University Press.

———. 1983. "The Study of Winchester: Archaeology and History in a British Town, 1961–1983." *Proceedings of the British Academy* 69: 93–135.

———. 1986. "Seasonal Festivals and Residence: Winchester, Westminster and Gloucester in the Tenth to Twelfth Centuries." *Anglo-Norman Studies* 8, 51–72.

———, ed. 2000. *King Arthur's Round Table: An Archaeological Investigation*. Woodbridge: Boydell Press.

Biddle, Martin, and David Hill. 1971. "Late Saxon Planned Towns." *Antiquaries Journal* 51: 70–85.

Biddle, Martin, and Derek J. Keene. 1976. "Winchester in the Eleventh and Twelfth Centuries." In *Winchester in the Early Middle Ages*, edited by Martin Biddle, 241–448, Winchester Studies, 1. Oxford: Oxford University Press.

Billot, Claudine. 1991. "Le message spirituel et politique de la Sainte-Chapelle de Paris." *Revue Mabillon* 63: 119–41.

———. 2004. "Des Reliques de la Passion dans le royaume de France." In *Byzance et les reliques du christ*, edited by Jannic Durand and Bernard Flusin, 239–48, Centre de recherche d'histoire et civilisation de Byzance, Monographies, 17. Paris: Association des Amis du Centre d'Histoire et Civilisation de Byzance.

Binding, Günther. 1965. *Pfalz Gelnhausen: eine Bauuntersuchung*, Abhandlungen zur Kunst-, Musik- und Literaturwissenschaft, 30. Bonn: H. Bouvier.

———. 1996. *Deutsche Königspfalzen von Karl dem Grossen bis Friedrich II, 765–1240*. Darmstadt: Primus Verlag.

Binski, Paul. 1986. *The Painted Chamber at Westminster*. London: Society of Antiquaries of London.

———. 1990. "The Cosmati at Westminster and the English Court Style." *Art Bulletin* 72: 6–34.

———. 1995. *Westminster Abbey and the Plantagenets: Kingship and the Representation of Power, 1200–1400*. New Haven: Yale University Press.

———. 2002. "The Cosmati and *Romanitas* in England: an Overview." In *Westminster Abbey: The Cosmati Pavements*, edited by Lindy Grant and Richard Mortimer, 116–34, Courtauld Institute Research Papers, 3. Aldershot: Ashgate.

Bise, Gabriel. 1984. *The Hunting Book by Gaston Phoebus*. London: Regent Books.

Bjork, Robert E., ed. 2010. *The Oxford Dictionary of the Middle Ages*. Oxford: Oxford University Press.

Blair, Claude, ed. 1998. *The Crown Jewels: The History of the Coronation Regalia in the Jewel House of the Tower of London*. 2 vols. London: Stationery Office.

Blair, John. 1993. "Hall and Chamber: English Domestic Planning 1000–1250." In *Manorial Domestic Buildings in England and Northern France*, edited by G. Meirion-Jones and M. Jones, 1–21, Occasional Papers from the Society of Antiquaries. London: Society of Antiquaries.

Bloch, Marc. 1961. *Feudal Society*. Translated by L. A. Manyon. 2 vols. London: Routledge and Kegan Paul.

Bloom, Jonathan M. 2011. "The Islamic Sources of the Cappella Palatina Pavement." In *Die Cappella Palatina in Palermo: Geschichte, Kunst, Funktionen. Forschungsergebnisse der Restaurierung*, edited by Thomas Dittelbach, 551–59. Künzelsau: Swiridoff.

Blunk, Julian. 2007. "Das Grabmal Ludwigs XII. in Saint-Denis: Zum sepulkralen Denkmalkrieg zwischen den Häusern Valois und Sforza." In *Grab—Kult—Memoria. Studien zur gesellschaftlichen Funktion von Erinnerung (Horst Bredekamp zum 60. Geburtstag am 29. April 2007; Tagungsakten des interdisziplinären Forschungskongresses vom 17.-19. Februar 2006 an der Humboldt-Universität zu Berlin)*, edited by Carolin Behrmann, 219–37. Cologne: Böhlau.

Boehm, Barbara Drake, and Jiři Fajt, eds. 2005. *Prague: the Crown of Bohemia, 1347–1437*. New Haven: Yale University Press.

Boëthius, Axel. 1960. *The Golden House of Nero: Some Aspects of Roman Architecture*, Jerome Lectures, 5th series. Ann Arbor: University of Michigan Press.

Bond, James. 1994. "Forests, Chases, Warrens and Parks in Medieval Wessex." In *The Medieval Landscape of Wessex*, edited by Michael Aston and Carenza Lewis, 115–58, Oxbow Monograph, 46. Oxford: Oxbow.

———. 1997. "Woodstock Park in the Middle Ages." In *Blenheim: Landscape for a Palace*. 2nd ed., edited by James Bond and Kate Tiller, 22–54. Stroud: Sutton Publishing.

Bond, James, and Kate Tiller, eds. 1997. *Blenheim: Landscape for a Palace*. 2nd ed. Stroud: Sutton Publishing.

Borsook, Eve. 1990. *Messages in Mosaic: The Royal Programmes of Norman Sicily, 1130–1187*. Oxford: Clarendon Press.

Boshof, Egon. 1991. "Aachen und der Thronerhebung des deutschen Königs in salisch-staufischer Zeit." *Zeitschrift der Aachener Geschichtsvereins* 97: 5–32.

Bosl, Karl. 1963. "Pfalzen und Forsten." In *Deutsche Königspfalzen, Band 1*, edited by Karl Hauck, 1–29. Göttingen: Vandenhoeck and Ruprecht.

Boucheron, Patrick. 2004. "*Non domus ista sed urbs*: Palais princiers et environnement urbain au *Quattrocento* (Milan, Mantoue, Urbino)." In *Les palais dans la ville: Espaces urbains et lieux de la puissance publique dans la Méditerranée médiévale*, edited by Patrick Boucheron, Jacques Chiffoleau, Theis Valérie, et al., 249–84, Collection d'histoire et d'archéologie médiévales, 13. Lyon: Presses Universitaires de Lyon.

Boumann, C. A. 1957. *Sacring and Crowning: The Development of the Latin Ritual for the Anointing of Kings and the Coronation of an Emperor before the Eleventh Century*. Groningen: J. B. Wolters.

Bove, Boris. 2003. "Les palais des rois à Paris à la fin du Moyen Âge (XIe–XVe siècles)." In *Palais et pouvoir: de Constantinople à Versailles*, edited by Marie-France Auzépy and Joël Cornette, 45–79, Temps et espaces. Saint-Denis: Presses Universitaires de Vincennes.

Bozóky, Edina. 2006. *La politique des reliques de Constantin à Saint Louis: protection collective et légitimation du pouvoir*, Bibliothèque Historique et Littéraire. Paris: Beauchesne.

———. 2007. "Saint Louis, ordonnateur et acteur des rituels autours des reliques de la passion." In *La Sainte-Chapelle de Paris: Royaume de France ou Jérusalem céleste?*, edited by Christine Hediger, 19–34, Culture et Société médiévales, 10. Turnhout: Brepols.

Branner, Robert. 1964. "Westminster Abbey and the French Court Style." *Journal of the Society of Architectural Historians of Great Britain* 23: 3–18.

———. 1965. *St Louis and the Court Style in Gothic Architecture*. London: A. Zwemmer.

Breeze, David John, Thomas Owen Clancy, and Richard Welander, eds. 2003. *The Stone of Destiny: Artefact and Icon*. Edinburgh: Society of Antiquaries of Scotland.

Brenk, Beat. 2010. "L'importanza e la funzione della Cappella Palatina nella storia dell'arte." In *La Cappella Palatina a Palermo = The Cappella Palatina in Palermo*, edited by Beat Brenk, Fabrizio Agnello, and Giovanni Chiaromonte, I, 27–78. 4 vols., Mirabilia Italiæ, 17. Modena, Italy: Franco Cosimo Panini.

——. 2011. "Rhetoric, Aspiration and Function of the Cappella Palatina in Palermo." In *Die Cappella Palatina in Palermo: Geschichte, Kunst, Funktionen. Forschungsergebnisse der Restaurierung*, edited by Thomas Dittelbach, 592–603. Künzelsau: Swiridoff.

Brenk, Beat, Fabrizio Agnello, and Giovanni Chiaromonte. 2010. *La Cappella Palatina a Palermo = The Cappella Palatina in Palermo*. 4 vols., Mirabilia Italiæ, 17. Modena, Italy: Franco Cosimo Panini.

Bresc, Henri. 1994. "Les jardins royaux de Palerme." *Mélanges de l'École française de Rome: Moyen Âge, temps modernes* 106 (1): 239–53.

Brightman, F. E. 1901. "Byzantine Imperial Coronations." *Journal of Theological Studies* 2: 339–92.

Brockmann, Joseph, Helmut Beumann, Franz Brunhölzl, et al., eds. 1966. *Karolus Magnus et Leo Papa: ein Paderborner Epos vom Jahre 799*. Paderborn: Verein für Geschichte und Altertumskunde Westfalens, Abteilung Paderborn.

Brown, Andrew. 1997. "Civic Ritual: Bruges and the Counts of Flanders in the Later Middle Ages." *English Historical Review* 112: 277–99.

——. 2006. "Ritual and State-Building: Ceremonies in Late Medieval Bruges." In *Symbolic Communication in Late Medieval Towns*, edited by Jacoba van Leeuwen, 1–28, Mediaevalia Lovaniensia, series 1, studia 37. Leuven: Leuven University Press.

——. 2011. *Civic Ceremony and Religion in Medieval Bruges c.1300–1520*. Cambridge: Cambridge University Press.

Brown, Andrew, and Graeme Small, trans. 2007. *Court and Civic Society in the Burgundian Low Countries c.1420–1520*. Manchester: Manchester University Press.

Brown, Elizabeth A. R. 1978. "The Ceremonial of Royal Succession in Capetian France: The Double Funeral of Louis X." *Traditio* 34: 226–71. Reprinted: Elizabeth A. Brown 1999. *The Monarchy of Capetian France and Royal Ceremonial*, no. 7, Collected Studies, 345. Variorum: Aldershot.

——. 1980. "The Ceremonial of Royal Succession in Capetian France: The Funeral of Philip V." *Speculum* 55: 266–93. Reprinted: Elizabeth A. Brown 1999. *The Monarchy of Capetian France and Royal Ceremonial*, no. 8, Collected Studies, 345. Variorum: Aldershot.

——. 1981. "Death and the Human Body in the Later Middle Ages: The Legislation of Boniface VIII on the Division of the Corpse." *Viator* 12: 221–70. Reprinted: Elizabeth A. Brown 1999. *The Monarchy of Capetian France and Royal Ceremonial*, no. 6, Collected Studies, 345. Variorum: Aldershot.

——. 1985. "Burying and Unburying the Kings of France." In *Persons in Groups: Social Behavior as Identity Formation in Medieval and Renaissance Europe*, edited by R. C. Trexler, 241–66. Binghampton: Center for Medieval and Renaissance Studies. Reprinted: Elizabeth A. Brown 1999. *The Monarchy of Capetian France and Royal Ceremonial*, no. 9, Collected Studies, 345. Variorum: Aldershot.

Brown, Michelle P., ed. 2007. *The Holkham Bible Picture Book: A Facsimile*. London: British Library Publications.

Brown, Peter. 1981. *The Cult of Saints: Its Rise and Function in Latin Christianity*, Haskell Lectures on History of Religions, new series, 2. London: SCM Press.

Brown, R. Allen, Howard Montagu Colvin, and Alfred John Taylor. 1963. *The History of the King's Works: Volumes 1 and 2: The Middle Ages*. London: HMSO.

Brubaker, Leslie. 1999. "The Chalke Gate, the Construction of the Past, and the Trier Ivory." *Byzantine and Modern Greek Studies* 23: 258–85.

Bruce-Mitford, Rupert L. S. 1975–83. *The Sutton Hoo Ship-Burial*. 3 vols. London: British Museum Publications.

Brühl, Carl-Richard. 1950. *Reims als Krönungsstadt des französischen Königs bis zum Ausgang des 14. Jahrhunderts: Inaugural-Dissertation zur Erlangung der Doktorwürde der Philosophischen Fakultät der Wolfgang-Goethe-Universität Frankfurt am Main*. Frankfurt: Druckerei Rud. Heil.

——. 1962. "Fränkischer Krönungsbrauch und das Problem der 'Festkrönungen.'" *Historische Zeitschrift* 194: 265–326.

Bryant, Lawrence McBride. 1986. "La cérémonie de l'entrée à Paris au Moyen Âge." *Annales: Économies, Sociétés, Civilisations* 41 (3): 513–42.

——. 2007. "From Communal Ritual to Royal Spectacle: Some Observations on the Staging of Royal Entries (1450–1600)." In *French Ceremonial Entries in the Sixteenth Century: Event, Image, Text*, edited by Hélène Visentin and Nicolas Russell, 207–45. Toronto: Centre for Reformation and Renaissance Studies. Reprinted: Lawrence McBride Bryant. 2010. *Ritual, Ceremony and the Changing Monarchy in France, 1350–1789*, no. 9. Collected Studies, 937. Farnham: Ashgate,.

Buccellati, Graziella, and Holly Snapp, eds. 1995–1999. *The Iron Crown and Imperial Europe*. 2 vols, Società di Studi Monzesi. Milan: Giorgio Mondadori.

Buren-Hagopian, Anne van. 1985. "Un jardin d'amour de Philippe le Bon au parc de Hesdin: le rôle de Van Eyck dans une commande ducale." *La Revue du Louvre et des Musées de France* 35: 185–92.

———. 1986. "Reality and Literary Romance in the Park of Hesdin." In *Medieval Gardens*, edited by E. B. Mac-Dougall, 115–34. Washington, DC: Dumbarton Oaks.

Burnett, Charles. 1994. "Michael Scot and the Transmission of Scientific Culture from Toledo to Bologna via the Court of Frederick II Hohenstaufen." *Micrologus*: 101–26. Reprinted: Charles Burnett 2009. *Arabic into Latin in the Middle Ages: The Translators and Their Intellectual and Social Context*, no. 8. Variorum Collected Studies Series 939. Farnham: Ashgate.

Burroughs, Charles. 2002. *The Italian Renaissance Palace Façade: Structures of Authority, Surfaces of Sense*. Cambridge: Cambridge University Press.

Byrne, F. J. 1973. *Irish Kings and High-kings*. Dublin: Four Courts Press.

Caldwell, D., and J. Lewis. 1996. "Linlithgow Palace: An Excavation in the West Range and a Note on Finds from the Palace." *Proceedings of the Society of Antiquarie of Scotland* 126: 823–70.

Cambridge, Eric. 1995. "Archaeology and the Cult of St. Oswald in Pre-Conquest Northumbria." In *Oswald: Northumbrian King to European Saint*, edited by Eric Cambridge and Clare Stancliffe, 128–63. Stamford: Paul Watkins.

Carile, Maria Cristina. 2012. *The Vision of the Palace of the Byzantine Emperors as a Heavenly Jerusalem*. Spoleto: Centro Italiano di Studi sull'Alto Medioevo.

Carlen, Louis. 1992. "Krönungskirchen." In *Studia in honorem eminentissimi Cardinalis Alphonsi M. Stickler*, edited by Rosalius Josephus Castillo Lara, 51–78. Rome: Libreria Ateneo Salesiano.

Caronia, Giuseppe. 1982. *La Zisa di Palermo: Storia e restauro*. Palermo: S.F. Flaccovio.

Carpenter, David A. 1996. "King Henry III and the Cosmati Work at Westminster Abbey." In *The Cloister and the World: Essays in Medieval History in Honour of Barbara Harvey*, edited by John Blair and Brian Golding, 178–95. Oxford: Oxford University Press.

———. 2002. "Westminster Abbey and the Cosmati Pavements in Politics." In *Westminster Abbey: The Cosmati Pavements*, edited by Lindy Grant and Richard Mortimer, 37–48, Courtauld Institute Research Papers, 3. Aldershot: Ashgate.

———. 2010. "King Henry III and the Chapter House of Westminster Abbey." In *Westminster Abbey Chapter House: The History, Art and Architecture of a 'Chapter House beyond Compare,'*, edited by Warwick Rodwell and Richard Mortimer, 32–39. London: Society of Antiquaries.

Carroll, Robert, and Stephen Prickett, eds. 1997. *The Bible: Authorized King James Version*, Oxford World's Classics. Oxford: Oxford University Press.

Carru, Dominique. 2004. "Le Palais des Papes d'Avignon: Essai de morphogenèse." In *Les palais dans la ville: Espaces urbains et lieux de la puissance publique dans la Méditerranée médiévale*, edited by Patrick Boucheron, Jacques Chiffoleau, Theis Valérie, et al., 189–212, Collection d'histoire et d'archéologie médiévales, 13. Lyon: Presses Universitaires de Lyon.

Carver, Martin O. H., ed. 1992. *The Age of Sutton Hoo: The Seventh Century in North-Western Europe*. Woodbridge: Boydell Press.

Carver, Martin O. H., and Angela Care Evans. 2005. *Sutton Hoo: A Seventh-Century Princely Burial Ground and Its Context*. London: British Museum Publications.

Catafu, Aymat, and Olivier Passarrius, eds. 2014. *Un palais dans la ville: vol. 1: le palais des rois de Majorque à Perpignan; vol. 2: Perpignan des rois de Majorque*. 2 vols. Perpignan: Editions Trabucaire.

Cavalera, Gabriele, and Guiseppe Cucco. 2007. *Urbino: Artistic Guide: Logical Path of a Tour of the Ducal Palace and Historic City Centre*. Urbino: Edizione l'Alfiere.

Cavallo, Adolfo Salvatore. 1998. *The Unicorn Tapestries at the Metropolitan Museum of Art*. New Haven: Yale University Press.

Caviness, Madeline Harrison. 1981. *The Windows of Christ Church Cathedral, Canterbury*, Corpus Vitrearum Medii Aevi, 2. London: Oxford University Press for the British Academy.

Cazelles, Raymond. 1982. *Société politique, noblesse et couronne sous Jean le Bon et Charles V*, Mémoires et documents (Société de l'École des Chartes), 28. Geneva: Droz.

Chaisemartin, Nathalie de. 2003. *Rome: Paysage urbain et idéologie, des Scipions à Hadrien (IIe s. av. J.-C.—IIe s. ap. J.-C.)*, Collection U. Histoire. Paris: Colin.

Champlin, Edward. 1998. "God and Man in the Golden House." In *Horti romani: Atti del convegno internazionale: Roma, 4–6 maggio 1995*, edited by Maddalena Cima and Eugenio La Rocca, 333–44, Bullettino della Commissione archeologica comunale di Roma. 6 Supplementi. Rome: "L'Erma" di Bretschneider.

Chaney, William A. 1970. *The Cult of Kingship in Anglo-Saxon England*. Manchester: Manchester University Press.

Chapelot, Jean, ed. 2004. *Vincennes: du manoir capétien à la résidence de Charles V*, Dossiers d'Archéologie, 289. Dijon: Éditions Faton.

———. 2011. "L'enceinte du château de Vincennes (1372–1380): La conception d'un grand projet architectural reconstituée par l'examen du bâti et les relevés de terrain." In *Châteaux et mesures: Actes des 17es journées de castellologie de Bourgogne 23–24 octobre 2010, château de Pierreclos*, edited by Hervé Mouillebouche, 100–23. Chagny: Centre de castellologie de Bourgogne.

Chapelot, Jean, and Elisabeth Lalou. 1996. *Vincennes, aux origines de l'État moderne: actes du Colloque scientifique sur "Les Capétiens et Vincennes au Moyen Âge."* Paris: Presses de l'École normale supérieure.

Charageat, Marguerite. 1950. "Le parc d'Hesdin, création monumentale du XIIIe siècle." *Bulletin de la Société de l'Histoire de l'Art Français*: 94–106.

Charanis, P. 1941. "Coronation and its Constitutional Significance in the Later Roman Empire." *Byzantion: Revue internationale des études byzantines* 15: 49–66.

Charles-Gaffiot, Jacques, Jean-Jacques Aillagon, Chantal Delsol, et al. 2011. *Trônes en majesté: l'autorité et son symbole*. Paris: Cerf.

Christys, Ann R. 2010. "The Meaning of Topography in Umayyad Cordoba." In *Cities, Texts, and Social Networks 400–1500: Experiences and Perceptions of Medieval Urban Space*, edited by Caroline Jane Goodson, 103–24. Farnham: Ashgate.

Ciampini, Giovanni Giustino, 1690–99. *Vetera monumenta: in quibus præcipuè musiva opera sacrarum, profanarumque aedium structura, ac nonnulli antiqui ritus, dissertationibus, iconibusque illustrantur*. 2 vols. Rome: Joannes Jacobus Komarek.

Claridge, Amanda. 1998. *Rome: An Archaeological Guide*, Oxford Archaeological Guides. Oxford: Oxford University Press.

Cohen, Kathleen. 1973. *Metamorphosis of a Death Symbol: The Transi Tomb in the Late Middle Ages and the Renaissance*, California Studies in the History of Art, 15. Berkeley: University of California Press.

Cohen, Meredith. 2010. "Metropolitan Architecture, Demographics and the Urban Identity of Paris in the Thirteenth Century." In *Cities, Texts, and Social Networks 400–1500: Experiences and Perceptions of Medieval Urban Space*, edited by Caroline Jane Goodson, 65–102. Farnham: Ashgate.

———. 2015. *The Sainte-Chapelle and the Construction of Sacral Monarchy: Royal Architecture in Thirteenth-Century Paris*. New York: Cambridge University Press.

Colgrave, Bertram, and R.A.B. Mynors, eds. and trans. 1991. *Bede's Ecclesiastical History of the English People*. Rev. ed. Oxford Medieval Texts. Oxford: Clarendon Press.

Collingwood, R. G., R. P. Wright, and R.S.O. Tomlin. 1995. *The Roman Inscriptions of Britain, Volume I, Inscriptions on Stone*. New ed. Oxford: Clarendon Press.

Collins, H.E.L. 2000. *The Order of the Garter 1348–1461: Chivalry and Politics in Later Medieval England*, Oxford Historical Monographs. Oxford: Clarendon Press.

Collins, Mark, Philip Emery, Christopher Phillpotts, et al. 2012. "The King's High Table at the Palace of Westminster." *Antiquaries Journal* 92: 197–243.

Colvin, Howard Montagu. 1983. "The 'Court Style' in Medieval English Architecture: A Review." In *English Court Culture in the Later Middle Ages*, edited by James Sherborne and V. J. Scattergood. London: Duckworth.

———. 1986. "Royal Gardens in Medieval England." In *Medieval Gardens*, edited by E. B. MacDougall, 7–22. Washington, DC: Dumbarton Oaks. Reprinted: Howard Montagu Colvin, 1999. *Essays in English Architectural History*, 1–12. New Haven: Yale University Press.

———. 1991. *Architecture and the After-Life*. New Haven and London: Yale University Press.

Cómez, Rafael. 2006. *El Alcázar del Rey Don Pedro*. 2nd ed., Arte hispalense, 66. Seville.

Copeland, Tim. 1988. "The North Oxfordshire Grim's Ditch: A Fieldwork Survey." *Oxoniensia* 53: 277–92.

———. 2002. *Iron Age and Roman Wychwood: The Land of Satavacus and Bellicia*. Charlbury: Wychwood Press.

Cormack, Robin. 2000. *Byzantine Art*. Oxford: Oxford University Press.

Cox, John Charles. 1905. *The Royal Forests of Medieval England*, Antiquaries Books. London: Methuen.

Cramp, Rosemary. 1993. "The Hall in Beowulf and Archaeology." In *Heroic Poetry in the Anglo-Saxon Period: Studies in Honor of Jess B. Bessinger, Jr.*, edited by Helen Damico and John Leyerle, 331–46, Studies in Medieval Culture, 32. Kalamazoo, MI: Medieval Institute Publications.

Creighton, Oliver Hamilton. 2002. *Castles and Landscapes*, The Archaeology of Medieval Europe. London and New York: Continuum.

———. 2009. *Designs upon the Land: Elite Landscapes of the Middle Ages*. Woodbridge: Boydell and Brewer.

Creighton, Oliver Hamilton, and Robert Higham. 2005. *Medieval Town Walls: An Archaeology and Social History of Urban Defence*. Stroud: Tempus.

Crossley, Paul. 2000. "The Politics of Presentation: The Architecture of Charles IV of Bohemia." In *Courts and Regions in Medieval Europe*, edited by S. R. Rees Jones, Richard Marks, and A. J. Minnis, 99–172, York Medieval Press. Woodbridge: Boydell.

Crossley, Paul, and Zoë Opačić. 2005. "Prague as a New Capital." In *Prague: The Crown of Bohemia, 1347–1437*, edited by Barbara Drake Boehm and Jiři Fajt, 58–73. New Haven: Yale University Press.

Crouzet-Pavan, Elisabeth. 2004. "Le palais des doges et Venise: les problématiques d'un effet de répresentation." In *Les palais dans la ville: Espaces urbains et lieux de la puissance publique dans la Méditerranée médiévale*, edited by Patrick Boucheron, Jacques Chiffoleau, Theis Valérie, et al., 231–48, Collection d'histoire et d'archéologie médiévales, 13. Lyon: Presses Universitaires de Lyon.

Crumlin-Pedersen, Olof, and Birgitte Munch Thye, eds. 1995. *The Ship as Symbol in Prehistoric and Medieval Scandinavia*. Copenhagen: National Museum of Denmark.

Cummins, John. 1988. *The Hound and the Hawk: The Art of Medieval Hunting*. London: Phoenix Press.

———. 2002. "Veneurs s'en vont en Paradis: Medieval Hunting and the 'Natural' Landscape." In *Inventing Medieval Landscapes: Senses of Place in Western Europe*, edited by John Howe and Michael Wolfe, 33–56. Gainesville: University of Florida Press.

Cunliffe, Barry W. 1971. *Fishbourne: A Roman Palace and Its Garden*. London: Thames and Hudson.

Ćurčić, Slobodan. 1987. "Some Palatine Aspects of the Cappella Palatina in Palermo." *Dumbarton Oaks Papers* 41: 125–44.

———. 2010. *Architecture in the Balkans from Diocletian to Süleyman the Magnificent*. New Haven: Yale University Press.

Curl, James Stevens. 2002. *Death and Architecture*. New ed. Stroud: Sutton.

Dace, Richard. August 2001. "The Foresters of Cannock in the Eleventh and Twelfth Centuries." *Prosopon: Newsletter of the Unit for Prosopographical Research* 12: unpaginated.

Dagron, Gilbert. 1996. *Empereur et prêtre: Étude sur le 'césaropapisme' byzantin*. Paris: Gallimard.

———. 2003. *Emperor and Priest: The Imperial Office in Byzantium*, trans. Jean Birrell. Cambridge: Cambridge University Press.

Dark, Ken, and Jan Kostenec. 2009. "The Haghia Sophia Project, Istanbul, 2004–8." *Bulletin of British Byzantine Studies* 35: 56–68.

Davies, Penelope J. E. 2000. *Death and the Emperor: Roman Imperial Funerary Monuments from Augustus to Marcus Aurelius*. Cambridge: Cambridge University Press.

Dawood, N. J., trans. 1968. *The Koran*. 3rd ed., Penguin Classics. Harmondsworth: Penguin.

De Franceschini, M., and G. Veneziano. 2011. *Villa Adriana. Architettura celeste: gli secreti degli solstizi*. Rome: L'Erma di Bretschneider.

De Franceschini, Marina. 1991. *Villa Adriana: Mosaici, pavimenti, edifici*, Bibliotheca Archaeologica, 9. Rome: "L'Erma" di Bretschneider.

Dectot, Xavier. 2009. *Les tombeaux des familles royales de la péninsule ibérique au Moyen Âge*, Histoires de famille: La parenté au Moyen Âge. Turnhout: Brepols.

Deér, József. 1959. *The Dynastic Porphyry Tombs of the Norman Period in Sicily*. Translated by Gerd Aage Gillhoff, Dumbarton Oaks Studies, 5. Cambridge, MA: Harvard University Press.

Delehaye, Hippolyte. 1933. *Les origines du culte des martyrs*. Rev. ed., Subsidia hagiographica, 20. Bruxelles: Société des Bollandistes.

Deliyannis, Deborah Mauskopf. 2009. *Ravenna in Late Antiquity*. Cambridge: Cambridge University Press.

Delorenzi, Paolo. 2011. *Venice: The Doge's Palace*. 2nd ed. Venice and Milan: Skira.

Demetz, P. 1997. *Prague in Black and Gold*. London: Allen Lane.

Demouy, Patrick. 2005. *Genèse d'une cathédrale: les archevêques de Reims et leur église aux XIe et XIIe siècles*. Langres: Dominique Guéniot.

Depreux, Philippe. 1991. "Saint Rémi et la royauté carolingienne." *Revue historique* 285: 235–60.

Derex, Jean-Michel. 1997. *Histoire du Bois de Vincennes: La forêt du roi et le bois du peuple de Paris*. Paris: L'Harmattan.

Devèze, Michel. 1966. "Forêts françaises et forêts allemandes: Étude historique comparée, première partie." *Revue historique* 235: 347–80.

Devroey, Jean-Pierre, and Nicolas Schroeder. February 2012. "Beyond Royal Estates and Monasteries: Land-ownership in the Early Medieval Ardennes." *Early Medieval Europe* 20 (1): 39–69.

Dickie, James. 1968. "The Hispano-Arab Garden: Its Philosophy and Function." *Bulletin of the School of Oriental and African Studies* 31 (2): 237–48.

———. 1981. "The Alhambra: Some Reflections Prompted by a Recent Study by Oleg Grabar." In *Studia Arabica et Islamica: Festschrift for Iḥsān 'Abbās on his Sixtieth Birthday*, edited by Wadad al-Qadi, 127–49. Beirut: American University of Beirut.

———. 1992. "The Palaces of the Alhambra." In *al-Andalus: the Art of Islamic Spain*, edited by Jerrilynn D. Dodds, 135–51. New York: Metropolitan Museum of Art.

Diederich, Toni. 1984. *Rheinische Städtesiegel*, Jahrbuch des Rheinischer Vereins für Denkmalpflege und Landschaftsschutz, 1984–5. Neuss: Neusser Druckerei und Verlag.

Dittelbach, Thomas. 1999. "Der Dom in Monreale als Krönungskirche: Kunst und Zeremoniell des 12. Jahrhunderts in Sizilien." *Zeitschrift für Kunstgeschichte* 62 (4): 464–93.

———. 2003. *Rex imago Christi: der Dom von Monreale: Bildsprachen und Zeremoniell in Mosaikkunst und Architektur*. Wiesbaden: Reichert.

———, ed. 2011a. *Die Cappella Palatina in Palermo: Geschichte, Kunst, Funktionen: Forschungsergebnisse der Restaurierung*. Künzelsau: Swiridoff.

———. 2011b. "The Ruler's Throne—Topology and Utopia." In *Die Cappella Palatina in Palermo: Geschichte, Kunst, Funktionen: Forschungsergebnisse der Restaurierung*, edited by Thomas Dittelbach, 534–43. Künzelsau: Swiridoff.

Dittelbach, Thomas, and Dorothée Sack. 2005. *The Lower Church of Palermo's Palatine Chapel*. Künzelsau: Swiridoff.

Dixon, Philip. 1996. "Design in Castle-Building: The Controlling of Access to the Lord." *Château Gaillard* 18: 47–57.

Dodds, Jerrilynn D. 1990. *Architecture and Ideology in Early Medieval Spain*. University Park: Pennsylvania State University Press.

———. 1992. "The Great Mosque of Cordoba." In *al-Andalus: The Art of Islamic Spain*, edited by Jerrilynn Denise Dodds, 11–25. New York: Metropolitan Museum of Art.

Dopsch, Heinz. 1995. "'. . . in sedem Karinthani ducatus intronizavi . . .': Zum ältesten gesicherten Nachweis der Herzogseinsetzung in Kärnten." In *Regensburg, Bayern und Europa. Festschrift für Kurt Reindel zum 70. Geburtstag*, edited by Lothar Kolmer and Peter Segl, 103–36. Regensburg: Universitätsverlag.

Dowling, Abigail P. 2012. "Landscape of Luxuries: Mahaut d'Artois's (1302–1329) Management and Use of the Park at Hesdin." In *Rural Space in the Middle Ages and Early Modern Age: The Spatial Turn in Premodern Studies*, edited by Albrecht Classen and Christopher R. Clason, 367–87, Fundamentals of Medieval and Early Modern Culture, 9. Berlin: De Gruyter.

Dragoun, Zdeněk. 2009. "Romanesque Prague and New Archaeological Discoveries." In *Prague and Bohemia: Medieval Art, Architecture and Cultural Exchange in Central Europe*, edited by Zoë Opačić, 34–47, British Archaeological Association Conference Transactions Series, 32. Leeds: Maney Publishing.

Driscoll, Stephen T. 2004. "The Archaeological Context of Assembly in Early Medieval Scotland—Scone and Its Comparanda." In *Assembly Places and Practices in Medieval Europe*, edited by Aliki Pantos and Sarah Semple, 73–94. Dublin: Four Courts Press.

Dubská, Gabriela ed. 2003. *The Story of Prague Castle*. Prague: Prague Castle Administration.

Duceppe-Lamarre, François. 2008. "Paysages et réserve cynégétique d'un lieu de pouvoir: Hesdin (Artois) à la fin du Moyen Âge." In *Le château, autour et alentours (XIVe–XVIe siècles): paysage, parc, jardin et domaine*, edited by Jean-Marie Cauchies and Jacqueline Guisset, 119–34. Turnhout: Brepols.

Duchesne, Louis, and Cyrille Vogel, eds. 1886-1957. *Le Liber Pontificalis: Texte, introduction et commentaire*. 3 vols, Bibliothèque des Écoles Françaises d'Athènes et de Rome, 2nd series. Paris: Ernest Thorin.

Duffy, Mark. 2003. *Royal Tombs of Medieval England*. Stroud: Tempus.

Dufraigne, Pierre. 1994. *Adventus Augusti, adventus Christi: Recherche sur l'exploitation idéologique et littéraire d'un cérémonial dans l'antiquité tardive*. Paris: Institut d'Études Augustiniennes.

Duggan, Joseph J., ed. 2005. *La Chanson de Roland*. 3 vols, The French Corpus. Turnhout: Brepols.

Duindam, Jeroen Frans Jozef. 1994. *Myths of Power: Norbert Elias and the Early Modern European Court*. Translated by Lorri S. Granger and Gerard T. Moran. Amsterdam: Amsterdam University Press.

Dunbar, John Greenwell. 1999. *Scottish Royal Palaces: The Architecture of the Royal Residences during the Late Medieval and Early Renaissance Periods*. East Linton: Tuckwell.

Durand, René, and André Bellessort, eds. 1948–57. *Virgile, Enéide*. 6th ed. 2 vols. Paris: Les Belles Lettres.

Durdík, Tomas. 1998. "A Few Remarks about the Structural Aspects of Karlštejn." In *Magister Theodoricus, Court Painter of Emperor Charles IV: Decorations of the Sacred Spaces at Castle Karlštejn: [Exhibition] Convent of St. Agnes of Bohemia, 12 November 1997–26 April 1998* edited by Jiří Fajt, 35–43, National Gallery in Prague Collection of Old Masters. [Prague]: National Gallery in Prague.

Dutton, Paul E., trans. 2004. *Carolingian Civilisation: A Reader*. 2nd ed. Peterborough, Ontario: Broadview.

Dutton, Paul Edward. 1983. "*Illustre civitatis et populi exemplum*: Plato's Timaeus and the Transmission from Calcidius to the End of the Twelfth Century of a Tripartite Scheme of Society." *Mediaeval Studies* 45: 79–119.

Duval, Noël. 1978. "Comment reconnaître un palais impérial ou royal? Ravenna et Piazza Armerina." *Felix Ravenna* 115: 27–62.

Dvoráková, Vlasta. 1964. "The Ideological Design of Karlštejn Castle and Its Pictorial Decoration." In *Gothic Mural Painting in Bohemia and Moravia, 1300–1378*, edited by Vlasta Dvoráková, Josef Krasá, Anez Cka Merhautova-Livorova, et al. London: Oxford University Press.

Dyggve, Ejnar. 1948. "The Royal Barrows at Jelling." *Antiquity*: 190–97.

Echevarria, Ana. December 2008. "Painting Politics in the Alhambra." *Medieval Encounters* 14 (2–3): 199–218.

Edwards, Nancy. 1990. *The Archaeology of Early Medieval Ireland*. London: Batsford.

Elias, Norbert. 1975. *Die höfische Gesellschaft: Untersuchungen zur Soziologie des Königtums und der höfischen Aristokratie mit einer Einleitung*. 3rd ed, Soziologische Texte 54. Darmstadt: Luchterhand.

———. 1983. *The Court Society*. Translated by Edmund Jephcott. Rev. ed. New York: Pantheon Books.

Elsner, Jaś. 1998. *Imperial Rome and Christian Triumph: The Art of the Roman Empire, AD 100–450*. Oxford: Oxford University Press.

Enderlein, Lorenz. 2001. "'In eternam et immortalem memoriam'—das Brückentor zu Capua und die Angiovinen." In *Burg und Kirche zur Stauferzeit: Akten der 1. Landauer Staufertagung 1997*, edited by Volker Herzner and Jürgen Krüger. Regensburg.

Enright, Michael J. 1983. "The Sutton Hoo Whetstone Sceptre: A Study in Iconography and Cultural Milieu." *Anglo-Saxon England* 11: 119–34.

———. 1985. *Iona, Tara and Soissons: The Origin of the Royal Anointing Ritual*. Berlin: Walter de Gruyter.

———. 2006. *The Sutton Hoo Sceptre and the Roots of Celtic Kingship Theory*. Dublin: Four Courts Press.

Ericsson, Ingolf, and Markus Sanke, eds. 2004. *Aktuelle Forschungen zum ehemaligen Reichs- und Königskloster Lorsch*, Arbeiten der Hessische Historische Kommission, new series 24. Darmstadt: Hessische Historische Kommission.

Erkens, Franz-Reiner. 2005. "Sakralkönigtum und sakrales Königtum: Anmerkungen und Hinweise." In *Das frühmittelalterliche Königtum: Ideelle und religiöse Grundlagen*, edited by Franz-Reiner Erkens, 1–8, Ergänzungsbände zum Reallexikon der Germanischen Altertumskunde, 49. Berlin: De Gruyter.

———. 2006. *Die Herrschersakralität im Mittelalter: von den Anfängen bis zum Investiturstreit*. Stuttgart: Kohlhammer.

———. 2009 (for 2008). "Königskrönung und Königsordnung im späten Mittelalter." *Zeitschrift der Aachener Geschichtsvereins* 110: 27–64.

Erlande-Brandenburg, Alain. 1975. *Le roi est mort: Étude sur les funérailles, les sépultures et les tombeaux des rois*, Bibliothèque de la Société Française d'Archéologie, 7. Paris: Arts et Métiers Graphiques.

Español, Francesca. 2014. "Le programme architectural: un palais pour vivre et gouverner." In *Un palais dans la ville: vol. 1: Le palais des rois de Majorque à Perpignan; vol. 2: Perpignan des rois de Majorque*, edited by Aymat Catafu and Olivier Passarius, I, 115–34. 2 vols. Perpignan: Editions Trabucaire.

Ettinghausen, Richard, and Oleg Grabar. 1987. *The Art and Architecture of Islam, 650–1250*. Harmondsworth: Penguin.

Everitt, Alan Milner. 1986. *Continuity and Colonization: The Evolution of Kentish Settlement*, Communities, Contexts and Cultures, Leicester Studies in English Local History. Leicester: Leicester University Press.

Ewert, Christian. 2009. "Spolien, ihre islamischen Nachschöpfungen und ihre Musterschemata in den Hauptmoscheen von Córdoba und Qayrawan." In *Spolien im Umkreis der Macht: Akten der Tagung in Toledo vom 21.-22.9.2006 = Spolia en el entorno des poder: actas del coloquio en Toledo del 21 al 22 de septiembre 2006*, edited by Thomas G. Schattner and Fernando Valdés Fernández, 287–304. Mainz: Philipp von Zabern.

Ewig, Eugen. 1976-79. "Les Ardennes au haut Moyen Âge." In *Spätantikes und fränkisches Gallien: Gesammelte Schriften, 1952-1973*, edited by Eugen Ewig and Hartmut Atsma, 523–54. 3 vols., Beihefte der Francia, 3. Munich: Artemis.

Fajt, Jiří, and Hlaváčová. 2003. "The Family of Charles IV in the Stairway of the Karlštejn Great Tower." In *Court Chapels of the High and Late Middle Ages and Their Artistic Decoration = Dvorské kaple vrcholného a pozdního středověku a jejich umělecká výzdoba*, edited by Jiří Fajt and Klášter Anězský, 16–20. [Prague]: National Gallery in Prague.

Fajt, Jiří, Markus Hörsch, Andrea Langer, et al., eds. 2006. *Karl IV. Kaiser von Gottes Gnaden: Kunst und Repräsentation des Hauses Luxemburg 1310—1437*. Munich; Berlin: Deutscher Kunstverlag.

Fajt, Jiří, and Jan Royt, eds. 1998a. *Magister Theodoricus, Court Painter of Emperor Charles IV: Decorations of the Sacred Spaces at Castle Karlštejn: [Exhibition] Convent of St. Agnes of Bohemia, 12 November 1997–26 April 1998*, National Gallery in Prague Collection of Old Masters. Prague: National Gallery in Prague.

———. 1998b. "The Pictorial Decoration of the Great Tower of Karlštejn Castle." In *Magister Theodoricus, Court Painter of Emperor Charles IV: Decorations of the Sacred Spaces at Castle Karlštejn: [Exhibition] Convent of St. Agnes of Bohemia,12 November 1997–26 April 1998*, edited by Jiří Fajt, 107–205, National Gallery in Prague Collection of Old Masters. Prague: National Gallery in Prague.

Fajt, Jiří, Jan Royt, and Libor Gottfried. 1998. *The Sacred Halls of Karlštejn Castle*. Prague: Central Bohemia Cultural Heritage Institute in Prague.

Falkenstein, Ludwig. 1966. *Der 'Lateran' der karolingischen Pfalz zu Aachen*, Kölner historische Abhandlungen, 13. Cologne and Graz: Böhlau.

———. 1981. *Karl der Grosse und die Entstehung des Aachener Marienstiftes*. Paderborn: Ferdinand Schöningh.

Faral, Edmond, ed. and trans. 1932. *Ermold le Noir: Poème sur Louis le Pieux et épîtres au Roi Pépin*, Les Classiques de l'histoire de France au Moyen Âge. Paris: Honoré Champion.

Farlati, Daniel, Philippus Riceputi, Jacopo Coleti, et al. 1751. *Illyrici sacri tomus primus [-secundus]: Ecclesia Salonitana ab ejus exordio usque ad sæculum quartum Ærœ Christianæ*. Venice: Apud Sebastianum Coleti.

Farrar, Linda. 1998. *Ancient Roman Gardens*. Stroud: Sutton.

Fawcett, Richard, ed. 2001. *Stirling Castle: The Restoration of the Great Hall*, CBA Research report, 130. York: Council for British Archaeology.

Fawcett, Richard, and C. J. Tabraham. 1999. *Stirling Castle*. London: B.T. Batsford Ltd./ Historic Scotland.

Featherstone, Jeffrey Michael. 2005. "The Chrysotriklinos Seen through *De Cerimoniis*." In *Zwischen Polis, Provinz und Peripherie: Beiträge zur byzantinischen Geschichte und Kultur*, edited by Lars M. Hoffmann and Anuscha Monchizadeh, 845–52, Mainzer Veröffentlichungen zur Byzantinistik, 7. Wiesbaden: Harrassowitz.

———. 2006. "The Great Palace as Reflected in the *De Cerimoniis*." In *Visualisierungen von Herrschaft: frühmittelalterliche Residenzen: Gestalt und Zeremoniell: internationales Kolloquium 3./4. Juni 2004 in Istanbul*, edited by Franz Alto Bauer, 47–62, Byzas, 5. Istanbul: Ege Yayınları.

Fenske, Lutz, Jörg Jarnut, and Matthias Wemhhoff, eds. 2001. *Deutsche Königspfalzen, Band 5: Splendor Palatii: Neue Forschungen zu Paderborn und anderen Pfalzen der Karolingerzeit*. Göttingen: Vandenhoeck and Ruprecht.

Fenucci, Fabrizio, and Marcello Simonetta. 2007. "The Studiolo of Urbino: A Visual Guide." In *Federico da Montefeltro and his Library*, edited by Marcello Simonetta, 88–101. Milan: Biblioteca Apostolica Vaticana.

Fenwick, Joe, and Conor Newman. 2002. "Geomagnetic Survey on the Hill of Tara, Co. Meath, 1998-9." In *Discovery Programme Reports* 6, 1–17. Dublin : Royal Irish Academy / Discovery Programme.

Fitzpatrick, Elizabeth. 2003. "Royal Inauguration Assemblies and the Church in Medieval Ireland." In *Political Assemblies in the Earlier Middle Ages*, edited by Paul S. Barnwell and Marco Mostert, 73–93, Studies in the Early Middle Ages, 7. Turnhout: Brepols.

———. 2004a. *Royal Inauguration in Gaelic Ireland c. 1100-1600*. Woodbridge: Boydell Press.

————. 2004b. "Royal Inauguration Mounds in Medieval Ireland: Antique Landscape and Tradition." In *Assembly Places and Practices in Medieval Europe*, edited by Aliki Pantos and Sarah Semple, 44–72. Dublin: Four Courts Press.

Fletcher, John. 2011. *Gardens of Earthly Delight: The History of Deer Parks*. Oxford: Windgather Press.

Fleury, Michel, Albert France-Lanord, and Annie Blanc. 1998. *Les trésors mérovingiens de la basilique de Saint-Denis*. Woippy: Gérard Klopp.

Foster, Richard. 1991. *Patterns of Thought: The Hidden Meaning of the Great Pavement of Westminster Abbey*. London: Cape.

Foster, Sally. 1998. *The St Andrews Sarcophagus: A Pictish Masterpiece and Its International Connections*. Dublin: Four Courts Press.

Foucher, Jean-Pascal. 1996. "Le bois de Vincennes du IXe au XVe siècle." In *Vincennes, aux origines de l'État moderne: Actes du colloque scientifique sur "Les Capétiens et Vincennes au Moyen Âge,"* edited by Jean Chapelot and Elisabeth Lalou, 23–51. Paris: Presses de l'École Normale Supérieure.

Fouracre, Paul, ed. 2005. *New Cambridge Medieval History: Volume 1, c. 500–c. 700*. Cambridge: Cambridge University Press.

Fradley, Michael. 2006. "Space and Structure at Caernarfon Castle." *Medieval Archaeology* 50: 165–78.

Fraser Jenkins, A. D. 1970. "Cosimo de' Medici's Patronage of Architecture." *Journal of the Warburg and Courtauld Institutes* 33: 162–70.

Fried, Johannes. 1997. "Kaiser Friedrich II. als Jäger." In *Jagd und höfische Kultur im Mittelalter*, edited by Werner Rösener, 149–66, Veröffentlichungen des Max-Planck-Instituts für Geschichte, 135. Göttingen: Vandenhoeck and Ruprecht.

Friedel, Birgit. 2007. *Die Nürnberger Burg: Geschichte, Baugeschichte und Archäologie*, Schriften des Deutschen Burgenmuseums, 1. Petersberg: Imhof.

Frodsham, Paul, and Colm O'Brien, eds. 2005. *Yeavering: People, Power and Place*. Stroud: Tempus.

Frolow, A. 1961. *La relique de la Vraie Croix: Recherches sur le développement d'un culte*, Archives de l'Orient chrétien, 7. Paris: Institut Français d'Études Byzantines.

Frye, Richard N., trans. 2005. *Ibn Fadlan's Journey to Russia: A Tenth-Century Traveler from Baghad to the Volga River*. Princeton: Markus Wiener Publishers.

Fulk, R. D., Robert E. Bjork, and John D. Niles, eds. 2008. *Klaeber's Beowulf and The Fight at Finnsburg*. 4th ed. Toronto, Buffalo, and London: University of Toronto Press.

Gaborit-Chopin, Danielle. 1987. *Regalia: les instruments du sacre des rois de France, les "Honneurs de Charlemagne,"* Monographies des musées de France, 0297–3995. Paris: Ministère de la Culture et de la Communication, Éditions de la Réunion des Musées Nationaux.

Gagnière, Sylvain. 1988. "Les jardins et la ménagerie du Palais des Papes d'après les comptes de la Chambre apostolique." In *Avignon au Moyen Âge: textes et documents*, edited by Hervé Aliquot, 103–09, Archives du Sud. Avignon: Aubanel.

Gajdošova, Jana. 2012. "Imperial Memory and the Charles Bridge: Establishing Royal Ceremony for Future Kings." *Kunstetexte.de* 5.

Ganshof, François-Louis. 1964. *Feudalism*. Translated by Philip Grierson. 3rd ed. New York: Harper and Row.

Ganz, David, trans. 2008. *Two Lives of Charlemagne*, Penguin Classics. London: Penguin.

Gasser, Stephan. 2007. "L'architecture de la Sainte-Chapelle: État de la question concernant sa datation, son maître d'oeuvre et sa place dans l'histoire de l'architecture." In *La Sainte-Chapelle de Paris: Royaume de France ou Jérusalem céleste?*, edited by Christine Hediger, 157–80, Culture et Société médiévales, 10. Turnhout: Brepols.

Gastgeber, Christian. 2005. "Die Heilige Lanze im byzantinischen Osten." In *Die Heilige Lanze in Wien: Insignie, Reliquie, "Schicksalsspeer,"* edited by Franz Kirchweger, 71–110, Schriften des Kunsthistorisches Museum Wien, 9. Vienna and Paris: Skira.

Gauert, Adolf. 1965. "Zur Struktur und Topographie der Königspfalzen." In *Deutsche Königspfalzen: Beiträge zu ihrer historischen und archäologischen Erforschung*, Vol. 2, 1–60, Veröffentlichungen des Max-Planck-Instituts für Geschichte, 11.2. Göttingen: Vandenhoeck and Ruprecht.

Gautier, Alban. 2006. "Game Parks in Sussex and the Godwinesons." *Anglo-Norman Studies* 29: 51–64.

Geary, Patrick J. 2011. *Furta sacra: Thefts of Relics in the Central Middle Ages*. Rev. ed. Princeton: Princeton University Press.

Gem, Richard D. H., and W. T. Ball. 1980. "The Romanesque Rebuilding of Westminster Abbey." *Anglo-Norman Studies* 3: 33–60, 203–7.

Gesbert, Elise. 2003. "Les jardins du Moyen Âge: du XIe au début du XIVe siècle." *Cahiers de Civilisation Médiévale, Xe-XIIe siècles* 46 (184): 381–408.

Giesecke, Annette Lucia. 2007. *The Epic City: Urbanism, Utopia, and the Garden in Ancient Greece and Rome*, Hellenic Studies, 21. Cambridge, MA: Harvard University Press.

Giesey, Ralph E. 1960. *The Royal Funeral Ceremony in Renaissance France*, Travaux d'Humanisme et Renaissance, 37. Geneva: Droz.

Gilbert, John M. 1979. *Hunting and Hunting Reserves in Medieval Scotland*. Edinburgh: John Donald.

Girouard, Mark. 1978. *Life in the English Country House: A Social and Architectural History*. New Haven: Yale University Press.

Given-Wilson, Chris. 2004. *Chronicles: the Writing of History in Medieval England*. London: Hambledon and London.

Glare, P.G.W., ed. 1990. *Oxford Latin Dictionary*. Oxford: Oxford University Press.

Gleeson, Patrick. 2012. "Constructing Kingship in Early Medieval Ireland: Power, Place and Ideology." *Medieval Archaeology* 56: 1–33.

Gockel, Michael. 1970. *Karolingische Königshöfe am Mittelrhein*, Veröffentlichungen des Max-Planck-Instituts für Geschichte, 31. Göttingen: Vandenhoeck and Ruprecht.

Godman, Peter, ed. and trans. 1982. *Alcuin: the Bishops, Kings, and Saints of York*, Oxford Medieval Texts. Oxford: Clarendon Press.

Götze, Heinz. 1998. *Castel del Monte: Geometric Marvel of the Middle Ages*. Translated by Mary Schäfer. Munich: Prestel.

Grabar, André. 1946. *Martyrium: Recherches sur le culte des reliques et l'art chrétien antique*. Paris: Collège de France.

Grabar, Oleg. 1987. *The Formation of Islamic Art*. Rev. ed. New Haven: Yale University Press.

———. 1992. *The Alhambra*. 2nd ed. Sebastopol, CA: Solipsist Press.

Grant, Lindy, and Richard Mortimer, eds. 2002. *Westminster Abbey: The Cosmati Pavements*, Courtauld Institute Research Papers, 3. Aldershot: Ashgate.

Grant, Raymond. 1991. *The Royal Forests of England*. Stroud: Sutton.

Graves, Robert, trans. 1957. *The Twelve Caesars: Gaius Suetonius Tranquillus*, Penguin Classics. Harmondsworth: Penguin.

Grewe, Holger. 1998. "Der Neubeginn archäologischer Ausgrabungen in der Königspfalz Ingelheim." In *Geschichte im Bistum Aachen, 4*, edited by Geschichtsverein für das Bistum Aachen, 7–22. Aachen: Einhard.

———. 1999. "Die Königspfalz zu Ingelheim am Rhein." In *799: Kunst und Kultur der Karolingerzeit: Karl der Grosse und Papst Leo III in Paderborn: Beiträge zum Katalog der Ausstellung Paderborn 1999*, edited by C. Stiegemann and M. Wemhoff, 142–51. Mainz: Philipp von Zabern.

———. 2001. "Die Ausgrabungen in der Königspfalz zu Ingelheim am Rhein." In *Deutsche Königspfalzen, Band 5: Splendor Palatii: Neue Forschungen zu Paderborn und anderen Pfalzen der Karolingerzeit*, edited by Lutz Fenske, Jörg Jarnut, and Matthias Wemhhoff, 155–74. Göttingen: Vandenhoeck and Ruprecht.

———. 2014. "Die Pfalz zu Ingelheim am Rhein: Ausgewählte Baubefunde und ihre Interpretation." In *Karl der Große, Charlemagne, vol. 2: Orte der Macht*, edited by Anon., 188–97. Dresden: Sandstein Verlag.

Grimal, Pierre. 1943. *Les jardins romains à la fin de la République et aux deux premiers siècles de l'Empire: essais sur le naturalisme romain*, Bibliothèque des Écoles Françaises d'Athènes et de Rome, 155. Paris: De Boccard.

Grogan, Eoin. 2008. *The Rath of the Synods, Tara, Co. Meath: Excavations by Seán P. Ó Ríordáin*. Dublin: Wordwell in association with the UCD School of Archaeology.

Grube, Ernst J., and Jeremy Johns. 2005. *The Painted Ceilings of the Cappella Palatina*, Supplement to Islamic Art, 1. Genoa: Bruschettini Foundation for Islamic and Asian Art.

Guérout, Jean. 1949–51. "Le palais de la Cité à Paris des origines à 1417: Essai topographique et archéologique." *Mémoires de la Fédération des Sociétés historiques et archéologiques de Paris et de l'Île de France* 1–3: 57–212 (vol. 1), 21–204 (vol. 2), 7–101 (vol. 3).

Guillaume, Jean, ed. 1991. *L'emploi des ordres dans l'architecture de la Renaissance*. Paris: Picard.

———, ed. 1994. *Architecture et vie sociale: l'organisation intérieure des grandes demeures à la fin du Moyen Âge et à la Renaissance: actes du colloque tenu à Tours du 6 au 10 juin 1988*. Paris: Picard.

Gussone, Nikolaus. 2000. "Ritus, Recht und Geschichtsbewusstein: Thron und Krone in der Tradition Karls des Grossen." In *Krönungen: Könige in Aachen: Geschichte und Mythos*, edited by Mario Kramp, I, 35–47. 2 vols. Mainz: Philipp von Zabern.

Gutkind, Erwin Anton, and Gabriele Gutkind. 1965–72. *International History of City Development*. 7 vols. London: Collier-Macmillan.

Gwynn, L. 1912. "De Sìl Chonairi Móir." *Ériu* 6: 130–43.

Hallam, Elizabeth M. 1982. "Royal Burial and the Cult of Kingship in France and England, 1060–1330." *Journal of Medieval History* 8 (4): 359–80, 393.

Halphen, L., ed. and trans. 2007. *Éginhard, Vie de Charlemagne*. 6th ed. Paris: Les Belles Lettres.

Hamerow, Helena, Helena Hamerow, David Alban Hinton, et al., eds. 2011. *The Oxford Handbook of Anglo-Saxon Archaeology*. Oxford: Oxford University Press.

Harris, Jonathan. 2007. *Constantinople: Capital of Byzantium*. London: Hambledon Continuum.

Harrison, John G. 2011. *Rebirth of a Palace: The Royal Court at Stirling Castle*. Edinburgh: Historic Scotland.

———. n.d. *King of the Castle: Stirling Castle's Landscape Setting*, Stirling Castle Palace: Archaeological and Historical Research 2004–2008. Edinburgh: Historic Scotland.

Harrison, Kenneth. 1998. *Sir Gawain and the Green Knight: A Verse Translation*, Oxford World's Classics. Oxford: Oxford University Press.

Hart, Vaughan. 2008. *Sir John Vanbrugh: Storyteller in Stone*. New Haven and London: Yale University Press.

Harvey, Anthony, and Richard Mortimer, eds. 2003. *The Funeral Effigies of Westminster Abbey*. Rev. ed. Woodbridge: Boydell Press.

Harvey, John. 1981. *Medieval Gardens*. London: Batsford.

Harvey, P.D.A., ed. 2006. *The Hereford World Map: Medieval World Maps and Their Context*. London: British Library Publications.

Hauck, Karl, ed. 1963a. *Deutsche Königspfalzen, Band 1*. Göttingen: Vandenhoeck and Ruprecht.

———. 1963b. "Tiergärten im Pfalzbereich." In *Deutsche Königspfalzen, Band 1*, edited by Karl Hauck, 30–74. Göttingen: Vandenhoeck and Ruprecht.

Haverkamp, Alfred. 1987. "'Heilige Städte' im hohen Mittelalter." In *Mentalitäten im Mittelalter: Methodische und inhaltliche Probleme*, edited by František Graus, 119–56, Vorträge und Forschungen, 35. Sigmaringen: J. Thorbecke. Reprinted: Friedhelm Burgard, Alfred Heit, and Michael Matheus, eds. 1997. *Alfred Haverkamp, Verfassung, Beiträge zur italienischen, deutschen und jüdischen Geschichte im europäischen Mittelalter: dem Autor zur Vollendung des 60. Lebensjahres*, 361–402. Mainz: Philipp von Zabern.

Heckner, Ulrike. 2012. "Der Tempel Salomos in Aachen—Datierung und geometrischer Entwurf der karolingischen Pfalzkapelle." In *Die karolingische Pfalzkapelle in Aachen. Material, Bautechnik, Restaurierung*, edited by Ulrike Heckner and Eva-Maria Beckmann, 25–62. Karlsruhe: Wernersche Verlagsgesellschaft.

Heckner, Ulrike, and Eva-Maria Beckmann, eds. 2012. *Die karolingische Pfalzkapelle in Aachen. Material, Bautechnik, Restaurierung*. Karlsruhe: Wernersche Verlagsgesellschaft.

Hediger, Christine, ed. 2007. *La Sainte-Chapelle de Paris: Royaume de France ou Jérusalem céleste?*, Culture et Société médiévales, 10. Turnhout: Brepols.

Heidenreich, Bernd, and Frank-Lothar Kroll. 2006. *Wahl und Krönung*. Frankfurt: Societäts-Verlag.

Heighway, Caroline. 1984. "Anglo-Saxon Gloucester to AD 1000." In *Studies in Late Anglo-Saxon Settlement*, edited by Margaret L. Faull, 34–53. Oxford: Oxford University Department for External Studies.

Helas, Philippa. 2009. "Der Triumph von Alfonso d'Aragona 1443 in Neapol: zu den Darstellungen herrscherlicher Einzüge zwischen Mittelalter und Renaissance." In *Adventus: Studien zum herrscherlichen Einzug in die Stadt*, edited by Peter Johanek and Angelika Lampen, 133–228, Städterforschung, Reihe A, Darstellungen, 75. Cologne: Böhlau.

Hemsoll, D. 1990. "The Architecture of Nero's Golden House." In *Architecture and Architectural Sculpture in the Roman Empire*, edited by Martin Henig, 10–38, Oxford University Committee for Archaeology monograph, 29. Oxford: Oxbow Books.

Henderson, Isobel. 1998. "*Primus inter Pares*: The St Andrews Sarcophagus and Pictish Sculpture." In *The St Andrews Sarcophagus: A Pictish Masterpiece and Its International Connections*, edited by Sally Foster, 97–167. Dublin: Four Courts Press.

Hernández-Núñez, Juan Carlos, and Alfredo José Morales. 1999. *The Royal Palace of Seville*. London: Scala Publishers in association with Aldeasa S.A.

Herren, Michael. 1991. "The *De Imagine Tetrici* of Walafrid Strabo: Edition and Translation." *Journal of Medieval Latin* 1: 118–39.

Hesberg, Henner von, and Silvio Panciera. 1994. *Das Mausoleum des Augustus: der Bau und seine Inschriften*,

Bayerische Akademie der Wissenschaften. Philosophisch-Historische Klasse, Abhandlungen, 108. Munich: Bayerischen Akademie der Wissenschaften.

Hill, Boyd H., trans. 1972. *Medieval Monarchy in Action: The German Empire from Henry I to Henry IV*. London: George Allen and Unwin.

Hiscock, Nigel. 2000. *The Wise Master Builder: Platonic Geometry in Plans of Medieval Abbeys and Cathedrals*. Aldershot: Ashgate.

Hoade, Eugene, ed. 1952. *Western Pilgrims: The Itineraries of Fr. Simon Fitzsimons (1322–23), a certain Englishman (1344–45), Thomas Brygg (1392), and Notes on Other Authors and Pilgrims*, Publications of the Studium Biblicum Franciscanum, 18. Jerusalem: Franciscan Print Press.

Holck, Per. 2006. "The Oseberg Ship Burial, Norway: New Thoughts on the Skeletons from the Grave Mound." *European Journal of Archaeology* 9 (2–3): 185–210.

Hollister, C. Warren. 2004. "Henry I (1068/9–1135)." In *Oxford Dictionary of National Biography*, edited by Lawrence Goldman, s.n. Oxford: Oxford University Press.

Homolka, Jaromír. 1998. "The Pictorial Decoration of the Palace and the Lesser Tower of Karlštejn Castle." In *Magister Theodoricus, Court Painter of Emperor Charles IV: Decorations of the Sacred Spaces at Castle Karlštejn: [Exhibition] Convent of St. Agnes of Bohemia, 12 November 1997–26 April 1998*, edited by Jiří Fajt, 46–93, National Gallery in Prague Collection of Old Masters. [Prague]: National Gallery in Prague.

Hope-Taylor, Brian. 1977. *Yeavering: An Anglo-British Centre of Early Northumbria*. London: HMSO.

Hope, William Henry St. John. 1913. *Windsor Castle: An Architectural History*. 3 vols. London: Country Life.

———. 1913–14. "The Funeral, Monument, and Chantry Chapel of King Henry the Fifth." *Archaeologia* 65: 129–86.

Hope, William Henry St. John, and Joseph Armitage Robinson. 1907. "On the Funeral Effigies of the Kings and Queens of England, with Special Reference to those in the Abbey Church of Westminster, with a Note on the Westminster Tradition of Identification." *Archaeologia* 60: 517–69.

Hornblower, Simon, and Antony Spawforth, eds. 2003. *The Oxford Classical Dictionary*. Oxford: Oxford University Press.

Howlett, David R. 2002. "The Inscriptions in the Sanctuary Pavement at Westminster." In *Westminster Abbey: The Cosmati Pavements*, edited by Lindy Grant and Richard Mortimer, 100–15, Courtauld Institute Research Papers, 3. Aldershot: Ashgate.

Hugot, Leo. 1965. "Die Pfalz Karls des Großen in Aachen." In *Karl der Grosse: Lebenswerk und Nachleben*, edited by Wolfgang Braunfels, 534–72. Düsseldorf: Schwann.

Hunt, Alice. 2008. *The Drama of Coronation: Medieval Ceremony in Early Modern England*. Cambridge: Cambridge University Press.

Hurlbut, Jesse D. 2001. "The Duke's First Entry: Burgundian Inauguration and Gift." In *Moving Subjects: Processional Performance in the Middle Ages and the Renaissance*, edited by Kathleen M. Ashley and Wim N. M. Hüsken, 155–86, Ludus, 5. Amsterdam: Rodopi.

Hvass, Steen. 2011. *Jelling-Monumenterne: deres Historie og Bevaring*. n.p.: Kulturarvsstyrelsen.

Impey, Edward, ed. 2008. *The White Tower*. New Haven and London: Yale University Press.

Ingstad, Anne Stine. 1995. "The Interpretation of the Oseberg-Find." In *The Ship as Symbol in Prehistoric and Medieval Scandinavia. Papers from an International Research Seminar at the Danish National Museum, Copenhagen, 5th–7th May 1994*, edited by Olof Crumlin-Pedersen and Birgitte Munch Thye, 139–47, Publications from the National Museum, Studies in Archaeology and History, 1. Copenhagen: Nationalmuseet.

Itgenshorst, Tanja. 2005. *Tota illa pompa: der Triumph in der römischen Republik: mit einer CD-ROM, Katalog der Triumphe von 340 bis 19 vor Christus*, Hypomnemata, 161. Göttingen: Vandenhoeck and Ruprecht.

Jackson, Richard A. 1984. *Vive le roi!: A History of the French Coronation from Charles V to Charles X*. Chapel Hill: University of North Carolina Press.

Jacobs, Paul W., II, and Diane Atnally Conlin. 2014. *Campus Martius: The Field of Mars in the Life of Ancient Rome*. New York: Cambridge University Press.

James, Tom Beaumont, and Chris Gerrard. 2007. *Clarendon: Landscape of Kings*. Macclesfield: Windgather Press.

Jarnut, Jörg. 1985. "Die frühmittelalterliche Jagd unter rechts- und sozialgeschichtlichen Aspekten." In *L'uomo di fronte al mondo animale nell'alto Medioevo*, 765–808, Settimane di studio del Centro Italiano di Studi sull'Alto Medioevo, 31. Spoleto: Centro Italiano di Studi sull'Alto Medioevo. Reprinted: Jörg Jarnut. 2002.

Herrschaft und Ethnogenese im Frühmittelalter: Gesammelte Aufsätze: Festgabe zum 60. Geburtstag, 375–418. Münster: Scriptorium.

Jashemski, Wilhelmina F., and Stanley A. Jashemski. 1979. *The Gardens of Pompeii: Herculaneum and the Villas Destroyed by Vesuvius*. New Rochelle, NY: Caratzas Brothers.

Johns, Jeremy. 2011. "The Bible, the Qur'ān, and the Royal Eunuchs in the Cappella Palatina." In *Die Cappella Palatina in Palermo: Geschichte, Kunst, Funktionen. Forschungsergebnisse der Restaurierung*, edited by Thomas Dittelbach, 560–70. Künzelsau: Swiridoff.

Johnson, Mark Joseph. 2009. *The Roman Imperial Mausoleum in Late Antiquity*. Cambridge: Cambridge University Press.

Jones, A.H.M. 1962. *Constantine and the Conversion of Europe*. Harmondsworth: Penguin.

———. 1964. *The Later Roman Empire, 248–602: A Social, Economic and Administrative Survey*. 2 vols. Oxford: Blackwell.

Jones, Graham. 2010. "A 'Common of Hunting'? Forests, Lordship, and Community before and after the Conquest." In *Forests and Chases of England and Wales to circa 1500*, edited by John Langton and Graham Jones, 36–67. Oxford: St. John's College.

Jones, Mark Wilson. 2000. "Genesis and Mimesis: The Design of the Arch of Constantine in Rome." *Journal of the Society of Architectural Historians* 59 (1): 50–77.

Jones, Michael E., ed. 2000 *New Cambridge Medieval History: Volume 6, c. 1300–c. 1415*. Cambridge: Cambridge University Press.

Jordan, Alyce A. 2002. *Visualizing Kingship in the Windows of the Sainte-Chapelle*, Publications of the International Center of Medieval Art, 5. Turnhout: Brepols.

Jørgensen, Mogens Schou. 1997. "Vikingetidsbroen i Ravning Enge: nye undersøgelser." *Nationalmuseets arbejdsmark*: 74–87.

Jotischky, Andrew, and Caroline Hull. 2005. *The Penguin Historical Atlas of the Medieval World*. London: Penguin.

Kaeuper, Richard. 1982-2004. "Forest Law." In *Dictionary of the Middle Ages*, edited by Joseph R. Strayer, V, 127–31. 13 vols. and supplement. New York: Charles Scribner's Sons.

Kantorowicz, Ernst Hartwig. 1944. "The 'King's Advent' and the Enigmatic Panels in the Doors of Santa Sabina." *Art Bulletin* 26 (4): 207–31. Reprinted: Ernst Hartwig Kantorowicz. 1965. *Selected Studies*, 37–75. New York: J. J. Augustin.

———. 1957. *The King's Two Bodies: A Study in Mediaeval Political Theology*. Princeton: Princeton University Press. Reprint, 1997, with a new preface by William Chester Jordan.

Kaspers, H. 1957. *Comitatus nemoris: die Waldgrafschaft zwischen Maas und Rhein: Untersuchungen zur Rechtsgeschichte der Forstgebiete des Aachen-Dürener Landes einschliesslich der Bürge und Ville*, Beiträge zur Geschichte des Dürener Landes 7. Düren and Aachen: Aachener Geschichtsverein and Dürener Geschichtsverein.

Kavka, František. 1998. "The Role and Function of Karlštejn Castle as Documented in Records from the Reign of Charles IV." In *Magister Theodoricus, Court Painter of Emperor Charles IV: Decorations of the Sacred Spaces at Castle Karlštejn: [Exhibition] Convent of St. Agnes of Bohemia, 12 November 1997–26 April 1998,* edited by Jiří Fajt, 15–33, National Gallery in Prague Collection of Old Masters. [Prague]: National Gallery in Prague.

Keen, Laurence. 2010. "The Chapter House Decorated Tile Pavement." In *Westminster Abbey Chapter House: The History, Art and Architecture of a 'Chapter House beyond Compare,'* edited by Warwick Rodwell and Richard Mortimer, 209–36. London: Society of Antiquaries.

Keevill, Graham D. 2004. *The Tower of London Moat: Archaeological Excavations 1995–9*, Historical Royal Palaces Monograph, 1. Oxford: Oxford Archaeology with Historic Royal Palaces.

Kelly, J.N.D. 1986. *The Oxford Dictionary of Popes*. Oxford: Oxford University Press.

Kemp, Eric Waldram. 1979. *Canonization and Authority in the Western Church*. Westport, CT: Hyperion Press.

Kempen, Matthias. 2012. "Statik und neuer Ringanker." In *Die karolingische Pfalzkapelle in Aachen. Material, Bautechnik, Restaurierung*, edited by Ulrike Heckner and Eva-Maria Beckmann, 229–36. Karlsruhe: Wernersche Verlagsgesellschaft.

Kendall, Calvin B., and Peter S. Wells, eds. 1992. *Voyage to the Other World: The Legacy of Sutton Hoo*. Minneapolis: University of Minnesota Press.

Kennedy, Hugh. 2010. "How to Found an Islamic City." In *Cities, Texts, and Social Networks 400–1500: Experiences and Perceptions of Medieval Urban Space*, edited by Caroline Jane Goodson, 45–64. Farnham: Ashgate.

Kerscher, Gottfried. 2000. *Architektur als Repräsentation: spätmittelalterliche Palastbaukunst zwischen Pracht und zeremoniellen Voraussetzungen: Avignon, Mallorca, Kirchenstaat*. Tübingen: Wasmuth.

⸻. 2002. "Le Palais des Papes, entre les palais des rois de Majorque et les palais italiens." In *Monument de l'histoire: Construire, reconstruire le palais des Papes XIV–XXe siècle*, 109–15.

Keynes, Simon. 2014. "Kingston-upon-Thames." In *The Blackwell Encyclopaedia of Anglo-Saxon England*, edited by Michael Lapidge, John Blair, Simon Keynes, et al., 277. 2nd ed. Oxford: Blackwell.

Keynes, Simon, and Michael Lapidge, trans. 1983. *Alfred the Great: Asser's 'Life of King Alfred' and Other Contemporary Sources*, Penguin Classics. Harmondsworth: Penguin.

Khoury, Nuha N. N. 1996. "The Meaning of the Great Mosque of Cordoba in the Tenth Century." *Muqarnas* 13: 80–98.

Kipling, Gordon. 1998. *Enter the King: Theatre, Liturgy, and Ritual in the Medieval Civic Triumph*. Oxford: Oxford University Press.

Kirchweger, Franz, ed. 2005. *Die Heilige Lanze in Wien: Insignie, Reliquie, "Schicksalsspeer,"* Schriften des Kunsthistorisches Museum Wien, 9. Vienna and Paris: Skira.

Kitzinger, Ernst. 1949. "The Mosaics of the Cappella Palatina in Palermo: An Essay on the Choice and Arrangement of Subjects." *Art Bulletin* 31 (4): 269–92.

⸻. 2001. "The Mosaic Fragments in the Torre Pisana of the Royal Palace at Palermo." In *Studies in Late Antique, Byzantine and Medieval Western Art; vol. 1: Studies in Late Antique and Byzantine Art; vol. 2: Studies in Medieval Western Art and the Art of Norman Sicily*, 1099–1119. London: Pindar.

Klaniczay, Gábor. 2002. *Holy Rulers and Blessed Princesses: Dynastic Cults in Medieval Central Europe*. Cambridge: Cambridge University Press.

Klein, Holger A. 2004. "Constantine, Helena, and the Cult of the True Cross in Constantinople." In *Byzance et les reliques du christ*, edited by Jannic Durand and Bernard Flusin, 31–59, Centre de recherche d'histoire et civilisation de Byzance, Monographies, 17. Paris: Association des Amis du Centre d'Histoire et Civilisation de Byzance.

Klein, Ulrich. 2010. "Forschungen zur Baugeschichte der Pfalz Gelnhausen." In *Burgenforschung und Burgendenkmalpflege in Hessen: Beiträge der Tagung in Bad Homburg, 4. und 5. April 2008*, edited by Christian Ottersbach and Rainer Zuch, 113–31. Marburg: Marburger Arbeitskreis für Europäische Burgenforschung.

Kleiner, Diana E. E. 1992. *Roman Sculpture*. New Haven: Yale University Press.

Knox, Brian. 1962. *Bohemia and Moravia: An Architectural Companion*. London: Faber and Faber.

Konstam, Angus. 2003. *Historical Atlas of Ancient Rome*. New York: Checkmark.

Kostenec, Jan. 1999. "Studies on the Great Palace of Constantinople, II. The Magnaura." *Byzantinoslavica* 60: 161–82.

⸻. 2004. "The Heart of Empire: The Great Palace of the Byzantine Emperors Reconsidered." In *Secular Buildings and the Archaeology of Everyday Life in the Byzantine Empire*, edited by Kenneth R. Dark, 4–36. Oxford: Oxbow.

Kramp, Mario. 2000a. "Krönungen und Könige in der Nachfolge Karls des Großen: eine Geschichte und ihre Bilder." In *Krönungen: Könige in Aachen: Geschichte und Mythos*, edited by Mario Kramp, I, 2–18. 2 vols. Mainz: Philipp von Zabern.

⸻, ed. 2000b. *Krönungen: Könige in Aachen: Geschichte und Mythos*. 2 vols. Mainz: Philipp von Zabern.

Kraus, Thomas R., ed. 2011. *Die natürlichen Grundlagen: von der Vorgeschichte zu den Karolingern*, Aachen von den Anfängen bis zur Gegenwart, I. Aachen: Aachener Geschichtsverein.

⸻, ed. 2013. *Karolinger–Ottonen–Salier 765 bis 1137*, Aachen von den Anfängen bis zur Gegenwart, 2. Aachen: Aachener Geschichtsverein.

Krautheimer, Richard. 1942. "The Carolingian Revival of Early Christian Architecture." *Art Bulletin* 24: 1–38. Reprinted: Richard Krautheimer. 1969. *Studies in Early Christian, Medieval, and Renaissance Art*, 203–56. New York: New York University Press, and in German as Richard Krautheimer. 1988. "Die karolingische Wiederbelebung der frühchristlichen Architektur." In *Ausgewählte Aufsätze zur Europäischen Kunstgeschichte*, by Richard Krautheimer, 198–276. Cologne: Dumont.

Kreusch, Felix. 1958. *Über Pfalzkapelle und Atrium zur Zeit Karls des Grossen* Aachen: W. Metz.

Krogh, Knud J. 1983. "The Royal Viking Age Monuments at Jelling in the Light of Recent Archaeological Excavations: A Preliminary Report." *Acta Archaeologica* 53–54: 183–216.

Krönig, Wolfgang. 1994. "Castel del Monte: der Bau Friedrichs II." In *Intellectual Life at the Court of Frederick II Hohenstaufen*, edited by William Tronzo, 91–108. Washington, DC: National Gallery of Art.

Krüger, K. H. 1971. *Königsgrabkirchen der Franken, Angelsachsen und Langobarden zur Mitte des 8. Jahrhunderts: ein historischer Katalog*, Münstersche Mittelalter-Schriften. Munich: Wilhelm Fink.

Krüger, Kristina. 2006a. "Die Palaststadt Madīnat al-Zahrā bei Córdoba." In *Visualisierungen von Herrschaft: frühmittelalterliche Residenzen: Gestalt und Zeremoniell: internationales Kolloquium 3./4. Juni 2004 in Istanbul*, edited by Franz Alto Bauer, 233–71, Byzas, 5. Istanbul: Ege Yayınları.

———. 2006b. "Fürstengrablegungen in Nordspanien: die 'Panteones' früh- und hochmittelalterlicher Kirchen." In *Grabkunst und Sepulkralkultur in Spanien und Portugal*, edited by Barbara Borngässer, Bruno Klein, and Henrik Karge, 33–63, Ars iberica et americana, 11. Frankfurt and Madrid: Vervuert and Iberoamericana.

Kühne, Hartmut. 2000. *Ostensio reliquiarum: Untersuchungen über Entstehung, Ausbreitung, Gestalt und Funktion der Heiltumsweisungen im römisch-deutschen Regnum*, Arbeiten zur Kirchengeschichte, 75. Berlin: Walter de Gruyter.

Kuhnen, Hans-Peter. 2003. "Kaiserresidenz Trier: der spätantike Palast und seine Ausstrahlung auf die Denkmalpflege." In *Palatia: Kaiserpaläste in Konstantinopel, Ravenna und Trier*, edited by Margarethe König, Eugenia Bolognesi Recchi-Franceschini, and Ellen Riemer, 162–73, Schriftenreihe des Rheinischen Landesmuseums Trier, 27. Trier: Rheinisches Landesmuseum.

Kuttner, Ann Lill. 1999. "Culture and History at Pompey's Museum." *Transactions of the American Philological Association* 129: 343–73.

Labbé, Alain. 1987. *L'architecture des palais et des jardins dans les chansons de geste: essai sur le thème du roi en majesté*. Paris: Champion-Slatkine.

Lachet, Claude, ed. and trans. 2010. *La prise d'Orange: chanson de geste (fin XIIe–début XIIIe siècle): Texte établi, traduction, présentation et notes*, Champion classiques, Moyen Âge, 31. Paris: Champion.

Laing, Lloyd R. 1969. "Timber Halls in Dark Age Britain—Some Problems." *Transactions of the Dumfriesshire and Galloway Natural History and Antiquarian Society*, 3rd series, 46: 110–27.

Lalou, Elisabeth. 1996. "Le vocabulaire des résidences royales en France sous le règne de Philippe le Bel (1285–1314)." In *Palais royaux et princiers au Moyen Age: Actes du colloque international tenue au Mans les 6–7 octobre 1994*, edited by Annie Renoux, 43–50. Le Mans: Université du Maine.

Lammers, Walther. 1971–2. "Ein karolingisches Bildprogramm in der Aula regia von Ingelheim." In *Festschrift für Hermann Heimpel zum 70. Geburtstag am 19. September 1971*, edited by Mitarbeiter des Max-Planck-Instituts für Geschichte, 226–89. 3 vols, Veröffentlichungen der Max-Planck-Institut für Geschichte, 36. Göttingen: Vandenhoeck and Ruprecht.

Lampen, Angelika. 2009. "Das Stadttor als Bühne: Architektur und Zeremoniell." In *Adventus: Studien zum herrscherlichen Einzug in die Stadt*, edited by Peter Johanek and Angelika Lampen, 1–36, Städteforschung, Reihe A, Darstellungen, 75. Cologne: Böhlau.

Lane, Alan, and Ewan Campbell. 2000. *Dunadd: An Early Dalriadic Capital*. Oxford: Oxbow.

Langton, John. 2010. "Medieval Forests and Chases: Another Realm?" In *Forests and Chases of England and Wales to circa 1500*, edited by John Langton and Graham Jones, 14–35. Oxford: St. John's College.

Lathoud, D. 1924. "La consécration et la dédicace de Constantinople." *Échos d'Orient* 22: 289–314.

———. 1925. "La consécration et la dédicace de Constantinople." *Échos d'Orient* 22: 180–201.

Lauer, Philippe. 1911. *Le palais de Latran: étude historique et archéologique*, École française de Rome. Paris: É. Leroux.

Lavéant, Katell. 2006. "Le roi et son double: a royal entry to late-medieval Abbeville." In *Symbolic Communication in Late Medieval Towns*, edited by Jacoba van Leeuwen, 44–64, Series Mediaevalia Lovaniensia, series 1, studia 37. Leuven: Leuven University Press.

Lavelle, Ryan. 2007. *Royal Estates in Anglo-Saxon Wessex: Land, Politics and Family Strategies*, British Archaeological Reports, British Series, 439. Oxford: Archaeopress.

Lavin, Irving. 1962. "The House of the Lord: Aspects of the Role of Palace Triclinia in the Architecture of Late Antiquity and the Early Middle Ages." *Art Bulletin* 44 (1): 1–27.

Le Goff, Jacques. 1996–98. "Reims, City of Coronation." In *Realms of Memory: The Construction of the French Past*, edited by Pierre Nora, 193–251. 3 vols. New York: Columbia University Press.

Le Jan-Hennebicque, R. 1980. "Espaces sauvages et chasses royales dans le Nord de la France (VIIe–IXe siècle): le paysage rural: réalités et représentations." *Revue du Nord* 244: 35–60.

Lehmann, Karl. 1945. "The Dome of Heaven." *Art Bulletin* 27 (1): 1–27.

Leistenschneider, Eva. 2008. *Die französische Königsgrablege Saint-Denis: Strategien monarchischer Repräsentation 1223–1461*. Weimar: Verlag und Datenbank für Geisteswissenschaften.

Leistikov, Dankwart. 2008. "Castel del Monte im Lichte der Forschung." In *Kaiser Friedrich II. (1194–1250): Welt und Kultur des Mittelmeerraums: Begleitband zur Sonderausstellung "Kaiser Friedrich II. (1194–1250): Welt und Kultur des Mittelmeerraums" im Landesmuseum für Natur und Mensch, Oldenburg*, edited by Mamoun Fansa and Karen Ermete, 142–57, Schriftenreihe des Landesmuseums fur Natur und Mensch Oldenburg, 55. Mainz: Philipp von Zabern.

Leithe-Jasper, Manfred, and Rudolf Distelberger. 1998. *The Kunsthistorisches Museum Vienna: the Imperial and Ecclesiastical Treasury*, Museums of the World. London: Scala.

Lentsch, Roberte. 1990. "La localisation et l'organisation matérielle des services administratifs au Palais des Papes." In *Aux origines de l'État moderne: le fonctionnement administratif de la papauté d'Avignon: Actes de la table ronde organisée par l'École française de Rome avec le concours du CNRS, du Conseil général de Vaucluse et de l'Université d'Avignon (Avignon, 23–24 janvier 1988)*, 293–312, Collection de l'École Française de Rome, 138. Rome: École française de Rome.

Lewis, Suzanne. 1995. "Henry III and the Gothic Rebuilding of Westminster Abbey: The Problematics of Context." *Traditio* 50: 129–72.

Ley, Judith. 2013. "Der 'Neue Salomonische Temple' in Aachen." In *Karolinger—Ottonen—Salier 765 bis 1137*, edited by Thomas R. Kraus, 209–46, Aachen von den Anfängen bis zur Gegenwart, 2. Aachen: Aachener Geschichtsverein.

———. 2014. "Warum ist die Aachener Pfalzkirche ein Zentralbau? Der Neue Salomonische Tempel as Vorbild herrschaftlicher Kirchenstiftung." In *Die Aachener Marienkirche: Aspekte ihrer Archäologie und frühen Geschichte*, edited by Harald Müller, Clemens M. M. Bayer, and Max Kerner, 95–112, Der Aachener Dom in seiner Geschichte. Quellen und Forschungen, 1. Regensburg: Schnell and Steiner.

Licinio, Raffaele. 2002a. "Castel del Monte: un castello medievale." In *Castel del Monte: un castello medievale*, edited by Raffaele Licinio, 53–108. Bari: M. Adda.

———, ed. 2002b. *Castel del Monte: un castello medievale*. Bari: M. Adda.

Liddiard, Robert, ed. 2007. *The Medieval Park: New Perspectives*. Oxford: Windgather Press.

Liebenwein, Wolfgang. 1977. *Studiolo: die Entstehung eines Raumtyps und seine Entwicklung bis um 1600*, Frankfurter Forschungen zur Kunst, 6. Berlin: Mann Brothers.

Lilley, Keith D. 2009. *City and Cosmos: The Medieval World in Urban Form*. London: Reaktion.

Litoux, Emmanuel, and Éric Cron, eds. 2010. *Le château et la citadelle de Saumur: Architecture du pouvoir*, Bulletin Monumental, Supplément, 3. Paris: Société Française d'Archéologie.

Litoux, Emmanuel, Jean-Yves Hunot, and Daniel Prigent. 2010. "L'édification d'un château-palais dans le dernier tiers du XIVe siècle." In *Le château et la citadelle de Saumur: architecture du pouvoir*, edited by Emmanuel Litoux and Éric Cron, 49–90, Bulletin monumental, Supplément, 3. Paris: Société française d'archéologie.

Littlewood, Antony Robert. 1997. "Gardens of the Palaces." In *Byzantine Court Culture from 829 to 1204*, edited by Henry Maguire, 13–38. Washington, DC.: Dumbarton Oaks Research Library and Collection.

Littlewood, Antony Robert, Henry Maguire, and Joachim Wolschke-Bulmahn, eds. 2002. *Byzantine Garden Culture*. Washington, DC: Dumbarton Oaks Research Library and Collection.

Livingstone, E. A., and F. L. Cross, eds. 1997. *The Oxford Dictionary of the Christian Church*. 3rd ed. Oxford: Oxford University Press.

Lobbedey, Uwe. 2014. "Beobachtungen und Notizien zum Königsthron." In *Die Aachener Marienkirche: Aspekte ihrer Archäologie und frühen Geschichte*, edited by Harald Müller, Clemens M. M. Bayer, and Max Kerner, 237–50, Der Aachener Dom in seiner Geschichte. Quellen und Forschungen, 1. Regensburg: Schnell and Steiner.

Lobel, Mary D., and W. H. Johns. 1989. *The City of London from Prehistoric Times to c.1520*. Oxford: Oxford University Press in conjunction with the Historic Towns Trust.

Loisel, Gustave. 1912. *Histoire des ménageries de l'antiquité à nos jours*. Paris: O. Doin et fils.

Longo, Ruggero. 2011. "The *Opus Sectile* Work in the Cappella Palatina in Palermo." In *Die Cappella Palatina in Palermo: Geschichte, Kunst, Funktionen. Forschungsergebnisse der Restaurierung*, edited by Thomas Dittelbach, 491–98. Künzelsau: Swiridoff.

Lorentz, Philippe, and Dany Sandron. 2006. *Atlas de Paris au Moyen Âge: espace urbain, habitat, société, religion, lieux de pouvoir*. Paris: Parigramme.

Lorenz, Sönke. 1996. "Der Königsforst (*forestis*) in den Quellen der Merowinger- und Karolingerzeit: Prolegomena zu einer Geschichte mittelalterlicher Nutzwälder." In *Mönchtum–Kirche–Herrschaft 750–1050*, edited by Dieter Bauer, Rudolf Hiestand, Brigitte Kasten, et al., 261–85. Sigmaringen: Thorbecke.

Loud, Graham A., and Thomas Wiedemann, eds. 1998. *The History of the Tyrants of Sicily by 'Hugo Falcandus,' 1154–69*, Manchester Medieval Sources Series. Manchester: Manchester University Press.

Loyn, H. R., and J. Percival, eds. 1975. *The Reign of Charlemagne*, Documents of Medieval History, 2. London: Arnold.

Luchterhandt, Manfred. 1999a. "*Famulus Petri*: Karl der Grosse in den römischen Mosaikbildern Leos III." In *799: Kunst und Kultur der Karolingerzeit: Karl der Grosse und Papst Leo III in Paderborn: Beiträge zum Katalog der Ausstellung Paderborn 1999*, edited by C. Stiegemann and M. Wemhoff, 55–70. Mainz: Philipp von Zabern.

———. 1999b. "Päpstlicher Palastbau und höfisches Zeremoniell unter Leo III." In *799: Kunst und Kultur der Karolingerzeit: Karl der Grosse und Papst Leo III in Paderborn: Beiträge zum Katalog der Ausstellung Paderborn 1999*, edited by C. Stiegemann and M. Wemhoff, 109–22. Mainz: Philipp von Zabern.

Lucy, Sam. 2000. *The Anglo-Saxon Way of Death: Burial Rites in Early England*. Stroud: Sutton.

Luscombe, D. E., ed. 2003a. *New Cambridge Medieval History: Volume 4, Part I, c. 1024–c. 1198*. Cambridge: Cambridge University Press.

———, ed. 2003b. *New Cambridge Medieval History: Volume 4, Part II, c. 1024–c. 1198*. Cambridge: Cambridge University Press.

Macalister, Robert Alexander Stewart. 1931. *Tara, a Pagan Sanctuary of Ancient Ireland*. New York: Charles Scribner's sons.

MacCormack, Sabine. 1981. *Art and Ceremony in Late Antiquity*. Berkeley: University of California Press.

MacDonald, William Lloyd. 1982–86. *The Architecture of the Roman Empire*. Rev. ed. 2 vols., Yale Publications in the History of Art, 17, 35. New Haven and London: Yale University Press.

MacDonald, William Lloyd, and John A. Pinto. 1995. *Hadrian's Villa and Its Legacy*. New Haven: Yale University Press.

Mackay, Angus, and David Ditchburn. 1997. *Atlas of Medieval Europe*. London: Routledge.

MacKenzie, John MacDonald. 1988. *The Empire of Nature: Hunting, Conservation and British Imperialism*. Manchester: Manchester University Press.

Mackie, Gillian Vallance. 2003. *Early Christian Chapels in the West: Decoration, Function and Patronage*. Toronto: University of Toronto Press.

Maclagan, Michael. 1968. *The City of Constantinople*. London: Thames and Hudson.

Magdalino, Paul. 2004. "L'église du Phare et les reliques de la passion à Constantinople (VIIe/VIIIe–XIIIe siècles)." In *Byzance et les reliques du Christ*, edited by Jannic Durand and Bernard Flusin, 15–30, Centre de recherche d'histoire et civilisation de Byzance, Monographies, 17. Paris: Association des Amis du Centre d'Histoire et Civilisation de Byzance.

———. 2007. "Medieval Constantinople." In *Studies on the History and Topography of Byzantine Constantinople*, edited by Paul Magdalino, 1–111. Aldershot: Ashgate.

Maguire, Henry. 1994. "Imperial Gardens and the Rhetoric of Renewal." In *New Constantines: The Rhythm of Imperial Renewal in Byzantium, 4th–13th Centuries: Papers from the Twenty-Sixth Spring Symposium of Byzantine Studies*, edited by Paul Magdalino, 181–98. Aldershot: Variorum.

———. 2000. "Gardens and Parks in Constantinople." *Dumbarton Oaks Papers* 54: 251–64.

Mâle, Émile. 1913. *The Gothic Image: Religious Art in France of the Thirteenth Century*. Translated by Doreen Nussey. London: J. M. Dent and Sons.

Mango, Cyril. 2000. "The Triumphal Way of Constantinople and the Golden Gate." *Dumbarton Oaks Papers* 54: 173–88.

Manzano Martos, Rafael. 1994. *La qubba, aula regia en la España musulmana*. Madrid: Real Academia de Bellas Artes de San Fernando.

Marafioti, Nicole 2014. *The King's Body: Burial and Succession in Late Anglo-Saxon England*. Toronto: Toronto University Press.

Marchi, Alessandro, and Maria Rosaria Valazzi. 2012. *La città ideale: l'utopia del Rinascimento a Urbino tra Piero della Francesca e Raffaello*. Milan: Electa.

Mark, Robert, and S. Cakmak Ahmet. 1993. *The Haghia Sophia from the Age of Justinian to the Present*. Cambridge: Cambridge University Press.

Marlowe, E. 2006. "Framing the Sun: The Arch of Constantine and the Roman Cityspace." *Art Bulletin* 88 (4): 223–42.

Martin, Jean-Marie. 2004. "Le cas du royaume de Sicile: Traditions et influences occidentales." In *Les palais dans la ville: Espaces urbains et lieux de la puissance publique dans la Méditerranée médiévale*, edited by Patrick Boucheron, Jacques Chiffoleau, Theis Valérie, et al., 77–93, Collection d'histoire et d'archéologie médiévales,13 Lyon: Presses Universitaires de Lyon.

Marvin, William Perry. 2006. *Hunting Law and Ritual in Medieval English Literature*. Woodbridge: Boydell.

Mattingly, H., and Sallie A. Handforth, trans. 1970. *Tacitus: The Agricola and the Germania*. Rev. ed., Penguin Classics. Harmondsworth: Penguin.

Mazzoli-Guintard, C. 1997. "Cordoue et Madīnat al-Zahrā: remarques sur le fonctionnement d'une capitale à double polarité." *Al-Qantara* 18 (1): 43–64.

McClendon, Charles B. 2005. *The Origins of Medieval Architecture: Building in Europe, A.D. 600–900*. New Haven and London: Yale University Press.

McCormick, Michael. 1986. *Eternal Victory: Triumphal Rulership in Late Antiquity, Byzantium and the Early Medieval West*. Cambridge: Cambridge University Press.

———. 1991. "Coronations." In *The Oxford Dictionary of Byzantium*, edited by A. Kazhdan, 533–44. 3 vols. Oxford: Oxford University Press.

McKitterick, Rosamond, ed. 1995. *New Cambridge Medieval History: Volume 2, c. 700–c. 900*. Cambridge: Cambridge University Press.

McLean, Teresa. 1981. *Medieval English Gardens*. London: Collins.

McTurk, Rory W. 1975–76. "Sacral Kingship in Ancient Scandinavia: A Review of Some Recent Writings." *Saga-Book: Viking Society for Northern Research* 19 (2–3): 139–69.

———. 1994. "Scandinavian Sacral Kingship Revisited." *Saga-Book: Viking Society for Northern Research* 24 (1): 19–32.

Meckseper, Cord. 1991. "Zur salischen Gestalt des Palas der Königspfalz in Goslar." In *Burgen der Salierzeit*, edited by Horst Wolfgang Böhme, 85–95. 2 vols., Monographien Römisch-germanisches Zentralmuseum, 25, 26. Sigmaringen: Thorbecke.

Mehofer, Mathias, Verena Leusch, and Birgitte Bühler. 2005. "Archäometallurgische Untersuchungen an der Heiligen Lanze in der Wiener Schatzkammer." In *Die Heilige Lanze in Wien: Insignie, Reliquie, "Schicksalsspeer,"* edited by Franz Kirchweger, 169–90, Schriften des Kunsthistorisches Museum Wien, 9. Vienna and Paris: Skira.

Meier, Hans-Rudolf. 1994. *Die normannischen Königspaläste in Palermo: Studien zur hochmittelalterlichen Residenzbaukunst*, Manuskripte zur Kunstwissenschaft in der Wernerschen Verlagsgesellschaft, 42. Worms: Wernersche Verlagsgesellschaft.

Meineke, E. 1995. "Forst, sec. 1, sprachliches." In *Reallexikon der Germanischen Altertumskunde*, edited by Anon., 345–48. 2nd ed. Berlin and New York: de Gruyter.

Meredith, Jill. 1986. "The Revival of the Augustan Age in the Court Art of Emperor Frederick II." In *Artistic Strategy and the Rhetoric of Power: Political Uses of Art from Antiquity to the Present*, edited by David Castriota, 39–56. Carbondale: Southern Illinois University Press.

———. 1994. "The Arch of Capua: The Strategic Use of *Spolia* and References to the Antique." In *Intellectual Life at the Court of Frederick II Hohenstaufen*, edited by William Tronzo, 109–28. Washington, DC: National Gallery of Art.

Mérindol, Christian de. 1993. "Clément VI, seigneur et pape, d'après le témoignage de l'emblématique et de la thématique. La chambre du cerf. L'abbiatiale de La Chaise-Dieu." In *Les décors des églises en France méridionale (13e–milieu 15e siècle)*, edited by Anon., 331–61, Cahiers de Fanjeaux, 28. Toulouse: Privat.

Mew, Karin. 2001 for 2000. "The Dynamics of Lordship and Landscape as Revealed in a Domesday Study of the Nova Foresta." *Anglo-Norman Studies* 23: 155–66.

Mierow, Charles Christopher, trans. 1915. *The Gothic History of Jordanes*. 2nd ed. Cambridge: Speculum Historiale.

Mileson, Stephen. 2009. *Parks in Medieval England*. Oxford: Oxford University Press.

Miller, Naomi. 1986. "Paradise Regained: Medieval Garden Fountains." In *Medieval Gardens*, edited by E. B. MacDougall, 135–53. Washington, DC: Dumbarton Oaks.

Moestrup, Katrina Lewinsky. 2011. *Vikingetidsbroen i Ravning Enge: en kort gennemgang af broens konstruktion*. Vejleegnens Museer.

Mommsen, Theodor, ed. 1894. *Cassiodori Senatoris Variae*, Monumenta Germaniae Historica, Auctores Antiquissimi, 12. Berlin: Weidemann.

Möseneder, K. 1981. "Lapides vivi: über die Kreuzkapelle der Burg Karlstein." *Wiener Jahrbuch für Kunstgeschichte* 34: 39–69.

Moulinier-Brogi, Laurence. 2003. "'Palais': la singulière fortune d'un mot." In *Palais et pouvoir: de Constantinople à Versailles*, edited by Marie-France Auzépy, and Joël Cornette, 295–308, Temps et espaces. Saint-Denis: Presses Universitaires de Vincennes.

Müller-Kehlen, Helga. 1973. *Die Ardennen im Frühmittelalter: Untersuchungen zum Königsgut in einem karolingischen Kernland*, VMPIG, 38. Göttingen: Vandenhoeck and Ruprecht.

Müller-Wiener, Wolfgang. 1977. *Bildlexikon zur Topographie Istanbuls: Byzantion, Konstantinupolis, Istanbul bis zum Beginn des 17. Jahrhunderts*. Tübingen: Wasmuth.

Müller-Wille, Michael. 1983. "Royal and Aristocratic Graves in Central and Western Europe in the Merovingian Period." In *Vendel Period Studies. Transactions of the Boat-grave Symposium in Stockholm, February 2–3, 1981*, edited by J. P. Lamm and H.-Å. Nordström, 109–16. Stockholm: Statens Historiska Museum.

Müller, Harald. 2014. "St. Marien als Pfarrkirche." In *Die Aachener Marienkirche: Aspekte ihrer Archäologie und frühen Geschichte*, edited by Harald Müller, Clemens M. M. Bayer, and Max Kerner, 191–96, Der Aachener Dom in seiner Geschichte: Quellen und Forschungen, 1. Regensburg: Schnell and Steiner.

Müller, Harald, Clemens M. M. Bayer, and Max Kerner, eds. 2014. *Die Aachener Marienkirche: Aspekte ihrer Archäologie und frühen Geschichte*, Der Aachener Dom in seiner Geschichte: Quellen und Forschungen, 1. Regensburg: Schnell and Steiner.

Müller, Harald, Judith Ley, Frank Pohle, et al. 2013. "Pfalz und *vicus* Aachen in karolingischer Zeit." In *Karolinger–Ottonen–Salier 765 bis 1137*, edited by Thomas R. Kraus, 5–408, Von den Anfängen bis zur Gegenwart, 2. Aachen: Aachener Geschichtsverein.

Müller, Silvinus. 2000. "Die Königskrönungen in Aachen (936–1531): ein Überblick." In *Krönungen: Könige in Aachen: Geschichte und Mythos*, edited by Mario Kramp, I, 49–58. 2 vols. Mainz: Philipp von Zabern.

Munby, Julian. 2007. "Reconstructing the Round Table: Windsor and Beyond." In *Edward III's Round Table at Windsor: The House of the Round Table and the Windsor Festival of 1344*, edited by Julian Munby, Richard Barber, and Richard Brown, 118–26. Woodbridge: Boydell and Brewer.

Munby, Julian, Richard Barber, and Richard Brown, eds. 2007. *Edward III's Round Table at Windsor: The House of the Round Table and the Windsor Festival of 1344*. Woodbridge: Boydell and Brewer.

Murray, Alan V. 1998. "'Mighty against the Enemies of Christ': The Relic of the True Cross in the Armies of the Kingdom of Jerusalem." In *The Crusades and their Sources: Essays Presented to Bernard Hamilton*, edited by John France and William G. Zajac, 217–38. Aldershot: Ashgate.

Murray, James M. 1994. "The Liturgy of the Count's Advent in Bruges, from Galbert to Van Eyck." In *City and Spectacle in Medieval Europe*, edited by Barbara A. Hanawalt and Kathryn L. Reyerson, 137–52. Minneapolis: University of Minnesota Press.

Musca, Giosuè. 2002. "Castel del Monte, il reale e l'immaginario." In *Castel del Monte: un castello medievale*, edited by Raffaele Licinio, 1–51. Bari: M. Adda.

Myhre, Bjørn. 1992. "The Royal Cemetery at Borre, Vestfold: A Norwegian Centre in a European Periphery." In *The Age of Sutton Hoo: The Seventh Century in North-Western Europe*, edited by Martin O. H. Carver, 301–13. Woodbridge: Boydell Press.

Nelson, Janet L. 1967. "The Problem of King Alfred's Royal Anointing." *Journal of Ecclesiastical History* 18: 145–63. Reprinted: Janet L. Nelson. 1986. *Politics and Ritual in Early Medieval Europe*, 309–28. London: Hambledon Press.

———. 1971. "National Synods, Kingship as Office, and Royal Anointing: an Early Medieval Syndrome." *Studies in Church History* 7: 41–59. Reprinted: Janet L. Nelson. 1986. *Politics and Ritual in Early Medieval Europe*, 239–58. London: Hambledon Press.

———. 1976. "Symbols in Context: Ruler's Inauguration Rituals in Byzantium and the West in the Early Middle Ages." *Studies in Church History* 13: 97–119. Reprinted: Janet L. Nelson. 1986. *Politics and Ritual in Early Medieval Europe*, 259–82. London: Hambledon Press.

———. 1977a. "Inauguration Rituals." In *Early Medieval Kingship*, edited by Peter Hayes Sawyer and Ian Wood, 283–307. Leeds: University of Leeds. Reprinted: Janet L. Nelson. 1986. *Politics and Ritual in Early Medieval Europe*, 283–308. London: Hambledon Press.

———. 1977b. "Kingship, Law and Liturgy in the Political Thought of Hincmar of Rheims." *English Historical Review* 92: 241–79. Reprinted: Janet L. Nelson. 1986. *Politics and Ritual in Early Medieval Europe*, 133–72. London: Hambledon Press.

———. 1982. "The Rites of the Conqueror." *Anglo-Norman Studies* 4: 17–132, 210–21. Reprinted: Janet L. Nelson. 1986. *Politics and Ritual in Early Medieval Europe*, 371–401. London: Hambledon Press.

———. 1987. "The Lord's Anointed and the People's Choice: Carolingian Royal Ritual." In *Rituals of Royalty: Power and Ceremonial in Traditional Societies*, edited by David Cannadine and Simon Price, 137–80. Cambridge: Cambridge University Press. Reprinted: Janet L. Nelson, 1996. *The Frankish World 750–900*, 99–132. Hambledon: London and Rio Grande.

———. 1994. "Kingship and Empire in the Carolingian World." In *Carolingian Culture: Emulation and Innovation*, edited by Rosamond Mckitterick, 52–87. Cambridge: Cambridge University Press.

———. 2000. "Carolingian Royal Funerals." In *Rituals of Power: From Late Antiquity to the Early Middle Ages*, edited by Janet L. Nelson and Frans Theuws, 131–84, The Transformation of the Roman World, 8. Leiden: Brill.

———. 2001. "Aachen as a Place of Power." In *Topographies of Power in the Early Middle Ages*, edited by Mayke De Jong, Franz Theuws, and Carine Van Rhijn, 216–41, Transformation of the Roman World 6. Leiden: Brill.

Neumayer, Heino. 2000. "Königliche Bestattungen—königliche Bücher: zur Publikation der Gräber aus Saint-Denis von Michel Fleury." *Germania* 78: 449–62.

Newman, Conor. 1997. *Tara: an Archaeological Survey*, Discovery Programme Monographs, 2. Dublin: Royal Irish Academy / Discovery Programme.

———. 2007. "Procession and Symbolism at Tara: Analysis of Tech Midchúarta (the 'Banqueting Hall') in the Context of the Sacral Campus." *Oxford Journal of Archaeology* 26 (4): 415–38.

———. 2011. "The Sacral Landscape of Tara: A Preliminary Exploration." In *Landscapes of Cult and Kingship: Archaeology and Text*, edited by Edel Bhreathnach, Ger Dowling, and Roseanne Schot, 22–43. Dublin: Four Courts Press.

Nicol, D. M. 1976. "*Kaisersalbung*: The Unction of Emperors in Late Byzantine Coronation Ritual." *Byzantine and Modern Greek Studies* 2: 37–52.

Niles, John D. 2007. "Beowulf and Lejre." In *Beowulf and Lejre*, edited by John D. Niles, with contributions by Tom Christensen, and Marijane Osborne, 169–233. Turnhout: Brepols.

Niles, John D., ed., with contributions by Tom Christensen, and Marijane Osborne. 2007. *Beowulf and Lejre*. Turnhout: Brepols.

Nussbaum, Norbert. 2000. *German Gothic Church Architecture*. Translated by Scott Kleager. New Haven: Yale University Press.

O'Meara, John, trans. 1982. *Gerald of Wales, The History and Topography of Ireland*, Penguin Classics. Harmondsworth: Penguin.

O'Sullivan, Muiris. 2005. *The Mound of the Hostages, Tara: A Pivotal Monument in a Ceremonial Landscape*, Archaeology Ireland Heritage Guide, 34. Bray: Archaeology Ireland.

Oakley, Francis. 2006. *Kingship: The Politics of Enchantment*, New Perspectives on the Past. Oxford: Wiley-Blackwell.

Orchard, Andy. 2004. *A Critical Companion to Beowulf*. Woodbridge: Boydell Press.

Osborne, June, and Joe Cornish. 2003. *Urbino: the Story of a Renaissance City*. London: Frances Lincoln.

Östenberg, Ida. 2009. *Staging the World: Spoils, Captives, and Representations in the Roman Triumphal Procession*. Oxford: Oxford University Press.

Owen-Crocker, Gale R. 2000. *The Four Funerals in Beowulf and the Structure of the Poem*. Manchester: Manchester University Press.

Packer, James E. 1997. *The Forum of Trajan in Rome: A Study of the Monuments*, California Studies in the History of Art, 31. Berkeley: University of California Press.

———. 2001. *The Forum of Trajan in Rome: a Study of the Monuments in Brief*. Berkeley: University of California Press.

Paravicini, Werner. 1997. *Zeremoniell und Raum, Potsdam, 25. bis 27. September 1994*, Symposium der Residenzen-Kommission der Akademie der Wissenschaften in Göttingen, 4; Residenzenforschung, 6. Sigmaringen: Thorbecke.

Pasquini, Laura. 2005. "L'immagine della croce come simbolo." In *Ravenna da capitale imperiale a capitale esarcale: Atti del XVII Congresso internazionale di studio sull'alto Medioevo: Ravenna, 6–12 giugno 2004*, edited by Fondazione Centro italiano di Studi sull'alto Medioevo, 1095–105. 2 vols, Atti dei congressi, 17. Spoleto: Fondazione Centro Italiano di Studi sull'Alto Medioevo.

Pastoureau, Michel. 2008. "Les ménageries princières: du pouvoir au savoir? (XIIe–XVIe siècle)." In *I saperi nelle corti: Knowledge at the Courts*, edited by Clelia Arcelli, 2–30, Micrologus, 16. Florence: SISMEL—Edizioni del Galluzzo.

Pawelec, Katharina. 1990. *Aachener Bronzegitter: Studien zur karolingischen Ornamentik um 800*, Bonner Beiträge zur Kunstwissenschaft. Cologne: Rheinland-Verlag.

Payne, Robert. 1962. *The Roman Triumph*. London: R. Hale.

Pedersen, Anne. 2006. "The Jelling Monuments: Ancient Royal Memorial and Modern World Heritage Site." In *Runes and Their Secrets: Studies in Runology: International Symposium on Runes and Runic Inscriptions*, edited by Marie Stoklund, 283–313. Copenhagen: Museum Tusculanum Press.

Pensabene, Patrizio, ed. 2010. *Piazza Armerina: Villa del Casale e la Sicilia tra tardoantico e medioevo*, Studia archaeologica, 175. Rome: L'Erma di Bretschneider.

Petit-Dutaillis, Charles. 1915. "De la signification du mot 'forêt' à l'époque franque." *Bibliothèque de l'École des Chartes* 76: 97–152.

———. 1929. "The Forest." In *Studies and Notes Supplementary to Stubbs' Constitutional History*, vol. 3, edited by Charles Petit-Dutaillis and Georges Lefebvre, Publications of the University of Manchester, Historical Series, 53. Manchester: Manchester University Press.

Petrů, Jaroslav. 2003. "The Chapel of Saint Catherine at Karlštejn Castle: Towards an Interpretation of its Purpose." In *Court Chapels of the High and Late Middle Ages and Their Artistic Decoration = Dvorské kaple vrcholného a pozdního středověku a jejich umělecká výzdoba*, edited by Jiří Fajt and Klášter Anězský, 35–42. [Prague]: National Gallery in Prague.

Picard, Tobias. 2004. "Königspfalzen im Rhein-Main-Gebiet: Ingelheim–Frankfurt–Trebur-—Gelnhausen–Seligenstadt." In *". . . Ihrer Bürger Freiheit": Frankfurt am Main im Mittelalter*, edited by Heribert Müller, 19–73, Veröffentlichungen der Frankfurter Historischen Kommission, 22. Frankfurt: Waldemar Kramer.

Plumpe, Joseph C. 1943. "Vivum saxum, vivi lapides: The Concept of 'Living Stone' in Classical and Christian Antiquity." *Traditio* 1: 1–14.

Poisson, Jean-Michel. 2004. "Le palais des papes d'Avignon: Structures défensive et références symboliques." In *Les palais dans la ville: Espaces urbains et lieux de la puissance publique dans la Méditerranée médiévale*, edited by Patrick Boucheron, Jacques Chiffoleau, Theis Valérie, et al., 213–28, Collection d'histoire et d'archéologie médiévales, 13. Lyon: Presses Universitaires de Lyon.

Posthoumis, Bernard. 2014. "Le palais des rois de Majorque: apports récents de l'archéologie du bâti." In *Un palais dans la ville: vol. 1: Le palais des rois de Majorque à Perpignan; vol. 2: Perpignan des rois de Majorque*, edited by Aymat Catafu and Olivier Passarius, II, 43–114. 2 vols. Perpignan: Éditions Trabucaire.

Pratt, David. 2005. *The Political Thought of Alfred the Great*, Cambridge Studies in Medieval Life and Thought: Fourth Series, 67. Cambridge: Cambridge University Press.

Price, S.R.F. 1984. *Rituals and Power: The Roman Imperial Cult in Asia Minor*. Cambridge: Cambridge University Press.

Pringle, Denys. 1989. *Linlithgow Palace* Edinburgh: H.M.S.O.

Rackham, Oliver. 1993. *The Last Forest: The Story of Hatfield Forest*. London: Dent.

Ragni, Marina Sapelli, ed. 2010. *Villa Adriana: una storia mai finita: Novità e prospettive della ricerca*. Milan: Electa.

Rahtz, P. A. 1969. *Excavations at King John's Hunting Lodge, Writtle, Essex, 1955–57*, Society for Medieval Archaeology Monograph Series, 3. London: Society for Medieval Archaeology.

Randsborg, Klaus. 2008. "Kings' Jelling." In *Nordic World: Prehistory to Medieval Times*, edited by Klaus Randsborg, 1–23, Acta archaeologica, 79, Centre of World Archaeology publications, 6. Oxford: Blackwell.

Reeve, Matthew M. 2006. "The Painted Chamber at Westminster, Edward I, and the Crusade." *Viator* 37: 189–222.

Renoux, Annie. 2001. *Aux marches du palais: Qu'est-ce qu'un palais médiéval? Données historiques et archéologiques: Actes du VIIe congrès international d'archéologie médiévale, Le Mans, Mayenne, 9–11 septembre 1999*. Le Mans: Publications du LHAM, Université du Maine.

Reuter, Timothy, ed. 2000. *New Cambridge Medieval History: Volume 3, c. 900–c. 1024*. Cambridge: Cambridge University Press.

Reynolds, N. 1980. "Dark Age Timber Halls and the Background to Excavation at Balbridie." In *Settlements in Scotland 1000 BC–AD 1000*, edited by Lisbeth M. Thoms, 41–60, Scottish Archaeological Forum, 10. Edinburgh: Edinburgh University Press.

Reynolds, Susan. 1994. *Fiefs and Vassals: The Medieval Evidence Reinterpreted*. Oxford: Oxford University Press.

Richardson, Amanda. 2005. *The Medieval Forest, Park and Palace of Clarendon, c. 1200–c. 1650: Reconstructing an Actual, Conceptual and Documented Wiltshire Landscape*, British Archaeological Reports, British Series, 387. Oxford: Archaeopress.

Richmond, I. A. 1933. "Commemorative Arches and City Gates in the Augustan Age." *Journal of Roman Studies* 23: 149–74.

Ricotti, Eugenia Salza Prina 2001. *Villa Adriana: il sogno di un imperatore*. Rome: "L'Erma" di Bretschneider.

Ridyard, Susan. 1988. *The Royal Saints of Anglo-Saxon England*. Cambridge: Cambridge University Press.

Roberts, Jane. 1997. *Royal Landscape: The Gardens and Parks of Windsor*. New Haven: Yale University Press.

Robinson, A. B., and Thomas Beaumont James. 1988. *Clarendon Palace: The History and Archaeology of a Medieval Palace and Hunting Lodge near Salisbury, Wiltshire*.London: Society of Antiquaries of London.

Robinson, Cynthia. December 2008. "Arthur in the Alhambra? Stories, Pictures and Nasrid Royal Self-Fashioning in the Ceiling Paintings of the Sala de Justicia." *Medieval Encounters* 14 (2–3): 164–98.

Roche, Helen. 2002. "Excavations at Ráth na Ríg, Tara, Co. Meath, 1997." In *Discovery Programme Reports* 6, 19–82. Dublin : Royal Irish Academy / Discovery Programme.

Rodwell, Warwick, and Richard Mortimer, eds. 2010. *Westminster Abbey Chapter House: The History, Art and Architecture of a 'Chapter House beyond Compare.'* London: Society of Antiquaries.

Rodwell, Warwick, Marie Louise Sauerberg, Ptolemy Dean, et al. 2013. *The Coronation Chair and Stone of Scone: History, Archaeology and Conservation*, Westminster Abbey Occasional Papers, 3.2. Oxford: Oxbow Books and the Dean and Chapter of Westminster.

Roesdahl, Else. 1987. *The Vikings*. London: Penguin.

Rolfe, John Carew, ed. and trans. 1998. *Suetonius*. Rev. ed. 2 vols., Loeb Classical Library 31, 38. Cambridge,MA: Harvard University Press.

Rollason, David. 1986. "Relic-Cults as an Instrument of Royal Policy c. 900– c. 1050." *Anglo-Saxon England* 15: 91–103.

———. 1989. *Saints and Relics in Anglo-Saxon England*. Oxford: Blackwell.

———. 2009. "Protection and the Mead Hall." In *Peace and Protection in the Middle Ages*, edited by T. B. Lambert and David Rollason, 19–35, Durham Monographs and Essays in Medieval and Renaissance Studies. Toronto: Durham Centre for Medieval and Renaissance Studies / Pontifical Institute of Medieval Studies.

———. 2012a. *Early Medieval Europe 300–1050: The Birth of Western Society*. Harlow: Pearson.

———. 2012b. "From Tintagel to Aachen: Richard of Cornwall and the Power of Place." *Reading Mediaeval Studies* 38: 1–23.

———. 2012c. "Palaces, Forests, Parks, and the Power of Place in the Early Middle Ages." *Early Medieval Europe* 20: 428–49.

———. 2015. "Charlemagne's Palace." *Archaeological Journal* 172 (2): 443–48.

Römisch-Germanischen Zentralmuseum Mainz. 1978. *Führer zu vor- und frühgeschichtlichen Denkmälern: vol. 35: Goslar, Bad Harzburg*. Mainz: Philipp von Zabern.

———. 1980. *Führer zu vor- und frühgeschichtlichen Denkmälern: vol. 32: Trier*. 2 vols. Mainz: Philipp von Zabern.

Rosario, Iva. 2000. *Art and Propaganda: Charles IV of Bohemia, 1346–1378*. Woodbridge: Boydell Press.

Rosenthal, Earl E. 1985. *The Palace of Charles V in Granada*. Princeton: Princeton University Press.

Rotthoff-Kraus, Claudia. 2000. "Krönungfestmähler der römisch-deutschen Könige." In *Krönungen: Könige in Aachen: Geschichte und Mythos*, edited by Mario Kramp, II, 573–82. 2 vols. Mainz: Philipp von Zabern.

Royal Commission on the Ancient Historical Monuments of Scotland. 1963. *Stirlingshire: An Inventory of the Ancient Monuments*. 2 vols. Edinburgh: H.M.S.O.

Royo, Manuel. 1999. *Domus imperatoriae: Topographie, formation et imaginaire des palais impériaux du Palatin (IIe siècle avant J.-C—Ie siècle ap. J.-C.)*, Bibliothèque des Écoles Françaises d'Athènes et de Rome, 303. Rome: École Française de Rome.

Royt, Jan. 2003. "The Dating and Iconography of the So-Called Relics Scenes in the Chapel of Our Lady at Karlštejn Castle." In *Court Chapels of the High and Late Middle Ages and Their Artistic Decoration = Dvorské kaple vrcholného a pozdního středověku a jejich umělecká výzdoba*, edited by Jiří Fajt and Klášter Anězský, 64–67. [Prague]: National Gallery in Prague.

Rubner, Heinrich. 1963. "Vom römischen Saltus zum fränkischen Forst." *Historisches Jahrbuch* 83: 271–77.

Ruggles, D. Fairchild. 2000. *Gardens, Landscape and Vision in the Palaces of Islamic Spain*. University Park: Pennsylvania State University Press.

———. 2004. "The Alcazar of Seville and Mudejar Architecture." *Gesta* 43: 87–98.

Ruiz Souza, Juan Carlos. 2001. "El Palacio de los Leones de la Alhambra: Madrasa, Zawiya y tumba de Muhammad V? Estudio para un debate." *Al-Qantara* 22: 77–120.

Ruiz, Teofilo F. 2012. *A King Travels: Festive Traditions in Late Medieval and Early Modern Spain*. Princeton: Princeton University Press.

Sack, Dorothée, Steffi Platte, Monika Thiel, et al. 2007. "Bauforschung in der Unterkirche der Cappella Palatina in Palermo." *Architectura. Zeitschrift für Geschichte der Baukunst* 37: 121–44.

Safran, Janina M. 2000. *The Second Umayyad Caliphate: The Articulation of Caliphal Legitimacy in al-Andalus*, Harvard Middle Eastern Monographs, 33. Cambridge, MA: Harvard University Press.

Salamagne, Alain. 2008. "D'Hesdin au Quesnoy: Jardins et parcs des châteaux de plaisance." In *Le Château, autour et alentours (XIVe–XVIe siècles): Paysage, parc, jardin et domaine. Actes du colloque international organisé au château fort d'Ecaussinnes-Lalaing, le 18, 19, et 20 mai 2006*, edited by Jean-Marie Cauchies and Jacqueline Guisset, 134–55. Turnhout: Brepols.

———. 2010. "Le Louvre de Charles V." In *Le palais et son décor au temps de Jean de Berry*, edited by Alain Salamagne, 75–138. Tours: Presses Universitaires François Rabelais.

Sanders, Paula A. 1994. *Ritual, Politics, and the City in Fatimid Cairo*, SUNY series in Medieval Middle East History. Albany: State University of New York Press.

Sauerländer, William. 2007. "Architecture gothique et mise en scène des reliques: l'exemple de la Sainte-Chapelle." In *La Sainte-Chapelle de Paris: Royaume de France ou Jérusalem céleste?*, edited by Christine Hediger, 113–36, Culture et société médiévales, 10. Turnhout: Brepols.

Saunders, Corinne J. 1993. *The Forest of Medieval Romance: Avernus, Broceliande, Arden*. Cambridge: D. S. Brewer.

Sawyer, Birgit, and Peter Hayes Sawyer. 2003. "A Gormless History? The Jelling Dynasty Revisited." In *Runica, Germanica, Mediaevalia. Gewidmet Klaus Düwelsbände zum Reallexikon der germanischen Altertumskunde*, edited by Wilhelm Heizmann and Astrid van Nahl, 689–706, Ergänzungsbände zum Reallexikon der germanischen Altertumskunde, 37. Berlin: de Gruyter.

Scarre, Christopher. 1995. *The Penguin Historical Atlas of Ancient Rome*. London: Penguin.

Schaller, Hans Martin. 2000. "Der deutsche Thronstreit und Europa 1198–1218: Philipp von Schwaben, Otto IV, Friedrich II." In *Krönungen: Könige in Aachen: Geschichte und Mythos*, edited by Mario Kramp, I, 398–406. 2 vols. Mainz: Philipp von Zabern.

Schalles-Fischer, Marianne. 1969. *Pfalz und Fiskus Frankfurt*, Veröffentlichung des Max-Planck-Instituts für Geschichte 20. Göttingen: Vandenhoeck and Ruprecht.

Schama, Simon. 2004. *Landscape and Memory*. London: Harper Perennial.

Schaub, Tanja. 2014. "Die 'Münsterthermen.'" In *Die Aachener Marienkirche: Aspekte ihrer Archäologie und frühen Geschichte*, edited by Harald Müller, Clemens M. M. Bayer, and Max Kerner, 29–41, Der Aachener Dom in seiner Geschichte: Quellen und Forschungen, 1. Regensburg: Schnell and Steiner.

Schenk, Gerrit J. 2003. *Zeremoniell und Politik: Herrschereinzüge im spätmittelalterlichen Reich*, Forschungen zur Kaiser- und Papstgeschichte des Mittelalters, 21. Cologne: Böhlau.

Schimmelpfennig, Bernhard. 1994. "*Ad maiorem pape gloriam*: La fonction des pièces dans le palais des Papes d'Avignon." In *Architecture et vie sociale: l'organisation intérieure des grandes demeures à la fin du Moyen Âge et à la Renaissance: Actes du colloque tenu à Tours du 6 au 10 juin 1988*, edited by Jean Guillaume, 25–46. Paris: Picard.

Schirmer, Wulf. 2009. "Archäologisch-baugeschichtliche Erforschung des Castel del Monte." In *Die Forschungsvorhaben der Heidelberger Akademie der Wissenschaften 1909–2009*, edited by Volke Sellin, Eike Wolgast, and Sebastian Zwies, 11–14. Heidelberg: Winter.

Schirmer, Wulf, and Wolfgang Zick. 1998. "Castel del Monte: neue Forschungen zur Architektur Kaiser Friedrichs II.: zweiter Vorbericht." *Architectura: Zeitschrift für Geschichte der Baukunst* 28: 1–36.

Schmid, W. 2012. "Heilige Städte, alte Städte, Kaufmannsstädte: zum Image deutscher Metropolen um 1500." In *Bild und Wahrnehmung der Stadt*, edited by Peter Johanek, 121–60, Städteforschung: Reihe A, Darstellungen, 63. Vienna: Böhlau.

Scholz, Berhard Walter, and Barbara Rogers, trans. 1972. *Carolingian Chronicles: Royal Frankish Annals and Nithard's Histories*. Ann Arbor: University of Michigan Press.

Schramm, Percy Ernst. 1937. *A History of the English Coronation*. Translated by Leopold G. Wickham Legg. Oxford: Clarendon Press.

———. 1954–56. *Herrschaftszeichen und Staatssymbolik: Beiträge zu ihrer Geschichte vom dritten bis zum sechzehnten Jahrhundert*. 3 vols., Schriften der Monumenta Germaniae Historica 13. Stuttgart: Monumenta Germaniae Historica.

Schreiner, Manfred, Vladan Desnica, and Dubravka Jembrih-Simbürger. 2005. "Naturwissenschaftliche Untersuchungen an der Heiligen Lanze." In *Die Heilige Lanze in Wien: Insignie, Reliquie, "Schicksalsspeer,"* edited by Franz Kirchweger, 191–207, Schriften des Kunsthistorisches Museum Wien, 9. Vienna and Paris: Skira.

Schulman, Jana K., ed. 2002. *The Rise of the Medieval World, 500–1300: A Biographical Dictionary*. London: Greenwood Press.

Schulte, Aloys. 1924. *Die Kaiser- und Königskrönungen zu Aachen 813–1531*, Rheinische Neujahrsblätter, 3. Bonn: K. Schroeder.

Schulze-Dörrlamm, Mechthild. 1991. *Die Kaiserkrone Konrads II. (1024–1039): eine archäologische Untersuchung zu Alter und Herkunft der Reichskrone*, Monographien, Römisch-Germanisches Zentralmuseum, Mainz: Forschungsinstitut für Vor- und Frühgeschichte, 23. Sigmaringen: J. Thorbecke.

Schütte, Sven. 2000. "Der Aachener Thron." In *Krönungen: Könige in Aachen: Geschichte und Mythos*, edited by Mario Kramp, I, 213–22. 2 vols. Mainz: Philipp von Zabern.

Schweers, Regine. 2009. "Die Bedeutung des Raumes für das Scheitern oder Gelingen des Adventus." In *Adventus: Studien zum herrscherlichen Einzug in die Stadt*, edited by Peter Johanek and Angelika Lampen, 37–55, Städteforschung, Reihe A, Darstellungen, 75. Cologne: Böhlau.

Semmler, Josef. 1991. "Der Forst des Königs." In *Der Wald in Mittelalter und Renaissance*, edited by Josef Semmler, 130–47, Studia humaniora, 17. Düsseldorf: Droste.

Sezgin, Fuat, Carl Ehrig-Eggert, and E. Neubauer, eds. 2008. *The Umayyad Mosque in Córdoba: Texts and Studies*. 3 vols., Publications of the Institute for the History of Arabic-Islamic Science: Islamic Architecture, 7–9. Frankfurt am Main: Institute for the History of Arabic-Islamic Science at the Johann Wolfgang Goethe University.

Shearer, Cresswell. 1935. *The Renaissance of Architecture in Southern Italy: A Study of Frederick II of Hohenstaufen and the Capua Triumphator Archway and Towers*. Cambridge: W. Heffer and Sons.

Sherrard, Philip. 1965. *Constantinople: Iconography of a Sacred City*. London: Oxford University Press.

Skre, Dagfinn. 2007a. "The Dating of *Ynglingatal*." In *Kaupang in Skiringssal*, edited by Dagfinn Skre, 407–29, Kaupang Excavation Project Publication Series, 1. Aarhus: Aarhus University Press.

———, ed. 2007b. *Kaupang in Skiringssal*, Kaupang Excavation Project Publication Series, 1. Aarhus: Aarhus University Press.

———. 2007c. "The Skiringssal Cemetery." In *Kaupang in Skiringssal*, edited by Dagfinn Skre, 363–83, Kaupang Excavation Project Publication Series, 1. Aarhus: Aarhus University Press.

———. 2011. *Things from the Town: Artefacts and Inhabitants in Viking-Age Kaupang*, Kaupang Excavation Project Publication Series, 3. Oslo: Aarhus University Press.

Skre, Dagfinn, and John Hines. 2007. *Means of Exchange: Dealing with Silver in the Viking Age*, Kaupang Excavation Project Publication Series, 2. Aarhus: Aarhus University Press.

Smith, E. Baldwin. 1950. *The Dome: A Study in the History of Ideas*. 1st paperback ed., Princeton Monographs in Art and Archaeology, 25. Princeton: Princeton University Press.

Smith, John Thomas. 1807. *Antiquities of Westminster: The Old Palace; St Stephens Chapel (Now the House of Commons)*. London: J. T. Smith.

Spain, Suzanne. 1977. "The Translation of Relics Ivory, Trier." *Dumbarton Oaks Papers* 31: 279–304.

Squatriti, Paolo, ed. 2007. *The Complete Works of Liudprand of Cremona*. Washington, DC: Catholic University of America Press.

Staab, Franz, ed. 1990. *Die Pfalz: Probleme einer Begriffsgeschichte vom Kaiserpalast auf dem Palatin bis zum heutigen Regierungsbezirk*, Veröffentlichung der Pfälzischen Gesellschaft zur Förderung der Wissenschften in Speyer, 8. Speyer: Pfälzische Gesellschaft zur Förderung der Wissenschaften in Speyer.

Staecker, Jörn. 2004. "Jelling: Mythen und Realität." In *Der Ostseeraum und Kontinentaleuropa 1100–1600: Einflußnahme–Rezeption–Wandel*, edited by Jens E. Olesen, Detlef Kattinger, and Horst Wernicke, 77–102. Schwerin: T. Helms.

Stammwitz, Ulf. 2010. "Geschlechtsspezifische Aspekte und historische Bedeutung der Nordhügelgrablege von Jelling." In *Zwischen Fjorden und Steppe: Festschrift für Johan Callmer zum 65. Geburtstag*, edited by Claudia

Theune, Felix Paul Biermann, and Gerson H. Jeute, 423–34, Internationale Archäologie, Studia honoraria, 31. Leidorf: Rahden.

Steane, John. 2001. *The Archaeology of Power: England and Northern Europe AD 800–1600*. Stroud: Tempus.

Stejskal, Karel. 1978. "Die Rekonstruktion des Luxemburger Stammbaums auf Karlstein." *Umeni* 26: 535–63.

Stella, Francesco. 2015. "L'historiographie en vers de 'époque carolingienne: la typologie politique des peintures d'Ingelheim." In *La Typologie biblique comme forme de pensée dans l'historiographie médiévale*, edited by Marek Thue Kretschmer, 25–52. Turnhout: Brepols.

Stephenson, Paul. 2009. *Constantine: Unconquered Emperor, Christian Victor*. London: Quercus.

Stiegemann, Christoph, and Matthias Wemhoff, eds. 1999. *799: Kunst und Kultur der Karolingerzeit: Karl der Grosse und Papst Leo III in Paderborn: Beiträge zum Katalog der Ausstellung Paderborn 1999*. Mainz: Philipp von Zabern.

Strayer, Joseph R., ed. 1982–2004. *Dictionary of the Middle Ages*. 13 vols. and supplement. New York: Scribner.

Strong, Roy C. 1979. *The Renaissance Garden in England*. London: Thames and Hudson.

———. 1984. *Art and Power: Renaissance Festivals, 1450–1650*. Woodbridge: Boydell Press.

———. 2005. *Coronation: A History of Kingship and the British Monarchy*. London: Harper Collins.

Stubbs, William, ed. 1874. *Memorials of Saint Dunstan, Archbishop of Canterbury*, Rolls Series, 63. London.

Studničková, Milada. 2009. "Karlstein Castle as a Theological Metaphor." In *Prague and Bohemia: Medieval Art, Architecture and Cultural Exchange in Central Europe*, edited by Zoë Opačić, 168–82, British Archaeological Association Conference Transactions Series, 32. Leeds: Maney Publishing.

Swanton, Michael J., trans. 1996. *The Anglo-Saxon Chronicle*. London: Dent.

Swoboda, Karl Maria. 1969. *Römische und romanische Päläste: eine architekturgeschichtliche Untersuchung*. Vienna, Cologne, and Graz: Böhlau.

Tabales Rodríguez, Miguel Angel. 2010. *El Alcázar de Sevilla: Reflexiones sobre su origen y transformación durante la edad media: Memoria de investigación arqueológica*. Seville: Junta de Andalucia.

Tatton-Brown, Tim, ed. 2003. *Westminster Abbey: the Lady Chapel of Henry VII*. Woodbridge: Boydell Press.

Taylor, A. J. 1989. *Caernarfon Castle and Town Walls*. Reprint ed. Cardiff: Cadw: Welsh Historic Monuments.

Thacker, Alan T. 1995. "*Membra Disjecta*: The Division of the Body and the Diffusion of the Cult." In *Oswald: Northumbrian King and European Saint*, edited by Clare Stancliffe and Eric Cambridge, 97–127. Stamford: Paul Watkins.

Thacker, Christopher. 1979. *The History of Gardens*. London: Croom Helm.

Thomas, Christopher, Robert Cowie, and Jane Sidell. 2006. *The Royal Palace, Abbey and Town of Westminster on Thorney Island: Archaeological Excavations (1991–8) for the London Underground Limited Jubilee Line Extension Project*. London: Museum of London Archaeology Service.

Thorpe, Lewis, trans. 1969. *Two Lives of Charlemagne*, Penguin Classics. Harmondsworth: Penguin.

———, trans. 1974. *Gregory of Tours: The History of the Franks*, Penguin Classics. Harmondsworth: Penguin.

Thurley, Simon. 1993. *The Royal Palaces of Tudor England: Architecture and Court Life 1460–1547*. New Haven: Yale University Press.

———. 1995. "Royal Lodgings at the Tower of London 1216–1327." *Journal of the Society of Architectural Historians of Great Britain* 38: 36–57.

———. 2003. *Hampton Court: a Social and Architectural History*. New Haven: Yale University Press.

Todd, A. Marden and Mark Wilson Jones, eds. 2015. *The Pantheon*. Cambridge: Cambridge University Press.

Toner, J. P. 2014. *The Day Commodus Killed a Rhino: Understanding the Roman Games*, Witness to Ancient History. Baltimore: John Hopkins University Press.

Tout, T. F. 1920–33. *Chapters in the Administrative History of Mediaeval England: The Wardrobe, the Chamber and the Small Seals*. 6 vols. Manchester: Manchester University Press.

Tracy, James D., ed. 2000. *City Walls: The Urban Enceinte in Global Perspective*, Studies in Comparative Early Modern History. New York: Cambridge University Press.

Tracy, Kisha G. 2010. "Representations of Disability: The Medieval Literary Tradition of the Fisher King." In *Disability in the Middle Ages: Reconsiderations and Reverberations*, edited by Joshua R. Eyler, 105–18. Farnham: Ashgate.

Triano, Antonio Vallejo. 2010. *La ciudad califal de Madīnat al-Zahrā': Arqueología de su excavación*. Seville: Junta de Andalucia / Almuzara.

———. n.d. *Madīnat al-Zahrā': Official Guide to the Archaeological Complex*. Seville: Junta de Andalucia.

Tronzo, William. 1997. *The Cultures of his Kingdom: Roger II and the Cappella Palatina in Palermo*. Princeton: Princeton University Press.

———. 2010. "L'architettura della Cappella Palatina." In *La Cappella Palatina a Palermo = The Cappella Palatina in Palermo*, edited by Beat Brenk, Fabrizio Agnello, and Giovanni Chiaromonte, 79–99. 4 vols., Mirabilia Italiæ, 17. Modena, Italy: Franco Cosimo Panini.

Tubbs, Colin R. 1986. *The New Forest*, The New Naturalist series. London: Collins.

Turner, H. 1970. *Town Defences in England and Wales*. London: John Baker.

Ullmann, Walter. 1966. *Principles of Government and Politics in the Middle Ages*. London: Methuen.

———. 1969. *The Carolingian Renaissance and the Idea of Kingship*. London: Methuen.

———. 1970. *A History of Political Thought: The Middle Ages*. Harmondsworth: Penguin.

———. 1975. *Law and Politics in the Middle Ages: An Introduction to the Sources of Medieval Political Ideas*. London: Sources of History.

Underwood, Paul. 1950. "The Fountain of Life in Manuscripts of the Gospels." *Dumbarton Oaks Papers* 5: 41, 43–158.

Untermann, Matthias. 1989. *Der Zentralbau im Mittelalter: Form–Funktion–Verbreitung*. Darmstadt: Wissenschaftliche Buchgesellschaft.

Vance, Eugene. 1970. *Reading the Song of Roland*. Englewood Cliffs: Prentice-Hall.

Vantuono, William, ed. 1999. *Sir Gawain and the Green Knight*. Notre Dame: University of Notre Dame Press.

Velímský, Filip. 2013. "Gründung, Struktur und Entwicklung der mittelalterlichen Bergstadt Kutná Hora/Kuttenberg aus der Sicht der Archäologie, der Montanarchäologie und der Geschichte." In *Die Frühgeschichte Freibergs im überregionalen Vergleich: städtische Frühgeschichte–Bergbau–früher Hausbau*, edited by Yves Hoffmann and Uwe Richter, 315–25. Halle: Mitteldeutscher Verlag.

Verbeek, Albert. 1965. "Die architektonische Nachfolge der Aachener Pfalzkapelle." In *Karl der Grosse: Lebenswerk und Nachleben, vol. 4: das Nachleben*, edited by Wolfgang Braunfels and Percy Ernst Schramm, 113–56. Düsseldorf: Schwann.

Verhoeven, Mariëtte. 2011. *The Early Christian Monuments of Ravenna: Transformations and Memory*, Architectural Crossroads, 1. Turnhout: Brepols.

Versnel, H. S. 1970. *Triumphus: An Inquiry into the Origin, Development and Meaning of the Roman Triumph*. Leiden: Brill.

Vespignani, Giorgio. 2010. *Hippodromos: il circo di Costantinopoli nuova Roma dalla realtà alla storiografia*. Spoleto: Fondazione Centro Italiano di Studi sull'Alto Medioevo.

Viarre, S. 1961. "Palatium 'palais.'" *Revue de Philologie* 35: 241–48.

Vikan, Gary, and Kenneth G. Holum. 1979. "The Trier Ivory, 'Adventus' Ceremonial, and the Relics of St Stephen." *Dumbarton Oaks Papers* 33: 113–33. Reprinted: Gary Vikan. 2003. *Sacred Images and Sacred Power in Byzantium*, 114–133. Aldershot: Ashgate.

Vílchez, José Miguel Puerta, Agustín Núñez Guarde, and Miguel Salvatierra Cuenca. 2011. *Reading the Alhambra: A Visual Guide to the Alhambra through its Inscriptions*. Translated by Jon Trout. Granada: Alhambra and Generalife Trust.

Vincent, Nicholas. 2001. *The Holy Blood: King Henry III and the Blood Relics of Westminster*. Cambridge: Cambridge University Press.

Vingtain, Dominique. 1998. *Avignon: le palais des Papes*, Le ciel et la pierre, 2. Saint-Léger-Vauban: Zodiaque.

Volk, Otto. 1999. "Von Grenzen ungestört—auf dem Weg nach Aachen: Die Krönungsfahrten der deutschen Könige im späten Mittelalter." In *Grenzen erkennen—Begrenzungen überwinden: Festschrift für Reinhard Schneider zur Vollendung seines 65. Lebensjahres*, edited by Wolfgang Haubrichs, 263–97. Sigmaringen: Jan Thorbecke.

Von Simson, Otto G. 1987. *Sacred Fortress: Byzantine Art and Statecraft in Ravenna*. Princeton: Princeton University Press.

Von Stackelberg, Katharine T. 2009. *The Roman Garden: Space, Sense, and Society*. London: Routledge.

Waddell, John. 2011. "Continuity, Cult and Contest." In *Landscapes of Cult and Kingship: Archaeology and Text*, edited by Edel Bhreathnach, Ger Dowling, and Roseanne Schot, 192–212. Dublin: Four Courts Press.

Wagner, Birgit. 2005. *Die Bauten des Stauferkaisers Friedrichs II: Monumente des Heiligen Römischen Reiches*. Berlin: dissertation.de.

Wander, Steven H. 1978. "The Westminster Abbey Sanctuary Pavement." *Traditio* 34: 137–56.

Ward-Perkins, Bryan. 1984. *From Classical Antiquity to the Middle Ages: Urban Public Building in Northern and Central Italy: AD300–850*, Oxford Historical Monographs. Oxford: Oxford University Press.

Ward-Perkins, John Bryan. 1956. "Nero's Golden House." *Antiquity* 30: 209–19.

Warden, P. Gregory 1981. "The Domus Aurea Reconsidered." *Journal of the Society of Architectural Historians* 40 (4): 271–78.

Weber, Max. 1947. *The Theory of Social and Economic Organization*. Translated by A. R. Henderson and Talcott Parsons. Rev. ed. London: William Hodge and Company.

———. 1968. *Economy and Society: an Outline of Interpretive Sociology*. Translated by Guenther Roth and Claus Wittich. 3 vols. New York: Bedminster Press.

Wehling, Ulrike. 1995. *Die Mosaiken im Aachener Münster und ihre Vorstufen*, Arbeitsheft der rheinischen Denkmalpflege, 46. Cologne: Rheinland-Verlag.

Wenskus, Richard. 1995. "Forst, sec. 2, historisches." In *Reallexikon der Germanischen Altertumskunde*, 348–50. 2nd ed. Berlin and New York: de Gruyter.

Whiteley, Mary. 1985. "La grande vis, its Development in France from the Mid-Fourteenth to the Mid-Fifteenth Centuries." In *L'escalier dans l'architecture de la Renaissance: Actes du colloque tenu à Tours du 22 au 26 mai 1979*, edited by Anon., 15–20, De architectura, Colloques, 2. Paris: Picard.

———. 1989. "Deux escaliers royaux du XIVe siècle: Les "grand degrés" du palais de la Cité et la "grande viz" du Louvre." *Bulletin Monumental* 147: 133–54.

———. 1992. "Le Louvre de Charles V: Dispositions et fonctions d'une résidence royale." *Revue de l'Art*: 59–75.

———. 1996. "Public and Private Space in Royal and Princely Châteaux in Late Medieval France." In *Palais royaux et palais princiers au Moyen Âge: Actes du colloque international tenue au Mans les 6–7 octobre 1994*, edited by Annie Renoux, 71–75. Le Mans: Publications de l'Université du Maine.

Wilkes, John Joseph. 1993. *Diocletian's Palace, Split: Residence of a Retired Roman Emperor*. Rev. ed. Ian Sanders Memorial Fund, Occasional Publication, 1. Sheffield: Department of Ancient History and Classical Archaeology, University of Sheffield.

Willemsen, Carl Arnold. 1953. *Kaiser Friedrichs II. Triumphator zu Capua, ein Denkmal hohenstaufischer Kunst in Süditalien*. Wiesbaden: Insel Verlag.

———, ed. 1973. *Das Falkenbuch Kaiser Friedrichs II*. Graz: Akademische Druck- und Verlagsanstalt.

———. 1988. *Über die Kunst mit Vögeln zu jagen: Miniaturen aus einer Handschrift des Falken-Buches von Kaiser Friedrich II*. 3rd ed. Frankfurt am Main: Insel Verlag.

Williams, Howard M. R. 1999. "Placing the Dead: Investigating the Location of Wealthy Barrow Burials in Seventh-Century England." In *Grave Matters: Eight Studies of First Millennium A.D. Burials in Crimea, England and Southern Scandinavia*, edited by M. Rundkvist, 57–86, British Archaeological Reports, British Series 781. Oxford: Archaeopress.

Williamson, G. A., trans. 1981. *Josephus, The Jewish War, with a New Introduction, Notes and Appendixes, by E. Mary Smallwood*. Rev. ed., Penguin Classics. Harmondsworth: Penguin.

Williamson, Tom. 2008. *Sutton Hoo and Its Landscape: The Contexts of Monuments*. Bollington: Windgather Press.

Wilson, Christopher. 1997. "Rulers, Artificers and Shoppers: Richard II's Remodelling of Westminster Hall, 1393–1399." In *The Regal Image of Richard II and the Wilton Diptych*, edited by Dillian Gordon, Lisa Monnas, and Caroline Elam, 33–59. London: Harvey Miller.

———. 2002. "The Royal Lodgings of Edward III at Windsor Castle: Form, Function, Representation." In *Windsor: Medieval Archaeology, Art and Architecture of the Thames Valley*, edited by Laurence Keen and Eileen Scarff, 15–94, British Archaeological Association Conference Transactions, 25. Leeds: Maney Publishing.

———. 2008. "Calling the Tune? The Involvement of King Henry III in the Design of the Abbey Church at Westminster." *Journal of the British Archaeological Association* 161: 59–93.

Wilson, Roger John Anthony. 1983. *Piazza Armerina*. London: Granada.

Winchester, Angus. 2010. "Vaccaries and Agistment: Upland Medieval Forests as Grazing Grounds." In *Forests and Chases of England and Wales to circa 1500*, edited by John Langton and Graham Jones, 109–24. Oxford: St. John's College.

Witney, Kenneth P. 1976. *The Jutish Forest: A Study of the Weald of Kent from 450 to 1380 A.D.* London: Athlone Press.

Wolf, Gunther G. 2005. "Nochmals zur Geschichte der Heiligen Lanze bis zum Ende des Mittelalters." In *Die*

Heilige Lanze in Wien: Insignie, Reliquie, "Schicksalsspeer," edited by Franz Kirchweger, 23–52, Schriften des Kunsthistorisches Museum Wien, 9. Vienna and Paris: Skira.

Wolffe, Bertram 1981. *Henry VI.* London: Eyre Methuen.

Wolters, Wolfgang. 2010. *The Doge's Palace in Venice: A Tour through Art and History.* Berlin: Deutscher Kunstverlag.

Wolverton, Lisa, trans. 2009. *Cosmas of Prague: the Chronicle of the Czechs,* Medieval Texts in Translation. Washington, DC: Catholic University of America Press.

Wood, Christopher S. 1999. *Albrecht Altdorfer and the Origins of Landscape.* London: Reaktion.

Woolley, Linda. 2002. *Medieval Life and Leisure in the Devonshire Hunting Tapestries.* London: V&A Publications.

Wormald, Patrick. 2004. "Alfred (848/9–899)." In *Oxford Dictionary of National Biography,* edited by Lawrence Goldman, s.n. Oxford: Oxford University Press.

Wortley, John T. 1980. "The Trier Ivory Reconsidered." *Greek, Roman and Byzantine Studies* 21: 381–94.

Wright, G. Sommers. 1974. "A Royal Tomb Program in the Reign of St Louis." *Art Bulletin* 56 (2): 224–43.

Yeates, Stephen J. 2008. *The Tribe of Witches: The Religion of the Dobunni and Hwicce.* Oxford: Oxbow.

Young, Charles Robert. 1979. *The Royal Forests of Medieval England.* Leicester: Leicester University Press.

———. 1985. "European Forests." In *Dictionary of the Middle Ages,* edited by Joseph R. Strayer, V, 131–36. 13 vols. and supplement. New York: Charles Scribner's Sons.

Young, Graeme. 2003. *Bamburgh Castle: The Archaeology of the Fortress of Bamburgh.* Bamburgh: Bamburgh Research Project.

Zara, Vasco. 2011. "Signatura rerum: le langage symbolique et musical dans l'architecture de Castel del Monte." In *Châteaux et mesures: Actes des 17es Journées de castellologie de Bourgogne, 23–24 octobre 2010, château de Pierreclos,* edited by Hervé Mouillebouche, 26–59. Chagny: Centre de Castellologie de Bourgogne.

Zettler, Alfons. 2001. "Gelnhausen als Gründung Friedrich Barbarossas." In *Burg und Kirche zur Stauferzeit: Akten der 1. Landauer Staufertagung 1997,* edited by Volker Herzner and Jürgen Krüger, 47–55. Regensburg: Schnell and Steiner.

Zotz, Thomas. 1990. "Palatium publicum, nostrum, regium: Bemerkungen zur Königspfalz in der Karolingerzeit." In *Die Pfalz: Probleme einer Begriffsgeschichte vom Kaiserpalast auf dem Palatin bis zum heutigen Regierungsbezirk,* edited by Franz Staab, 71–101, Veröffentlichung der Pfälzischen Gesellschaft zur Förderung der Wissenschften in Speyer, 8. Speyer: Pfälzische Gessellschaft zur Förderung der Wissenschaften in Speyer.

———. 1991. "Präsenz und Repräsentation: Beobachtungen zur königlichen Herrschaftspraxis im hohen und späten Mittelalter." In *Herrschaft als soziale Praxis: Historische und sozial-anthropologische Studien,* edited by Alf Lüdtke, 168–94, Veröffentlichungen des Max-Planck-Instituts für Geschichte, 91. Göttingen: Vandenhoeck and Ruprecht.

———. 1996. "Die Goslarer Pfalz im Umfeld der königlichen Herrschaftssitze in Sachsen. Topographie, Architektur und historische Bedeutung" In *Deutsche Königspfalzen: Band 4: Pfalzen–Reichsgut–Königshöfe,* edited by Lutz Fenske, Veröffentlichungen des Max-Planck-Instituts für Geschichte, 11. Göttingen: Vandenhoeck and Ruprecht.

———. 1997. "Beobachtungen zu Königtum und Forst im früheren Mittelalter." In *Jagd und höfische Kultur im Mittelalter,* edited by Werner Rösener, 95–122, Veröffentlichungen des Max-Planck-Instituts für Geschichte, 135. Göttingen: Vandenhoeck and Ruprecht.

Zotz, Thomas, Karl Heinemeyer, and Elsbet Orth, eds. 1985–. *Die deutschen Königspfalzen: Repertorium der Pfalzen, Königshöfe und übrigen Aufenthaltsorte der Könige im deutschen Reich des Mittelalters, vol. 1, Hessen.* Göttingen: Vandenhoeck and Ruprecht.

Illustration Credits

Index